STORMY WEATHER

There are no golden ages and no dark
ages. There is the oceanlike monotony
of the generations of men under the
alternations of fair and foul weather.

—THORNTON WILDER,
The Eighth Day

STORMY WEATHER

Crosslights on the
Nineteen Thirties
an informal
social history
of the
United States
1929-1941

BY J.C. FURNAS

G.P. PUTNAM'S SONS · NEW YORK

For H.S.G.
who persuaded the amoeba to split.

Copyright © 1977 by J. C. Furnas

SBN: 399-11842-X

Library of Congress Cataloging in Publication Data:

Furnas, Joseph Chamberlain, 1905-
   Stormy weather

   Bibliography.
   Includes index.
   1. United States—Social conditions—1933-1945.
I. Title.
HN57.F874   1977   309.1′73′0917   77-6467

PRINTED IN THE UNITED STATES OF AMERICA

ACKNOWLEDGMENTS

The writer is deeply indebted first and foremost to the Princeton University Library; then to the New York Society Library and the New York Public Library; then to the Dartmouth University Library, the Pennsylvania State University Library, the Pomona College Library, the Vassar College Library, the Dayton Public Library, the Easton Public Library, the Flemington Public Library, the Hunterdon County Library, the Phillipsburg Public Library, the Free Library of Trenton; and to the Chicago Historical Society, the Museum of Modern Art, the Tennessee Valley Authority, the Wine Institute of California and many other institutions obliging with incidental help. Individuals heartily thanked for data or consultation include Mrs. Lloyd Lewis, Helen Papashvily, Mrs. Wallace Richards, Clark Kinnaird, Robert J. Landry, Freeman Lewis, David E. Lilienthal, Scott Nearing, Frank Schoonmaker, Robert B. Thorpe, Philip Wagner ... and many, many others. None of these people or institutions has any responsibility for the writer's opinions or interpretations.

I also owe admiring thanks to Miss Ethel Watters for the way she sang the 1930s song that gave the book its title.

Gratitude for permission to quote is due: Brandt & Brandt for "Listen to the People" by Stephen Vincent Benét from *Selected Works of Stephen Vincent Benét,* Pub: Holt, Rinehart & Winston, copyright, 1941 by Stephen Vincent Benét, copyright © 1969 by Thomas C. Benét, Rachel Benét Lewis and Stephanie Benét Mahin.

University of Missouri Press for passages reprinted from *An Artist in America* by Thomas Hart Benton by permission of the University of Missouri Press. Copyright 1968 by Thomas Hart Benton.

Alfred A. Knopf, Inc., for passages reprinted from Harold Clurman, *The Fervent Years,* copyright 1976.

Houghton Mifflin Company for passages reprinted from Archibald MacLeish, *A Time to Speak.*

Norma Millay (Ellis) for a passage from *Three Plays,* "Aria da Capo," copyright 1921, 1949 by Edna St. Vincent Millay.

Coward, McCann & Geoghegan, Inc., for a passage from Alice Duer Miller, *The White Cliffs,* copyright 1940.

CONTENTS

INTRODUCTION   9

BLACK SQUALLS TO WINDWARD   11

THE DYNAMIC DECADE?

    A. The Arts   26
    B. The Media   104

THE REAL THING WAS BAD ENOUGH   182

SELF-SENT MEN   192

THEY DIDN'T JUST STAND THERE   288

THE LITTLE RED FOXES   336

WHAT THEY SAID ABOUT DIXIE   377

WHERE ANGELS FEARED TO TREAD   399

OZYMANDIAS IN WASHINGTON   438

FIRE UNDER THE ELMS   512

SOME CORNER OF A FOREIGN FIELD   538

THE POT AND THE CRADLE   573

"THERE WILL BE NO TOMORROW"   596

APPENDIX OF DEFINITIONS   603

NOTES   606

NONPERIODICAL SOURCES QUOTED   626

INDEX   643

INTRODUCTION

In *The Americans* (1969) the writer described our forebears' circumstances, habits and ways-of-doing from the time of the Lost Colony to 1914. The book sought to follow George Macaulay Trevelyan's definition of social history as "history with the politics left out." Inevitable lapses made it clear that, as common sense had already hinted, complete adherence to that is necessarily impossible.

The successor, *Great Times* (1974), found this difficulty heightened because during its period—1914 to 1929—politics were more deeply permeating the American climate. This third and last of the series must deal with political concerns to an even greater extent. It is by no means political in either intent or substance. But its field of interest takes in a great national calamity twisted by such agencies as the radio, the collective impulse, the shift in relative size of age-groups—all, plus a dozen others, carrying political overtones or repercussions. Hence Americans in the 1930s were probably more political-minded than they had been since ... well, since the Revolution of 200 years before.

It should also be mentioned that this was the decade in which the writer got his feet on the ground so far as they ever have been there. He was at least a fly-on-the-wall during much of what the book covers, sometimes personally involved, occasionally more or less personally acquainted with this or that figure coming onstage. So his personal views must color the text. This involvement has some virtues. It may lend sharper definition to the shadows cast by the crosslights promised on the title page. Other crosslights may come of the reader's recognizing parallels between what went on then and what the headlines took to be new kinds of goings-on in the last ten years.

In this attempt to illuminate the climate of the 1930s—stormy indeed but with what the British weatherman calls "bright intervals"—the *crosslights* motif dominates. Both responsibly and irresponsibly the mass miseries of the Great Depression have been thoroughly covered in the several subsequent decades. Time and accumulating folklore have blurred, distorted and even suppressed many angles of significance. The 1930s were stimulating and stimulated as well as bitter and stagnating. By now that too can be gone into.

The reader may find this or that aspect of the day omitted. The reason will be that either (1) the writer is unaware of it; or (2) its origins and much of its developments were already described in his *Great Times;* or (3) he knows he is so numb to its connotations (those of ballet, say) that he should not try to handle it; or (4) he believes its leverage on the times was too slight to warrant the required space.

BLACK SQUALLS TO WINDWARD

IT IS A PERILOUS THING FOR ANY GENERATION TO MISJUDGE
ITS IMMEDIATE PAST.

—MURRAY KEMPTON,
Part of Our Time

A traditional parable to begin with: A certain German headsman
was so deft that the condemned man with his head on the block was
likely to tire of waiting and beg to be put out of his anticipatory
misery. The headsman would smile and administer a pinch of snuff.
The victim, unaware that his neck was already severed, would
sneeze. . . .

Late in 1929, as shadows gathered but few discerned them, New
York City's Greenwich Village acquired a fashionably "modernistic"
building designed by Joseph Urban for the New School for Social
Research founded by radical-minded social scientists and noted for
radical-tending adult education. One of its lecture rooms was to be
decorated with mural paintings by Thomas Hart Benton, then a
coming painter of known radical bent. They are still there. A few
years ago the New School published an official description of them,
commending their distillation of "those early depression years . . . on a
subway, in the cornfields of Kansas, workingmen in a shipyard, people
on a breadline . . . the faces [Benton] has painted carry a look of
sorrow. . . . " [1] Depression years? Breadline? Look of sorrow? Alvin
Johnson, head of the New School who commissioned the work, said
that the public's first look at it produced complaints "that Benton . . .
depicted the gigantic, inhuman machinery of industrialism with never
a pathetic note for the wage slaves . . . the operators . . . look
triumphant." [2] Today's visitor studying these paintings looks in vain

for a breadline. It hasn't been painted out. It was never there * except in the unwary imagination of whoever wrote that description. Having read the right things about the notorious Great Depression, he assumed that any radically inclined artist painting Americana in any year numbered 193- would necessarily put in a breadline, whereas all Benton did was tuck in a small bit of a coffeepot and emaciated hands clutching for it.

Maybe a year or so later he would have put in a breadline, a Hooverville, an apple seller. ... But in those early months of 1930 to the extent that those things existed they were not yet solid in the national consciousness. What this able painter-reporter's antennae picked up and recorded instead was speakeasy, burlesque show, oil derrick, stock ticker, airplane—epitomizing the 1920s, no hint of the 1930s. Later compilers would telescope it all, making it seem as if the Depression as social force-in-being had begun to be warpingly felt as soon as the stock market closed on October 24, 1929. Since history is seldom neat, it didn't happen that way.

A revolution in women's fashions that fall and winter may have provided minor but probably helpful distraction from the potential disintegration that 20/20 hindsight so astutely discovered long after the fact. Within a few months the breastless, hipless, low-belted androgynous chic of the Jazz Age gave way to a "natural waistline" candid about buttocks and the natural bulginess of bosoms, and skirt lengths crept downward, reaching the lower shin in a couple of years. Then to garnish this winsome, if somewhat corn-fed, look, the longish, bouncy "pageboy bob" deposed the shingled haircut that, from behind and above the neck, had had both sexes looking curiously alike. This sudden decision of millions to look like girls again was well suited to taking minds off the persistent erosion of stock values. It was probably not, however, as amateur anthropologists eventually suggested, a cyclical symptom of economic change, or impending war, or tactical retreat in the struggle for freedom for women. In less pretentious terms it looked like just another of those seismic shifts periodically recurring in women's fashions when the international dressmaking industry concludes that its economic health calls for suddenly "making everything in a woman's closet look unwearable"—as the late Larry Aldrich, eminent dress designer, once formulated it for me. He

---

* Benton confirmed this for me: "You are absolutely correct about the New School mural. It represents the life of our country as I directly experienced it in the twenties ... before the 1929 crash, the year the mural was commissioned and conceived. ... I do not protest interpretations of my performance because, as I see it, the purpose of art is not to impose meanings but to generate them. If the interpretations are cock-eyed, what's the harm? People like you will correct them in the course of time." (Personal communication, August 15, 1974.)

thought it needed trying every seven years or so. The 1929 try was a sweeping success just in time to keep Seventh Avenue afloat in the shoal waters ahead. It also gave the brassiere industry, originally dedicated to flattening the upper salients that God gave women, the profitable task of reemphasizing them.

Had this sartorial shift held deeper significance, men's garb would probably have changed, too, maybe not so drastically but more than it did as the New Era sagged into Depression. As it was, the daytime uniform remained the three-piece suit, collar-attached shirt with necktie, snap-brim felt hat; changes were confined to slight fluctuations in width of lapel or trouser leg. The open-necked "sports shirt" with rudimentary tails dangling, a contribution from Hawaii's parasitic beach boys, was well in the future. It was all so long ago that for some years after the Great Crash many golfers still wore knickerbockers, the long, baggy, plus fours kind that the Prince of Wales (later and briefly Edward VIII) sponsored in the early 1920s; and the "boiled shirt," stiff and shiny as sheet metal, topped by a viciously starched wing collar, remained *de rigueur* with black as well as white tie. So long ago that only males below the age of thirty left off sock supporters, miscalled garters, a negligence originated by the Jazz Age's Joe College, and not synthetic nylon but genuine, worm-created silk enhanced the shapeliness of American girls' famously long legs. So long ago that electric refrigerators were by no means standard equipment and rival refrigerators powered by a gas flame, allowing simpler and quieter works, held a large part of the market. So very long ago that Robert Hutchings Goddard of Clark University and the Russian and German scientists working the same side of the street had barely got their teeth into the rocketry that eventually put men on the moon and automatic laboratories on Mars.

Yet to the reminiscent mind maybe the most luminous sense of far away and long ago comes of memories of the shipping that was the bridge to overseas. The *Queen Elizabeth 2* still makes some transatlantic passages to remind Miss Liberty of the old days of midnight North River sailings and the ship-news reporters going down the Bay on the cutter to interview incoming celebrities. But such vestigial survivals lose money hand over fist. Only the jejune cruise industry keeps a number of large passenger vessels, mostly degenerating retreads sold downriver by first-class maritime nations to low-wage operators, sailing from Manhattan's new Marine Terminal and the rootless facilities of Port Everglades. The *United States,* greatest self-powered ship ever built, her underwater lines the culminating miracle of 1,000 years of growing subtlety, has lain rusting at Norfolk these 10 years. Labor problems and deficits scuttled the *France* in 1974.

On pleasant Saturday mornings in 1930 we went down to the Staten

Island side of the Narrows just above Quarantine in time for the noon sailings. Toward half past twelve, as we chatted and peered northward, the sunlight would evoke from the upriver haze one after another bluff white superstructure backed by a majestic funnel. One by one in line ahead, seven, eight, ten if it was a busy season, they came gliding and looming higher, then growing longer and longer as, effortlessly silent at half speed, they slipped past procession-wise only a few hundred yards from shore—huge, lofty, multiplex and yet so shapely that even at close range one realized their implausible size only by the gnatlike scale of the passengers waving from the starboard rail. Kipling said, "The liner, she's a lady." He could have said noblewoman.

Or on Friday before the weekend cluster of first-class sailings we took the Hoboken ferry—that's gone, too—climbed to the Stevens Institute grounds and saw berthed across the water and at the Hoboken piers below to the right the great princesses—*Aquitania, Ile de France, New Amsterdam;* the elegant duchesses—*Rochambeau, Kungsholm, Saturnia;* the hospitable countesses—*Scythia, Bergensfjord;* the one-class baronesses—*Pennland, Minnewaska;* and a dozen or so others, all counters to the stream and bows shoreward like a teeming litter of 500-foot seagoing pigs suckling a five-mile sow. We knew their silhouettes and funnel paint like friends' faces, never confusing Cunard's brick-red with the Compagnie Générale Transatlantique's crimson, distinguishing the Panama Pacific's white rings in black from the Royal Netherlands' different version, and White Star's beige from the North German Lloyd's cream yellow. . . . As midnight neared and the boarding passengers' taxis clogged West Street, stay-at-homes returning from the movies would glimpse floodlighted funnels, high and heart-stopping, at the western end of cross streets, and soon the heart stopped again as the *Majestic*'s or the *Resolute*'s whistle let drive, sounding as if the constellation Taurus were bawling for his freedom. Ting-ting-ting-*ting* on the steward's portable chimes. "All ashore that's going ashore!" *Da capo, da capo.* . . .

Those passengers were bound not only for Southampton, Cherbourg or Bremen but also in other ships for Rio, Palermo and Oslo, Glasgow and Paramaribo. Today people go to those places by entering an overgrown bus station, whence they are herded into a long, low-ceiled tunnel filled with several hundred seats all facing the same way as if in a Hollywood megalomaniac's projection room. There they sit in deadly dullness for a few hours and are then evacuated into a second overgrown bus station at their overseas destination. A passenger sailing in the *Conte Biancamano* in 1930 would soon see a gap widening between broadside and pier as the tugs cast off dutifully tooting and puffing away to the next job. Lower Manhattan's skyscrapers and Governors Island and the Brooklyn side of the Narrows would slide past—no Verrazano Bridge yet—then the widening Lower Bay and the freshening breeze and presently that climactic gentle jostle underfoot, only half perceptible but signifying that the imperative North Atlantic had taken over, a buoyant universe relegating this steel monster of so very many thousand tons to her proper place relative to the high seas. That bobbly lurch was something to celebrate in the bar—wide and richly lighted, now gradually filling with persons some of whom could prove worth getting to know, a process requiring days, not a few hours in the air.

Today's fat-cat cruise ship feels that premonitory jostle, too. But it doesn't mean the same. She isn't going anywhere in any intelligible sense, merely out and back, as aimless as her passengers' plans for getting a tan and shopping ashore. The lady liners carried bankers, cardsharps, professors, Cabinet officers, prima donnas, engineers, bishops, newspaper correspondents, expatriates, impostors, honeymooners on their more or less lawful, specific occasions *one way*. Even the liner's unqualified tourists, their numbers varying with the season, were going somewhere far away and different, and the five to ten days of the voyage made it easy for them to grasp the fact of major displacement, of changing hemispheres, of distances between cultures and histories, whereas Robert Graves tells of sitting on a London bus behind two typists. One asked the other, "Where did you spend your holidays?" "Mallorca." "Where's Mallorca?" "How should I know? I flew there." *

Nor was the lady liner merely the seagoing hotel that her elegant withinsides resembled. In spite of cables and radio and the very new transatlantic telephone, she was still in 1930 the chief means of human communication between hemispheres, for airmail was not yet a transoceanic practicality. A letter specially marked "Via RMS *Aquitania*" taken to the Morgan Annex Post Office at the close of business on Friday would, with a touch of luck, be delivered in London Saturday week. Archaically slow in today's terms? Modern improvements in handling mail have now so fouled up both the US Postal Service and HM Post Office that any airmail from London usually takes five days sender to me, and vice versa.

Transatlantic airmail had to wait until 1939. But the omens were pretty plain early in the 1930s. Young folks were driving their secondhand Model As out to the major airports just to stand with their mouths slightly open in observation galleries and watch the planes take off.

The victim's unawareness that decapitation had occurred was evi-

* In a radio interview on WOR some years ago. Tom Wolfe also uses it in *The Electric Kool-Aid Acid Test*.

dent in Wall Street's immediate response to the cataclysm. Black Thursday was preceded by one curious bit that seems to justify superstitious explanation. No doubt the cultivated (or anyway Ivy-League-educated) chiefs of *Time* magazine *c.* 1929 had heard of the ancient Greeks' notion of *hybris*—an overweeningness that, when too flagrant, tempts the gods to apply persecutory discipline. That had been a shopworn cliché for 2000 years. Yet Henry R. Luce and his staff probably did not mean to call down disaster on the American economy when, in *Time* for October 21, 1929, they announced the unveiling of a consort magazine—a fat-cat monthly to be called *Fortune* dedicated to the "generally accepted commonplace that America's greatest achievement had been Business ... [giving] to the record of Modern Industrial Civilization a distinction comparable to the intelligence which business now attracts ... [reflecting] Industrial Life in ink and paper and word and picture as the finest skyscraper reflects it in stone and steel ... [attracting] those active, intelligent and influential individuals who have a relatively large stake in U.S. Industry and Commerce ... directly or indirectly ... the executive ... also his friends (able doctor, politician, lawyer or wife) who are increasingly concerned with Business and with Businessmen." 3 Meaning, presumably, that like him those friends of his were up to their ears in the stock market.

Five-year-old *Time* was already making money and conspicuous for brash journalistic innovation. But its bright young men would hardly have taken the weight of Luce's empire-to-be seriously enough to think of knocking on wood after that rhapsodical ode to the New Era. Nevertheless, an ancient Greek might have seen it as the crucial, the too provocative flaunting of the emotional axioms of those then in charge of America—the series of attitudes lumped by Henry F. May as "the ultra-practical, anti-intellectual, pseudo-idealistic gospel of Prosperity First." 4 For within three days of that issue of *Time* the Great Bull Market, the outward and visible sign of that gospel, struck one of the worst sell-offs in the rackety-rockety-rickety history of Wall Street, and within eight days blue chips were smothering in a vacuum offering no bidders at all at any price. That went into the folklore of disaster along with the Johnstown Flood and the *Titanic*. The cult of Business, alias the New Era, was, like Polycrates, getting its comeuppance. That is just American for Nemesis.

That is, suppose John Bunyan had been an ancient Greek. For the protagonist of this drama was unmistakably a direct descendant of Mr. Worldly Wiseman of *Pilgrim's Progress*. He might be a San Francisco shipping man or a La Salle Street commodities man or a Philadelphia machine-tool man instead of the proverbial Big Man in Wall Street, but all those usually had in common a sleek self-esteem and a costume signifying it—stiff collar, dark suit with white piqué edging in the V of the vest, two-dinted gray felt hat and velvet-collared, charcoal gray Chesterfield overcoat. When that breed of cat was interviewed for the *American* magazine, the photograph that went with it was the most strong-chinned of a new batch of proofs from Bachrach. (Those cozily adulatory interviews in the *American* were beginning to be considered corny, however; what *Fortune* was up to was outfitting the generic Businessman in the special, platinum-plated kind of class associated with Morgan partners.) W. W. Businessman might still be self-made, up from stockroom or roundhouse, but the odds were increasingly against it. The law was probably his bridge to the seat of power. He did prefer to be honest when it was at all practical. And his knack with men and things in his own segment of the economy was often impressive enough to blunt the abuse and ridicule that Babbitt baiters heaped on him. And in the heady climate of the Great Bull Market he could hardly have seen any reason to heed the epitaph that incisive young Walter Lippmann enjoyed writing for him—most prematurely as it proved—c. 1912:

" ... this nation ... sixteen years ago [that is, in the gathering good times of the McKinley administration] vibrated ecstatically to that magic word 'prosperity'; today ... [it] induces little but excessive boredom. If you wish to drive an audience out of a hall, tell it how right America is." [5] And the next year: "The business man has stepped down from his shrine; he is no longer an oracle whose opinion on religion, science and education is listened to dumbly as the valuable by-product of a paying business. We have scotched the romance of success." [6]

That should have gone on the spike for printing in 1932 when events of twenty years would have made it dismally accurate. Halfway between, in the mid-1920s, Lippmann's misgivings about W.W.'s credentials as prophet-king could sound no better than hopeful, magic-making incantation, as though stating one's dearest wish helped bring it about. For W.W. came out of the post-Armistice slump into the early 1920s generous with assorted wisdoms—after the examples of Andrew Carnegie and Henry Ford—on international affairs, public and private morals and the intimate, providential affinity between his economic sagacity and the eternal verities. And the habit grew on him. "In the early days of capitalism," Charles A. Beard, pontiff of America's school of history-as-economics, noted in 1931, "bankers and industrialists were men of deeds rather than words ... paid little attention to what the public was supposed to think ... many years ago [there was] a change.... Magnates of business suddenly became oracles of destiny ... their opinions ... [were] sought by eager reporters on everything under the sun from prosperity to ping-pong. ... When the whole country went into a frenzy of speculation in 1928 and 1929, these high councillors, with a few honorable exceptions, were all on the side of more frenzy ... a double discredit ... business leadership had failed to lead and it had given false counsel." [7]

Thus W.W.'s willingness to let big moneymen lead him up the garden path in a haze of financial self-celebration and euphoria is not hard to understand. For a long while they had been telling him that the economic wonders of the new productivity were not only America's new contribution to history (true) but also the doing of big-shot businessmen like themselves (dubious) and that the seemingly limitless buoyancy of stock prices confirmed not only their but also his, W.W.'s, validity. True, he as well as they often did show a canny ability to do his own thinking in his own buy-and-sell bailiwick, and it was naturally exhilarating to hear that it was himself and his likes who had built the glorious New Era—a belief the deeper for being so showily shared by the eminent bankers and mighty industrialists whom he hero-worshiped.

In view of how stocks had behaved since 1924 it would have taken skepticism more bilious than most W.W.s commanded to doubt that such kings and councillors of the earth knew what they were talking about, even knew what they were doing. Jubilantly W.W. followed his culture heroes into the stock market, and every time his margin-bought RCA and United Corp. spiraled up again his faith deepened. One cannot doubt either that most of those influential cheerleaders—the Andrew Mellons, Samuel Insulls, Irving Fishers, John J. Raskobs *et al.*—sincerely believed their own doctrine of eternal economic bliss. In that they even had a certain justification of the extrapolatory sort. The American standard of living, the cultural fluid that floated the New Era and wafted it upward as in a canal lock, had risen sharply since Sarajevo. "Prosperity was real," wrote liberal economists William T. Foster and Waddill Catchings in early 1931. "The profits of capital were not mainly paper profits. The profits of labor were scarcely paper profits at all. During [1913–1928] ... the real wages of all workers in all manufacturing concerns went up about thirty-four per cent." [8] About the same time George Soule of the *New Republic,* no admirer of the New Era and its sycophants, admitted that in terms of real wages the American of the Crash year was "on the average, nearly one-fourth better off than before the [First World] war." [9]

For all that, W.W.'s conclusions from those data, his bayings of the harvest moon in a sky that was the limit, amounted to an extremely rash asking-for-it that was duly requited. As self-admirer he had shown little classic dignity. Once *hybris* brought down on him the usual result, he showed less still, and his supernal leaders were in the unhappy position of the spotlighted inventor whose perpetual motion clanks to a halt. But then whoever said that anything the Greeks had a word for must be necessarily dignified?

The timing of the birth of *Fortune* was not the only way in which the Luce organization helped keep America from realizing that the New Era's neck was severed. The cover of *Time* for October, 1928, carried the foxy face of Ivar Kreuger, the Swedish match king, world-shaking international operator whose grandiose schemes and eventual collapse and suicide in 1932 showed that America was not alone in New Era-mindedness and Gargantuan thimblerigging. The cover the following week serenely pursued the same anomalous (we know now) motif with the flabby face of Samuel Insull, the New Era's most conspicuous demigod of the electric power industry. The securities representing his lofty house of cards were a major ingredient in the Great Bull Market, and the best that could be said of the collapse of his empire, also in 1932, was that it did not smell quite as bad as Kreuger's in the nostrils of economic morality. On the cover of the issue of November 11 was the charmingly shrewd face of Thomas W. Lamont, presumed mastermind of the Morgan firm's famous effort to restore stability to Big Board stocks. "He felt the helm respond," said the caption. "Thus did Confidence win its subtle race against Panic." [10] *Time* further quoted impressive persons, from John D. Rockefeller, Sr., to Stuart Chase, most ingratiating of radically skeptical economists, to the effect that the sequelae of Black Thursday were no more than what the *Dictionary of American History* would still call "a stock-market panic exclusively" [11] thirty years later.

Only in the issue of November 18, four weeks after unshirted hell broke loose on the Exchange floor, had wisdom matured enough for *Time* to gather a nosegay of expert accountings for this technically interesting disaster. It no longer hinted at the culpability of a few bears such as William H. Danforth of Boston who had sold conspicuously short at a certain juncture. Now the dust was settled—a symptomatic assumption—*Time* blamed the clumsy haste with which large corporations playing banker with their surpluses had got the wind up and called in their money, which unnecessarily pulled the rug from under otherwise sound brokers' accounts. It hinted that recent financial reports from major companies had been so overcautious that speculators were tempted to overvalue their stocks and blamed the newfangled movement to sell to employees stock in the companies they worked for because it made "hundreds of thousands newly stock-conscious." [12] All that was regrettable, of course. But now that the amateurs were shaken out and the wise guys licking their wounds, reliable forces like the Rockefellers and Lamont would hold the New

Era's bows firmly into the teeth of the storm and stay on the bridge while she rode it out.

So, late in January, 1930, the maiden issue of *Fortune* went unabashed to its business-minded charter subscribers, fifty-one ounces of costly paper, elegant printing and judicious admiration of what Business had done for the nation. For comment on Black Thursday one had to turn all the way back to page 109. There blame was put on amateur dabblers in stocks and also on underscrupulous brokers failing to determine whether those opening new accounts could afford the risks of speculation. The New York Stock Exchange itself was reproached with rashly creating "a tremendous market in securities by extending its ticker system all over the country" and "listing a multitude of stocks" [13] as bait tempting all tastes. Apparently the editors OKing that copy had curiously exalted ideas of how stock-brokers of the 1920s should have regarded their responsibilities. More to the point, as the New Year got under way—few then knew it would be the first year of the Great Depression—*Fortune* nibbled gingerly at things that the glitter of the New Era and the chatter of the tickers had kept most economic statesmen from appreciating at the time. Late in spring, 1929, for instance, business indices had fallen off, and though stocks rose during the summer, building starts did not.

Other such disregarded portents would be gradually exhumed as impatience with the New Era's self-sent prophets deepened. But as the slide toward puzzled frustration began, a contributor to Beard's symposium on technological America, *Toward Civilization,* could confidently cite recent improvements in railroad freight service, enabling industry to reduce inventories, as a chief reason why "the story following the financial panic of 1929 in Wall Street [has not been] ... widespread disaster." [14] In John O'Hara's Gibbsville, Pennsylvania, that same year "the good day's work of October 29, 1929, continued to be known as 'a strong technical reaction.'" [15] Wallace Stegner was well justified in describing the Great Depression as "an event that most Americans comprehended only in retrospect, by its trickle-down consequences." [16]

In some instances relative failure to grasp what had happened came of Nemesis' mills' grinding slowly because her attention centered on one particularly flagrant set of culprits. It was a matter of two years before the slightly less flagrant Insull had to pay for that picture on the cover of *Time.* By the time the storm broke over him the buzzwords "Morgan," "Mellon," "Black Thursday," even to some extent "Hoover" were sagging stimuli. Indeed, for a while it had looked as though she had forgotten him and he might go unscathed.

For a generation he had been the pattern of strive-succeed-and-benefit-thy-fellowman in a situation where that genial motif had begun outwearing its welcome. Born in Britain's lower middle class, facing the lean future of the City clerk, Insull had come young to the notice of Thomas A. Edison, who fetched him to New York City as indispensable secretary and financial errand boy. When the Morgan interests ousted Edison from his Eastern enterprises (they became the General Electric Company), Insull went to Chicago to manage the local Commonwealth Edison power company. Within a few years his skills in organization and finance had him controlling electricity production in the vastly important Chicago area,* as well as the local elevated transit system, taken over because it could no longer meet its bills for electricity to power its trains.† The advent of Edison's tungsten-filament electric bulb was now making electric lighting far cheaper as well as brighter than the gas mantle. This not only greatly increased use of electricity, but made millions of households customers of the electric power industry, aware of its expanding presence with every monthly bill and every new electric gadget—toaster, fan, percolator to begin with and then vacuum cleaner, stove. . . .

Insull's remarkable sense of economic strategy led him into successive rate reductions, realistic (if often underhanded) dealings with organized labor and a handling of public relations that, looked at two generations later, resembles much of what most American big shots never learned until the New Deal made them. Well before World War I he was acquiring and consolidating small power plants in the country around Chicago in order to put electric water pumps and washing and milking machines into dwellings and barns far out in the bushes where such facilities had not been previously dreamed of. In his own way he was anticipating the Rural Electrification Administration that did so much to make the New Deal popular among country folks a generation later. "It must be said for Insull," John T. Flynn, no admirer, pointed out, "that while he built unsoundly—financially—he built well physically . . . [as] he added other utility companies in the Mississippi Valley. . . . He modernized their equipment, applied his principle of mass production, dismantled their old plants, put up new ones. . . ." [17] His skill at weaving local plants together for lower operating costs and mutual support to keep kilowatt supply steady got

---

* This account of Insull depends gratefully on Forrest McDonald's *Insull* (1962), presumably the official biography but in my judgment admirably judicial, and on John T. Flynn's "Up and Down with Sam Insull" in Alexander Klein, ed., *Grand Deception,* 1955. Those wanting antidotal crosslights may be referred to Matthew Josephson, *The Money Lords* (1972).

† Pertinent business folk tale: A bank customer, letting the banker know that the note due the first of the month will not be met, says wistfully: "You know how it is in the pickle business." Banker: "I've never been in the pickle business." Customer: "No? You are now."

him called to England to show his mother country's publicly owned power developments how to set up their renowned "grid system." Eventually that was the pattern on which the TVA worked out its distribution of New Deal-inspired juice in the Tennessee Valley.

This unprepossessing little man—puffy mustache, bulgy eyes, rather like a London taxi driver—was not the only such large frog in America's power puddle. Free-swinging financial jugglers like Howard Hopson, Harrison Williams and the Morgan interests had formed conglomerations of kilowatt capacity that sometimes jostled his. The managements of most of them disapproved of Insull's heretical habit of lowering rates as it grew economically possible in order further to increase use of current. Insull paid little heed. His first principle—and probably one cause of his eventual downfall—was that he was sure that he did what he did better than anybody else, a drift toward the sense of omnipotence that apparently overtook him late in the New Era. His second principle, on which he felt as strongly as Henry Ford, was to stay away from Wall Street bankers, the crew that had done wrong to his patron, Edison. Insull and his allies in his Midwestern bailiwick took a parochial pride in independence from the Effete East's money changers, which incidentally left him free to do unorthodox things that other utility magnates, banker-ridden, sometimes banker-created, were not allowed. Much of the capital behind his growingly complicated network-pyramid of operating companies and holding companies and then holding-companies-holding-holding-companies came from securities retailed to individual Chicagoans in small parcels by Chicago brokers close to Insull. Much of his equity capital came from his fondness for "customer ownership" of the stocks of his companies—the financing device that would make him the most reprehended man within 500 miles of the Loop.

He began that in 1914. Just when the outbreak of World War I froze normal financing, Insull needed $400,000 for equipment to expand a small company new in his stable. The bright young man in charge whipped up an issue of $400,000 in 6 percent preferred stock and sold it door to door to the company's customers, corporate and individual, who were aware of Insull's well-deserved reputation of efficient, profitable operation of El lines, gas companies, powerhouses and so on. It was as simple as that. So in 1920, when strains consequent on the *end* of World War I again made money awkward to come by, Insull remembered and set a door-to-door sales force peddling stock to individuals whenever financing was needed. By the end of the 1920s a million or so persons, including a great many who had never owned any other securities and never dreamed of buying any until Insull's personable henchmen knocked at the door, had a tiny piece of Middle West Utilities or Insull Utilities Investment

Corporation. This was no part of the concomitant rise in amateur speculation in stocks bought on margin or anyway with quick resale in mind. Most of it was self-endowment, nest-egg buying, relying on the Insull reputation for consistent, sound profits from the growing use of electricity. In consequence, when the worst happened, many hated his name as though he had stolen their money from under the spare-room mattress.

Certain other great economic entities, such as the American Telephone & Telegraph Company, were then seeking, for defensive purposes, to distribute their stocks widely and permanently among very small investors. To give so many a sense of partaking in AT&T's welfare was good public relations, sound precaution against perennially hostile public opinion—a point that Insull grasped, too. Besides, the more voting stock was held by atomized hordes of hard-to-organize individuals obligingly sending proxies to management on request, the less danger of trouble from antimanagement forces. Insull's example of tapping individuals at doorstep level was taken up by the brothers Mantis and Oris van Sweringen (those really were their given names) of Cleveland, fast-stepping, strive-and-succeed organizers of a fantastic railroad-and-real-estate empire of the 1920s, and A. P. Giannini, financial *padrone* of California's immigrant-flavored Bank of Italy, who snowballed it into the Bank of America and a famous national network of banks owing fealty to his Bancitaly Corporation. When the storm came in 1929, Bancitaly took it green over the bows but weathered it well thanks to the ethnic loyalty with which Giannini's thousands of Italo-American depositor-customer-stockholders sent him their proxies through thick and thin. When the Van Sweringens came disastrously apart, their myriad mom-and-pop stockholders were naturally bitter. Indeed, the high-riding brothers had so abused the holding-company device, so tortuously diluted accountability through layer on layer of ownerships, that they had to confess even they couldn't find their way through the maze. But it was Insull who, as aforesaid, caught the worst of public excoriation.

He had made himself so personal a matter in the Chicago area. No matter how local reformers denounced him as a "gold-plated anarchist," [18] the efficiency of his services, the sweet savor of his frequent reductions in rates, the local relish for the way he paddled his own canoe through corruptible politicians and economic hazards, his vaunted independence of the predatory money powers kept sharp tongues from doing much damage. Toward the end of the 1920s he capped it all by creating for Chicago a Civic Opera housed in a lordly skyscraper, the high tower and two lower wings of which got it called Insull's Throne—offices of his enterprises in the upper stories, opera house in the lowest seven. This harmonized with Chicago's recurrent hopes of becoming a cultural city equal to New York City. In line with his usual mass methods of financing, Insull proclaimed this opera for the people instead of primarily the silk-hatted and diamond-studded. Of 3,200 guarantors of the enterprise, only 600-odd put in more than $100. The balcony seats were nearer the stage than in any other major opera house. It had only thirty-odd boxes instead of the traditional diamond horseshoe, and they only on three-year lease, not owned.

The grand opening came only a week after the Great Crash. No repercussions were visible on Insull's great night. Flashlight powder was burned by the bushel, Lake Shore Drive limousines sleeked multitudinously up to the covered entrance of Insull's Throne and deposited as representative patrons of the people's opera a platoon of McCormicks, a corporal's guard of Swifts, both the Dawes brothers ...

Still, for a while, though bankers and brokers were running for cover, utility securities generally, including Insull's intricate, inter-locked pyramids of watered stocks held together by surface tension, were in less trouble than those of other segments of the economy. But in time growing pessimism and forced liquidation of portfolios caught up with them. The market values of Insull's holding companies melted away. He tried to "peg" them by buying them in himself at given levels but succeeded only in undermining what credit he had left. Middle West, once over $50 a share, went down to 25 cents, a mere two bits. Even Commonwealth Edison, wheelhorse of the operating companies, sources of the actual revenues that had long kept the pyramids coherent, sank from $450 to $50. A raid attempted by Cyrus M. Eaton in 1931 forced Insull to admit New York banks to his emergency financing. Now in baleful 1932, as irregularities in his jugglings of assets from one Insull company to another came to light, Wall Street moved in. After he went personally bankrupt, he was indicted by Illinois for embezzlement and by the federal government for fraud. He fled to Europe, moving from country to country as extradition papers followed him, finally giving up the game in Istanbul and returning in custody to stand trial.

It made him Exhibit A among those whom even financier-baiting Matthew Josephson called "finance capitalists and bankers who [in effect] were put on trial *because they had lost so much money for the public,* though in all but a few cases, they had done nothing unlawful according to the statutes of the time." [19] In court Insull was sometimes tearful; Westbrook Pegler, sharpest-tongued of newspaper columnists of the day, pilloried him as "Sobbing Sam * ... Crying Croesus of the

* A reference to a radio commercial of the day advertising a popular shaving goop: "Singin' Sam, the Barbasol Man. No brush, no lather, no rub-in. Wet your razor, then begin. ... "

Utility Trust." [20] Pegler had grown up in Chicago among the kind of lower-middle-income people who were backbone of Insull's "customer ownership" program. They had been largely unaware that any stock buying, even in so well-regarded and substantial enterprise, carries more risks than savings in the sock, and many of them could ill afford the massacre of assets that his downfall brought. Their exasperation is thoroughly understandable. But the state's case proved so weak that, in spite of the public's sense of disillusioned outrage, the jury was out for only two hours, and that was mostly stalling to mask its having known after ten minutes of deliberation that it would acquit.

One of the unfortunate things about the *hybris* scenario is that in the course of giving the overweening hero his comeuppance, Nemesis may wipe out whole subject populations who had nothing to do with his presumptuous actions. So it was here, and for unedifying contrast, Insull fared much better than Oedipus or Polycrates. Acquittals and dropped indictments cleared him of criminal charges, and he had assets enough overseas to get by on. He went into self-exile. Not until five years after his great trouble did he die, suddenly felled by a heart attack in the Paris Metro subway. Only small change was found on him, so the newspapers had him dying poverty-stricken. Actually he was known always to carry a bankroll of the order of $1,000. It is likely that, as a last flick from a Nemesis suddenly remembering him, she arranged for him to be rolled as if he were a derelict drunk.

THE DYNAMIC DECADE?

A. The Arts

FOR ME ... THE DEPRESSION WAS A TIME OF ELATION. ...
THE HARD TIMES OF THE THIRTIES SERVED MANY OF US AS AN
INCUBATOR.

—HAROLD CLURMAN,
All People Are Famous

Maybe one reason why many Americans neglected their historic duty promptly to feel the cold breath of the Depression was its inconsistency. Though it thickened and spread dismally, it did so on a highly irregular front. Certain forces and things of pre-Crash origin came pushing through into vigorous adolescence without being stunted by the frustration and lethargy that hard times gradually brought on. Indeed, those blithely anomalous developments were often so successful that with both ears and one eye shut one can see the early 1930s as an admirably dynamic period.

It was, for instance, the time when such recent inventions as book clubs, newsmagazines and radio were shaking down into supersolvency and great national significance.* And only a few days after Black Thursday three women whose resources ranged from affluence to the heights of plutocracy regardlessly launched in a New York City office building only five miles from Wall Street the money-hungry, aesthetically momentous Museum of Modern Art. "Regardlessly" may leave a false impression. At the time the public mind as these women knew it gave little reason to wonder whether those stock market difficulties downtown had much bearing on the advisability of launching their pet scheme. That was the very period when John D. Rockefeller, Sr., father-in-law of the chief of the three lady founders, was, as previously

---

* Their genesis in the late 1920s is covered in my *Great Times* (1974).

mentioned, announcing that he and his son, her husband, supremely confident in the future of America, were eagerly buying stocks at the prevailing bargain prices.

Daughter-in-law was, of course, Abby Aldrich Rockefeller, daughter of Nelson W. Aldrich, US Senator from Rhode Island, banker symbol of classical tariff-addicted Republicanism. Traveling in Egypt late in 1928, she encountered a friend, Lizzie P. Bliss of New York City, a spinster with a sizable fortune left by her textile-magnate father. She and Mrs. Rockefeller shared a taste for what was then loosely but recognizably called modern art—the Postimpressionist-through-Dada tradition that had first burst on America through the illustrious Armory Show of 1913. Much of its financing had come from her through her good friend, painter Arthur B. Davies. Her own personal collection ran Degas-to-Picasso. She used her leverage in the proper quarters to chivy the staid Metropolitan Museum into an exhibition of such work in 1921. Mrs. Rockefeller's purchases were the same sort of thing plus unconventional work by Americans controversial then, now part of the national canon—Georgia O'Keeffe, Louis Eilshemius, Charles Burchfield. . . . In Egypt the pair agreed that America needed, and they should provide, a museum to heighten public interest in Modern Art. In the ship going home Mrs. Rockefeller found another like-minded friend, Mrs. Cornelius J. Sullivan, a Hoosier-born, European-trained former art teacher in New York City schools who in middle age had married a prominent Manhattan lawyer and with him bought Modern. Though he was not even Bliss-rich, just pretty well off, the low prices then prevailing for such work enabled them to afford such a taste.

Three Graces? Three Fates? Three Weird Sisters? None fits the tripod that supported MOMA. Its staff called them the Ladies. Only in the United States could three women of whatever degree of influence and affluence have hoped to set up and control any such institution as MOMA became—"the most important taste-making institution in the world,"[1] said Aline Saarinen. They seem to have had no more misgivings than if they had been planning a luncheon—a striking case in point for alien visitors decrying the American woman's then-notorious and still-lively stranglehold on serious culture. It is also an example of how effective "womanpower" could be before Women's Liberation came along like Chanticleer commanding the sun to rise.

Not that only women marched in this auxiliary avant-garde. Certain moneyed American men fond of their own heresies had also admired and acquired. Sizable collections of Modern belonged to John Quinn, lawyer, friend of Sullivan and generous subsidizer of writers; Sam A. Lewisohn, art- and uplift-minded mining magnate; Stephen C. Clark, whose fortune came from O.N.T. sewing thread. Dr. Albert C. Barnes of Philadelphia's Main Line, wealthy from having invented Argyrol, a preparation of silver then widely used for nose-and-throat ills and venereal prophylaxis, bought staggering numbers of Modern canvases that he allowed practically nobody to see. A. Conger Goodyear, lumber magnate, former colonel in the AEF, collected Modern and, as president of the Albright Gallery in Buffalo, New York, had outraged its directors by sinking $5,000 of its money in a Picasso. The Ladies chose him as their organizer. MOMA's first board of directors included Lewisohn and Clark; Frank Crowninshield, editor of *Vanity Fair,* the shiny-chic magazine that had been full of Modern; Paul J. Sachs, forward-minded director of Harvard's Fogg Museum and den father of many young curators; and Mrs. Rockefeller's close and windily open-minded friend, Mrs. W. Murray Crane of the Crane Paper fortune.* Paper, copper, textiles, thread, lumber, mucous membrane medicine. . . .

Eventually the crass-minded suggested an economic purpose for MOMA—wider acceptance of Modern would enhance these director-collectors' investment in paint and canvas. That was probably unjustified. During the Great Bull Market people of their financial resources did not have to dabble in marginal works of art to get a run for their money. Doubtless the major force was the Ladies' nagging cultural consciences, their eager hopes of teaching others to respect what touched their own aesthetic hearts. And though minor shows of Modern had come and gone every year or two since the Armory Show, acceptance was still hesitant. Modern's reliance on distortion and flight from the representational still repelled people almost as much as when Marcel Duchamp's "Nude Descending a Staircase" rivaled Paul Chabas' "September Morn" as America's painting scandal of 1913. Nor was this just Babbitt snorting that his grandchild could do better, or the cynic telling of the donkey switching his pigment-laden tail against a canvas. Only a few months before Mrs. Rockefeller visited Egypt, *Harper's Bazaar,* usually achingly modish, printed cultivated Emily Post's sarcasms about "the kind of [paintings] that look like a cross between algebra and lightning." [2] And Edna St. Vincent Millay, Greenwich Village's pattern woman poet, anything but a Philistine, had her Pierrot fleeringly pose as a painter seeing his Columbine as

> "Ah, yes!—six orange bull's eyes, four green pinwheels,
> And one magenta jelly-roll—the title
> As follows: Woman Taking In Cheese From Fire-Escape!" [3]

* This section gratefully owes a great deal to Russell Lynes' recent and fascinating *Good Old Modern.*

It shows how great MOMA's impact was that within a few years of her birth even women's clubs in Dubuque knew of Matisse and Picasso as well as Reynolds and Millet. Modern Art had a strong ally in Europe's newly improved techniques of color-photography and -reproduction that brilliantly exploited its intense colors and blocky compositions. By the late 1930s van Gogh's sunflowers in full color had replaced the sepia halftone of "The Isle of the Dead" on the cultivated bachelor girl's wall. In *Virginibus Puerisque* R. L. Stevenson said he "always suspected public taste [meaning not mass taste but the consensus of upper social strata] to be a mongrel product, out of affectation by dogmatism." [4] All too true; yet the young lady's flat was more cheerful for the change. So was schoolroom art. Teachers were pleased and pupils gratified by the affinity—Babbitt had already noted it—between much Modern work (say Marie Laurençin, Henri Matisse, Paul Gauguin) and what colored crayons do for children on paper. As color reproductions of Modern works multiplied on classroom walls, affinity became dilute resemblance. It apparently embarrassed nobody that eight-year-olds of both sexes subconsciously aped Raoul Dufy just as their great-grandmothers in ladies' seminaries had consciously aped Currier & Ives prints. For some this confirmed the doctrine of Progressive Education that the Child, left to its own devices, has high creative powers. To others it meant that what the French call the *faux-naïf* is much the same whether deliberate or not.

Despite Mrs. Rockefeller's leaning toward American art, MOMA's early missionary work concentrated on newish European materials. Creation of prestige for American work coming up after John Marin and George Bellows was the specialty both of the Harvard Society of Contemporary Arts in Cambridge, Massachusetts, an early project of Lincoln Kirstein, a precocious undergraduate as rich (department store money this time) and intensely cultivated as a Belgian truck farm, and, after 1931, of the Whitney Museum of American Art, child of Gertrude Vanderbilt Whitney, a capable sculptress as wealthy as her name implied. In a world of transatlantic telephones and airplanes, cultural parochialism had less place than ever before. From a cosmopolitan point of view American painting was only part, and not a leading one, of the Western world's new approach to creation. Nevertheless, MOMA's early policies did have rather the air of a schoolgirl crush on Europe *qua* Europe. The effect deepened when, only two years after the place opened, it embarked on missionary work in architecture—specifically a groundbreaking project in public education called Modern Architecture, International Exhibit.

This show would have been important had it done no more than teach cultivated Americans the phrase *machine à habiter*. Among fifty architects covered were America's Frank Lloyd Wright and Raymond

Hood and a few Europeans practicing in America. But primarily it celebrated what Europeans of several nations, Walter Gropius, Le Corbusier, for instance, were doing with steel, glass and concrete in the movement thenceforward identified as the International Style. In a way it was American, too, for its roots lay deep in the Chicago School of thirty years earlier. But transplantation had quickened the organism, and America had neglected the potentialities of what it had begun.

This coup completed MOMA's election as the nation's aesthetic governess. She owed it to young Henry-Russell Hitchcock, a Harvard-trained scholar for whom the new European architecture was aesthetic history-to-be so compelling that he had to tell posterity what to think of it, and to his collaborator, younger Philip Johnson, fresh from Harvard College and gripped by the same passion though he would not be a qualified architect for ten years yet. After World War II, of course, he became one of the nation's best-known architects, a trend leader as crucial in that world as, say, Christian Dior in women's fashions. In the early 1960s when the president of a bank in a cow-country state capital accepted an architect's sketches for a new building looking like a honeycomb set on edge, he did so because thirty years earlier Hitchcock & Johnson had boiled Louis Sullivan's "Form follows function" down with the *machine à habiter,* served it with a sauce of Mies van der Rohe's "Less is more" and made the banker's elders and betters like it.

Lewis Mumford had long been preaching to fellow Americans the European-born dogma that "there is more aesthetic promise in a [Thom] McAn shoe store front [already mostly glass and steel] ... a Blue Kitchen sandwich palace [already mostly glass, steel and white enamel] than ... in the most sumptuous showroom of antiques." [5] At the time that was healthily corrective talk. All too soon, of course, it became overcorrection and cliché. The gospel written by Alfred H. Barr, young director of MOMA, for the Hitchcock & Johnson show denounced the "setback" silhouette then fashionable for skyscrapers as "at best pseudofunctional" [6] and suggested that sound planning would place skyscrapers far enough apart to rise straight to the top without needing setbacks for light and air. Enter the United Nations Building and others that make hay of the historic purpose of the skyscraper—to get maximum use of a valuable plot of land. Barr did have kind words for Hood's most recent work—"the spectacular verticalism of the Daily News building" [7]—and the less massive, ingeniously tinted, glass-emphasizing McGraw-Hill Building. He even noted that some few European masters admitted influence from and residual respect for America's already-patriarchal Frank Lloyd Wright. But the burden of the song was the advanced architects of the Netherlands, Germany,

Scandinavia and France whose structural grasp and aesthetic acuity were producing a Wave of the Architectural Future based on a Post-Functionalism.

Functionalism he defined as building for "utility-and-nothing-more" as in a railroad water tank—the sort of thing that Charles Sheeler loved to paint. Post-Functionalism added to such clean engineering "space enclosed by thin planes or surfaces as opposed to the suggestion of mass and solidity; regularity as opposed to symmetry or ... obvious balance ... dependence upon the intrinsic elegance of materials ... fine proportions as opposed to applied ornament." Do all that in glass, steel, concrete and plywood and lo! the promised International Style so welcome to those "appalled by the chaos" [8] of setback skyscrapers tricked out in the Art Deco then fashionable. Two years later Philip Johnson worked up for MOMA a show of unadorned utilitarian artifacts called Machine Art—ball-bearing assemblies, simple hand tools, ship's hardware and so on—persuading many who had never thought of it before that objects undistractedly devoted to function may in consequence be handsome. But enthusiasm cannot make this universally applicable. A wad of engine-room waste is both utterly adapted to its purpose and one of the ugliest things in the world.

The International Style was at its best in factories—it had learned much from well-engineered industrial buildings—office buildings and certain dwellings resembling the superstructure of a ship come adrift and washed high ashore. Much of its momentum from MOMA's show was necessarily specious because a museum exhibit of architecture is a contradiction in terms. Unable to fetch the Taj Mahal indoors, it must use models, which unfairly dwarf the originals; or drawings, which convey too little to laymen; or photographs, which distort, are partial and intrude the values of an alien medium. The International Style's affair with the camera was so brazen that, as industrial designer Walter Dorwin Teague used to complain, architects came to regard neither the client's needs nor sound architectural values, concentrating instead on how well the photographer's prints would look to the editors of architectural magazines.* It was also glass-addicted. That made some sense in relatively sunless northern Europe where it was born. In sun-smitten North America before air conditioning and double-pane glass came along, it was dysfunctional.

* Apropos, Lars Porsener, the radical Swedish architect cited by Paul Jennings *(I Said Oddly, Diddle I?,* 101), was bitter about "the Photographic Fallacy; most of the arguments for [Functional International Style] houses ... turn out to be photographs in glossy magazines taken on cloudless days in Israel or Brazil."

The readiness with which the Depression-ridden decade took to the International Style probably had much to do with its economic virtues. Never mind its highfalutin aesthetic tenets, the simplicity of its designs and the low cost of its materials gave more edifice for the money than one got from gussying things up in either traditional or Art Deco style. Janet Malcolm recently objected in the *New Yorker* to "the bland, money-pinching rigidities of glass office buildings." [9] Walter Gropius, *primus inter pares* here, was annoyed to find that "we were often held down to a minimum of expenditure by a public which could only be sold on modern architecture when it promised to be cheaper." [10] Yet he was also so adept in this aspect of it that the house he built for himself in Lincoln, Massachusetts, was a brilliantly seminal and charming example of how to make the most of its thriftiness.

In his native Germany even before World War I Gropius had fertilely explored such promising new things as cantilever construction, lavish use of fixed glass, functional criteria. In the 1920s he was the illustrious chief creator at the Bauhaus—post-Versailles Germany's great school of crafts-design-architectural engineering. Among his eminent associates there were Marcel Breuer, Josef Albers, Ludwig Mies van der Rohe, Paul Klee.... Two of its basic notions were particularly notable: It insisted on training its adherents in pertinent basic skills, so they knew from within the materials and techniques needed in working out their designs. And it sought to fuse industrial mass production with aesthetic integrity, designing chairs, say, to exploit the structural and economic virtues of aluminum tubing in shapes that would also express both the nature of this nontraditional material and the function of the chair. In the atmosphere of the Weimar Republic—permissive, novelty-minded, cosmopolis-oriented— the Bauhaus and its aims naturally flourished. Just as naturally the Nazis' Third Reich proved poison to it. One way or another Breuer, Albers, Mies van der Rohe, Gropius left Germany and settled in America, much to the improvement of the aesthetic atmosphere of their refuge.

In 1937 Gropius became chief of Harvard's Graduate School of Design, Breuer working with him. Almost overnight the two made what had been a stronghold of traditional architecture into a white-hot source radiating doctrinaire teachings into the sluggish tissues of American practice. As dazzled students learned the gospel of Post-Functionalism and the high technical standards that went with it, they went out into the world to multiply examples of Bauhaus-inspired character, small and private as well as large and public. Until then the new architecture had been primarily associated with office buildings, apartment houses, megalomanic plans for ideal cities—the sort of thing that Gropius' own Graduate Center contributed to Harvard's unmatchable architectural hodgepodge. But he made other waves by building for his own use, smack in the middle of the Currier & Ives belt, not far from where the rude bridge (a highly Functional structure by all accounts) had arched the flood, nearer still to the site of Thoreau's defiant (and doubtless also extremely Functional) cabin on Walden Pond, an ideological jewel of a small dwelling incorporating most of what Bauhaus principles taught about single houses intelligently mindful of the twentieth century in the temperate zone.

Deliberately Gropius put into it as little as possible that was not ready-made available in America's lumberyards, steel warehouses, builders' supply catalogues. Dimensions were in terms of standard precut lengths and widths. Sheathing was mostly standard tongue-and-groove. The glass brick freely used in some internal partitions and a pellucid screen between the front door and the prevailing wind were already much used and highly available. All this contrasted cogently with the special millwork and hand fitting required in most building of the time. White paint outside slightly tempered the rip-roaring summer sun that plagues American dwellings even in New England's latitudes. That was an old idea supplementing modern insulation. Bauhausery contributed cleverly positioned "eyebrows" and fixed louver baffles oriented against summer sun heights further to protect a house so lavishly glazed on the sunny side. From the aesthetic standpoint the admirable proportions of these sun-checking devices, including an insubstantial screened porch (that venerable American invention), elegantly break up the austerity of the basic building. Otherwise Chez Gropius would have to be included in what came to be called "filling station modern." It was more than a gibe. The large oil companies early recognized the economic advantages of the Bauhaus clichés and strewed the country with unimaginative but practical white boxes well before the occasional disciple of Gropius/Breuer could persuade more than a very few private clients to let him try something with Bauhaus flavor.

That too was long ago. Just how long came home to elder architecture buffs when the august Society for the Preservation of New England Antiquities took Chez Gropius under its wing in 1974. Disturbing as the thought is in terms of the calendar, the arrangement has logic. As Ada Louise Huxtable commented at the time, this house, "an instant landmark when completed in 1938," is now "a handbook of the new rules of 20th-century domestic architecture grown old gracefully ... the fireplace stripped of traditional mantel trim and frame ... the wall of bracket-held bookshelves ... rooms that flow into each other ... the house is as much a period statement as any Bulfinch treasure ... a symbol of a moment when esthetic rebellion was seen as a social need. ... The rationale of its acquisition by the

Society is incontestable." [11] So is her observation that it has "grown old gracefully." Some of that comes of the trees grown up roundabout to complement its severe lines. It also comes of the action of time on the eye of the beholder. By now one is so used to Functionalism's clichés that he can more keenly feel the Gropius/Breuer distinctively nice sense of proportion. Not only did they show the way for emulation, but at once and permanently they outdid subsequent sedulous imitations.

Nevertheless, the gospel that the Bauhaus and Hitchcock & Johnson took to the heathen has the disadvantage of many another missionary dogma: In the anthropological sense of "culture" it is culturally sterile. The trees and the genial attrition that comes of being lived in do not altogether mask the connotations of the doctrinaire. The components of even Chez Gropius, harmonious as it is, originate in intellectual deductions that have no more flesh on their bones than the algebra that calculates the stresses of the structure. An architect using such terms for anything but straightaway engineering—the elementary Functionalism that produces the beauty of, say, the Golden Gate Bridge—is in the position of the poet confined to a table of logarithms or of Oliver Wendell Holmes' student of dentistry who celebrated his girl's charms in rhapsodies about her dental formula.

That may be what Frank Lloyd Wright meant when reproaching Mies van der Rohe's high-rise buildings—though he granted them some virtues—with springing from "head-made" instead of "heart-made simplicity." [12] Some seek to minimize this flaw by saying that Post-Functionalism "derives its sanctions from both Greek and Gothic architecture, for in the temple as in the cathedral the aesthetic expression is based on structure and function." [13] This is specious. The lovely details of the finest Doric architecture have little to do with the engineering imposed by its ingredient stone slabs and column drums. Indeed the frieze, capitals and columns of the Parthenon are the reverse of Functional. They are slavishly traditional, imitative vestiges of the beam ends, peg heads, planking and upended logs headed with horizontal slabs that go back to the time when Greece built its temples of wood, not stone—and pretty crudely too.* The medieval master

* For a recent analogy take the design of the short-order "diner," home of the hamburger and legends of countermen shouting, "Sweep up the kitchen!" when hash is ordered. The diner was born of the "dog wagon"—the gypsyish quick lunch on wheels that appeared every night on Railroad Avenue to cater to cabdrivers, railroad men, reporters and others hungry in the small hours. Then obsolete horse-drawn streetcars were converted to that use; then discarded railroad coaches, seats torn out and galley and counter installed, were permanently sited in likely places. By association with railroad dining cars they got called diners, and custom being stubborn, for decades now the design of new-built roadside "diners" still recalls the spacing of dining-car windows, the curved-down eaves and long, narrow floor space of the original.

builder working in the Gothic context paid a thousand times more attention to what stone might and might not be asked to do. For in Post-Functionalist terms a good Doric temple is as false as a log cabin made of molded concrete. But the shape of what Greek tradition required, refined by generations of affectionate modification, offering ample scope for non-Functional emotion-rich ornament, carries an aesthetically fleshed-out quality that no Post-Functionalist edifice—for that matter, no self-conscious imitation of the Greek because it is "classic"—can present.

Such captiousness need not be carried too far. Post-Functionalism had the good taste, however frigid, to undermine the jagged, epicene excesses of Art Deco's influence on building and permanently to smother Academic Gothic. Indeed, it made its case so chillingly cogent that for good or ill it still negatively shapes and inhibits much of today's building. Those vistas of glass slabs on end *are* at least in better taste than the once admired Singer Building or the Ruskinian monstrosities lining Edinburgh's Princes Street. Pity that they are also a crashing bore. The end result of Mies van der Rohe's "Less is more" has been a vast, bland banality. It was not realized that what made that gleaming, upended slab look so good was not so much its own virtues, which are largely and pallidly negative, as the contrast that the obsolete fussiness on both sides afforded it. The Seagram Building desperately needs St. Bartholomew's.*

Much of that applies not at all or to a lesser degree to the other force that long since made it difficult for cultivated persons to commission Tudor manor houses or lovingly reproduced saltboxes— that turbulent force, Frank Lloyd Wright, who considered himself more than counterweight to all Post-Functionalists. His reaction to being included among them in the Hitchcock & Johnson show was to try to make himself a one-man anti-International Style movement. For that he had several reasons, some good, anyway all cantankerously characteristic of the Frank Lloyd Wright phenomenon and of the times in which it so flamboyantly flourished.

To begin with, he was considerably the elder of Gropius, Le Corbusier, Eliel Saarinen, Alvar Aalto *et al.* His generation was that of Henry Ford, Thomas A. Edison, John Dewey. Born when Andrew Johnson was in the White House, zealous disciple of Chicago's Louis

---

* This was even better said by that most refreshing student of architecture Osbert Lancaster: " ... while a modern office block may be an architectural masterpiece if viewed in isolation (which it most certainly never will be), when flanked and faced by other office blocks, conceived in the same idiom, it becomes an anonymous bore. But ... even a comparatively undistinguished example alongside an old brownstone or a bit of General Grant Gothic acquired a certain vitality and may well achieve a visual interest beyond that originally envisioned. ..." (*Cartoon History of Architecture,* 190.)

Sullivan, who, in the late 1880s, was founding modern architecture, by 1910 Wright already had an influential international reputation as a great innovator-designer. At his death fifty years later he was still breaking new ground with his spiral-shaped Guggenheim Museum. Meanwhile, he had passed through four or five aesthetico-technological phases, mostly important. Soon after striking out on his own toward the values leading to his remarkable "Prairie Houses" phase, he had announced that he meant to be "the greatest architect of all time" [14] and, as a recent biographer observes, "those ... irritated by the remark are also haunted by the thought that he may have made it come true." [15] Years later on the witness stand he was asked by hostile counsel whether he really did consider himself the greatest known architect; he said yes, he did. Afterward, the story goes, his wife told him he should have been more modest. "You forget I was under oath," he said. [16]

The older he grew, the more bitterly he denounced America. But he also considered himself intensely American, so one of his most direct complaints about the International Style was that it was exotic, a European cuckoo in the American nest. It only deepened the heinousness that much of its theoretical basis had come from either Sullivan, his revered Master, the only man he ever honored with that term, or from himself. He set up an invidious distinction between this imported "autocratic" architecture and the indigenous "democratic" sort of which he was exponent. The latter was plastic, free-formish and based on the horizontal lines he had been fond of since his Prairie period c. 1905–10. The former was non-American because stiff, geometric, committed to post-and-beam structure—the perpendicular motif that resists nature, or so he said. "Vertical is vertigo, in human life," he told the International Congress of Architects in Moscow in 1937. "The horizontal line is the lifeline of human kind." [17] He called Le Corbusier more of a painter than an architect and fired many a hot shot into Mies van der Rohe and Gropius, who were sowing what he considered subversive tares in America—his native land, not theirs.

The point could be overplayed, but it is tempting to see here an architectural parallel to the Midwest's chronic isolationism always specially strong in Wright's—and the La Follettes'—Wisconsin. It fits so well with his fervid approval of Colonel and Mrs. Charles A. Lindberghs' Wave-of-the-Future isolationism in the late 1930s and then with the anarchistic pacifism in which he persisted throughout World War II with an impunity highly creditable to his neighbors and the federal authorities. In other terms, however, the thing had other faces: The warm welcome that cultivated Americans gave the International Style doubtless showed that in spite of generations of resentment, the old cultural colonialism still lives; that, as Wright said apropos of Mies van der Rohe's great success in America, "our provincials feel that culture comes from abroad if at all." [18] In this respect the self-conscious Midwesterner tended to be more wary than the Easterner because he was struggling to keep from being sucked into the ever-growing cultural monopoly of New York City, all too accessible to European infections. Thus, here was architecture cajoled by Manhattan into seeking its stimuli in alien perversions of honest American precedents created in Chicago—the same sort of intercultural snobbery that made it advisable for a young singer from Oshkosh named Mary Hunter to· study in Milan and make her career billed as Maria Cacciatore.

From that point of view the Bauhaus exiles' contribution, however substantial and valid, looked like an aesthetic parallel to the New Deal's borrowings of Old World measures and economic assumptions—Marx's economic determinism, John Maynard Keynes' manipulative fiscal gospel, Otto von Bismarck's social security programs, Ebenezer Howard's garden cities.... No matter how American economic and technological power grew, the urge toward independence that buoyed up the Boston Tea Party and Noah Webster was still obliged, like the White Queen, to run like mad in order to stay in the same place. Then assume another point of view: Though it took European sensibility—or pedantry—to found the serious cult of American jazz, say, there was mutuality in that very fact, an invigorating swapping back and forth of data and techniques that happened far less a few generations earlier when the Atlantic was largely one-way westbound. That was the good-natured way—not Wright's—of regarding what Europeans did to Sullivan and his ideas. The world was not yet much smaller than it had been in 1890 with "ocean greyhounds" and transatlantic cables. The great shrinkage came with long-range bombers and commercial transport planes. But the spread of literacy and democratic political machinery was vastly accelerating interchange of ideas and skills. It was possible to hope, more so than now, for the rise of a less parochial and even more harmonious world.

Wright's work in the 1930s showed sharp and sometimes constructive contrasts with the International Style, particularly because in this decade he was deep in what his latest biographer calls a "continuous and almost compulsive attempt to build the perfect house." [19] Some of the terms were curiously archaic. Though he worked steadily toward greater simplicity of elevation and closer affinity to site, in details he stayed reminiscent of the artsy-crafty ideas fashionable in his youth when his mother and aunts, schoolteachers all, kept putting John Ruskin and William Morris in his hands. Further, in his early independent practice he "talked art, crafts and philosophy by the hour," [20] said one of his sons, with Elbert Hubbard, the advertising man turned handicraft-cultist sage whose self-promoted career was an inadvertent parody of turn-of-the-century aesthetics. As late as 1940 this influence is evident in the table lamps for the Lloyd Lewis house, and his rejection of Gropius' endorsement of mass production is just as evident in his having them specially made, all but the electric sockets and bulbs and the screws that hold them together. Chez Gropius had little ornament for its own sake and few details about which one could ask what's that here for without getting a Functionalist answer, whereas in the fireplace chimney breast of Wright houses the flat stones jut out a bit here, recede there in patterns pleasantly resembling weather-worn strata but for no other purpose. Such a thing was necessarily laid not with the relative speed and insouciance of a bricklayer dealing with standard bricks but with the deliberate slowness of a Yankee farmer laying up a dry wall of no-two-shaped-alike stones from his pasture. And if the resulting effect was not exactly what Wright had in mind—or if he changed his inner vision while the job was doing—it all had to be redone. The inner vision was what counted.

Because it was his inner vision. He attained an extreme degree of the professional arrogance that suffuses twentieth-century architects of stature. He liked to tell about the lady who asked Louis Sullivan to design her a "Colonial" house. "Madam," Sullivan said, "you'll take what we give you." [21] As a cub Wright managed to meet clients' wishes for wooden "Queen Anne" villas with multiple verandas and corner towers with conical roofs. But as soon as he got his professional feet under him, the tendency was toward not what the man paying for it wanted but what Wright wanted to try out at his expense. If lucky, the client succumbed to Wright's explanations gradually enough to be allowed minor suggestions. However that went, he usually ended with a highly livable house willy-nilly. Consider Falling Water, the masterpiece built for Edgar Kaufmann, Pittsburgh department-store millionaire. The Kaufmanns chose the site in their nobly wooded country estate in order to get the best view of a lovely waterfall in the local stream. Wright built the house *over* the waterfall with no window bearing on it because, he said, if one could always look at it, its beauty would become banal,* whereas if one had to go out on the balcony and lean over the balcony to see it, one would always appreciate it at full value. The resulting edifice—basically two superimposed "trays" of reinforced concrete cantilevered over the fall—is

* Princess Ruth of the royal house of Hawaii felt differently. In the 1880s she built herself a magnificent wooden mansion of Victorian gimcrackery in Honolulu, lived in it awhile, then rented the house across the street and moved into that. Because, she said when they asked why, when she lived inside her beautiful house, she couldn't see it and admire it as it deserved.

deservedly famous for dramatic asymmetry the more striking for its background of forest trees. Its generous living room centers on a fireplace—Wright's atavistic love for fireplaces usually had admirable consequences—based on a great boulder shouldering up through the floor; out from that focus spreads one of the finest examples of his harmoniously informal uses of space. The incessant rush and rumble of the waterfall belowside do sound like a gigantic air conditioner in bad repair, but curiously, the effect soon becomes pleasant.

So far not just so good, excellent. But Falling Water's guest-room ceilings are impractically as well as oppressively low—a fault common in Wright's dwellings; he candidly admitted that had he been taller than five feet eight inches he might have scaled things differently. The tinting of the concrete surfaces of Falling Water is a pastellish tan that is—in our culture—disconcertingly reminiscent of the free-form plaster entrance to the House of Fun in an amusement park. And inevitably the concrete has cracked and stained into the shabbiness apparently inseparable from the medium. " ... once ... simple concrete begins to age," Russell Lynes has noted in *The Taste-makers,* "it [looks] even more terrible than when it was new, and it seems to age awfully fast. A crack in a clear surface [shows up] like a scar on a woman's cheek." [22] Not that Wright was to blame for that architectural fact of life. Only, like many of yesterday's and today's architects, he seemed to learn little from experience in that respect. For the next twenty-five years he occasionally used vast concrete surfaces likely to seam and blotch. He was far better off with the weathering wooden siding of the smallish, long-overhang Usonian dwellings growing out of the ground like horizontal mushrooms, snug as a Hobbit's hole withinsides, that he put his artsy-crafty soul into in the 1930s.

"Usonian" leads back into the crankishness that afflicted him during the latter half of his amazingly active long life. The tendency was in the family: His father, a rolling stone of more charm than stability, doubled as preacher and music master in New England and Wisconsin and then abandoned his growing family when Frank was fifteen years old, leaving the boy only a lifelong passion for Bach and Beethoven. The wife thus left to secure a divorce was one of a large family clan of Welsh farmers settled in southern Wisconsin. In his adolescence Frank did much old-fashioned farmhanding and never lost his pride in a knowledgeable grasp of everything a farm involved. One of his mother's many brothers, Jenkin Lloyd-Jones, became a prominent Unitarian minister in Chicago, consistently supporting liberal and latitudinarian causes; his Lincoln Center was a Chicago institution, his remarkable white beard an ornament of Henry Ford' Peace Ship foray to Europe in 1915. Frank's mother and two of her sisters were early committed to what came to be called Progressive Education. Among them they brightened the boy's childhood with the gaily colored gadgets developed by the great German Friedrich Froebel, plied him, as aforesaid, with Ruskin and Carlyle and assured him that he would grow up to be a great architect. A sub-vegetarian food crankism of the cracked-wheat-and-cold-carrots sort was another of Mrs. Wright's notions.

Late in the 1920s, as he was rounding his sixtieth year, Wright gathered a shifting group of architectural disciples to sit at his feet and absorb architectural wisdom in a new-built homestead on one of the Lloyd-Jones family's hilltops in Wisconsin. He called it Taliesin,* the name (meaning "shining brow") of a Welsh prophetic bard, for he always made a great deal of his Welsh descent. Gradually his growing overweeningness and his young men's devoted subservience blended into a vague cult of the Good Life to be lived in elegant, thriftily planned houses, each on its own acre of intensively cultivated land, by families closely bound one to another in a diffuse cooperative community. Wright called this Usonianism.† Broadacre City was the name of the projected settlement for which he and his pupils worked out an elaborate model, including a number of his previous designs, that was displayed here and there in the 1920s. Edgar Kaufmann, son of the Falling Water client, gave the money to make it. "City" was a misnomer. The scheme envisaged four square miles of a bucolic extended village that, though it sought to make use of the automobile and the power grid, retained many of the archaic Hubbard-Roycrofter overtones that—happily on the whole—Wright never sloughed off.

---

* This first Taliesin, of markedly Japanesy design, burned out when a manservant ran amok, set fire to it and killed Wright's incumbent mistress, her two children and several craftsmen working on the place. The second also burned when near completion. The third, still used in summer by the student fellowship that Wright's widow supervises, may be Wright's work at its most typical and winning. It is known as Taliesin East to distinguish it from Taliesin West near Phoenix, Arizona, the highly stylized complex of desert-oriented buildings that Wright built much later to house the fellowship in winter. This account of the Taliesins is necessarily scamped. The extraordinary and often traumatic marital and legal troubles that made Wright front-page news in the 1920s are altogether omitted. My chief concern is with the public Wright of buildings and public soundoffs—that is, with him as cultural phenomenon.

† This had nothing to do with the Production for Use slogan of many radicals of the 1930s. He derived it from *U*nited *S*tates *O*f *N*orth *A*merica and apparently hoped it would emphasize both the American quality of his ideas and be polite to Canada and Latin America by ceasing to monopolize "America." He said *(Autobiography,* 35) that Samuel Butler invented "Usona" as proper designation for the United States. Twombly's recent biography of

" ... a marvellously engaging flight of fancy," Peter Blake of the *Architectural Forum* called it, " ... a society devoted to leisure and pleasure ... pursuit of the arts ... a sort of modern Garden of Eden, complete with vineyards, baths, facilities for physical culture, a circus, stables ... nine sectarian temples surrounding a central edifice devoted to universal worship. . . ." [23] How long had it been since Blake had last seen the Garden of Eden? He was sounder attributing some of the special flavor of Broadacre City to Wright's third wife, a Montenegrin lady adherent of the consciousness-enhancing movement founded in France in the early 1920s by a probably Russian quasi-guru known as Gurdjieff. Thus, the economics of Broadacre City leaned on the Social Credit cult fashionable at the time and endorsed by both Gurdjieff's disciples and Ezra Pound. The emotionally and physically hygienic dances that Gurdjieff taught were part of the fellowship's regimen along with dabblings in spiritualism and blister-raising sustenance farming. Less definitely Broadacre City also showed traces of the artsy-crafty communes that certain anarchists envisaged. But such references, however valid, are not indispensable. Wright was capable of dreaming up the Broadacre kind of doctrinaire whimsicality on his own without outside prompting.

Broadacre City never got beyond the model stage, but it did pose problems in small-house design that bore fine fruit in the Usonian group of dwellings. Critics are justifiably respectful about the administration building, all glass tubing, fluid shapes and load-bearing piers shaped like Gargantua's golf tees, that Wright built during this period for Johnson's Wax at Racine, Wisconsin,* and about his contemporary churches that play pyramidal games with the basic design of the old Methodist preaching house. George Nelson included Wright's chapel for Florida Southern University in his list of "fourteen great American structures." [24] But properly to gauge Wright as a force affecting his and our time, one must note primarily that among them the Usonian

---

Wright locates the term in Butler's *Erewhon;* only it isn't there. Not that it matters; Erewhon was an imaginary country to begin with. John Sergeant of University College-London, close student of Wright's work, considers Usonianism a key to his career after 1929.

* The adjacent laboratory tower, to my mind more successful aesthetically, was not built until after World War II. Here the wrongheaded disregard of intended use that so often crops up in Wright's work is represented by design of the work floors so that light from the windows is square in the eyes of those seated at the built-in desks. Wright's dwellings often show that same flaw. Then the Lewis house has a doorway into the master bedroom too narrow for a size 40 man. And Wright's favorite and pretty device of lighting a corridor with wooden cutouts in abstract shapes and glazing them leaves the glass very hard to clean.

houses so fruitfully developed (this is Blake's summary) "the car-port,*
the floor with integral radiant heating, the built-in furniture, the open
kitchen, the utility core, the modular plan, the pinwheel growth of that
plan out of a central fireplace ... realistic and beautiful solutions to
living in America in our day." [25]

So Usonianism left a fertile residue. In contrast, nothing at all came
of the visions that Chicago's projected Century of Progress fair
inspired in Wright in the early 1930s. His admirers in New York City
held a meeting to protest failure of the directors of the fair to include
him among its architects. To give them something to chew on, he
made a speech about how, if asked, he would have gone about
designing it. Why not a 245-story, 2,500-foot skyscraper to dwarf the
just finished Empire State Building and remain after the fair along
with a gigantic auditorium at its foot as permanent civic assets? That
could be, he promised, "beautiful as the Eiffel Tower never was (and
the Eiffel Tower would reach only well below its middle) ... clouds
might artificially or naturally drift across its summit ... beacons from
the top would reach adjoining states...." [26] Or, suppose that inadvisable—it did have an ominous feel of the Tower of Babel—put the whole
show under a 500-foot square canopy slung on multiple cables
drooping from 500-foot pylons; † the rainwater could gush out of
interior fountains fed by draining the low-swagged center. Or float the
whole show on light metal pontoons connected by floating bridges and
interspersed with huge fountains and floating gardens: " ... three
ideas, genuine and practical," [26] he told Alexander Woollcott, Lewis
Mumford, Raymond Hood and the other protesters, and 300 more to
be whipped out on demand.

It sounds like Cyrano de Bergerac, whom Wright admired, telling
De Guiche about his several plans to reach the moon. Yet Wright was
an originally able engineer. His pinned-together concrete slabs for a
"Mayan" house in California and his fragmented cantilevering for the
Imperial Hotel in Tokyo ** proved as practical as they were new and

---

* The West's builders of motor courts' roofing over the spaces between
cottages to begin the evolution toward the modern motel probably also had a
hand in developing the carport; cf. my *Great Times,* 360.

† This may be regarded as expanding a serious proposal *c.* 1850 from James
Bogardus, inventor of the iron column-and-girder buildings that sired the
steel-skeleton skyscraper. He wanted to house New York City's Great
Exhibition (on the site where Bryant Park now is) within "an iron-framed,
glass-lighted sort of circus tent with a sheet-iron roof hung on cables." (Cf. my
The Americans, 624.)

** It was not true, as the public heard, that this building was the only one
in Tokyo to withstand the disastrous earthquake of 1923. Some dozens of
other buildings constructed on more workaday principles also held together;
cf. Farr, *Frank Lloyd Wright,* 169–70. The reason for all the talk about it at

celebrated. So did the golf-tee columns in the Johnson's Wax project. Had those in charge of the Century of Progress taken him up on one of those fantasies, it is not unthinkable that he'd have made it stick. Less imaginative architects remained in charge, however, and then the financial pinch of the Depression turned their fashionably pretentious plans upside down. Whether or not he was at all serious about them, Wright's pontoons and pylons were never tested.

Obviously much of his genius—and genius he was—came of his ability to choose to take seriously anything he did, felt, thought or said. He was hardly susceptible to youthful exuberance when, already middle-aged, he told Hubbard of his purpose to become superior to all previous architects as well as to those to come. Blake described this hypernarcissism as "a delight to ... all who knew him." [27] Twombly postulates a twinkle in the eye modifying self-admiring pronouncements. Mrs. Lloyd Lewis, who, with her distinguished journalist husband, knew him well a long time and went through house building with him, concurs. Indeed, this extravagance in self-assertion tempts one to surmise that most of it was trademark showing off like Mark Twain's white suit, Oscar Wilde's knee breeches, George Bernard Shaw's Jaeger costume. Thus, Wright did go in for billowing tweed capes and to the end of his days tied his wide, soft cravats Roycrofter-fashion. Shaw's twinkle may well have been there when he described himself as greater than Shakespeare. But it is also possible that Wright's case may have been more like that of W. C. Fields or Muhammad Ali, the ebulliently egocentric personality simultaneously letting itself soar spontaneously while deliberately understanding the promotional value of building up a towering image of an universally recognizable "character" like Mickey Mouse in the Macy's parade. After a while the twinkle, suppose it ever were there, loses pertinence. Even the sympathetic Twombly suggests that Wright early developed "a mild paranoia," [28] having cited his attacks on rivals threatening to gain stature as too corrosive for twinkles to neutralize. His friend Carl Sandburg's admiring biography of Abraham Lincoln roused him to feverish denunciation of "The great fanatic who invented conscription-in-a-democracy, and by way of white slavery drove black-slavery into the body-politic instead of banishing it ... [waving] the Stars and Stripes over a devastated South, where a culture might have taken root that would have cured its own evils from within if any real help had come from the North." [29] The flavor of that peevish amateur revisionism is unmistakably paranoid.

And its windiness is as notable as it is symptomatic. One need only visit the two Taliesins and browse in Wright's printed works to discern

---

the time was that the earthquake showed there had been no grounds for the grave misgivings about Wright's unorthodox design.

how often he was in deadly earnest about his own superlative qualities and the "organic architecture" that he prescribed for the social and spiritual regeneration of humanity. Thus:

> The Usonian citizen ... on his own acreage [will be] no longer a man to be afraid or to be afraid of ... because [he] will learn how expanded light, spacious openness and firm cleanliness of significant line in oneness of the whole may be his own, and how all may add up to his stature as a man among men ... beauty is concerned with him and he with beauty. With a sense of rhythmic quality in the appropriateness of plane to quiet length of line, he is able to trace the flowing simplicity of melodious contours of structure as he sees them in what he does to the land itself. ... The Usonian ... will have truth of form or he will have none! This goes out from him to his familiars and to establish better social and economic relations with other nations. ... The simplicities of Laotze and Jesus would dawn afresh. ... "[30]

Or:

> ... the real seeker for Truth ... with rectitude, amplitude and impartiality lets the shallow surf of erudite self-assertion break upon itself and roll back where it came from. Bred to greatness and splendor by Art and Science, Architecture has cosmic destinies yet undreamed of ... by the critics.[31]

Such megalomanic logorrhea shows Wright to be in one sense a bridge between the confident Victorian times in which he was born and the frustratingly self-conscious times when he defied conventional engineering in the Johnson's Wax project. Rhetorically such stuff has significantly familiar odors: Ruskin and Carlyle, yes, and the almost equally extravagant pronouncements of Louis Sullivan. But the context of the 1930s affords him palliation. By then numerous architects of stature were talking and writing almost as windily, building up an aesthetic habit of interminable theorizing and arrogating to one or another art hegemony over its matrix society. Gropius, too, for instance, in spite of the cool pragmatism of his techniques, came around presently to this sort of thing: " ... our society ... has apparently forgotten the importance of the creative artist. ... His Apollonic work is of the greatest significance for the development of a genuine democracy. ... To become fully mature a democracy must bestow the highest prestige upon the artist." [32] That is the same overweeningness coming around to meet Wright's from the other direction. Maybe the most generally familiar expression of it is in Ayn Rand's *The Fountainhead,* in terms that sound like Elinor Glyn plagiarizing Irving Stone.

Molière presumably thought it joking fantasy to set the dancing master and music master of *Le Bourgeois Gentilhomme* persuading themselves that if only everybody learned dancing—no, music—the world would suddenly turn all prosperous and peaceful.* But in our time the artist hoping to be taken seriously may find it advisable to treat a considerable number of people—they are often all too willing—to his views on art as key to social and moral and emotional validity. Wright can hardly be blamed for all that, only for setting a lamentably prolix and conspicuous example. In fairness one must note that he was also sometimes pithy. He told a Los Angeles audience that their city was "much worse than the average American city because there is so much more of it to be ugly" [33] and some University of Chicago students that "they went into college plums and came out prunes." [34] Nevertheless, to the wreath of superlatives that he awarded himself should have been added a claim to have been the greatest amateur windbag of all time—the greatest, that is, who was neither philosopher, writer, politician nor minister of the gospel. They are professionals.

The delusions of grandeur plaguing architects were the more ironic because the profession failed to make itself significant in an apparently promising field much discussed at the time—prefabricated housing. That was assumed to be the next great field for assembly-line manufacturing wedded to ingenious streamlined design. Once the dwelling is the *machine à habiter,* it follows that it not only can but should be mass-produced in a limited range of models with interchangeable parts like the automobile or the harvester. Some saw in it the dynamic new industry that would rescue the nation from the Slough of Depression.

Such talk rose higher when Buckminster Fuller, early in his career as technological Messiah, exhibited his Dymaxion House—a sort of habitable Japanese lantern made of impeccably modern materials; floors and roofs cantilevered out from a central pier that contained the heating and plumbing arrangements. The prospective saving in labor costs was immense, for the structural elements arrived on the site ready-shaped. The whole thing could be disassembled and erected elsewhere with nothing like the trouble needed to build a conventional house. Not all of Fuller's high-flying swans of keenly thought-out ideas have proved wild geese. His later geodesic dome, for instance, made

* *Maître de Danse: Tous les malheurs des hommes ... tout cela n'est venue que faute de savoir danser....*
Maître de Musique: Et si tous les hommes apprenaient la musique, ne serait-ce pas le moyen de s'accorder ensemble et de voir dans le monde la paix universelle? ...

itself a place. But this answer to the prefab housing riddle appealed far more to the kind of people who frequent art galleries than to the kind who build and sell houses. The rival efforts of hardheaded business fared no better. Little came of the elaborate plans of the American Radiator Corporation (interested in the heating and plumbing aspects) and the Celotex Corporation (makers of wallboard) to develop a line of prefab houses of more conventional foursquare shape. Even practically infallible Sears, Roebuck & Company tried and came a cropper, too. Each aspirant had duly employed capable architects to design something that would exploit the obvious engineering and economic possibilities while also appealing to a substantial number of people as something to live in. But by 1939 the disinterested report was that though there were fifty-odd companies in the field, large and small, the outlook was highly discouraging: consumer acceptance was dismally low.

The chief blame, however, was laid, probably justly, on the building unions, which naturally resisted anything that would lower the number of man-hours required, and the municipal building codes, which, little changed for decades, served union purposes so well that effective revision was about as likely as a visit to the moon. In the mid-1930s, however, while prefab-minded engineers calculated and architects still tried to make the most of wallboard and modular units, real prefab housing by another name was born and growing lustily right under their noses as a by-product of the cult of the automobile. Its germ was the two-wheeled trailer cobbled up by the Tin Can Tourist of the 1920s * to haul his tent and heavier baggage in his gypsyings to Florida and California. As improved highways made heavier trailers feasible, he tried making them big enough to sleep in, eliminating the tent. Making it tall enough to stand up in led to a coal or kerosene stove ... a folding table ... a water tank and sink, an evolution that in a few years eventuated in a towed "touring trailer" or "rolling home"—it took awhile for the nomenclature to settle down.

Some attributed the rapidity of this development to the Depression as unemployed men loaded wives and belongings into homemade trailers and cruised the nation's highways, looking for work without having to pay rent. But crude as they were, these contraptions appealed to the prosperous, too. Attracted by the open-road footlooseness of taking your house with you like a snail, people of substance, particularly retired couples, ordered from men trained in automobile bodywork more elaborate jobs. Small companies—the Aerocar Company of Detroit, the Covered Wagon Company of Mount Clemens, Michigan, and so on—pushed the infant industry along. Their products

---

* See my *Great Times* (1974) pp. 320–21.

ran up to eighteen feet long, six to seven wide, with not only stoves
and beds and sinks but showers, refrigerators, even air conditioning.
The basic material was plywood for strength and lightness on a steel
frame with dead-air cells in the roof as elementary insulation.
Flamboyant Senator Robert R. Reynolds of North Carolina found it
good publicity to tour far and wide in his Aerocar "Land Yacht." In
the presidential campaign of 1936 the Democrats sent all over the
country forty such trailers painted red, white and blue, each containing
two spellbinders and the best obtainable public address systems. The
attention that they attracted was just as good publicity for the rising
trailer cult as for FDR. The US Public Health Service sent into
underprivileged areas trailer-borne dental and venereal disease crews.
They made fine traveling showrooms and temporary headquarters for
scientific and engineering work in desolate places. But the chief
purpose was domestic, usually Mom and Pop enjoying wanderlust.
The affluent intellectual showing off his new trailer in Lionel Trilling's
Middle of the Journey says, "I must have Scythian blood. You know,
the ancient Scythians went around with little wicker houses. ... " [35]
Some of those fancy jobs cost up to $5,000 in Depression dollars.

Motorists on narrow, winding roads were bitter when either slowed
down for miles and miles behind a dawdling, weaving car-and-trailer
ensemble or committed to the nasty risk of passing its inordinate
length. Traffic authorities had new problems in keeping the things off
congested or limited-access highways. But production was already at
least 60,000 a year by 1935, and manufacturers, scenting the big time,
were reaching for 1,000,000, whipping up capacity as fast as they could
manage and their banks permit. Within a few years the consequent
output potential became important in supplying emergency housing
for workers in new-created war industry in outlandish places.

Meanwhile, the question of what to do with hundreds of thousands
of these cumbrous vehicles was reaching solution—of a sort. They
could not be left to clutter the margins of highways. First in California
and Florida, gradually later in less favored parts of the country, arose
the trailer park—a dry-land marina where scores and soon hundreds of
these minimum habitable boxes for people could come to a mooring
among their kind and hook up to city water and electricity at a few
dollars a day. Evolution took charge again. Having hauled that ton-
and-a-half Aerocar 1,000 miles at an embarrassingly slow pace and
great cost in gasoline, Mom and Pop saw no good reason to take to
the road again at once. They stayed a week ... a month.... Presently
Mom planted zinnias around the door, and Pop went to Sears,
Roebuck for an awning to sit under in camp chairs after supper. Soon
he put jacks under the corners and suppressed the pneumatic-tired
wheels. Now the trailer was a fixture. The car was used for hither-and-

yonning but never again hooked up to haul it back to Sandusky. The owner of the trailer park turned landlord of a new kind of real estate subdivision, renting sites and facilities and often also dealing in new and secondhand trailers. As the things grew still larger, owners wanting to move grew less likely to put the wheels back on and tow it themselves, more likely to hire a professional trucker with an over-the-road tractor. Indeed, the new models ran so large that the family car could no longer haul one. At this point, just when the thing had practically lost mobility, the term "mobile home" took over. Though the specimens one meets towing along the interstate with WIDE LOAD on the stern are menacingly mobile at the moment, once they reach their destined slots in a trailer park, odds are 20 to 1 they will never move again, just sit there constituting the low-ticket prefabricated housing toward which architects and big industry struggled in vain. As Nathaniel Owings, one of the founding partners of the illustrious firm of Skidmore, Owings & Merrill, has glumly written, the deadlock between entrenched influences and progressive floundering "squeezed out from between the trailer and the house the worst of both—the mobile home." [36]

One reason why uncoordinated groping thus outdid organized planning was that the planners had taken things by the wrong end. Fuller and the big companies envisaged prefabricating the elements, maybe even some subassemblies, for final assembly at the site, which was bound to stir up the building trades. As late as 1936 William B. Stout, the imaginative engineer who designed those trimotor airplanes for Henry Ford, was cooking up a trailer made specially to carry the components of a prefab house to be put together here today, there tomorrow, like an uncommonly substantial tent, whereas what the lackadaisical collaboration of the Tin Can Tourist, the Depression and the appeal of playing house-on-wheels came up with—the house trailer all assembled before it reached the site, which left the unions no leg to stand on—had got at it the other way. Now the things squat there by millions, made mostly of spit and cheese, housing whores here, contractors' crews there, honeymooners and Mom and Pop everywhere, collective eyesores and occasions of savage community backbiting. Hypertrophy has now gone so far that one hears of a mobile home in Palm Springs, California, costing $150,000 and including "a grand piano and 17th century French chandelier ... a basement and a sun deck and an elevator connecting the two." [37] Never mind that absurdity, however; the run of large mobile homes represents the best output-per-man-hour value in habitable cubage that the American economy—or any other—ever saw. It makes one wonder what good it is having brains and taste—which, of course, many architects do have.

* * *

In 1939 MOMA had grown out of her quarters in a Fifth Avenue office building. The new ones were her own palace designed in International Style a few blocks away. The Rockefellers provided the site in the shadow of their towering new Rockefeller Center. It is not clear (or really outsiders' business) how much of the support that MOMA had through Mrs. Rockefeller came from her husband's family and how much from Senator Aldrich's daughter's considerable private fortune. But one can say that in view of what midtown Manhattan real estate was worth even in the 1930s, that parcel of land was an extremely handsome birthday gift from John D., Jr., to an institution about which he felt lukewarm. Picasso *et Cie*. were not for him. Indeed, Rockefeller Center seems to have been occasion for an amiable aesthetic tug-of-war between him and his staff and his wife and their son Nelson, who shared his mother's tastes, over what kind of art would ornament it.

Son's great victory was the recruiting of Diego Rivera, then at the height of his fame as king of Mexico's revolutionary muralists, to paint the focus of interest in the lobby of Rockefeller Center's chief building, and that—see later—blew up in his face. The decor of the whole project, most particularly the Radio City Music Hall, was nontraditional Art Deco. But John D., Jr., continued respectfully to disagree with his clever wife until, as the Depression got under way, she began to amass, under guidance of art critic Holger Cahill, her illustrious collection of "American primitive" art, now housed in its own suavely Georgian building as adjunct to her husband's Colonial Williamsburg. It is gratifying that the two worked out this bridge to aesthetic harmony. For Colonial Williamsburg was John D., Jr.'s, monument to his loyalty to traditionalism. The family's persistence in building Rockefeller Center in the teeth of hard times had a strong, commendable flavor of economic pump priming about it. But the resurrection of Williamsburg was already under pick and shovel when Black Thursday struck and remained a stubbornly fostered luxury through thick and thin.

Though the Rockefellers were blown-in-the-bottle Baptists, the man who turned John D., Jr., into the prince who kissed Williamsburg awake was a parson of the more august Episcopalian persuasion—the Reverend Dr. W. A. R. Goodwin, professor of biblical literature at Williamsburg's College of William & Mary (oldest seat of more or less higher learning south of the Charles River) and rector of its venerable Bruton Parish Church. The decay of the town distressed him. Though never more than a sizable village, it had nevertheless been laid out by a royal governor as Virginia's pre-Revolutionary capital and was focus of the doings that made the Old Dominion southern pivot of Independence. *C.* 1925 its broad main street was disfigured by telephone poles and a central strip of concrete. Bruton Church and the main college building, reputedly built from sketches by Sir Christopher Wren, were falling apart, though still used for the original purposes. The governor's palace, once one of the Colonies' best edifices, had disappeared, replaced by an ice plant and a powerhouse. The main line of the Chesapeake & Ohio ran where its garden had been. Most buildings surviving from the great days were masked by or build into newer construction, usually slatternly. The handsome brick powder magazine, for instance, was part of a corrugated-iron garage with a sign: *TOOT-An-Kum-In."* *

Goodwin had learned fund raising in work for William & Mary. At annual meetings of the council of Phi Beta Kappa (founded there) he cultivated the acquaintance of a fellow council member, the younger Rockefeller. Never was the belief that it pays to belong to the right fraternity better justified. Having long been natural targets for every good cause in America, the Rockefellers were formidably skilled in evasive action. But Goodwin hooked and played his man subtly well. Within two years John D., Jr., was financing the rebirth of Williamsburg, beginning with the taverns and the capitol, vanished like the palace.

In the form and on the scale contemplated the scheme had no precedent, or maybe Goodwin had read the last chapter of H. G. Wells' *The World Set Free* (1914), in which the highly civilized persons building a hygienically rational culture in a world just devastated by atom bombs—yes, Wells had such things nicely anticipated—in 1933 are "clearing up what is left of London ... to repair the ruins and make it all as like as possible to its former condition. ... Westminster ... suffered badly ... but there are plentiful drawings to scale of its buildings. ... Already [in 1960] it becomes difficult for us to recall the old times. ..." [38] Wells' society of 1960 could embark on so elaborate a toy because it had on tap inexhaustible atomic energy and almost inexhaustible human leisure to guide it. Goodwin's patron-collaborator had neither, but his expenditures on Williamsburg were an awesome demonstration that, no matter how Depression blasted and paralyzed upstarts, the Rockefeller fortune was in its own way inexhaustible, too. For a guess this scheme reverently to revive the good old days—or their empty shells—cost fifty times what Abby Aldrich channeled into MOMA's first ten years.

Observing fanatic secrecy to keep Rockefeller's name out of it—a stipulation carried out in the teeth of probability—Goodwin himself

---

* It probably must be explained that this was part of the fashionable hullabaloo of the early 1920s over the extravagantly publicized opening of Tutankhamen's tomb in Egypt. Among other consequences were Grauman's Egyptian Theater in Los Angeles and "King Tut" textile designs.

handled the buying of pertinent real estate. It made talk when the incumbent of Bruton Parish, whose lack of worldly goods was known, began to write a stream of checks that, by the time all requisite parcels were assembled, totaled more than $2,000,000. Gossip provided a lightning rod by hinting that the source of it all was Henry Ford, another symbol of boundless wealth, known to be rehabilitating the Wayside Inn at Sudbury, Massachusetts. The suspicion was so strong that the local Ford dealer tried to curry favor with Henry by offering to let Goodwin buy the first of the new Model As to be released in Virginia.

Digging began in 1926. Six years later, at the very bottom of the Depression, the reborn Raleigh Tavern opened as first demonstration of what the past was like. Delay was implicit in the meticulous archaeology and craftsmanship on which John D., Jr., Goodwin and their hired experts insisted. Once the railroad was relocated—at Rockefeller expense—the site of the palace was sifted, as intensively as if gold were being panned, for bits of crockery, brick, glass, hardware, plaster, anything study of which would help toward authenticity. Craftsmen were trained in obsolete skills without which the new-burnt bricks, for instance, would lack proper texture. Archives on both sides of the Atlantic were ransacked for illuminating data, maybe just a few words in a diary about garden layout. From the Huntington Library in California came Jefferson's sketch of the palace; from the Bodleian Library at Oxford engravings of 1740 showing the exteriors of palace and capitol. . . .

In its first twenty years this zealous and ghastly expensive program demolished 625 post-1800 buildings; completely rebuilt 341 of which only foundations were found; rehabilitated and partly rebuilt 70-odd pre-1800 buildings; replanted in authentic fashion 75 acres of pre-1800 gardens. Two miles of concrete sidewalk were replaced by brick, gravel or whatever research shows was there in Patrick Henry's time. Hitching posts were restored, the wires of the telephone system decently buried. Even now, decades later, outlying quarters are still getting conscientious finishing touches.

In the several revived taverns waiters serve in knee breeches and loose-sleeved shirts. Bills of fare offer some dishes that Patrick Henry would recognize. The gentlewomen-hostesses who herd the tourists through the palace and George Wythe's compactly elegant house wear paniers and lace caps. In the detached cookhouse of the palace black cooks tend the wood fire in the great fireplace and skillfully juggle all those wrought-iron devices for roasting, baking, boiling, toasting, frying, broiling. The blacksmith shop forges them in the old shapes. All up and down the manicured streets new-painted but authentic hanging signs proclaim gunsmith, silversmith, baker, cooper, cordwainer, cabinetmaker *et al.,* showing how our forefathers made the artifacts that our museums reverently preserve. Elsewhere are printer printing, apothecary dispensing—also in knee breeches and buckled shoes.

Such things are common now in many contexts coast to coast. All follow the seminal example of Williamsburg. The previous few efforts at responsible restoration had been fragmentary. Maintenance, let alone restoration or reconstruction, of august old buildings such as Independence Hall and Mount Vernon was never so conscientious. As Williamsburgery has spread, however, one now visits revivified buildings once housing eccentric German sects at Ephrata, Pennsylvania, and New Harmony, Indiana; admirably restored old ironmaking colonies at Allaire, New Jersey, and Hopewell, Pennsylvania. Artificiality is more candid at Sturbridge, Massachusetts, and Shelburne, Vermont, eclectic collections of buildings from several periods that nevertheless seem to have group validity of their own. Nor does frank artificiality put one off much in the reconstructions of the Pilgrims' grim little hamlet at Plymouth, Massachusetts, the Lost Colony's stockade at Roanoke Island, North Carolina.... Some of those come near Williamsburg's standards of authenticity. But few have commanded the order of resources that enables Williamsburg to be obsessively thorough.

Rockefeller's two major contributions were the funds to pay the pipers of such elaborate tunes—and probably that thoroughness. No bricks-and-mortar work began until he had mastered the details. No garden was planted until he had studied it out with the landscaper on the spot. His and Goodwin's aim, an associate said, was to create *"visual history* ... based on truth and accuracy ... a vivid picture of the men and women who lived in [Williamsburg], their way of life, their sense of proportion, their love of beauty, their self-reliance." [39]

That seeks too much. Doubtless those virtues were shown by the great Virginians who spent a few months a year in Williamsburg for social and public purposes. But that the run of Williamsburgers—lesser planters, craftsmen, white and black servants and their progeny—were consistently high-minded and sensitive is questionable. Even Washington, Jefferson, Wythe and George Mason—the cream of Williamsburg's great names—got into their breeches one leg at a time. To evoke them as always stately clothed and sententious figures from a pseudohistorical movie—such as that with which Williamsburg briefs the tourists—prevents intelligent idea of them. Williamsburg was created by royal governors from overseas who were sometimes venal, petty, stupid or numb, sometimes several of those at once. Stand in the rebuilt capitol as a way to insight in what Jefferson was and did?

His *Notes on Virginia,* which relatively few visitors ever read, convey twenty times as much at far less expense.

To operate Colonial Williamsburg and satellites (the noble Carter's Grove mansion and Mrs. Rockefeller's Museum of American Primitive Art) has recently cost more than $11,000,000 a year. Admissions, sales of artifacts and so on cover maybe two-thirds of that; the rest comes from endowment income. The Rockefellers bought more for their money when endowing the University of Chicago in the 1890s and in the vast sums distributed by their General Education Board. That flaw is inseparable from the rich-man's-hobby natures of Williamsburg. Granted, other rich men's hobbies—yachts, women, pleasure domes, horses—often have educational value only insofar as they are warning examples that never sink in, and at Williamsburg at least a certain educational effect must persist, particularly for children, in the demonstrations of the old crafts and the anachronistic elegances of the buildings and their contents. Even the quiet that persists in spite of the troops of tourists is in itself a subtle lesson. But it cannot be pretended that the place lives up to its official purpose: "To recreate accurately the environment of the men and women of 18th-century Williamsburg." [40] The children giggling at the pillory, staring at the turning windmill and the cannon outside the courthouse, depart unaware of how often their forebears *c.* 1760 let the knocker go untarnished, the hedge untrimmed—and spat tobacco juice on the floor of the publick gaol.

For unless Williamsburg was unlike other Colonial towns 200 years ago, its streets were often foul as a barnyard and its housekeeping year round lacked any of today's primness. Where are the loose poultry, the vagrant dogs, the straying cows and the garbage broadcast behind the taverns? A few horse-drawn vehicles ply the streets, but their droppings quickly disappear. Where are the flies with which Lord Dunmore and Edmund Pendleton must have been familiar? Those reconstructed privies are fresh-painted and lack the stench that must have been the most noticeable feature of the originals. Some of that is unexceptionable. The hostesses can hardly be forbidden to bathe or use deodorants lest they fail to smell as Colonial dames undoubtedly did. But Williamsburg's choosing to be all deliberate elegance, all polish and no spit, leaves it a three-dimensional Kodachrome with colors acceptable only till one happens to think how many of them are untrue. It shares the flaw brought up by Edison when they showed him his old laboratory moved to Henry Ford's Greenfield Village so conscientiously that they had even dug and brought along the very earth from the dooryard. Wonderful, Edison said, "only our floor was never as clean as this." [41] It is a relief in Williamsburg to come on the fire in the cookhouse, for wood ash and greasy iron are incurably and reassuringly untidy, and to see that somebody had the historical sense to let the fence around the windmill stay half fallen down as Colonial fences so often were.

The Greenfield Village that acquired Edison's laboratory and a bewildering myriad other things has an affinity with Williamsburg, but the differences are sharp, and no imitativeness is implied. Henry Ford was at this game before Dr. Goodwin took Rockefeller in tow. Soon after World War I the motor billionaire had embarked on his own strange kind of archaeologizing by creating a filial tribute—restoring to its exact condition *c.* 1880 the demure farmhouse west of Detroit where his mother had reared him. In person and through agents he ransacked antique stores, junkyards, dumps, roadsides and private houses for the very model of wood-burning stove on which Mother had cooked, the very pattern of carpet that lay in her parlor. When he could not recall the exact design of Mother's best china, he had her yard dug up and found enough broken bits to identify it; a complete set of it, correspondingly costly, now fills the rebuilt shelves. Soon it was all spick-and-span, just the way she always kept it—a fire laid in the stove, a new washer in the kitchen pump, the coal oil lamps full, wicks clean and chimneys shiny bright. Nobody lives there but Henry's memories, of course. That, however, amply justified all the pains and expense, which were nothing to him while the tribute to his ego was great. For Mother's shrine was really a monument to the sparse, diligent, ingenious culture from which he sprang, that he did more than any other American to ruin. Not that such a reproach was likely to occur to him. His obsession with that culture's details came of his colossal self-esteem. It made the tiniest thing that had helped shape Henry Ford a very important matter.

This narcissism-by-artifact rubbed off on the famous McGuffey school readers on which Henry's one-room schooling had been based. He led a movement reverently to exhume and reprint them as obviously better for children than the newfangled textbooks of the 1920s—hadn't McGuffey's moral tales and didactic verses resulted in sterling characters like Henry's? Motoring in New England, he came on the disused stage tavern where Longfellow set his *Tales of a Wayside Inn,* including those of Paul Revere and the Birds of Killingworth, both in McGuffey. Henry bought the place in 1923 to refit it as solicitously as he had done Mother's house. Warming to this hobby, he rebuilt complete with working artisans the grist- and sawmills and blacksmith shop that the neighborhood had once supported and moved to a nearby knoll a richly McGuffeyish find—the little red schoolhouse alleged to have been the scene of "Mary's Little

Lamb." For the next twenty years it housed the first four grades of the local school.

To accommodate his fancy, he paid $330,000 to relocate the main highway to Boston; the rest of it cost about $1,000,000. His personal search for the requisite genuine candle snuffers, hoof parers and so on addicted him to antique shopping. He began to buy complete antique dealers' stocks and ship them to the disused tractor plant near Dearborn, Michigan, where he now housed things that had interested young Henry Ford—old steam tractors, old plows, old clocks, old telegraphers' "bugs"—"snowing himself under with duplicates," [42] wrote William C. Richards, shrewdest of his sympathetic biographers. To carry on the spirit of his Wayside Inn he hired a married couple expert in archaic dances—the Victorian schottische and mazurka as well as minuet and Virginia reel—to teach them to the Fords, their guests and staff. Eventually he moved these teachers to Dearborn to instruct Ford executives and their wives. If a certain aide proved clumsy, Henry might drop into his office next morning saying, John, last night you had trouble with that five-step polka, let me show you again—and a billion dollars clutched John around the waist, and off they went, bowing and dipping and capering sidewise. In the private school system that he set up around Dearborn to embody his educational crotchets, Henry had about 22,000 children in dancing lessons. He hoped thus to blunt the effect on them of the jazzy fox-trotting that otherwise was all they would know.

Sidebar buggies, harvesting cradles, shoemakers' lasts, pewter tankards kept piling up in Dearborn. During a transatlantic voyage Henry mentioned to an architect among the passengers that he needed a building properly to house his collections; what would be fitting? Reproduce Independence Hall, the architect said. Today a duplicate Independence Hall screens fourteen acres of floor space displaying Henry's accumulations. Decades of sorting them into something like intelligible order has yet to disguise the highly personal basis on which they were acquired. In the central tower where, in the first Independence Hall, hung the bell that proclaimed liberty unto all the land is a display of Ford memorabilia. Those preparing working drawings in Philadelphia found that the original windows and pilasters were often an inch out of line and suggested correction. No, Henry said, reproduce every error.

Soon he fetched in bodily, Wayside Inn-style, what seemed to him significant buildings for a village with Mother's house as nucleus. The schoolhouse he had sat in as a boy, a chapel built of brick from Mother's birthplace.... The underlying feeling is that of the mid-1800s when he was born. But packrattery soon precluded any Williamsburgish consistency. The guiding principle was: "That interests Mr. Ford, get it for him." Here higgledy-piggledy are the bicycle shop in which the Wright Brothers cobbled up the airplane; an antique covered bridge; a Cape Cod windmill; an old stone cottage from Britain's Cotswolds 3,000 miles away; the courthouse in which Lincoln pleaded his early cases; the railroad depot at which Edison was fired as train newsboy because his chemical studies set the baggage car afire; a cotton gin; an eighteenth century jeweler's shop from London; buildings associated with Luther Burbank, Noah Webster, Charles P. Steinmetz, Stephen Foster. Scholars cast doubt on the authenticity of the alleged Foster cottage. Having had similar trouble about Mary's schoolhouse, Henry shrugged this off stubbornly and caused to be dug near the probably spurious cottage a circular Swanee River, bearing on its narrow bosom a Mississippi type of steamboat. The log schoolhouse associated with McGuffey contained that great man's desk and corner cupboard and—a gesture toward reality—was used in some of Henry's educational projects. But children learning the three Rs in it were spared the cold feet and eyestrain of genuine log-schoolhouse days. It has indirect incandescent lighting and is heated by modern air conditioning, not by a wood fireplace or stove.

Similarly his steamboat, which he sometimes piloted around the circular Swanee like a sternwheel Flying Dutchman, had internal-combustion, not wood-fired steam, engines. A Detroit newspaperman calling on him by appointment in Greenfield Village one evening was directed to the Foster shrine and found Henry seated at its old-timey parlor harmonium "Alone with himself, picking out with one finger ... *Old Folks At Home* with a concentration that excluded all ... the assembly lines everywhere making bread and butter for him and thousands of men he'd never know." [43] Doubtless it also excluded the overtones of the Depression that made Greenfield Village almost as expensive a demonstration as Williamsburg that hard times could not handicap a really superlative fortune.

Thus Ford's rich man's hobby, even more personal than Rockefeller's, reflected his egocentricity and incoherence as Williamsburg did its founder's primness. And here again this immense cost was at least better use of money than chartering quixotic Peace Ships and the financing of anti-Semitic garbage that Henry went in for at the same time he was restoring the Wayside Inn. From the one afternoon I spent with him in 1939, I doubt whether he was capable of making any such distinction in quality; he seemed to me to be verging on the psychotic. Anyway, there is this to be said for Greenfield Village: That past that it conveys is more pertinent to the average American tourist-visitor than Williamsburg's Valhalla of silver-buckled shoes and quill pens. And add that both make more sense than the chewing-gum mock-ups of Disneyland and its imitators.

*   *   *

Seekers after sociological syndromes might see in the timing of American nudism,* which gained its first solid foothold in the 1930s, a subtle result of the Depression—a period during which many unable to afford clothes got together to learn how to do without them? Actually this grim ingenuity is untenable. Black Friday was still two months ahead when, on Labor Day, 1929, a German zealot, Kurt Barthel, having recruited three married couples by advertising in the German-American press, set up the first American nudist colony on the edge of the Great Swamp in northeastern New Jersey. Within two years the nudist gospel was so much in public consciousness that Stuart Chase had to pay his disrespects to it. Notably open-minded, he had long been among many other things an apostle of the 1920s' cult of sunbathing. But nudism, his keen sense of logic discerned, was another matter. Writing for the *Nation* on "If I Were Dictator . . .," he suggested "sunbathing reservations near all large cities" but with the proviso that "the instant one of them turns into a nudist cult it will be summarily abolished." [44] That is, he felt a sharp distinction between his fellow heliophiles, stripped and toasting because they thought it physically hygienic, and doctrinaire nudists, stripping because they thought nakedness part of the Good Life.

Thus stated, the line is easy to draw. But it was an advantage for nudist propaganda that even Chase's sort strayed beyond it. In theory the health-minded sunbather had no need to expose genitalia or mammaries. A girl in a bra-and-G-string bikini gets whatever systemic benefits sunlight affords; so does her boyfriend in briefs. Yet Chase and his heliophile comrades lay on their secluded beach stark naked without the kilted towel usual in locker rooms. One suspects a hint of cryptonudism, a slight relish in exposing before others in the open air what convention held to be immodest. No more than a hint, true, so long as sunbathing company was segregated by sexes. But the thing was unmistakable when the two segregations self-consciously merged with the joys of sunbathing as bridge to the subtle freedoms of coeducational nakedness. In the late 1920s this was reinforced by the sex educationists' urging of parents to strip for their children's psychic edification. Earlier ideological preparation appeared in Edward Carpenter's widely influential *Love's Coming of Age* (first published in America in 1911), which recommended not only homosexuality but

---

* "Nudism" is, of course, an abhorrent Nice Nellyism using a Latinism for the English root "naked," which is the exact equivalent of the Romans' *nudus* and its several Romance derivatives. Since the term is by now as much part of the language as "Christian Science," however, this text uses it to mean "the cult of deliberately going naked in company composed of both sexes in the belief that to do so is somehow positively virtuous and psychologically as well as physically healthy." I balk at calling a naked human being "nude"—in this book he will appear as naked as he was born.

also social nakedness as beautiful and spiritually rewarding. Impatience with the code of the bathing suit probably underlay Jazz Age youth's occasional forays into moonlight skinny-dipping to be giggled about in the dormitory afterward; Greenwich Villagers sometimes did it too just as self-consciously. And the serious enthusiasts had august precedent to point to: The heroine of *Lady Chatterley's Lover* went swimming naked with German university boys even before World War I; add the comradely mixed naked bathing in the early USSR. . . .

Actually formal, idea-fraught nudism—ambivalently ascetic/hedonistic, stuffily/romantically nature-happy—as a social cult was born in Germany. In Germany, George Sylvester Viereck, persistent warhorse of German propaganda, told the pre-World War I world, "Nudeness [is becoming] an accomplishment," particularly in the performances before Berlin's Society of the Friends of Beauty by a certain Olga Desmond "perfectly nude . . . [in] a series of beautiful poses." [45] Already in 1903 one Richard Ungewitter had published at his own expense a book about *Die Nacktheit* (= nakedness) with illustrations that gained attention and converts, and one Paul Zimmermann had set up a resort for people of all ages and both sexes who, for the highest motives, wanted to go naked outdoors in mixed company—which is a fair definition of organized nudism. Within twenty years it had 50,000 devotees, mostly German. Soon called *Freikörperkultur* (= free body culture), it also taught vegetarianism, aesthetic group calisthenics, eschewing alcohol and tobacco, a syndrome persisting in today's nudism. By 1913 a missionary of the cult was discussing it at Mrs. Mabel Dodge's ever-memorable salon on Lower Fifth Avenue. But the formal assault on America's taboo on nakedness except for statues, paintings and lovers in private waited until July, 1927, when New York City saw its first nudist documentary movie, an importation from Germany billed as *The Way to Strength and Beauty*—"a strange outbreak," wrote Oliver Claxton in the *New Yorker,* "one's chief recollection . . . is bodies, mostly nude and only occasionally handsome." [46] The next year E. P. Dutton & Company, a staid house, found itself publishing, in a series of pamphlets written by speculative British intellectuals, *Lady Godiva: The Future of Nakedness* by John Langdon-Davies, a minor pundit with an established American public.

His particular contribution was inextricably to confuse what he called insolation (= sunbath therapy) with German-style ideological nudism. In his view the alleged panacean virtues of the first were inseparable from practice of the second. This confusion also permeated an equally influential paper in the *Psychological Review* by Howard C. Warren, chairman of the Department of Psychology at Princeton, spelling out his conclusions from his elderly dabbling in sunbathing and consequent visit to Zimmermann's nudist ashram in

Germany. He saw no necessary affinity between nudism and vegetarianism but had no misgivings about the Germans' other assumption, that those sunbathing stark naked should stage what amounted to a continuous Sunday school picnic that had lost its clothes: games, community sings, inspirational lectures and enthusiastic, if decorous, camaraderie. Nudist propagandists exploited these gaps in logic. Barthel soon renamed his nudist operation the American Sunbathing Association—the name still survives. The turbulent Reverend Dr. Ilsley Boone's conspicuous nudist resort founded in 1935 at Mays Landing, New Jersey, was called Sunshine Park. His post-World War II nudist magazine he called *Sunshine and Health.**

By then nudism was so much in the public eye that the "World a Million Years Ago" concession at Chicago's Century of Progress supplemented its rearing, snorting dinosaurs with a nudist wedding ceremony. The best man was the show's press agent stark naked, giving all for his art; the parson wore nothing but a tiny goatskin apron; the happy couple nothing whatever. Nudist resorts proliferated, their names often evincing the inspirational naturophile tone that neophytes seemed to like: Sky Farm, Elysia, Zoro Nature Park.... None will be surprised to hear that the largest number of nudist resorts and clubs enrolled in the American Sunbathing Association are located in California. This is not a matter solely of favorable climate. Florida, with a climate as well or better suited, has only five to California's twenty; Arizona only one.

The bohemian overtones marginal in the early movement have now worked up an underground life of their own that undermines the cult as the 1930s knew it.† But for most of its life it has been a curiously bourgeois affair stiff with the asceticisms of its German preceptors. The typical nudist park barred intoxicating drinks, forbade members to touch one another unnecessarily, excluded homosexuals and those belonging to subversive organizations. As in Alcoholics Anonymous, surnames were taboo to prevent embarrassing identifications off the reservation and to promote the leveling camaraderie of looking just as much like a plucked chicken as everybody else. Stripping on arrival was "getting into uniform" or donning "the one-button bathing suit." Menstruating women preferring not to use tampons were allowed shorts. Footgear was permitted; indeed, anybody feeling chilly could

* This section gratefully owes many details to the authoritative *Nudist Society* (1970) by William E. Hartman, Marilyn Fithian and Donald Johnson. None of its authors is responsible for or should be expected to agree with my interpretations.

† This comes chiefly from Sheila E. Johnson, "The New Nudism vs. the Old Nudism, as seen by a Non-Nude Female Anthropologist," *New York Times Magazine,* June 4, 1972.

wear anything he chose, provided there was no taint of taboo modesty in his motivation. Lodgings were simple, food plain, activities centered on swimming pool, volleyball and singing around the campfire. Barring the uniform, it might all have been under the auspices of the YM/YWCA.

Apropos of this atmosphere, nudist resorts claimed and apparently had great success in suppressing men's libidos. Many practicing male nudists told the authors of *Nudist Society* that the prospect of lots of naked women to look at had much to do with drawing them to the movement. Yet, unless all outside observers always lied, the rarest thing in a nudist camp was an observable example of what Warren delicately called "the uncontrollable virile reflex." [47] Study of genuine nudist-cult photographs of the faithful doing nip-ups and standing chow line (not pseudonudist shots of commercial models) suggests that this numbness may be at least partly ascribed to the generous nudist principle laid down in *Nudist Society:* "... physical beauty is not a prerequisite for membership participation." [48] Yet a number of women shapely and smiling enough are also usually in the picture. Maybe the explanation in the *Encyclopedia of Sexual Behavior* is better: "Desexualization ... has been from the beginning one of the major aims of nudism." [49] The animals—God's creatures, often beautiful, always innocent—go genitals exposed and think nothing of it. Why not men and women? The answer—that few animals are monogamous and none shares *Homo sapiens'* unfortunate trait of being in potential heat all the time—is not the sort of thing likely to impress the romantic/ascetic nudist mind.

The cult's dreary respectability was a great help in keeping clear of the law. The early years saw a few police raids, some fines paid, some time spent in jail—particularly where nudists setting up new resorts failed candidly to explain beforehand to local authorities what standards they would enforce and what precautions they would take to avoid scandalizing the neighbors. When the sheriff came checking up, it also helped when he found that these naked folks at Camp Gymnosphere were solid old American stock named Jones, Brown, McIntyre and Hoffman. New Immigrants, blacks, Chicanos and Indians have yet to take much to nudism. Sheriff and nudists sometimes hit it off so well that he deputized a few of their huskiest men so they could arrest and hold trespassing Peeping Toms until he arrived.

Above local levels tolerance took longer to develop. In several states the Catholic Legion of Decency, founded primarily to clean up the movies but also recognizing other menaces, got legislatures to pass antinudist laws—only to see them sluggishly ignored or, when convictions were got, disallowed at one or another level of appeal. The US Post Office fought long and fruitless battles with the Reverend Dr.

Boone's *Nudist* magazine until it learned to stop wasting time and money. One of the handicaps was that in such publications photographic cuts with ventral exposure had pubic hair and genitals brushed out, leaving them no more indecent than the allegorical figures on stock certificates and post office pediments. Thus, inadvertently the postal inspectors jostled nudism symbolically toward its goal—taking the lewdness out of nakedness.

Fifty years ago the lovely girls wearing so little in the *Ziegfeld Follies* moved Gilbert Seldes to deplore misguided efforts to contrast "nudity . . . with nakedness . . . [implying] a sort of Y.M.C.A. aesthetics [holding] that the nude is always pure." [50] Benton, long accustomed to naked bathing at Martha's Vineyard, found himself dismayed by the self-consciousness with which, as the notion spread, "literary folks . . . very emancipated ladies . . . even . . . bankers . . . [trying] to show that they also . . . are capable of free behavior" [51] stood around after dropping the beach robe. I owe another crosslight on nudism to the small daughter of a neighbor who observed her baby brother in his bath and said it was a good thing that hadn't grown on his face. Those airbrush artists had not only kept Boone out of jail, but also tidied up God's creation in His own image by obliterating the most grotesque detail in the whole mammalian morphology—except possibly the painted mandril's blue and red behind.

Nudist theory, rigidly uncompromising, gets little crèdit for the early 1930s' acceptance of men's stripping to the waist on beaches or for the slightly later timid, protobikini display of two inches of female midriff that gave new meaning to the term "two-piece bathing suit." * Those came directly of the sun cult with an assist from cryptoexhibitionism. But there were certain inner consonances between nudist attitudes and what was taken at the time to be another significant breach in conventional erotic morality—Judge John M. Woolsey's famous *Ulysses* decision. For one thing, like nudism and so on, it showed the world stalking ahead on an already projected course heedless of the Depression clouds blackening outside the windows of museum and courthouse. For another, its assumption that lewdness is susceptible to rational analysis, that Priapus can be tamed by intelligence to lie down with the lambs without risk to them or the public good, was not unlike the illusions of nudism.

"The new deal in the law of letters is here," proclaimed Morris Ernst, of counsel for the victorious defense in *United States of America*

* It had meant what is now called a tank suit (in the 1920s an "Annette Kellerman" after the vaudeville and movie star who exploited it in swimming acts), with a tiny attached skirt masking the shape between navel and upper thigh.

v. *One Book Called "Ulysses."* " . . . a major event in history of the struggle for free expression . . . it should henceforth be impossible for the censors legally to sustain an attack against any book of artistic integrity." * His exultation was premature. The decision applied only to the US Customs' procedures without direct effect on the US Post Office's criteria of what should be barred from the mails or local handling of pornography under the police power. And in general it long remained true that, as Charles Rembar, one of the lawyers who has almost succeeded in tidying the matter up, recently wrote: "The *Ulysses* case impressed the literary world but not the other courts." [52] It would be thirty years before one could assume that—Rembar again— "no matter what the courts and legislatures . . . traditionally deemed 'obscene'—no matter what the term meant to laymen or lawyers—the government could not suppress a book if it had merit as literature." [53] For actually Woolsey had only hinted at and then backed away from the criterion of aesthetic quality. Nowadays it looks as if that had been good judgment, for when conscientiously applied, that criterion may prove either impertinent or evanescent.

In 1932 probably hundreds of copies of James Joyce's flagship novel were in the United States, but none was there legally. Since 1920, when the *Little Review* was fined for printing parts of it, it had been on the US Customs' *Index Expurgatorius*. Nobody had sought to publish a licit, expurgated version. The author would certainly never have given permission to clean it up. In any case, to excise its improprieties would have left a disorganized jumble even more baffling than the original seemed to most readers. And to do so would have eliminated much of the prurient appeal that made most potential purchasers want it. One might as well have cut the fighting out of *The Three Musketeers*. Random House, a young firm prospering on the Modern Library, wished to publish *Ulysses* in America and, hoping to clear the track, arranged in early 1932 to import a copy, have it stopped at customs and take the matter to court. Consequently, late in 1933 Judge Woolsey delighted the firm, its lawyers, Joyce and most right-feeling, if confused, persons by deciding that the law against importation of obscene matter did not apply. It was taken to be a victorious culmination of a nibbling away of elder standards of what was legally publishable that had been going on in the courts since the early 1920s.

Woolsey's opinion dealt with two successive issues. As to whether *Ulysses* was pornography: No such thing, he said; its text and most of the critical comment on it persuaded him that it lacked the "leer of

---

* In this section quotations from Ernst and from Woolsey come from the front matter of the Random House-Modern Library edition of *Ulysses*.

the sensualist" and was not "written for the purpose of exploiting obscenity." (Doubtless he meant "economic purpose," for much of the book patently exploits for literary purpose what its characters would certainly have considered obscenity.) Then he drifts into a sort of *obiter dicta* book report—this part was what so pleased Ernst—concluding that though "In many places it seems to me disgusting," it was "sincere and honest ... an amazing *tour de force*...." As for the second issue, whether it tended to "stir the sex impulses or to lead to sexually impure and lustful thoughts"—the legal test of obscenity derived from British and American precedents—he summoned up the hypothetical "reasonable man" to whom the law often refers in tort cases. For a live equivalent he went to two friends of his who were, in his judgment, qualified referees of "average sex instincts." Each read *Ulysses,* and each, asked separately—neither knew the other was being consulted—said, "It did not tend to excite sexual impulses or lustful thoughts." Woolsey added his own "considered opinion [that] whilst in many places the effect on the reader is somewhat emetic, nowhere does it tend to be aphrodisiac. 'Ulysses' may therefore be admitted into the United States."

Observing angels who had kept straight faces while nudism undermined the lust of the eye probably broke into giggles at this well-meant denial that Gertie MacDowell's exhibitionism and Molly Bloom's soliloquy could, in Rembar's phrase, "get you in the groin." [54] For Woolsey's sample of the reading public—two referees and himself—was statistically and sociologically absurd. The three were no better qualified to pronounce on the matter than many other more or less normal and cultivated, presumably middle-aged men. Indeed, to the extent that they were particularly objective and stable—and, for that matter, middle-aged—they were less suitable testing reagents. Having thus mishandled these aspects of the case, Woolsey went on to muddle the issue that Ernst proclaimed taken care of—does aesthetic merit exempt from censorship? Suppose that his two referees or even a statistically adequate sample of *hommes moyen sensuels* had said hell yes, Mrs. Bloom's reminiscences of derring-do could very readily stir one up and the leer of the perverted sensualist is all over a lot of Joyce's stuff about the whorehouse. Would that have been grounds for denying Americans access to so significant a literary work? For it can hardly be maintained that the aesthetic necessarily precludes the prurient.

Woolsey failed to say no, letting it roll to the outfield instead. Augustus N. Hand, the great federal judge who handled the consequent appeal, accepted the chance and exonerated *Ulysses* on the quantitative grounds that "The erotic passages are submerged in the book as a whole and have little resultant effect." [55] That was hardly heads-up ball, however. It raised the problem of degree. What proportion of nonprurient verbiage is necessary to insulate the reader from being turned on? That is, how much aesthetic merit neutralizes how much lewdness? In the succeeding decades the courts, growingly timid about holding that at some point the wings of Art might be clipped, have steadily retreated under inexorably logical lawyers' fire, finding in effect that the slightest hint of artistic merit ransoms any degree of foulness. That practically renounces curbs on pornography, for aesthetic merit is necessarily a matter of subjective opinion. If anybody wants to say so in court, practically anything spelled legibly and getting all the four-letter words in the right syntactical slots may claim enough vestigial merit to qualify.

At least that relieves the absurdity of denying that Chaucer's "Miller's Tale" is a dirty story in order to secure it licit publication. But it also opens the way to leather-and-chains movies about sadomasochism and coprophilia, both highly insanitary one way or another. By now certain advertisements in the amusement section of most newspapers would make Chaucer and Rabelais throw up. No wonder that this moral vacuum has grown so stifling that the US Supreme Court seems inclined to turn the whole insoluble problem back to legislators, lawyers and laymen on a municipal basis. None of them, however, is likely to be of much help because it is the essence of the problem that it is unsolvable on logical grounds. From the angels' point of view the whole frustrating tangle is just another example—angels have been around a long time—of what happens when well-meaning application of obviously civilized thinking is misdirected. And the worst of it is that while the law can throw up its arthritic old hands and abdicate, society cannot.

Woolsey's decision had precedent in less august courts. Much earlier (1933) New York City's famous Society for the Prevention of Vice had had Erskine Caldwell's *God's Little Acre* prosecuted on the usual grounds. Dozens of eminent literary folks testified that it was a serious work of art, portraying significant actuality and so on and on and on. City Magistrate Benjamin E. Greenspan loosed his intellectual powers and found for the defense on grounds that the book did not "tend to incite lustful desires in the normal mind ... if the courts were to exclude books from sale merely because they might incite lust in disordered minds ... literature would very likely be reduced to a relatively small number of uninteresting and barren books. The greater part of the classics would certainly be excluded." [56] It makes one wonder what His Honor thought classics were, for such a criterion would obviously leave the great bulk of Western literature unscathed. Just at random: no hazard for most of Hesiod, Virgil, Shakespeare, Milton, Goldsmith, Jane Austen, Wordsworth, Coleridge, practically all the great Victorian novelists, and on our side of the water *Moby Dick, Walden, Huckleberry Finn, The Red Badge of Courage* ... how disordered one's mind would have to be to get an erotic charge out of the presumably classic works of Henry James!

This repulse by a cultivated jurist apparently so disheartened the society that the following year it let go unchallenged such taboo words as "fucking" in John Steinbeck's *In Dubious Battle.* Other old four-letter favorites were popping up elsewhere not as lavishly as they do today but breaking precedents in a fashion that steadily, if very gradually, let down ancient bars. When, in 1937, the society tried again by hauling James T. Farrell's *A World I Never Made* into court, Magistrate Henry S. Curran, a notably urbane local figure, listened respectfully to such defense witnesses as Bernard De Voto and Carl Van Doren and ruled that the book was obviously not written as "dirt for dirt's sake ... I do not think it obscene ... the defendant is discharged." [57] By then the agenda as well as the premises were widening. Already Sinclair Lewis' *It Can't Happen Here* had been explicit about epicene orgies polluting the White House at the instance of the chief aide of the book's fascist dictator. By 1941 even the *Ladies' Home Journal* boggled not at an article from the house psychiatrist on erotic inversion that said not only "homosexual" but also "fairy" right out and counseled mothers on what to do about that sort of emotional emergency among their young.

A premonitory hunch that bluenosery was wasting away may have encouraged the launching of adventures in unusual raunchiness in 1933 well before the *Ulysses* decision. There was the birth of *Esquire* magazine deliberately aimed at men—a minority previously ignored except for hunting, fishing and boating periodicals for the out-of-door sort and the shootin'-an'-kissin' pulp magazines for the bunkhouse and hallroom trade. In some ways *Esquire* was a mirror image of the long-flourishing women's magazines. It carried expensively illustrated palaver about men's fashions—indeed, in its pupal stage it was a slick paper quarterly aimed at the men's wholesale garment trade—and fiction and articles of better than pulp standards. But its special pitch assumed that Sex was all men's hobby in terms theretofore confined to the French naughty weeklies that Joe College brought home from Paris. Full-color cartoons overplayed harem scenes clotty with voluptuous houris and captions about eunuchs. Its cover mascot was "Esky," a dwarfish, white-tied elderly roué with a puffy mustache and roving, boiled-fish eyes and what those times thought of as penthouse habits. Its tutelary deity was "the Petty Girl"—a full-page, pneumatically pink, impossibly leggy, smirkingly blond, airily draped fantasy—as though somebody had given a precocious adolescent an airbrush to play with and then his big brother had come along and given him a few pointers. In twelve monthly manifestations assembled in a wall calendar or just carefully slipped from the magazine, she became chief exemplar of the new term "pinup." The formula was eventually borrowed and expanded into *Playboy* and on into *Hustler*, with the photograph centerfold in the Petty Girl's slot. Such recent lust-of-the-eye publications make the *Esquire* of 1933 look fumblingly innocent. But *mutatis mutandis*, it had the same purpose: to pour on as much crude come-hither as the traffic of the day would bear.

Also in 1933 a version of come-hither known to the stage as Mae West began loosening up the movies by bursting on the screen in *She Done Him Wrong.* She had been trying to loosen up show business for twenty years—ever since her "muscle dance" (alias the cooch, alias belly dance today) done in a sitting position had been part of her act in small-time vaudeville. Its engineering must have been curious. When the shimmy grew fashionable just after World War I with Gilda Gray its ranking exponent, Miss West's version, though apparently convulsive, caused no proportionate sensation. She was probably ill advised ever thus to go violent; in her later great days the merely robustly sinuous was to be one of her two long suits. The other had been censured as far back as 1916 by *Variety*, reviewing a turn she did with her sister: "She'll have to clean up her style—she has a way of putting dirty meanings into innocent lyrics." * To that sympathetic advice she paid no heed whatever, and the rest is history.

As the 1920s built toward the New Era, she began writing plays in which to star herself as missionary of the leer and smirk on Broadway. *Sex* was the fair-warning title of the first: ". . . a nasty red-light district show," said *Variety*, ". . . would be tolerated in but a few of the stock burlesque houses." The reference to burlesque was sound, but the plot was more complicated than the Minskys' audiences would have liked. Miss West's role was that of a noble prostitute shacked up with a blackmailer. She rescues from his clutches a New York society matron and then, vexed because she has been arrested by the police, gets her revenge on society by seducing the lady's son. Its odor was so strong that Burns Mantle, dramatic critic of the New York *Daily News,* blamed it for being what finally drove the district attorney to raiding dirty shows that season. Miss West drew a $500 fine, ten days in the workhouse—and headline publicity. The next season she wrote and starred herself in *Diamond Lil*, a slightly less gamy affair about the white slave traffic and a handsome police captain posing as an officer of the Salvation Army. Many members of the carriage trade decided

---

* This and many of the following details I owe to Abel Green and Joe Laurie, Jr.,'s *Show Biz from Vaude to Video*, which distills the essences of *Variety*'s first fifty years.

that the heroine's undulations were "amusing"—the term "camp" was not yet invented—and their patronage laid the foundation for the triumphant movie phase of her career.

She had poor luck with her 1928 entry, *Pleasure Man,* which ornamented the murder of a Times Square Don Juan with Skid Row jokes and a group of transvestites billed as "The Bird of Paradise," "The Cobra," "Madam Goddamn," but then more publicity came of its being raided and closed the second night. Already her net effect on her times was, though maybe inadvertent, not unimportant. Every such stretch-the-limit-till-it-snaps book or stage production that got public exposure knocked a chip or two more off the public's shock reflexes. Because *Pleasure Man* and *Sex* caused talk, it was likelier that within a few years the stage version of *Tobacco Road* could run 3,192 performances on Broadway.

So far Miss West's image was largely confined to the five boroughs of New York City, except for occasional photographs of her in police court in the west-of-the-Hudson press. When Hollywood took her up for *She Done Him Wrong,* however, she could exert the same latitudinarian effect on neighborhood screens throughout the land. It probably meant something in itself about ongoing changes in screen morals that this movie was barred only in Australia. There she was, busty, slithery, deliberately overblown travesty of what acne-tormented adolescents and YMCA managers in Iowa thought the madam of a sporting house would be like. The script did no more than some others of the day to drive a horse and wagon through the famous Hays Code regulating screen morals. Her Gay Nineties costumes were no more absurd, only differently so, than those of certain contemporary she-stars. But the code could set down no criteria controlling her specialty—her ability to read "Beulah, peel me a grape" so it sounded as lewd as the innuendo she put into her soon nationally celebrated signature line: "Come up and see me some time." When she played opposite Charley McCarthy in 1939 in a radio skit about Adam and Eve, nobody but the studio audience could see her. The breathy rasp of Eve's colloquy with the serpent was all the juicier for it. Both Protestants and Catholics screamed sacrilege! and she had another publicity coup to hang in her tepee.

For a while this gradual unbuttoning of taboos—presumably clearing the air, assuaging guilt, complementing Repeal and growing acceptance of divorce and birth control—remained minor in scale and seemed to promise the self-limitation that Heywood Broun had confidently promised in 1923: "Let the State say to the average author, 'Go ahead and abandon all reticence and set down the most intimate things on paper, ... [and] nothing in particular would happen. This flood of outrageous and devastating expression ... supposed to be threatening the community ... simply doesn't exist.' " [58] Twenty-odd years later Dorothy Parker, just as liberal-minded as Broun, just as good an alumna of the gloriously unstuffy Algonquin Round Table, was aghast at the failure of that sanguine expectation: "[Today's] ruling that no word is unprintable has ... done nothing whatever for beautiful letters. The boys have gone hogwild ... the effect is not of shock but ... tedium. Obscenity should be taken out of the safe on special occasions only." [59] A more plaintive indignation comes from Anatole Broyard, recently reviewing a run-of-mine bed-and-buggery novel in the New York *Times:* "One would think that the honeymoon would be over by now, that American fiction would have tired of its new toy ... we brought it on ourselves by leaving all protesting to the Protesters, we've created the impression that we'll put up with anything. And here it is." [60] A sense of betrayal is just as evident in Fred M. Hechinger's distress over the movie of *Portnoy's Complaint:* "... those of us who fought hard and long against both political and moralistic censorship are being rewarded, not by the release of previously fettered creativity but by an outpouring of vulgarity." [61] Add Irving Kristol's dismay: "... the real disasters ... begin when you get what you want ... this was not what [censor fighters] meant at all. They wanted a world in which 'Desire Under the Elms' could be produced ... without interference by philistine busybodies ... they have ... got a world in which homosexual rape takes place on stage." [62]

It might be fun to take Magistrate Greenspan and Judge Woolsey to *Let My People Come* or on a general tour of Times Square; only since both of them certainly meant well, it would also be a dirty trick. As in the matter of the nudists' don't-look-now nature-faking, sweet reason has gone down swinging again. The ---- has its reasons. Now that the same kind of mind that sees nothing disturbing in *Deep Throat* is recommending removing legal curbs on whoring, we elders are inevitably reminded of a toast that seemed extravagant as well as raucous fifty years ago: "Here's to crime! May prostitution prosper and son-of-a-bitch become a household word!"

As may happen, however, an unanticipated side effect now somewhat redeems that major failure. The new freedom to print taboo words encouraged the nation's first realistic campaign against venereal disease. Its hero was Dr. Thomas Parran, brilliant surgeon general of the US Public Health Service, who had been New York State's commissioner of health during FDR's last term in Albany. Previously such programs had been sporadic, fumbly and cumbered with euphemisms and old wives' tales. The college medical officer gingered up his diffident lectures for freshmen with lurid hints about the sequelae of vice and jokes about the practical impossibility of contracting VD in any way except intercourse or, as to syphilis, inheritance; if he did know better, he thought it better propaganda not to say so. The extent of hush-hushing about such ailments is hard to believe nowadays. In *Ruggles of Red Gap* (1915) Harry Leon Wilson's narrator can only owlishly describe Oswald in *Ghosts* as "a youth who goes quite dotty ... for reasons ... better not talked about." [63] Quacks and the microorganisms of syphilis and gonorrhea both flourished when, as Dr. Parran said, the nation was committed to "the widespread belief ... that nice people don't talk about syphilis, nice people don't have syphilis, and nice people shouldn't do anything about syphilis." [64] They even wanted the word itself ignored. Just then Dr. Parran was particularly exasperated because New York State's Division of Social Hygiene's proposal to change its euphemistic name to "Division of Syphilis Control" was opposed in the New York State Senate because "this word is not decent ... there is a limit to our modern ideas. The bill would only be giving our children a new word to talk about" [64] and presumably chalk on fences.

"Modern ideas" hints strongly at the association between the courts' new tolerance of "dirty" words and the approaching breakthrough in this field. The first leak in the dam was the work of Paul de Kruif, a word-slinging biologist whose breathless journalistic panegyrics of the great pioneers in microbiology and epidemiology made them folk heroes in the popular mind and developed into several best-selling books; he also acted as adviser, indeed almost collaborator, for Sinclair Lewis in developing *Arrowsmith.* In mid-1932 De Kruif's characteristically overheated account of the discovery of the organism of syphilis and of "606" to cure it appeared in *Forum* magazine and called the disease straight out by name. This precedent was useful when Parran began preaching his crusade. Its largest fruits were in the Chicago *Tribune* and its giant corporate cousin, the New York *Daily News,* which began splashing the words "syphilis" and "gonorrhea" all over public consciousness. The *Daily News'* Carl Warren got a well-deserved Pulitzer Prize for his featured series on causes, cure, prophylaxis and so on of what Parran labeled "The Nation's No. One Killer." By summer, 1936, the *Reader's Digest,* queen of popular-information media, was condensing from the *Survey-Graphic,* monthly Bible of the world of social work, Parran's masterly summary of the grisly facts about VD, syphilis particularly, and popular neglect of its dangers. Maybe 10,000,000 cases, active or arrested, among Americans. Incidence as high as 30 percent among blacks in the Deep South. Doomed babies, heart disease, insanity all owing to syphilis, imposing intolerable burdens from a disease readily detectible by serological tests, readily cured when the patient stayed with the tedious treatment....

A great incidental service to an ill-informed public lay in Parran's own highly authoritative estimate that only half the cases of syphilis came from coitus. The old wives and wise guys were wrong, it seemed; it was not true that contracting it was inevitably associated with fornication, adultery and those other ugly words. In addition to those all too numerous babies with congenital syphilis, it could come of merely kissing a person with syphilitic mouth lesions; of other contact with such lesions, a standing threat to doctors and dentists; from plumbing contaminated by a syphilitic's excretions. "... it may be taken for granted," wrote this great medical statesman, "that when it was assumed as self-evident that all victims of syphilis were guilty of sexual misconduct ... when free discussion of the disease was ... a serious breach of taste if not actually forbidden ... it was difficult to teach people to avoid syphilis." [65]

The *Ladies' Home Journal,* showing what may have been even more editorial courage than the newspapers and the *Reader's Digest,* opened its pages to Parran. *Parents' Magazine* lent generous support. *Collier's* sent Quentin Reynolds, one of its most renowned reporters, to cover the campaign to take serological tests and treatment to the appallingly threatened black population of Dixie. The bandwagon rolled on like Byron's deep and dark blue ocean. Late in the decade antibiotics weighed into the pharmacopoeia and proved even more effective and far less patient-wearying than Salvarsan (606). Between education and better therapy it could be confidently anticipated that even though VD was tied to the animal creation's least governable impulse, its future was bleak. That's what we thought then. In time the high effectiveness of antibiotics began to make VD seem less calamitous than the propaganda asserted. Then the Pill convinced the fornicating public that they need no longer bother with the condoms that had been fairly reliable preventers of VD as well as pregnancy. So today in spite of Mr. Justice Hand and Dr. Parran—two most distinguished gentlemen who deserved mighty well of the Republic—what is one of the chief health hazards in the United States? S-p-i-is. And another, only less calamitous because its sequelae are not systemic, g-n-r-h-a.

The Germans' taste for the "natural" even at the price of undermining human dignity led to another importation flourishing in spite of Depression alongside nudism—candid photography. The agent was Erich Salomon, an earnest Berliner who had spent most of World War I in a French prison camp * and then prospered doing publicity for the great German publishing firm of Ullstein. The means were newly perfected German cameras much superior to the photographer-

---

* *Who Was Who,* IV, noting that the information could not be verified, says that Salomon is reported to have died in Auschwitz in 1944.

reporter's previous equipment. The new lenses were so subtly sharp, the new mechanisms so precise that they could stop most action in not too good light even indoors. Skillfully handled, they cut out most of the need for time exposure, cumbrous incandescent lights and the recently invented flashbulbs that, though better than the risky old flash powder, still shed unnatural glare and made subjects blink and start. They were also small and more easily smuggled into situations where the standard bulky news camera of the Speed Graphic type could not go.

Not only were they a blackmailer's dream, but their ability to take (in both senses) people unawares suggested instead to Salomon a higher purpose—to "record history as it was being made, at its sources." [66] Having mastered the use of the new cameras, he disguised himself as waiter, musician, house painter or whatnot to snap notables and others in expressively unposed behavior in social situations. Soon it was fashionable for the great and near great of the Continent to give him the run of conferences, parties and such in order to photograph the participants looking like human beings instead of stuffed shirts intent on the birdie. Salomon was, as his sponsors in America boasted, "persona grata with most European big wigs." [66] Behind and below his success came a new photojournalism garnishing already existing picture papers with lively shots of mothers whacking children, boys tousling girls, sopranos straining for high notes—not to mention eminent persons looking tipsy, petulant or unwontedly and disarmingly or scandalously vivacious. The eventual *reductio ad obscenum* was Rome's notorious *paparazzi.* But that potentiality was strong from the beginning. It was as "the *candid* camera" that these new tools and their professional consequences impinged on America.

Already in 1931 Edward Steichen, America's leading portrait photographer, was extolling Salomon's "fine stolen shots of subjects unconscious of the event ... adding a new feature to the hitherto purely objective News Camera." [67] In its first year *Fortune* brought Salomon to America and set him salting down history with "candid photographs" of rooters rooting at a Harvard football game, diners formally dining at a Cabinet member's in Washington, French Premier Pierre Laval gesticulating in private [sic] conference with President Hoover. The resulting illusion of immediacy was the sensation of the American and other publishing worlds and a great spur to nonstudio photographers, who rushed out to buy Leicas, Zeiss Ikons and such and borrowed from overseas heady talk about "photo-reportage." It all flowered showily in Luce's *Life,** a new kind of picture weekly for

---

* Use of the name involved buying out the old humorous weekly *Life* that had fallen on evil days partly through inept editing after Charles Dana Gibson bought it in the mid-1920s, partly through competition from the chipperly rising *New Yorker.*

America relying on the candid-camera approach. Not that the new cameras provided all the material or that of the not-quite-so-slick rival *Look*. But the difference between these new publications and the Sunday rotogravure sections that they replaced was a heightened expectation of caught-in-the-actness as the still camera moved into the territory of the newsreel with a flexibility and versatility that newsreels could not manage. The roaring success of *Life* and *Look* in spite of the Depression looks as if the public had been subconsciously eager for just this extra pepper in the dime's worth.

An unlooked-for result was heightened falseness in journalism. Steichen's "purely objective News Camera" had already become suspect. The New York *Daily News'* Paul Gallico wrote half-admiringly of the ingenuity behind that photograph of, say, two slum kids taking flowers to ailing Babe Ruth: "You can almost hear the photographer saying: 'Hey! wouldn't it make a swell shot to get a couple of dirty-faced kids ... Jack, run down to the corner ... there's a florist's shop there ... get a couple of bunches of cheap flowers. We'll get 'em to hold 'em and look up at the Babe's window....' " [68] And that the resulting heartbreaking halftone in the paper was a phony probably never crossed the mind of one in a thousand seeing it. Reenacting the event for the newsreels, maybe in advance of its actual occurrence, had long been as common as the results were banal. Basic integrity suffered further when Luce's *March of Time,* a synthesis of reenactment of news events first merely heard on radio, then going visible on the sound screen in the movie house, used fictional scripts and actors in both media, and heaven knows how many thought they were seeing or hearing the real thing. But now the renown of the candid camera, taking the public fancy like the Abominable Snowman or the Flying Saucer, tripled the likelihood that viewers would assume that the images printed there on paper were genuine.

Even when the shots were genuine, their tenor was often false. Photographers learned to exploit the rapid-fire feature of the new cameras to take many successive shots of a given episode or person and then choose those making the subject look most absurd or impressive or beautiful or intrepid—whatever the boss had in mind. Those accidental grotesqueries or beauties created through lens, shutter and film by the vagaries of chance have won many a lucky photographer a prize. Then one began to hear of the "photo-essay" described by *Life*'s experts as "a new art form.... [Formerly] single images had sufficed. But now ... photographs were selected and arranged to tell a complete story ..." [69]—at least the story that said selectors and arrangers had in mind. Where the subject was a person or group—say, a filling station owner or a school board—the chance that mere multiple shutter clicking would secure a spontaneous record of everything needed was too low. So, setting up his shots to look as if "candid," the photographer turned the subjects into actors playing roles illustrating what he thought—or preferred to assume—their lives or functions were like. The latent acting ability that often comes out under those circumstances helped keep the public from wondering how it happened that a man with a candid camera was only six feet away when the girl subject of the photo-essay accidentally encountered her estranged boyfriend on the street and tearfully embraced him.

All that was far from Salomon's hope to deep-freeze authentic history as it happened. A second untoward fruit was further erosion of the printed word, which had already begun with the picture-emphasizing tabloids and would soon be catastrophic with TV. In a *New Yorker* cartoon one of Luce's picture editors was asking another "Is it all right to refer to our subscribers as readers?" That allegedly Chinese dictum "One picture is worth a thousand words" applies to only a limited range of statements and narratives. Pictures can convey the copybook values of *The Rake's Progress* but could never handle the ironies of *Le Rouge et le Noir*, can explain how to don a life jacket but not what the author of *Walden* had on his mind. *Life* and *Look* implicitly confessed as much when, after the first decade or so, they went far more verbal, carrying magazine-length articles. But that did not keep the immediacy of their photographs from being more misleading than most verbal misrepresentation achieves. How much did the press photographs of Hitler looking his most absurd have to do with the world's failure to take his Nazis seriously enough? The two most evil technical innovations, W. H. Auden said, have been the internal-combustion engine and the camera. That may be unfair to Detroit. Gasoline at least did liberate horses. The camera undermined the graphic arts, weakened writing as a social tool and infected architecture with a new set of false values. Louis Jacques Mandé Daguerre should have stuck to scenery painting.

The candid camera, like nudism, could be blamed on Germany, the Old World. Mexico, the New World, afflicted post-Crash America with the propaganda mural painting, a specially vigorous version of the picture-as-statement. The three prongs of the penetration were José Clemente Orozco, Diego Rivera and, less influentially, David Alfaro Siqueiros—the giants of the "anti-esthetic ... aggressively proletarian, ... nationalist art movement" [70] (John Canaday's recent evaluation) of the 1920s known as the Mexican Renaissance. Though varying in extent and duration of formal adherence to Communism, they shared the Marxist hope of making art primarily a revolutionary force, the tactical judgment that huge murals in public places used art more effectively than easel painting and hatred of the gringo's capitalism so woundingly conspicuous within Mexico through economic involvement as well as on the American side of the Rio Grande.

Influences from these culture heroes' impressive works in Mexico City might well have got into the American bloodstream anyway. Significant Americans were already making pilgrimage to Mexico to savor its edifying contrasts with crass, neurotic America. But the infiltration was greatly furthered when, just before the Crash, Rivera and Orozco separately arrived in California with reputations so great that both were invited to adorn gringo capitalism's walls with pretty much whatever they chose to paint. Naturally that came out as allegorical or symbolic but bludgeon-blunt denunciation of the society that was financing them. The logic now seems skewed. As *Art News* said of the consequences at Dartmouth College, suppose Georgetown University had sprouted murals extolling Martin Luther and caricaturing the Medici Popes? But c. 1930 such anomalies were already familiar, and this example may help in the understanding of subsequent developments.

Ford and Rockefeller will again be key names, but not in the first round. That was California II's * and Orozco's. In Mexico he had studied architecture, shifted into graphic arts, drawn newspaper cartoons, had several years after World War I in self-exile in Paris—and by the time he reached Los Angeles had acquired apocalyptic radical† feelings and a devouring urge to express them high and wide on immense walls. (This kind of urge, implicitly associated with leanings toward psychosis, is well described in Joyce Cary's *The Horse's Mouth*.) Hispano-American art experts found him an opportunity near Los Angeles at Pomona College, a coeducational Congregational campus of good standing that had a new dining hall with large blank interior wall spaces. Faculty and students raised money to support him while he covered those enticing expanses with his notion of Prometheus "upsetting the ancient times by giving knowledge to mankind" [71]—that is, bringing fire down from heaven. Coolly considered, the major panel is like the cover of a comic book drawn by a rash admirer of El Greco. The side panels—Zeus, Hera, Io and assorted centaurs dismayed by Prometheus' presumption—disconcertingly suggest Disney. But its chief sponsor-critic respectfully called it "Expressionism ... on a monumental scale ... the first 'modern' fresco in the United States." [72]

---

* Following use in my *Great Times* (1974), this book will treat California as two culturally distinct entities: California I having San Francisco as capital and extending south to the Tehachapis; California II running thence to the Mexican border with its capital at Los Angeles.

† Working definition of "radical" and the several other ideological labels used in this book will be found in the Appendix of Definitions following the text.

Both parts of that were true. The art of fresco (method of Giotto and Michelangelo, done directly on fresh plaster, making the work a bitten-in part of the wall, not a canvas cut to fit and painted) had been little attempted in America for generations. Aside from its merits or lack of them, the Pomona work was thus bound to draw the notice of technique-minded artists. That served Orozco well two years later, when the fine arts people at Dartmouth invited him there to demonstrate fresco painting. He did them a small (for him) and low-keyed (for him) panel at the head of a stair in the college's new library. Zealously observing students took a liking to him; he seems to have been a man of some charm. Faculty were impressed. And Orozco was ravished to find in the lower reading room of the library 3,000 square feet of irresistibly blank wall in large parcels, a vacuum that his nature yearned to fill. For the next two years he was a special member of the Dartmouth faculty, doing just that.

A previous stay in New York City, doing murals to go with Benton's at the New School, had strengthened his already radical leanings, welcome in the art- and Depression-minded circles he frequented. So the content of what he put on Dartmouth's walls was far more raucous than what Pomona got. Half the panels were Mexican—the vigor of pre-Columbian Mexico and its shattering by predatory whites. The other half were gringo America—bloodlessly mechanistic, bloodily war-minded, intellectually sterile. The key panels showed the revolutionary Latin-American peasant harassed by scrawny capitalists and crassly brutal officials, civil and military; and anemic scholars attending a lady skeleton spraddled on a pile of learned volumes to give birth to a skeleton baby. In an adjacent panel about the Unknown Soldier the wreaths obscuring most of the corpse look like extruded entrails—all in the spandy-new pseudo-Georgian building given to Dartmouth by George Fisher Baker, chairman of the board of the First National Bank of New York City.

In that long and rather low room the roaring, shouting and screaming of these lurid charades provide a curious background for an environment presumably meant for undistracted study. But that architectural issue had been lost sight of at the start. The radical-tending fraction of Dartmouth's faculty and students was ecstatic. A faculty member wrote to Orozco that he and his likes were "greatly moved. ... [the frescoes] put before us what we were trying to shape into words ... always I shall be seeing the horrible grinning skeleton of intellectualism against the lovely brown muscles of the [Aztec] man working his maize. For there, *without the necessity of confusing words* [italics mine] is the thing." * The student toastmaster at a banquet

---

* Letter signed "A.M." in Orozco file, Dartmouth University Library. This is an admirable early example of the self-reproachful inferiority feelings that

celebrating the completion of the work in 1934 told Orozco: "I think I speak for every one of [2,000 students] ... it has contributed so much to our growing concern with the world about us ... teaches us to face the world with no illusions ... to be cynics, but always with the reservation that the greatest cynics are the greatest idealists." [73] The staider alumni were aghast, of course. The conservative National Commission to Advance American Art deplored the choice of alien, radical Orozco to decorate that room when so many right-thinking Americans were eligible and available and needed the job. They were hotly rebutted by John Sloan, who was mighty radical then, for the Society of Independent Artists. The college administration took the high ground—that the aesthetic and technical importance of the frescoes was ample defense, no matter what their content. Whether or not their aesthetic content was ample defense, those pictures-as-statement—grim, boneless Yankee schoolmarm, Cortes, Christ, Quetzalcoatl looking like John Brown pantomiming "They went thataway!"—are still there for a new generation of undergraduates to experience and assess.

Cyclonic disturbances centering on Rivera may have encouraged Dartmouth to stand firm about Orozco. In Mexico's new mural art Rivera was probably the more important, certainly more closely linked to Communism. In 1929 he had come to California in order, he said, to test "the reaction between my painting and the great masses of industrial workers ... [and to learn how] to produce painting for the working masses," [74] as, presumably, he could not in relatively underindustrialized Mexico. He never explained how that purpose squared with his first job in San Francisco—a mural for the stairwell of the San Francisco Stock Exchange Club—or for that matter, with the second—a mural for the San Francisco Art Institute. The first summarized California's economy to remind the brokers, he wrote, that "what they eat and what enriches them are the products of the toil of the workers and not of financial speculation." [74] Asked why he hadn't at least put Tom Mooney in, Rivera said that would be out of harmony with the club—an unassailable point. The fresco itself is admirable, rich-textured decoration, a sort of visual fruitcake. The chief decorative feature of the Art Institute mural is an amusing rendering of the artist's own ponderous behind high on a painted scaffold as he paints away at the wall.

Such tact and whimsicality were false dawns. William P. Valentiner, German-born and -trained director of the Detroit Institute of Arts,

---

many radical-minded, cultivated Americans developed as the Depression deepened, an intellectual fashion brilliantly analyzed in Richard F. Hofstadter, *Anti-Intellectualism in American Life.*

took advantage of Rivera's visit to invite him to decorate the institute's new garden court. Valentiner got money and sponsorship for this artistic coup from his loyal patron-friend and artistic protégé Edsel Ford, who was not only his father's uneasy right hand but also a poet of some talent and a fair Sunday painter. Rivera consented, ostentatiously immersed himself in a study of Detroit's economy, decided to concentrate on the automobile, pharmaceutical and aviation industries and by midsummer—when the Bonus Army was still making headlines—began to paint. His assistant was amateur painter Lord Hastings, eldest son of the Earl of Huntingdon, who, fresh from eloping to Tahiti with an Italian marchese's daughter, had met Rivera in San Francisco and become a disciple. Movie cameras were to record their work. The papers were all agog. Rivera, who looked like Sancho Panza come into his kingdom, made a rewarding photographic subject and was generous with dramatic statements—including denials that he was still a Party-lining Communist. The Detroit *Free Press* promised that through his eyes and skills "Detroit will see itself in a pictorial light entirely new, devoid of any sentimentality, real to the degree of pain, and honest to the core." [75]

Eight months later the new light was hardly blinding. The two chief panels showed automobile assembly as a clutter of machine tools that looked as if they were made of plastic, not steel, swarmed over by boneless workmen, a high proportion of whom had profiles unaccountably similar to those of Aztec carvings. Above them brooded hulking human figures of Mongolian cast to express semiabstract concepts identified for those who cared by the institute's reverent brochure. The effect certainly was sturdier than that of the elder tradition of murals—Beauty wearing little but a wreath leading Truth wearing a Hellenistic nightgown toward the Place of Knowledge. But only the smallest, monochromatic panels really had bones in them, and the whole was fumbly-busy trying to convey things in a fashion appropriate to predominantly illiterate societies—say, medieval Europe, doubtless Mexico *c.* 1920—but not America *c.* 1930.

A minor panel, for instance, showed a womb containing a human embryo fed by stylized blood vessels unknown to anatomy but explained as starting point of Rivera's picture lecture on evolution from "the most primitive forms of life to the complex industrial society to which we belong." [76] At the time Detroit's public and academic libraries certainly contained plenty of sound books on biology and economics. Most Detroiters could read, and in 1932, God knows, many of them had ample spare time. Anybody needing to learn about evolution from Rivera's mural—done by a man more versed in use of brush and pigment than in embryology—was ill prepared to understand. Nor was such a student likely to see Rivera's mural to begin with. This, Rivera's third step in coordinating his genius with America's toiling masses, was visible only in an institution of which 90 percent of Detroit's workers were imperfectly aware, which few of them would ever visit. Instead, most of those seeing it would be the run of visitors to such places—fat-cat women, art students and captive schoolchildren. And that teeming womb presided over by a brace of cozily limber, nakedly mammarian women was bound to offend as soon as somebody with good eyesight made out what it represented. Detroit city councilmen were soon saying such things should be confined to medical textbooks.

Rivera had not abandoned all tact. One panel deferentially showed Edsel Ford looking brightly thoughtful and Valentiner looking gratified. Another had the Ford trimotor airplane—the famous Tin Goose that had much to do with early commercial flying—to symbolize aviation. But Rivera must have been aware that it was gratuitously provocative for his panel about immunology to mock the conventional sticky picture of the Holy Family. Its Three Wise Men in laboratory coats, its hints of halo on the insipid blond nurse and the central imbecilic baby, its very composition made up a vapid bad joke that, coming from an acknowledged Red, was bound to stir up the Catholics of Detroit—a city stiff with Poles and well supplied with Irish. Even before Rivera's work was finished, Catholic students were denouncing that panel as "insulting to Christians" and the whole as "atheistic and communistic." [77]

Rivera painted on. The tumult grew. Eventually the Detroit *News* and the Michigan Civic League supported a movement to whitewash the fresco over as the "vulgar, incongruous and grotesque" [78] result of allowing an alien to interpret America for Americans. (There was precedent: In 1932 Los Angeles had thus whitewashed a mural done for its Fine Arts Center by Siqueiros, youngest and most stubbornly Communist of the leading Mexicans; it showed a Latin-American peasant dying on a cross surmounted by an American eagle.) A local liberal rabbi reminded Detroit that Rivera was known to be bright Red and cantankerous before he was invited in and said that, in view of the man's candid feud with capitalism, he had let the city down easy: "He might have painted soup kitchens, bank failures, riots . . . he seems to have gained such respect . . . for Detroit's mechanical genius that he had room for nothing else." [79] Others deplored his having made Detroit out altogether materialistic. From afar radical-minded, eminent artists, notably Rockwell Kent and John Sloan, protested against whitewashing to the Detroit Fine Arts Commission, with which the decision lay.

Rivera had already left for New York City to execute a new commission—a mural in the lobby of the Rockefellers' new-built RCA

Building. The Detroit Commission formally accepted the fresco and thanked Edsel Ford for paying for it. By now things have so cooled off that the guidebooks mention the once-notorious Rivera mural as merely a minor sight to see. Nobody recalls the one broadly intelligent, nonaesthetic judgment passed on it at the time: The Very Reverend Kirk B. O'Farrell, dean of Detroit's Catholic cathedral, said that his chief objection was to the place it was situated in—it would have been unexceptionable in the General Motors Building.

In a few weeks Rivera was bearing down harder and having better luck with baiting Rockefellers than he had had with Fords. The result was a most gratifying martyrization of one of his renowned works of art. As he worked in the RCA Building, his radical-minded admirers paid daily admission to gape upward while he and assistants (one was Ben Shahn, a sounder artist with a surer grasp of radical art) endowed humanity with a slab of social-comment peanut brittle sixty feet tall. The RCA Building was the core of Rockefeller Center, the family's well-meant demonstration that enlightened capitalism need not succumb to Depression blues. If this project was to pull its symbolic and economic weight, the last thing it needed was a figurehead carved by a dogmatic artist pledged to antiplutocrat propaganda. What the Rockefellers thought they were doing is hard to guess. They were certainly aware that one of Rivera's class-baiting murals in Mexico City showed John D., Sr., Henry Ford and J. P. Morgan making a greedy meal of gold coins and ticker tape. At least the Rockefellers were not alone in their folly. General Motors had also asked Rivera to decorate its exhibit at New York City's already-projected World of Tomorrow Exhibition in 1939. Had some GM PR man taken Dean O'Farrell's suggestion seriously? Rivera must have pinched his pudgy self every time it came home to him that the *Rockefellers,* the classic international symbol of exploitative wealth, were paying him $21,000— purchasing power at the time equal to at least $65,000 today— permanently to spread his contempt for them and their world over 117 square yards of their own premises.

On the other hand, had this work been left intact, its fervid revolutionary influence would have largely bounced off those seeing it most often—the major and minor executives and clerical help working in the building, among whom potential impulses to man barricades were probably rare. Indeed, this context was even worse suited to his annnounced purpose than the Detroit Institute of Arts. Was he using capitalism's walls and dollars to force his enemy into an explosive demonstration that it was callous about art as well as about the miseries of the masses? Anyway, as his cluttered, energetic design grew, it began to include the kind of thing the lack of which had puzzled the Detroit rabbi—demonstrations of the unemployed, the Red flag.... On May Day, the great Red festival, he worked in a small but poignant portrait of Lenin. On behalf of the family Nelson Rockefeller asked Rivera to substitute somebody else. Rivera offered to balance Lenin with Abraham Lincoln, whom the Communists were then trying posthumously to enlist. The Rockefellers called the whole thing off, paid him his full fee, masked the fresco with burlap and, as the hubbub dwindled, had it chipped into rubble. General Motors withdrew its invitation. And up frothed acrid casuistry about whether the owners, which the Rockefellers certainly were, of a great work of art, which the fresco may have been, had a right to destroy it. The net result, of course, was to make them look bad and cast Rivera as a thwarted victim of both Philistinism and reactionaryism.

Rubbing it in, he used his fee to finance painting for the Party-lining New Workers' School a twenty one-panel "Portrait of America" picture history that included unflattering portraits of John D., Sr., and John D., Jr. Most of those panels ended up in a vacation resort in the Poconos maintained for members by the International Ladies Garment Workers' Union.* Only thus, lamely and anticlimactically, did Rivera approach that promised interaction between his art and the downtrodden people of America. But the RCA Building episode probably did help preserve Orozco's strident frescoes, Dartmouth preferred not to look as silly as the Rockefellers and as historical document about the ideological vagaries of the 1930s that Baker Library job is well worth houseroom. Rivera further left a mark on American culture by strengthening the association in painters' minds between murals and social comment. International Style; candid camera; nudism; Mexican propaganda-by-symbol.... America's avidity for exotic innovations was persisting as though it were still quasi-colonial.

*   *   *

Some tried to discern a reaction against that cultural inferiority feeling. They saw the Depression encouraging American writers to set novels not on the Left Bank or Côte d'Azur but on Tobacco Road or Greenpoint or Monterey. Wherever two or three forward-minded young couples gathered together, folk song and square dancing were on the upbeat. The virtues of the latter, whether as exercise or

---

* The ILGWU's panels were destroyed when the resort burned in 1969. A few scattered into other hands may survive. (John Canaday, "Sic Transit Infamia Mundi," New York Times, July 6, 1969.) Rivera eventually got into the papers again as star turn of the Artists in Action exhibit at San Francisco's Golden Gate Exposition of 1939–40, putting in conspicuously long hours painting a mural (not a fresco this time) and hamming it up by lunching on the job on the torn-out insides of loaves of French bread (Life, July 29, 1940).

something fun to do or merely observe, in contrast to the prevalent modified fox-trot, constituted one of the decade's few indubitably admirable changes. But it was notable that though out-for-the-evening fashionables were also trending away from the Jazz Age's kind of dancing, the innovation they chose was the imported Cuban rumba to the omnipresent tune of "The Peanut Vendor"—a calamitous choice; one could only mercifully avert one's eyes from the spectacle of a middle-aging matron trying to rotate her behind as enticingly as the law allowed. Mixed and ambiguous results also came of the chronic art colonists' trek southwestward. Most notable at Taos, New Mexico, those who had once sought the Good Life Aesthetic in France were now flourishing on the cross-cultural stimulus of breathing the same rarefied air as genuine, indubitably indigenous Indians. The consequent shortcomings were testily but fairly described by Thomas Craven, critic-apostle of an independent spirit in American art: "As perfect illustrations of the ineffectualness of the love of art as ... stimulus ... I may cite ... Woodstock, Provincetown and Santa Fe. Working in typically American ... environments, but working servilely from European forms and without organic interest in their subjects, these rustic Bohemians produce only imitations ... the New Mexican desert resembles the Provençal landscape of Cézanne, and the Indian is chopped into the cubes and cones of Picasso." [80]

Actually the connection between the sporadic vogue of Americana and the Depression was often deceptive. Thus, though folk song took on a radical tinge as plaintive or indignant work- and jailhouse items gained favor, the cult in general was already stirring back in the 1920s. A trend toward "social significance" was clear in imitators of John Dos Passos and John Howard Lawson, Mike Gold, *et al.* But they too were pre-Crash. The Taos artist's idealizing of kiva, adobe and peyote was merely a new shoot from the romantic anti-Main Streetism going back even before World War I. The most deliberate reaching for indigenous materials occurred among painters. Benton, John Steuart Curry, Grant Wood, Edward Hopper, Charles Burchfield, Charles Sheeler, Reginald Marsh, Henry Varnum Poor, Ben Shahn all preferred to handle American phenomena, and for several of them—particularly the first three—the other side of the coin was articulate revulsion against the fashionably exotic. But here, too, the case lacks consistency. Most of them were already exploring the local, the chewily immediate before the Depression sent the self-exiles home and focused America's attention on its present troubles and their roots in the past.

At the turn of the century "regional" had meant novelists exploiting the "local color" of this or that cultural backwater—the postbellum South or the decayed towns of maritime New England. It persisted as narrowed down to the Dixie less respectfully handled by T. S.

Stribling, Caldwell, William Faulkner, Paul Green. . . . But in painting, art journalism of the early 1930s applied the term "Regionalists" to Benton, Curry and Wood. The region involved seemed well defined, for they came respectively from the contiguous states of Missouri, Kansas and Iowa, and as their talents matured, all returned to their native trans-Mississippi Midwest to settle. All had been young aspirants in Paris and there experienced more or less of the artistic climate they would react against, which Lippmann ably defined: "The modern artist . . . [specializes] on some aspect of form, exaggerates some quality of line . . . produces art that only a few would miss if it disappeared. Then he denounces the philistine public . . . a school is no sooner founded than there is a secession. The usual manifesto is published (they all say about the same thing); authority and classicism are denounced in the name of youth and adventure. . . . " [81] Sixty years later Daniel Boorstin accurately sized up the Regionalists as "a few strong talents . . . united in revolt against the new dogma of novelty. . . . [They] had all been to Paris and come back to live in their American hometowns spiritually as well as physically. . . ." [82]

Since he could write better than most painters, indeed better than many professional writers, Benton was the most articulate, not to say aggressive, about Regionalist aims. His road to Damascus had been World War I. Home from Paris full of the clichés of the time, living in New York City on potboiler portraits, he joined the US Navy in 1917 and was put to doing drawings for the architectural engineers of the Norfolk Navy Yard. Out of this drab duty he gained a new grasp of reality, coming to value subjects—traveling crane or dockside shack or knot of assorted gobs—for their own sakes, not for the fillip they might give to this or that finicky variation in subjective technique. After the war he tackled the great wide world of gandy dancers, fiddlers, short-order joints, drummers, choir sopranos, decrepit railroad stations and jalopies. His qualifications to interpret it were impeccable. His great-uncle was Thomas Hart "Old Bullion" Benton, the elder statesman of pioneer Missouri who winged Andy Jackson in a frontier brawl over politics and later helped him fight both the Bank of the United States and the inflationists. Great-nephew's father was up to his ears in backcountry Missouri politics and was known locally as The Little Giant of the Ozarks.

The boy's apprenticeship began at the age of seventeen in a cartoonist's job on a Joplin, Missouri, newspaper. The Chicago Art Institute, Paris, an instructorship at the New York Art Students League and years of wandering and sketching in the remote crannies of the Southeast all contributed to the development of what his obituary in the New York *Times* called "a cocksure, crusty, craggy, tobacco-chewing, whiskey-drinking, profane, pugnacious product of the Middle West." [83] But this was no case of what the 1920s called "the mucker pose" flaunting a self-conscious scorn of polish. It was just Tom Benton, the man who, when Frank Lloyd Wright suggested designing a house for him instead of what Wright called the "rat-trap" pseudo-Spanish mansion that Benton lived in in Kansas City, said no thanks, your roofs leak. At the age of eighty-three he finished a vigorous set of murals for Joplin. At eighty-five he was hard at murals for the Country Music Foundation of Nashville, Tennessee. He died that year half an hour after having a martini at 11 A.M. because, in spite of his chronically ailing heart, he felt like having one.

In an age reluctant to leave any large wall space plain plaster, Benton's murals for the New School in 1929–30 had made him a stimulus second only to the great Mexicans. And in his indigenous way he spontaneously caused as many ructions as Rivera, Orozco and Siqueiros put together. His murals for the Indiana building at Chicago's Century of Progress—Craven called them "one of the landmarks of modern painting" [84]—had to be rerouted on the way to Chicago because they were too tall for railroad overpasses. One kind of Hoosier objected to their unflattering depiction of the Ku Klux Klan, dead but all too recently the mainspring of Indiana politics. Another kind finally headed him off from painting in James Whitcomb Riley, the "Children's Poet" (but also Indiana's most renowned heavy drinker) as chief toper at the bar of Indianapolis' august Claypool Hotel. His later murals for the Missouri State Capitol drew screams of anguish because they celebrated among the state's cultural monuments Frankie & Johnny and Kansas City's noisome Boss Thomas Pendergast. Headline-conscious clergymen in St. Louis went out of their way to denounce his easel painting, "Susannah and the Elders," showing the lady most explicitly naked and the elders' leers much too juicy for even an apocryphal sacred subject.

While working on the Missouri murals, he shifted base from New York City to Kansas City, returning only now and then to give Manhattan the rough side of his tongue: "a highly provincial place" where "humane living was no longer possible." Museums, he maintained, were artistic graveyards and should be abolished. He had already fallen foul of the amateur Marxists whose numbers were growing so fast in the early 1930s. In his time he had been as radical as the next callow young artist conforming to nonconformity. Now, as knowing his own mind became a free-swinging habit, he protested against forcing art into "stereotypes of propagandist patterns." [84] His series of murals for the Whitney Museum (1932) showed Mutt (of the Mutt & Jeff comic strip) leading a "Literary Playboys' League of Social Consciousness," including the *New Masses,* the *New Republic,* the *Nation* and so on, and advertising a "Greenwich Village Proletarian Costume Dance ... Expressing American Class Solidarity." To make his contempt scatologically clear, the whole composition is labeled "The Eagles They Fly High in Mobile." A woman visitor hearing him hauling off on some person or thing asked, "Mr. Benton, why are you so mean?" "You're not mean, Tom," interposed his wife and quondam pupil. "You're vulgar but not mean!" Nor was he lax about confessing error. Settling in Kansas City, he had hopes that it would be less queasy-making than Manhattan about important things like art. Within a few years he glumly admitted losing any illusion that "the cultivated people of the Middle West [could] be less intellectually provincial ... the same 'educated' ladies and the same damn bores whom I tried to escape in New York ... lisp the same tiresome aesthetic jargon."[84] Craven called him "one of the few living artists ... with a first-rate mind ... and a painter with the ability to think is something criticism has not had to reckon with for many a day." [85]

Whether his artistic achievement measured up to his extraordinary personal integration is doubtful. Craven found him a great draftsman. Critics suggest marked influence of El Greco in the spiraling energy of his best figures. But many and many a time he slipped below that best, particularly in murals, which often contain figures deserving the pejorative term "rubberoid" applied by James Mellow.[86] But then the same would apply to Rivera *y Cia.* There must be something about mural painting that vitiates the arm and eye. Only a few have had Giotto's and Michelangelo's magnificent ability to escape it. Where Benton outdid his contemporaries was in composing large wall spaces. Too often the miscellaneous political or cultural ingredients to which muralists feel committed lead to an effect as of an overpacked suitcase—there's a corner not quite full, jam into it a Chinese baby in a red diaper playing with a hand grenade. Benton could get everything in apparently higgledy-piggledy and yet make a picture stronger than anything it contained, answering Picasso's criterion—that the quality of an able painting will be unmistakable from far away at the other end of the gallery. Or maybe his best contribution was what Canaday recently described as the "de-sentimentalization" of his materials.[87] None of the hulking, clear-eyed abstract Worker of proletarian art for Benton, or yet the sunbonneted Pioneer Mother with a string of Covered Wagons in the background. His myriad figures manage to be unmistakably individuals and smell of sweat at the same time that they vigorously represent the indicated strata of the nation that he knew and loved well.

John Steuart Curry's career was shaped like a biographical movie. Kansas farm boy hipped on drawing whatever he sees studies at Chicago Art Institute, becomes well-paid illustrator for slick magazine stories in the *Saturday Evening Post, Country Gentleman,* the better

Western pulps. But after some years his talent gets restless, and simultaneously editors complain that his work is getting too much like gallery painting, isn't illustrative enough. This sends him off to Paris on borrowed money to learn to transcend hackwork. There by a strange catalysis the effect of the Left Bank is to richen his awareness of the country he came from and ripen his already able draftsmanship. On his return he shows at the Corcoran Gallery in Washington a dramatic canvas, "Baptism in Kansas," widely taken to be a manifesto proclaiming new values in graphic Americana. Mrs. Gertrude Vanderbilt Whitney, lady Maecenas and capable sculptor, buys it for her new Whitney Museum of American Art, grants Curry a livelihood stipend for two years and in 1930 arranges him a highly successful one-man show. After teaching at the Art Students League, he treats himself to a whole season with the Ringling Brothers-Barnum & Bailey Circus, drawing and painting his heart out to do justice to elephants and aerialists. As times get tougher, he takes shelter in the New Deal's subsidized art projects; the murals he does for them are high among the best. And then here is the University of Wisconsin making him artist-in-residence at its College of Agriculture. He can teach when he likes, paint when he likes. The John Brown he paints as focus of an aborted series of murals for the Kansas State Capitol is the outstanding, though maybe not the best conceived, consequence of his relish in knowing his own country.

Yet among the Regionalists' works it was neither Benton's slab-sided mule skinners nor Curry's rapt Holy Rollers that brought the nation to a sudden gasp of recognition. That was reserved for Grant Wood's "American Gothic." It was the talk of the show at the Chicago Art Institute's annual exhibition in 1930. At Chicago's Century of Progress in 1933, where it attracted more attention than "Whistler's Mother" and almost as much as Sally Rand, it became third in America's gallery of proverb paintings after "Washington Crossing the Delaware" and "The Spirit of '76." Its superiority to either as a work of art had nothing to do with it. But its conspicuousness probably did owe much to Wood's method of painting. For twenty years dealers, critics, art teachers, museum staffs and reproductions in popular magazines had been weaning—or trying to wean—the American mind away from art-as-representation. It was gospel that to paint painstaking detail doomed the twentieth-century artist never to rise higher than Norman Rockwell's ingenious folksiness. And now here was the conscience-relieving arrival of a canvas taken seriously by critics that carried recognizable detail to fanatic lengths, that looked exactly, *exactly* like what you just knew its models were in real life. The worn area on the overalls bib, the potted plants on the side porch, the cameo at her throat, the stray lock of lank hair were near trompe l'oeil in quality and consonant with that first feeling as though one had come around a corner on two long-lost cousins. Beneath—or beyond—those factors was the artist's coolly valid style as unobtrusive and yet as indispensable as the Peychaud bitters in a Sazerac cocktail.

The last generation, well aware of "American Gothic" as a cultural monument, has been taught to take it as primarily satire, hostile and bitter. A recent description—"Fundamentalist in religion, anti-intellectual by tradition . . . the salt of the earth, the backbone of the country, the originals of Grant Wood's 'American Gothic' pair standing with pitchfork in front of their farm, their faces set against progress, Jews, foreigners, Eastern bankers, newfangled nonsense, and, of course, sin" [88]—is a typical piling on of material that isn't there. Actually the originals of that famous pair were the artist's sister, with whom he was on excellent terms, and an obliging kinsman; the pitchfork is not a weapon but an indispensable part of the brilliantly conceived composition as well as a necessary implement in the most peaceful of barnyards; and how Jews, foreigners, progress and sin got into the act along with these obviously timid but well-meaning persons is a puzzle. The answer may be that in 1932 Wood showed his second most discussed canvas, "Daughters of Revolution," which *was* devastatingly satirical and received with deserved whoops of joy to match. It shows three middle-aged-or-more princesses of small-town respectability peering suspiciously and stuffily out at the viewer, and on the wall behind them is a faithful copy of "Washington Crossing the Delaware." Louis Untermeyer said it was "a complete Sinclair Lewis novel." [89] Anyway, one can say it would have made Honoré Daumier grin. Postcards of it outsold even "American Gothic" at the Century of Progress. In my view its astringency rubbed off on "American Gothic" and got it mistakenly regarded as similar in tenor. But the main significance of both canvases is, of course, that painting is like the other arts, a craft that, when all the circumstances are right and the painter's skills ripe enough, can get airborne.

In Wood's case the skills came by way of a strictly exotic influence farther away in time and space than the direct ancestries of either Benton's or Curry's work. After his time in Paris, Wood had come home to Cedar Rapids, Iowa, and through friendly patronage from local people—one the top-ranking undertaker, another a prince of the local oatmeal industry—became the local artist figure selling his recognizable workmanlike paintings for modest sums; he was also occasional interior decorator for prosperous local families. In the mid-1920s Cedar Rapids wanted a symbolic stained-glass window for its War Memorial. Though he knew nothing about stained glass, Wood, as the town's house artist, was naturally chosen to design and execute it. That took him to Munich, home of the best stained glass of the time. There artists were preaching a *neue Sachlichkeit* that may have soaked into him in spite of his knowing little German, but more to the point, there he encountered the solicitously intense, highly detailed work of the great German and Flemish painters of the sixteenth and seventeenth centuries. In the light of what they had done Wood's strong instinct of craftsmanship seems to have undergone something like a religious conversion. And that's how "American Gothic" was born, out of Quaker Oats by Hans Memling and the Cranachs. It sounds strange only if one's faculty of cultural discernment is overdeveloped and tunnel-visioned. In other contexts and on a smaller scale it was like the effect of impertinent West African artifacts on the techniques of Picasso, Modigliani *et Cie.*

In Wood's case it led to what has been called "an unreal realism," but then, one way or another, realism is always unreal. The phrase applies best to his later landscapes, which turn the rolling topography of eastern Iowa into a blend of upholstery and atmospheric depths. It is only one's first impression that this toy universe, like an aquarium full of liquid glass, could be wound up and started going with the windmill turning and the little horses heaving their shoulders into their collars. For, though the trees are conventionalized blobs, they indubitably grow from roots; the distant buildings are playthings, yet habitable; the tiny people look like dolls but would prove warm to the touch. Then in such work as "Death on the Ridge Road" there is a nudging toward something like abstraction.

His liking for folks-back-home material probably has much to do with the way interest in his work has fallen off in the last decades. The memories of fewer and fewer people, particularly of those whom *Women's Wear* calls "fashion victims," are intimately jogged by such data as the hired man combing his wet hair in the bit of mirror hanging over the washbasin on the back porch. Outside the narrow Regionalist category—which never meant as much as its users intended—another Midwesterner, Charles Burchfield, had better luck with his passion for decaying, isolated specimens of pre-1900 mansarded dwellings, jigsawed railroad stations and so on. Most of the country still lived with, if not in, the stained, skewed degenerations of that architecture, and by leaving out the people who had built it, the artist could dwell almost lovingly on its bleariness without resorting to nostalgic self-reference. That he was a canny, zestful feeler of bleak shapes and lugubrious color schemes helped a great deal, of course, but people and pictures being what they are, that remained secondary.

The human presence as ingredient—though he sometimes used it— was also unimportant to Edward Hopper, dean of the list, who, to put it simply, was likeliest to retain permanent place in the canon of American art. Had a young Vermeer studied for a while among

Manhattan's Ashcan School of pre-World War I days, something like "Early Sunday Morning"—that apotheosis of an empty, sordid street—might have resulted. Unlike Benton and too many others, Hopper was a standing frustration for interviewers and critics who expected painters to follow the growing custom of eloquence about what and how they painted and why, interminably why, and its place in the shaping of life and civilization. Hopper just painted and kept his mouth shut as firmly as Winslow Homer's. Asked to comment on a canvas for a forthcoming exhibition, he wrote: "This picture is an attempt to paint sunlight as white, with almost or no yellow pigment in the white. Any psychologic idea will have to be supplied by the viewer." [90] He had little use for the self-conscious categorizing implicit in talk about Regionalism and so on: "I hate the word American Scene," said this great specialist in it. "It has been applied to American painters who definitely tried very hard to be American and I never did. I just tried to be myself." [90] Yet such admirable reluctance to wag the tongue cannot be set up as essential to extraordinary work. Ben Shahn sounded off as glibly as anybody, yet was a formidable artist. This childhood immigrant from Lithuania came to art through journeyman work in lithography—another parallel to Homer—and made his luck in 1932 with a brilliant series on an indubitably American theme, the Sacco-Vanzetti case. His gnarly emotions and superb drawing even survived the ordeal of muralism in his tribute to the Jewish garment worker painted in the schoolhouse of the garment workers' cooperative colony at Roosevelt, New Jersey.

In this dubious game of seeding painters as if they were tennis players Hopper and Shahn may not quite rank with George Bellows, John Marin, Maurice Prendergast of the preceding generation. But they were leading edge of a cluster of painters richer in cultural texture than any appearing since in America and in quality by no means mediocre. They also lack whatever significance would come of showing the marks of the Depression. Though most of them were more or less involved in the New Deal's art projects, none seems to have derived much beyond temporary livelihood from the experience. Reginald Marsh's federally financed murals in the New York Customs House seem vapid disappointments in contrast with the energy of his previous semicaricatures of Manhattan's lower orders, at once funny and ferocious. It was left largely to the minor painter-pensioners of WPA to celebrate the working-class hero and the sweatshop.

For that matter, the most widely recognized art of the decade—the magazine covers of Norman Rockwell and what Gutzon Borglum did to Mount Rushmore—came from men whose careers were already well in motion in 1929. Rockwell's nimbly painted felicities, four-color equivalents of the Rogers groups of the 1880s or maybe O. Henry's short stories of 1910, had been a national institution since the Armistice. Not even a Great Crash could alter a detail in his genial observations, as accurate as they were specious, of small boys, elderly grandparents, callow striplings against small-town backgrounds. Borglum had warmed up for Mount Rushmore by bringing to partial completion a colossal high relief of the chief heroes of the Confederacy on the flank of Stone Mountain in Georgia. Blasting began in 1927 on his even huger project of carving the nation's most eminent Presidents on that natural wall of granite in South Dakota. Fourteen years and almost a million mostly federal dollars later, as the Depression bowed out and the war boom took over, it was a consummate *tour de force*—a phrase most literally applicable to a work of art involving so much cleverly applied dynamite. Its four great men are better identifiable than Ozymandias—so far, anyway—but still look rather queer from the viewing platform. Washington is like the Houdon bust carved in soap. Lincoln has a touch of Jack Benny, and Jefferson a disconcerting resemblance to Miss Helen Hayes. Borglum was much better off with profiles in relief for Marse Robert and Ole Jack riding so gracefully-spookily there across the vast bulge of Stone Mountain.

Ever since the first shipyard craftsman roughed out the first figurehead for an American-built ship more than 300 years ago, the new nation, however inchoate, had been producing something like sculpture. As the 1800s spun imitative webs between New and Old Worlds, American cities and towns acquired provincial equivalents, sometimes the work of Americans born, of the statues that provided points of political-historical, aesthetic and funereal interest in Old World urban vistas. The skills of such renowned American statue makers as Augustus St. Gaudens and Daniel Chester French were comparable to those of their transatlantic opposite numbers; indeed, they had often trained in the same ateliers. Borglum's megalomanic efforts may have represented the effort of a not-too-formidable talent to transcend, in scale anyway, the limitations of the transplanted Old World sculpture. But it was the privilege of the 1930s to titillate the Old World with the work of an American sculptor doing things that Europe had not yet thought of.

The net gain to the world's permanent store of indispensable art cannot yet be intelligently estimated. In cultural history, however, Alexander Calder, man of mobiles and stabiles, impressing the same strata in Paris, London and Manhattan for whom Picasso, Cocteau and Brancusi were the law and the prophets, was the same sort of cosmopolitan news in his time as Poe, Walt Whitman, Louis Sullivan, Frank Lloyd Wright and jazz were in theirs. He was the only major

American artist since Mary Cassatt so well rooted in France that international renown clung to him as if by investiture the rest of his varied career. After blooding in Montmartre, Benton went back home and stayed there. After his neophyte years on the Left Bank, Calder kept one foot in a converted old farmhouse in Roxbury, Connecticut, the other just as firmly in a much older farmhouse in Saché, Indre-et-Loire.

His paternal grandfather, son of an emigrant Scotch stone carver, had become a prominent conventional sculptor 100 years before, best known for his colossal figure of William Penn that looks so small up there on the central tower of Philadelphia's gimcrack City Hall. His sculptor father had been about as conventional, but a striking vigor of execution kept his best work from going cliché. His wife, Sandy's mother, was a professional portraitist, so there was any amount of studio talk and artists' company in the boy's childhood. His early hobby of cobbling up ingenious toys with wire and wood was no doubt premonitory. But at first he took his mechanical bent to the Stevens Institute of Technology, where, as erratic but brilliant student of engineering, he kept his clever hands and ingenious mind busy with both tools and drawing materials. After some years of odd-jobbing he went to Paris in the momentous mid-1920s on a bare-subsistence allowance. Gradually word got round on the Left Bank about this genial young American who, duly mindful of the fashionable cult of the circus as aesthetic stimulus, had made out of wire and odds and ends a whole toy circus—trained animals, trapeze artists, ringmaster and so on—and put it charmingly through its paces on the floor. This was his bridge to acquaintance with great ones, particularly Joan Miró and Piet Mondrian, the sources of the seminal hints that led to his own aesthetic radicalism.

In 1933, apprehensive of the future in Europe, he returned to America. His circus came along in a couple of suitcases. Again it proved useful as passport to the right people who had heard of it from their counterparts overseas. At a pretentious Manhattan party Thomas Wolfe thought it a deplorable bore and went out of his way to say so in *You Can't Go Home Again*. The movie of it shown at the Whitney Museum in 1976 along with many of the original figures and props seemed to confirm that verdict, but then maybe the diffuse museum atmosphere was unpropitious. The important part is that once across the bridge into acceptance, Calder made himself an innovative institution.

The validity of his talent is indisputable. During his studies at the perennially fertile Art Students League, he did drawings of animals that for sureness of grasp and straightforward economy of line would not be out of place in the prehistoric cave of Lascaux—than which, of course, no praise is higher. A few years later in Paris, working with wire—his favorite medium since boyhood—he produced three-dimensional caricatures, whole little figures or life-size heads, sharp as a bamboo splinter, light and spare as a discarded snakeskin, graceful as a leaping fish. Then he made drawings *as if* of wire flattened on paper, an unnecessary fusing of media but apparently answering the impulse toward new approaches that he felt in common with the inventors of Cubism, collage and Dada. Then, struck by polygons of pure color in Mondrian's studio, he suggested it would be rewarding to set them in motion. Mondrian didn't think much of that. But thus "mobiles"— name supplied by Duchamp—were born, bringing, says Hilton Kramer, "movement and a certain playful humor to the abstract conventions of constructivist sculpture." [91]

Calder's mechanical bent could whet itself against the problems of levers and weights activating disks, squares, balls, strings and rods that danced in the slightest drafts or responded to motorized or hand-cranked mechanism. His love for primary colors was embodied in the near-and-yet-so-far juxtapositions among brightly colored spheres and so on, circling and circling as if forever; these "mobiles" carry a distinct reminiscence of the orrery of the 1700s, the clockwork model of the motions of the solar system. And the relatively simple ingredients of these ever-shifting compositions fitted with what seems to have been a subadult quality in his temperament. They evoke him at the age of ten months, say, lying on his back in his baby buggy, gurgling and clutching at the red celluloid pacifier and blue celluloid teething ring suspended from its canopy and jiggling and swaying as he is wheeled along. That element is either a most valuable or a somewhat offputting aspect of his later work, depending on point of view. His admirers gloried in it. A French critic (Michael Seuphor) called him "This giant child"; an American (Barbara Rose) "the eternal child, the naïf whose vision never goes stale, who brings to each experience the ingenuousness of the innocent eye." [92] Yet there is also the uneasiness of *Newsweek*'s Mark Stevens about "a kind of Rube Goldberg cuteness." [93] That may be what irked Wolfe as he watched "Piggy Logan" on his knees trundling his wiry puppets through their paces and giggling at their mishaps. Such artifacts are less likely to arrive at the unflawed vision of the ideal but improbable child postulated by Blake and Wordsworth as at that uncomfortable *faux-naïf.* That flavor was strong in the Paris of Calder's formative years: Dufy, Laurencin. . . .

While his mobiles proliferated, Calder began moving into stabiles— name supplied by Hans Arp. These were growingly abstract constructions of monotone sheet metal that, instead of moving, depended on first rousing in the onlooker and then resolving tensions among interconnected irregular shapes. The New York *Times'* John Russell attributes to them "the look of gigantic stalking creatures, part insect and part extravagant vegetable, that [have] made a momentary landfall in places that [do] not expect them." [94] Those who had delighted in mobiles also delighted in stabiles. Eventually the press and people buying prestige for municipalities and large corporations followed along as usual. By now Calder's stabiles are conspicuous in plazas, courtyards, lobbies and so on pretty much all over the Western world.

They are often imposing. Originally more or less man-height, they grew as acceptance grew until the culminating specimens run sixty to eighty feet tall, often just as wide. In my own view none does more or even as much as one derives from looking with the same eyes at the voluptuous, huge, richly metallic symmetries of, say, the propeller of a great ship or a large steam locomotive, and the engineering meaning of those adds a validity that a Calder stabile lacks. Prevalent expert opinion is, of course, different. Jean Lipman of the Whitney Museum: " ... many ... believe [Calder] ... the most important living sculptor in any country. No other American artist has had a greater impact on the art of his time. He alone of our major American artists is an international figure." [95] Probably nine in ten qualified critics would agree with that, even though so many French ones supply counterpoint for this unanimity about Calder the cosmopolite force by expatiating on how American he was. Arthur Miller clearly transcends mere aesthetics by saying, "If anybody could understand what Sandy Calder is saying, I would have cast him as God." [96] Consonantly Calder himself said in 1951, "The underlying sense of form in my work has been the universe, or part thereof ... rather a large model to work from. [97]

Yes indeed. Not even Frank Lloyd Wright could have gone cosmic more sweepingly. The two had more in common than American birth and international renown. Learning that Calder planned a stabile for the Guggenheim Museum, Wright sent word it should be golden. Calder replied, "All right, I'll make it of gold but I'll paint it black." [98]

But no matter what future generations do to tread down these estimates of him, keep the eye firmly on those early drawings of dog, porcupine, lioness.... They are all the escort to Parnassus that anybody need have.

The years straddling the Great Crash, in which Calder gave sculpture the new dimension of motion, saw a parallel momentous new faculty, the sound track, added to the movie camera. That is, the thing began jerkily and clumsily to try its wings in 1927, and by 1930 "talkies" outnumbered "silents" among Hollywood's new releases. The movie industry was one of those, like automobile making and house building, ominously slacking off in 1927-29. Lack of spare change in most pockets and competition from free entertainment over radio would make the going rough enough for Hollywood in the 1930s as it was. But how it would have survived without a fresh technological shot in the arm was a problem that never had to be faced, for the sound track gave it enough extra buoyancy to keep afloat. It was out and away the key technological-cultural innovation of the decade. After all, it midwifed the techniques that would marry radio and screen into television after World War II.

It had been hovering in the wings for some years. Since before World War I experimenters (Edison among them, of course) had tried to synchronize movie projector and phonograph well enough to give the illusion that the black-and-white image on the screen was singing, talking, rattling its chains or whatever. In 1926 Warner Brothers came out with an unprecedentedly successful version, Vitaphone, amplifying to fill a whole theater with the recorded sounds coming from huge phonograph discs geared to the unrolling film. Dipping its toe in public notice with short subjects—singers singing, fiddlers fiddling, Mussolini making a speech and so on—these movies that one actually heard! roused the same sort of sideshow curiosity that had met the first silent movies—photographs that actually made gestures! There were mishaps. When the needle slipped a groove, the heroine might suddenly bark like a dog or the dog hum a tune. But it was Vitaphone that scored the epochal icebreak late in 1927, when it put Al Jolson in *The Jazz Singer,* a schmaltzy tearjerker, not only overpowering the audience with his strenuous singing style but also going briefly into dramatic dialogue. Though quality of reproduction was still sketchy, obviously movie heroines could soon be saying, "But you don't understand!" and "Won't you ... sit down?" just like real actresses behind footlights.

Only it was not obvious at the time. Late in 1926 Robert E. Sherwood reported "a general opinion ... that ... talking movies will be an interesting novelty" but about on a par with colored movies, and "the real backbone of the industry" [99] would continue to combine silence, subtitles and sympathetic music (canned and used as accompaniment) much as always. Sherwood regretted this but knew he was in a weak minority. Even after *The Jazz Singer* most moviemakers—except Warner Brothers—went on describing the new tool's chief usefulness as in saving the cost of live musicians in movie palace and grindhouse alike. Interpolated songs? Yes, yes, in their place. Here came the "theme song," to brew which a segment of Tin Pan Alley moved to Hollywood—an *ad hoc* number usually plugging the title of the movie,* often sung off screen or maybe by a character on screen and reprised at strategic intervals. Themes that became song hits were excellent promotion. "Marie," for instance, which crops up now when radio goes nostalgic, was theme song of a vapid movie with Anna Sten as an artless peasant girl in an artful peasant blouse. Fortunately "Wild Party Girl of Mine," theme of *The Wild Party,* proved less popular. The eventual descendant of this was the special mood score worked out by Dmitri Tiomkin taking a full orchestra through goozly reprises of a theme so permeating the consciousness that it pays to record and sell it all by itself with no movie to guide it—like Alice's dream of the smile without the cat.

Hollywood's reluctance to board what would be the greatest movie bandwagon since the close-up was invented was rather like legislators' dread of reapportionment. Having mastered the ins and outs of their districts, they naturally shrink from having to learn strange new terms to play the game in. Once movies went in for give-and-take speech, story lines and shooting scripts had to be cobbled up differently. The demands of dialogue would inhibit the flexible old practice of improvising while shooting. Most experienced movie directors had had no opportunity to handle dialogue. The lovely superstar from the Texas Panhandle whose normal speech sounded like a bandsaw striking a knot would have to be trained out of it, which would take costly time, or be dropped, which would ruin a screen property worth millions a year. Gorgeous balls of fire imported from Europe would be out of action while learning workable English, suppose they ever did manage it.

A dismaying prospect. But as Hollywood kept hoping that the nonmusical, spoken-speech aspect of the sound revolution would go away, screen-and-sound systems far better than Vitaphone became inexorably available. These new methods, abandoning the wax record, turned sound into shadow, photographing the vibrations of the actor's voice in jiggly markings on the edge of the same film that depicted his actions. As the film rolled through the projector that threw his image on the screen, a separate beam of light also played on the passing jiggles—out of sight of the audience—and activated a speaker system reproducing in indissolubly accurate timing what he said as he clouted the villain. Further, this direct reproduction lent itself to improving the quality of sound as engineers learned their way about in it. The talk of the entertainment world in 1928 was Movietone's short subject of

* Essentially an old device. In the silent early 1920s movie promoters might get Tin Pan Alley to cook up a song the title of which coincided with that of an upcoming movie, in hopes it would become popular and thus plug its namesake. The first example that comes to mind is the very popular song "Mickey" hung on the Mabel Normand movie thus titled.

George Bernard Shaw in Norfolk jacket and knickerbockers mugging like a bearded Pantaloon and speaking like a cultivated angel.

For public consumption the industry remained hesitant. "Movie men are now considering," the *New Yorker* reported in mid-1928, "whether people could like dialogue throughout fictional films, but nobody seems inclined to find out yet." [100] Actually the panic was already on. Secretly swallowing statesmanlike words about sound's being a useful supplement but nothing that would ever change the basic art of the silent screen, ahem, the studios were diving helter-skelter into "the talkies" while the movie-theater chains scrambled to install sound systems. In an amazingly short time, in view of the technological problems, "ALL TALKING! ALL SINGING!" releases crowded into the sound sweepstakes that founded the dynasty of screen musicals so popular in the 1930s. Warners had entered *The Desert Song* in mid-1929; British all-talkies weighed in later that year. Heads rolled as Prescott Profile proved incapable of reading a line of dialogue either intelligibly or intelligently and Marya Kielbasy's tongue refused to cope with *sh* and *w*. (The "dubbing" techniques that now enable Eliza Doolittle instantly to sound like a duchess were perfected too late to save Marya.) Joseph P. Kennedy, then one of the screen's dominant moneymen, hired Laura Hope Crews, veteran stage actress, to teach Gloria Swanson to sound as elegant as she looked. John Gilbert, Pola Negri sank without a trace. Some salvage occurred. Greta Garbo's smorgasbord accent was made palatable by choosing for her first talkie—the marquees shouted, GARBO SPEAKS!—Eugene O'Neill's *Anna Christie* about the trollop daughter of a Swedish bargeman. And Ronald Colman's pound-of-plums British accent valuably heightened the ravishing suavity of his silent-screen image.

As engineering improved, the hampering immobility of the early sound-and-film recording equipment gave way and flexibility returned. By mid-1929 King Vidor's *Hallelujah* showed that a fine silent director could bring special qualities out of a sound track (not only music and dialogue specifically but also a wide range of what radio already knew as sound effects) by blending it with the continuity in motion in ways that no live stage could touch. As the international film industry fumbled with these new opportunities, most talkies came out pedestrian or flimsy—as indeed most silents had been, and most stage plays before them. Today's hindsight often calls John Ford's *The Informer* (1935) the watershed sound movie that first made sound a naturalized cinematic tool. It was great work, but as a matter of history, the idiom was well developed before that. France's René Clair had been handling it with wit and fencer's timing. Ernst Lubitsch, the great German director well tucked into Hollywood, had shown the same order of grasp of sound's possibilities in three genres—musical comedy, satiric farce, pacifist tract. His "Blue Horizon" sequence in *Monte Carlo,* his impish duets of motion-sight and sound in *Trouble in Paradise,* his ironic use of those tools in *The Man I Killed* (idiotically billed as *Broken Lullaby)* made it clear that the new medium was *new,* not just a screening of the way the stage did things.

Beyond those fancy considerations the talkies persisted after the novelty wore thin because by and large they were meatier and more entertaining than their tongue-tied predecessors. This was more than the mere mechanical advantage of being free of the stop-and-go of subtitles. Only two groups had reason to deplore the change: Lip-readers could no longer enjoy knowing that what the heroine said to the hero as they embraced was by no means "Darling! Alone at last!" as the subtitle said; and diehard pure-movies fanatics remained miffed. Well into 1933 Dalton Trumbo, soon one of the screen's outstanding writers and eventually anchorman of the famous Hollywood Ten, was still laying down the law that a movie "must be unfolded primarily through motion, secondarily through music" and use the spoken word only sparingly as mere subtitle replacement. Had the sound track waited until 1940 to perfect itself, he said, "the silent cinema would have established itself sufficiently to resist the whole capitulation to speech which has beggared it." [101]

Actually without the sound track the screen would have been stuck in adult infantilism. Already for a generation it had been allowed to keep telling itself and the public—with all too good reason—that it was yet in its infancy. "Film characters [in silents], like the screen, were only two-dimensional," said A. R. Fuller's history of the movies thirty years after sound came in. "Complex characterization [had] to wait until the screen took on the dimension of sound." [102] This was not all general gain. Sound enabled the screen even more seriously to cripple live theater. Following Hollywood's habit of overdoing things, it saddled movies with overobtrusive sound effects and theaters with gimmicky, overblown, super-sound systems. Yet it is difficult to fault Kenneth Macgowan's judgment in 1964: " ... see ... any famous silent film [he duly made some exceptions *] ... and you will wonder why people thought it at all bearable. ... Compared with the talkies of thirty years ago [that would be specifically *A Night at the Opera, The Thirty-Nine Steps, The Informer, Of Human Bondage*] the great majority of [silents] seem ... obvious ... puerile. ... " [103]

Further—but this is no afterthought—sound did for the animated cartoon what Tom Collins, whoever he was, did for lemonade. The

---

* They were much of Chaplin, Harold Lloyd, Raymond Griffith, Buster Keaton, Laurel & Hardy; *The Birth of a Nation;* parts of *Greed, Grass,* Flaherty's documentaries and "a few German and Russian productions." I wish he had also excepted certain parts of *The Big Parade.*

best silent cartoons, such as Paul Terry's *Aesop Fables* and Pat Sullivan's *Felix the Cat* series, which Sherwood called "Near relative of the immortal Krazy Kat," [104] were very engaging. Their frank artificiality blended with quasi-human or -animal behavior gave the best of them the surefire, innocent amusingness of the puppet show. They also founded the convention, still ruling the jejune glut of derivative cartoons under which TV smothers today's children, of pseudoanthropomorphic animals as staples of the genre. When sound came in and animators snatched for it (thereby helping develop the dubbing methods that enabled talkies to go clumsily international), Flip the Frog, the more or less canine Bosco, *et al.*, croaking and barking, were invented to exploit it, often with tasty results. But Walt Disney's Mickey Mouse was, of course, the most shining example of the salutary effect of the early sound track on the screen. Possibly it was the pungent fancy with which Disney and his crew handled sound for Mickey and his crew that gave Clair and Lubitsch fertile hints to build on.

Mickey would have been inconceivable without the hyperadolescent voice that fitted his chuckle-headed person so well. Such aural trademarks were the breath of life for several members of his stock company: Donald Duck's furious gabble, making him the national symbol of irascibility; Pluto the Pup's lugubrious snuffle; Horace Horsecollar's laugh like a defective pump. . . . The indescribable sound gags that went with these creatures' surrealistic doings honed up the rowdiness—a quality in which, except for early silent slapstick, movies have always been deficient—that was one of the early Disney's best traits. The unladylike antics of Claribel Cow's udder brought down on her censorship from both local authorities and the Hays Office. And every frame of the artfully accumulating drawings whisking on and off screen gave the customer the feeling of encountering mastery of a medium, of skill rejoicing in knowing exactly what to do.

It wasn't too good to be true, but it was too good to last. The canker invaded the rose when Disney ventured into sight-and-sound fantasy shorts called *Silly Symphonies* that played music-and-motion games with oddments animal, vegetable and mineral. In *Springtime,* for instance, potato bugs danced on the petals of various flowers, a landscape of daisies went into a ballet routine. Though the first of these were jauntily refreshing, as they went into color—the waxy-pastelish colors of plastic bathroom gadgets—they seemed to acquire, as I noted in a regretful review at the time, a sort of candy-box prettiness, and empty-calorie sweetness alien to Minnie Mouse's coy leering and boding ill for Disneyism. Give some blame to the intellectuals who had been breathing down Mickey's neck. H. G. Wells, Thornton Wilder *et al.* spoke of him and his creators in the same breath as Chaplin—not unjustifiably but with the same risk of inducing megalocephaly.

Mickey's head did not swell. But his nose, what there was of it, went lamentably out of joint in 1933, when Disney's most elaborate effort up to then, *Three Little Pigs,* was the screen sensation of a year that also offered *M, Cavalcade* and *King Kong.* The three bouncy little heroes were better-than-average *Silly Symphony* stuff, and grave people interpreted the chief song, "Who's Afraid of the Big Bad Wolf?," as morale-building defiance of the Depression thought to be sneaking away discomfited because the nation was rid of Hoover. *Pigs* rather than the elder shorts was the occasion of Disney's getting a special certificate of honor from the Academy of Motion Picture Arts and Sciences in 1933, a thing previously accorded only to Chaplin, as general recognition, and to Warner Brothers, for bringing in Vitaphone. Presently Disney, maybe affected by the adulatory chorus,* moved on into full-length, more elaborately drawn and colored features based on other children's stories, beginning with a fusion of "Snow White" with "The Sleeping Beauty." The advanced techniques of animation that went with it were astonishing, and sometimes the old impish style stuck out a reassuring tongue. These productions gave parents splashy things to take offspring to. There was some august muttering about what the witchy sequences might do to small fry's psyches but little evidence that the trauma was real. The substantial damage was more serious: The candy box had now burst open and spilled daintily colored goodies made of corn syrup all over the place. The contrast was sharp between such goop and Mickey Mouse's battle on the beach with the cross-eyed octopus only a few years earlier. Recently, apropos of the fiftieth anniversary of Disney's animations, Canaday let *Snow White* have both well-deserved barrels: " . . . that mawkish, vapid, gooey-colored, rubber-bodied specimen of animated vanilla custard . . . those cutey-pie dwarfies straight out of a Bavarian souvenir shop . . . I still believe that Walt Disney was two people, the one I loved [for Mickey Mouse & Co.] and the one that makes me sick to my stomach." [105]

Say that *Snow White* had a greeting-card simper. At the time, however, the New York *Times'* review headed a tumult of approval, calling it one of "the ten best pictures of 1938" [106] though it was only January. The box office rendered the same verdict. Irresistibly drawn

---

* I understand that economics, too, may have had something to do with the shift into full-length features—that is, the low rentals that short subjects, of whatever quality, commanded from exhibitors could not cover cost of production and marketing for *Mickey Mouse, Silly Symphonies* and so on, whereas Disney's features commanded rentals that triumphantly floated the organization into its present extraordinary position.

on, Disney followed with *Pinocchio, Dumbo, Bambi.* ... It all got into the national bloodstream. Ever since Disney tampered with them, the "Three Little Pigs " and "Pinocchio" have been primarily his versions, not the originals from back there in horse-and-buggy, storytelling times. Numerous girl babies born in 1942 were named Bambi. Every other schoolchild's Christmas loot included a Mickey Mouse watch. Reactionary blue-collar lugs sang to the tune made famous by Snow White's dwarfs: "Hiho, hiho, hiho! / Don't join the CIO / And pay your dues to a bunch of Jews / Hiho! Hiho!"

The climax came in 1940, when Disney reached for the stars with *Fantasia,* a group of supercolossal *Silly Symphonies.* "Genius at Work" was the implicit theme of the publicity. After the press preview the reviewers' respectful superlatives confirmed it. Here were Leopold Stokowski and the Philadelphia Symphony Orchestra doing eight renowned pieces of music—Bach, Beethoven, Stravinsky and so on—accompanied by or as accompaniment to colored animations. The best of them illustrated Paul Dukas' *The Sorcerer's Apprentice* with Mickey Mouse! Himself! as the blundering drudge overwhelmed by implacably marching brooms and pails to match the implacable score. Good *Silly Symphony* work—an engaging dance of Chinese mushrooms, a ballet of Russian thistles—went with *The Nutcracker Suite* but were worse than canceled out by bedroom-eyed tropical fish and naked dragonfly sylphs that resembled what the drippiest girl in the class used to draw in the back of her notebook. For the *Sacre du Printemps* dinosaurs were shown feeding and fighting in a style like a misguided natural history museum's promotion pamphlet for circulation in kindergartens, and the mating amoebas were ineffably dreadful. So were the high jinks parasitic on—or as Disney's PR men had it, inspired by—Beethoven's Sixth (Pastoral) Symphony. Baby centaurs and teething satyrs; adult he- and she-centaurs of the same paper-doll breed as Snow White and her Prince, as if the YM/YWCA had chosen them Couple of the Year....

Shakespeare played by Kewpie dolls. That was the hero sandwich of tasteless anomalies that the New York *Herald Tribune* saw as "a brave and beautiful work." [107] The public showed what might have been but probably was not better taste by failing to give *Fantasia* Disney's accustomed box office success. Fortunately he had already told a meeting of the National Board of Review that he did not expect it to be profitable. The outstanding refusal to shout hosanna took it by the wrong end. *Fantasia* gave acute aesthetic indigestion to Dorothy Thompson, earnest foreign correspondent and columnist for the New York *Herald Tribune* and the *Ladies' Home Journal.* At the time she was far gone, and with reason, in anxiety about the world situation. The Battle of Britain was still on; Hitler had not yet trimmed his enemies' ship by attacking the USSR. And the lady's Cassandra-like single-mindedness converted the churning of her cultural insides into terms of alarmist politics. At least that is the best way to account for her column complaining that *Fantasia* sent her retching into the night because it was essentially Nazism, "perverted betrayal of the best instincts, the genius of a race turned into black magical destruction. . . . " [108]

It really was almost as bad as that; only that was not the way it was bad in.* If Miss Thompson wished to venture into comment on movies, she'd have done better to celebrate how generously within so few years the sound track, though run into the ground by Disney & Co., had generally matured the movies as technique and to a considerable degree as art form. There at the end of the 1930s Hollywood had just shown the world two astonishingly able achievements that were the essence of the new talkies skills: *Gone with the Wind* and *Citizen Kane.* Then, for the indigenous fun department, simultaneously came *The Great McGinty,* first of Preston Sturges' demonstrations of blithe virtuosity inconceivable without plenty of audible human speech to keep it bubbling. No three productions could have differed more widely in tone and intent. The dark was coming, for the moment the war was over, TV would begin that gradual smothering of the screen that has been as socially wasteful as the airlines' and truckers' smothering of the railroads. Nor were those items sporadic freaks. They were heirs of a young but already solid tradition of new technical skills born of the union of sight and sound. That is why so many of the movies of the 1930s hold up so well on the Late Show.

In spite of all the attention that the early 1930s paid airplanes and flying at the Century of Progress and elsewhere, the public tended to remain in a paradoxical attitude about air transportation. Its reluctance to try it personally was about as strong as its fascination with the persons and machines that did the flying.† While motorized airframe

---

* One can only surmise what Disney would have thought of what happened to *Fantasia* a few years ago. Reissues of it attracted large far-out audiences, many of whom combined it with marijuana. Billed as "THE ULTIMATE EXPERIENCE," it grossed many millions. (New York *Times,* April 21, 1974.)

† To call what an airplane does "flying" is, as we have now completely forgotten, a misnomer if one insists on the original meaning—that is, what a bird does, using wings to sustain and propel it through the air. What a balloon does is to float like a fish in water; what an airplane does is to soar, like a circling hawk; only for the airplane the necessary air resistance is artificially created by the propeller or, squid- or fart-fashion, by the gases evacuating from the jet motor. No man can properly be said to have "flown" until he has built and used some equivalent of wings activated by his own muscle power in reaching forward and pulling air behind him.

aviation was distinctly an American invention, until World War I Europe was far ahead of America in using the air for either military or civilian purposes. Even in 1927, the year of Lindbergh's triumph, the *New Yorker* could still justly complain that America had only five airlines, of which only one served New York City and went only to Boston while Europe was well covered by such routes. Just the previous year had William B. Stout's all-metal, eight-passenger *Maiden Dearborn* embarked on the nation's first reliable scheduled airlines flight—all the way from Detroit to Grand Rapids, Michigan. Nor might that have come to pass had not Stout's patron, Henry Ford, become a flying fan, who stiffened his belief in reincarnation with a faith in aviation so great that he thought people taking up flying would be first to come back to earth in any resurrection.

The process of getting the American traveler into the air was gingerly gradual. By 1930 air taxis (50 cents a mile) were growing in number at fields near large cities. In 1931 the Santa Fe Railway and the fliers worked out an amphibious schedule that halved travel time coast to coast, yet gave the customer horizontal sleeping room—he had a Pullman berth New York City to Columbus, Ohio; flew thence to Waynoka, Oklahoma; had another Pullman berth to Clovis, New Mexico; flew thence to Los Angeles. Soon they dropped the Pullman part, and he made the whole trip in the air with several refueling stops; the planes had a few sleeping bunks for the highly affluent, as readers of *The Last Tycoon* may recall. In June, 1932, when FDR not only broke political precedent by going to the Democratic convention to make his acceptance speech in person but also *flew* to Chicago to do so, he did a great deal to make passenger aviation seem reliably practical. If a man just nominated for the presidency trusted flying that much.... The time was ripening, and late in 1935 came the tool to harvest it—the Douglas DC-3, first transport with heated cabin, soundproofing and power brakes, able to go coast to coast in fifteen hours nonstop and so sturdily reliable that numbers of those built for workhorse chores in World War II are still flying in odd parts of the globe.

It took time for such aircraft's reliability to soak in, however. Meanwhile, though air fares were higher than those the fast trains charged, it was clear that, as one of the new industry's wits said, it was "fear not fare" * that was keeping the bulk of the public on the ground. Ten years after Lindbergh came to fame the airlines admitted that only 250,000 Americans had ever used their services; Pullman-passenger miles were still twenty times air-passenger mileage. Number and size of emergency landing fields were growing, thanks to the New

---

* This section draws heavily on my "Mr. Milquetoast in the Sky," *Scribner's*, September, 1938; unattributed quotations are from it.

Deal's various work-relief programs. Weather reporting was improving; pilots were gaining experience; plane design was taking safety more to heart. The plane passenger's chance of getting killed was 21,000 to 1 against per trip—that is, he had to fly every day for sixty years for the odds to catch up with him. The reassuring life insurance policies sold in slot machines in airports paid $5,000 a death on a 25-cent premium. Yet it was also true that the odds were 120 times better still by rail, indeed practically infinite in Pullmans. What the airlines complained about, however, was not the potential passenger's sense of odds but the tall headlines that plane crashes always received. That, in their view, was what kept businessmen, who were the industry's potential basic customers, from trying the skyways even once. Once usually did it. After a first flight, surveys showed, the inhibition was likely to vanish and a steady patron was born, chattering knowingly on the commuting train about getting socked in at Wichita and the best seat to choose in a DC-3.

Women were supposed to be part of the problem. Consistent lady customers such as Mrs. Roosevelt and Dorothy Thompson were a great help but few in numbers. Customer service researchers asking W. W. Businessman why he didn't fly instead of wasting all that time on the train were often told that he'd like to but his wife wouldn't hear of it. When they went behind him to Mrs. B, it might prove that she had never objected to his flying—that was just his way of masking his own fear. Or her resistance proved real but disappeared when she was assured that the life insurance companies had seen the light and his insurance would pay off if death occurred on a regularly scheduled airline. When her antipathy was deeper, and particularly when W.W. was important enough for his example to influence others, she might be cajoled into a "courtesy flight" in an elegantly plushed-up new plane along with a dozen or so other unreconstructed wives of her stripe. Three out of four times that measure made steady patrons, often Mrs. B as well as her husband. More directly, in the low-booking month of February, 1938, three major airlines gave Mrs. B free passage when accompanying her spouse. In a single weekend one New York–Chicago service thus deadheaded 250 presumed wives, many probably genuine.

Half fare for the kids to catch them early; air conditioning to match the crack trains; free meals to reduce the rails' cost advantage—gradually they grew more elaborate. But the best businessman bait, the stewardess, was already part of the Boeing exhibit at a Century of Progress in 1933. Said to have been introduced by Stephen Simpson, a promotion man for United Airlines on the Coast, she was originally required to be a registered nurse not because such skills were likely to be needed—though there she was in case of hemorrhage or miscarriage—but because she presumably had learned how to handle children and obstreperous adults and to carry out strict orders. In time other requirements arose—under five feet four; under 115 pounds; age twenty-one to twenty-seven; standards of looks so demanding that not one in fifty otherwise qualified was taken for training. The purpose was patently double: If these mere slips of girls blithely flew day in and day out, and they were well trained for blitheness, no large, important man had much excuse for nervousness. And having one of them fetch a magazine, point out the scenery down there—in those primitive planes most seats were next to windows—give you a pillow for a snooze, fetch your dinner, chat for a few flattering, dimply minutes gave him a mild but pervasively pleasant association with flying more positive than anything to be got from the Pullman's black man in a white jacket, however genial and efficient.

Eventually the RN requirement was dropped, for as both planes and air travel grew, the supply of eligible nurses dried up. But the levels of good looks and solicitous charm were, if anything, upgraded until now, as David Daiches, the eminent literary critic, has pointed out, the air hostess is the Western world's equivalent of the geisha.

A decade that could come up with that was dynamic indeed.

B. The Media

IT'S STRANGE, BUT ALMOST EVERYBODY WHO WRITES ABOUT
THE THIRTIES, WRITES ABOUT THEM DEFENSIVELY.
                                        —THOMAS LASK, review
                                        of ALBERT HALPER,
                                        Good-Bye, Union Square

The dynamic decade's yeastiness also took it into meddling with the Constitution—not directly by way of formal amendment but subtly and indirectly by way of cultural attrition reshaping and supplementing what it says there in print. The minor example is the emergence of the presidential press conference as a major bridge between the White House and the people. The thing was not invented by FDR. Its elementary, occasional forms went back to his cousin Theodore at least. It was Calvin Coolidge who invented the ectoplasmic "White House spokesman" as transparent mask for the President, saying in effect to reporters, "This is off the record, but go ahead and use it anyway; only keep me off the hook." Hoover tried it occasionally but without success enough to encourage expanding its function. FDR, of course, found it so handily suited to his charm and nippy footwork that he made it a regular executive function like the State of the Union message or throwing out the first ball of the baseball season. No such development could have occurred, of course, unless that remarkable and utterly unofficial body, the White House correspondents, had responded to his virtuosity so cordially that doing it oftener and oftener was well worth his while. In effect the Fourth Estate ratified the unwritten amendment "The President shall, from time to time, that is, as often as his nervous system will stand, convene duly constituted representatives of the news media and, exercising such control as in him lies, answer questions propounded by them in hopes of eliciting something that is or may be made to sound important." And the unprecedentedly long stay in office of the maestro so embedded the press conference in the system that his successors, no matter how ill suited for it temperamentally, are saddled with the obligation to follow the custom frequently enough to keep up appearances. Cabinet members found themselves well advised to imitate the example; governors; mayors of large cities ... indeed, the thing went international, and even Charles de Gaulle felt impelled to put on his own frozen version of it.*

Probably far more important in the long run was the public opinion poll, which, looked at now, seems to have been a cultural attempt to supply the Constitution's failure to provide for public referenda. In the loosening up of state constitutions that went with the muckraking era, many states set up one or another kind of referendum, but the terms differed between states so widely that no gauge on national sentiment was arrived at. On all levels politicians, however acutely aware that they sank or swam according to their constituents' opinions, had to rely chiefly on the primitive device of the ear to the ground. Among experienced professionals that organ can be sharp but is necessarily nonobjective and readily distracted by mail, telegrams and personal visits from cranks and lobbyists, overt or in disguise.

The first effort to fill the gap was made by the Fourth Estate. Just before an election or during a hot controversy over local public policy—sewers or allegedly salacious movies or whatever—a local newspaper might take a "straw vote," printing an unofficial ballot to be clipped, marked and mailed or fetched in for tally by office help with nothing better to do at the time. Even in honest hands that reached only the paper's special public—in those days, remember, important cities had three or four to nine or ten competing dailies—a sample certainly skewed in favor of its editorial views on candidates or issue. And in any case it was an open invitation to ballot stuffing by groups exploiting the bandwagon theory of elections—that a significant number of wavering voters tend to come down on the side that they

---

* The extent to which the presidential press conference is now a permanent institution is unmistakable in the comment of Arthur M. Schlesinger, Jr., on President Nixon's behavior c. 1972: "... he feels he can ignore Congress, invade and bomb other countries with impunity and *even* [italics mine] dispense with regular Presidential press conferences." (*New York Times Magazine,* July 30, 1972, "How McGovern Will Win.")

have reason to believe will win.* Nor in view of the strong partisan-ships often involved was there any guarantee that the staff of the *Daily Meteor* would not cook the returns to suit its own purposes.

In 1916 the *Literary Digest,* a diffuse precursor of today's news-magazines, gave the straw vote national scope on presidential nomina-tions and elections and on such issues as Prohibition and reduction of income taxes. Ballots were mailed to millions of telephone subscribers or automobile owners or both; some such polls drew a gratifying 25 percent of mailed returns. The procedure acquired a treacherous reputation for dependable accuracy when, in 1928 and 1932, it predicted the actual popular vote for the presidency within a few percentage points. There were elements of sound public service in it when polls on Prohibition eight years apart (1922, 1930) showed a sharp increase in the number of Americans wanting it repealed. Doubtless legislators found that a datum fruitfully to ponder. But those among them accustomed to truckling to the Drys still had room for doubt. Weren't militant Wets likely to be overnumerous among those bothering to mark and mail a ballot? What about the millions receiving ballots who hadn't bothered? And the other millions lacking telephone or automobile? Nevertheless, these much-discussed *Literary Digest* straw votes gained the magazine great prestige—and circulation, for attached to each mailed ballot was a subscription blank that the voter was urged to fill in, as many did. This greatly helped the stodgy old publication hold its own against the rising competition from those vigorous, newfangled upstarts *Time* and *Newsweek.*

Then in the mid-1930s Madison Avenue got into the act and soon turned it upside down into a far better social tool. For some years advertising agencies, hoping to keep their clients persuaded that their money was well spent, had been developing "market research" to guide product design and sales approach by determining what the potential customer wanted or thought he wanted or could be jockeyed into wanting. This led into fairly subtle demographic and statistical methods. Say the Widget Corporation was considering making a new line of widgets less expensive but also of limited range of use. Would lower retail cost offset that? So Space & Billings sent out canny hirelings armed with clipboards to interview actual or potential widget users. They found it was best done not at random but in particular neighborhoods representing specific income brackets as indicated by analysis of census returns, incidence of previous sales of widgets and

---

* Several studies by polling organizations have demolished the bandwagon, but it still rolls on, full of tootling brass and clashing symbols. See George Gallup, *The Sophisticated Poll Watchers' Guide,* 31–41.

other guides worked out as experience grew. More and more they relied on the mathematicians' theory of probability, the same guaranteeing that even an honest roulette wheel makes money in the long run if it doesn't pay off on only one of thirty-six numbers. As such theory came to bear, it grew clear that interviewing only a few thousand properly situated persons came as near as dammit to the same result that working through the whole population would secure. The analogy would be diagnosis through analysis of a few sample drops from the entire bloodstream. And to make it better still, such statistically sound sampling not only was better for the Widget Corporation's purposes than earlier methods, but it also cost less.

Elsewhere in this fast-stepping field a specialist, Archibald M. Crossley, began using telephones to find out for Madison Avenue how well the new art of radio advertising was reaching the potential customer. In those less begadgeted days telephones and radios went pretty consistently together; relatively few households without telephones had radios. Thus, to learn what proportion of radio owners was listening to the A&P Gypsies, Crossley's staff had only to place calls to a given number of telephones at the right hour in locations duly chosen on demographic and statistical bases. By 1930 Crossley was working this unusually reliable oracle nationally for a Cooperative Analysis of Broadcasting paid for by the American Association of Advertising Agencies, the Association of American Advertisers and the flourishing radio networks. Questions asked over the phone, times of day and so on were varied widely and subtly depending on the exact purpose of the survey and the lessons of experience, and Madison Avenue and Radio City had very good reason to take a radio show's "Crossley rating" seriously.

At the same time academic researchers, notably Claude E. Robinson of Columbia, were applying statistical theory to straw votes and fusing them with the new methods of market research. From that union was born the public opinion poll (hereinafter referred to as POP) an American invention as momentous as, and probably more useful, on balance probably more beneficent, than the martini. Yet it too presents dangers when misused. Set its birth in 1933, when George Gallup, research director for the mighty advertising firm of Young & Rubicam, began experiments culminating in the American Institute of Public Opinion. Late in 1935 his weekly reports on scientifically sampled, expertly digested public feeling on current social and political issues began to be released to newspapers subscribing to the new service. It paid well, for the papers jumped at it, making the "Gallup Poll" a national byword. In a pleasant side effect it also gave a new kind of interesting part-time work to the several thousand interviewers—mostly married women, mostly with high school or better education—whom it trained to elicit useful answers from statistically significant witnesses. Earlier that same year *Fortune* began its Quarterly Survey of Public Opinion based on such methods by Elmo Roper, another crack market researcher; overnight it became the most talked-of part of the business world's most gilt-edged publication. Soon Crossley was doing POPs for the King Features syndicate of the Hearst publishing empire.

This intense public interest in POPs was spiked with skepticism. How did sample-minded pollsters know that such relatively small dips into the stream of public sentiment gauged it accurately? Scientific palaver about demographic groupings and cross sections was all very well, but this new thing needed checking up on. How? The pollsters saw the presidential election of 1936 as their chance to do just that. Variously and separately they would work their magics, predict the popular vote—and the day after election the actual totals would confirm or deny the validity of their methods as astronomy used the sun's obscuration of a star to check on the Einstein theory. As the campaign heated up, *Fortune,* Gallup and Crossley all were thus poaching on the *Literary Digest*'s preserves. To make it worse, Gallup not only predicted that the *Digest*'s unscientific methods doomed it to go wrong this time, but even said that while it would show Alfred M. Landon winning with 56 percent of the popular vote, actually FDR would win in a walk. He based that on test postcard samplings of the magazine's "tel-auto" lists compared with results from his own staff's sounder methods.

Confident from having called the turn before, the *Digest* took up this cheeky challenge, recommended its poll as "the Bible of millions" and scoffed at the notion that statistical finaglings could prognosticate as reliably as the massed voices of millions of Americans. It was ill advised. On election eve, sure enough, the *Digest* promised Landon victory with almost 54 percent of the popular vote. All three of its rivals called for FDR—who won sweepingly. The trouble probably was that the "tel-auto" category did not include true proportions of the mass of Americans in straitened Depression circumstances—on relief or dreading what defeat for FDR might mean—who voted for him. In the previous elections in which the *Digest* had done well enough, it was suggested, economic strata had been much more realistically distributed between Republican/Democratic voters, making the tel-auto segment of the population a more reliable gauge of sentiment.*

---

* In 1948 the POPs got their comeuppance. In the 1948 election they misfired for the first time, albeit not as disastrously as the *Digest* in 1936. The best-reputed POPs promised Thomas E. Dewey victory with some 49 percent of the popular vote to Truman's 45 percent; among major party voters the

Roper's *Fortune* POP had come nearest the exact results. All three had reason to be gratified with the vindication implicit in the contrasting findings. The continuing need for such checks has been one reason for the persistence of election polls ever since. This battle of slide rule vs. mailbox had so caught public attention and the *Digest's* failure had been so striking that the magazine went into an immediate and soon fatal decline. It had put all its prestige in one basket, and the basket fell off Humpty Dumpty's wall. Conversely the POPs soon built themselves on the ruins a new organ of modern democracy, a kind of connective tissue between the people and their governors that the Constitution founders had no inkling of, supplied unsought by the private enterprise editor, presently supplanted by the inquisitive huckster. Gallup's weekly feature about public opinion on a given issue was appearing in seventy-odd newspapers, none insignificant, led by the cream of the key-city dailies: the Atlanta *Constitution,* the Baltimore *Sun,* the Memphis *Commercial Appeal,* the Miami *Herald,* the Cincinnati *Enquirer,* the Chicago *Daily News,* the Louisville *Courier-Journal,* the Los Angeles *Times,* the Salt Lake *Tribune,* the New York *Times.* ... By 1938 *Fortune* carried a Roper survey twelve instead of four times a year, and the *Ladies' Home Journal* was using elaborate, Gallup-procured data to tell American women what they were thinking about social and civic issues.

For reasons not yet understood, POPs are relatively useless in predicting primary results. They do best on the first Tuesday in November after the last round of asking, "How would you vote if the election were held today?" Usually coming within the probably irreducible error of 2–3 percent, they confirm both the public's and the pollsters' confidence in the method. Conversely, when there is a really wide discrepancy between their findings and the announced actual totals, it probably means that the precinct captains have been up to the old-fashioned tricks of invalidating genuine ballots or voting the residents of local graveyards. Maybe the fairly high reliability of POPs the day after election means that the amount of dirty work is lessening. That in itself would be a good reason to encourage them. This high accuracy may also reflect the clean-cut, open-and-shut, Box-or-Cox nature of the question asked—free of the ambiguities and ever-

---

actual result was Truman 49.9 percent, Dewey 45.7 percent. Gamely taking it to heart, the POPs shifted the basis of their samplings from emphasis on particular social groupings to random selections. Since then the Gallup Poll's average deviation from accuracy in national elections has been 1.6 percent—better than the 4.0 percent of the period 1936–48. But note that even that still leaves plenty of room for being wrong about a fairly close race.

present risk of inadvertent word weightings that plague the attitude/ opinion kind of POP. To make sure that no unconscious bias gets between him and his responsibilities, Gallup has refrained from voting in national elections ever since he got into this work.

Nevertheless, he calls election POPs "the least socially useful form of polling," [109] and much prefers the attitude/opinion assignments. From the beginning Roper, Gallup *et al.* were refining phrasing of questions and interviewing methods to reduce accidental influence on respondents' answers. Questions are regularly tested to show up flaws. Interviewers are carefully chosen and subtly trained in the avoidance of pitfalls such as diffidence and the pull of fashionable ideas. Their raw results are also "weighted"—a sort of statisticians' windage—when necessary to allow for known or suspected distorting factors. In 1938, for instance, the Gallup Poll was a whopping 12 percent too low in gauging the Californians' primary vote for Upton Sinclair and EPIC— an error that proved on investigation to reflect the opposition's colossal campaign of ridicule, which "led many of his supporters to conceal their true voting intentions. In succeeding public studies of [Sinclair's campaign as Democratic nominee] this factor was controlled." [110]

Here, of course, polling becomes as much art as science. That is not necessarily a reproach when skill and conscience are reliable and always being honed sharper by responsible experience. But such integrity is not always found. Today's multiplicity of POPs and pollsters leaves undue room for somebody with a bill of goods to sell or a powerful interest to appeal to working within a hitherto ethical organization—or a polling outfit set up *ad hoc* by a group willing to count on the public's rising confidence in such activity. Add the less smelly but also likely possibility that substandard phrasing and interviewing—mail and phone pollings, for instance, remain woefully suspect—and stupid weighting will skew reports of the national verdict on some vital issue. Newspapers, the best pollsters complain, are too likely to print anything calling itself a POP without looking into the soundness of its methods.

That is serious not so much because it may affect the bandwagon-minded—if they exist—as because politicians in high office too often, to quote Lester Markel, retired editor of the *New York Times Magazine,* "look upon polls not as indications but as conclusions." [111] Roper once protested that the ups and downs of credibility to which POPs are subject are largely the fault of politicians hiring "a research organiza-tion to prepare a poll and then [releasing] only the results that reflect favorably on their own interests." [112] The Gallup people say, "Polls serve the same function for government ... as the intelligence division of the army does for the army staff. [It] does not make the final

decision ... merely supplies information which enables the commanding general to make better decisions. ... The President ... must follow
... his own judgment but that judgment is likely to be improved by
objective data about the state of public opinion." [113] Or, says Markel,
polls, which should be taken merely as "straws in the wind [are] too
often mistaken for the wind itself." [111]

Within those limits here probably is the "new instrument" that
Gallup described forty years ago as narrowing "the gap between
the people and those responsible for making decisions in their
names. ... " [114] It is certainly superior to the trustworthiness of the
telegrams, letters and chats with the boys on the store porch on which
the harassed legislator had to rely previously in deciding what
Buncombe County really wanted. By 1939 a magazine reporter asking
members of the US Congress whether they took POPs seriously got
the invariable, emphatic and prayerful answer "Very!" Yet many a
Senator or Congressman seems unable to shed the old habit of putting
weight on the trend of his daily mail. The senders are obviously from
self-selected, special-interest minorities, meaning samples so skewed as
to cause acute pain to anybody with a notion of statistical validity.
This probably reflects inadequate knowledge of mathematics among
Congressmen. Indeed, they sometimes seem to be allowing validity to
POPs in direct proportion to the degree to which they approve of the
findings. In May, 1940, Senator Bourbon obviously thought he was
falling back on sound horse sense when denouncing Gallup for trying
to tell him, on the basis of asking no mo' than 1,500 pussons, suh, that
only 18 percent of the American people wanted the Wagner Act
repealed. Yet he probably believed eagerly when in November, 1936,
Gallup told him that 82 percent of Americans thought a woman
should not fill a paying job when her husband could support her.

This technological lag among legislators persists so stubbornly that it
may be set down as incurable. It is encouraged by the man in the
street or the lady of the house, both also innocent of statistical theory,
who express chronic doubt by saying, "Well, no pollster ever came
asking me, and I don't know anybody in town ever got asked either!"
It helps little for the pollster wearily to reply that the odds against a
given individual's being thus approached in his lifetime are more or
less 200 to 1, but that this does not vitiate the scientific reliability of
the results. A sort of impersonal hurt feeling may keep that attitude
lively. Over the years only some 10 percent of those approached have
refused to answer somehow. But recently there has been some reason
to believe that people are less likely to cooperate than they were back
then, fouling up the statistics. It also skews recent results that with
more wives working, neighborhoods changing faster in sociological

character, it is more difficult and more expensive to catch the necessary kinds and numbers of witnesses at home when the interviewer can get there.

Thirty-seven years ago the importance of integrity among pollsters led Gallup to propose a trade organization like the Audit Bureau of Circulation (ABC) in the world of publishing "to check ... polling procedure ... the nature of sponsorship ... where the money comes from ... methods used ... margin of error within which the published figures 'are to be interpreted.... "[115] Twenty years later two POP-watcher associations did arise. Doubtless their codes of professional conduct have done something to stiffen the members' backbones. But like most such organizations, they lack the teeth to keep Caesar's sleazier wives as straitlaced as the most virtuous. The other approach, often suggested since POPs first came into favorable notice, is that in view of their influence and the risk of manipulation, they should be taken away from private hands and monopolized by government. Some have even proposed making them binding instant mini-referenda using impeccable scientific samplings inexpensively—and authoritatively?—to turn into law public approval or disapproval of birth control or offshore drilling.

In view of the self-serving character of all governments, that may be inadvisable. But that anybody thought of such a thing does reflect the extent to which the POP, once only a provocative journalistic novelty, is now part of the democratic process. And not only in America. The thirty-six nations now somehow utilizing it include all western Europe except Portugal—even Switzerland, where the formal national referendum is a chief agency of legislation—plus a scatter of nations on other continents. The US Census and US Bureau of Labor Statistics rely on POP-like samplings for the data on population shifts and cost of living on which many laws and wage contracts are based. Yet no responsible American pollster recommends POP as substitute for national elections or possible national one-man, one-vote referenda. He is too well aware of that irreducible margin of potential error that, in a close run, may throw the result the other way. Living with the ironbound implications of the theory of probability breathing down his neck, he knows better than laymen that certain as it is that well-managed POPs will be right and useful most of the time, it is just as certain that occasionally they will be wrong.

The social impact of scientific attitude sampling soon reached far beyond political judgments. Crossley's early work in radio enabled—or tempted—advertisers, broadcasters and federal authorities firmly to commit the publicly owned air, the national property, to mass-created values, sometimes fairly rank, in the interests of private enterprise. In 1932 *Fortune* could still describe radio advertising as, though leaping forward, still second fiddle to print. By the mid-1930s Crossley's Cooperative Analysis had played a crucially large part in diverting advertising toward radio, away from print. The new tail was wagging the old dog. The abject commercialization of the air was completed.

For whether or not radio advertising was always more effective per dollar spent—a thing hard to gauge since effectiveness varied with relative skill of presentation within the medium—it at least had the advantage that facts about its impact were easier to come by. In a magazine, for instance, how many readers did a given ABC figure really mean? Provided one could estimate the number intelligibly, how many readers even glanced at the Widget Corporation's half page opposite the runover of the Damon Runyon story? Such matters lent themselves to exploration but only through exacting and expensive processes, whereas pollsters' skilled telephone crews could elicit with far less cost and trouble plausible answers to: How large was the size of the potential radio audience on a given day at a given hour? How much of it was tuned to the Widget Corporation's program? How well did its content create an urge to buy or at least valuable goodwill? What might improve its effectiveness? And so on and on.

Still more stimulatingly, Crossley's staff regularly released a top-to-bottom percentage rating of what proportion of listeners tuned in to *Amos & Andy,* say, rating it three points ahead of the Widget Wacketeers orchestra, which in turn was two points ahead of the Gasparilla Cigarettes' Gaucho. Soon a radio performer's "Crossley rating" was as important in his cosmos—and his sponsor's—as a baseball player's batting average. Madison Avenue had always leaned toward mass-market goods sustained by mass-appeal advertising; that was where the big billings grew. Now Crossley's unimpeachably objective service so publicly pilloried relative failure of mass appeal and so glorified success that national advertisers' tactics grew analogous to those of the football coach who plans every play so that if it works perfectly, a touchdown results. Thenceforward the radio shows dominating America's air had little hope of rising above a least common denominator roughly cognate to that of the booming comic strips of the period, the same that brought in Dick Tracy and Blondie and Dagwood. Maybe vague premonitions of this cultural erosion had prompted the generalized objections to radio's acceptance of advertising made in the early 1920s by not only conscientious Herbert Hoover and chipperly liberal Bruce Bliven but also by Raymond Rubicam, guiding genius of the great agency that gave birth to Gallup's career.

Research by telephone had certain disadvantages. Once the public was used to radio, listening might be so perfunctory as to defeat some of the purposes of a survey. It proved that one in five persons answering the telephone and saying yes, the radio is turned on, could not identify the program tuned in; one in eight could not even name the station. Checking disclosed that about half the presumed listeners were actually playing cards or reading or doing some other distracting thing that would keep their awareness of the content of a broadcast at best subliminal. Once those factors were known, proper discounts were applied. Difficulties less easy to cope with appeared as the retail price of radio sets sank with the widening market. Many households acquired a second set for the kids, maybe a third for Grandma—hence complications in reaching all three sources of data with one phone call—and the spread of automobile radios put another joker in the deck. Then the handy equation phone subscriber = radio owner no longer held good. With cheaper radios millions of families without phones joined the radio audience. In 1930 only 2,000,000 of the 18,000,000 American families who had no phones owned radios. By 1938 3 out of 4 nonphone families had them. Only cumbrous and expensive door-to-door work could properly cover their listening habits. No wonder that this widening discrepancy shifted research away from tried-and-true telephone work into a new, more vulnerable approach—the mechanical gadget installed on the radio set automatically showing what station was tuned in when.

Households thus relied on were chosen with careful scientific criteria for location, income group and so on. No cash involved at first: The inducement went no farther than promise of a copy of the eventual report on listening habits and a little present for Mom, say half a dozen steak knives or a set of table napkins. The obvious grave risk was that the household would go self-conscious, tending to tune in on what it felt the survey wanted or what would look better on the record than WWVA's racket-ridden hillbilly whinings. That was minimized, it was hoped, by never monitoring a given family longer than a month. No volunteers—and plenty offered—were accepted. Nevertheless, this was acknowledgedly ticklish ground. The best that could be said for it was that something had to replace the unreliable telephone method and recording gadgets did supply Madison Avenue and the networks with a consistent basis, whatever its shortcomings, on which to shape strategy and tactics.

For thirty-odd years now that realism has been embodied in the dominant ratings techniques worked out in the late 1930s by a fast-stepping market-research company founded by A. C. Nielsen, a Chicago engineer who got into this field by way of surveys of retail merchandising. For radio data his weapon of choice was the Audimeter, a superior recording gadget created by two professors at MIT. First used on a large scale in 1942, now apparently a fixture in the TV industry, its successor refinements pipe viewing data instantaneously to computerized compiling centers in a system that neglects some of the elder precautions against listeners' self-consciousness. Many of the participating households are paid a few dollars a month ostensibly to recoup the cost of electricity for the TV. They may be kept in the sample for up to five years. What with the normal attritions of moving, family breakup and so on, three to four years are normal expectation. A. C. Nielsen & Co. say and obviously believe that not only are the 1,200–1,300 households making up their national sample at any given time chosen by the most exacting standards but tests show that no distortion of viewing habits results from their knowing that Big Brother has an eye on them. In 1974, however, Dick Adler of the Los Angeles *Times* scored a beat on all the TV reporters who had been trying for years to find and talk to some of Nielsen's hyper-carefully shielded guinea pigs. Four of them in the Los Angeles area successively volunteered some or much information about their relations with Big Brother's tube. At least two candidly admitted that a wish to encourage what they considered worthy or engaging programs had a good deal to do with what they tuned in for the Nielsen box to record, whether or not anybody was in the room to look and listen. If that ratio of datum cooking to total number of guinea pigs holds good in other metropolitan areas, the possibility of considerable distortion becomes a probability.

In any case this is a curious situation—the content of the nation's TV frequencies, as much the nation's property as the ships of the US Navy, are determined primarily by 1,200-odd jurors faceless so far as Nielsen can keep them so and, to judge by many of their decisions, witless, too. The rating pundits disclaim responsibility, of course. In an address Nielsen made to the august Newcomen Society in 1964, he insisted, "The programming decisions are not made by us; they are made by networks, advertisers and agencies. Our role is quite analogous to that of the box office accountant in a theatre. He counts the attendance ... and the fate of the show is decided by its owner." [116] In view of the uneasiness still widely felt not only by TV producers whose shows fail to get good ratings but also by certain kings and councillors of the world of POPs, that is not quite good enough; what they are questioning is the accuracy of the treasurer's accounting system. But at least it can be said for Nielsen's method that it is not quite as absurd as Hollywood's traditional reliance on the sneak preview. That hangs large or small decisions about a new movie on the reactions of an audience self-consciously aware they are playing guinea pigs in California II. Of all places.

The spread of radio owning into low-income groups that spoiled Crossley's polling method was part of one of the Depression's most striking inconsistencies—the way the new radio industry bucked the ebbing economic tide. In little more than a decade broadcasting had become America's weightiest cultural institution, eclipsing even public school and church in numbers reached and probably in influence exerted. Few were like Titus Moody, the testy Yankee character in Allen's Alley, who, twitted with seldom listening to radio, said, "I don't hold with furniture thet talks." [117] It was triumphantly true that "The writer for radio who has something to say and says it well can have, in a single half hour, a larger audience than Shakespeare had in a lifetime." [118] The antidote to that statistically correct boast from Arch Oboler, one of the ablest radio writers, is the reflection that the same could be said of the writers of soap opera who had little to say and said it with intentional flabbiness and discursiveness.

The rise of radio coincided roughly with the gradual shift from President Hoover's hesitant anti-Depression measures over to the sweep and scale of the New Deal. Thus, in the nick of time radio gave FDR the communications tool that best suited the nation's emotional needs—and, also to the purpose, his rhetorical style. The aspect of his career on which students best agree is that it depended critically on his broadcasts bypassing the previous main channels of contact between Chief Magistrate and citizen. Time was when that had consisted at best of a distant glimpse of the great man far away on a bunting-draped platform. Now one sat in one's own living room within a few feet of the apparent source of the frank, soothing, amazingly clear voice of a man who understood very well how to exploit the consequent illusion of close personal touch. Warmly he dwelt on the metaphor of the "fireside chat," avoiding the mistake of saying "Ladies and gentlemen of the radio audience" as if the room were large and full of people strangers to one another. He said "My friends" to keep it small and cozy. During his four presidential campaigns that virtuosity was an immense advantage over opponents who, though also extensively using radio perforce, sounded over the air like ordinary political speechmakers.

So far that is mere campaign tactics. But in view of the New Deal's lasting social consequences, it was further important that FDR's skills as living-room confidant persuaded crucial millions into approving or at least suspending judgment on measures that would have curled their forebears' hair—the Tennessee Valley Authority, the Wagner Act. ... It may not be true that without radio the chief evangelist of the New Deal could never have brought it to birth. It may well be true what without that cohesive lubricant the New Deal could never have accomplished half as much and the marks it left would have been different and shallower. Nor was FDR sole conduit for this lubricant. Father Charles E. Coughlin's and Senator Huey P. Long's peevish-to-vicious appeals to unreason exploited the public almost as ably as FDR's calls for energetic goodwill spiked with occasional cultivated sarcasms.

This new relation between President and citizen—or, when perverted, between demagogue and easy mark—was, in the purest sense, democratic. So was use of statistical ratings to guide what Americans would hear over radio during the 8,000-odd hours a year when politicians were not using it to manipulate them. The elder kind of furniture that talked and sang and played musical instruments—the phonograph—had been less arbitrary. Within the limits of his stock of records its owner could choose for himself *The Washington Post* to suit one mood, "The Two Black Crows" for another, *Eine Kleine Nachtmusik* for another. Radio gave out with only what its several managers believed a substantial public would want at a given time. The basis of judgment was usually Crossley or, after Crossley quit the field because its terms had changed, the "Hooperating" of a given effort. Yet, however shaky it sounds to the lay mind thus to take the tastes of a few thousand as a gauge to the nation's preferences, the probability is high that the results were seldom grossly skewed. Democracy was probably not too ill served. Though it could never be said that broadcasting was certainly giving America what it positively wanted, it seldom gave what the ratings showed was *not* wanted. The public's fingers changing stations amounted to voting against broadcasts that it found less attractive than something earlier or later or right or left on the dial.

By federal law broadcasters' licenses depended on their serving "public interest, convenience and necessity." The kind of "interest" meant thereby was ignored or scamped most of the time. But in another sense "public interest" was the chief determinant of what got on the air. Here was a perpetual popularity contest among competing kinds of music—jazz, opera, symphonic, country, religious, potted-palm—among competing dramatic genres—detective, science fiction, love, family troubles, adventure, religious—all complicated by the kinds of listeners available at this time of day, day of week, season of year, all modified by considerations of regional tradition and the waxing or waning popularity of this or that microphone personality.

Given the overriding needs of advertisers, the findings of the ratings services, the tastes of various strata of the population, the skills of the growing caste of broadcasting technicians (engineers, writers, producers, music directors and so on), this is how the 1930s worked it out in radio's new art form—the soap opera, which Gilbert Seldes called "the great invention of radio, its single notable contribution to the art of fiction." [119]

Naturally it had ancestors in other media. Newspapers and magazines had long relied on the continued-in-our-next serial to keep readers buying, to keep circulation large and advertisers happy. In the silent days Hollywood's weekly two-reel cliff-hanger serials had done well. The newspaper comic strip, bulwark of circulation, had addicted readers to the daily doings of synthetic and seldom subtle characters—first funny (Happy Hooligan, Mutt & Jeff, Jiggs) in self-contained episodes, later appealing or dashing (Walt Wallet, Little Orphan Annie, Dick Tracy) in scenarios overlapping from day to day through several weeks to make sure the public stayed hooked. In fact, one radio producer trying to warn a new writer how soap opera was put together showed him three months' worth of a newspaper comic strip and said, "Do it like that." Just when and where soap opera was born of these forebears is uncertain. But one of the beginnings definitely occurred when the Chicago *Tribune*'s WGN asked a minor vaudeville blackface team, Charles Correll and Freeman Gosden, to work up a radio serial cognate to a comic strip. From this substitution of ears for eyes came *Amos & Andy,* the endless story-in-dialogue-and-sound-effects of two Southern blacks in a Northern big city. It struck the national fancy as hard as any comic strip ever had. The material was reminiscent of the very popular short stories by Octavus Roy Cohen in the *Saturday Evening Post* about the black community of Birmingham, Alabama, centered on dandified, glib Florian Slappey, pretentious lawyer Evans Chew and the black burial-society lodge called The Sons and Daughters of I Will Arise. Amos & Andy had their lodge, the Mystic Knights of the Sea; their high-prestige friends Madame Queen and the Kingfish (Huey Long's *nom de guerre* derived from him); their precarious Fresh Air Taxi Company; and the farcical contrast between Amos' earnest simplicity and Andy's misguided and often disastrous efforts to be shrewd and knowing.

Correll & Gosden's local success drew such attention that in August, 1929—score another for those momentous few months just before the Great Crash—Pepsodent toothpaste made broadcasting history by putting them on the national network of the National Broadcasting Company in the early evening six days a week for only fifteen minutes of japery-plus-entertainment instead of the usual half hour. For the next decade *Amos & Andy* was a national cult. People planned their lives not to conflict with the show. When it was on the air, use of telephones dropped 50 percent. In Atlantic City shopkeepers found it necessary to install loudspeakers at street corners so the tourists wouldn't have to stay in their hotel rooms to keep up with the Kingfish. It taught broadcasters that, for a minor thing, listeners would accept a mere crisp quarter hour of dialogue story; for a major thing, that popular radio personalities in perpetual-motion continuity would bring the advertising sponsor's customers back day after day as loyally as admirers of *Tillie the Toiler* or *The Gumps* in the daily paper. Madison Avenue, home of the hucksters' axiom that "Repetition is reputation," found this admirably suited for building loyalty to a particular brand or trademark. By September, 1932, *Fortune*'s summary of radio advertising practice said, "The serial can currently present a pretty strong case for itself as the ideal program." [120]

The lesson had been taught again when, three months after *Amos & Andy* went national, NBC gave the ethereal audience *The Rise of the Goldbergs,* an evening serial based on the juicily mangled English and pungent family doings of New York City's Eastern Jewish enclave with its heart in the Lower East Side and its pocketbook in the newly developing garment district south of the Broadway theaters. This bubbly mash had previously been distilled into more stimulating form by Montague Glass' stories and plays about Potash & Perlmutter and even more momentously by Milt Gross' *Nize Baby* dialogues and drawings in the New York *World,* and Mike Gold, corrosive star of the Communists' *New Masses,* was about to pay his respects to the same subculture in a notable novel, *Jews Without Money.* But Molly Goldberg, written and played for the next twenty years by her creator, Gertrude Berg, was a sweetly jolly, pithily sententious embodiment of the ideal sympathetic mother with appeal far wider than that of Gross' accounts of the remarkable things Mrs. Feitlebaum said to Mrs. Yifnif across the tenement airshaft. The nation affectionately condescended to Amos & Andy, for in those days the word "stereotype" was seldom heard outside the printing industry. Molly Goldberg's public found her not only entertaining but a source of emotional comfort—and for many women, Gentile as well as Jewish, a figure to identify with. In the evolution of soap opera that was crucial.

Back to Chicago, where, the next year, the basic structure was practically completed with *Clara, Lu & Em,* a serial about three women—a mother of five, her housekeeper and a widow neighbor. Their temperaments were folksily differentiated; their successive daily troubles, engagingly homey. Doubtless many women were better able to see themselves in this audible mirror because it broke away from what we now call "ethnic" material in favor of the Midwestern WASP references and speech habits of the mainstream that American advertisers most sought. Thenceforward the typical soap opera was set in a small town; its chief characters were named Thompson or Brown. Note that to make the most of women, *Clara, Lu & Em* came on five days a week in the *afternoon*—when most men were away at office or factory, while womenfolks used the radio to beguile the tedium of household chores or, as automobile radios came in after 1930, drove to and from shopping. The one ingredient of classic soap opera still lacking at this point was its utter humorlessness—not a smile in a year's worth of *Stella Dallas*—whereas an occasional chuckle surfaced in *The Goldbergs* and *Clara, Lu & Em.* Otherwise, the statesmen of radio production had already filled out the formula that Aristotle would have deductively arrived at had he studied American radio *c.* A.D. 1936 instead of Greek drama *c.* 320 B.C.: "The species *Opera saponacea* consists of a daytime, quarter-hour serial daily narrating, largely in dialogue, the vicissitudes of a fictitious, closely related group of WASP persons centered on female characters for women listeners to identify with in spite of—or because of?—their and the program's complete lack of sense of humor."

Or from a contemporary student of the genre, James Thurber: "Between slices of advertising spread twelve minutes of dialogue, add predicament, villainy, and female suffering in equal measures, throw in a dash of nobility, sprinkle with tears, season with organ music, cover with a rich announcer sauce, and serve five times a week." [121] Or from within the studios, Mary Jane Higby, specialist in playing soap opera heroines: "Soap opera may well have been the lowest point ever reached by dramatic art, down deep beneath 'Nellie, the Beautiful Cloak Model' ... but ... as *advertising,* it was just plain great ... habit-forming ... and cheap." [122] Within a few years it was swamping the major networks between 11 A.M. and 6 P.M. It was mass produced by Elaine Carrington, a known writer in women's magazine fiction; Irna Phillips, a former normal-school teacher of how-to-tell-stories-to-the-kiddies, who made $250,000 a year doing five soap operas simultaneously; and Frank and Ann Hummert, husband and wife working into radio producing through bright young careers in advertising. Their script factory where salaried hacks turned story lines into dialogue and sound effects, stuffed an eighth of all available major radio time with canned heartbreak and leased it out to advertisers hoping to profit from the magic wrought by this warlock and witch. Others nibbled around the edges of the gold mine, but those three sources, all Chicago-developed, were the big time. The generic "soap opera" was, of course, spun off from Hollywood's "horse opera" (= the movies' Western genre) plus the enthusiasm with which the nation's large soap makers used it to imprint on the housewife's subconscious the names and merits of their entries in the laundry, bathing and face-washing sweepstakes. True, cosmetics, staple groceries and home remedies, even life insurance, were also in there. But soap powders and cake soaps enhancing one's charm were the backbone of the bonanza.

Except in profit-and-loss-statements the magic was rather limp. Story line and characters might derive from printed originals: *Stella Dallas* was expanded from a lugubrious best-seller of the 1920s by Olive Higgins Prouty. Cracker-barrel folksiness was provided by adaptation of E. N. Westcott's *David Harum* (1898), about a wryly humorous small-town banker, and by extrapolation from Clarence Budington Kelland's Scattergood Baines ("Well, I got to be gittin'!") stories for the slick magazines. *The Light of the World* made soap opera of the Bible; Adam shouted at Eve, "Don't tell me what the serpent said! I'm tired of hearing about him!" [123] Max Wylie's textbook on radio writing granted that radio versions of Bible stories "always command large radio audiences" but warned that "few ... can be transferred to radio without serious reorganization. They are either too diffuse and ill-assembled or too compact or too fragmentary."[124] So most soap opera was built from scratch formula like the old Westerns and the ten-twent-thirt melodramas, some of the values of which were retained. Not all: Bertha, the Sewing-Machine Girl, at least came out the other side of her successive ordeals and was about to live happily ever after the fifth-act curtain. At the end of the Western He and She rode off into the sunset hand in hand, leaving the corpses of Mexicali Pete and his Indian accomplice, Horse Feather, to the buzzards. The troubles of the she-protagonist of the soaps never ended. Whether harassed widow or mother of a calamity-addicted family or winsome girl trying to make her way without getting made or made away with, she would gamely survive two months of five-day weeks of one set of miseries and misunderstandings only to be rinsed off, patched up and sent right back into the ring against another set of interlocking catastrophes, emotional and physical.

That was just like the comic strips. Another such borrowing was indifference to the effect of the passage of time on the characters. Just as Little Orphan Annie stayed four feet tall and some ten years old for forty years, so was the basic problem of the heroine of *The Romance of Helen Trent* daily stated as: "The story of a woman who sets out to prove what so many other women long to prove in their own lives, that romance can live on at thirty-five and even beyond...." [125]

Before it was over, Miss Trent, a dress designer by trade but always too busy fending off admirers and enemies ever to get near a drawing board or a fitting room, was pushing Cleopatra and Ninon de Lenclos for the age-cannot-wither-her title. Fortunately, being invisible, she had no need for plastic surgery.

The earlier preferred setting was a town of a few thousand people called Mapleville or Martinsburg. The good, though often wrong-headed, characters were local bred, just like yourself. The bad ones, sometimes learning better under the influence of Mapleville's fine people, but never really their sort, usually came from the big city. Eventually the source of their viciousness was usually New York City, though while this Chicago-born idiom still felt its ancestry strongly, the Loop was probably where the headstrong daughter went to seek her own life and find it far too hot to handle. As the soaps multiplied, folksy situations wore thin and competition for the housewife's adrenals sharpened, Mapleville folks were likely to be precipitated into highly unusual vicissitudes borrowed from suspense fiction—kidnappings, blackmail, manslaughter. . . . Ma Perkins' daughter Fay once suffered simultaneously from amnesia, paralysis below the waist and arrest for murder.

Dope, rape and bastardy were present only as potential factors not specifically spelled out; it was TV that made them face cards in the soap opera deck. But good old amnesia—the easy way into the Enoch Arden situation beloved of the Victorian servant girl's novel—was as common as athlete's foot in Mapleville. Few soap opera husbands or boyfriends got through without at least one dose of it. The "God box"—the control room's name for the pipe organ indispensable to bringing on and signing off—went groan, whooffle, ooh-ooh-ooh, and then past the announcer's tonsils, lissome and tender as creamed sweetbreads, flowed the come-on: "Will Marvin Mandrake recover his memory before he and his new sweetheart, lovely Sonia Spandrel, are entangled in the unwitting crime and irredeemable tragedy of bigamy? Tune in tomorrow at this same time to . . . Happiness Haven! brought to you by the makers of Thistledown Soap. . . ."

Presently the more advanced practitioners dropped the folks-in-the-next-block motif and went in for high life, or anyway what sounded like it to the lady unloading the washer. Helen Trent dwelt somewhere in the Hollywood sphere of influence, and most of her entanglements had a flavor of the film colony, elegant and glamorous by definition. Stella Dallas' troubles, all whine, gurgle and stiff upper lip, originated in the marriage of her serenely beautiful daughter, Laurel ("Lollie baby!"), to the son of a high-chinned family of millionaires unable to overlook Stella's wrong-side-of-the-tracks origin. *Our Gal Sunday's* problem was even more flagrantly caste-minded: ". . . the story of an orphan girl named Sunday from the little mining town of Silver Creek, Colorado, who in young womanhood married England's richest, most handsome lord, Lord Henry Brinthrop.... Can this girl from a mining town find happiness as the wife of a wealthy and titled Englishman?" [126] For twenty-odd years of trying that question went unsolved.

On the fringes of soap opera there was good work in, for instance, Paul Rhymer's remarkably human *Vic and Sade* in their "small house halfway up in the next block" and, for a few years after World War II, in Peg Lynch's genuinely sparkling *Ethel & Albert*. But those were never true, identification-or-bust examples of the genre, partly because they worked from valid observation embodied in chewy dialogue, partly because they stuck to self-limited episodes, not overlapping long plots. The earmark of the real thing was its ingenious stringing out of a single incident for a week, recapitulating daily so that the lady of the house could tune in any time, even miss an installment because the cat scratched the baby, and still know just what was going on. The comic strips' past master of that was Harold Gray of *Little Orphan Annie* stalling through the weekday strips without losing the addict's attention while saving the big punchy action for the Sunday full page.

This recurring parallel with comic strips even carried over into minds usually impatient of undisguised banality. Just as certain subscribers to the *New Republic* seldom missed *Gasoline Alley,* so soap operas were curiously familiar to many, men as well as women, whom the advertisers did not have in mind at all. I recall the dismay with which the wife of a middle-aged psychiatrist learned at a talkative luncheon that her presumably deep-thinking, cultivated husband was inexplicably well versed in what currently went on in *Just Plain Bill's* barbershop and how *Amanda of Honeymoon Hill* had recently got out of Jam No. 39. His lady still looked perplexed after he explained plausibly enough that three times a week he drove sixty miles to a teaching clinic and the radio in the car offered little else. But this understandable low-grade fascination, like that of the compulsion to listen for rhythmic patterns in dripping water, could not mask the alarming things that soap opera meant about a large segment of American womanhood. Listeners not only obligingly identified with matriarchal Ma Perkins and Ellen Brown (of *Young Widder Brown,* whose peevish children kept her from marrying her best beloved for at least two decades) but developed quasi-hallucinations about their actuality. There all alone in the kitchen, maybe a little drowsy as the day wore on and soap opera succeeded soap opera, gradually slipping into fantasy, many beglamored women came to believe these were real people and their troubles genuine. The proof was that they acted on it—they sent wedding presents by the thousand when a nice-girl subsidiary character married; baby clothes when she had her firstborn; home remedies when she fell sick; dollar bills when she was penniless in that grim boardinghouse in Chicago; black-bordered cards of condolence when her mother died. . . .

One such woman told market researchers that she used a certain face cream because Helen Trent used it and "she's way over thirty and has all those romances. . . ." [127] Sponsors pushed this imbecility farther by causing the writers to work up gradual interest in a particular ring or brooch that the dialogue represented the heroine as wearing; after some weeks of such buildup the announcer's spiel offered duplicates for sale mail order at, say, $1, plus a wrapper from a large cake of Thistledown Soap—think of it, only $1 for a genuine simulated gold True Love brooch just like the one Marvin gave Sandra when he got back from his run-in with the gangsters. The purpose was not so much profit from dime-store junk, though presumably that was welcome, as getting a gauge on how seriously how many women were taking *Happiness Haven.* The results were usually ungodly gratifying.

In some other aspects of radio the identity of the performer was as important as in other kinds of show business. Photographs of newscasters, crooners and comedians were all over the papers indissolubly tied to their voices and individual microphone mannerisms. In the movies for a generation the identity of the star had so overshadowed the role that only scriptwriters paid much attention to its name. For fan and reviewer alike it was Norma Shearer married to John Gilbert in this picture. Soap opera reversed that. The housewife's relation to the Sonia Spandrel voice was so intimate that the actual actress standing there at the mike in the studio dropping mimeographed sheets on the floor was altogether obliterated by the fictional persona. She knew those voices so well that if a soap opera actor had to leave the cast for a better job or some private purpose, a death or disappearance for him had to be written into the script to account for his absence; no replacement could fool the women. The whole muddle was summed up in a letter from a housewife who realized from voice alone that the young husband in *Just Plain Bill* and Larry Noble, the matinee-idol husband in *Backstage Wife,* were being played by the same actor. She threatened to expose him to one or another of his wives unless he stopped leading this shameless double life—a thing that soap opera had taught her was very common. Frightening?

Students of soap opera surmise that such thoroughly hooked listeners * visualized these audible phantoms rather vividly. Even the

---

* The comic strip analogy holds here, too: Fans of *Dick Tracy, Little Orphan Annie, Mary Worth's Family* and so on have been known to take the economic and medical emergencies of the principal characters with this same

nonhooked occasional listener did some of that. For me, another car-radio captive, Helen Trent was dark, widemouthed, rather like a more willowy Joan Crawford; Just Plain Bill like the photographs of William Dean Howells in his sixties; Larry Noble a more limber version of the young FDR; Stella Dallas pudgy, hair done à la Mrs. Calvin Coolidge. ... In 1948 Thurber predicted that these millions of conflicting visualizations would probably make it impossible to transfer *Big Sister* or *Pepper Young's Family* to TV with disillusioningly visible actors, so, since "their intense and far-flung audience would never give them up easily," [128] those and other such valuable radio properties could go on forever—sight unseen on radio. He was wrong probably not because listeners' loyalties slackened but because as TV soaps came in—as they inevitably did with new characters and story lines gradually getting much more lurid—the sponsors concentrated their dollars on them, not on radio, which had to drop them. They hung on for some years after the handwriting was on the wall. In 1959, however, CBS killed off *Backstage Wife, Our Gal Sunday, Road of Life, This Is Nora Drake.* ... I happened to be in the car on the afternoon in 1960 when the hemlock was served successively to *Young Dr. Malone, Ma Perkins, Helen Trent.* The networks actually went to the trouble to work it out that at last, at last Miss Trent was marrying her sturdy and abjectly long-suffering politician-suitor and that the parole board had finally sprung the wayward son of *Right to Happiness,* so no more downbeat premonition of agonies to come could spoil the family's last Thanksgiving. Thus knocked in the head after twenty-five years of faithful service, these wheelhorses shuffled off into the boneyard of show business, along with the old Chautauquas, minstrel shows, magic lantern lecturers and courthouse medicine shows.

Thus, radio (that is, radio's advertising clients, paying the piper and calling the tune) directly exploited the American housewife as household purchasing agent. It soon also got at her indirectly by creating leverage from her own children on her purchases of what they ate. In 1932, for instance, Frank Hummert set Robert Hardy Andrews, a famously prolific source of radio scripts, concocting "a soap opera for

---

seriousness. Yet, though the audiences of the strips are about as wide as those of the radio soaps were, the incidence of such illusions among them is probably less proportionately. Note that fans of TV soap opera behave about as imbecilically in this respect as radio listeners ever did, and things are now complicated by their knowing what the characters look like; cf. two excellent books, Chris Chase, *How to Be a Movie Star or, a Terrible Beauty Is Born* (1968), and Madeleine Edmondson and David Rounds, *The Soaps* (1973), both by those who have written or acted or both in soaps.

kids." So he begat *Jack Armstrong, All-American Boy,* dedicated to cajoling teenagers into badgering Mom into buying them Wheaties for breakfast because they were the secret of Jack's glorious stamina and intelligence. He began as a painfully recognizable type out of those pre-World War I series of books-for-boys—a *Motor Boys* high school hero-athlete and big-man-in-the-corridor with a cheerful but bumbly crony, Billy Fairfield; Billy's sister, Betty, who decorously admired Jack and always tagged along; a dastardly enemy Jack's own age up to any dirty trick with—this was an innovation—an equally dastardly sister named Gwendolyn.... But just as soap opera had to move into melodramatic calamities, so Jack had to liven things up by leaving football field and baseball diamond for exotic perils and complications in jungles, marine depths, lakes of fire, aided and abetted by the Fairfields' Uncle Jack, a retired intelligence officer who always had an amphibian plane or bathysphere or dirigible at his disposal. Out of those ingredients grew long, looping episodes good for weeks of "What's that thing creeping over there?" and "No time for that now!" and shrieking or explosive sound effects, and once the treasure was found or the Worm Ourobouros foiled, they no sooner touched home base than some fresh quest of the Aztec Alligator sent them off again.

This was a long established genre, of course, a staple of the new kind of noncomic comic strips and of the consequent "comic books" that replaced nickel and dime novels as kids' widely deplored favorite reading—if that is the word. Behind Hummert's germinal request for what became *Jack Armstrong* probably lay the success in the very early 1930s of radio serials based on adventure comics already popular in newspapers. For several years before radio gave him another dimension as cheerleader for Cocomalt, Buck Rogers, intrepid young king of space-navigating rocket ships in the twenty-fifth century, had done very well on newsprint. His rival in the goop-up-your-milk world was Ovaltine's Little Orphan Annie of the Harold Gray adventure strip disporting herself on the air with Sandy's "Arf!" duly prominent among the sound effects. Toward the end of the day, as Mom grew too busy getting supper to pay requisite heed to soap opera, the kids home from school could settle down with Buck, Jack, Annie and their dozen or so rivals for the acne set's attention—and the networks' revenues never skipped a beat. Even the Old West was exploited. Silvercup Bread's brand was on *The Lone Ranger's* great white stallion: "Hi-Yo Silver! Awaaaay!" *Tom Mix's Straight Shooters* opened with:

> Hot Ralston for your breakfast
> Starts the day off shining bright,

Gives you lots of cowboy energy
With a flavor that's just right. . . .[130]

Radio commercials made America almost certainly the first culture in which a major factor in pediatric nutrition was the young telling their dam what to buy them to eat and drink.

Inevitably Edgar Rice Burroughs' free-swinging *Tarzan* jungle yarns, already well worn in books, movies and comic strips, were a formidable contender in this lucrative sweepstakes. Also inevitably the souvenir gadget grew in this field with special rankness. Just as in soap opera, alleged use of the dingus by the hero (or heroine) was pretext for making the listener crave that membership badge or code-interpreting device or magic ring with a secret compartment, each glowing in the dark, for a box top (or reasonable facsimile thereof to meet pointless federal regulations), plus 10 cents. And unlike the soap opera heroine's lavaliere, these gizmos were of fair quality, good enough to work and last, or so says *Great Radio Heroes,* a valuable recent study by Jim Harmon, who was the right age at the time and lovingly kept them all. Collectors now pay well for them. At last hearing a *Terry and the Pirates* nose ring would bring $25, and it was largely all bid, little ask for *Little Orphan Annie* ceramic mugs inscribed "Gee, Sandy, isn't Ovaltine great for you?"

Those mail-order True Love brooches infiltrated the national networks with a style of broadcast advertising otherwise scantily represented on radio's big time—call it the Two-to-Take-Him school. It had several aspects—the religious, the magical-medicinal, the occult-mystical, the nasty-paranoid, the straight-hustler pitch—but all were aimed, usually with dismaying success, at those too ignorant and in many cases obviously too dim to be allowed at large unattended. One contribution of the rise of radio was to warn the nation of previously unsuspected shortcomings in the distribution of common sense—basic savvy, the quality that the countrymen of the Yankee peddler, the Mississippi river gambler, the Philadelphia lawyer and the ubiquitous salesmen of gold bricks and green goods should have developed in self-defense. The soap opera housewives were by no means the only presumed adults thus showing alarming lack of sense of reality. During the same enterprising 1930s the rise of mail-order ballyhoo on the air argued comparable gullibility concentrated among a far larger segment of the population—the low-income, mentally and often physically undernourished millions living in the half of the country below the fortieth parallel—historically the once-slaveholding South and the once-Mexican Southwest. Down there susceptibility to ethereal cheap-jackery was equaled only by the appetite for country music, hot gospel religion and bitter social suspicions.

Not that any region of the United States then had or now has a monopoly on chumps. Manhattan Island is chronically infested with pitchmen and hawkers of allegedly hot furs. Charles Ponzi's financial perpetual-motion machine did well in Boston in the early 1920s. Winter vacationists from all over fell hard for Florida real estate and California oil wells. But the new ease of access to the sucker's ear afforded by radio was most flagrantly exploited by purveyors of genuine simulated diamonds and electric-lighted bow ties in the area where snuff sells best and boys are likely to be named Joe Billy instead of James William. It probably also means something about that area that the pitch was primarily aimed at whites. Mail orders are color-blind, so there is no knowing how many requests for packages of scraps to make patchwork quilts with came from blacks. But the whole tone of the racket neglected appeal to any but red-necks and hillbillies. The preachers and hymns were white; the music was country, not jazz; the politics were nasally Fascistic; the sales talks never offered the hair straighteners, skin whiteners or race records that the black press advertised so extensively. The prime audience was probably typified by the displaced white sharecroppers in John Faulkner's *Men Working* who spent their first WPA checks to buy radios.

The aristocrats of this broadcasting were WWVA-Wheeling (West Virginia) and WCKY-Cincinnati (actually in Covington, Kentucky), spraying come-ons over the Border states. Dozens of low-powered local stations throughout the Deep South and the Southwest fed chiefly on the same kind of programming, hoping that the Federal Communications Commission wouldn't notice—a hope well founded on what it already let WCKY and WWVA get away with. But the lowdownest giants of the racket were half a dozen powerful to superpowerful stations operating under Mexican license just south of the border but broadcasting altogether in English and concentrating on the fatback belt to northward and eastward.* The signal of XERA-Villa Acuna (across from Del Rio, Texas) was so powerful that when atmospheric conditions were just right, its broadcasts came in clear and loud in Alaska and Nova Scotia. Listeners in Minneapolis or Buffalo picking up this bootleg station over which the FCC had no jurisdiction suddenly learned how mistaken they had been in thinking that soap

---

* Much of the following comes from my "Country Doctor Goes to Town," *Saturday Evening Post,* April 20, 1940, and "The Border Radio Mess," *Saturday Evening Post,* September 25, 1948.

opera and laxative commercials had plumbed the depths of inanity and offensiveness. Its rivals at other border towns, such as XELO and XENT, were no better. At the height of it all an officer of the Better Business Bureau at Laredo, Texas, was got out of bed late one evening by a strange voice on the telephone: "Finally reached you. Great what the phone company will do when challenged. I'm an astronomer on night observations at the Harvard Observatory in Cambridge, Massachusetts. I kill the time with radio, and I've learned not to expect much, but my God, man, I've been listening to a station in your town for two hours, and it hasn't carried anything but squalling and drivel yet. How can you people down there put up with it?"

The Texan explained that no matter what the announcer said, that station was across the river in *Nuevo* Laredo, Mexico, and Texans also thought it stank. Actually hordes of other Texans out in the water-tank-and-cactus country made up a prime market for the sort of radio sales pitches that advertised bargain gravestones, $9.95, name already engraved, with a vocal quartet singing "I Hear You Callin' but I Don't Believe You, So I'm Gonna Leave You Now." Certain other Texans owned large interests in those X-Over the Border stations or freely used them to advertise mail-order gimmicks with addresses in Fort Worth or Dallas. The commercial would go: "Now, friends, here is your chance for a limited time to get an all-steel, genuine portable typewriter suitable for small business, wonderful for children's homework and a great help in getting them good marks, for just two dollars and ninety-eight cents. Please don't confuse these with any other typewriters on the market. No, sir, this typewriter has a separate key for each letter of the alphabet. It has capital and small letters and is built on the good old rotary system. Anybody who can write and read can operate it. No need to spend hours learning. Send no money, just your name and address on a postcard to TYPEWRITERS, Box 000, Fort Worth, Texas, and pay the postman only two dollars and ninety-eight cents plus a few cents COD charges...." What was sent was of course, one of those rotary-disk kids' toys that look as if they were made of the tops of baking powder cans. But it was, as advertised, portable and did have capital and small letters and the advertiser was always careful to send a refund in case anybody stupid enough to believe had the enterprise to send it back, so the postal inspectors stayed out of his hair. Other such irresistible bargains might be a $1.98 candid camera, a burial-insurance policy, a jukebox bank that lit up when a coin dropped in, a collection of thirty-eight fruit trees and berry bushes for $3.95....

The staple come-on entertainment was gittar-and-vocal quartets often represented as family groups, whining and plunking their way into the country music that, though already indispensable in the hominy grits area and causing cultural revolutions in Nashville, Tennessee, did not become a national cult until after World War II. Secular numbers big on the X frequencies and their W competitors would be: "Why Did I Teach My Wife to Drive?," "If You Got the Money, Honey, I Got the Time," "If You Want Your Freedom PDQ, Divorce Me COD" and, always and forever, "The Yellow Rose of Texas." They all sounded pretty much alike to outsiders. For the next quarter hour another family, holy this time, with a musical evangelist on the gittar, his wife on the bull fiddle, his daughter on the accordeen tore into such gospel specialties as "From Blues to Blessings" ("I was just as blue as blue could be / Till Jesus come and set me free"); "The Converted Cowboy" ("At the set of sun when life's race is run / With my Saviour I'll take a ride; / Just to dine with me there as we meet in that air / Who could ask to be more satisfied?"); or "I'm Free from the Chain Gang Now."

As the radio has succumbed to rock, plus old-time religion, one can hear a great deal of tuneful blather of not much better quality on the air nowadays; did you ever hear the Lundstroms' little boy render "Why Doesn't Daddy Come Home?" But the interspersed pitch for contributions or for mail-order records of this or that Sacred Trio or books of their favorite hymns is more subdued. The Reverend J. Charles Jessup, one of a troupe of six preacher brothers, each mighty handy with gittar or banjo, used to pour it on: "Folks, please keep this lil ole boy from the clay hills of Alabama on the air! I'm your brother, I'm doin' the best I kin. Won't you, friend, send your offerin' today? Now that's care of Station XERF, Del Rio, Texas. . . ." On such programs after the plug for the large-type, red-letter Bible for dear old mother, send-no-money, just pay the postman $1 and a few cents COD charges, the Chuckwagon Boys might favor the ether with "God's done thrown me and branded me, I'm hisn forever and ever . . ." and a plug for their latest album. But when the singer was Gene Autry or Red River Dave in some favorite of the day, records were never mentioned. Management told me they'd rather let listeners keep their illusions: "When we got Autry on that turntable, those folks think we got Ole Gene right there in the studio."

When the Reverend J. C. Bishop of Dallas moved up from radio evangelism to long-range faith healing he took to promising the listener not only to pray that he be healed but also to send him an individually anointed and blessed "prayer cloth" to apply to the afflicted spot. Thousands of bits of cheesecloth daubed with olive oil and blessed in weekly job lots were duly mailed out. No charge; that part was covered by the take from contributions simultaneously begged for on the air. For those who wanted their spiritual nourishment in non-Bible-thumping terms a self-created seer grandly named Koran whose metaphysical attainments were vague but impressive over the radio used it to sell the literature of his occult Mayan Order. His wife, Rose Dawn, whose pink Cadillac picked out in pistachio green was one of the sights of Del Rio, sent X-station listeners either a prayer shrine to unfold the soul or a special perfume to effect changes of a strongly hinted-at nature in others' behavior. Such fast-talking "mystics" and hot-gospelers were greedily following the leads given them in the late 1920s by the Reverend Aimee Semple McPherson and the Reverend Bob Shuler, whose broadcasts from Los Angeles had vividly demonstrated the uses of radio in working up support— meaning revenue. The top X stations were now charging preachers up to $150 per quarter hour, both parties confident that enough bread would float back on the airwaves to leave a good profit. The small FCC-licensed stations through the South might ask only $35 to $50, but then their signals covered smaller areas with smaller returns. Some station managers were uneasy about selling time to preachers. It was felt that the public that liked hymns and hellfire were not the best prospects for the worldly kind of gadgets and records that bulked large in the station's operations. But preachers paid cash on the barrelhead, whereas the mail-order advertisers were there on the contingent basis of commissions paid the station on sales and inquiries.

Since X stations were neither under FCC regulation nor members of the American broadcasters' associations, their standards of what kind of material was unacceptable and how much time to allow for commercials were lower than those of the American-based competition for the suckers. Hence out-and-out aphrodisiacs and contraceptives were about the only things never plugged on the bootleg X air. Rheumatism cures (the slogan of one such, "You have nothing to lose but your pains," would have been better had any of the listeners ever heard of Marx); "Yer kidneys need a good flushin' out, so you don't have to git up nights ... Dr. Comeon's Swamp Root with its wonder-working ingredients"; the Mayo Brothers' (that was a neat one) miracle tooth powder ... genuine 12-carat gold-plated wedding rings designed by a famous artist and ordered from The Diamond Man, Box Such-and-such, only $2.95. ... Interviewing one such operator, I began by saying I'd come to see him because the US authorities had told me he was one of the biggest phony jewelry radio-mail-order specialists in the country. "One of the biggest!" he answered hotly. "Boy, I *am* the biggest. Nobody else can't come near me."

As the 1930s progressed, the no-holds-barred advantages of the X stations drew a constellation of racist-minded, homegrown-Fascist preachers trying to emulate the power that Shuler had developed in Los Angeles. They all sounded like Donald Duck calling hogs: the Reverend Harvey Springer (The Cowboy Evangelist), the Reverend Wendell Zimmerman (The Flying Evangelist), the Reverend J. A. Lovell, whose anti-Semitism took the form of preaching that the English-speaking and Scandinavian peoples are the true seed of Abraham, whereas those now known as Jews are spurious, actually descendants of the heathen Canaanites on whom the Old Testament is so severe. Their variations on anti-Catholicism, pro-Axisism, anti-Modernism, white supremacyism and other basic philosophies popular at the forks of the crick were in a forensic style well typified by what one of them called the Federal Council of Churches when he suspected it of stirring up opposition to his broadcasts: ". . . this mad dog from hell, this green-eyed monster, this hydra-headed Frankenstein, this destroyer of the faith . . . the best friend the devil has in America today. . . ."

Among those thus soaring in the spiritual climate of the X stations were several hate mongers going on to national prominence as the approach of World War II caused isolationism to close ranks and double-charge its epithets—for instance, the Reverend Gerald Winrod of Wichita, Kansas. That aspect of bootleg broadcasting was not funny. Nor, once one gets beyond grinning about the $2.98 typewriter with a key for every letter, was the cold-drawn effrontery of advertisers thus counting on ignorance and malnourished apathy to coax dollars previously unattainable from millions previously unreachable because they didn't read even the two-line ads in the back pages of pulp magazines. The best that can be said for those sharp operators was that they made the commercial manners of soap opera look good. At least the soap did lather.

A special kind of listeners' naïveté came to bloom in the mid-1930s in a special kind of radio sharp practice—the amateur hour. Its ancestor was the old-time Amateur Night of shabby vaudeville theaters and honky-tonks *c.* 1900—a weekly contest offering small cash prizes to local amateurs eager to compete in singing, dancing, juggling, playing ragtime piano or whatever. Success was gauged by volume of applause from the beery audience—more tumultuous for the smirking girl singing "Where the River Shannon Flows" than for the pimply youth of eighteen doing a conscientious buck-and-wing. The penalty of failure was to be howled at, maybe have things thrown at you, while from the wings a huge hook on a pole dragged you offstage. A dreary and rather brutal institution, but it entertained the customers, and out of it now and again real talent went upward to professional vaudeville.

As radio singers and musicians developed standing, Perry Charles, a radio jack-of-all-trades, adapted Amateur Night to the air. Though inability to see the performers ruled out dancers and jugglers, amateurs eager to get into radio were plentiful. A gong replaced the hook. Instead of applause, listeners telephoned in their approval; maybe this feeling of personal participation helped make the thing popular. The rest was the attraction of the Cinderella motif, "human interest" fascination with the possibility, implied by the announcer, of seeing a great career start. Within a year or so the nation's evening airwaves were top-heavy with amateur hours, the most high-powered of which, attracting 30,000 votes a week from all over the country by mail and telegram as well as telephone, was Major Edward Bowes' Original Amateur Hour sponsored by Chrysler.

The Major (the title, which he insisted on, was from a commission in the US Army Reserve) had greatly prospered in San Francisco real estate, then in Eastern theatrical real estate, including a piece of the Capitol Theater, the great Broadway movie palace that went early into radio for publicity. His liking for titles and publicity eventually made him honorary fire chief in fifty-five cities, honorary police chief in fifty-seven, a member of twenty-four small-time yacht clubs, mostly freshwater (but he used his own saltwater yacht to commute from the Jersey shore to Manhattan), and honorary governor of three states. His tailor was suavely expensive, his credit rating unimpeachable, but his nimble, wary step, cold eyes in a head shaped like a battered tomcat's and glib speech suggested the essential con man. In his routine as master of ceremonies of his *Amateur Hour* he even opened with the old carnival barker's come-on for the Wheel of Fortune: "Round and round she goes! and where she stops nobody knows! . . . If you think you have talent, why not try for this program? Obey that impulse— don't be timid! A letter mailed from New York or vicinity will bring you a prompt invitation. It's easy and pleasant and you're doing us a favor. . . ." *

That drew 10,000 inquiries a week to what Ben Gross, radio observer for the New York *Daily News,* called "the apotheosis of the hillbilly and the musical saw." [131] As a side effect the bus terminals and help-the-stranded agencies of Manhattan overflowed with derelicts, mostly young, who had taken it all too seriously. A woman from Toronto spent her all to get herself and two small children (they played the bagpipes) to New York City and, failing to secure an audition from the Major, came into the hands of the Travelers Aid. A

---

* Much of this section is from my "Terrified Amateurs," in *Life* (its last pre-Luce issue), November, 1936.

Chicago boy whose railroad-worker father sent him to New York City on a railroad pass to sing for the Major got no audition, and when the Aid telegraphed his father to pay his passage home, the reply was that the kid could just stay there and support himself singing in nightclubs. A high school girl in California sang "The Rosary" so sweetly that her brother, a gas pumper in a filling station, persuaded a party of motorists from New York City to take her there for the Major to hear. For a miracle, she arrived *virgo intacta* and for another got an audition—but when rejected, she was pitiably stranded. ... Every week the Aid and the Salvation Army did what they could for 3,000 to 4,000 such hapless paragons of gullibility. An acquaintance of Bowes' on the board of the Aid wrote to "Dear Eddie" asking for money to help it look after his leavings. Bowes sent a check for $100. At the time Chrysler was paying $5,000 a week for his show, and his net annual income after taxes was $185,000. A landlady saddled with a penniless girl reject who telephoned Bowes' office to ask that something be done about her was told, "My good woman, she's nothing to us."

Requiring a postmark from in or near New York City enabled the Major to avoid moral responsibility for return transportation even for those managing to get auditioned. Every week, after all, he needed another dozen not-too-impossible fresh amateurs. He also needed to keep his millions of listeners agog over that potentiality of glittering success for God-given talent wherever found, maybe this time for the dewy-eyed local girl who sang "The End of a Perfect Day" so winningly at the PTA banquet. If such Pied Pipering was the best way to keep Eddie Bowes' program the most popular show on radio with a thundering Crossley rating of 27 percent, never mind the human breakage concentrated among those obviously least able to fend for themselves. Indeed, in his own view Bowes was a benefactor. He told the *New Yorker*'s Morris Markey that the whole elaborate *Amateur Hour* apparatus was eminently worthwhile if, in the hard times of the mid-1930s, it supplied work for only twenty new entertainers a week.

The average level of talent among candidates was so low that the Major could not afford strictness about lack of precious professional experience. He paid talent agents a bounty of $5 a head for likely "amateurs." One showman said Bowes' definition of an amateur was somebody who had not yet played the Palace—top rung of vaudeville. Anybody getting past the audition and actually appearing on the air in the weekly contest got a free meal in a cafeteria, $10 and the privilege of being photographed with the Major, glossy print going to the hometown newspaper. The most that winners, whether genuine amateurs or ringers, could expect was eight weeks in one of the Major Bowes Amateur Hour troupes that, missing no chance of extra profit, went touring what was left of vaudeville and movie houses in those times. Nor could the aspirant be sure of a square shake from the national jury of listeners. The Major gathered extra publicity by dedicating the weekly doings to one large city after another. The week it was Madison, Wisconsin, for instance, it meant a Madison girl was in the contest, Governor Philip La Follette, a neo-Progressive who should have known better, proclaimed Bowes temporary governor of the state and presented him with a Wisconsin cheese *and* Madison's Boy Scouts were deployed door to door urging Madisonians to telephone in votes for the local girl while the service clubs stirred up the PTAs and the University of Wisconsin fraternities to the same end ... what chance had the other contestants on the great night?

Rival amateur hours were a touch more scrupulous. The one handled by Fred Allen, the brilliant stand-up comic (only the phrase was not coined yet) with the unmistakable gravelly voice, advised all applicants from outside New York City to stay home. At first the amateur hour sponsored by Feenamint chewing gum did the same; then it tried to protect candidates from dislocation by organizing preliminary local contests and paying the winners' transportation to New York City and back. (Eventually Bowes had to do something like that.) The weekly winner of Allen's show appeared for a week in the stage presentation at Broadway's Roxy Theater—a good break for anybody with real talent.

The federal authorities had had good reason to put the Reverend Bob Shuler off the air. But his racist slaverings were no more flagrant than the Major's abuse of the "public interest" to which broadcasting was presumably dedicated. The immense popularity of his show and his own faculty for knowing the right people were probably what made the difference. But part of the responsibility also lay with the gullible public. In any case it would probably have done little good to bar the Major from federally controlled air. In a week he'd have made a deal with a Mexican border X station: "Just so your letter has a postmark from any town on the Rio Grande River. . . ."

Out of vaudeville came more evidence unflattering to radio listeners with the tremendous success of the phenomenon known as Walter Winchell. On "the Pan time"—the second-rate vaudeville circuits of Alexander Pantages—this rabbi's grandson had learned to eke out a living as more or less of a singer and rather less of a dancer. His notable traits included an aggressiveness special in even that sharp-elbowed world and an itchy curiosity about others' affairs—chiefly love and money—that led him uninvited to post on theater call-boards tags of flippant gossip about his fellow performers interspersed with current jokes. Then he sent such bits to the lower strata of the show business trade press; they drew attention. Then he quit footlights to do legman's chores and a column of gossip for *Vaudeville News,* house organ of the Keith company union of vaudevillians. From this minor vantage point on Broadway he elbowed himself into the newborn New York *Evening Graphic,* an outrageous tabloid excreted in 1924 by Bernarr Macfadden, the wealthy, egocentric, vegetarian publisher of *Physical Culture* and several confessions and detective magazines. The paper's original staff was captained by Fulton Oursler, destined to be a Macfadden stalwart, and George Sylvester Viereck, then catching his breath between the two World Wars that set him leading cheers first for Wilhelm II's Germany, then for Hitler's. But the yappy youngster thus hired eventually overshadowed those established jacks-of-all-writing-trades, even grew better known than the publicity-addicted Macfadden. At his death in 1972 the Associated Press obituary rated Winchell as in his day "the country's best known and most widely read journalist . . . most influential." [132]

While skipping around as the *Graphic's* weekly columnist, play reviewer and solicitor of amusement advertising, Winchell improved his already-wide acquaintance with the seamy underside of Broadway and kept trying to feed gamy news tips to Emile Gauvreau, the managing editor. For what looked like but probably was not professional scruple Gauvreau ignored the pushy amateur. One day, when short of copy for his weekly column, Winchell fell back on his stock of such rejected bits about Broadway figures and filled in with bits like those in his old vaudeville bulletins: "Helen Eby Brooks, widow of William Rock, has been plunging in Miami real estate. . . . It's a girl at the Carter De Havens. . . . Lenore Ulric paid $7 income tax. . . . Fannie Brice is betting on the horses at Belmont. . . . S. Jay Kaufman sails on the 16th via the Berengaria to be hitched to a Hungarian. . . . Report has it that Lillian Lorraine has taken a new husband again. . . ."

Broadway name-dropping columns were not new. Through the King Features Syndicate, for instance, O. O. McIntyre's "New York Day by Day" had long favored readers in Portland and Springfield and so on with vacuous comments on his famous-name frequenters. Once a week Franklin P. Adams' "The Conning Tower" in the New York *World* consisted largely of "The Diary of Our Own Samuel Pepys" rich with mentions of persons whose names knowing people knew. Nor was there lack of precedent for printed gossip skirting libel but trusting in the proverb about getting into pissing matches with skunks. Scandal sheets like *Town Topics* had long used that sort of thing to levy blackmail. Not that Winchell was a blackmailer in the hush-money sense. But as he hit his stride, he managed to give his column a flavor, sometimes genuine too, of keyholes and bribed chauffeurs that did for the Broadway column what Tabasco does for a cocktail sauce. Then from *Variety,* show business' weekly newspaper, he borrowed and corrupted the trick of coining and flaunting one's own private slang. *Variety*'s autogenic lingo sometimes added usefully to the language and usually expressed what was on its mind with an inimitable, pungent, accurate concision. Winchellese was euphuistic, diffuse, often grotesque, used mainly to add false zest to intrinsically dull data about people who didn't matter much or at all. A birth was "a blessed event"; to marry was "to middle aisle it"; hard liquor was "giggle water"—all phony as a $3 bill even when by keeping on trying he occasionally struck wit: "Wildeman" for homosexual, "Renovated" for getting divorced.

Most of the Big Town, however, thought it all racily authentic. In the rest of the nation readers had no way of knowing it was nothing of the sort. Winchell's booming popularity was probably the chief factor keeping the *Graphic* afloat. When he left it in mid-1929 for the Hearst tabloid *Daily Mirror,* which gave him access to Hearst syndication and potential circulation of 30,000,000, the *Graphic*'s efforts to replace him spawned a dynasty of not unsuccessful imitators—Ed Sullivan, who soon took his Winchell-like column to the dominant tabloid, the New York *Daily News;* Louis Sobol, who soon moved to the Hearst *Evening Journal.* Later imitations, with slight variations, were the columns of Dorothy Kilgallen, Frank Farrell, Earl Wilson. Winchell even imitated himself by supplying the *Morning Telegraph,* the national racing and show-business daily, with a pseudonymous "Beau Broadway" column. No rival ever matched his breathless style. Ben Hecht, dean of Chicago's rowdy newspaper Bohemia, likened it to "a man honking in a traffic jam." [133] But his vicious overtones, the more nauseating for frequent fits of baby-shoe sentimentality, were unforgivable.

A recent biographer * lists Winchell's unscrupulous sleights of hand as the Blind Item—"What married producer of three B'way musicals pays rent for a chorus girl in each?"—the Pointed Question—"Are the Clark Gables seeing a lawyer?"—the Ambiguous Phrase—"Billy Rose and Eleanor Holm are on the verge"—and goes on: "Sometimes his items were inaccurate." That put it mildly. In 1940 St. Clair McKelway applied a responsible newspaperman's criteria, analyzed for the *New Yorker* the 239 items appearing in five successive Monday

---

* Bob Thomas, *Winchell* (1971), 158. I rely heavily on this, as well as on St. Clair McKelway, "Gossip Writer" *(New Yorker,* June 15; 22; 29; July 6; 13, 1940), and somewhat on Ed Weiner, *Let's Go to Press* (1955). My own acquaintance with Winchell in the late 1920s consisted of sometimes feeding him a gag with a performer's name attached.

columns of Winchell's, checked them out where possible and summarized: 108 were "blind" (names missing or identification so blurred that a check was impractical); 54 completely inaccurate; 24 partly so; only 53 completely accurate. That is an overall breakage rate of 78 percent; of 60 percent among explorable statements. Winchell retaliated by printing anything even remotely derogatory that he could find about McKelway and Harold Ross, editor of the *New Yorker.* Sherman Billingsley, operator of the Stork Club, the former speakeasy that was Winchell's headquarters and relied on his frequently mentioning it in print and on the air, refused to serve Ross when he came in one night—and with a movie star, too.

Not that Winchell needed to strike back. He was just reacting to *lèse majesté*. Few among the millions of his readers and (by then) radio fans read the *New Yorker*. Many of those who did probably shared a strange, fashionable tolerance for the twitchy little monster. For instance, Stanley Walker, famous city editor of the New York *Herald Tribune,* praised his "perfect equipment" for his job and "refusal to be fuddled by ... what some people would have thought good taste" and went far out on a limb by saying that though "[Winchell] made a few mistakes ... he is [usually] ... uncannily right." * Walker also liked his hellbent passion to become a newspaperman. But Winchell's own view of the emotional rewards of that career would disquiet many sound reporters. "The newspaperman," says the last paragraph of his autobiography, "can sit at his window and review the Passing Parade. He sees everyone he likes and doesn't ... everyone who likes him and doesn't. ... He can either drop a flower. Or a flowerpot." [134]

The social leverage that his bulging readership gave him was immense. The mutual admiration society made up of Winchell and J. Edgar Hoover, then riding high as chief of the gangbusting Federal Bureau of Investigation, was as conspicuous and gratifying to both as Winchell's columns and Hoover's visits to nightclubs could make it. The least ingratiating thing I know about FDR is that as World War II came near and while it lasted, he cultivated Winchell far more cordially than was necessary, giving him private interviews of a sort no other newspaperman had—even though Winchell had previously come to the White House' notice with rude printed remarks about Eleanor

* Actually the man's inability to get things straight, even when substantially correct, went right on down to the end. In a hasty reading of the posthumously published autobiography, *Winchell Exclusive* (1975), I found such errors as: "Woodrow Wilson went on Henry Ford's Peace Ship ..." (he didn't); the British aristocrat whom Beatrice Lillie married was Sir Robert Peel, not "Lord Peel"; the publisher-founder of the New York *Daily News* was Captain Joseph M. (not James) Patterson.

Roosevelt's buckteeth. As war became a fact: "During a typical evening at the Stork," wrote a respectful biographer some years later, it was "not unusual for Winchell to have at his table at one time or another generals, admirals, important industrialists, labor leaders, stage and screen stars, high government officials, novelists, playwrights and correspondents." [135]

The pull toward delusions of grandeur had become irresistible when success in print was squared and cubed by unprecedented success in radio. Civilization owes that to William S. Paley, creator of the Columbia Broadcasting System, who seems to have decided in 1932 that public interest, convenience and necessity would be well served by putting Winchell's kind of newspapering on the air. For WABC-New York he teamed up Winchell and the Gimbel Brothers department store for fifteen-minute weekly broadcasts of what seemed juicy enough to report. That went well and came to the attention of George Washington Hill, the American Tobacco Company's genius of advertising, and Winchell found himself advertising Lucky Strike cigarettes weekly on a national network. Soon the makers of Jergens Lotion launched him as voice of *Jergens Journal* every Sunday evening—a venture that was almost instantly a national institution "with lotions of love" as the sign-off.

To dramatize newsiness and urgency, Winchell opened this spasm of dynamic frenzy by hammering on a telegraph key with irregular vigor to make the insistent chirping that the radio audience associated with press dispatches and SOS signals. Winchell knew no Morse code. His dots and dashes were, as old-time telegraphers and radiomen complained, mere hasty gibberish. Nicely symbolic, for nothing really coherent or significant followed his shrill: "Good evening, Mr. and Mrs. America and all the ships at sea ... let's go to press!" Twelve minutes later he signed off with, say, "... this is your New York correspondent, Walter Winchell, who knows that all the lights on Broadway are never as bright as the candle in the window when you come home." The terminal aphorism or wisecrack changed weekly. The filling, consisting largely of bits that would make up his Monday news column in the *Daily Mirror*, was followed, as he got his teeth into the new medium, by yelpings about national and international affairs, for he was now making himself a commentator, a younger statesman, and the size of the hat that he always wore at the microphone, like a stage reporter out of *The Front Page*, steadily swelled. He was eventually capable of believing that Joseph Stalin made a certain speech about the USSR's peace-mindedness in reply to a Winchell column two days previously, and that it was a cable from him to Sir Neville Chamberlain that moved HM Prime Minister to state publicly that Britain was declaring war not on Germany as such, but on Hitler and the Nazis.

Thus, radio enabled him to add his bit to the growing impression that Americans were easy marks. His printed stuff had already shown that if it were dished up with the right wise-guy hints, an ungodly number of newspaper readers would welcome word of the gamy doings of showgirls, mobsters, fat cats, Manhattan politicians even when the subjects were thousands of miles away and few outside Manhattan had ever heard of them. That was the Big Town-legend part of it. The hix in the stix—credit *Variety*'s second greatest headline—took it for granted that Times and Longacre squares were a prime locus of what they called "glamor" of the same order as Hollywood and Parisfrance. On radio Winchell not only distanced the field in exploiting this vapid yearning of the cabbage butterfly for the Great White Way, but spread it among those who never read newspapers large enough to buy his column. In Bugtussle Courthouse and Choctaw Bottom the crickets and bullfrogs had only to hush their own racket of a Sunday evening and one heard through the open door of the shack Winchell letting Ma, Pa, Joe Billy and little Urea May in on how the Lionel Eveningstars—he was her fifth Lohengrinning—had phfft. That was important and very likely sinful, too, else why was the man kicking up such a fuss about it? And it was a change from "The Yellow Rose of Texas" on XERA.

Against charges that Winchell (1) befouled newspapering by inventing the lowest form of the Broadway column, (2) committed atrocious assault on the American vernacular, that prime national asset, and (3) made so many of his countrymen look even more disheartening than God had created them, weigh one substantial good deed: In 1932 he was one of the first American journalists to take seriously and sustainedly attack Hitler and the Nazis, whom he called Ratzis. Moreover, he seems to have done so not so much because he was Jewish as because some insightful quirk of his sharp-elbowed temperament warned him of what many of his betters were dangerously slow to see—that here was a thing as dangerous as it was vicious, however ridiculous its mustache. Between that and his warm support of FDR and the New Deal many liberals made him rather a hero. It lasted until, as the Cold War blew in, he went frantically anti-Stalin and became a principal partisan of Senator Joseph McCarthy's sinister travesty of security-mindedness. This mistake among liberals was just another of their frequent wishful judgments. Minds of that sort were unlikely to understand that the Winchell who now trotted proudly up with a bit of ordure, maybe accurate, maybe not, it didn't matter to him, about some hapless fellow-traveler-innocent was the same as the brash pseudocrusader who had hauled off on Hitler. Right about Hitler, wrong about McCarthy, what difference? It was just "Mrs. Winchell's little boy Walter," dropping flowerpots.

Paley's CBS supplied another demonstration that the American public just couldn't be trusted around radio any more than Madison Avenue could. The reference is to the famous panic set off on October 30, 1938, by the Mercury Theatre of the Air's fantasy about Martians devastating New Jersey, an adaptation for the ear alone of H. G. Wells' science-fiction *The War of the Worlds*. This colossal and significant hoax was, of course, not intentional. Its fantasy character was duly brought up in the first minute of the broadcast and again at the half hour break. But by then it was far too late. Dubious whether its dramatic quality would be adequate, its creators—Howard Koch, Orson Welles, John Houseman—had gone out of their way to pile up convincing detail, and overdone it. The actor cast as the radio reporter succumbing to Martian death rays modeled his reading of his lines on the choked horror of the radio reporter at the destruction of the German dirigible *Hindenburg* the year before, and the rest of the script was as near as ingenuity could get to that kind of radio-now-takes-you-there, this-is-going-on-right-before-my-eyes news-coverage with which the public was already familiar.

In Morristown, New Jersey, a newlywed couple turned on the radio after dinner, not caring what frequency it was tuned to. Out came a pleasant enough, Spanish-sounding orchestral number—they let it ride. After announcement of "slight atmospheric disturbance over Nova Scotia," another Spanish number came along. Then a more peremptory bulletin about an astronomer in Chicago reporting a gas explosion on the planet Mars. The next number, "Stardust," was quickly interrupted by an interview with Princeton University's Professor Pierson (played by Welles) prefacing an announcement that "At 8:50 P.M. a huge flaming object ... fell on a farm in the neighborhood of Grovers Mill, New Jersey ... the noise of the impact was heard as far north as Elizabeth. ..." With the bit about the explosion on Mars, that could have been a tip-off, for by then it was only a few minutes after 8 P.M. But as the professor and interviewer rushed to Grovers Mill and found the state police keeping curiosity seekers away from a huge cylinder making a hissing sound, excitement built too high to allow looking at clocks. The top of the cylinder was unscrewing itself, and out was coming "something wriggling ... like a gray snake ... large as a bear and it glistens like wet leather ... that face ... indescribable. I can hardly force myself to keep looking at it. The eyes are black and gleam. . . . The mouth is V-shaped with saliva dripping from its rimless lips. . . ."

So the death ray annihilated the reporter, and other voices and sources took up the story of how the creatures out of the cylinder deployed a sort of super-Tin Woodman monster inside which they went on the rampage after massacring 7,000 national guardsmen who attempted to contain them. "The monster is now in control of the middle section of New Jersey," burning and demolishing, laying down clouds of poison gas; other such cylinders were reported landing here and there all over the country, while the New Jersey contingent was approaching Morristown, ignoring salvos from National Guard artillery and straddling the Pulaski Skyway en route to Manhattan, whence 3,000,000 people had already fled. . . .

That Martians could do all that in twenty minutes might be conceivable to overheated imaginations. But that the New Jersey National Guard could get 7,000 infantry and a regiment of artillery mustered, let alone transported anywhere, in any such time was not. The Morristown newlyweds, however, glancing nervously out the front window saw sudden flames and smoke—by fantastic coincidence a nearby barn had chosen just that minute to catch fire. They were in their car and driving hell-for-leather away from extinction when the car radio interrupted doom and destruction with "You are listening to a CBS presentation of Orson Welles and the Mercury Theatre. . . ." And here came on Professor Pierson, having miraculously survived the trouble at Grovers Mill, reminiscing years later about what had happened next: The Martians had died quickly of our bacteria to which they had no immunity, the world had recovered. . . .

Sheepishly the Morristown newlyweds promised each other never to tell how they had been taken in. * They felt better on learning that as the nationwide broadcast took effect, hundreds of thousands had panicked without the excuse of a burning barn or—as happened in Concrete, Washington—a local power failure at just the right time. The wildest behavior naturally struck heavily populated northern New Jersey so clearly identified as the scene of the Martians' horrendous capers. But pretty much all over the country police stations were swamped by frantic phone calls, parishioners besought clergy for last-minute shrift, church services were disrupted, highways clogged with automobiles packed with instant refugees. Sociological surveys done within a few weeks showed that of 6,000,000-odd people listening to

---

* Recollection of Ruth Gilbert of the staff of the Hunterdon County (New Jersey) *Democrat,* November 4, 1970. Otherwise, this section leans heavily and gratefully on John Houseman, *Run-Through;* Howard Koch, *The Panic Broadcast;* Hadley Cantril, *et al. The Invasion from Mars.*

Welles' show, 1,000,000 or so had either actively panicked or experienced grave emotional disturbance. God knows what would have happened if most of the nation had not been following its Sunday evening custom of listening to the highly popular Edgar Bergen-Charlie McCarthy program on NBC, hence failed to learn in time that Martians were destroying them.

After Professor Pierson put civilization together again at 8:58, Welles' terminal announcement tried to get the egg off the face by reminding listeners that the date was October 30 and this was "The Mercury Theatre's own radio version of dressing up in a sheet ... saying Boo! ... if your doorbell rings and nobody's there, that was no Martian ... it's Hallowe'en!" Apparently he had confused October 30 with April 1. The FCC took cognizance by sternly slapping CBS' wrist with one finger of the velvet glove kept for such purposes. The newspapers, long resentful of the way radio was attracting advertisers' money and apprehensive about its rising importance in the field of news, naturally enjoyed themselves denouncing radio's irresponsibility. Dorothy Thompson wrote that Welles deserved a medal for "one of the most fascinating and important demonstrations of all time ... [of] the appalling dangers and enormous effectiveness" of radio as a potential tool of unscrupulous propaganda and added that it also "cast a brilliant and cruel light on the failure of popular education ... the incredible stupidity, lack of nerve and ignorance of thousands ... uncovered the primal fears lying under . . . so-called civilized man. . . ." [136]

Miss Thompson was a bit of a Chicken Little, as has been shown by her alarm about *Fantasia*. Those seeking other accountings for this bizarre episode found less momentous ones. It appeared that Charlie McCarthy's opening routine had been succeeded by a change-of-pace vocal number, which led many listeners to turn the dial to CBS for something livelier until Charlie came back on the air. That pitchforked them into the full horrors of the hell that was popping at Grovers Mill—and much screeching and scrambling ensued. Further light came when investigators using POP and other techniques interviewed not only those who had taken it all seriously but also listeners who had either taken it as fiction or soon got their bearings. Most of the 6,000,000 tuned into CBS had done so because they actively preferred the Mercury Theatre's able adaptations of well-known plays and stories even to Bergen-McCarthy, so they were in no danger. Among others, those paying reasonable attention to the opening announcement were also immunized; still others recognized Welles' distinctive voice as soon as Professor Pierson came in. Even among people momentarily taken in, those levelheaded enough to get the newspaper and check the radio listings read: "Mercury Theatre—War of the Worlds" and could relax. Still more capably some bethought themselves to turn the dial to other stations and conclude that WOR or whatever wouldn't still be blatting or yapping away if the Martians really were devastating the Garden State.

Among the 1,000,000-odd failing to exercise any common sense, Hadley Cantrill and associates, studying the episode as scientifically as circumstances permitted, found a high proportion of rather primitively religious-minded persons well prepared to accept what they heard as that confidently predicted end of the world or maybe God turning supernal power loose on America for His own good reasons. But the majority of those hoaxed showed no such traits. Among them, the study suggested, it was "lack of critical ability" [137] that sent cases of shock to crowd Newark's hospitals and people running up tenement stairs to hammer on doors. And there was marked correlation between this trait and extent of formal education. Some college graduates panicked; some fourth-grade dropouts had the gumption to take it as "all just a play." But by and large those who had at least finished high school showed up better. One can read that several ways: Miss Thompson was right; it showed failure of popular education. Or wrong: It showed failure to apply popular education far and well enough. Or the impulse to get educated, as opposed to that to quit school, goes along with inherent savvy, so that, in large statistical groups, the higher the average level of intelligence, the higher the average level of education. However that may be, Miss Thompson did well to point out the troubling implications of what Wells & Welles had done by accident: "If people can be frightened out of their wits by mythical men from Mars, they can be frightened into fanaticism by fear of Reds, or convinced that America is in the hands of sixty families, or aroused to revenge against any minority." [136] This sounds like the same shortage of residual gumption so profitably counted on by the Diamond Man, Major Bowes and the soap opera industry.

Yet the technological instead of the sociological mind might lay the triumph of Welles' Martians to the chief flaw of broadcasting as communication—the spoken word is evanescent. An armchair newspaper reader can go back over the permanent, explicit print to explore what it does *not* say and for confirmation of his once-over-lightly impression of what it has already told him. The armchair radio (or TV) listener has only the moment, with his memory of what his ears fed to his attention already fading, and if alarming data keep streaming in, they preclude him from even reconsidering what survives from the fading.* Did what the announcer said really amount to a six-month money-back guarantee? Did the newscaster say the rioters were Communist-led or Communist-Red or was it something about Communist dead?... Or ... well, Communist was in it somehow, no chance of a playback to get it right—that is reserved for football. Such ambiguity and data loss have long made broadcasting the happy hunting ground of the propagandist and the pitchman-huckster, skilled in buzzwords and cognates. Add that standing vexation of the industry, the audience's slovenly listening habits. It pays little or no heed to opening announcements, including commercials. It uses what comes out of the speaker, talk as well as music, for background to cards or conversation, relating to it not exactly subliminally but in a blur of underalertness—and then suddenly, DID YOU HEAR WHAT I HEARD? Add that at the time of the Martian incursion the public was already nervous about a series of potentially explosive international crises preliminary to World War II. News of them frequently flashed as bulletins into run-of-mine programs had predisposed them to hear the worst any time. Indeed, numbers of those panicking were found to have had a rattlebrained impression that the Nazis were somehow attacking America.

In any case Wells & Welles had dramatized by *reductio ad absurdum* the grip on the nation's attention that news broadcasting had in 1938—only eighteen years after it had begun in the Harding-Cox presidential campaign in 1920. Just as one's parents assumed that if something burstingly important happened, a newspaper extra would suddenly appear on the streets, now it was taken for granted that the radio would make the pulse skip a beat with "We interrupt this program with a bulletin just in from ..." and the voice-on-the-spot would create sudden intimacy with riot, earthquake or assassination. It was all the best possible buildup for the Mercury Theatre's script. In wider terms it had already made broadcasting the prime source of spot news. Gradually newspapers were being relegated to supplementary details and primarily dependent on comic strips, elaborate palaver about

* Donald Barr *(Who Pushed Humpty Dumpty?*, 142) maintains ably that even microfilm and tape recording can never serve intelligence as well as the printed page: "The book is the unique repository of free culture ... will never be replaced by such devices as spools of tape—*unless* we want to make learning a matter of submitting ourselves to control by the 'writer.' Anyone who has ever used microfilm can understand this. It is too hard to skim and search in microfilm, too hard to go back and forth, to compare parts. One tends to go through microfilm as one submits to a speech—as an experience organized *for* one in time."

sports and magazinelike features to keep the circulation pumping. Even before World War II taught America to hang on the radio like a diver to his air tube, the invariably tuned-in "six o'clock news" was a major pivot for the American day. Product of the newspaper wire services and the radio industry's own growing staffs of legmen and rewrite men, such a program was necessarily a very narrow selection of tomorrow morning's headlines over compact leads—and nothing further, as if a newspaper consisted of only a crowded front page, no runovers.

Reporting-for-the-ear, with the human voice as medium, also intruded personality disastrously into journalism. It was more and more "Now here is Andrew Asterisk with the WHAT six o'clock news ... Andrew! ... Thank you, Pete...." Thus, forty years ago radio news showed newspapers the way to becoming the happy hunting grounds of by-lines that they now are. Long before the TV anchorman's face became important, radio knew how much the public valued the newscaster's name attached to the voice they counted on hearing evening after evening. As in soap opera or comedy shows with masters of ceremonies, it was the gravitational pull of the recurring personality, real or synthetic, that brought the listener back every twenty-four hours—and sponsors' money flowing in.

The voice might be Boake Carter's plum-puddingish boom, Edwin C. Hill's incisive whine, Lowell Thomas' casual tenor. The radio public recognized and valued each as a dog recognizes master's footstep. (At least one dog in New York City insisted on joining master in listening to Carter every evening.) Gradually the rewrites of what came over the wire or phone took on idiosyncrasy of word to match that of voice and reading style, and the single-personality broadcasts became half-editorial. Leader in this was H. V. Kaltenborn, whose newspaper job on the Brooklyn *Eagle* was his springboard into broadcasts for WEAF-New York as "lecturer" on current events in the mid-1920s. His well-balanced copy style, floating on his grainily cultivated, clearly precise voice, earned him international fame. "He always gave listeners a sense that they had glimpsed, through his analysis, the true complexity of an issue; but in the end he also provided a clarifying feeling," [138] says Eric Barnouw's judicious history of broadcasting.

Thus, that new kind of journalist, the radio commentator, came to be. The FCC still forbade broadcasting companies to express corporate opinions directly, as newspapers always had and, since that rule was relaxed in 1949, TV as well as radio now does. But in the 1930s nothing kept growingly popular newscasters, like Gabriel Heatter ("There's good news tonight!") from verging ever nearer to radio equivalents of the syndicated, general comment, by-lined newspaper column that proliferated so lushly and on the whole usefully in the same period. Then the two genres diverged as they reflected the difference between the relative responsibility of the printed word, however subtle between the lines, and the fluidly streaming radio text rippling with indefinable, unrecapturable innuendo both verbal and vocal—for tone of voice and tiny quirk of emphasis or slur on "deficit" or "military expert" could make a vast difference. In both departments—news bulletins and commentary—Winchell's antics on the air showed how to make a fortune by carrying to extremes the sins of radio-as-journalism.

Not that it was all deplorable. A democracy had reason to welcome the way newscasting conveyed what was going on to many who had seldom heeded even the headlines of newspapers. It was certainly healthy when what Elmer Davis said nightly went as far to shape opinion as what Lippmann said in the Zenith *Morning Herald* and what Eleanor Roosevelt said in the Zenith *Evening Register.* For that meant Davis' civilized, shrewd attitudes were, thanks to radio, at least occasionally impinging on those immune to newspaper editorials or by-line columns. As things heated up in the late 1930s, it was a dizzying privilege to listen to twelve minutes of Fulton Lewis, Jr., playing hatchetman to the New Deal's splintery totem pole, and then with a flick of the hand bring in Davis' astringent, ironical common sense stinging inflamed areas but also nourishing sound tissues. He had been writing that way in print for years. But print would never have found him a hearing as wide as this, his words reinforced by the voice that exactly matched their quality—"the droll voice of America's best instincts," [139] said James Wechsler in retrospect. His twenty years in the effete East had little affected its Hoosierish quality. Deep and slow, heavy-voweled, unmistakably warm and yet rueful, he sounded as trustworthy and keen as the generic Man from Home—much more so than Wendell Willkie ever managed with the same raw materials.

In the radio producer's terms—showman's terms—the fact that Davis really was what he sounded like was neither here nor there. The individual personality as it came across in a broadcast was soon so dominant that it was disproportionately identified even in on-the-spot bulletins: "Seven passengers are believed dead in a derailment on the Gotham & Zenith main line in Tracktown, Pennsylvania. We take you now to the scene of the accident where WSIN's Harry Hassle has the story. Come in, Harry.... Thank you, Andy, this is Harry Hassle in Tracktown, Pennsylvania. Seven passengers are known to have died in...." Then after another sentence or two: "This is Harry Hassle returning you to Andrew Asterisk for WSIN, New York.... Thank you, Harry, now...."

The strong affinity between newscasting and show business was long since recognized when the American Federation of Television and Radio Artists forced membership on even nationally renowned TV anchormen on the same basis as if they were walk-ons in soap opera. Twenty years ago Gilbert Seldes complained that in newscasting fact "is delivered in competition with . . . radio's vast quantity of entertainment; one daytime serial leads off with an actual news broadcast, from which a reporter proceeds to her daily quota of fictional crime [the long-defunct Wendy Warren show] . . . the singing of Bob Crosby leads into the news analysis of Edward R. Murrow for the same sponsor . . . [in sponsored news] the atmosphere of the commercial is the same as that on a comedy show . . . [news] may be distorted by omissions, by suppressions, by exaggerated emphasis, by the use of charged words, by the tone of voice . . ." [140] which last, growingly abused, was a tool no unscrupulous newspaper ever had.

Maybe what Providence was trying to convey by turning those Martians loose on New Jersey was that by 1938 the process of fusing news and show business had got so far that when show business imitated news, millions of people couldn't tell the difference.

The huge popularity of the Bergen-McCarthy radio show, which rose even higher when W. C. Fields got into the act, illustrates a minor addleheadedness of the radio audience: The act was primarily ventriloquism—a "sight gag" depending on amusing the house by half persuading it that the obviously wooden dummy is talking back to the obviously flesh-and-blood straight man. Yet Bergen made the most lucrative success any ventriloquist ever knew in a medium that kept the audience from seeing him or the dummy. Another case in point was the smaller but substantial success on the air of the Mills Brothers—engaging black men who imitated with ungodly accuracy a jazz combo, using only their vocal cords. The indispensable wonder of their act was that, standing there empty-handed, they almost made one believe they were playing saxophone, clarinet and so on. If one didn't see them, there was no occasion for wonder. The sound that came out of that studio a long way off would have been the same had they used instruments.

Presumably the presence of a studio audience prevented fraud; its laughter and applause reassured living-room listeners. Actually, however, they existed so that Kate Smith's admirers could be invited to write in for tickets so they could see her in the emphatic flesh and enjoy semibackstage acquaintance with how a broadcasting studio looked and worked. The tickets were free, but show business being what it is, a scalper's market in admission to the high-rating shows promptly developed. Besides, some former vaudevillians found it hard to work without a live audience guffawing and applauding to assure them that the act was getting across. This led to abuses: They were likely to throw in sight gags that made the house giggle but exasperated living-room listeners, who heard the reaction without seeing what caused it. Those studio audiences were sheepishly docile, readily obeying the announcer's preshow instructions to clap like mad when he raised the APPLAUSE sign.* If their laughter proved inadequate, the control room had only to put on the air one of the several kinds of canned laughter kept in stock. As it developed that it helped persuade living-room listeners that what they were hearing was funny, it became the curse of the airwaves. And sponsors hearing such gales of hilarity were also likely subconsciously to feel that they were getting their advertising dollar's worth. The only real resentment came from the hard-of-hearing who were prevented by instantaneous crashes of laughter after each of Bob Hope's wisecracks from understanding any of them.

Canned merriment was only one of thousands of canned "sound effects" kept on tap to create any desired illusions. At first studios went to great lengths to serve up supplementary sounds fresh, partly because some felt it infra dig not to, partly because in some cases a recording of the real thing didn't sound real over the air. Genuine rain recorded on a disc, for instance, made noises inferior in verisimilitude to what was produced by pouring birdseed into a hopper to dribble through, bounce off a swinging table-tennis ball onto a slanting sheet of tin and slide down through a windshield wiper into a berry box on the floor; the late Rube Goldberg could have worked it out no better. It was undesirable to get the sound of a club crushing a human skull by actually doing it to a studio page; instead, one whacked a watermelon with a softball bat. A blunt bayonet and a head of cabbage sounded like stabbing a man. A real gunshot might ruin the mike's sensitive insides, so one whacked a cardboard box or leather cushion with a wooden slat. Specialists in imitating crying babies, dogs in various frames of mind, lions, banshees and so on were much in demand and for certain purposes remained so. But as costs mounted and the shine wore off such ingenuities, they relied more and more on recordings of locomotive whistles, the thundering, thumping rush of a steam locomotive, automobile horns, sizzling bacon. ... Specific sound effects began to cluster into symbol clichés to which listeners were

---

* In Norman Corwin's *Man with a Platform* radio fantasy, a special award went to Beulah Benlak of Winthrop, Massachusetts, who, "when the announcer cued the audience for cheers ... refused to applaud." Asked why, she said, "I didn't like the show." (*Thirteen by Corwin*, 193.)

trained. Thus, a combination of (recorded) crickets, spring peepers, faint wind in the trees and faint running water meant He and She had parked down by the old millstream. The grunt and whine of a self-starter meant they were driving home—the motors of radio characters' cars always had noisy motors for the same reason that the character at the wheel in a movie keeps jiggling it, to make it clear he is under way and steering.

Back to Fields and the invisible stage: His avatar as Charlie McCarthy's boozy, abusive antagonist rounded out a unique professional history. He began as a world-renowned vaudeville headliner who never uttered a sound onstage, just juggled better than anybody else ever did—a masterpiece of merely visible skill. Then he broke silence and became one of the American stage's and Hollywood's greatest funnymen by inimitable use of spoken words blended with his previous genius for gesture and sight gag—a masterpiece combining eye and ear. Then he took to radio and, with voice alone, all his previously indispensable, riotously hilarious person now invisible, outdid or equaled such established princes of radio laughter as Fred Allen, Jack Benny. ....

Never forget that they and dozens of others whom radio exploited had been, like Amateur Hours and *Amos & Andy,* cannibalized from dying vaudeville like transplanted kidneys. Indeed, the laughter department of broadcasting rather morbidly resembled an all-star benefit staged by the Friars Club in Wells' *Country of the Blind.* The precedent was the old one-sided 78-rpm records *c.* 1910 that made Uncle Lester laugh himself black in the face over traditional vaudeville routines from Weber & Fields ("My son Heinie went to college ...") or "No News, or What Killed the Dog." Now in the same terms—all ear, no eye, no tune, just words—the chronic lunacies of Allen's Alley, Jack Benny's parsimony, Gracie Allen's sudden volubilities proved just as effective in the evening as soap opera in the afternoon at bringing listeners loyally back show after show. On secondary levels people were addicted to "Hello! Duffy's Tavern ... Archy the manager speaking. Duffy ain't here ..." or the surrealistic prattle of *It Pays to Be Ignorant* with Tom Howard, master of gritty gift-of-gab from years in burlesque and vaudeville, using whip and chair on a turbulent troika of veteran vaudevillians—Lulu McConnell, Harry McNaughton ("I have a poem, Mr. Howard!") and George Shelton ("I useta woik innat town ...") in a travesty of quiz programs as effervescent as a hangover cure. But all necessarily suffered from anemia owing to the need for a new script each week, new lines week after week and next weaker still as the writers bled white. Every three to seven days a vaudeville act had shifted to a different town and different audience. Even if it had the same routine as last year, the customers had had 358 days to refresh in. Radio's funnymen had the whole United States as audience once a week, no change of venue admitted.

Where would radio have got grist for its greedy mills had vaudeville not been ripe for cannibalizing at the right time? Soap opera was the largest autogenous response, of course. "Sustaining"—that is, unsponsored, hence non-revenue-producing—programs might supply others. Their first job was to fill unpopular, hence unsalable quarter or half hours; their second to provide "good" music or "public service" broadcasts handy when it was time to tell the FCC how mindful WSIN had been of public interest, convenience and necessity; their third to develop new programs that, with much luck, might develop audience enough to attract sponsors—"using the wilderness of unsold periods," wrote Barnouw, "to grow new crops of value yet to be determined." [141] The process sometimes worked in what had seemed unlikely contexts. NBC's broadcasts of Arturo Toscanini's symphony concerts became what Robert J. Landry, dean of *Variety*'s coverage of broadcasting, described in 1941 as "a nation-wide Saturday night fiesta . . . radio's most clear-cut contribution to the elevation of taste in musical matters . . . the concert world and the opera owe their present prosperity to the tonic effect of broadcasting." [142] The "opera" reference was to the regular-as-payday Saturday afternoon broadcasts of grand opera from the Metropolitan Opera House in New York City knowledgeably described and framed by the elegant voice of a former conservatory tenor, Milton Cross, doing on the air for *La Bohème* and *Aïda* what Ted Husing was doing for baseball. Since Cross' audience numbered some 12,000,000, it was well worth the Texas Company's while to write handsome checks in return for dignified sponsor credits.

The soap opera formula of tell-it-in-dialogue-and-sound-effects was soon applied to other kinds of plot less cozy than blackmail, amnesia and kidnapping. One of the noisiest general-audience serials was Phillips Lord's *Gangbusters,* which had nominal endorsements from genuine heads of major police forces. That encouraged the listeners' illusion that its unceasing spatter of machine-gun fire, howling sirens, agonized groans, exploding pineapples, smashing windowpanes and so on and so forth genuinely represented high-powered law enforcement—a cacophony indeed. Lord was a versatile man. His previous great success had been a down-amongst-us-homey-folks series built around a synthetic New England sage named Seth Parker; it leaned heavily on hymns and homilies. That was for Mom and Pop, of course, but *Gangbusters* greatly attracted their young. So did another noise-and-violence serial, *I Love a Mystery,* that seemed to be aimed at all ages from early adolescence through wolf-whistling maturity to cackling senescence. Here was a comradely, raunchy (so far as radio could hint at carnalities) group of soldiers of fortune gallivanting all over creation ostensibly to ride herd on elaborate villainy but actually to work in a maximum number of knock-down-drag-out fights and irresistibly slithery women. The general line of country is clear in the titles of some of their adventures: "Blood on the Cat," "I Am the Destroyer of Woman," "My Beloved Is a Vampire," "The Thing Wouldn't Die." This 100-proof spin-off from pulp magazines and comic strips, said a reminiscing admirer, "seems to have been specially designed to outrage the PTAs ... and ... whiten the hair of child psychologists." [143]

By then the PTAs and child psychologists had reason for their hair not only to whiten but stand on end—in terms of the time, of course, which were archaically innocent. The same thing was going on as the same PTAs and psychologists wrung their hands over the effect on small fry of movies of lissome ladies in tenuous costumes wrapping themselves around sleek, glib gentlemen and swarthy fellows in tight overcoats filling one another with lead for flagrantly illegal reasons. This was double trouble: The sort of story best adapted to movie and radio has always been, in Western cultures anyway, what one of Henry James Forman's underprivileged witnesses defined for him as the kind of movie he liked to see: "Shootin' and kissin'," he said, and was immortalized in Forman's dreary study *Our Movie-Made Children.* Nothing wrong with those terms; the result can be *High Noon, The Blue Angel, Brief Encounter.* But that is not the sort of condiment suited for the kiddies' daily nourishment, and radio not only dished up violence and man-is-fire-and-woman-is-tow in terms even more vulgar than the run of movies but fed it to the child within easy reach of a radio at least weekly and often daily. That is the second factor in the double trouble: It is probably unhealthy for any human organism, particularly the inchoate, subadult sort, to have access to the artificial stimulus of unlimited entertainment in all leisure hours. Entertainment should be occasional, like going to a party, not daily at the same time like breakfast. Those shaking their heads today about small fry gluing themselves to TV should remember that, pernicious as it unquestionably is, it's nothing new. Their parents, in some case even their grandparents, glued themselves to the radio exactly the same way.

Among broad hints of better things in radio in the 1930s there was the success of Mary Margaret McBride, an able and well-established magazine free lance who did winsome morning chats thick with interviews for just-us-girls.* It sounds sticky and was, and the several direct imitations that also greatly prospered were stickier. But the format—helpful babble about women's minor problems, interviews with the staider kind of author and the more ingratiating kind of do-gooder and stage figure—was a demonstration that soap opera had no strong hold on the American housewife. That is, in spite of her strange little-girl voice and personality as billowy-smothery as her person, Mary Margaret and her imitators made far more sense than *Stella Dallas.*

Her materials, however, were much the same as those of women's magazines, so in a sense radio was here still cannibalizing, drawing on elder idioms and media for stuff to adapt or predigest. The same was true of the overworked dodge of adapting (à la *War of the Worlds*) stage plays or novels, usually in truncated hour-long, even half-hour-long, form that discarded most of what had made them good in the first place. But presently radio began verging on its own new forms— one sign of a newborn medium's getting its wobbly legs under it—with the panel quiz shows of which *Information Please* was leader. It was also a hint that impromptu mental agility neglecting to be stuffy had a certain place in the public heart—hence on the air. Call it a cross between the old-time spelling bee and the Categories parlor game popular in the Depression years. The cast was several New Yorkers fast on their mental feet and unusually well informed—Adams of "The Conning Tower," John Kieran, incisive and wildly omniscient sports-writer, Oscar Levant, a versatile and prickly pianist who got around a great deal—playing verbal badminton with Clifton Fadiman, one of the nation's deftest book reviewers. Fadiman served, and they put back over the net answers to listener-contributed questions about almost anything. When a question "stumped the experts," the contrib-utor got a complete *Encyclopaedia Britannica.* If the experts knew the answers, the consolation prize was a few dollars—none of the huge accumulating sums that tempted the *$64,000 Question* to make a spectacle of itself on TV awhile ago.

Those encyclopedias moved slowly. Collectively the panel knew much about many things, and the questions were, of course, sifted to avoid dull overspecialization. But the special fun lay in the incidental

---

* This presents difficulties in identification: The lady first went on the air as a pseudonymous "Martha Deane" and then, shifting to a major network, continued under her own name. The name "Martha Deane" remained with her original outlet and after some vicissitudes became an on the whole intelligently successful national institution with Marian Young as "Martha Deane" for years and years, never deserting radio for television.

garnish of splattering wisecracks, puns, side references and outrageous
nonsense usually helped along by a shrewdly chosen guest celebrity
from an interesting background: Dorothy Thompson or Gracie Allen
or playwright-producer Howard Lindsay or his equally genial collaborator, Russell Crouse. The show was, as Gilbert Seldes truly said,
"more a conversation than a quiz." [144] It was like sitting in on an
amusing, good-natured party. Week after week the listeners came back
not only because the experts were consistently entertaining but because
the subject matter varied engagingly.* In some ways it telescoped the
soap opera, for no sooner had the experts extricated themselves from
one chipper five-minute predicament than they were plunged into
another and frisked about in it like so many gleeful otters. Almost
equally popular in its time was the *Quiz Kids* panel of bright-eyed
child prodigies answering the damnedest questions to which preadoles-
cents were ever subjected and bringing out the vicarious proud parent
in millions.

Better still, for a while there a major breakthrough into a specific
new radio art form seemed to be shaping up. The wishful promised an
autogenous radio drama of high aesthetic quality, particularly employing poets and reaching for poetry. It was true that by the mid-1930s
commercial broadcasting, however crass and tenuous, had worked up
the necessary technical means. Between soap opera and improvement
in adapting plays and novels, radio could call on a wide range of
mood- and locality-evoking sound effects, some specific, some subliminal, and respectable skills in getting optimum impact from dialogue
without reinforcement—or distraction—from visible action. Why could
not the same tricks that brought out the idiocy of Jack Armstrong be
used for purely auditory equivalent of Great Art? The obvious
ancestor was strangely stuffy, of course, the nineteenth century's closet
drama, verse plays admittedly unsuited for a stage cluttered with sets
and actors, instead written by Percy Bysshe Shelley or Lord Tennyson
or Algernon Charles Swinburne primarily as poetry for print—but
sometimes read aloud to respectful private groups.† That genre,

* Sample questions: Why would the planet Jupiter be a favorite hangout for
lovers? ... Identify or explain Redeye, Redhanded, Redhorn, Redback, Red
Tape.... Name four comedians of the talkies who never talk.... Name the
man and the scientific discovery associated with each of the following: a
bathtub, a teakettle, a frog's leg, a cathedral lantern, a hungry dog.... What
popular or once popular dances are named for a fruit, a city, an animal, a
state, a vehicle?

† The form is by no means nonsense. Fanny Kemble, brilliant member of a
great acting family, a renowned Shakespearian star in her youth, in later life
came to believe that Shakespeare was too good to be mauled behind footlights
by any supporting company she had ever seen. She turned to a long career (in

however, lacked some of radio's tools. It had no sound effects, could not use different voices for characterization (as is currently done in stage readings of Shaw and so on) or the powerful weapon that broadcasting shares with the sound screen—an immense range of background music, sentimental here, aggressive there, an invaluable development from the old movie-palace orchestra. John Houseman described this new tool, with which he had had much early experience: "Working in the single dimension of sound, it became a highly effective narrative medium which allowed full scope to the listener's imagination." [145] Nor need he have thus confined it to narrative.

Here again "who was first" is cloudy. But one indubitable parent was Archibald MacLeish, a poet of stature regularly publishing well-received, rather free-form verse, who was also part of the no-by-line writing team that made *Fortune* magazine readable. Experiment-minded, he had done a successful ballet scenario, *Union Pacific,* and in 1935 had attracted literate attention with an expressionistic verse play, *Panic,* on the Wall Street crash. His manifesto-preface for its printed version called for bold ventures into a theater handling great public and moral-emotional themes in a vernacular verse exploiting the virtues of the angular American tongue. With its knowing changes of prosodic pace, its chewy verse that actors could get their teeth into and its limberly shifting, quasi-Greek chorus of assorted everyday people, *Panic* interestingly exemplified the possibilities that he preached. In 1936 he took to the air. Irving Reis of CBS, who had so whooshed, boomed, crackled and screamed the interplanetary Buck Rogers serial that he was made supervisor of the Columbia Workshop (experimental), received from MacLeish a verse script for radio based on the principle later set down in its preface that "the ear is already half-poet." [146]

Reis did it up brown. To give the required effect of an emotion-gripped crowd in the huge city square, he produced *Fall* not in a studio but in a National Guard armory with a real crowd of students and faculty from City College of New York. For the dominant Announcer, filling in the listener on action and describing reactions— "the most useful dramatic personage since the Greek Chorus," [147] MacLeish said—he cast Orson Welles, then merely a hopeful radio performer. The way Welles imposed MacLeish's harsh, driving, sprung-rhythm verse on listeners' consciousness made the boy a name

---

the mid-1800s) of reading Shakespeare play by play, stem to stern, to entranced audiences with no support other than a reading desk, her own voice and her own extraordinary person. From all accounts her ability to stand out of the way and give Shakespeare his head resulted in evenings that people remembered with awe and gratitude the rest of their lives.

among radio people long before the Martians made him one nationally. Note, too, that *Fall* was two years ahead of the Martians in using a simulated newscast for dramatic purposes. Its content was simply, gruesomely disquieting. In growing tension the people of a sort of Aztecish city-state come to dread and then perversely welcome an invading tyrant-stranger. At the end, while they felicitate themselves because "Freedom's for fools.... Chains will be liberty!" [148] the Announcer and the listeners, not the populace, become aware that the vaunting savior-conqueror up there on the platform is only a suit of armor with nothing inside. The verse was well up to the effect sought, and it helped greatly that only a few months earlier Franco had staged his rebellious invasion of Spain.

In a matter of months this vigorous *succès d'estime* had other established poets—Stephen Vincent Benét, W. H. Auden, Edna St. Vincent Millay, Maxwell Anderson, Carl Sandburg, most of whom had already won some acclaim with verse plays—either writing for radio or planning to do so. Just then American poetry was well on its way to self-destruction, sliding into an esotericism soon to wall Calliope, Erato, Euterpe, Thalia and even Polyhymnia off from all but the most infatuated or doctrinaire of their admirers; poor girls! In the 1920s the same people who bought and read *Main Street* and *The Sun Also Rises* also bought and read *John Brown's Body* and *The Buck in the Snow*. Only a few years later, however, the leading edge of American poetry was Hart Crane's posthumous and hypercryptic *The Bridge*—the sort of thing that people tended to read *about* in pretentious reviews instead of tackling the actual text on their own. Certain magazines, the *New Yorker* most commendably, went on giving brief lyrics of one or another degree of comprehensibility houseroom. But beyond that a willfully deepening obscurity made the prognosis bleak. Now it struck the thoughtful as reassuring that radio—medium of huckstering vulgarity—should be thus exposing millions to recognizable poetry. Hope was higher yet in 1940, when Norman Corwin's radio version of Earl Robinson and John Latouche's "Ballad for Americans" (written for the Federal Theatre's topical revue *Sing for Your Supper*) developed such prestige that, in spite of its maverick ancestry and New Dealish associations, the Republican Party had it sung at its nominating convention.

It did not elect Wendell Willkie. Actually much of its effectiveness was due to its being usually sung by Paul Robeson, the great black baritone whose voice could have made *The Revised Statutes of Ohio* sound like *Paradise Lost*. Without him "Ballad for Americans" was just Whitman-and-water with an ill-advised dash of Vachel Lindsay. Under the electronic prod some of the poets listed above did rather better. But even in them the new medium fostered a discursive diluteness, and the most renowned item resulting, Carl Sandburg's *The People, Yes,* was so windy that his being Chicago's unofficial poet laureate was all too fitting. What virtues its text had depended, like those of "Ballad for Americans," on being strained through an actorish voice. Maybe this lack of sticking to the ribs, as in the proverbial Chinese dinner, was the reason why this radio-roused flurry on Parnassus aborted, leaving American poetry to slide on downward into a self-fascinated catatonia. The other reason probably was the distraction of World War II and, once that was over, the smothering effect on radio of the rise of television.

In any case it was soon clear that this new genre was better handled by writers of radio's own begetting and nurture who had ingrained experience of what sound could do, whether in verse or prose. One shining example was CBS's Norman Corwin, who had broken into radio as a news announcer in New England and the Midwest; the other was NBC's Arch Oboler, who, as a radio-struck kid, had pestered Chicago radio stations into letting him try writing scripts. Fadiman, primarily a bookman but by then radio-minded, noted in admiring amazement about the product of Corwin's first few years that he had written successes a good seven times out of ten. Carl Van Doren, learned academician as well as amateur of popular arts, said, "He is to American radio what Marlowe was to the Elizabethan stage." [149] His prose dialogue was workmanlike, but he often used verse, and though he hardly wielded "Marlowe's mighty line," the versemen he echoed in fitting contexts—W. S. Gilbert, T. S. Eliot, Whitman—were discerningly chosen and pleasantly recognizable. And the contexts were happily varied. His first success was a nippy rehandling of Mother Goose to begin a series of poetry broadcasts—he called them "word orchestrations" of Benét, Sandburg *et al.*—skillful enough to please even such eminent members of the *genus irritabile.* As chipper change of pace some of his best work was fast-stepping spoofing of standard radio fare and radio techniques in a tone anticipating the later work of Henry Morgan, Bob & Ray and Stan Freberg. At the same time he led in using radio as propaganda weapon against the Axis well before World War II began. His *They Fly Through the Air with the Greatest of Ease,* produced in February, 1939, was a telling revulsion against Vittorio Mussolini's brutal comparison of the observed effect of an aerial bomb exploding among Abyssinians as like the spreading of the petals of a flower. Again and again Corwin used anti-Fascist themes—good preparation for the hands-across-the-sea propaganda of his assignments when war came.

Oboler, recruited by NBC to fill the dead listening time opposite

CBS' Jack Benny on Sunday evenings, had been specializing in Chicago on horror fictions with brilliant, if morbid, sound effects: For instance, warm spaghetti was sozzled with a "plumber's friend" plunger to make a sound like a man being turned literally inside out. In the climate of Radio City he stayed ingenious while taking out after the new kind of horror manifest in Nazis and Fascists. Where Corwin burned brown- and blackshirted leaders in effigy, Oboler went etiological: Vivaciously he hammered into listeners the theory that the chief villains of such movements were not the strutting front men but the self-serving plutocrats who financed them. One of his best, *Bathysphere,* had a freedom-minded engineer about to asphyxiate a Hitler-like leader along with himself but dissuaded by the intended victim on the grounds that "you're dying quite in vain ... the conditions ... were such that other men sitting in wealth came to the decision that I alone could keep them there ... privilege ... seeks to live no matter what the cost! ... when I am dead [those] who gave me power will find a new leader to stop the rumblings of rebellion with all the tricks that I taught them! A new Leader, you hear me, fool— Leader!" [150] In *The Man to Hate* a devoted, idealistic assassin, lurking where he can shoot the dictator, is thwarted by suspecting he will do no good; another such will be along to exploit the same social strains. In *Profits Unlimited* a ruthless entrepreneur has set up on a remote island an industrial company manned by colonized workers seeking security at the implicit cost of social freedom. Between natural selection and apathy they have gradually grown vegetatively reconciled.... These simplistic views confusing the motives of Fascism's subsidizers with Fascism's deeper pathologies were fashionable in the late 1930s.

Those were limited fashions, however, and it would be wrong to think of Corwin, Oboler *et al.* making significant inroads on the great radio audience's attention. Both *Fall* and Oboler's early work were broadcast at times when, because of immensely popular funny stuff on the competing network, it was assumed that no sponsor would buy the time because everybody would be listening to the competition. Even in the pressure-clogged year of 1941 most of these two men's work was aired in the summer months when potential customers were scattered away from their usual habits and advertisers were less likely to buy time. The following year all such talent went into the war effort the more willingly because Hitler, Thyssen & Co. were the chief enemy, and after the war the epitaph of hopes for radio drama of intelligence and significant form was supplied by the durable soap opera actress Mary Jane Higby: "Radio developed a small group of glamor writers ... writing documentaries, experimental, unsponsored 'sustainers,' and paeans for the American Way. At their best they wrote tellingly for the ear ... dialogue, sound and music ... made authentic radio drama. On the other hand much of their output might nowadays seem self-conscious, pretentious, or even windy." [151]

And so it does. But for a little while there it looked good.

Even as radio commentators proliferated and rose to glory in the 1930s, newspaper columnists waxed fat in parallel. The gathering momentum of each group probably supported that of the other. For both encouraged the growing national habit of relying on self-elected oracle-personalities for opinions and catalytic analysis. Doubtless the deepening bewilderment of the post-Crash years had a hand in this as anxiety sought communion with wiser, better-informed heads. Anyway, just as Portland, Maine, and Portland, Oregon, and Portland, Indiana, all listened assiduously to Kaltenborn, so did the boom in syndicated columns deliver Eleanor Roosevelt, George Sokolsky and Heywood Broun to millions of breakfasters from Miami to Seattle. One of the most pungent of the lot, Westbrook Pegler, contemplated the field, himself included, with dismay:

> Of all the fantastic fog shapes that have risen off the swamp of confusion ... the most futile, and at the same time, the most pretentious, is the deep-thinking, hair-trigger columnist or commentator who knows all the answers just offhand and can settle great affairs with absolute finality three or even six days a week ... this trade began as a sort of journalistic vaudeville intended to entertain the customers and exert a little circulation pull of a slightly higher tone than that of comics.... You might think that once in a while we would run out of intelligence, and I often marvel at my own inexhaustible fund of knowledge, but it just keeps on bubbling up....[152]

Some of this was nothing new. In 1831 Honoré de Balzac's gabby Parisian journalist described the staff of a new paper founded to oppose Louis-Philippe as "captious spirits ... whose perspicacity exposes the intentions of Austria, England or Russia before Russia, England or Austria had formed any intentions...." * But the elder form of it seldom depended on personality played up for the reader as do the daily arrays of syndicated columnists in large American papers today—those managing to survive. Fifty years ago few such columns

* "... *ces esprits frondeurs ... dont la perspicacité découvre les intentions de l'Autriche, et de l'Angleterre ou de la Russie, avant que la Russie, l'Angleterre ou l'Autriche aient des intentions....*" (*La Peau de Chagrin,* Livre de Poche, 66, 68.)

existed; few papers ran them. Newspaperdom stayed with the "editorial we" tradition that a paper expressed its own views only in anonymous editorials and allowed backtalk only in certain kinds of news stories, such as reports of speeches, and maybe in letters to the editor. Much of Louisville was aware that Colonel Henry Watterson slashed out those editorials in the *Courier-Journal,* but they were not signed. In many other cities, where editorial chiefs were less resounding characters, not one in fifty readers of the local papers knew who Ye Ed was. One of the few exceptions was Hearst's big-city papers, on the front pages of which usually ran "Today," an editorial column from headquarters signed by Arthur Brisbane. Through it this testy son of a Utopian reformist told the hundreds of thousands bothering with it—few of Hearst's public got beyond the comics and the sports pages—what his reactionary chief wished them to think and feel. And after all that the one teaching of Brisbane's that anybody remembers is his dictum, after the Dempsey-Firpo fight, that a reasonably fit gorilla could have licked both of them at once.

Nevertheless, Brisbane's persistent, opinionated by-line may have been what broke the way for columnists of many stripes. The New York *World,* once Joseph Pulitzer's means for outdoing Hearst in yellow journalism, eventually the nation's most brilliant Democratic newspaper, encouraged the every-other-day short column of fiction or comment—grave or gay as moods and subjects varied—from regular contributors likely to be welcome in Washington Square, Gramercy Park, Central Park South and Morningside Heights. The chief pioneer was Heywood Broun, member of the wit-smitten Algonquin Hotel's Round Table luncheon clique and star of the *World*'s op-ed page; indeed, a biographer speaks of "his major journalistic invention—the modern column of opinion which is sometimes at odds with the editorial policy of the newspaper in which it appears." [153] In 1927 these occasional divergences grew frequent, and in the end the *World* suppressed him for several months because he took the execution of Sacco & Vanzetti harder than his employers did. Or as he sometimes maintained, he voluntarily abandoned his column for several months in what Ralph Pulitzer, for the management, called a witch's Sabbatical. The nominal or actual occasion for the paper's finally firing him was his accusing it in its own columns of cowardly truckling to the Catholic Church. The Scripps-Howard chain of middle-sized papers, then still practicing some of the muckracking tactics of the decade before World War I, snapped him up and most profitably for all concerned gave him his head in wide national syndication.

In 1931, when the *World* died of hard times, its editorial chief, Walter Lippmann, went to the New York *Herald-Tribune* with a sociopolitical, scatter-gun column, "Today and Tomorrow." There, too, was a great catch. At his best he wrote like Edmund Burke filtered through Samuel Butler, and his integrity was as marked as his intelligence. In the *World* lack of by-line had kept him from being widely known outside the magazines of ideas and the spines of shrewd, sober books on the society around him. Now his signed studies of what went on and why and what it might mean moved out from the split page of the *Herald-Tribune* to dozens of other papers through syndication. This made him an elder statesman of the same order as Justice Oliver Wendell Holmes—an eminence so marked that Broun once fired off a column deploring what seemed to him the nation's feckless fondness for sitting at Lippmann's feet beseeching him to tell America what to think.

Maybe Broun felt a symptomatic divergence between his and Lippmann's careers. Both belonged to the amazing generation of Harvard graduates *c.* 1910 including Dos Passos, Robert Edmond Jones, Robert Benchley, John Reed, Bronson Cutting.... For years after the Armistice Broun had been letting a sloppy radicalism fester beneath his newspaper writings. Eventually it took him into formal affiliation with the left-wing Socialists and then into acting as the Communists' catspaw in gaining temporary control of the Newspaper Guild, of which he was a chief founder. Lippmann, however, beginning as an overt Socialist of Fabian flavor, came to feel lack of relation between Socialist postulates and social actualities, cut loose from dogma and examined for his readers both the FDR-baiting Liberty League and the New Deal with the subtlety of a responsible Socrates and the gingerly sympathy of an unusually commonsensical psychiatrist—an intellectual feat that led disgruntled radicals to accuse him of going conservative. Broun's tell-us-what-to-think gibe was impertinent. Lippmann's style of statement was: "My thinking in the light of what I discern leads me in this direction. Come along, provided the initiative is yours." That was far from Broun's partial views and flouncing self-righteousness. "I will never be a good reporter," he told his readers. "I never feel minded to call for a bowl of water and ask, 'What is the truth?' "[154]

It was also far from the tastes of many readers of the *Herald-Tribune* who valued the paper for its conservative editorials and the Washington column of Mark Sullivan, once a keen Bull Mooser, then one of President Hoover's inner circle, now remembered chiefly and gratefully as a genial and able social historian. Here was the pregnant novelty of a paper featuring writings not only often controverting its editorial policy but usually expressing such heresies better than its own editorial page expressed its orthodoxies. Today one thinks nothing of seeing William F. Buckley, Jr., and Joseph Kraft on the same page of the Zenith *Morning Herald,* each in his own way devastating the editorials. This may well be progress. It gives the public access to abler writing reflecting a wider range of experience and information than a given paper could favor its readers with fifty years ago. Yet there may also be the sinister connotation that competition from broadcasting has now bled the newspaper press so debilitatingly that it has ceased to care about integral responsibility.

The relative size of Lippmann's public could never match that of the most highly spiced columnists. All the more to the credit of hundreds of thousands of Americans that their appreciation of his work made him a national institution. Credit also the publishers and editors who went on printing and paying for "Today and Tomorrow," even though none pretended that it would drastically raise circulation. As years passed, the drag of that thrice-weekly deadline often kept Lippmann's style from doing itself justice. Some of his money-on-the-line judgments were as wrong as the next man's—his rueful description of the pre-Chicago FDR was: "No tribune of the people . . . no enemy of entrenched privilege . . . a pleasant man who, without any important qualification for the job, would like very much to be President." [155] But he consistently left readers with a salutary sense, particularly valuable under Depression conditions, that to see things as whole as one can and as steadily as possible was still conceivable among civilized people.

Less salutary was the extent to which interest in what the St. Paul *Pioneer-Press* or the Zenith *Evening News* said about a weighty event became obscured by interest in what Lippman thought about it. Here, too, news and its bearing on the nation and the citizen were cloggingly intertwined with an aggrandizing name and style. The point is clear in the running title of Broun's column, "It Seems to Me." True, in the 1850's Horace Greeley *was* the highly opinionated New York *Tribune;* in pre-World War I days Finley Peter Dunne's "Mr. Dooley" had an immense public. But neither precedent fits well. Greeley's name seldom appeared, and in the southern half of the country few read him. Mr. Dooley was a fictitious Chicago barkeep and halfway through his career quit newspaper syndication for weekly and monthly magazines.

In some ways the atmosphere of Lippmann's column was over-rarefied. Late in 1933 Scripps-Howard redressed the average toward down-to-earthiness with Pegler's syndicated column. He had made his name with a "Speaking Out on Sports" column for the Chicago *Tribune* syndicate so sourly effervescent that literate liberals made it fashionable. Though Broun too had served a successful stretch in ball-park press boxes, he also had the advantage of a comfortable, cultivated rearing and of being a valued alumnus of the "creative writing" course of Charles Townsend Copeland and George Pierce Baker at Harvard. Pegler's education had consisted of two years at a Jesuit high school in Chicago; listening to his father, a harshly capable veteran of police beat and rewrite desk; and an apprenticeship on his own in Midwestern city rooms.

His new assignment to comment on anything and everything was tagged "Fair Enough." Its third appearance—a defense of the lynching of kidnapper-murderers in California—brought instant notoriety. It had not been a racist affair but a flare-up of the grim old tradition of vigilante impatience with fumbly law. Thirty years earlier Pegler's position would have caused less, if any, outcry. But by 1933 moral fashion, for once changing for the better, had imbued any kind of lynching with an intolerable stench. The attention thus drawn to "Fair Enough" seldom wavered during several stormy decades. The same hair-trigger bent that thus set him off on the wrong foot kept getting Pegler into noisy scuffles-in-print that, there is small doubt, he enjoyed.

A generation later, toward his dismal, probably paranoid end, it was assumed that he had always been an atrabilious reactionary. Earlier, however, before years and the knee-in-the-groin tactics of his smellier ill-wishers had sharpened his native peevishness, his political coloration could not be deduced from his choice of targets. He pursued Winchell with whips of scorpions, calling him a "gents' room journalist" [156] as much because he thought the man's love affair with the New Deal nauseating as because he was fouling up the newspaperman's prideful profession.* Yet nothing Winchell threw at Hitler was as effective as Pegler's piece in 1936 on what Nazism did to Germany's Jewish children: "... the child's first attempt at spelling out public notices on the billboards will inform him that he is not a human being ... but a beast whose parents were ... loathsome animals ... the few hours of innocence given to us all ... [have] been destroyed by a man with a mustache ... seriously nominated by some of his followers ... for God the Redeemer of the German race. It would be a mistake to call him a baby-killer. You can't torture a dead child." [157] Covering the Winter Olympics at Garmisch-Partenkirchen, he devastatingly

---

* When Winchell learned that Pegler had attended Broun's funeral, he printed in his column instructions specifically barring Pegler from his (Winchell's) funeral. Pegler seems to have said this was the most valued honor ever accorded him. (Jack Alexander, *Saturday Evening Post*, September 14, 1940.)

detailed the strangely soldierly behavior of the "work battalions" and "security guards" infesting what was meant to be a jolly carnival of peace-minded sportsmanship. He followed up with:

"The Nazi press bureau released a ... despatch to the New York Times intimating that anyone reporting ... troops at the Olympic Games was a liar. I guess that's me, but the report was natural. ... When thousands of men seem to march but don't in clothing and tin hats that seem to be military uniforms but aren't, and carry harmless utensils that appear to be bayonets but ain't, any stranger is likely to make the same mistake." [158] His earlier attacks on *Fascismo* and Mussolini—he called the Ethiopian War of 1935 a conflict between "The King of Kings" [as Haile Selassie was styled] "and the Bum of Bums—" [159] were so stinging that the *New Masses* invited him to contribute to an anti-Fascist symposium. His column decrying efforts to equate Catholicism with support for Franco was so blistering that his syndicate refused to distribute it: "I ask whether it is intended to drive the Spanish masses back to the Church at the point of Franco's bayonets, some in the hands of Mahommedans, some in the hands of pagan Nazis. ..." [160] As for domestic Fascism, he duly praised the neighborly generosity and pluck with which Evansville, Indiana, took a horrible flood but also reminded readers that Evansville had been "the point of [Indiana's] infection with the Ku Klux Klan ... Fascism at its worst," and these very same splendidly behaving people "formerly had stayed up nights scheming ways to gang up on their neighbors ... stewing in the smelly juice of hatred." [161]

He also endeared himself to unwary Reds by calling J. Edgar Hoover "a night-club fly-cop." [162] Disrespectfully he nipped at the Rockefellers' staid heels. His Philippics against Insull sounded as if written for the *Daily Worker*, and their lively feeling for the hundreds of thousands who lost their small savings in Insull-empire securities certainly identified him as no knee-jerk reactionary. A trip to Florida in the late 1930s set him off on a column, "Behind the Pleasure Coast," about Sunshine Land's blacks and poor whites:

> It would be interesting ... to hear what ... an Albanian goatherd would have to say about the vaunted American standard of living after observing the foul poverty of so many Americans, white and black, and the wretched, swaybacked, windowless cabins in which they live and beget and dissolve ... shacks in which an Abyssinian leper would not keep his dog, or even his wife ... the homes of so many American families are no better than the tin shanties ... on city dumps in the days of the Long Panic.[163]

Yet in the same period his original admiration for FDR was changing into bilious suspicion of his motives and supplementary snoot cocking at conspicuous New Dealers, particularly Harry Hopkins and Harold Ickes. Further to dismay liberals who had been hoping this stridently cogent voice would be on their side, he persisted in stating early, late and at lunchtime that in his view Communists were just Red-shirted Fascists, and fell foul of organized labor. He had a large hand in exposing the corrupt leadership of the International Association of Theatrical and Stage Employees in Hollywood. Thenceforward, even though IATSE's bosses smelled to heaven and the case against them was ironclad, Big Labor treated Pegler as poison, and year after year he fought back harder until he could not be distinguished from a committed labor baiter. Further, he took to the public his war against Communist infiltration of the new Newspaper Guild, which Broun, its chief creator, defended by saying, "You have to have Reds in a labor organization." [164] At the height of the ensuing feud, which coincided with the Hitler-Stalin pact, Broun took to bed and died of pneumonia. Many of his admirers hinted that Pegler's refusal to believe in Broun's last-minute renunciation of Moscow was partly responsible.

Presently Pegler's intolerance of the way organized labor operated led him to drop all restraint in attacking Eleanor Roosevelt. For some years he had been tossing brickbats her way, particularly for her and her family's willingness to get handsomely paid for amateur writings the primary value of which came from association with the White House. "No false, old-fashioned sense of propriety," a supposititious new President wrote to his son in a Pegler column, "is to fetter [the President's wife and daughter] from the exploitation of an office which belongs to the Nation ... for the private enrichment of the family. Your mother will seek and accept at the highest figure engagements to deliver public addresses as the wife of the President ... cashing in on the Presidency ... by selling [a great volume of writings] at the highest possible figure." [165] When Mrs. Roosevelt proclaimed that she couldn't bring herself to cross a picket line, fair or unfair, Pegler declared war. She became "the Gab," "La Boca Grande": coarsely he celebrated her buckteeth. This was part of a falling off in content and style, gradually spiraling downward to where Scripps-Howard set him adrift. The Hearst interests picked him up, but eventually they did the same. Before the end he was swinging so wildly that even Robert Welch, founder of the John Birch Society, refused to print what Pegler wrote when invited to contribute to the Birchers' house organ. It almost looked as if the devil were deliberately turning him into the monster that readers of that lynching column had suspected him of being.

Years earlier, however, when his temperature was running lower and his writing skills were at their peak, he was powerfully engaging. On hiring him, Scripps-Howard had advertised him as combining "the drollery of Ring Lardner, the iconoclasm of Henry Mencken, the homely insight of Will Rogers," an absurdly tall order, yet one must say he was the only other member of the guild of columnists who wrote in the same league as Lippmann, disparate as their purposes and methods were. It was also absurd for a biographer to imply that one reason for his troubles with Broun was envy of Broun's ability to knock off his next day's column in half an hour sandwiched into a poker game, whereas Pegler's daily 800 words cost him hours of paper- and temper-destroying toil. Broun could play the piccolo of whimsy pretty well and sometimes beat a big drum effectively but day in and day out seldom came level with Pegler on even marginal topics, such as the crassness of dog breeders and shows; the shade tree that died in his arms after the experts had shaken their heads and tiptoed away; what they did to the wisteria that wouldn't bloom; the new breed of wine snobs springing up after Repeal; the hazards presented by amateur cooks.... Pegler's analysis of French political parties and French technique with eating tools was based on observations made while he was a war correspondent in England and France in 1918. Inevitably he came brashly athwart the hawse of first Rear Admiral William S. Sims, USN, and then General John J. Pershing, USA.

In the early 1940s he created a man-in-the-street spokesman named George Spelvin *—not a whimsical essayist's usual alter ego but a lower-middle-income family man whose grumblings and fantasies rejoiced many recognizing in them what was biting themselves and their wives. Such nonprofessional readers had no reason to see that these prickly bits going straight to the heart—or often the spleen—were written in a masterfully accurate and evocative medium, talk in print that muttered and slurred and yet bounced true. Mr. Spelvin was frequently called before congressional committees to testify on the state of the nation (usually under examination by Senator Nilly, Ind., Ind.), and sometimes Mrs. Spelvin was the witness. She was as dizzying as her spouse with surly banalities and open-ended syntax that simultaneously travestied congressional hearings, expressed with

---

* The name traditionally set down in the program for the actor playing a given role when he has already been onstage in an earlier role under his regular name. Doubtless the original George Spelvin was an ubiquitous utility man, but I know nothing definite about it. Pegler would probably have protested—and Actors' Equity should have—when they used "Georgina Spelvin" on the marquee for the girl playing the central character in the very X-rated The Devil in Miss Jones.

candor what Spelvinistic types had on their minds and showed how well their creator understood how little sense they made at the same time he agreed with them down among his hormones. Yet much of Pegler's best irony came not from tangled statements—though he knew that trick as well as any—but from cadence, the curl, stretch and twist of the vehicle sentences themselves. Read one to a Kamchatkan who knew no English, and he would somehow feel its bite anyway. For the rest Ben Hecht, up from Chicago newspaperdom himself, no reactionary but no collectivist either, tasteless but wary of enthusiasms, did him a worthy epitaph:

> [Pegler] often clouted at targets dear to me. . . . He was a sort of one-man counter-revolution . . . fought . . . mushrooming statism . . . and another concentration of power . . . labor unions. He took swipes at the Catholic Church and even at a few Jews. He slipped occasionally, for he fought on muddy ground. And when his eyes fogged he was apt to knock over a few innocent bystanders. Pegler's cheering section is shy of people I admire. But when he finishes his stint . . . he will emerge as one of the brightest of the prose lighthouses in a time darkened by the pall of government.[166]

One trouble with unusual skills in print is that brains to match may not go with them, or vice versa. Thus, the order of John Dewey's intelligence was far higher than the way he wrote about or lectured on his ideas. The reverse case was Henry David Thoreau. In Lippmann, of course, the levels were close; word and brain sang together, peers of exalted rank. As for Pegler, though he was sound on Winchell, Nazis, hangovers and mooching park pigeons, the quality of his hagridden opinions on many other matters was inferior to his remarkable way of expressing them, also to his reporter's skill in gathering and mustering data. That mattered less in the 1930s, however, because that decade had a growing taste for newspapermen who wrote well but thought with the backs of their necks. The hero-reporter, particularly the foreign or war correspondent, had come into his own—indeed, rather more than his own.

Apotheosis had been cooking up. In the old days before by-lines only newspapermen themselves were aware how well the ablest correspondents had covered the Civil War in spite of menacingly uncooperative generals as well as flying lead. The next few decades made little use of that wistful phrase "gentlemen of the press." Gradually, however, newspapermen developed their own belief that, dim a view as society might take of reporters and their Paul-Prying function, they were collectively the salt of the earth, the only segment of the human race who, when you came down to it, really knew the score. They had to. Mark Twain and his widely read works were full of that. Before World War I David Graham Phillips, muckraking reporter and high-flying novelist, was saying, "I'd rather be a reporter than President." [167] In the *Light That Failed* sort of thing the equally popular Rudyard Kipling built up the legend of the archangelic war correspondent riding the storm and telling the weather bureau afterward where and how it could have sharpened up the performance. America's Richard Harding Davis and his imitators applied clay on the right parts of this armature. Out of World War I came Sir Philip Gibbs, bullet-dodging British reporter on war in the front lines but just as much at home among the brass at GHQ; once the shooting died down, he could unleash his analytic faculties to make a career of telling the world how stupid it had all been, you know. Cruder but just as famous was America's Floyd Gibbons, whose eye patch was as well known as Dick Davis' dimpled chin ever was; the story was that eye had been knocked out by a German bullet in Belleau Wood and he had caught it in his hand. Both he and Frazier "Spike" Hunt covered international politics and fighting as if they were college football games.

In the 1920s a new crop was led by Vincent Sheean, six feet two and handsome, only a few years out of the University of Chicago, who got through the lines to cover from the Moslem-native side the fight that Abdel Krim was putting up against colonial Spain—such pluck and resourcefulness obviously had a future. A crucial ingredient in Hemingway's personal climate—the musketeerish aura that did his literary career no harm at all—was those oblique firsthand bits about the Greco-Turkish War and, for press-table statesmanship, the absurdities of the Genoa Conference. One way or another, at least metaphorically and sometimes actually, such reporter-errants photographed well, and the gloss prints were handy publicity for their lecture tours. Inevitably the type got into the movies, trench coat, binoculars, portable typewriter and all. A home-stable running mate was added when Hollywood borrowed from Broadway (*The Front Page, Gentlemen of the Press* and so on) the stereotype of the raffish big-city reporter, pint of whiskey in hand, snap-brim hat on back of head, wisecrack in mouth, heart of gold gradually cropping out on sleeve. Soon he mutated into terms of the other sex—girl reporters usually played by Jean Arthur or Rosalind Russell. . . .

With these burgeoning personae came an epidemic spread of byline, indispensable in the dashing foreign correspondent's kit. Time was when he had no more flavor of his own than clung to "From Our Special Correspondent." Nowadays an advertisement lists 243 members of the staff of the New York *Times* accorded by-lines. Even before World War II the public had four classes of by-lined agents personally interpreting the news: radio commentators, columnists, foreign correspondents/war correspondents and radio and screen actors reacting to fictitious but recognizable newsworthy situations. It began to feel as though the Nazis' seizure of Austria and the Moscow trials were primarily opportunities for Miss Thompson, Kaltenborn and Walter Duranty to be impressive.

For the more sociable kind of foreign correspondent radical-mindedness verging on and sometimes culminating in stooging for Communism was an occupational hazard. During his prejournalism career as a fixer in Moscow, Negley Farson contracted that ailment, and it permeated his best-seller autobiography, *The Way of a Transgressor.* Hemingway's case developed severely enough to send him to Spain in 1937. At first he stayed nominally within the intent of his correspondent's credentials but later did overt Communist propaganda in the script for the movie *The Spanish Earth* and let the Party-lining League of American Writers use him as a major exhibit. His "reputation for under-statement," said a recent pro-Loyalist historian, "was not earned by the things he wrote about the Spanish Civil War." [168] In view of the low resistance to Red collectivism then prevalent among Sheean's playmates, his dismay with the world of Hitler, Mussolini, Daladier, Franco and Chamberlain—so unlike that of his offbeat hero, Gandhi—might well have persuaded him had he never met Rayna Prohme, the hard-line lady Communist who played Vivian to his willing Merlin. By the time he got to the war in Spain he not only was slanting his copy to move the outside world to help the Loyalists, but was proudly aware he was doing so. Such flavoring above or anyway beyond the call of a reporter's accepted duty was not rare among correspondents covering Spain's pitiful ordeal. The rarity was Sheean's honestly admitting to himself and others what he was up to.

Such "advocacy journalism" is nothing new, though the term is. Its origins lie back there somewhere among the newsletters of the 1600s. The woefully slow, never complete process of getting rid of it was a major thread in the history of American reporting in the 1800s. Here the point is that the cult of the magnetic personality-with-a-typewriter imposing on its admirers news of its own cooking came just in time to give disguised, often unconscious, propaganda a new lease on life.

Dorothy Thompson's obvious right to a place among the topmost personalities-with-typewriters shaping public opinion in the 1930s has double significance. Here was a woman considered so well worth listening to on foreign and domestic affairs that the *Herald-Tribune* alternated her thrice weekly "On the Record" with Lippmann's column. This was indeed a novelty. A few American women correspondents had already shown they could file cables from overseas as meaty as any male competitor's. Anna Louise Strong was one of the least creditable examples, Anne O'Hare McCormick of the New York *Times* one of the best in spite of a curious leaning toward *Fascismo* and *Il Duce*. As if to nail this cultural wonder down, Eleanor Roosevelt simultaneously had superb success with her "My Day" column syndicated by Scripps-Howard's United Features and a monthly question-fielding chat with the *Ladies' Home Journal's* millions of readers that drew as much or more attention than Miss Thompson's generously proffered opinions in the same magazine. *Time* understated in calling this pair of queens back to back "the most influential women in the U.S." [169] No previous American women had wielded such influence overtly and explicitly, not Frances Willard, queen of the Women's Christian Temperance Union, or Jane Addams, queen of pacifism and the settlement house, or Harriet Beecher Stowe of *Uncle Tom's Cabin*. For none of them had access to either newspaper syndication or radio.

It was a good time for the experiment. Otherwise American feminism would have had little to show for itself between the World Wars. Where was the brave new world to which Votes for Women was to have given birth? If it existed, it was well hidden under the vulgar excesses of the New Era and the grim realities of Hooverville. A major, though hardly dominant, hand in effecting Repeal was the only solid coup that post-Nineteenth Amendment Woman had racked up. And there was dissension among her as to strategy. Thus, the American Women's Party, persistent, militant and in the 1930s miniature core of doctrinaire feminism, denounced one of Miss Thompson's earliest columns because it scolded the US Supreme Court for disallowing a New York State law setting minimum wages for women in factory work. The AWP position, then as now, was that legislation specifically protecting women as such is insultingly discriminatory. The social-worker background that Miss Thompson and Mrs. Roosevelt shared helped them see that that position was graceless, and both had more than dabbled in orthodox feminism. Now both were doing far more than the AWP to show society that certain women's observations and opinions were to be taken far more seriously than such pickthank rigidity.

Reared in upstate New York, daughter of a Methodist parson of British background, Miss Thompson was born to plain living and thinking as high as the local high school and Methodist-supported

Syracuse University afforded.* In middle age she put much of a handsome professional income into very comfortable living and could and did put away scotch whiskey all evening in a fashion outdoing many men, but she never altogether sloughed off the values of the campus YWCA. Tall, wholesomely nice-looking, with a peaches-and-cream complexion, effortlessly capable, she gravitated less toward boys than toward other capable girls and after college toward amateur social work and writing for newspapers. Soon after World War I she made a free-lance reporting foray into Europe and within a few years was Central European bureau chief for the New York *Evening Post* and the Philadelphia *Public Ledger.* No woman had ever held such a post before. Astringent George Seldes, in Berlin for the Chicago *Daily News,* deplored other women correspondents' horizontal methods of securing interviews but testified that "Dorothy was different ... the only woman 'newspaperman' of our time." [170]

Her judgments of persons and situations were hardly infallible. When she went to the USSR in 1927 to cover the vastly ballyhooed celebration of the tenth anniversary of the October Revolution, she apparently failed to grasp that Anna Louise Strong and Albert Rhys Williams, her chief guides and companions, were not just cordial American fans of Communism told to be nice but long-standing, paid press agents. Yet her resulting newspaper pieces and book (*The New Russia,* 1928) were better than most of the fatuous writing that came out of the doings. She was reporter enough to manage to see some of the forest in spite of the warped trees that Comrade Potemkin set up all over the landscape. Soon after World War II she learned in dismay that the highly trusted German refugee whom she had hired to monitor the European press and radio for her had been a Communist agent all along.† And she also muffed a diagnostic opportunity of great moment when, after seven years of trying, she finally secured an interview with Adolf Hitler. This was 1932, when he was waiting in the wings with everybody assuming he would soon come crushingly to power. "When I walked into the room," she reported, "I was convinced I was meeting the future dictator of Germany. In something less than fifty seconds I was sure that I was not. It took just about that time to measure the startling insignificance of this man who has set the world agog. . . ." [171]

* This section is much indebted to Marion K. Sanders' workmanlike *Dorothy Thompson: Legend in Her Time* (1973). Its judgments and mine do not necessarily coincide.

† Her account of this is informative about the atmosphere of liberal opinion after Hitler attacked the USSR: ". . . in a time when many people are suffering from having had associations with Communists . . . it may be useful to show how this can occur innocently, and even through our better nature. Moreover, at a

Within a year His Insignificance was in the saddle, of course. At the time her verdict was convenient for the Nazis, but they resented her contemptuous view of their man as well as her frank horror at the Nazis' Jew baiting. In 1934 they made her a martyr-heroine by expelling her from Germany. She commented, "My offense was to think that Hitler was just an ordinary man," [172] and framed the expulsion order to hang on the wall of her office in New York City. The silver lining in her miscue was a rush of writing and lecturing as qualified expert on the Nazis that set off her heady career in America. She wrote and broadcast about morals and home politics, but her specialty was playing Cato to the Third Reich's Carthage for the next decade. Some thought her "a dangerous warmonger and incendiary," [173] Margaret Case Harriman wrote in the *New Yorker*. Sir Wilmot Lewis, Washington correspondent of the London *Times,* said she had "discovered the secret of perpetual emotion." [174] But she was an admirable antidote to the American Firstism behind which the nation's proto-Fascists sheltered themselves as World War II drew nearer. In that role she not only wrote and spoke tirelessly but also inspired Sinclair Lewis, her second husband, to write *It Can't Happen Here,* the story of how out-and-out Fascism might come to America. Superficially the political demons of the book resembled Huey P. Long, Father Coughlin ... but the mechanism by which boots, banners and blackjacks took over, the homosexuality of the Corpos' cleverest leader, the tactics of the underground resistance were all watermarked "Made in Europe." Had it happened here, the way of it would have been less imitative. Nevertheless, there was more America than Europe about the moral drawn by Lewis' newspaperman-protagonist: that "the world struggle today is not of Communism against Fascism, but of tolerance against the bigotry ... preached equally by Communism and Fascism." [175] The trouble was not that this was unsound but that it disagreed with the polarizing gospel already being preached by both stripes of authoritarian and already dangerously fashionable: Red/Black, Communism/Fascism, take your

---

time when others are describing Communist infiltrations as a 'red herring,' and the exposure of it as 'red-baiting,' my own experience demonstrates the fact of such infiltration...." She was warned early about her employee, she said, but only by ex-Communists and "In those days I was inclined to mistrust all 'disgruntled' ex-Communists. I held to the theory that a man is innocent unless proved guilty ... none [offered] conclusive proof. I therefore dismissed them as 'red-baiters' attacking an innocent man." ("How I Was Duped by a Communist," *Saturday Evening Post,* April 16, 1949.) She noted also that at this time her former monitor-researcher, Hermann Badzislawski, was now a professor of sociology at the (East German) University of Leipzig and doing journalistic and radio chores for the USSR's armed forces.

choice. The next year, when Spain exploded, the both-your-houses position became more heretical than ever. It was significant that no such speech as that quoted above survived in the dramatization of *It Can't Happen Here*, produced that year by the Federal Theatre.

Whether or not she was more than a Cassandra built like Brunhilde, Miss Thompson was certainly a magnetic model for bright, well-meaning girls to emulate as they matriculated in Limbo University's School of Journalism. She even showed that such careers as hers did not require abdicating from traditional femininity. As she swirled from make-a-speech dinner to radio broadcast to late party with the Sheeans, the John Gunthers, Hamilton Fish Armstrong of *Foreign Affairs*, she was womanly in deep-dish chiffons from Bergdorf Goodman. She also retained Woman's proverbial privilege of changing her mind. In 1940 what seemed to her the shortcomings of FDR and the New Deal led her to throw her considerable weight into backing Willkie for the Republican nomination. As his campaign grew troublingly bitter, Morris Ernst persuaded FDR to invite her, just back from a transatlantic reconnaissance, to the White House to tell him what she had observed. The interview so impressed her with FDR's firmness and grasp of affairs that she changed course 180 degrees and wrote a column saying Willkie was all very well but FDR was indispensable, vote for him. Aghast, the Republican-committed *Herald-Tribune* suppressed a follow-up column enlarging on that advice, but the lady had the bit in her teeth and was soon helping write FDR's speeches. Sherwood, head of the speech-writing task force, said she supplied more and better angles than anybody else except Dean Acheson.

"Who wrote President Roosevelt's speeches?" was one of the questions that FDR's wife answered in the *Ladies' Home Journal* just after World War II. Her answer showed that she sometimes subordinated candor to image preservation: "Mr. Roosevelt wrote his own speeches but he, of course, called on all the experts to furnish him with facts and to go over them with him. . . ." [176] This smooth denial of most of what Sherwood, Samuel Rosenman *et al.* did may hark back to the lady's traumatic first major publicity. During World War I young FDR was assistant secretary of the Navy and his tall young wife chatelaine of their well-staffed mansion in Washington. Apropos of Herbert Hoover's Food Will Win the War movement, the New York *Times* sent a woman reporter to ask Mrs. Roosevelt how to go about conserving food. Earnestly—so much that she did was earnest—she explained that she "does the shopping [herself], the cooks see there is no food wasted, the laundress is sparing in her use of soap . . .

all [servants] are encouraged to make helpful suggestions on the use of 'left overs.' ... Making the servants help me do my saving has ... been highly profitable." There were "guffaws all over Washington," says her major biographer. Her absent husband sent a letter about his pride in being married to "the Originator ... of the New Household Economy for Millionaires!" Her dismay was honest: "I do think it was horrid of that woman to use my name in that way ... yet some of it I did say. I never will be caught again, that's sure. ..." [177]

Negatively that pledge was fairly well carried out. Positively she eventually became the schoolgirl crush of the distaff side of the Washington press corps. From the men's side Raymond Clapper, a highly respected Washington correspondent of the 1930s, admiringly called her one of the ten most important people in the nation's capital. It was not so much that she learned fast as that when she did, she learned solidly. The other outstanding thing about her remarkable career is that it bloomed so vigorously in the very 1930s when everybody said the strive-and-succeed story was as dead as the New Era. For, child of affluence though she was, she had to come up the hard way, and her success owed as much to her own strength as to that of her bootstraps.

The crucial bending of this not too promising twig was the work of Marie Souvestre, a cultivated and, for her time, radical-minded French schoolmistress conducting a girls' school near London. She was a Dreyfusard, a pro-Boer, a member of the English Positivist group led by Frederic Harrison, and given to grave discussion of "the religion of humanity" and the virtues of labor unions. Her pupils tended to come from affluent liberal-to-radical British families. That atmosphere is probably the chief explanation of how Eleanor Roosevelt became, as the *New Yorker* said many years later, "a liberal by conviction, from above, and not by aching protest, from below." [178] She was sent there, instead of to a standard, high-ticket American "finishing school" for the daughters of established wealth because a strong-minded aunt had greatly valued having been schooled there. It is always sad to have to say of anybody that schooldays were the happiest. The available data make it clear that this was true of Eleanor, not least because the place was sealed off from male society, so this tall, big-footed, overtoothy, wistful girl was free from having to contrast herself with those whose prettier faces and surer poise better drew men and boys.

Eleanor became a favorite of her preceptress, singled out to accompany her on vacation travels on the Continent as well as in much tea and talk during school terms. In middle age she gratefully identified Mlle. Souvestre as "the most interesting and unforgettable person [I've] ever met." [179] Spiritually the lady was certainly mother of the person who within thirty-odd years would be called, only half-amusedly, the Great White Mother of America. From these formative years came even Eleanor's manner of speech—not the pseudo-British yap and drawl of the finishing school but a mannered incisiveness Britishly rich in broad As, rather as if an aristocratic Englishwoman had spent much of her childhood with an American grandmother. It spoke well for her unmistakable integrity that this high-pitched, outlandish accent, soon conspicuous over the radio and on many and many a platform, failed to flaw her popularity among the millions who mattered—to her.

Supplementary touches were added when they fetched her home at the age of eighteen to do the things that girls with names like Roosevelt were then supposed to do—debutante balls, weekends on relatives' estates, summers in Europe, the Berkshires or Bar Harbor. She was miserable at the balls, not much happier at the picnics. But by then one of the things one did was join the Junior League, which exposed debutantes to marginal good works. That put Eleanor, by an inevitable magnetism, into what was already known as "social work" at the Rivington Street Settlement House on Manhattan's Lower East Side. Jane Addams' Hull House in Chicago was the best-known such institution in America, but most large cities had one or more. Like so many American social devices, this was borrowed from Britain, where for some decades tender consciences had sought constructively to alleviate the miseries of industry-swollen slums. The charter of Hull House was in English-sounding terms: ". . . to provide a center for a higher civic and social life, to institute . . . educational and phil-anthropical enterprises, and to investigate and improve the conditions in the industrial districts." [180] Beyond that American settlements soon took on specialized form as emollients for the difficulties of the masses of recent immigrants handicapped by illiteracy, lack of English and other cultural misfittings. Zealous to ease and promote assimilation, settlement workers waded in to teach Italians, Poles, Greeks, Eastern European Jews and others workable English and train them in new notions of sanitation, schooling, law and family ties while also reinforcing their self-respect—which meant keeping up their own cuisines, dances. . . . Their teeming progeny also needed activities absorbing enough—music, handicrafts, theatricals and so on—to keep them from vicious street influences.

As settlements proliferated and the ideas of their staffs, salaried or volunteer, widened with experience, "settlement interests and strategy [extended] into . . . large scale public housing, city and regional planning, systemized social insurance, internationalism and world peace . . . they struck out against sweatshops, insanitary workrooms, child labor, low wages, overwork of women. . . ." [180] Out of those attitudes came Florence Kelley's National Consumers' League, which looked into the conditions under which consumer goods were made and pledged members to buy only from manufacturers and retailers whom it "whitelisted"—a negative boycott that, though it lacked much economic impact, was nevertheless one of the eggs from which today's consumer movements were hatched. Naturally Eleanor worked with and for the Consumers' League; it was part of the syndrome manifest in her public life. She was also deep in the League of Women Voters, victorious feminism's most realistic effort to make the Nineteenth Amendment count. Another part was her loyalty to Prohibition. It is often surmised that alcoholism in her family was responsible here. Actually the settlement house mind, acutely aware of what alcohol did in the slums, never averse to manipulating people for their own good, typically supported the Dry cause and often, like Eleanor, stuck with it to the bitter end. Ten years after Repeal, though admitting that Prohibition had failed as a social reform, she still wrote: "I would be glad to see all the hard liquor in the world at the bottom of the sea." [181]

How fitting that, barring her membership in the Women's Christian Temperance Union, much of this sounds like a read-through of the New Deal! For many key New Dealers—Harry Hopkins, Rexford G. Tugwell, Harold Ickes, Frances Perkins, Aubrey Williams—had at one time or another been in or close to settlement house or "social agencies," sharing their assumptions. Tugwell called the species "holists," saying, "[We] know each other somehow and . . . are recognized by those . . . on the other side. One of us cannot be picked out on the street any more than . . . a Rotarian, a Mason, an Iowan . . . a Methodist, a merchant or a salesman. But let one of us work for a week in any group, and even if we have been most circumspect . . . there will be an identification . . . in special situations where some members of our persuasion happen to have responsibility, we may be favored. . . ." [182] As chief public relations missionary for the New Deal, FDR's "Missus" (as he rather patronizingly called her when discussing her findings with his high command) was only pursuing Mlle. Souvestre fleshed out with Rivington Street, generous in intent, emotionally rewarding. Such work among slum-smothered immigrants was particularly educational for affluent women, probably did most of their objects of solicitude little harm, maybe helped a fair number. But the catch was well stated by David E. Lilienthal, master magician of the Tennessee Valley Authority: He recognized her earnest charm, respected her highly, but thought her "social worker angle" ill suited to "a world that is tough and bitter and hardly amenable to such tampering with symptoms." [183]

At least she was not toploftical about it, as some of her fellow workers were. She so enjoyed teaching Rivington Street's tattered kids the dancing and calisthenics she had learned at school that she actually welcomed it when a colleague's absence forced her to work double shifts. Ten years later, as wife of the governor of New York State, she so enjoyed teaching girls of her own special stratum in the Todhunter School in New York City that she commuted weekly from Albany, New York for two and a half days—110 miles by rail. It is daunting to learn that she handled classes in literature, American history and drama from Aeschylus to Eugene O'Neill,* though her schooling had stopped when she was eighteen and her published writings make it clear that she had little better grasp of literature as such than Aeschylus had of atomic physics. Secondary-school teachers can be like that, however, and the primary purpose of such classes is to cajole pupils into reading certain items. In history Eleanor tried to tie the past in with modern concerns à la Souvestre: "Give your reason for allowing women to actively participate in ... government. . . . How are Negroes excluded from voting in the South? . . ." [184] Borrowing from the already modish Progressive Education, she took the girls to courtrooms, police lineups and, beamingly, settlement houses. "Teaching gave her some of the happiest moments in her life," said her partner in the school. "The girls worshipped her." [185]

In a way it was a pity that the emotional pattern that married her to handsome Cousin Franklin kept her from what might well have been a happier life for her—that of a growingly confident, devoted teacher, forming with other teachers friendships of the girls-together sort that always meant much to her; graciously recalling her pupils' names when they came to see her as young matrons; never required to handle children of her own and risk the corrosive difference between the teacher's solicitous but partial and the mother's total concern. As it was, fate combined with her and his conventional rearings and some quirk of his young hormones to trick them into a mutual misfit. It seems to have thwarted his destiny less than hers. Even poliomyelitis did not keep him from going about as high as he could possibly have had in mind, whereas the demands that his terms and career made on her were, in this view, warping. Gallantly and capably as she coped, her conspicuous achievements probably never exorcised the (doubtless subliminal) blueprint of Miss Roosevelt's School for Girls somewhere in the East Eighties that her mind and temperament hankered after. Just as, when pondering the New Deal, it helps to think of Eleanor as

---

* This section obviously owes a great deal to Joseph Lash's invaluable *Eleanor and Franklin.* I should make it very clear that many of the judgments that his data suggest to me are probably nothing he would agree with.

epitome of the settlement house mind, so it helps to understand her to think of her journalism as a duet sung from a national lectern by a superior schoolteacher and a settlement house worker.

In popular legend the creatrix of the "My Day" newspaper column and the question page in the *Ladies' Home Journal* was a previously obscure woman utilizing for purposes she deemed worthy the spotlight necessarily shining on the First Lady of the Land. Others admired her for putting the opportunity to well-meaning uses. Either way her behavior was unprecedented. No previous First Lady had ever held her own regular press conferences or gone on the high-paid lecture circuit. Nor was it likely that either United Features or the Curtis Publishing Company would have bought her opinions and daily doings had her husband remained the merely well-connected young Wall Street lawyer whom she married. But "obscure" was no word for her long before they took over the White House. The name Roosevelt, to which she had double title, had been a national eye-catcher for thirty-five years. And her President-uncle's magnification of the name had been supplemented in a minor but real way by FDR's Navy Department job in World War I; his nomination and able campaigning for the vice presidency in 1920; his conspicuous support of Al Smith in the Democratic conventions of 1924 and 1928, Eleanor organizing women right behind him; his imaginative governorship of New York State. With the innocence of ladylike ambition she had exploited that name by dabbling in by-line print for ten years before she had the White House for springboard.

When the *Ladies' Home Journal* offered a $50,000 prize in 1923 for the best plan to stabilize world peace, Mrs. Franklin D. Roosevelt wrote the kickoff article and then toiled conscientiously on the steering committee of the contest. She wrote for the popular *Redbook* magazine on women's place in politics—about which she had a good right to speak—and for *Success* magazine on "What I Most Want Out of Life." In 1928 the august *North American Review* let her put the case for Al Smith; *Current History,* identifying her as on the Women's Committee of the New York State Democratic Committee, made her the only woman among eleven Republican and Democratic stalwarts in a symposium on the Hoover-Smith election. She was one of nine women of national prestige on the board managing the Leslie Commission fund that was nucleus of orthodox American feminism. Her ardent, if responsibly moderate, feminism probably had much to do with her efforts to get her ideas and name published for what seemed to her good purposes. This was no do-good Pallas born suddenly from the creative headache of the New Deal's initial Hundred Days.

Nevertheless, it took the fierce light that beats on the White House as well as on thrones to make her a major phenomenon. It also tempted her, it appears, to manifest the serious flaw in her personal sense of discretion—strange in one who was indubitably a lady and shy to boot. In personal matters her developing skill in public relations, so serviceable to the New Deal, often lapsed. While wife of the governor of New York State, nominally the nation's second most important elective office, she saw no harm in endorsing Simmons beds in an advertisement complete with an obviously phony photograph of her own bedroom. She signed up for commercial radio broadcasts for cosmetics and consented to be nominal editor of a new magazine for mothers to be published by Macfadden (of the noisome New York *Daily Graphic*) called *Babies, Just Babies;* it was first published in October during the Hoover-FDR election, so obviously its editor would be First Lady within a few months. At the time the irony of its field of fire was not clear. Only gradually over the years did it become clear that, like many another woman embarking on motherhood with small talent for it, she mishandled her own progeny. But it hardly lessened the indiscretion of the deal that it included a generously salaried position for her daughter, Anna, a complete newcomer to journalism. The outcry was sharper then than it would be now, when Presidents' daughters, exploiting the breach that Mrs. Roosevelt innocently made, can take it for granted that highly paid magazine jobs are theirs on request. The height of her clumsiness came later when she joined her son Elliott in a radio program thick with commercials.

Her mistake about *Babies, Just Babies*—fortunately for her and for journalism it soon succumbed to infantile disorders—persuaded her to renounce teaching, writing about politics and use of her name in advertising while she was in the White House. That was a gain for public decorum. Within no time, much to Pegler's indignation, she was making about $54,000 a year from lecturing and writing—pre-World War II dollars, call it $125,000 now—but she could not be censured too heavily for thus exploiting her husband's position because she gave most of it away to public or private good causes. And it was completely creditable that with such meager skill in writing she could turn out printed and spoken texts exerting such wide influence. Miss Thompson's professional style had an easy swing and a lawyerlike logic. The 1930s' third principal female influence in print, Clare Boothe Luce, slipped rhetorical spitballs across the corners in a fashion worthy of her experienced past as glamor-magazine journalist and playwright. But all the writer of "My Day" had to offer her sixty-odd newspapers coast to coast was the vapid settlement house vocabulary and a rhetorical pace best described by what Arthur "Bugs" Baer said of an overbland dish new to him: "It tastes like my foot's asleep." She struck that vein in her first book, *It's Up to the Women* (1933), telling them what to do about the Depression: "Older people should be able to give to younger people a sense of values and make them realize what really matters and what does not matter in social relations, and one of the great benefits which should come to us with advancing years is the realization that after all anything we really want to do can be accomplished." [186] Six years later she told the American Youth Congress, chock-full of tough-minded Communists, "It is all very well to have a great many nice ideas but if you can't say them so any child of five can understand them, you might as well not have them." [187]

In the early 1940s her monthly page in the *Ladies' Home Journal* answered questions put by readers. It made striking pronouncements on topics not suited for the daily diary column: "All young civilizations are slow to recognize the value of their artists.... It is rare to find an Englishman who does not know the classics...." [188] Her intellectual innocence was harmless in such contexts.* But it was less so where it kept her from knowing what she was talking about in more practical concerns. Yes, she told one reader, some labor leaders are corrupt, but "Of course, if the members of a union really begin to be discontented and feel their leadership is poor ... [they] can use their ballots in the union elections.... Leaders could never remain in office unless the rank and file of the union members allowed them to remain." [189] Or when the settlement house reformer-feminist popped up: Should girls be allowed to smoke and drink in public bars with men? "If girls behave themselves and men behave themselves I see no reason why they should not go to any place which is decent. Places that are not decent should be closed and neither men nor women should go there." [190] Yet now and again one wanted to shake her hand for fumbling out something revealing the integrity that was her saving grace. What did she mean when she wrote she had never advocated "social" equality for blacks? "I meant that it is impossible to advocate social equality for anyone. Social equality is a personal relationship. You or I can associate with anyone we like, and when we do, we associate as friends and neighbors, but you cannot 'advocate' that for anybody." [191]

* The one good thing about Pegler's one-sided feud in print with Mrs. Roosevelt was his parody of "My Day" (July 13, 1942) uncannily like the real thing: "In the afternoon a group of young people came in for tea and we had a discussion of the effect of early environment on the efficiency of war workers. I am afraid environment is more important than many of us think and I have asked the Department of Agriculture to make a survey. Of course some people have more than others but then, I am afraid, very often the reverse is true and that is something that one cannot dismiss lightly these days...."

Anne O'Hare McCormick, an eminent woman staffer on the New York *Times,* attributed Mrs. Roosevelt's appeal to the America of the 1930s to the implicit presentation in "My Day" of FDR as "the many-sided father of a family ... [slipping] in and out of the diary of the accomplished White House character who manages to sublimate the typical American woman in the person of the First Lady of the Land." [192] What there is in that has little to do with the actual First Lady whose likeness to the American woman went little beyond her eagerness to advise others on how to rear children. I get more feel of reality out of a terse answer-to-question reflecting her social grain—not only part teacher, part social worker but also part quasi-royal Roosevelt: "Suppose you found yourself beside a stranger at dinner with no conversational clues to follow. How would you begin talking?" Answer: "I think I would begin by asking him what he was interested in." [193]

THE REAL THING WAS BAD ENOUGH

HISTORY A DISTILLATION OF RUMOUR. . . .
—THOMAS CARLYLE,
The French Revolution

If the Depression years were so dynamic and constructive, what was all the complaining about? Yes, Virginia, there was a miserable plenty of cause for suffering, fury, frustration and despair of the Republic. But in view of how legend has been allowed to encrust the whole period and of how spottily its effects were understood at the time—or even now, forty-odd years later—it may be advisable to look at what it wasn't and what it tried to be and couldn't before going into what it *was* like.

First the most lurid detail: those suddenly bankrupted Wall Streeters jumping out of skyscraper windows. The origin of this is hopelessly obscure, but likely enough it came of spontaneous combustion among the crowds gathered outside the New York Stock Exchange on the ever-memorable day when, against all precedent, blue-chip shares could find no bidder at any price. If large and small operators caught in that speculative fire storm were not jumping out of windows as the obviously handiest way of ending it all, they should have been; *ergo,* they were. This grisly fiction seized on the public mind and still grips it. It is the one thing that those now middle-aged and younger associate with the Great Crash. That is probably the doing of the writers of the 1930s of all calibers who always tucked it in as people always bring up the Watergate affair when mentioning former President Nixon. For instance, Carl Sandburg in *The People, Yes:* "Why when the stock crash came did the man in blacksilk pajamas let himself headfirst off a fire escape ten floors to a stone sidewalk? His sixty million dollars had shrunk to ten ... he didn't see how he could get along." [1] Or Jack Conroy, introducing *Writers in Revolt:* "... the thud of stock broker suicides jumping from 18-story windows, the reverberations of banks bursting in air, could be heard...." [2] Or Clifford Odets in *Awake and Sing:* "... still jumping off the high buildings like flies.... I saw it happen ... they shoveled him together ... brains ... all over the sidewalk...." [3] And so on—they were revengefully ghoulish about it.

Corollary legends concerned the epidemic of evictions for unpaid rent, of which there were horribly many but not as implied by Gene Smith, a usually reliable writer, in: "There was hardly a block of New York City that each day did not see at least one family numbly sitting on a couch on the sidewalk...." [4] I lived in Manhattan then under circumstances that took me into a variety of neighborhoods and testify that this is a huge exaggeration. Smith also says of the winter of 1931–32: "Only half a dozen Broadway shows were playing. Half a hundred theaters were dark...." [5] Actually the *New Yorker* directory of available shows for the weeks of January 23 and February 13, 1932, shows eighteen to twenty-one open, including such evidence of theatrical dry rot as Philip Barry's *The Animal Kingdom,* Katharine Cornell in *The Barretts of Wimpole Street,* Elmer Rice's *Counsellor-at-Law,* Ferenc Molnar's *The Good Fairy,* Noel Coward's *Hay Fever,* Sherwood's *Reunion in Vienna,* Eugene O'Neill's *Mourning Becomes Electra....* But the suicidal margin customers were the star turn. Only there was little, if any, substance to them. The curve of the American suicide rate between 1900 and 1940 can be made to show some correlation with economic vicissitudes. But the rate had actually begun to rise—that is, more suicides per capita—five years *before* the Great Crash, *upward with the Big Bull Market, rising in the teeth of the euphoric New Era* and continuing to rise during the first three years of the Depression.* Nor was the suicide rate higher in New York City, where despairing bulls should have been most plentiful. If those alleged hundreds and hundreds did jump, their remains escaped the attention of the police and the medical examiner's office.

---

* For discussion of suicides in Western cultures relative to hard times see *Suicide* (1963) by Louis I. Dublin, the Metropolitan Life Insurance Company's great statistician. He thought hope of correlating the two valid, yet saw no "simple causal relations.... Economic stringency is ... only one factor among many ... inner contributions of the individual ... [make] the difference." Anita Loos (*Kiss Hollywood Good-Bye,* 16) made a possibly pertinent contribution to this by injecting the sex angle: "... the adjustment [to the stock-market Crash] was much easier on women.... I can't recall a single headline: ... KEPT GIRL LEAPS FROM LOVE NEST."

The second major legend of the Depression is not subject to statistical check. Its substance was well stated by a North Carolina millhand interviewed by the Works Progress Administration-Federal Writers Project in mid-decade: "I believe we'd a had a rebellion back when Roosevelt come in if the government hadn't done like it did. A man jest couldn't hardly keep goin' when Hoover was in; you can't live on no dollar a day like he said to do." [6] In her highly privileged observation post Eleanor Roosevelt too remained persuaded that "at the time of the depression ... parts of this country were [very nearly] ready for revolution. If there had been a leader in the coal mining areas in the spring of 1933, a revolution could easily have been started. ..." [7] That obviously reflected not her own findings but the considered opinion of early New Dealers closer to the mines than she was at the time. New Dealers were likely to maintain that FDR and they had saved the nation from some such catastrophe; to have done so was a feather in their loyal caps, and who then or now could say that it was not true? Nor were conscientious relief administrators alone in dreading the worst at the time. One often encountered actual characters like those whom F. Scott Fitzgerald tucked into the first chapter of *The Last Tycoon,* doubtless from memory, the young actress saying that come the revolution "mother and I are ... coming out to the Yellowstone ... to live simply till it all blows over. Then we'll come back. They don't kill artists, you know;" the lawyer with a boat hidden in the Sacramento River for a quick disappearance; the director with "an old suit, shirt and shoes waiting ... he was going to Disappear into the Crowd. ..." [8]

Yet at the time first-class observers, while allowing that revolutionary outbreaks would be understandable, could also see little evidence that such things were brewing. Yes, there were at least 10,000,000 out of work in a population of 120,000,000-odd; steel mills at one-eighth capacity; whole communities reverting to barter, as between bank failures and shrinking payrolls, the cash economy broke down; sporadic farmers' milk strikes and the march of the Bonus Army showing hard-hit segments of the population how to open the ball; public confidence in its leaders lower than the government was designed to endure.... But take Frederick Lewis Allen, whose *Only Yesterday* was deservedly famous for its accurately astringent picture of the Jazz Age; now he was marveling at the patience—or was it apathy?—with which the country was taking its three years of hard, harder, hardest times. It was inexplicably evident, he thought, that Communist and other radical, violent outlets for exasperation were getting nowhere. The political conventions that had just renominated Hoover and pitted FDR against him had spent most of the assembled politicans' time disputing what to do about Prohibition instead of what to do about the Depression.

True, he said, people were bitter about moneymen. Their fall from their previous prestige was "a shift of power and place almost as significant as that which accompanied many a violent revolution." [9] This was no matter merely of losers in the stock market snarling at those who had misled them. Benton, tramping through the backwaters of American life, was finding that "the potentates ... who ran the country in the days of mounting prosperity" were the targets of "derisive jokes about 'their majesties'... from backwoods stores to ... the legislatures." [10] But even in hard-nosed New York City, the mood in late 1931, *Fortune* reported, was "friendly facetious rather than downright dejected." [11] At much the same time Morris Markey, an admirable reporter motoring coast to coast to observe the complexion and take the pulse of Depressed America, found plenty of serious strains but small sense of major mass menace.

The radical-minded tended hopefully to anticipate barricades, but few were unable to suppress the meaning of what they saw under their puzzled noses. George Soule, a radical mainstay of the *Nation,* rather scornfully observed in mid-1932 that "If you want to hear discussions of the future revolution ... do not go to the bread lines and the mill towns but to Park Avenue ... or ... young literary men. Most of those who really suffer from the depression are, according to the best informed reports, simply stricken down by it." [12] Gardner Jackson, chronically radical, if a bit of a maverick about it, testified *c.* 1931 that "despite the swift accentuation of the unemployment and financial crisis, there seems to be nothing but apathy and dull acceptance among the American workers...." [13] And Edmund Wilson candidly, if ruefully, reported a conversation with an American Communist settled in Russia at this period; he said that when he spoke at meetings and told the comrades about the Depression, they asked whether Communist propaganda was illegal in America and when he said no: "Well, why isn't there a workers' revolution?" "Maybe you think that's an easy one to answer," he said. "I thought so ... till I tried." [14] For summary of these reports from competent sources made at the time, not after some years of tendentious rationalizing, Allen saw "the average American's attitude [was] not that of a patient who implores the [Red or Fascist] doctor to try anything, but that of a patient who warns the doctor not to try any strong medicine because it might kill him." [9] And this in spite of "the cruel and unjust" fact that "adversity has fallen not only upon the callous and extravagant and greedy, but upon the prudent and generous and kindly; upon the supersalesman's victim as well as on the supersalesman...." [9]

The third legend needing scrutiny is that of the sharp contrast between do-nothing-but-talk Hoover and government-to-the-rescue FDR. This is largely residue from the 1932 presidential campaign. The actual scenario was: Sequence I: much blather in hopes the ship would right herself as a rising tide of talk-stimulated new confidence seeped under her keel. At that early stage it was still tenable to contemplate the Spartan doctrine of Secretary of the Treasury Andrew Mellon: "Liquidate labor, liquidate stocks, liquidate the farmer, liquidate real estate." [15] Thus, to let the economy go through the wringer in the belief it would come out chastenedly healthy and ready for another upward spiral had worked eventually—or something had—to exorcise the great panics of 1873 and 1893. As blather failed to pay, however, as the wringer closed too many banks in which too many voters had deposits and foreclosed on too many farmer voters, a new tune ushered in Sequence II; its refrain was "Shift the blame overseas." Elsewhere in the world, particularly in Europe, hard times were erasing what hope there had ever been for post-World War I economic health, and the consequent international repercussions, it was held, were prolonging America's ordeal. In 1931 President Hoover saw "The main cause of the extreme violence and the long continuation of this depression [coming] not from within but from outside the United States. Had our wild speculation ... loose and extravagant business methods ... been our only disasters, we would have recovered months ago." [15] Maybe there was something in it. Anyway it enabled Hoover to recommend economic self-containment as America's road to lasting recovery and future immunity to debilitating infections from Over There. And at least it was preferable to reliably fatuous Henry Ford's latest doctrine: "These are really good times but only few know it.... The average man won't really do a day's work unless he ... can't get out of it.... There's plenty of work to do if people will do it." [16]

In the same speech Hoover, who had disliked the archaic hands-off-the-wringer approach from the beginning, went on: "For the first time in history the Federal government has taken an extensive and positive part in mitigating the effects of depression and expediting recovery." [17] What he meant was hardly revolutionary, though unprecedented it was: not only expanded federal aid to farmers but federal encouragement of state-level public works. Within a year Uncle Sam, egged on by Congress, was playing Mr. Fixit directly. Federal-owned wheat and cotton acquired through measures to bolster farm prices went to the Red Cross to give to the unemployed in the shape of flour and clothes—a program momentously close to direct federal relief. Earlier in 1932 precedent was broken by the establishment of a Reconstruction Finance Corporation (RFC) lending federal millions to shaky banks and industrialists. Now it was authorized also to lend to states no longer able to finance relief. And a Federal Home Loan Bank, (FHLB) was set up to refinance mortgage-ridden small farmers and homeowners.

Little of it worked well. The theory of the RFC—that revival of credit and confidence among businessmen would crack the downward spiral, maybe nudge it up again—disintegrated in the pandemic of bank failures in early 1933. Besides, public distress had long been too acute for any more waiting to see whether what rained on the parson would drip on the clerk. Too many clerks were already dehydrated. Hindsight can now see, however, that in his last disastrous year, between Uncle Sam's turning emergency banker in the RFC and FHLB and his all-but-direct part in relief, President Hoover gingerly abandoned moneymen's classic prescription. Maybe stumblingly and grudgingly he thus set the stage for the New Deal that would make him look derisory in posterity's eyes. He had, so to speak, put the ship on the other tack. It was for FDR to crack on sail until the hair of old sailors, Hoover included, turned white.

Thus, the sidewalks of New York were not paved with bodies of self-defenestrated plungers. President Hoover was not an icy-do-nothing. The nation probably was not on the brink of revolution when FDR and the New Deal galloped up just in the nick of time. The intent here, however, is not, repeat not, to paint the Depression as anybody's Good Old Days, but to pay a little more attention than usual to the relative weights of the factors of the time. It can readily be overdone. I was strangely edified recently to read in a piece about photography in the New York *Times:* "... the disasters of the thirties were succeeded by evils so much greater, and so much more discouraging, that the thirties by contrast seem almost idyllic." [18] Exclamation point. Nevertheless, even the matter of how the millions of down-and-outers, the supersalesman's victims, who should have been far more on his conscience than they were, got nourished should be looked into for necessary corrections.

Here, too, the specific hardships of the Depression seem to have been somewhat warped by well-meaning alarmists. God knows the problem was hideously real. And the lengthening breadlines, the growing number of pitiful panhandlers who were so obviously not chronic bums, the crushing, unmanageable loads on local charitable relief agencies, the failures of underfinanced local and state relief to cope naturally led to rising clamor among those closest in touch—social workers, labor organizers, certain politicians on several levels—about a national epidemic of starvation, a famine attributable not to act of

God or the weatherman but to the shortcomings of private-enterprise economics. Hence a semantic crisis unnecessarily embittering a situation already intolerable. "Starvation," always a shocking word, was specially so in God's country even when used, consciously or unconsciously, to startle Americans into doing something effective about their guiltless countrymen's unprecedented difficulties.

President Hoover, whose Surgeon General kept telling him what was a fact, that public health statistics showed steady improvement, rejected the term. "Nobody is actually starving," [19] he said. The Metropolitan Life's Dublin, who, in that haphazard day, knew more about the nation's vital statistics than Washington bureaus could, saw "no evidence whatever that anybody in the United States is starving." [20] Such talk outraged social workers and their allies as inhuman denial of the grim privations they saw every day. They fired off rolling broadsides of cases of genuine, ghastly death from hunger and backed them with the likely point that since the malnourished are specially liable to infections and systemic breakdowns, many deaths certified as pneumonia, heart failure, the then still-common "children's diseases" and so on were primarily attributable to sheer lack of food. The first issue of *Common Sense,* young Alfred Bingham's magazine for a wide range of radical comment, carried a piece by Lillian Symes, a responsible witness, adducing a 6 percent rise in malnutrition cases in New York City's public schools and predicting disastrous things for the nation's health as such children came to warped maturity. That was for the already convinced. More important was the impact of a piece in *Fortune,* September, 1932, at the crucial point of the election campaign, a scathing survey headline: "NO ONE HAS STARVED ... which is not true ... Twenty Five Millions in Want...." [21] The business community read that.

That switch from "STARVED" to "in Want" contains the semantic trap. For Hoover, Dublin and the dictionary the basic meaning of "to starve" is "to die of hunger." In that sense they probably were right: No significantly unusual number of Americans were dying of that specific cause. Yet social workers could fall back for shock value on a secondary meaning: "to suffer severely from hunger," as in the Bright Young Thing's affected hyperbole "My dear, I'm absolutely starved!" or the opening of the English version of "The Internationale"—"Arise, ye prisoners of starvation!" Any such appeal to the dictionary as against well-meant emotion was, of course, vain. Hoover's really having said, "Nobody is actually starving," probably did him as much harm at the polls as the prosperity-is-just-around-the-corner thing that he never did say. It was exquisitely inept for an overweight man with a large private fortune who smoked costly cigars in a rent-free mansion to get pedantic about whether the absolute worst came of having to prowl garbage dumps for decaying scraps because the local relief office had run out of money; * no less so because he was the same man who had been internationally famous as volunteer creator of the admirably managed operation that fed German-occupied Belgium in World War I. The social workers' indignation was as understandable as the apprehension expressed in the *Woman's Home Companion* by Ray Lyman Wilbur, president of Stanford, not at all an hysterical do-gooder making a point: "The present depression is like a forest fire which kills many trees and sears all. In some the scars are so deep that no future growth can cover them." [22]

Not until years later, as the data got compiled and shaken down, was it clear that such justifiable fears were unnecessary, at least not as to the general population. For throughout the Depression (1930–33), when presumably hunger just this side of lethal was undermining the health of stricken millions, deaths-per-capita were slightly but steadily falling. Nor was this a legacy from better feeding pre-Crash. It did not begin until 1930, went on down until the New Deal began, then perversely rose to peak in 1936; after the New Deal's show-piece, the National Recovery Administration was abandoned, it resumed the downward trend.† Even nonwhites—mostly blacks, who presumably fared worse in hard times on the whole—showed much the same pattern. A famine in which the death rate *improved?* And those were the same years in which economic and emotional errors exacerbated by punitive policy really did carry off several million Russians by

---

* Municipal efforts to feed those in hard luck varied widely in method and effectiveness. Tulsa, Oklahoma, was proud of a (pre-New Deal, of course) program that fed those in need for six cents a day, overhead included. Its weekly ration for a child, for instance, sounds adequate if dull: Two lb. whole wheat, ½ lb. oatmeal, 4/10 lb. sugar, one lb. beans, two lb. potatoes, supplemental carrots, cabbage, onions, ½ lb. bacon, 4/10 lb. lard or equivalent, one lb. powdered milk, ¼ lb. cocoa, supplements of tomato juice, codliver oil.... Adults got 2120 calories daily including hamburger ground from whole carcasses, sausages part beef, part pork, part powdered milk.... Volunteers trained wives and mothers in preparing these supplies. When checkups showed children failing to do well with no medical reason, nonsupport proceedings were entered on. Children thus nourished began to show health better than that of the average pre-Depression population. This shining example is obviously not to be taken as typical. (Gove Hambidge, "Meals at Six Cents a Day," *Ladies' Home Journal,* October, 1932.)

† This picture is somewhat complicated by simultaneous widening of the "reporting area" for national vital statistics, but there is no reason to believe that seriously affected the general trends.

starvation while America's liberal-to-radical public looked loyally and resolutely the other way.

Some seeking to account for this anomaly in America suggest that it took a long time for the dire sequelae of hunger to show up in the death data—that is, had the Depression not intervened, the death rate would have declined still more sharply. Possible but indemonstrable. Others surmise that improvements in medical care and public health measures were more than overcoming the results of malnutrition. Plausible maybe; only one cannot point to any such deployment of drastic improvements during those years; sulfas and antibiotics, for instance, did not weigh in until the very late 1930s. Or, since during New Era prosperity many Americans probably had eaten unwisely too much, a Depression-forced reduction in gluttony had proved a salutary use of adversity? In that case, however, the death rate would not have dropped among nonwhites, already notoriously ill fed even in good times, whereas actually the decline among them was as sharp or sharper.

Gross sequelae to be expected from unusually widespread malnutrition also failed to show up among the youngest presumed victims. World War II's recruits consisted chiefly of boys who had been between the ages of six and twelve when hard times and scanty market baskets struck. Four years of growing deprivation should have at least left them with malnutrition-based disabilities. Yet they averaged slightly taller and ten pounds heavier than those drafted in World War I, and they showed an average of physical defects no higher. Or take men processed for the Korean War, a good many of them conceived or born from 1930 to 1933, the depth of the Depression. Malnutrition should have given them a particularly bad start. But only 13 percent were disqualified on physical grounds; only 2.2 percent were below Army requirements of height.

Some of the above is not necessarily cheering news after the fact. As was pointed out in 1933 by Mauritz Hallgren in the radical *Nation:* ". . . the proletarians, who suffered in silence through [the New Era] were relatively little worse off after three years [of Depression] than they had been at any time during the Golden Age." [23] "He who is down need fear no fall," sang John Bunyan's shepherd boy. By "proletarian" Hallgren meant the 22,000,000 Americans whom Paul H. Nystrom, studying consumer economics, had rated at "Bare Subsistence" or worse. Presumably that included not only his 1,000,000 "public charges" and 2,000,000 "Tramps, Work-shy, etc." but also the worst rewarded of many gainfully employed—millions of blacks everywhere; Southern sharecroppers and field hands, black or white; migrant fruit-and-vegetable harvesters; many textile workers (mostly white); coal miners drowning economically in the flood of woes that technological change imposed on their ingrown livelihood.... Add further millions from those and better-off strata dislocated by the vicious spiral of decreasing demand ... fewer jobs ... demand decreasing further.... A side effect of the Depression was to call attention to the plight of the country's worst-off strata by forcing into the same hand-to-mouth, frustrated miseries so many once better-off citizens. In analogous effect the Industrial Revolution of the early 1800s concentrated into growing industrial towns, hence made far more noticeable, the unspeakable squalor of Britain's worst-off rural population that had previously been scattered and tucked away out of most people's sight.

SELF-SENT MEN

... THE ENEMIES OF CIVILIZATION, APART FROM THE UNCOM-
PREHENDING PRIMITIVES, ARE THE SOCIALLY IRRESPONSIBLE
AND THE NEUROTIC SIMPLIFIERS.

—NORMAN F. CANTOR,
Medieval Civilization

Allen was probably right that, as the Depression deepened, the generic American grew ever warier of presumably responsible experts. Most of them, however, could not bring themselves to burn their books of divination and give up the cherished trade of economic wizardry. Instead, with an almost heroic effrontery, they went right on pontificating as if Black Thursday and Blacker Tuesday had never made them look bad. John J. Raskob, generalissimo of the Empire State Building that gave the New Era its loftiest gravestone, celebrated the New Year's Day after the Great Crash by assuring the nation that early spring would see a steady business upturn beginning. In early spring Secretary of Commerce Robert P. Lamont said that within two months business would be back to normal. In late spring Harvey S. Firestone, chief of the great rubber company, was confident that fall would set off the greatest prosperity America had ever known. And all the while things got worse and worse.

A Technocrat—see later for description of the species—writer called such men rainmakers beating tomtoms. His contempt was understandable under the circumstances. Yet their behavior was not altogether nonsense. In the past their likes really had had some success at rainmaking, for magic that everybody believes in sometimes works. Several times in the late 1920s such talk from on high in Washington or from the chief of some great bank did stimulate the economy or, psychologically the same thing, the stock market that was understood to be its prognostic index. Some put money where their words were. Sears, Roebuck & Company guaranteed its employees' brokerage accounts to prevent their being wiped out by margin calls. Henry Ford gamely dramatized his confidence by raising the nominal minimum wages in his plants from $6 to $7 a day. That soon cost so much without visibly affecting the economy that he dropped it, $15,000,000 out of pocket. It was a discouraging time, and at the end of thirty months the only eminent economist who seemed to be making much sense was F. W. Taussig of Harvard, a staunch expounder of Adam Smith's copybook maxims, who was reduced to telling the readers of *Harper's* with a most becoming candor that economists knew no more about the etiology of the crisis than physicians knew about cancer— that is, just enough to make it dismally likely that all therapies being suggested were quackery or otherwise useless, and yet one couldn't be dead sure about that because for no predictable reason one of them might work.

In those conditions it was small wonder that the intelligent impulse not to just stand there but to *do something* had everybody swinging rather wildly. There was, of course, sense in a statement made in the touch-and-go-year of 1930 by Ogden Mills, then Undersecretary of the Treasury and a prominent moneyman privately, that anticipated the doctrine with which FDR heartened the nation in 1933: "There is more to fear from frozen minds than from frozen assets." [1] Anything tending to slow down the Depression's mounting pandemic of decisions to retrench, foreclose, reduce payrolls, drop plans to rebuild or retool or expand services, was worth trying, and the more devoutly anybody bucking that trend believed in what he was doing, the likelier that he would influence other managers enough to make a therapeutic difference. But the brash, newish public relations industry took a hand with, to put it politely, mixed results. Loring Schuler, editor of the *Ladies' Home Journal,* foregathered with Edward L. Bernays, son-in-law of Sigmund Freud and most cerebral of American PR sages, in hopes of reviving the grand old days of the *Journal's* social-minded, constructive crusading. The elder targets had been patent medicines, Fourth of July fireworks, obscurantism about Sex—now economic defeatism?

"It's Up to the Women" was the motto of the magazine's consequent campaign early in 1932, which flatteringly nominated American women as the sense-making half of the nation that would get the economy back on the track. In another anticipation of FDR the kickoff editorial said, "There is nothing to fear except fear." [2] Eleanor

Roosevelt joined Elizabeth Arden, symbol of the cosmetics industry, and Mary Roberts Rinehart, redoubtable writer of wholesome mystery stories, in endorsing the new "Pocketbook Patriotism" as the follow-up editorial called it. Its kindergartenish gospel was outlined in a letter from a reader: ". . . my older little girl . . . not yet three, [watches] my face to see whether she should laugh or cry when she falls down. When I laughed and said, 'Jump up darling . . . ,' she laughed and jumped up. If women now will say 'Jump up!' to the world, I think the world will respond." [3] The method was to start spending as if nothing had happened except gratifying reductions in price. To this end Bernays organized an Economists' Committee for Women's Activities, including Professor Irving Fisher of Yale, a widely revered prophet of the New Era, glib as ever. Samuel Crowther, veteran writer for the great 5-cent weeklies on economics and politics, assiduous collaborator with Ford, Edison, Firestone *et al.,* supplied the *Journal* an avuncular piece on "Why Traitor Dollars Prolong the Depression." These were hoarded dollars, stashed away in mattresses, old stoves, teapots instead of getting out there to help the nation. The proper kind of hoarding would be goods bought with previously withheld dollars. Another of those superpertinent letters: "I'm hoarding—and proud of it. I'm hoarding . . . a between-season coat . . . shirts, shirts, shirts for Bob . . . whole cases of canned foods . . . that coffee table I've wanted. And if you don't think that's smart hoarding, go out and compare today's prices with those of a year or two ago." [4]

It was true that food prices were down 28 percent since 1929, shoes 13 percent, silk stockings 41 percent, cars only 8 percent, but new gadgets and refinements made them worth far more than 1929 models. For those of hedonistic bent the editors sounded like Thorstein Veblen under the influence of Omar Khayyám as they praised "Many women . . . [who] have discovered that the best investments are not dollar-wise, but soul-satisfying, and that it is better to live richly than too cautiously." [5] With that sermon on the text *carpe diem* went an elaborate story-cartoon spelling the whole campaign out: In one panel sourpussed Mrs. Depression goes to the bank, takes out her money and buries it in the backyard while in the background stand smokeless factory chimneys. In the larger panel Mrs. Prosperity cashes a fat check at the bank and skips patriotically from dress shop to grocery store to florist's to beauty shop (for a morale-raising permanent), while the several merchants with whom she has dealt rush to make deposits in the bank and her husband roars off in the family car to the factory which has just put up a sign: MEN WANTED.

Bernays' account of it all says: "Loring Schuler was enthusiastic." [6] As promotion it was probably worth his fee. But though many millions of women read the *Journal,* there was little discernible effect on the economy. Prices slid on downward, but also more husbands were laid off or having to take pay cuts that made spending seem, to say the least of it, inadvisable for too many. The vicious circle remained the order of the day.

In those days symbols were even less reliable than usual. The heavenward climb of Raskob's and Al Smith's Empire State Building continuing stubbornly after the Great Crash should have betokened that the New Era refused to let financial famine stunt it. Seen from across the Jersey meadows or up from the sidewalk, it looked triumphantly consummated. But actually and notoriously at the time a fourth of its 102 stories above the jangly Art Deco lobby were empty, bankruptcy-smelling sham. The elevators never stopped between the forty-second and sixty-seventh floors because no part of them was rented. Indeed, hopes of rental income were so slim that much of the thing was left unfinished in the girder and flaking plaster stage. As a whole it was half unoccupied.

A mile farther uptown an even more presumptuous fiasco-to-be was hurrying toward frustration in the shape of two huge sister theaters meant to ornament the complex of interlocking office buildings that flaunted the names Rockefeller Center/Radio City. The Rockefellers were pushing these icily regular, splendidly null skyscrapers onward and upward regardless of head shaking about good money after bad in considerable part as a make-work-when-people-needed-work project. The office buildings eventually paid off. The family did not even shrink from abandoning its long, loyal support of the Dry cause by, in effect, going into the saloon business with the Rainbow Room on top of the whole complex. One of Pegler's best early columns was written after he attended the opening of what he called "Jack's Place" to advise John D., Jr., that success in running a gin mill required the owner to be there every night to keep the customers in line and prevent the help from robbing him blind. But the $15,000,000—say, $50,000,000 plus now—that went specifically into the Radio City Music Hall and the RKO-Roxy (movie-and-stage-show) Theater eventuated almost instantly in fulminating cases of fallen proscenium arch.

Both opened in the second week of the dreadful winter of 1932–33 that ended with all the nation's banks closed. What the Rockefellers meant to accomplish with these show shops was made disastrously clear at the opening of the RKO-Roxy in the speech of Will H. Hays, Republican politician and limber-souled front man for Hollywood: "... this is not the dedication of a theatre—it is a reaffirmation of faith in America's indomitableness and fearlessness.... [It] rises like a

Pharos out of the blinding fogs of irresolution and bewilderment to proclaim that leadership has not failed us ... the bravest declaration of faith in their country's stability that the Rockefellers, father and son, America's most useful citizens—have yet offered.... Let us rise and salute them and all their works." [7] It took some special quality, maybe courage, to tell an American audience that bleak December that leadership had not failed it.

At the just-as-splashy opening of the Music Hall three days earlier the house included Al Smith, President Nicholas Murray Butler of Columbia University, Gene Tunney, Amelia Earhart, Walter P. Chrysler, Leopold Stokowski *et al. ad infinitum* admiring its determinedly Art Deco interior, which the cultivated today seek to have preserved as archaeologically significant, as no doubt it is. The guiding spirit of the whole was S. L. "Roxy" Rothafel, who for twenty years had midwifed and bedizened a whole dynasty of growingly super-colossal movie palaces in New York City—Strand, Rialto, Rivoli, Capitol, the "old" Roxy, the nose of which the new RKO-Roxy was meant to put out of joint. As its name implied, the Music Hall was meant to be the world's most celebrated showcase for vaudeville. It seated 6,200 customers in an auditorium so large that those in the front seats could not see the whole stage at once, and to those in the most remote balcony seats the performers looked like Cracker Jack prizes. It had thirty-one "rest and powder rooms" and dressing rooms for 600 performers, which in view of Roxy's Romanly megalomanic production ideas, were none too many. The opening show included not only tremendous production numbers of the sort that made him famous but a ballet of eighty; the Tuskegee choir doing spirituals; for a highbrow touch the symbolic dancer Harold Kreutzberg in a portentous number called "The Angel of Fate"; two high-ranking opera singers; for nostalgic liaison with the elder vaudeville the ineffable comedy team of (Joe) Weber & (Lew) Fields; for current vaudeville the remarkable one-man medical school taught over the footlights by the impudently great Doc Rockwell ... such riches that the last curtain did not fall until 12:30 A.M.

Only this time Roxy's hunger after piling one thing on top of another—not a bad parallel for pre-Crash America—betrayed him. Not the plethora of the opening bill—that could be trimmed—but the Brobdingnagian scale of the house inevitably made human performances Lilliputian. The audience could hear rather too well, for the microphones were well placed and the new sound system was efficient, but the sense of personal response between audience and performer, essential in vaudeville, was unattainable. "... simply too big ... too long and too wide," said one critic, who suggested "building a smaller theater inside it and tearing down the outside." [8] Within days it was clear that, as e. e. cummings jeered, "A Roxy is a fabulously birdy.... Roxies lay eggs ... not ordinary eggs...." [9] After two weeks the two-a-day-vaudeville policy gave way to Roxy's old formula of first-run movies with stage shows dominated by mass dancing and singing and huge orchestras—the formula that persists today along with the ill-fitting "Music Hall" name. The change pulled the rug from under the RKO-Roxy a block away. In a Manhattan where movie theaters were already in straits because public spending was dwindling, the increment of 10,000 new cash-demanding seats in the Broadway area (Music Hall 6,200; RKO-Roxy 3,700) was unthinkable. The least understandable thing about the whole strange project, so flashily un-Rockefeller, was that it was the shipshape RKO-Roxy, not the overblown Music Hall, that was thrown to the Depression wolves.

Some wild swings pay off, of course. Eight hundred miles west of Radiofeller Center Chicago face-lifted the stated purpose of a huge pre-Crash project, made a fair wind of a foul one and sailed it into the first FDR year as cheerily as though it had always been planned as harbinger of the New Deal. It was born as one of W. W. Business-man's most sanguine New Era dreams. Indeed—back to *hybris*—omen readers of 1930 would have had cause to say Chicago should have known better. Forty years previously, within the memory of those fathering this Century of Progress scheme, Chicago's other world's fair—the memorable Columbian Exposition—had coincided with the grim panic of 1893 that Justin Kaplan recently described as having "the same formative meaning for [the muckraking] generation that [the Depression] had for the generation coming to social awareness in the 1930s.... [It] dramatized corporate irresponsibility, the appalling gap between the rich and the poor, the failure of government to regulate an economy run wild." [10]

In 1927, when the phrase "New Era" was young and seductive, Rufus C. Dawes, electric utility magnate, responsible civic leader, collaborator with his brother, Charles G. Dawes (Coolidge's Vice President) on the Dawes Plan that was supposed to solve the insoluble problem of German reparations, became aware that six more years would bring the centennial of Chicago's incorporation as a village on the bank of a sluggish, swamp-fed little river. He and some well-placed friends began to muster influence and money to celebrate that. On July 9, 1929, just when the Great Bull Market was beginning its summer surge to nowhere, they announced that the title theme would be "A Century of Progress." Scheme and name show how they shared the faith that things were in such good shape that they would go on getting better and better forever, amen. Dawes played the early tricks well. The architects, corporations and cultural groups approached were mostly the right ones. He secured official countenance from Mayor William H. "Big Bill" Thompson but kept the scheme under the largely autonomous Parks Department, so City Hall could not get sticky hands on it. "There are no grafters in this show," Milton Mayer reported in wonder. "... politicians, racketeers and sly old boys are on the outside, dolefully watching the pickings go untouched." [11] In 1929, too, it heightened the public impression of able integrity behind the scheme that Insull managed the campaign by selling Chicagoans $5 books of admission tickets in advance. By 1933, when the show opened, Insull's name was mud. But meanwhile, the money was there, and the tickets were honored.

The goose hung high that year. If Chicago had only first incorporated in 1829.... But 1933 was four years too many. By 1931 the side effects of hard times forced drastic changes. The first round of plans had called for a vast explosion of Art Deco—"Sunday supplement Chrysler Building architecture," [12] as a participant now recalls it. That blurred as the Depression eroded corporate and public resources. Dawes' group's financial pledges stayed solid enough to get some sort of show built and opened. But after that—contrary to older traditions of continuing subsidy for world's fairs—it had to float itself on admissions and revenue from concessions and exhibits. And in order to get the coat cut of far less costly cloth with fewer major furbelows, new tailors were called in to design a new kind of world's fair. Chief among them were young Louis Skidmore and young Nathaniel Owings, both born and reared in next-door Indiana, though with European and Eastern experience, nucleus of the still-towering firm of Skidmore, Owings & Merrill, and Joseph Urban, an Austrian well established in America as a stage designer combining taste with opulence splashy enough to mount Florenz Ziegfeld's *Follies*. Further recognizing the facts of Depression-mindedness, the project, though keeping A Century of Progress (ACOP) on the letterhead, struck up a new song making a public relations virtue of the ominous memories of 1893. For Chicago was shaking its head at the strange sight of work bustling forward on the new-made land on the lakefront while the economic indices kept sinking and the breadlines kept lengthening.

"Hard times?" said a probably PR-inspired piece in *Collier's* magazine in mid-1932. "What are these men thinking of, planning a World's Fair just now? Well, in the first place, they aren't expecting hard times in 1933 ... in the second place, looking backward ... times ... in 1893 ... were just as hard.... Homeless men were sleeping in the corridors of the Chicago City Hall ... thousands of families [were] fed by charity ... but the [1893] fair opened ... and 22,000,000 persons paid to see it. And good times came again." [13] Magic, magic. Having possibly brought on the Depression by planning a world's fair, Chicago would now atone by dancing widdershins around the economy with nods, becks and wreathed smiles and reassuring exhibits demonstrating the glories of the immediate future. That cluster of queer-looking edifices on the lakefront was to be a crucially heartening, three-dimensional equivalent of the "Happy Days Are Here Again" that was FDR's campaign song that summer. And by the time the show opened in late spring, 1933, it looked as if the magic were working. The sense of relief at getting rid of Hoover, heightened by the flashy first Hundred Days of FDR, had many Americans' psyches propitiously off dead center for the first time in some years.

Some of ACOP's large buildings retained much Art Deco—for instance, the Travel & Transportation Building (designed by E. H. Bennett, Hubert Burnham and John Holabird) with a spiky sunburst glorifying the façade and a circumvallation of gigantic prisms—but the great interest lay in its roof slung from exposed tripods of structural steel by catenary cables. Thrift obliged the replacement crew of architects to eschew the expensive but essential shady tricks customarily used to make a world's fair look permanent. They made a striking virtue of necessity with huge windowless expanses of rockbottom-cheap wallboard painted like Joseph's coat. Only 20 percent of these wall surfaces were of the expected white. The rest showed skillfully varied combinations of the twenty-four different colors that Urban splashed around with a boldness that the International Style would never have tried and that made the much admired pastel palette that San Francisco had used in 1915 look maiden-ladylike.

By no means everybody liked it. Milton Mayer called the buildings "windowless and hollow and inarticulate. Some are angular and stark, some are sylphlike and flossy, and some are sloppy and elephantine ... painted like a new saloon.... After four or five raucous pinks and greens have been thrown at the uncomplaining walls ... conflicting hues ... are applied in the form of demure stripes about three feet wide." [11] But the prevailing reaction was about that of E. M. Delafield, a lightly shrewd British writer: "Buildings all ... modern and austere ... coloring ... inclined to be violent but, as a whole ... effective and impressive and much to be preferred to customary imitation of ancient Greece." [14] Lack of windows prompted resort to the new air conditioning previously confined largely to theaters and, rather recently, railroad trains. Though ACOP could fairly be described as, to quote a recent critic, "a triumph of paper [= utterly temporary] architecture," [15] it nevertheless left a deeper mark on American notions of building than any American fair since 1893. The consequences of our running air conditioning into the ground are, we now see, pernicious, meaning those windowless cubes completely dependent on artificial ventilation. But forty years ago the designers of ACOP had reason to think the uses of financial adversity sweet and themselves creatively ingenious. Looking back, Owings says that ACOP was "the first almost non-architecture for people ... the big show was the people with architecture for background," for in his view Urban was "the best of all things for the fair.... [He] added a great new vocabulary for us all who followed him." 12

Another future was there in exhibits of mechanized cotton pickers that would soon complete the dislocation of Southern blacks that boll weevils and World War I had begun. Repeal of Prohibition was presaged in the 3.2 percent beer, newly made legal by simple amendment of the Volstead Act—one of the New Deal's first measures—flowing from the exhibits of Pabst, Schlitz *et al.* on such short notice that it was obvious somebody had been making a lot of beer right along. The same summer heat that sold so much beer on the grounds also caused visitors to marvel at the Black Forest Village's open-air ice-skating rink and peeled weight off the college boys who had summer jobs trotting between the shafts of jinrikishas provided for individual hire. The most popular free entertainments seem to have been the Great Atlantic & Pacific's concerts of gypsy dancing, Tony Sarg marionettes and the jolly gourmet patter of George Rector, son of the founder of Broadway's once-glittering lobster palace, and the Sinclair Refining Company's life-size dinosaurs wriggling, snorting and bellowing to dramatize the venerable age of fossil fuels. The Skyride, a half-mile swing over the grounds in pseudostreamlined cable gondolas shuttling between 600-foot towers, one of ACOP's own enterprises, took in more money than most of the concessions on the Midway—a name for the amusement area recalling the great 1893 fair.

ACOP also had hog-calling contests and draft-horse-pulling contests from the county fair idiom; and George Washington's false teeth; and at the Indiana State exhibit Benton's murals showing a grateful public that historical subjects need not consist of either allegorical vapidity or tooth-gritting anticapitalism. Art was further served by a rich exhibit of European and American painting and a mock-up in fireworks—that's what I said—of Jean François Millet's "Song of the Lark," from the Chicago Art Institute, billed as "America's Best Loved Painting." The Midway had the assembled freaks, live and otherwise, of Robert Ripley's Odditorium and a miniature village busily peopled by 60, count 'em 60, midgets. But the core of the Midway was what *Billboard,* newspaper of the circus, carnival and Tin Pan Alley segments of show business, called "nude shows to satiation ... never in the history of expositions has there been such a deluge of vulgarity," [16] observing that whereas in 1893 it had been the fair that made the Midway, now it was the other way around.

Small, neatly shaped Sally Rand is inextricably entwined with this aspect of ACOP. She came out of vaudeville; her ballet company of nine had once played the Palace on Broadway, peak of such careers. But vaudeville was dwindling, and she was taking bookings in minor Chicago nightclubs when, in 1932, she was hired to do Lady Godiva wearing only a long wig at a Beaux Artsy ball for the benefit of ACOP. In rehearsal she explained that riding a horse was new to her; she was primarily a fan dancer. She demonstrated on a skyscraper roof. Chicago's notorious wind blew her fans about so provocatively that she was recruited to do her act next year at the fairgrounds—it was promisingly breezy down there by the lake. With a sound view to publicity she eschewed the G-string and net brassiere that civic outcry demanded. There were headline-making arrests and scenes in court when still with no costume but what she put on with a powder puff, she performed in a Loop movie house between stints at ACOP. In a few weeks her name was as well known as that of Admiral Richard Evelyn Byrd, the handsome explorer of the Antarctic whose ship was one of the exhibits. Little girls skipping rope in New York City were singing:

> Sally Rand has lost her fan.
> Give it back, you nasty man! . . .

Heavy wear and tear on ACOP turnstiles ensued.* And as things gradually shaped up along lines laid down by a local judge who, hearing a case involving indecent exposure at the fair, told his court, "Some people would want to put pants on a horse," [17] fan dancers and naked posing overran the Midway. Lloyd Lewis, drama critic of the Chicago *Daily News,* hailed it as "The Rout of the Puritans." [17]

Miss Cati Mount posed as Manet's "Olympia" with a hand carelessly disposed to hide the pudendum. One judge ordered her to put rose petal pasties on her nipples; another, in a trial that made her runner-up to Miss Rand, ruled she could leave them off. The ACOP staff explained that the nakedness didn't trouble them so much as the barker's spiel: "Ladeez and gentlemen! You will see inside a reproduction of the world's most notorious and infamous painting—Olympia!

---

* Miss Rand's own account of her rise to fame at ACOP is already familiar to millions in Studs Terkels' *Hard Times.*

There she lies undraped and unashamed, so close to your eyes that it's uncomfortable. It's a $50,000 education that will take ten years off your life, give you fifty new ideas, clean and press your suit, curl the brim of your hat...." [17] Voyeurism so engulfed the Midway—"Salome and the Virgins in Cellophane," "The Greenwich Village Art Shop," a device that rolled a naked girl out of bed when a customer hit a target with a baseball and so on—that even staid concessions had to enter the lists. In ACOP's successful second year the replica of Shakespeare's Globe Theater offered a peep show on naked doings in "The Notorious Limehouse District."

Miss Rand's momentum carried her on into her "Dnude Ranch" the biggest grosser on the midway at San Francisco's Treasure Island exposition in 1939. When I last visited the Chicago Historical Society, the featured display was her fans twirling and flailing away inside a glass case—no Sally inside, though, just a soulless machine with an electric motor. As late as 1975 the real Sally, at the age of seventy-one, was doing her old stuff in Seattle for $1,500 a week and asking the press, "What in heaven's name is strange about a grandmother dancing nude? I bet lots of grandmothers do it." [18] And in this day of anything-goes-in-naked-peepshows, she is probably right.

A wild swing itself, ACOP sponsored certain others, some technological; false dawns in air transport, for instance. At the time, of course, exhibits such as Boeing's were all agog about heavier-than-air work, bragging up its new single-engine transports taking ten passengers in luxurious reclining seats, cruising at 180 mph, New York to Chicago in five hours, coast to coast in twenty! Fare-paying, long-distance travel was still, however, dominated by the express liner and the sleek, air-conditioned railroad cars on display on the other side of the Transportation Building. Nor, supposing the air had a future, was the hegemony of heavier-than-air yet established. Thus, the architects of the Empire State Building provided it with a mooring mast for the rigid dirigible balloons of the day; nobody but King Kong—and after World War II, the TV industry—ever made any use of it, but its existence is significant of once-bright hopes. Among distinguished visitors that ACOP and the nation took very seriously was the *Graf Zeppelin* of the famous German family of dirigibles. Disasters to the dirigible in which Umberto Nobile explored the North Polar regions and to the US Navy's great dirigibles had already cast grisly doubts on the practicality of even the most impressive lighter-than-air craft. But the (nonrigid) Goodyear blimps taking sightseers over ACOP were reassuring sights, and while ACOP was still going on, the *Hindenburg,* imposing successor of the *Graf* in Germany's bid for commercial use of the air, set up a strikingly regular transatlantic schedule.

A woman editor of the *Ladies' Home Journal* went abroad in the *Hindenburg* in 1936 and pointed out its record of 128 on-time crossings. She celebrated the coziness of its tiny individual staterooms with hot and cold running water, its glass-enclosed, "spacious, even luxurious" [19] dining room and lounge, wherein two child passengers played several thousand feet above the ocean as unconcernedly as if on a lawn at home. Back and forth the *Hindenburg* shuttled as reliably as a Cunarder. Then the pitcher went to the well once too often. While coming to a mooring at her customary berth, the US Navy base at Lakehurst, New Jersey, she caught fire and disintegrated. That celebrated catastrophe was reported live on radio by a gaspingly horrified newsman who had expected only the usual handshaking, interview-seeking routine. It also made ghastly pictures for the newsreels and newspapers. After all that catastrophic publicity lighter-than-air was dead except for very special uses—sightseeing, advertising and submarine hunting in World War II. The daunting effect of those shots of the *Hindenburg* burning like crumpled newspaper was heightened by other considerations: Dirigibles were unlikely ever to exceed speeds around 100 mph, which transport planes were already doubling. Noninflammable helium gas, of which America had the world's only substantial supply, took care of the fire hazard, but as the US Navy's troubles showed, a tough thunderstorm could twist dirigibles apart like breaking a loaf of French bread. Even today some imaginative engineers hope somehow to keep lighter-than-air alive. To them buoyancy still seems a sounder principle than artificial creation of the air resistance producing the aerodynamic effect on which airplanes soar.* That is a good commonsense judgment. Only beyond a certain point common sense does not always apply in aviation.

Thus, it was also common sense that an airplane intended to fly over water should have a fuselage boatlike enough to land safely on water when necessary. Such a "flying boat" was first made practical by Glenn H. Curtiss, who would have been the father of early American flying had Wilbur and Orville Wright not gone to such momentous pains a few years earlier. In 1919 it was the NC-4, a US Navy-Curtiss flying boat, one of three taking off for the trip, that first crossed the Atlantic by air, struggling from Long Island to England by way of the Azores and Spain as stepping-stones. Better flying boats enabled the infant Pan American Airways to schedule service between Miami and

* For instance, see "Airships Deserve a Second Look," *Newsweek,* June 2, 1975.

Havana in 1931. And for ACOP's large contribution, Mussolini almost stole the show from Sally Rand in midsummer, 1933, when his General Italo Balbo set down on Lake Michigan twenty-four military flying boats fresh from Italy by way of the Netherlands and Ireland— 6,100 miles, six refueling stops. In 1935 Pan Am's further improved flying boats brought Hawaii within hours, no longer days, of the mainland. In World War II the slow, ugly PBYs were indispensable for rescues and reconnaissance. But as VJ-Day neared, the flying boat principle was already heavily undermined by the gathering speed, widening cruising range and improved reliability of the great four-engine, land-based bombers. Streamlining, however subtle, could not reduce the air drag of the flying boat's hull to the extent that would let it compete with the hypertrophying passenger transports developed from military prototypes. Like the dirigibles, the flying boat died except for minor special uses such as taking fat-cat sportsmen to isolated wilderness lakes.

Balbo's showy transatlantic foray was less politeness to ACOP than celebration of the tenth anniversary of Mussolini's gaining power in Italy 4,000-odd miles away. Like most of *Il Duce*'s flashy pre-World War II spectacles, the gesture was well staged. Only one out of twenty-five flying boats in the squadron came to grief on the way. Late on a July afternoon the surviving twenty-four swooped past the fairgrounds in a tight formation of threes and settled on the blue lake waters like so many migrating waterfowl. After a formal reception on the US Navy pier the crowd at the fair cheered as Balbo was driven up its Avenue of Flags. A major Chicago street leading to the lakefront is still named Balbo Drive. And a flight of US military planes spelled out "ITALIA."

The advance work had been excellent. The *World's Fair Weekly,* official drum beater, had been heralding the flight for months, eloquent about the significance of Italy's huge exhibit building shaped like an airplane and dominated outside by a tower shaped like the Roman fasces, symbol of the Blackshirt Revolution, inside by a hulking, scowling, mump-jowled portrait head of *Il Duce.* It was pointed out that whereas in 1893 Italy's exhibit had relied on lovely works of art, in 1933 it emphasized "a new Italy, the fascist Italy of scientific discovery, engineering, aeronautics, and social and governmental reconstruction [that] ... energetically drained the Pontine marshes ... [taught] farmers the use of tractors, fertilizers. ..." [20] And so on and on in a tone that, queer as it now sounds, then met considerable acceptance—three years before *Il Duce* sent his legions to imitate conquering heroes in Ethiopia, ten before he was publicly hung by the heels like a dead hog awaiting dismemberment in a Chicago packing plant. This tolerance, not to say admiration of the man and his works, was part of the tendency of many Americans—no majority but a weighty minority—to palter with Fascism or some cognate as a possible answer to their perplexities—a wild swing indeed.

The only jarring note during Balbo's triumph in Chicago was leaflets distributed at the fair by the tiny anti-Fascist minority among the city's huge Italian colony—most of whom were out there leading the cheering. At the official dinner in his honor the official toastmaster reading out the cordial messages from the Pope and FDR was Richard Washburn Child, an old acquaintance of Balbo's, who had been President Coolidge's ambassador to Italy and seen the Fascists' takeover at first hand. It so delighted him that, already an author-journalist of standing, he appointed himself Mussolini's volunteer press agent in America and ghost-midwife of the great man's autobiography (1927). Tirelessly, winningly, Child's speeches and articles explained the gallant motives and statesmanlike realism of *Il Duce*'s destiny-fraught policies. On the other side of the coin the same sort of emotional-political crush made tub thumpers for the USSR out of John Reed, Anna Louise Strong, Jerome Davis, Maurice Hindus, George S. Counts. . . .

Kenneth Roberts, then spot-reporting wheelhorse of the *Saturday Evening Post,* later a best-selling historical novelist *(Rabble in Arms, Oliver Wiswell),* was one of those supplying appealing corroborative detail on just how *Fascismo* had made the trains run on time, run on time, run on time. . . . When he promised that *Il Duce* would restore the Italian railroads to private ownership whenever he found anybody trustworthy to take over, Roberts evinced his devout belief, to which W. W. Businessmen lent a ready ear, that, as Mussolini said not long before the March on Rome: "If the Fascisti party governs . . . [the] State will only attend to purely State functions . . . justice, the army, public security, and foreign policy." [21] That was well before the most exophthalmic statesman in history created the Corporate State to coordinate "Everything within the State. Nothing without the State." [22]

That trains-on-time motif owed some of its immense success in America to a latent (sometimes woundingly overt) xenophobia. Any man who could whip those millions of dagos into responsible effi-ciency, make them pull up their socks, stop screaming and milling about and knifing each other and get down to business must be a man to tie to. Even while trying to score points for Fascismo in 1934, *Fortune* defined its basic purpose as "to unwop the wops." [22] Roberts' respect for it, as John P. Diggins notes in his recent *Mussolini and Fascism,* obviously "implied a low regard for the Italians themselves." [23] And George Santayana's good opinion of what *Il Duce* had wrought was rooted in the great philosopher's "utter scorn of Italians." [24]

The $100,000,000 that the Morgan bank lent Mussolini's new regime may help explain why Thomas W. Lamont, high among the Morgan partners, took up his cause in America. It is more notable that something, maybe the sheer gravitational pull of candid power, also converted Lincoln Steffens, goateed Socrates-Pied Piper of radical America, quondam quarterback of the muckrackers of the early 1900s. Having known Mussolini as a Socialist fellow journalist, Steffens kept up the acquaintance and in 1923 had told readers of the liberally inclined *Century* magazine, apropos of the March on Rome, that "the first and perhaps the best form of government [is] a dictatorship founded on the organized minority." [25] Another of his dicta: "A strong man, however bad, is better than a weak man, however good." [26] Even after Steffens was high on the Communist bandwagon—the apparently rising Red tide that was *Fascismo*'s chief pretext for being—even after Mussolini's struttings in the newsreels had grown almost as absurd as the known methods of his Blackshirt bully boys were foul, Steffens' autobiography (1931) was blasphemously admiring: *Il Duce* was "a romantic figure ... thunder on the right ... as if the Author of all things ... seeing the physical, mental, moral confusion here ... said, 'I will have a political thunderstorm ... that will strike down their foolish old principles, burn up their dead ideas and separate the new light I am creating from the darkness men have made. And so he formed Mussolini out of a rib of Italy." [27] After that none should be surprised to learn from Diggins' soundly researched book that Henry Morgenthau, FDR's liberal Secretary of the Treasury, thought *Fascismo* a promising "receivership" under which Italy would recover republican health; that Charles A. Beard, liberal dean of America's economics-minded historians, candidly admired it for its polity-wide planning and disregard of class lines; that as late as 1938, Philip F. La Follette, governor of Wisconsin, political heir of the momentous Progressivism of an earlier time, kept hung on his wall an autographed photograph of Mussolini as companion piece to one of the great liberal Justice Louis D. Brandeis of the US Supreme Court.

All that is good explanation for Chicago's and the nation's cordiality toward Balbo's *Fascismo*-glorifying stunt. It meant that America had been given too few and too weak antidotes for a widespread attitude toward *Il Duce* that, though not usually as warped as Steffens' and Child's pleasure in cleaning up after the man-on-horseback's horse, had an ambivalent yearning about it—a half-condescending envy of what lesser breeds without the law could do about economic dislocation and Red efforts to exploit it. Soon after *Fascismo* gained power, for instance, *St. Nicholas,* magazine for the most genteel young people, its current events section eager to inculcate what proper parents wished their children to think, endorsed the Blackshirts' boast that they had indeed saved Italy from anarchy and chaos caused by Communist subversion. Their methods "do not appeal to us as practical in this country, but [they] fit the chivalrous Italian character.... We cannot see anything wicked in [their motto] 'Concord, Discipline, Work.' The Italians are solving their problems in their own way ... a good, safe and profitable way for Italy." [28] With that ran an appealing photograph of Mussolini's three children looking almost like one's schoolmates.

Soon E. S. Martin, cultivated and fairly levelheaded editorialist of *Life,* then the nation's chief cartoon-and-comment weekly, approvingly likened a free-swinging crackdown on the Ku Klux Klan in Oklahoma to Mussolini's example and later called him "a very instructive person" [29] for his willingness to use compulsion where persuasion failed. Such use of the supralegal fist would never do with us but wouldn't it be nice to have such tools handy when dealing with Kluxers ... and Wobblies ... and gangsters? *Fascismo*'s campaigns against the Mafia and sister barbarisms in Sicily and the Mezzogiorno might alone have earned him cordial opinions in America. This might be merely *Fascismo*'s jealous reluctance to let any disparate organization rival it anywhere within Italy. But it sounded good to American newspaper readers who knew where Al Capone, Johnny Torio, Frankie Yale *et al.* came from. Reporting on law enforcement in America, President Hoover's Wickersham Commission quoted approvingly the Chicago *Tribune*'s relish for the way the *Fascisti* harassed Italy's gangsters, even though one result was that many of them were seeking refuge in America.

Hence probably the lack of dismay when *Claire Ambler* (1928), latest novel from Booth Tarkington, whose works usually neglected politics, cast as appealing martyr an idealistic, patrician Fascist foully done in for organizing for *Il Duce* against the Mafia in Sicily. He tells the American heroine, who knows little of Italy and thinks politics nothing to fret about, "I am one of the men who believe Italy is being saved by a great leader and his great ideal; and any of us is ready to make sacrifice to help bring all the people to serve this ideal." [30] Not even Dorothy Parker, so soon to be a broodily active quasi-Communist and Fascistophobe, showed any uneasiness when reviewing this. For more exalted traces of the same quirk influencing that long-ago period, snarling affinities with *Fascismo* infested the minds and verses of Ezra Pound and Robinson Jeffers. It was unprofessionally stupid but not altogether fantastic of Roberts to write: "The indications in America ... justify shirt factories in installing enlarged and improved machines for the manufacture of black shirts." [31]

The Balbo sort of gesture was meant generally to impress Americans, specifically American moneymen, with Italy's new stability, anti-Red militancy, military strength and technological prowess—necessarily interdependent—in order to maintain the flow of credit that *Fascismo* needed for armament and auxiliary industry. That was more or less in the open, taken for granted, like the preliminary banter between boy and girl in a parked car that may or may not turn into substantial doings. What was not thus in the open and taken for granted was the continuous effort to make *Fascismo* a power in the Italian enclaves of American cities. They contained 4,000,000-odd Italian-born, many of whom had done nothing about acquiring citizenship, all of whom *Il Duce* considered Italian nationals on the same basis as if still in Taranto or Palermo. Assuming that another great war was inevitable, *Fascismo* wished to be able to repatriate many of these overseas Italians for soldiering, to command the economic and political leverage of the rest in America's affairs, to keep them sending the really important sums that they remitted yearly to their folks in the old country.

Some of that resembled the aims of the National German-American Alliance between 1910 and 1917 and the parallels clumsily attempted by the German-American Bund in the mid-1930s. *Il Duce*'s followers managed to keep a lower profile than German tactlessness worked up. But some of it was cryptoaggressive. *Fascismo* was bold within the invisible boundaries of Little Italys, trying to set up an underground Fascist government with its own schools and courts and even extralegal taxes. Each member of the Fascist League of North America (FLNA), wearing the black shirt and tasseled cap of Italian prototypes, paid $1 a month and took an oath mingling Italian chauvinism with watery pledges of loyalty to America. Such "Fascios" made up the Blackshirt guard of honor at the lying-in-state of Rudolph Valentino in 1926. In older times the Sons of Italy, counterparts of Irishmen's Ancient Order of Hibernians, had promoted citizenship and Americanization among its 300,000 members. As *Fascismo* took the helm, all that came to a halt. Only two of the nation's dozens of Italian-language newspapers resisted. Italian businessmen failing to advertise in *Fascismo*'s new publications, *Giovenezza* (= Youth, the Fascist slogan, title of its marching song) and *Il Grido del Stirpo* (= The Cry of the Race), were unlikely to secure stocks from their usual Italian-American suppliers or credit from Italian-American banks. A member of the FLNA who got the message so poorly that he took out first citizenship papers was expelled and reminded that he still had relatives back in Italy, and suppose he lost his job in that firm importing olive oil and Parmesan cheese?

Copies of *Il Duce*'s organizations for children, the Balilla and the Avanguardista, herded Italian-American small fry (mostly born American citizens, of course, but not in *Fascismo*'s view) into classes in Italian in rooms borrowed in public as well as parochial schools. In 1929 the Italian ambassador came from Washington, D.C., to smile upon 160 Balilla, drilled to within an inch of their lives and wearing uniforms blending Blackshirtery with Boy Scoutery, sailing for a summer of indoctrination in camp in Italy. But such capers within range of news cameras were tactfully rare outside Italian enclaves, and America's Red press, the logical source of expository protest, paid strangely little attention. No alarm was effectively raised until late 1929—by Marcus Duffield, a surgically able newspaperman, in a piece in *Harper's* spelling out the purposes and practices of the FLNA and its allied Italian embassy and consulates.

For a short while it looked as if the fat were properly in the fire. Loud protests came from Senators William E. Borah and J. Thomas "Tomtom" Heflin and Representative Hamilton Fish, Jr.* The FLNA hastily disbanded. But, as Diggins says, its demise did not "seriously hinder"[32] *Fascismo*'s continuing nibbling at Little Italy. The Sons of Italy had a revolutionary schism that merely purged it of elements lukewarm about *Fascismo,* so it was a better organ of Blackshirt propaganda than ever. And the Dante Alighieri Society, a grave institution meant to impress America with the superlative virtues of Italian culture, was warped into becoming a deliberate source of infection in Academe and the highbrow press.

For a while it looked promising no doubt. In mid-1934 *Fortune,* sounding much like *St. Nicholas* eleven years earlier, had respectfully given a whole issue to *Il Duce*'s new Italy, builder of the longest double-track railroad tunnel in the world, the fastest liners on the Atlantic, the new manifestation of "ancient virtues ... Discipline, Duty, Courage, Glory, Sacrifice ... no man who really loves liberty could ever endure the Fascist state.... But the Italians do like it...."[33] Apparently *Fascismo* had succeeded in taking the high road for the general American public as restorer of order and hard work among a frivolous, friably chaos-addicted people—and for the Italian-

---

* In liberal terms the leaders of reaction to the Duffield piece should have been outstanding liberals. That label does not fit even Borah well, and by the 1920s both Heflin and Fish were grotesque reactionaries each in his own fashion. All three illustrate the inadvisability of trying to impose imported left/right terms on American politics.

American enclaves the low road as restorer of discipline and Italy's previously nonexistent international prestige. There were minor unfavorable indications, true. With the Depression Italian-Americans had less spare cash to support their ethno-chauvinist cause. Italian refugee intellectuals who fled to America inveighed against the reactionary, sadistically organized repression that forced them into exile. Some Americans hearkened with shivers up their spines, and doubtless numerous others came gradually to wonder what Mussolini's ostentatious rearming had to do with putting Italy back together intramurally. But the decade was half over before the bulk of WASPs inclined to concentrate on trains running on time began to glimpse what the score really was. Mussolini did that for them himself. In 1935 he blew the gaff by invading Ethiopia.

Obviously *Fascismo* hoped that America would sprout a sister movement handily sympathetic like the Nazism infesting Germany. This was apparently the less likely because most Americans felt that any radical therapy required by Italy's special needs was probably impertinent to societies with other complaints. Yet there was a possibility of something native filling that niche. Thus, only a week or so before Balbo arrived, ACOP had drawn to Chicago a showy meeting of an American-flavored movement often suspected of Fascist overtones—and for our purposes, a highly instructive example of the wild swings into which the Depression tempted intelligent Americans. How far the suspicions were justified depends to some extent on how one defines Fascism. The movement's defenders said in injured tones that all they intended was to ward off future depressions by abandoning the price system and giving society the full benefits of modern technology. For the few years it lasted, chiefly in the Northeastern Quadrant and on the Coast, it drew as much attention as flower-childishness did in the same areas some years ago. Enter Technocracy.

In Chicago several groups had been talking it up. One was led by a quack doctor who had substituted harmonious living for the germ theory of disease; another, by a former organizer for the once-formidable Wobblies. Support came chiefly from certain minor-to-middling professional and industrial persons. At this plenary conference in Chicago, Technocracy, Inc.—organizing arm of the movement—introduced its elegant new emblem, half gray, half vermilion, a version of the wriggly yin/yang disk borrowed from Eastern mysticism and still revered by amateur occultists in blue jeans. Technocrats reverently called it "the monad" and said it signified "unity, balance, growth." [34] Despite its unifying powers the great Technocratic dinner crowning the proceedings broke up in a quarrel.

The cause was a rash statement by the movement's great man, Howard Scott, advising use of bayonets on "those who willfully refuse to join" Technocracy's imminent, inevitable triumph.

The word "Technocracy" was sired by a British-reared professional engineer, William H. Smyth of Berkeley, California, for a social panacea that was his reaction to World War I. In 1919 he published in a professional magazine, *Industrial Management,* a series of essays urging the nation to take a lesson from its experience in organizing to fight. To build a better life for all, society should depose moneymen and the credit system from their economic hegemony and coordinate its technological resources of experts and machinery War Industries Board-style. The nature of that better life was to be determined by popular needs and wishes arrived at by questionnaires attached to the US Census; hence TECHNOlogy + demoCRACY = TECHNOCRACY. In 1926 Smyth managed to get publication (by the high-prestige house of Alfred A. Knopf) for a muzzy book propounding it all in an elaborate fable about a hairy, beetle-browed caveman called Irascible Strong, his wife Trixy Cunning and their posterity, who down the generations gradually evolved the economic and technological mess of modern times. The book drew little attention. Smyth blushed more or less unseen until late in 1932, when the San Francisco *Chronicle* and the *Nation* printed his letters complaining that Scott had stolen his thunder, his name for it, and perverted both. For Scott read "Technocracy" to mean dictatorial rule by engineers with no room for democratically determined social goals. That was nearer the actual meaning of those two Greek roots, but it also had a strong smell of Fascism, no doubt of it.

Whether Smyth's charge of stolen thunder was as sound as his identification of the flaw in Scott's gospel is uncertain. Maybe Scott had read *Industrial Management?* As Technocracy chipped the shell in the East, observers credited it to Thornstein Veblen, august old curmudgeon of American economics, who had revised the dismal science's naïve psychology and applied his great talent for cynical analysis to industry, schools and other targets of opportunity on his horizon. In 1921 his *The Engineers and the Price System* went beyond his usual merely iconoclastic romps on the disquieting undersides of things. It taught that the efficiency of American industry had dangerously outstripped the money system that presumably guided it. Technologists—engineers, researchers and so on—who necessarily knew the world of machines better than moneymen could, should organize what he fashionably called a soviet—meaning a deliberate, not necessarily secret conspiracy—to take over before moneymen's wrongheadedness brought the whole thing crashing down. Around these doctrines gathered after World War I an informal group of self-conscious social surgeons called the Technical Alliance—Charles P. Steinmetz, General Electric's renowned inventive genius; men of stature in architecture, physics, economics; sometimes Stuart Chase; and the aforesaid Scott as Apostle Paul of Veblen's new gospel.

Many Technocrats had it the other way around: that Veblen had learned from Scott that America had better turn its affairs over to the engineers. Anyway, Scott was full of it when he first surfaced in Washington just after the Armistice of 1918; presently he shifted the focus of his missionary work to Greenwich Village. There serious-minded free souls knew him as a tall, rugged, often harsh young man in a leather overcoat and broad-brimmed hat, necktie and handkerchief both red, who had been engineering assistant to the famous Colonel Hugh L. Cooper in building the great wartime hydroelectric plant at Muscle Shoals. For admirers at Lee Chumley's speakeasy he sometimes allusively sketched a European boyhood: His father was chief engineer of the Berlin-to-Baghdad railway project. Trained in German technical schools, son went to Canada during World War I to build that nation's only acetone plant. Having played soccer in Europe, he once won a close football game for Notre Dame. He had had to leave Mexico hurriedly because he had inadvertently shot an archbishop who had intrigued against him lest his plans deprive the Church of its vast wealth. Delusions of persecution, often in reference to Catholics, occasionally peeped out of him. In connection with his often-persuasive accounts of "places he had never seen, people he had never met, and dams he had not built" [35] (thus, Margaret Mead described his conversational habits) this suggests a strong possibility of a tendency toward psychosis.

At Technocracy's height in 1932 Allen Raymond, crack reporter for the New York *Herald-Tribune,* checked into Scott's accounts of himself. The only hard fact ascertained about him was that he had once been partner in a small factory in New Jersey making floor polish—good polish too, the *Herald-Tribune*'s maintenance man said. Nobody concerned with acetone in Canada had ever heard of him. The German technical schools where he had trained had no record of him. (He told Dr. Mead in a candid moment that he had never got beyond the ninth grade.) When Raymond asked him why he passed as Dr. Scott when he held no such academic degree, he said, well, he was often up at Columbia where everybody was Professor or Doctor. A congressional committee investigating the building of the Muscle Shoals plant did, however, hear of a construction foreman—not engineer—named Howard Scott whose work in pouring footings had been so poor as to rouse suspicions of sabotage. And for a while after the Armistice he had tried to interest the hot-revolutionary Wobblies in hiring him as economic consultant.

Such revelations seemed not to trouble him. Indeed, it was he who advised Raymond to look into that Muscle Shoals investigation. He went right on waving charts garnished with esoteric mathematical symbols and talking the hind legs off the assembled donkeys with what, to judge from results, was a mesmeric impressiveness. Maybe he was one of those men of patent ability but unstable personality who sometimes manage to pose as doctors on hospital staffs and handle routine medical practice well enough not to expose themselves to genuine MDs. Anyway, Dr. Mead remembered him as quite a person in spite of his windy yarns. Stuart Chase, who had known him thirteen years before writing the best of the many pamphlets that took Technocracy seriously, said that flaws in his past—or lack of discernible past—didn't matter. It was his figures and analyses that counted. Even Raymond felt that this demonstrable phony might have "elements of greatness.... It matters little what the facts of his career have been. If he has some unique contribution to make ... his place in the history of his time is fixed." [36] Such talk from witnesses of high intelligence helps one understand how, by 1932, Professor Walter Rautenstrauch of Columbia's Department of Industrial Engineering took it on himself to recruit fifty jobless architectural draftsmen to draw up under Scott's direction a master Energy Survey of North America with which to dot the *is* and cross the *ts* of the heady mix of threat and promise that was Technocracy's story.

Scott and his Technical Alliance, child of immediate post-Armistice strains, had dropped out of sight as Harding-Coolidge prosperity reassuringly took over. Maybe he played his Notre Dame football and shot his archbishop during this period. Under the strains of Hoover's last two years, however, the survivors of the group (Veblen and Steinmetz had died) bubbled up again, calling themselves Technocrats. They were gloriously severe on the moneymen who had inflicted hard times on the nation and now could only counsel patience until time and impersonal forces remedied economic ills: "Would we accept as rulers ... medicine-men ... [running] our society ... by charms, shibboleths and the beating of tom-toms? ... throughout this worst of all depressions about all [the bankers] have been able to do is to call on their financial rainmakers. We are still awaiting the shower." [37] The positive message was that "capitalism and the price system by which the present order distributes ... [are] tumbling into the abyss ... constitutional government and the rights of private property [will] have to be abandoned ... a new 'energy state'... set up ... nobody [is] going to have to work very much any more. Everybody, man, woman and child, [is] ... to have an income which, measured in 1929 dollars, would be about $20,000 a year...." [38]

This purchasing power was to lapse unless soon expended. It was expressed in terms of "ergs" and "joules" (units in which physicists measure energy) as gauge of the energy that society put into items of economic value, so much into shoes, so much into machinery for making replacement shoes. In return each person between twenty-five and forty years, say, was to work four hours a day, four days a week, on whatever his home community set him at. North America would have some 20,000 such highly integrated communities—a borrowing from anarchism—each with a particular production task, forestry here, fishing there, airplane motors here, oil there, loosely coordinated not by bankers calling the tunes of a money system but by a high command consisting of the 300,000 technology-wise engineers who had created the mass-producing world to begin with.*

Most of this had been most conspicuously anticipated forty-five years earlier in Edward Bellamy's immensely successful Utopian novel *Looking Backward.*† It described as of A.D. 2000 an America saved by abandoning the price system and giving ample, equal, guaranteed incomes to all willing to work a small number of hours per year. It exploited the realization, new then, two generations old by the time Technocracy took it up, popularized meanwhile by widely read idea-midwives such as H. G. Wells and Bertrand Russell, that modern technology enabled the human race generously to house, feed and clothe all its members with one hand tied behind it. Technocracy's part was to emphasize the morbid effects of the price system such as technological unemployment with its privations and emotional dislocations. It warned that an already-huge discrepancy, worsening yearly, between the guiding theories of finance capital and the facts of modern industry was so extreme that any day the system would crash, taking America back to cave life or thereabouts. In 1931 zealous Technocrats gave the nation only two years, or eighteen months ...

* Some writers on Technocracy, including Scott at diffident moments, shied away from hazarding definite schemes of organization. Details above are mostly from a conspicuous small book written with approval of the Continental Committee for Technocracy by Harold Loeb, who had taken Scott seriously since they had lived in the same Greenwich Village apartment house in the early 1920s. Son of the famous New York City banking family, Loeb was editor-publisher of *Broom,* a well thought-of avant-garde magazine of the 1920s and led the slightly more levelheaded, Scott-mistrusting faction among Technocrats. He is thought to have been the original of the punch-throwing Robert Cohn of Hemingway's *The Sun Also Rises.*

† Those unacquainted with *Looking Backward* or who find it dull reading may be referred to my short account of it in *The Americans,* 724–28.

better let the engineers take over now! Conversely, if society stayed stupidly hesitant, the engineers should band together, throw all switches, close all valves and bring society to its knees begging to be forced to make sense. Even before the Depression became a disquieting force, Beard was near enough to the Technocrats' attitude to cite Oswald Spengler's warning that "if a few hundred thousand engineers should quit work ... modern society would come down around our ears" and to describe engineers collectively as a potential "fifth estate in the modern order, perhaps the first." [39]

From World War I Technocracy inherited the practical precedent of which Smyth had already made so much. Scott, Chase, Harold Rugg, radical-minded professor of education at Teachers College-Columbia University, led in describing how Bernard Baruch's War Industries Board had thrown out traditional notions of cost, profit and competition to streamline the whole economy for the single purpose of waging war. Shift the purpose to waging peace in economic and social harmony and presto! Technocracy exploited the isolationism that flourished after World War I by promising to confine itself to North America, leaving the rest of the world to sink or swim in its own shiftless, wrongheaded way. It taught that the continent's natural resources and unique technology would keep the Technocratic good life at full steam ahead for any foreseeable future. Nobody explained where tin, manganese, rubber and other essential items scarce or unavailable in North America were to come from or how Mexico and Canada were to be brought into line. Scott was the only Technocrat crude enough to mention bayonets. But Loeb's autarchic Fortress North America was represented as safe from attack from lesser economies overseas because state control of energy meant that "such a tremendous capacity to destroy could be so quickly improvised, that no nation such as those now existing would dare to open hostilities." [40] Anybody from the old War Industries Board could have told him how little sense that "so quickly" made. But Technocrats, like others, took from the numerous lessons of World War I only what suited their emotional thirsts.

Olympian engineers sifting subtly organized data of high accuracy would lay down how much of the continent's annual use of energy went to how much and what kinds of shelter, clothing, food and such social services as medicine and education, how much into research and new and replacement plant. Though the individual would have no say on what jobs he spent his sixteen hours per week, psychologists using refined techniques would see that round pegs got into round holes. Any refusing assignments would first be imprisoned at the dirtiest kinds of useful hard labor; those staying recalcitrant would be welcome to starve,* for all means of livelihood would be in the hands of the public work force. For the conformists working hours would be so short and income so far above minimum needs that there would be much individual moonlighting, much of it producing with materials got from the state with one's spare ergs familiar things that had economic value in price-system times. A could paint pictures and sell them if anybody cared to buy; B grow fancy flowers ditto; C organize a repertory theater with members clubbing their ergs to build and equip it; D organize a church.... Creative-minded Loeb confidently hoped for a boom in artsy-crafty self-expression—and not only to bring beauty and satisfactory skills into life, but also to prevent so much leisure from fostering alcoholism, quack cults and feckless *dolce far niente.*

A likely source of many of Loeb's decorations on the Technocratic blackjack was Wells' *The World Set Free* (1914), about a proto-Technocracy encouraging handicrafts and horticulture "to keep the less adaptable out of mischief." [41] But the best thought-out use for such time-on-one's hands was suggested by an elderly, affluent woman sage, Prestonia Mann Martin, in 1932 before Scott's gospel had much public notice. Eleanor Roosevelt was among those taking very seriously the book *Prohibiting Poverty,* setting forth Mrs. Martin's two-ply version of a technological heaven of plenty-for-all. Its faint flavor of common sense contrasted with not only Technocracy but also the lady's early background. She had sat at the feet of the wide-eyed old Concord School of Philosophy and founded a New Hampshire summer colony patterned after the Brook Farm experiment of the 1830s.† Now married to a British-reared Fabian Socialist on the faculty of Rollins College in Winter Park, Florida, she admiringly crossed Henry Ford's windiest talk about the glories of mass production with William James' famous notion of organizing young persons for a "Moral Equivalent of War." The hybrid offspring was a Technocracy-like scheme promising to keep alive the best features of

---

* Here Technocracy was less humane than Bertrand Russell, whose ideal society, so well organized technologically that it had ample resources to spare, allowed a "vagabond wage," a bare dole livelihood for those unwilling to do the work society prescribed.

† Upton Sinclair was curiously peevish about her; he usually glowed with sympathy for such people: "... wealthy utopian, who for many years had turned her ... camp into a place of summer discussions—incidentally making her guests practice cooperation in kitchen and laundry.... When I met them they were both on the way to reaction; Prestonia was writing a book to prove that we had made no progress in civilization since the Greeks. Both she and her husband are now [1931] good, old-fashioned tories...." (*American Outpost,* 193.)

laissez-faire capitalism and the price system. ". . . far from seeking to destroy capitalistic exploitation, providing a field for . . . individual initiative and personal ambition, and leaving room for the acquisition of Private Wealth in any amounts." [42]

Like this: Up to age eighteen all American children were to be trained in the three Rs, handicrafts and basic science in national schools like Henry Ford's private system in Dearborn, Michigan. For the next eight years all (known in this phase as Young Commoners) were to be drafted into an industrial-agricultural labor corps using modern technology efficiently enough to give every American man, woman and child the basic necessities—food, shelter, clothing, transportation and so on—free. Young Commoners would get only that basic living plus a little pocket money. After age twenty-six they left the corps entitled to that free livelihood the rest of their days. They could loaf if they liked or go in for artsy-crafty hobbies of small or no economic consequence. But Mrs. Martin, aware that amateur painting and fishing would hardly keep her busily competitive countrymen in good shape for long, provided for a second economy floating on the free-subsistence economy. Any post-twenty-sixers, of the sort hungry for luxuries or rat races (significantly called Capitals at this stage), could engage in the whole range of private enterprise that provides the suprabasic needs—finer clothes and food, show business, the major arts generally, fancy resorts, shiny automobiles and so on. The market would be all those whose successes in this business world supplying luxuries enabled them to afford first-class goods and services—all on a money basis with competitive prices reflecting a free supply/demand situation. The only restriction forbade the Capitals' world to traffic in basic necessities.

For analogies: The Young Commoners' progression was rather like that of the British paupers of Colonial times who sold themselves into temporary slavery livelihood as indentured servants in exchange for a passage to America and eventual freedom to better themselves in the New World's catch-as-catch-can conditions. Or put the basic livelihood in terms of cash handout, not commodities in kind, and it recalls recent proposals of an income floor under poverty. Some of the lady's efforts to be practical were not as clever as her recognition that many people would be unhappy settling for mere plain living, high thinking, dancing on the green and joy in one's fellowman—a realism never shown by any other Utopist I know of. As for the Commoners' love life, for instance, she seems to have persuaded herself that schooling and social pressure would keep the program from being embarrassed by inconvenient pregnancies. If she counted on the birth control of the day, fairly efficient in its best forms but always handicapped by the impulsive ways of young men with maids, she failed to say so. Her notion of proper command for the Commons' economic empire— factories, farms, forests, fisheries and so on—was a completely authoritarian executive and scientific management staff, the chief of which was chosen once, at the beginning. Thereafter he and his chief lieutenants appointed their successors as occasion required from the likelier persons in both the Commons' and the Capitals' world—as lively a temptation to mankind's empire-building streak as any of the polities created by Plato, Lenin or Mussolini. But those shortcomings were not what kept her scheme from drawing better than secondary attention. The prime reason for its obscurity was that just when her little book appeared in August, 1932, Technocracy's tempest of publicity blew up and half smothered it.

For that was the moment Scott chose to summon the press to Columbia to hear him being sourly persuasive about his apocalyptic bill of goods. The association with Columbia, though tenuous, gave an air of august auspices, and what Beard called its "melodrama" [43]—that odor of trenchant science fiction—did the rest. "Magazine editors leaped like trout," Raymond said. ". . . Blasé directors of worldwide press services shot their news sleuths up to Columbia." [44] Chase glowed as "the newspaper boys, swarming like bees, made technocracy a household word." [45] In a few months a dozen quickie books and pamphlets explaining the new gospel were selling briskly. Upton Sinclair, soon to borrow from it for his End Poverty in California (EPIC) campaign, assured the world that it was "the most important movement which has shown its head in our time." [46] The *Nation* called it "the first step toward a genuinely revolutionary philosophy in America." [47] A talk with Scott so impressed Theodore Dreiser that for some years Technocracy supplanted Communism in his muddled affections. When Albert Einstein held his first press conference in America, the first question asked was: "What do you think of Technocracy?" [48] With a modest tact that he sometimes failed to show later when issues outside his field came up, he begged off from answering.

Frank A. Vanderlip, retired president of the National City Bank, long hoping to be an economic elder statesman, had Scott out for the weekend at his country estate. Mrs. Vanderlip, a power in her own right, projected a National Planning Board including Scott and key industrialists such as Gerard Swope, chairman of the board of General Electric, who had been making statesmanlike noises, to think the country out of the Depression. Carleton H. Palmer, president of E. R. Squibb & Company, an enterprise of the sort Technocracy deplored, gave a dinner at New York City's gilded Metropolitan Club with

Scott—most of the guests thought he was Professor Scott—as chief speaker. Rautenstrauch took the gospel to the 1932 convention of the American Association for the Advancement of Science in a speech that stirred up the most violent reactions which that body of savants would see until the Movement tried to take it over a few years ago. Most significantly the jokesmiths of show business exploited and so widened its household currency. Will Rogers asked over the air whether Technocracy was a new mouthwash or a new corn plaster. Colonel Stoopnagle & Budd, the sharpest zanies on radio in the early 1930s, tucked cracks about it into broadcast after broadcast. Even Skid Row knew about it. Burlesque comics got laughs by calling to the soubrette from offstage, "Honey, I'm a Technocrat!" Virgil Jordan, president of the National Industrial Conference Board, had reason to say—and not approvingly—that the country had gone "technocrazy." [49]

To account for it, William Soskin, well-known bookman of the day, said that the movement shrewdly used "the American community's own language ... engineering, man-hours of work, technological efficiency...." [50] A good try, but no explanation of why it attracted not only self-consciously open-minded big shots but also what was so widely being called the intelligentsia. Their cordiality probably meant a collective-mindedness long presaged first by *Looking Backward* and kindred fantasies and then by the sanguine cult of Planning brewing up before World War I. The loose but earnest brotherhood of Planners looked on competitive profit seeking, the alleged lifeblood of the new production economics, as, in Lippmann's representative words *c.* 1914: "an antiquated, feeble, mean and unimaginative way of dealing with the possibilities of modern industry." [51] They preferred deliberate coordination of industries to satisfy projected demands to make a plenty-for-all Good Life attainable. They deplored trust-busting, the muckrakers' weapon of choice, as artificial and wrongheaded, for the healthy growth of national, monopolistic trusts obviously prepared the way for public takeover of key industries—coordinated Planning next step.

In this context Technocracy and Prohibiting Poverty were only two of dozens of demands for Planning that sprouted out of the festering compost of the Depression. Harold Clurman is a good witness here: "... so deep was the crisis [*c.* 1931] ... that virtually every conscious person was attempting to find some basic answer to society's jitters ... ready to consider any idea that promised a solution, no matter how extreme or unpopular." [52] But no matter how they varied otherwise, all required a Plan if only planned planlessness. A year before Technocracy made the headlines Beard had fathered a potent symposium, *America Faces the Future,* in which weighty names zealously endorsed Planning as the only intelligible reaction to Depression. Even Nicholas Murray Butler, president of Columbia, hardly a committed radical, deplored "A Planless World" and said, "A man with a plan, however much we dislike it, has a vast advantage over a group sauntering down the road of life complaining of the economic weather and wondering when the rain is going to stop." [53] Within three months he was recommending federal control of basic industries "to control production within the limits of a proper balance with an expanding power of consumption." [54] An arm of the Federal Council of Churches of Christ in America not only proposed womb-to-tomb social se-curity—two years before the New Deal began groping toward it—but also laid it down that "we shall have to see ... a new ... organization of society ... a system of national planning adjusted to world-wide trends." [55] Beard—and Butler—plumped for repeal of antitrust laws and a national planning agency working with and through manipula-tion of basic industries "affected with public interest" [56]—meaning to treat not only transportation, electric power and all communications but also fuel, iron, steel, lumber, building materials and food packing as public utilities subject to unlimited regulation.

Matthew Woll, president of the National Civic Federation as well as vice-president of the subradical American Federation of Labor, wanted the USSR's then-vaunted Five-Year Plan of industrialization matched with an American "warm-blooded, ten-year plan of demo-cratic idealism." [57] That reference dovetails with the other reasons why Technocracy—essentially collectivist Planning done by engineers—was warmly received by little groups of serious thinkers. *Looking Backward* was influential, yes. The War Production Board was a hearteningly hard-nosed precedent, yes. Certainly the Depression was a sound occasion for reexamining the catch-as-catch can economics that—whatever scapegoat one or another economist might select—was gen-erally responsible for the crisis. But for many temperaments the detonator for the Planning rocket was the emotionally contagious Russian example. The scores of more or less pro-Bolshevik books and pamphlets bedeviling the early Depression were awestruck by the USSR's gigantic achievements—some actually existing in fact as well as in the Kremlin's promises and figures—in consequence of Planning. Knowing persons were aware that "Gosplan" was shorthand for the USSR's Communist-led planning agency and called its masterpiece, known to the laity as the Five-Year Plan, the *Piatiletka.* Soule was writing in the *New Republic* that in view of how the USSR's industrialization borrowed American machinery and engineers, it was a pity "we cannot make use of her economic inventions." [58] On the other side of the street President Hoover's speech to the Indiana

Editorial Association in mid-1931 accurately, if grumpily, ascribed much of the current vogue of Planning to "an infection" from Russia's struggle "to redeem herself from ten years of starvation and misery." [59] And in between Beard found it necessary to proclaim that Planning "had nothing Russian about its origin ... would have gone forward inexorably even if the Russian revolution had not borrowed and dramatized it." [60]

Maybe so; yet none who knew firsthand the intellectual-emotional climate of Technocracy's ephemeral career fail to recall how the USSR had imbued the word "Planning" with a special, glowingly pink magic. The association had its own inner affinities. For, though few mentioned it, the other side of the Planning coin was collective Coercion. Plans are meaningless unless carried out at more or less cost in accustomed freedoms. Fifty years earlier *Looking Backward* confessed as much by describing its beautiful society as organized like a self-sustaining peacetime army. Soule's *A Planned Society* openly suggested that "a great and world-wide depression [is] too large a price to pay for what [anti-Planners] choose to call liberty." [61] * Scott's bayonets were the corollary. His arrogant, though not illogical, choice of engineers as the dictator elite to bring Technocracy's plenty-for-all to pass was like the elite of guardian educators proposed in Rugg's *The Great Technology* (1932). Molière's dancing master all over again, of course. For Rugg the educationist, the world should obviously be run by experts in pedagogy. Scott, the Walter Mitty who longed to be an engineer, naturally chose engineers to straighten things out and then keep people straightened out to match. Old Bolshevik Lenin not only preferred Old Bolsheviks for such purposes but saw to it that they got and kept the jobs.

Well before Scott mentioned bayonets in Chicago, Loeb's blueprint wrote off democracy's chances in the Technocratic camp: "Administration, in a technocracy, has to do with material factors ... subject to measurement. Therefore, popular voting can largely be dispensed with. It is stupid deciding an issue by voice or opinion when a yardstick can be used." [62] Such authoritarianism inseparable from effective Planning was already getting Technocracy called Fascist. "... a dictatorship of engineers ... is fascism," said Norman Thomas, not yet in his phase of

---

* It was more openly stated at a debate *c.* 1932 between Everett Dean Martin, the veteran libertarian, and John Strachey, then Communism's most active missionary-ambassador to the American *bourzhui*. Martin was warning of the hazards to liberty in Communist polity when a little man popped up in the back of the house and shouted, "What good is liberty to a man out of work?" The question is, of course, unanswerable in terms of anybody who propounds it to begin with.

acknowledging Stalin's right to *carte rouge,* "or at least it lends itself beautifully to fascism." [63]

Today "Fascism" is, as Naomi Bliven recently wrote, only an "all-purpose term of abuse." [64] C. 1932 it still meant usually the sum of what Mussolini had done and hoped to do in Italy—order imposed by *force majeur* on a polity threatened by chaos as misery-sharpened radicals, dominated by Communists, clawed at a bewildered government and a stupidly predatory economy running down like a watch. It was a nasty nonsolution for a morbid problem complicated by local weakness, but it attracted notice in a world understandably nervous about Communist aggressiveness.

What an American meant by using "Fascist" as pejorative depended on the values of the speaker. For Reddish-to-Red minds Fascists were foul primarily because they had bullied, beaten, jailed, exiled, tortured, assassinated and reduced to political impotence Italy's Reds—the sacrosanct Chosen Segment of politics who had seemed in a fair way to turn Italy into the world's second Communist-dominated nation. For those aware that Communist street fighters were no prettier than Fascists and that democratic freedoms were as scarce in Moscow as in Rome, the Blackshirts and their puffy, strutty little leader were self-swindled confidence men promising small shopkeepers pie in the sky that could never get baked and viciously enjoying the brutality that kept *Fascismo* in power. Communism deplored Technocracy; it competed for the favor of the collectivist-Planning mind. Decent people smelled Fascism in it because it so eagerly abandoned democratic values to create a self-aggrandizing elite vowed to omniscience and omnicompetence. This preceded Technocracy's second blooming on the Coast that took it into paramilitary uniforms and flourished somewhat among the harassed white-collar elements of California II's lower-income strata—opposite numbers of Fascism's stalwarts in Italy and Germany. When, in 1935, Lawrence Dennis, able casuist and former collectivist, applied to America in his *The Coming American Fascism* lessons he derived from Mussolini and Hitler, 99 percent of it could have been a Technocratic tract. Yet Scott's narcissistic arrogance kept him from seeing allies in *Fascismo*. He ridiculed what he thought its bad strategy in "consolidating all the minor [Italian] rackets into one major monopoly" and called Italy a country of too poor resources for the "industrial energy civilization" [65] that Technocracy's monolithism promised.

Maybe because of the buoyancy of the New Deal, the glory of Technocracy waned within a year of Scott's kickoff press conference. Early in 1933, for instance, a great dinner for him in New York City soured when his speech proved incoherent and harsh—"We do not bother with critics," [66] he said—and led to the schism opposing Loeb's CCT to Scott's own Technocracy, Inc. Backing water, he began to reply to questions about how elitist-minded Technocracy would take over: "Technocracy is merely placing the problem before persons who must deal with it." [67] It began to occur to previously dazzled observers such as Vanderlip that it was unscientific to have arrived at diagnoses and prognoses ten years in advance of the great Columbia Energy Survey that was to supply their foundations. "Sentence first, verdict afterwards," said the Queen of Hearts. Columbia's President Butler disclaimed university sponsorship of Scott. Rautenstrauch resigned from the steering committee. . . .

Two years later, however, Scott found his second windiness in the more elastic atmosphere of California II, Washington State and western Canada. Thither he took not only the esoteric monad, a gimmick of the sort to which Los Angeles County was suspectible, but also the new Technocrat uniform—a double-breasted gray gabardine suit, gray shirt, blue tie, monad emblem in the buttonhole—and the faithful were now encouraged to paint their automobiles gray with the monad on the driver's door panel. The Los Angeles *Daily Illustrated News* had already set things rolling with a series of favorable articles on Technocracy and called it potentially "as important as the great American Revolution of 1776." [68] Late in 1935, 10,000 adherents mustered in the Hollywood Bowl to greet Scott. Whittier College, a steady-going Quaker institution nearby, let him lecture and invade classes. The local branch of the American Association of Engineers dined him at the University Club of Los Angeles, and though he spoke for three hours, *Technocracy* magazine reported, "not a soul moved" [69]—notable control of sphincter muscles among California II's engineers. The San Diego Exposition of 1935 had a Technocracy Day. As he moved northward, Scott predictably found California I less fertile. But Seattle was so apt a culture medium that for years it harbored branches of both Technocracy, Inc. and the rival CCT.

Thence Scott invaded Canada with similar success—no overwhelming numbers but a striking local willingness to hear him seriously. In 1938, for instance, the Regina (Saskatchewan) *Daily Star* called this "tall, scowling American engineer . . . speaking in a cold, metallic style . . . terribly effective" [70] as he told an audience of 600 that soon Technocracy would be so powerful that neither Canada nor the US could discuss war without permission of his organization. The following year he telegraphed the prime minister of Canada to line Technocracy up against overseas service for Canadians. North Americans "who conspire to make war off this Continent," he proclaimed, "are guilty of Continental Treason." [71] Ottawa actually found it advisable to proscribe Technocracy, a measure rescinded when, after Pearl Harbor, Scott reversed himself and went baldheaded for an anti-Fascist war. Now he wanted the continent's decks cleared by letting Technocracy take over French-dominated Quebec and "the hacienda culture south of the Rio Grande." [72] He also demanded that FDR appoint him dictator to organize the United States' war effort and took full-page advertisements calling for "TOTAL CONSCRIPTION" of all persons, machines, money and materials and a campaign of extermination for pro-Fascists in America. Such gestures were a tall order from a man whose following at no time much exceeded 10,000 persons.* After V-J Day he gradually dribbled on into xenophobe slaverings about sinister aliens and paranoid nonsense about a conspiracy of Roman Catholic nations to dominate the United Nations—an intensification of symptoms familiar to the psychiatry of psychosis. But apparently he had not yet come completely apart when he died in 1970, and tiny fragments of Technocracy still survive on the Coast, hanging on with no future like the vestigial remains of the Wobblies.

At least Scott did secure a year or so's livelihood for those fifty unemployed draftsmen whose Technocratic charts were so widely admired. It was most understandable that the bedraggled unemployed man in the street found enticing promise in the Technocrats' plenty-for-all described in the newspaper he fished out of a trash can. But it was, if not exactly shocking, at least morbidly symptomatic that so many well-grounded people of presumably mature judgment should have been at all drawn to so flimsy and obviously tyrannical a way out. The ease with which Scott recruited them while his luck was running betokened the alarming degree to which the Depression-harassed nation's leaders might lose their heads.

Of wild swings Technocracy might have been the noisiest but probably not, to be fair, the strangest example. In 1931, just before Scott's great period, Britian sent over an economic panacea called Social Credit fathered by a Scottish engineer-soldier, Major C. H. Douglas. In Britain its adherents, including for a while the Very Reverend Hewlett Johnson, Dean of Canterbury, wore green shirts. In America its chief missionary was A. R. Orage, a handsome, self-made British intellectual, once a Guild Socialist, who looked and handled himself like the ideal psychiatrist. By 1934 the same publications that had talked up Technocracy were printing elaborate coverage of Social Credit. Its basic tenet, shared with many open-minded economists, was

---

* This is the authoritative estimate of Henry Elsner, Jr., to whose *The Technocrats* (1967) this section is gratefully indebted, particularly as to the movement on the Coast and in Canada. I should add that Professor Elsner sees much less Fascism in Technocracy than I do.

that a chief cause of the worldwide Depression was maldistribution of purchasing power. The cure was for government to take over banking and pay every citizen a monthly stipend in paper money that lapsed if not soon spent, a proposal likely to meet with favor among those in hard luck and some whom their troubles distressed. Whatever its economic merits, however, Social Credit depended most on the snarling mistrust of banks that, though understandable in view of recent trauma, has long been a symptom of potential anti-Semitism, as in the cases of Henry Ford and the giddier Progressives of the 1890s. Charles Norman described the Social Credit example well; it began with: "... the 'real credit' of a nation resides in its people, but ... a perversion had set in ... the 'cornering' of money.... Enter, of course, the Rothschilds, the de Wendels, the Comité des Forges.... What kept Douglas and his associates warm ... was the hot lamp of anti-Semitism.... This man delivered himself of sentiments worthy of the lowest rabble-rouser ... the Douglasites recommended to [their] readers 'The Protocols of Zion'...." [72]

That odor goes far toward accounting for Ezra Pound's adhesion to Social Credit as presage of his subsequent infatuation with *Fascismo*. It fails to mean much in the different, if strange, cases of Graham Munson, competent literary scholar; James Laughlin IV, rich boy from Pittsburgh who begot the New Directions publishing firm for avant-garde writings; Archibald MacLeish; Bronson Cutting, literate, able and liberal US Senator from Arizona—none anti-Semites to my knowledge. For such anyway temporary admirers of Social Credit one can, however, also refer to the Svengali-like talents of Orage. He had previously entangled himself in the gospel of that maybe Russian, highly pretentious mystic named Gurdjieff who maintained a soul-calking colony at Fontainebleau in France. His soul-shattering methods of leading neophytes into supernal values—and a fascinated obsession with the master's tyrannical self *—were notoriously successful with cultivated Britons in the 1920s. Orage's methods had more charm mingled with the cunning of Eve's serpent and less sadism, but much guruistic magic had evidently rubbed off on him and obviously helped him persuade well-placed New Yorkers that Major Douglas' green goods were genuine.

---

* Llewellyn Powys (*The Verdict of Bridlegoose,* 162–63) left a pungent little sketch of Gurdjieff and his public demonstrations in Greenwich Village in the 1920s: "... a high bald head, with sharp black eyes. His general appearance made one think of a riding-master, though there was something in his presence that affected one's nerves in a strange way. Especially ... when his pupils came into the stage, to perform like a hutchful of rabbits under the gaze of a master conjurer." The reader has already heard of him in connection with Mrs. Frank Lloyd Wright.

A generation later Arthur M. Schlesinger, Jr., named among the probably healthy consequences of Technocracy "a sense of infinite technological possibilities; a susceptibility to new approaches; a readiness to break with the past." [73] Certainly genes from such cults were traceable long after they themselves ceased to be fashionable topics. Social Credit leapfrogged northwestward to stiffen the Populism of Canada's William "Bible Bill" Aberhart, and a new Social Credit Party actually took power in the prairie province of Alberta; though it did little to carry out Douglas' ideas, it stayed until 1971. Both Social Credit and Technocracy—Dreiser probably should get an assist here—contributed to Californa II's ephemeral but temporarily huge Utopian and EPIC movements and to the generalized collectivism in Bingham's *Common Sense* magazine and its off-and-on ally, the League for Independent Political Action. In those circles Technocracy's "balanced load" (= production geared to ascertained need unperverted by a price system) bolstered and blended with the long-familiar Socialist goal of "production for use and not for profit." [74] Shortened to "Production for Use," this was another of those slogans like "Learning by doing" invulnerable because self-recommending. Who would defend production for nonuse? Only the same kind of fumbler who would tolerate unbalanced loads.

There was something upper-class about Social Credit and Technocracy (at least in its pre-Coast phase), an appeal to the cultivated or anyway well-informed mind. Maybe that kept both from exploiting the Depression-formed anxieties and exasperations seething among the blue- and lower-white-collar strata. But those unhappy millions did not go neglected. They were well and truly ministered unto when the governor of (later junior US Senator from) Louisiana and the parish priest of Royal Oak, Michigan, each in his own jangling way went lurching toward a home-brewed, low-down, grass-roots Fascism. Fortunately for them, unfortunately for the rest of the nation, the ideal medium for tampering with this potential following was already developed. In its unregulated infancy radio had shown a pimply affinity for quacks and hog-calling opportunists. At one time the most listened-to station in the country was KFKB, mouthpiece of "Dr." John R. "Goatgland" Brinkley; * with its facilities he twice almost got elected governor of Kansas and also carried several counties in neighboring Oklahoma, where, of course, he was not a candidate at all. The Honorable Huey P. Long and Father Charles E. Coughlin carried that tradition on with spirit. One might even say that their

* See my *Great Times*, 455–67.

showing how to use airwaves to sell bills of goods—never mind differences in quality—pointed the way for FDR's politically and socially indispensable "fireside chats." Particularly Coughlin's voice like a crystalline trumpet and candidly clear enunciation were harbingers of FDR's forensic virtuosity.

Not that the two had similar speech habits. They differed as markedly as their personalities. FDR was a rather testy but basically generous well-wisher of his fellowman and his own power-relishing self. Coughlin was an egocentric, pontifical dreamer of dreams and seer of visions all too ready to hate anybody and anything obstructing them. As for enunciation, FDR's was pure WASP-prep school. Coughlin's marked him down as a variety of the golden-voiced Irishman. His rhetorical presence reminded Frank Kent, veteran newspaperman who had heard them all, of both "the vibrant personal charm of the lamented William Jennings Bryan" and "the deeply stirring voice of the [Irish-born] late Bourke Cochran * ... that indescribable timbre that touches the emotions ... a rare gift." [75] The words that rang so clear in FDR's plangent tenor were put together by one or more staff writers and finally shaped by his own revisions. So far as I know Coughlin's communiqués from on high were all his own work. In spite of their often discussing economics—that is, Coughlin's version of it—they were often rhapsodical in a fashion well suited to his almost operatic vocal style.

Coughlin came honestly by his Irish tongue. His father was Irish-American, his mother Irish-Canadian; his preceptors in small Catholic schools and colleges were largely Irish, too. The province of Ontario reared him in an atmosphere favorable to latent suspicions and potential hatreds. Local Irish Catholics were usually under pressure not only from the dominant Scots Presbyterians but also from a militant minority of Scotch-Irish—the Orangeman kind retaining in all its virulence the bitterness between Ulster and the rest of Ireland. Many such Irish of both stripes filtered over into southeastern Michigan. Coughlin crossed the Detroit River as part of this cultural drift. His ecclesiastical patron, Bishop Michael J. Gallegher of the diocese of Detroit, sent him to build up the new parish of the Shrine of the Little Flower (St. Theresa) in Royal Oak, an inchoate suburb of Detroit.

To begin with, he had only a jerry-built church and twenty-five Catholic families. It was Ku Klux times, and although the Klan never really flourished in Michigan, it was active enough to burn a fiery

* Congressman from New York State famous for spellbinding and behind-the-scenes juggling within the Democratic Party; died 1923.

cross on the church lawn. (Legend sometimes has it that it was the church they burned and Coughlin's subsequent grandoise basilica was the replacement.) He got the better of the Klan, according to his own story, when, on a wet, windy day he saw a Klan funeral passing, dashed out, marched with its leaders to the cemetery and took a hand in the graveside rites; thereafter the hooded chivalry let him alone.* A not-impossible but implausible story. Give it due weight, it remains true that what probably spared the young priest further molestation was his growing prestige among Detroit's blue-collar elements as the voice of vicarious, respectable righteousness.

This was no matter of his regular sermons drawing Catholics. True, the parish grew sturdily but at least partly because Royal Oak was doing the same; the rest was his radio prowess. Soon after taking over, Coughlin had told the owner of WJR-Detroit how hard it was to get an infant parish off the ground. The radioman advised religious broadcasts to work up local support and cash contributions—the same thing that canny Protestant preachers, usually Fundamentalist Bible thumpers, were doing here and there at the time. The suggestion bore fruit as momentous—at least temporarily so—as that of whatever prompted Aldous Huxley to try peyote. Interviewers dwelled on Coughlin's imposing physical presence—burly, bright blue-eyed, curly-haired, emanating energy and assurance. No doubt all that helped at congressional hearings and mass meetings. But of the millions who for the next dozen years counted on him to express their frustrations and vague hopes of vengeful redress, not one in a thousand ever saw him in person. The rest owed their sense of his avuncular support to the ear alone, to that sense of bristling imminence that his deep-dish, word-caressing voice gave as it rolled and tumbled, cajoling, denouncing, scorning, deploring out of the faceless radio set. When Long called Coughlin "just a political Kate Smith ... they'll get tired of him," he was only half right. Years later, when Coughlin left the air for good after Pearl Harbor, many, many Americans had not yet tired of the combination of that tutti-frutti voice and the reassuring toxins that it released on the neutral air.

For its first few years *The Golden Hour of the Little Flower* seems to have dealt chiefly with life and its problems. The voice made it growingly popular. Late in 1929 WMAQ-Chicago and WLW-Cincinnati, an important early station, thought it worth picking up and gave

---

* This is one of the invaluable touches in Sheldon Marcus' *Father Coughlin* (1973), to which I am much indebted. Also useful have been Charles J. Tull, *Father Coughlin and the New Deal* (1965), and Geoffrey S. Smith, *To Save a Nation* (1973).

him hundreds of thousands of delighted new listeners. As the Great Crash set the nation groping for scapegoats and panaceas, he began to show a previously muted social-mindedness. This pleased Bishop Gallegher, who had studied in Austria and acquired from fellow clergy there a strong sense of the Church's social responsibilities; he was a firm friend of Engelbert Dollfuss, the Catholic quasi-Fascist Austrian politician assassinated in 1934. Coughlin's warnings to Americans against letting the woes of the Depression trick them into Socialism or Communism were particularly lurid. "Christ and the Red Fog" was his title for one such broadcast. When it drew strong protests from both camps attacked, Coughlin shouted back so lustily that Congressman Hamilton Fish, Jr. (Rep., N.Y.), soon made him star witness at the Detroit hearings of his committee to investigate Communist activities. The brisk new Columbia Broadcasting System enlisted Coughlin as a regular Sunday feature of its big-city network. As he went on to accuse international bankers of promoting Communism and to demand a living wage for all labor, the flood of approving mail—often including contributions to support the good work—kept fifty-five clerks busy sorting and replying. Money left over after covering their salaries, overhead and so on went into the new Shrine of the Little Flower, an ornate cross between a mosque and a modern theater-in-the-round. Its purpose, Coughlin said, was to give workmen badly needed jobs. In a cell at the top of its lofty tower he concocted and sent out over the air his statesmanly messages to mankind.

Midway in his contract CBS grew nervous and cracked down on his planned broadcast blaming the nation's ills on the Treaty of Versailles. Coughlin substituted a text denouncing CBS for muzzling him. After the dust settled, he was free of CBS and had his own network anchored on WOR-Newark; it eventually had twenty-seven outlets coast to coast. Economics had been his weak subject in school. Now he was an expert on that as well as on Communism. "For Coughlin," Arthur M. Schlesinger, Jr., has soundly said, "economics was a minor branch of rhetoric." [76] Zealously he supported efforts of legislators from silver-producing states to revive the old Bryan-Populist inflationary stimulus of unlimited coinage of silver on a footing equal to that of gold. As a fast-talking friend of the common man, he pleaded before a congressional committee for the veterans' bonus not only because it would redress a great injustice to "our boys" but also because the proposed payment in greenbacks would help get the gold standard off Uncle Sam's back. As he spiced his case for silver with pungent diatribes against the international bankers for whom alone the hegemony of gold and the downgrading of silver were profitable, he proved almost as effective as Bryan himself at making the quantity theory of money a topic entrancing the man in the street. Indeed, he went Bryan's "bimetallism" one better with "symmetallism" to mingle 25 percent of gold with 75 percent of silver in the same coins—an alloy that harked back to the ancient world's pale yellow "electrum" coinage. Half a dozen US Senators, including Long and Henrik Shipstead of Minnesota, and five dozen Representatives actually urged FDR to appoint the wise man of Royal Oak to the American delegation to the London Economic Conference of 1933.

Mounting ever higher on the wings of notions then pervading the air, he sometimes sounded like the poor man's Scott: "My friends, there is no need with modern machinery for you to work more than thirty hours a week ... you and your family are deserving of a comfortable and permanent living by working only so long as production is needed to meet the ... needs of the consumers ... 'Plenty for all!' is our battle-cry! ... This nation must become the United States, Incorporated, and cease being Wall Street, Incorporated.... Call this new system 'socialized capitalism' or 'state capitalism' if you will. But do not identify it with the radicalism of the extreme right or ... the extreme left, both of which eventually meet at the equator of chaos." [77]

He must sadly have puzzled foreign embassy staff trying to decide whether to class him, in European terms, right or left. A recent biographer calls him a "frustrated, disgruntled demagogue lashing out at the world" [78] and impossible thus to categorize. He accused FDR, as governor of New York State, of wantonly persecuting James J. Walker, jauntily corrupt mayor of New York City, and compared the alleged victim with innocent Susanna in the Apocrypha falsely accused of fornication by the lecherous elders to whom she denied favors—a reference that must have made even the harassed Walker grin. But he also dismayed the Fish Committee by calling Henry Ford Communism's best friend because his personnel policies were irresponsibly heartless. He sought to get labor's right to organize buttressed by law but used only nonunion labor in building his costly church. He went all out for FDR in 1932, warning his millions of listeners that it was "Roosevelt or Ruin." His ties with the candidate had been fostered by Frank Murphy, mayor of Detroit, later a liberal Justice of the Supreme Court, and Hall Roosevelt, FDR's brother-in-law, comptroller of Detroit. Joseph P. Kennedy helped keep the connection strong.* FDR called Coughlin "Padre." But the next year Coughlin

* In 1936 Kennedy joined liberal Father John A. Ryan in attacking Coughlin as irresponsible rabble-rouser. (Geoffrey S. Smith, *To Save a Nation*, 50.)

joined Long, Hearst and Will Rogers in stirring up the isolationist whirlwind that smothered FDR's attempt to affiliate the United States with the World Court—which was, in Coughlin's view, a creature of the international bankers begotten in "secret sessions when the abortion of the League of Nations was cradled by those determined to protect injustice." [79]

Set down much of that to a proud man's resentment, sometimes justified, at being cynically used; the vagaries of an egocentric with more gift of gab than brains, that always deplorable combination; and the normal antics of American demagoguery. In those respects Coughlin belongs not so much with Bryan as with such strident old Progressive feuders as Ignatius Donnelly, Thomas E. Watson and Charles A. Lindbergh, Sr. But there are other ugly smells here: While he was demanding monetization of silver, a measure bound to raise its market price, a woman on his staff was heavily buying silver futures with contribution dollars. The dummy corporations got up to blur Coughlin's responsibility for his later ancillary organizations—the National League for Social Justice, the Christian Front and so on—were as crooked as any devices that international bankers' lawyers ever dreamed up. He even had the effrontery to tell a correspondent protesting against the Christian Front's anti-Semitic violence that he refused to comment on "this organization. I have nothing to do with it." [80]

By 1933 Frank Kent called him "the most ... effective propagandist of the Roosevelt policies," remarking in wonder, "the first time a priest [has played] this role in this country." [81] No Protestant clergyman, neither Theodore Parker nor Henry Ward Beecher nor John Haynes Holmes, though all were renowned orators and meddlers in politics, ever wielded influence so wide. In view of America's chronic anti-Catholicism, recently so effective in keeping Al Smith out of the White House, it was an even greater wonder for a Catholic priest to be thus applauded by so many outside his own faith for gratuitously advising the nation on matters fiscal, international and social. Coughlin himself referred his acting as elder statesman to the two famous encyclicals—Leo XIII's *Rerum novarum* (1891) and Pius XI's *Quadregesimo anno* (1931)—in which the Papacy asserted the Church's duty to deal with social questions and its misgivings about the morality of capitalism's basic values. As Coughlin read them, they permitted any priest to promulgate to any society any advice that seemed good in his eyes.

The only member of the hierarchy, except the Pope himself, who could curb Coughlin's tongue was the admiring Bishop Gallegher. Now and again the Church press reflected rumors that the Vatican was uneasy about the situation. But nothing came of them, and the bishop never faltered. He once said publicly that had radio and Coughlin been available in Russia at the time, the Russian Revolution would have been prevented. Returning from a trip to Rome, where presumably he had discussed his rambunctious subordinate, he told the press, "It's the voice of God that comes to you from the great orator of Royal Oak. Rally round it!" [82] One who rallied was a factory worker in Geneva, New York, who happened to tune Coughlin in one Sunday in 1935 and was deeply impressed by what he said about the international bankers. That very night he met the Virgin in his sleep; she told him to go to Royal Oak to serve Coughlin. He secured the job of maintenance man at the Shrine of the Little Flower, in which capacity he came gradually to believe that his reverend employer represented Christ's second coming, a hypothesis apparently not too severely discouraged. The death of Archbishop Edward Mooney of Detroit, who had put Coughlin off the air in 1942, happened on Coughlin's birthday. He said to the awed maintenance man, "My Father has given me a birthday present." [83]

Late in 1934 his evident megalomania supplemented the Radio League of the Little Flower (payee for checks and money orders from listeners) with a National League for Social Justice open to all of any faith willing to pledge "to follow the example of Jesus Christ Who drove the money changers from the temple because they exploited the poor." [84] The manifesto laid down for its branches blamed all problems of the 1930s on "the harsh, cruel and grasping ways of wicked men who first concentrated wealth into the hands of a few ... then [pitted] state against state in the frightful catastrophes of commercial wars." Then a sort of Populist creed: "I believe ... that every citizen willing to work shall receive a just, living annual wage.... I believe in nationalizing the public resources ... too important to be held in the control of private individuals ... in ... a government owned central bank ... to maintain the cost of living on an even keel ... in the cost of production plus a fair profit for the farmer ... in ... the duty of the Government ... to protect [labor] organizations against vested interests of wealth and intellect ... in conscription of wealth [in event of war]...." It ended in this magnificent tangle: "I believe in preferring the sanctity of property rights; for the chief concern in government shall be for the poor because, as it is witnessed, the rich have ample means of their own to take care of themselves." A seven-clause codicil soon added was a skewed sketch of FDR's National Recovery Administration—"... there can be no lasting prosperity if free competition exists in any industry ... if necessary, factories shall be licensed, and their output limited ..." [85]—with a denunciation of strikes and lockouts that managed simultaneously to sound prolabor and recommend compulsory arbitration.

At this stage he was cozying up to Long, whose radio-promulgated Share-Our-Wealth movement (founded in January, 1934) and catchword "Every Man a King!" had much in common with Coughlin's ideas. Long was at least willing to be courted. His substantial following, strongest in the South and Southwest, complemented Coughlin's, strongest in the Old Northwest and the Northeastern Quadrant. The two egocentrics would probably have fallen out in the end. But at the time rational observers had reason to view this conjunction with alarm. The quiet doctor who killed Long for private reasons in September, 1935, did his country a great favor. He spoiled whatever interlocking plans came of Coughlin's many visits to Long's hotel suite in Washington. Thus forced to seek other allies and springboards, Coughlin explored Social Credit. He invited to Detroit both Dean Hewlett Johnson and Alberta's newly installed Premier Aberhart. Apparently neither persuaded Coughlin that Social Credit was a horse worth saddling. Within a few months he went back a square, broke with FDR publicly and abusively and put in motion what Long and he probably had in mind—an eclectic third party to mass the nation's fears and hates in a backlash against both New Deal and Republicans in the election of 1936. Its emotional foundation can be felt in Coughlin's remarks in late September, 1936: ". . . one thing is sure. . . . It is either fascism or communism. We are at the crossroads." He was asked which road he preferred. "I take the road of fascism," Coughlin said.*

Long's death took much of the bounce out of Share-Our-Wealth, but his second-in-command, a bull-voiced jackleg preacher from Dixie, the Reverend Gerald L. K. Smith, had kept way on the ship. For new momentum he threw in with the pitiful Townsend Old-Age Pension Plan recently arisen in California II, of which more later; it was millions strong. Further fuel lay in the bad feeling among farmers in the upper Midwest and Great Plains where old-timey Populism-isolationism was gathering new strength as the New Deal's measures failed to take hold out there; much of the area was still in Dust Bowl conditions. This diffuse but considerable force was informally gathered behind veteran North Dakota Congressman William Lemke, high in

---

* Geoffrey S. Smith, *To Save a Nation*, 47–48. The author goes on to suggest that in view of Coughlin's base in the blue-collar strata, his might be a "fascism of the left" like Perón's in Argentina. In the terms of Coughlin's time, of course, a Fascism-of-the-left was as fantastic a contradiction in terms as dry water; nowadays, however, it is worth pondering.

the neo-Populist Non-Partisan League and chief parent of recent federal laws meant to shield the farmer from distress foreclosure.

Mixing those three, like charcoal, saltpeter and sulfur in gunpowder, was supposed to make something explosive enough to enable Coughlin's National Union for Social Justice to reshape the nation with power and glory for all involved. Clumsily, warily, warily, the allies cobbled liaison together. On his national network and in the NUSJ's house organ, *Social Justice,* first appearing in 1936, Coughlin and his minor mouthpieces manned the National Union Party's chief propaganda machine. Had his birth in Canada not ruled him out, the nation might have seen its first Catholic cleric running for President. As it was, Lemke, as colorless as he was earnest, bore the standard. In sheer decibels Smith was the outstanding spellbinder. But in person on platforms, particularly at the separate conventions through which the mutually jealous ingredient movements ratified the alliance, Coughlin seemed almost able to rival him in corrosive clamor. Shucking his clerical coat and button-behind collar as though symbolically to renounce the virtues associated with his calling—or maybe to assuage the traditional dread of the Pope and his minions among prairie farmers, Dixie red-necks and Methodist old folks—he glowed and shone with sweat and hatred as he explicitly called FDR liar and swindler and whooped it up for a political Armageddon.

In November the theoretically powerful mixture fizzled miserably. National Union attracted less than 2 percent of votes cast and had only the slim consolation of coming in at least ahead of both Socialists and Communists. None of the participant movements was ever the same again. Coughlin had again and again promised audiences to stop broadcasting forever if the Lemke ticket got fewer than 9,000,000 votes. For some ten weeks he actually did go off the air, even though, he assured his public, Bishop Gallegher besought him to go on. *Social Justice* kept hammering away at the money changers in print under nominally separate direction. Then, in January, 1937, Bishop Gallegher died. It should have been fatal to Coughlin, too. American cardinals and the Catholic intellectual press in America had been hotly snapping at his heels of late. Now his indispensable shield and sponsor was gone. Making a fair wind of a foul one with an audacity that almost commands admiration, Coughlin made this catastrophe his pretext for going back on the air. That had been Gallegher's dying wish, he said. When the successor, Archbishop Mooney, tried to curb Coughlin's new broadcasts, he got such a storm of protests from listeners—and apparently little support from Rome—that he let the matter slide.

Thenceforward Coughlin put more and more pepper in the soup.

Was this from exasperation with defeat? Or a tactical awareness that he had to beat the drum louder to keep his audience? Or what a psychiatrist might see as a deepening of paranoid impulses that would probably have set in, defeat or not? Some of his doings had already been as unfitting as Gallegher's grotesque passivity. During the bitter battle over one of Lemke's farm bills in 1936, a good Catholic and very powerful Congressman, John J. O'Connor, was so irked by Coughlin's slandering of its opponents that he telegraphed: "You are a disgrace to my church ... please come to Washington I will guarantee to kick you all the way from the capitol to the White House with clerical garb and all the silver in your pockets you got from speculating in Wall Street...." [86] Coughlin's acceptance of the challenge was read on the floor of the House. No meeting occurred, however, even though Kid McCoy (Norman Selby), former light heavyweight champion, apparently an admirer of Coughlin, offered to fight O'Connor in his stead. At a news conference in the 1936 campaign a reporter from the Boston *Globe* challenged Coughlin's identification of Felix Frankfurter and David Dubinsky (of the International Ladies Garment Workers Union) as Communists. Coughlin snatched the man's glasses off and landed a solid punch before he could be pulled away. And in consequence of a radical crank's trying to scramble to the platform presumably to attack Coughlin at a Union Party meeting, he carried a Smith & Wesson .38 during the rest of the campaign.

Some of the added pepper came of letting the anti-Semitism always latent in *Social Justice* now boil over. "International bankers," Coughlin's favorite targets, had long been the Populists' mask word for Jews, as much of his public already understood. As the light grew stronger: "Avariciously and greedily they gloated over their pounds of flesh—their precious bonds, their dishonest dollars, their confiscated homes and farms—while Shylock-like they prated of financial rights in the ears of a prostrate nation.... Inflation, my friends, as interpreted by the Baruchs, Warburgs and the rest of them only begins when there are ... 50 cents in the domestic purchasing dollar!" [87] Time was when he had named the Morgan or Mellon interests along with the Rothschilds and Kuhn, Loeb to blame for all the world's ills, but now the cast was exclusively Jewish. Zestfully he endorsed the story that Kuhn, Loeb had fomented and financed the Russian Revolution, staffed it with Jews and now steered all of Stalin's evil doings. The boys selling *Social Justice* on the street were trained to start weeping bitterly and, when asked what's the matter, sonny, wail, "A big Jew hit me!" Coughlin's new "Workers' Council of Social Justice," a projected labor union promising to persuade the Ford Motor Company to supply its employees with consumer goods at cost, barred Jews—and, in a ridiculously transparent dodge to soften criticsm, also Brahmins and Buddhists.

As his broadcasts grew nauseating, first WOR and then his successor outlet in New York City, WMCA, dropped his Sunday program. Soon he had lost his outlets in Chicago and Philadelphia.... Though forty-six stations still carried him, none was west of Kansas or south of Maryland. Naturally he blamed this shrinkage on Jewish influence. That was at least a touch more plausible than the Kuhn, Loeb-Stalin alliance, for as it happened, the dominant figures in all three national networks were Jewish at the time. But as if to scotch any suspicion of respect for fact, *Social Justice* now republished the *Protocols of the Elders of Zion,* the threadbare forgery about the Jewish conspiracy to take everything over already so thoroughly exposed that even Henry Ford had to admit it was utter fiction.

About the Spanish Civil War, hot potato of the latter 1930s, Coughlin was rather slack. Like much of America's Catholic public, he sided with the Insurgents but sounded off about it less than the fashionable radicals on their side of the ideological street. He made up for it, however, by noisiness about other international issues as he spun toward the isolationist/Hearst/Fascist syndrome. He applauded Hitler's takeovers of Austria and the Sudetenland and Japan's mus-clings into the Asian mainland. He espoused the America First movement. After war struck Europe, he wildly denounced each of FDR's efforts to help the anti-Axis powers. Down to the day of Pearl Harbor he was accusing FDR as hotly as any of today's revisionists of deliberately teasing Japan into striking in righteous self-defense.

Pearl Harbor tore it, of course. Hoping to avoid divisive screeching while doing the needful, FDR's Attorney General, Francis Biddle, sent certain eminent lay Catholics to expostulate understandingly with Archbishop Mooney. For reasons some of which are obvious, some probably too Byzantine for lay surmise, Mooney obliged this time. He silenced Coughlin. No more broadcasts. No more *Social Justice;* actually it was about to lose its mailing privileges because of subversive content, the same thing that had happened to the radical *Masses* in 1918. The "ecclesiastical Huey Long," [88] as the Detroit *Free Press* described Coughlin, withdrew passively into his parish and stayed there. Now retired, he tells occasional interviewers that he regrets neither what he said and did in the old days nor his present inactivity. The psychological stamina—or muscle, or whatever it is—that this anticlimax implies is a formidable trait. Just as one cannot really think it altogether bad that Huey Long was eliminated, one can count

America lucky that Charles E. Coughlin was Catholic and born in Canada.

Those reproaching Canada for having fouled up the United States with the mephitic Coughlin need to be reminded about the contemporary born-Americans working the same side of the street. True, of indigenous proto- or quasi- or semi- or pseudo-Fascists of the 1930s only Long loomed as large as Coughlin. But the smell of the small fry, if less pervasive, was even ranker, and in fairness to the Church, note that all were Protestants, at least not Catholics.

For thumbnail summary lump them as the Shirt-smitten. Giuseppe Garibaldi knew not what he did when he deployed his renowned Redshirts in the cause of a liberalized and rationalized Italy in the mid-1800s. The imitative example of Mussolini's Blackshirts soon strengthened by Hitler's Brownshirts proved as tempting to America's dictator-minded crackpots as it did to Britain's Sir Oswald Mosley. The area around Atlanta, Georgia, sprouted an American Fascist Organization of Black Shirts that had nothing at all to do with Mussolini's propaganda, instead promised to make Dixie safe for white supremacy and had picked up 25,000 members at $1 a head when the Macon *Telegraph* denounced it as a misbegotten revival of the Ku Klux and blew it to smithereens. The Khaki Shirts were a side effect of the Bonus Army momentarily ominous but aborting in a few months. At the other extreme of elegance just then were the Gray Shirts, first Fascistic gesture of Philip Johnson, then finishing his first brilliant work at MOMA, not yet one of the nation's most renowned architects. A distinctly affluent victim of this infection, he designed for his few score adherents special-order shirts of gray Oxford cloth, button-down. Gray seems not to have been a dynamic color. He and Alan Blackburn, his colleague organizer, soon manifested their inner sympathies by offering their services to Long. He snubbed them. They turned to Coughlin, who made some use of them but never eagerly. Nathanael West's *A Cool Million* contained a Leather Shirt movement, alias the National Revolutionary Party, with a noisy leader named Shagpoke attacking "the Jewish international bankers and the Bolshevik labour [*sic*] unions." [89] George S. Kaufman and Morris Ryskind had good reason to weave into the highly topical *Let 'Em Eat Cake* (1933) a Blueshirt—not blue-collar—movement meant both to revive the sluggish needle trades and to set up a dictator in a renamed Blue House. The notion was so pervasive that even the War Resisters League, pacifist and radical as its name implies, made the tactical error of committing its well-meaning members to *green* shirts.

Eventually the most striking of such chemise-begotten groups was the Silver Shirts, strongest on the Coast and in the Northeastern Quadrant, though headquarters were in Asheville, North Carolina. "Strong" is misleading, of course. Under oath before the Dies Committee (US House of Representatives Special Committee for Investigation of Un-American Propaganda—hereinafter referred to as HUAC) in early 1940 William Dudley Pelley, its founder, said it had local organizations in only twenty-two states and over the seven years of trying had signed up only 25,000-odd full members. At no given time could the roster have been above 10,000—absurd in a national population of 130,000,000. Pelley was as strange a figure as any crawling out from under swastika-shaped stones in this decade. He was a known writer of folksy short stories and serials for the *American* magazine, which paid well. In 1929, while living in Altadena, California, he had an emotional crisis that culminated one night in his dreaming—only he knew it was no dream—that he died in his sleep and went for seven minutes to a chastely elegant next-world limbo, apparently designed by H. G. Wells and Pierre Puvis de Chavannes, where everybody he had known was walking about behaving in a fashion more charming and refined than their behavior on earth. He described it in an article for the *American* that brought a flood of mail from readers valuing this preview of the hereafter. It also made a changed man of him, he said. In token of change he turned to writing about the occult. That led to a correspondence school giving $60 courses in "metaphysics," meaning a diffuse spiritualism. He called it Galahad College and allowed the susceptible to buy $50 shares in its future. He also created the Galahad Press, publishing the house organ of his League for the Liberation of America (from Radicalism) and an even vaguer Foundation for Christian Economics.

Hitler's coming to power in 1933 seemed to Pelley to fulfill a complicated prediction that a woman-seer had vouchsafed him earlier. As soon as he heard of it over the radio, he announced the founding of the Silver Shirts, militant arm of his mystic starfish. Its members' uniform carried a scarlet *L* for Liberation. From Jewish dominance, of course. Pelley had none of Coughlin's dwindling diffidence about anti-Semitism. His bulletins to local branches said this month, "The Jews have the money but the Gentiles have the numbers. No matter what measures may be taken in the sacred name of preserving existing institutions, it will be a very fine thing in that hour not to be a Jew." [90] Next month: "The only man in Europe who understands the tie-up between Communism and the predatory elements among the Hebrews is Hitler. He is maligned in this country because Hebrews are determined the stark truth shall not be known and use every agency of publicity to disparage and vilify him." [91]

Four years before Pearl Harbor he called FDR's handling of Japan "wholesale defense of Jewish communism facing disaster in a world that has finally had its convincing demonstration of exactly what Jewish communism is. SHALL THE UNITED STATES GO TO WAR AT THE FANAGLING [sic] OF A KOSHER PRESIDENT TO MAKE THE WORLD SAFE FOR JEWISH BLOODGUT [sic]?" [92] He put Martin Dickstein, the Jewish congressman conspicuous in congressional harassment of groups favoring Hitler, at the top of a list of public figures whom, on coming to power, the Silver Shirts would consign to life imprisonment—with the same penalty for any who "shall interest himself in their liberation or work for their release." [93] The Silver Shirts' first meeting in New York City was held in German-dominated Yorkville jointly with the Friends of the New Germany, which soon became the German-American Bund. Several times Pelley made fumbling efforts to get direct or indirect financial as well as moral support from the Nazis.

There were also George W. Christians' White Shirts, alias Crusaders for Economic Liberty; and the Paul Reveres; and the American Vigilante Intelligence Federation; and George S. Deatherage's Knights of the White Camellia, another effort to revive the old KKK game; and the American Christian Defenders, founded by Colonel E. N. Sanctuary—some of these strutting fretters had very strange names—and Edmund James Smythe's Crusaders of Americanism, almost as anti-Catholic as anti-Jewish. In 1937, when Deatherage summoned leaders of such monuments to folly to meet in Kansas City to unite their powers in an American National Confederation, the Friends of Democracy, an organization watchdogging this sort of thing, had data on more than 400 in one or another phase—coming to birth, actively recruiting, aborting or turning into something else. So add the Clerical Reservists of Christ the King, the Honest Money Foundation, the Knights of the Flaming Heart and Purple Robe, the Order of the Blue Lamoo, Washington's Bodyguard and the World Alliance Against Jewish Aggressiveness.

The Friends of Democracy (FofD) was organized by the Reverend L. M. Birkhead, a Unitarian minister whose All Souls Church in Kansas City, Missouri, was known as the Liberal Center. He had helped Sinclair Lewis work up background for *Elmer Gantry* and learned Fascist-baiting as a leader in the fight to keep the Reverend Gerald Winrod, a prize Fundamentalist bigot, from getting nominated for US Senator in Kansas. In the late 1930s Birkhead operated in New

York City a useful clearinghouse for information—in the nature of things usually discreditable—about Shirtist and ancillary movements. On occasion it also did counterpropaganda and -organization. Thus, when Coughlin's Christian Fronters grew violent in the South Bronx and Brooklyn, smashing the windows of Jewish-owned shops, roughing up Jews on the street and so on, the FofD recruited neighborhood watchdog squads of responsible residents of all faiths to put the lid back on. Then a large, handsome Texan, Joseph E. McWilliams, found the Christian Front too watery and formed his own Christian Mobilizers, who specialized in street-corner meetings addressed by inflammatory goons from the tailgate of a Hollywoodish covered wagon drawn by white horses. Consequent anti-Jewish violence usually sent the FofD to City Hall, demanding a little more law and order and usually getting it. When McWilliams ran as an independent (the American Destiny Party was his label) for Congress in the heavily Teutonic Yorkville district, the FofD contributed to his ignominious defeat by saturating the area with leaflets giving the criminal records of his henchmen and describing his own cozy relations with the already discredited Bund. That affinity could, of course, be taken for granted. And McWilliams' guiding ideas, as he gave them to a reporter during this campaign, are a sound epitome of what ailed Shirtists:

> Adolf Hitler is the greatest leader in the history of the world. Herbert Hoover is mentally deficient. . . . Roosevelt is an amateur Englishman, a Jew and the leader of the Fifth Columns. . . . I intend to . . . run the government like a factory. . . . I may not be President but I will have absolute control. . . . I would ship all the Jews to some such place as Madagascar. . . . I look on every newspaperman as a prostitute. I have a blacklist of the worst ones and they will be taken care of. The newspapers and magazines will be run with a firm hand . . . a real free press. Once in power, I will down all dissident opinion.[94]

"Handsome Joe" said he had been something of a technology-minded inventor, and his "run the government like a factory" again brings in that slight odor of Technocracy. Several of the better-known Shirtist leaders were small-time industrial engineers, Scott-style, before their shingles began to loosen. To the credit of the US armed forces one should remark that the roster of these would-be dictators included no admirals and only one general, Major General George van Horne Moseley, USA (ret.), who could listen raptly when some freshwater Hitler came telling him he could be the American Ludendorff. It is not at all to the credit of the Fundamentalist movement that, as Richard

Hofstadter once pointed out, there were strong "historic links between the radical right of the depression ... and ... fundamentalism.... Many ... leaders of right-wing groups had been preachers, or ex-preachers, or sons of preachers.... Some ... associated with Billy Sunday ... later turned up as quasi-fascist agitators.... Gerald Winrod began as a crusading anti-evolutionist.... Gerald L. K. Smith was a minister's son and a preacher for the Disciples of Christ...." [95] Through their ungodly skilled use of radio, in which they almost rivaled Coughlin, as well as their lurid publications, such as Winrod's consistently noisome *Defender,* they made a deep mark on public consciousness, if not on formal political power.

Some of that may unfortunately have been the doing of well-meaning people seeking to discredit the whole deplorable crew. "In the short run," says Smith's *To Save a Nation,* "the liberal crusade against American fascism helped create in the national mind a domestic threat where none existed, stimulated the egoism of men like Pelley, and slightly augmented membership in groups like the Silver Shirts." [96] That needs some modifying. Coughlin and Long did have enough mass potential to constitute a genuine "domestic threat." But the likes of McWilliams, whose following the knowledgeable set at about 600, was quite another matter. Yet the FofD's cries of warning and the newspaper coverage ensuing made him sound like hordes of Assyrians coming down on the democratic fold. When HUAC finally got salt on Pelley's tail, it took it several days to manipulate him through his delusions and jugglings of money and inchoate alliances with like-minded, self-styled crusaders. The committee gave him a bad time of the same sort it gave suspected Communists and fellow travelers, and no liberals saw fit to protest that this ineffable living dead man's civil liberties were being infringed. But there he was in the spotlight, and for such as he any exposure is usually better than none. By the time it was over headline scanners from Key West to Seattle knew who William Dudley Pelley was and what he stood for; hence the tiny minority whom his gospel attracted were somewhat likelier to gravitate into his orbit or that of the next amateur Fascist who came along.

Consider, too, that though denunciation of Shirtist ideas was all very well, prolonged clamor about them might do harm by overalarming public opinion. This period was understandably jumpy. It was NRA sick-chicken time; Spanish Civil War time; court-packing time, hate-Roosevelt time, and all the while both Party-liners and reactionaries were shouting, with too little responsible correction, that it was now Marx or Mussolini-Hitler, no third alternative conceivable. So over-awareness of the Silver Shirts or Winrod was a propaganda advantage also for the Party-lining Popular Front. To any objection that such movements were feckless, tiny and friable, it was replied rather effectively that that's what they said about the Nazis in their early days. So it can't happen here. Famous last words! All power to the League Against War and Fascism! Any grumbling about its being a front for the Kremlin was just Tory sabotage. Somebody should have persuaded Coughlin, McWilliams *et al.*—and Congressmen Dickstein and Dies and the FofD*—that what they were variously doing might make it easier for the Popular Fronters.

The ill-advised antics of alien-inspired Shirtists probably also did much for the Comintern in the same direction. For once the chief clown was not Mussolini. His crass adventure into Ethiopia in 1935 was such a public relations disaster that the several sorts of Italian-American pseudo-Blackshirts seem to have been told to seek and maintain a very low profile. During the latter 1930s thunderously scowling pictures of *Il Duce* continued to decorate shops and offices in well-encapsulated Little Italys, but the rest of the nation saw little of them. As soon as Hitler gained power in 1933, however, the German talent for walking on others' feet with no notion it may be resented, which had so vitally affected World War I, revived in all its arrogant glory. To complete the resemblance, the first man sought out as pilot of the Nazis' interests in America was George Sylvester Viereck, inept storm center of German propaganda here in 1914–17. American-born, German-educated, single-mindedly devoted to *Deutschtum* right or wrong, confirmed in unrepentance by the revisionist climate of the 1920s, this time he tried to be skillfully modern in his assignment—to change the repulsive image that the Nazis had in the outside world, goose-stepping, Jew-baiting, mass-hysterical street brawlers.

On his advice the German government through state-owned railroads and tourist agency hired the prominent public relations firm of Carl Byoir & Associates to help mix the whitewash. As his plans developed, Viereck used funds from the German embassy to create a publishing house called Flanders Hall, which was to issue books and pamphlets making a case for the Third Reich, as clandestine support for the official propaganda clipsheet, which Viereck edited. Through him Germany also bought *Scribner's Commentator,* a struggling, no-connection successor to the old and august *Scribner's Magazine,* and set its American editors to making it the house organ of isolationism.

---

* At the time I was marginally involved in helping the Friends of Democracy make their case. In spite of the above considerations, I do not regret it. Never mind the accidental tactics and strategy, their instincts were civilized and their findings responsible.

Viereck developed cordial relations with hot-isolationist Senators and used their free mailing privileges to have sent out under their franking signatures speeches by Senator D. Worth Clark (Idaho), Robert M. La Follette (Wisconsin), Henrik Shipstead (Minnesota), Representatives John Rankin (Mississippi), Jennings Randolph (West Virginia) *et al.*; extracts from isolationist writings by Quincy Howe and Beard; and long passages from the official German White Book defending Hitler's invasion of Poland that were included in an isolationist speech that Viereck prepared for Senator Ernest Lundeen of Minnesota, who duly delivered it in the Senate.

The same effort at subtlety is evident in choice of front men. In 1915 the leading lecturer sent to persuade America that Wilhelm II's Reich was sole hope of world civilization and that, in effect, Belgium had invaded Germany, was Dr. Bernhard Dernburg, a high-ranking veteran of the German Colonial Service, in America as accredited representative of the German Red Cross. In 1934 it was a minor radio commentator, Douglas Brinkley—no relation of either David or Dr. "Goatgland" John—sent on a tour of the Third Reich and home to assure Americans, not in Dernburg's sauerkraut accent but good United States, that Hitler's Germany was "no longer owned by wealth and property, rather by character and work . . . has seen the end of the labor agitator who lives in luxury on the contributions of the worker . . . has placed a new dignity on labor." Its anti-Jewish measures were aimed chiefly at "the professions, which had become predominantly Jewish. . . . Many Jews [are] still doing business without molestation. . . ." [97] "In the years before the Nazi revolution positions of authority in government, law, the schools and the professions were coming increasingly into the hands of the Jews. Now Germany is being reforged for the Germans." [98] As for the other sore spots: ". . . more people [are] attending church in Germany today than ever before"; the inmates of concentration camps he visited were "uncomplaining"; and Hitler was "one of the great psychologists of the day . . . and [had] poured magic into the soul of his people and raised them from the dead . . . the only leader in Europe with the courage to save the whole continent from communism." [97]

The prelude to Brinkley's lecture in Detroit was "Die Lorelei" rendered by the local Young Heidelberg band. He was introduced by Fritz Julius Kuhn, a machine-gunner lieutenant in the German Army in World War I, now a chemist at the Ford Motor Company and stalwart of the Detroit branch of Friends of the New Germany. The stated purpose of this organization was to improve America's understanding of German doings. It went about this by studding Brinkley's audience with husky ushers in a black-tie, white-shirt uniform and by operating conspicuous summer camps where adolescents of both sexes from Nazi-minded families got military drill in quasi-Nazi uniforms led by the swastika flag and learned not only German folk songs but also the "Horst Wessel Lied" anthem of Nazi strong-arm squads. At the Friends' meetings of adult full members the most emphatically uniformed were the brownshirted *Ordnungsdienst* and the honor guards in full German Army kit. Their publications consisted largely of extracts in German as well as English from the homeland Nazi press.

Washington eventually protested to Berlin about this chauvinistic militia containing at least a majority of not-yet-naturalized German immigrants. The Friends were converted into a successor organization requiring American citizenship, or first papers, for admission. The new name, presumably chosen to allay uneasiness, was the German-American Bund! Kuhn quit his job with Ford to be its full-time *Führer;* his citizenship was vintage of 1933. The citizenship requirement disappeared as soon as the heat was off. Since a certain kind of militant Irish-American, reviving the terms of World War I, was concluding correctly that Hitler was likely to be the worst news for Britain since Napoleon, the rosters of the Bund, for all its Teutonic flavor, came to include toward 40 percent of members named Clancy, O'Toole, Riley. It collaborated eagerly with McWilliams because, as Kuhn said, "we sponsor [his ideas] 100%." [99] The number of youth camps modeled on Camp Siegfried at Yaphank, Long Island, and Camp Nordlund at Andover, New Jersey, doubled and tripled.

Inevitably, Kuhn found himself in HUAC's witness chair. His official position about the Bund's doings was that all were utterly consistent with Article II of its cynically hypocritical constitution: ". . . to uphold and defend the Constitution and laws of the United States. . . . To respect and honor the flag and institutions of the United States and to cultivate their lofty ideals." [100] For such another suit of ideological peacock feathers worn with equal impudence one turns to the Comintern's Popular Front slogan of the late 1930s: "Communism is twentieth century Americanism." Indeed, as the Nazis occasionally admitted among themselves, they were consciously following the Communist example. Just as the Popular Front tried to recruit Jefferson and Lincoln, so did the Bund make a great show of holding its 1939 mass meeting in Madison Square Garden on Washington's Birthday. It would take very clever casuistry to justify analogues between Camp Siegfried and Valley Forge, however, and Kuhn was not at all clever in any context. When being interviewed for a mass-circulation magazine, he asked the reporter Joseph Dinneen, "Are you an Aryan? You look Jewish." "I know," Dinneen said, "but, as it happens, I'm Irish." [101] "Who do you write for?" "The *American* magazine." "We don't read American magazines," Kuhn said. But rancid as the Bund's anti-Semitism was, it let Pelley outdo it. When he suspected a taint in an applicant for membership, he burned a lock of his or her hair and studied the ash to detect Jewish genes.

As for size, the Bund, too, was much-cry-and-little-wool. Once Kuhn spoke of a membership of 200,000 but, when pressed, admitted it was more like 25,000 enrolled members and maybe three times as many sympathizers supplying warm bodies and contributions of small change at meetings. The Federal Bureau of Investigation estimates never exceeded 8,500 members. Surveying the nation's ethnic enclaves for the *American* in 1937, William Seabrook, after studying St. Louis, Milwaukee and so on, as well as Yorkville, called "this Nazi stuff in America ... no more than a pimple on the face of German Americanism" [102] and analyzed German-Americans' opinion as 70 percent indifferent about Hitler, 20 percent actively anti-Nazi, only 1 percent strongly pro-Nazi. The evident purpose—to make the millions of German-descended Americans into a Fifth Column brake to keep America from helping anti-Nazi powers in case of war—was plainly nonsense. After World War II German files showed some pretty bitter comments about those renegades in the United States pretending to be just 100 percent Americans even though their names were Schmidt and Hauptmann. Yet public revulsion from the Bund did lead to demands for legal curbs. The American Civil Liberties Union duly pronounced existing laws adequate to check any serious getting-out-of-line and said that efforts to penalize "opinion or activities not associated with violence, coercion or preparation for violence ... would be indefensible in a democracy" and too useful a precedent for illiberal forces eager to crack down on labor and liberal movements. All the ACLU's *ad hoc* committee * could suggest was federal laws banning "private military forces and ... private military training." [103]

Indirectly, however, government managed some effective measures. In 1935 Pelley was convicted of fraud, conspiracy and violation of North Carolina's "blue sky law" by his freewheeling stock selling. Sentence was suspended, but that kind of wide publicity did his cause little good. New York State arrested and convicted Kuhn of embezzling some $20,000 of Bund funds; he justified this on "the *Führer* principle" that gave him prescriptive right to whatever he, as embodiment of the Bund, might need. The faithful screamed "Jewish frame-up," but his sentence, five years in the penitentiary, not suspended, was a hard blow to the Bund's prestige. Had he not thus come to grief, HUAC was about to ask federal indictment of him for perjury

---

* This admirable statement patently reflects the fact that the committee included little or none of the ACLU's then strong Communist element.

before it and failure to register as a foreign agent. For that matter, merely being summoned before HUAC, as Kuhn was several times, was in itself a minatory or at least cautionary penalty probably exerting a certain braking effect.

Mention of HUAC or "the Dies Committee" today usually connotes indecent bullying of dauntless liberals. Few remain aware that it sometimes exercised common sense and restraint; else it would never have given the ACLU a clean bill of health in spite of its having several known Communists on its board or got from the Reverend Dr. Harry F. Ward, ardently fellow-traveling chairman of the (Party-lining) League for Peace and Democracy, a voluntary admission that even though he was a hostile witness, he had not received any of the browbeating associated with HUAC. Further, it spent more time than is now remembered working over Shirtists *et al.* Geoffrey S. Smith's recent study estimates that some 25 percent of the committee's activity was directed at reactionaries. Running down the lists of witnesses at one or another HUAC hearing one finds higgledy-piggledy Anna Damon, national secretary of the (Party-lining) International Labor Defense; Wilbur C. Keegan, counsel for Kuhn; Joseph Cadden, executive secretary of the (Party-lining) American Youth Congress; report on Dr. Colin Ross (registered German agent, frequent speaker at Bund meetings). The treatment that J. B. Matthews, renegade fellow traveler and chief investigator for HUAC, gave to incommunicative Party-liners was no rougher than that given the likes of Deatherage and Pelley by Representative Jerry Voorhis (Dem., Calif.); or by Representative J. Parnell Thomas (Rep., N.J.), who eventually almost eclipsed Dies as a hissing and a byword among the best people.

One might even maintain that this failure to narrow its field in the 1930s, this tactless interleaving of flagrant Red and dirty Black, targeting both as obviously "Un-American," was one of the things that gave HUAC so lasting a bad name. It was dismaying enough to have turncoats like Matthews and Benjamin Gitlow describing the Party's infiltration game from the inside and publicly naming so many well-meaning and eminent persons as either snakes in the grass or round-heeled innocents. It gave an extra sting that these courthouse politicians on HUAC considered Earl Browder, Stalin's anointed, as just as septic as Fritz Kuhn, and the Park Avenue hostess of a party for the Abraham Lincoln Brigade as the same kind of chump as the Hartford heiress who sent such substantial sums to Pelley.

Pelley's organization in Los Angeles was hijacked in 1935 by his Coast viceroy, a minor soldier of fortune, "Captain" Eugene Chase, seceding in order to keep the pickings himself instead of sending them east. The Silver Shirts, Chase told an interviewer, needed several posts thereabouts: One "plays for ... what the Communists call proletarians.... Another ... for the nuts—the kind that go to fortune tellers and seances ... our mainstay ... there are more nuts in this part of the world than any place you can name outside of an asylum." [104] That was tactless. That "part of the world" was where Pelley had taken his momentous little trip into the beyond. It was also a generalization of a sort that, though tenable then and still today, needs responsible handling to keep the following discussion valid. Nothing subsequent means or is meant to mean that in the 1930s the emotional climate of California II was as eccentric and unstable as its detractors agreed it was. To say Sweden contains more beautiful blondes than Switzerland does not mean that practically all Swedish women are beautiful blondes or that Switzerland too cannot show a certain number of such. This is a question of relative incidence. Given that, the shady Captain Chase could rely on his assumption that the Los Angeles area offered an unusually large proportion of persons susceptible to cults, crank ideas and palaver about karma.

For sixty years observers have tried to account for this phenomenon. The usual hypothesis is that it has something to do with a disproportionate accumulation of retired old folks presumably lacking what they should do, hence giddily exploring the occult, the deliriously specious and the self-aggrandizing. There is probably something in that. Yet it does not explain why much of the same kind of old folks in much the same circumstances, also lacking emotional anchors, never showed the same vulnerabilities to the same extent in southern Florida. It might be attributed to smog, far more of a problem in Long Beach than in Fort Lauderdale; only the thing was notorious before internal combustion took over in California. On the chance that more than mere geriatrics is involved, Carey McWilliams, radical but knowledgeable and usually coherent critic of California II, tosses in the suggestion that some far subtler environmental element—doubtless analogous to the Delphic priestess' tongue-lubricating gas—nudges local settlers toward the suprarational and ecstatic. He adduces the allegedly demonic experiences of William Butler Yeats' wife, a known medium, during a visit to Los Angeles; D. H. Lawrence's relation there with a Rosicrucian sage expert on Atlantis; * Christopher Isherwood's succumbing there to swami-flavored asceticism in the desert.

Anyway, in the stumbling quest for orientation in the 1930s California II lived up to its reputation on a wider and lower level than that. It became the Land of Wild Swings *par excellence,* even the land

---

* Should this be credited to California I? The Rosicrucian headquarters shrine, their mail-order ashram, like something strayed from a minor world's fair, is at San Jose. But Lorenzo's case seems to have involved the catalytic climate of California II as well as the Rosicrucian sage.

where wild swings almost came true. Its tiny minority welcoming Shirtism were presumably those most given to paranoid impulses. Its Technocrats presumably shared an affinity for authoritarian *Gleichschaltung.* Neither group, however ugly, carried much weight. But Technocracy and probably emanations from *Social Justice* and Share-Our-Wealth did waft in infectious attitudes. And in at least indirect consequence there was astonishing weight in the End-Poverty-in-California movement, the Townsend movement, the Utopian and Ham-and-Eggs movements—all variously showing how pathetically vulnerable millions in Calfornia II could be sucked into one or another kind of cross between the South Sea Bubble and the Children's Crusade. In pondering this, add to the possibly halluci-nogenic climate the unsettling invasion of the Okies. Add the preda-tory ballyhoo artists who seized on EPIC, Townsendism and so on for pickings. The overheated local tradition of real estate and oil-stock rackets made sure that plenty of such talent was at loose ends in consequence of the Depression. But personalities also took a hand. It was, for instance, specifically unlucky that Upton Sinclair had trans-planted himself thither in 1919.

In loose usage "extraordinary" is a complimentary term. In the stricter sense at least here was an extraordinary man—a character out of Chekhov? Or Gogol? As chronic Socialist and temperamental sympathizer with the USSR, yet never exactly a Marxist, he was hard to pigeonhole. His salient traits were utter confidence that whatever he thought was first and last word on the matter, a sincerity of the same purity, minor delusions of persecution and a lifelong bad habit of writing prolix, jejune novels with social messages, exposés of journal-ism, the oil and coal industries, education. . . . He opposed America's entry in World War I but, once it came, supported it on the at least ingenious grounds that to get rid of the Kaiser would hasten the Revolution. The California motif appeared when he became a friend of Gaylord Wilshire, a dressy little man with a waxed mustache who made his pile in Los Angeles billboard advertising and real estate—hence Wilshire Boulevard—converted himself to Socialism, got into local hot water and went East to put his money into a Socialist magazine. Then he launched a gold-mining venture run on allegedly Socialist lines that soaked up much money from sympathetic readers.

While acclimatizing in California after World War I, Sinclair met George Sterling, then the ranking local poet, who interested him in Dr. Albert Abrams, a San Francisco savant who used an electrified box called an oscilloclast to diagnose disease by scanning blood samples. It determined, for instance, that Dreiser had tuberculosis and his mistress a sarcoma, but that, Abrams said rather airily, was really nothing to worry about. His chief interest was in syphilis, which he considered, in hidden or latent forms, the cause of most human ailments; one acquired it from polluted smallpox vaccine. The oscilloclast was also able to pick up data from one's handwriting, so Adams could tell what had ailed Edgar Allan Poe, Oscar Wilde *et al.* Sinclair wrote a fulsome piece for *Pearson's Magazine* declaring his complete confidence that Adams' was "an infallible method of diagnosing disease." [105] Syphilis-minded himself, he had violently denounced James Branch Cabell's conspicuous erotic fantasy *Jurgen* as likely to tempt youth into lewd behavior that entailed venereal infection. He was also, like many radicals of his time, a vegetarian, a teetotaler, an eschewer of tea and coffee.

As Sovietophile he interested himself in the visit to America of Sergei Eisenstein, the USSR's most renowned movie director, and encouraged him to produce a great social-minded movie in Mexico. To finance it, Sinclair shook down all available sources of good-cause money in the film colony and elsewhere, while Eisenstein went extravagantly on shooting film as fast as it could be procured, apparently no likelier ever to finish than Penelope was to finish her weaving. In the end all that came of it was bad feeling all around, a few short subjects and a cobbled-up editing of one theme of that huge quantity of film released as feature-length *Thunder over Mexico.* By then Sinclair had ample distraction from his celluloid adventure. He had run for Congress in California on the Socialist ticket in 1920; ditto for the US Senate in 1922; ditto for governor in 1924, never making much impression on the public mind. But now, in 1934, he was running as the regular Democratic nominee for governor, albeit on a platform that made Huey Long sound realistic and responsible.

California, particularly California II, had probably gone farther than any other state with the so-called self-help response to the privations of the Depression—of which a full account later. Sinclair's movement, casting him as shrewd, experienced and trustworthy social engineerspearhead, expanded self-help with trappings borrowed from Technocracy and Social Credit. Its slogan, "End Poverty in California!," gave the acronym EPIC—at home in the magnetic field of Hollywood, which had spread that noble word so thin. The glue that held EPIC together was Sinclair's omniscience and omnicompetence. There was nothing self-effacing about the title of his chief campaign document, *I, Governor of California, and How I Ended Poverty,* a sixty-page tract with the merest skin of fiction as lubricant.* Not that narcissist egos were scarce among the wild swingers of the day. Scott, Coughlin,

---

* Note that a year later Huey Long borrowed this device for his *My First Days in the White House;* thanks to his ghostwriter's giving good value, it was much livelier reading.

Long, Pelley were all ego trippers at bottom. But in California Sinclair's spelled-out fantasy took on such ominous substance that even many hardheaded observers wondered whether he might not make it to Sacramento after all.

I, Governor wrote: "I say positively without qualification ... we can end poverty in California. I know exactly how to do it, and if you elect me, I will put the job through—and it won't take more than one or two ... years." [106] Never doubt that, whatever impelled some of his lieutenants, Sinclair himself was Olympianly sure that his plan would work every bit as fast and well as he promised. After all, how could a brainchild of his not make sense? George Creel, also a veteran of pre-World War I muckraking, who had opposed him in the Democratic primary, complained: "Facts and figures were a disturbing and irreligious noise to which he closed his ears. [But] I could not attack Sinclair's sincerity, branding him a cheap demagogue playing on credulity ... he believed ... implicitly in his nostrums." [107]

EPIC promised a California Authority for Production to put the unemployed to work in factories that hard times had closed, their wages paid out of the proceeds of selling their output—shoes, shirts, nails or whatever—through publicly owned chain stores for a new state-secured scrip currency. A California Authority for Land would settle more unemployed on farmlands that the Depression had thrown out of use, to raise the dairy stuff, vegetables, fruits, cereals and so on (meat was rather played down) that CAP would process. Each farm colony would be a serene center of the Good Life with a community kitchen and laundry to spare women drudgery, a community day-care center so they could do more rewarding work, a free hospital, a hall for free lectures, concerts and culture-bearing movies—and all air-conditioned at a time when that amenity was largely confined to movie theaters and Pullman cars, a curious confession that at times the climate of California II was not quite all the Los Angeles Chamber of Commerce said it was. A California Authority for Money would issue bonds to back the scrip and finance heavy investment, such as the great water-management project in the Great Valley. Those working on it would be fed by farmers contributing produce for credit against eventual charges for irrigation water. Taxes would be lifted from those in low-income brackets, raised for others. But all would benefit from restoration to use of facilities that private owners had been unable to keep going. With the economic potential of the state thus pivoted on Production for Use, how could there fail to be Plenty for All? To a Sacramento editor who called it "wild, fanciful, chimerical. Neither [Sinclair] nor any other governor can keep such promises. And Upton Sinclair knows it," he loftily replied, "Upton Sinclair not merely does not know that he cannot keep his promises ... he knows ... quite positively that he can ... it has never occurred to me to consider any other possibility." 108

Exposing the weak spots was, of course, like shooting fish in a barrel. The bare beginning of such changes would annihilate the state's credit; how could major construction be financed? Sinclair relied on all right thinkers to withdraw their money from banks to buy small-denomination bonds: "Let your money work for you instead of against you!" 109 That would break the banks, he noted with relish, another step toward the day—within two years of his inauguration—when the old economy would crumble "like a rotten log" 110 under the attrition of the new and confiscatory taxes on private enterprise. Next, how could California, oil-rich but metal-poor, find the wide range of raw materials necessarily implied by so autarchic a program in a single state? And so forth and so on. But Los Angeles alone had 300,000 unemployed, nine-tenths white collar. Sinclair's frenetic propaganda so ably exploited their desperation-fueled will to believe that—doubtless the local crackpot climate helped—he beat Creel in the primary by 100,000. Going East to raise moral support, he secured endorsement from an assortment of serious thinkers, including Chase, Clarence Darrow, MacLeish, Dreiser, Ernst, John Haynes Holmes, and a warm welcome from Coughlin, who apparently got a gratifying whiff of mass panic from EPIC.

EPIC clubs arose by the hundreds, mostly in California II. *I, Governor* and sister tracts sold well enough to finance much of the campaign-to-come, enabling Sinclair to reject offers of lump sums with hidden strings implied. It is a backhanded index of how well California deserved its name for lacking sense of reality that his Republican opponents thought him as serious a threat as he said he was. The growing possibility that he would soon be making state appointments so appalled those in charge that they put through a civil service measure taking all but fifty-nine of the state's thousands of appointive jobs out of the governor's hands. As things looked worse, they went in for overkill, raising a huge war chest, and sought help from Hollywood, where studio heads were already saying that if EPIC came in, they would move the industry out of California. They shook their high-paid stars down for large contributions and filled the state's movie theaters with faked newsreel interviews with alleged out-of-state derelicts planning to start for California as soon as EPIC won,* and

---

* Sinclair had asked for this. To objections that EPIC would bring more and more job- and food-hungry people to California, his literature said it would—and a good thing too: "All persons will bring with them their heads and their

quavery old folks determined to vote against Sinclair to save their little homes from his radical taxes. Lord & Thomas, one of the nation's most renowned advertising agencies, was retained to flood the state with anti-EPIC literature, some of it forgeries purporting to come from Communist sources endorsing Sinclair, some of it—and this probably more damaging—massing genuine quotations from the flabbily foolish things that his books were so full of.

Flagrantly fighting crankism with crankism, Frank P. Merriam, Republican candidate for governor, endorsed both the Townsend Old-Age Pension Plan, which had recently got airborne, and Social Credit. Merriam won, but it was close. Had he not cultivated the Townsendites, had not several hundred thousand votes gone to a "Progressive" third candidate from California I, Sinclair might have won his game. It was not the kind of result of which one could say after all, the basic common sense of the grand old Golden State had responsibly asserted itself. That commodity existed but was usually in short supply at election time in the loose, personality-ridden structure of California politics. EPIC candidates took twenty-nine seats in the legislature. Several members of Sinclair's ticket went on to higher things. Sheridan Downey, his running mate for lieutenant governor—so the pair were caricatured as "Uppie and Downey"—ran 125,000 votes ahead of his much-maligned chief and eventually got elected US Senator by espousing Townsendism as soon as EPIC died. In this Townsendite phase Downey earned the undying reproach of having invented the term "senior citizen." EPIC also paved Cuthbert L. Olson's way to the governorship and Jerry Voorhis' into the US House of Representatives, where his literate liberalism made him conspicuous on HUAC.

Even more important was the demonstration of what Madison Avenue could do in politics if given its head. Ever since then the matter of what public relations firm a candidate hires has been almost as important as his track record. For there is no denying that what probably beat Sinclair was PR dirty pool supplemented by cynical manipulation. *Time,* no admirer of appealing crackpots, likened the ethics of it all to those of a big-city gashouse precinct. Revulsion from that unsavory fact may, however, be tempered by asking oneself to imagine what in God's name might have happened had Sinclair got elected. In view of California's chronic leaning toward vigilante values, guerrilla civil war would have been only one of several unspeakable results.

---

hands. They ... will produce the equivalent of what they consume. This will help to make prosperity in California. ..." ("Epic Answers," in *End Poverty in California,* 20.) That was particularly ill advised in a state just then feeling the first major impact of the Okies and Arkies.

For another qualification, Sinclair himself hardly comes out scathe-
less. His comment on defeat had a splendid condescension to it: He
said he had contemplated the possibility of being governor with "acute
boredom.... But I was prepared to go through with it; to give four
years of my life for helping the people of our State to peace and
security ... to put my own tastes and desires aside...." [111] It is not
easy to forgive him for not only knowing all the answers and knowing
he could make them work but also for tempting throngs of needy,
frightened people to take the appalling risk of letting him try to show
he could. The one reason for forgiving that would be the plea that he
couldn't help it; he was made like that. True, but treacherous: It also
applies to Hitler, Coughlin, Franco....

There was probably less ego, though as much California II, in Dr.
Francis E. Townsend, focus and matrix of the Townsend Plan, alias
Old Age Revolving Pensions, Ltd., the nightmare of legislators and the
object of wonder among economists of all persuasions. Few could
believe anybody would seriously propose it. This gaunt, demure
oldster had spent his first sixty years not exactly as a ne'er-do-well,
rather as a halfway misfit. Farm-born in Illinois, he drifted westward
as ranch hand and mine worker, salesman of cookstoves, hay dealer.
At the age of thirty-one he decided to turn doctor. In the sorry state of
American medical education in the 1890s an aspirant altogether
lacking college education could still acquire an MD in numerous
marginal medical schools that, though not quite diploma mills, taught
little and that badly. Townsend worked his way through and hung out
his new shingle in the Black Hills country of South Dakota. His
income from local practice was about as skimpy as his training for it.
After serving in the Army in World War I, he moved himself and
family to Long Beach, California, for its less exacting climate. Returns
were niggardly there, too, but dabbling in real estate on the side kept
him afloat. During the early Depression he had a steady-paying job in
the county health department. In 1933 a change of guard at the
courthouse deprived him of that.

The sudden bleakness of his personal prospects at the age of sixty-
six coincided with that of hundreds of thousands of other elderly
Midwesterners come to California for the climate and potential good
life—and now more or less resourceless. Banks failed; the bottom
dropped out of real estate; rashly bought oil shares were worthless;
mom-and-pop little businesses went broke; sons and grandsons back
home were out of work and could contribute nothing. Long Beach and
dozens of its sister communities in California II were a world of old
folks on their uppers. "... despoiled professional men, retired farmers,

skilled workers and small businessmen ... had exemplified the rewards of and belief in the prevailing system," says Abraham Holtzman's study of Townsendism, "... yet they were as hopelessly broken on the economic wheel as were their less fortunate brethren." [112]

Townsend's own—or a ghostwriter's?—account of what he did about it was that one morning in 1933 he saw some old women searching a garbage can for edible refuse and broke into a wild rage of pity and exasperation, causing him to vow to stop such miseries. It would hardly be strange if his own hopeless future had something to do with that emotional storm. Actually, however, the distressing hard-luck cases he saw in his county job seem to have set him pondering such matters a good deal earlier. Years previously in the medical school a Socialist of the classic American cracker-barrel stripe had instilled into his favorite student indignation against society's heartless shortcomings. Whatever lay behind it, late in 1933 he put his ideas into a letter in the Long Beach paper headed "A Cure for Depressions." At the time self-help was gaining momentum, Sinclair was cranking up EPIC and the Utopian movement was making its first gestures. Townsend's differed from all those schemes in being national in intended scope and providing a leaky sketch of Keynesian economics.* Money, he said, wasn't circulating healthily, and machines had cut down the number of jobs—hence the Depression. Uncle Sam could and should fix all that by paying everybody over sixty $150 a month on condition that he stop working and looking for work and spend it all in a month. A federal 2 percent sales tax would finance it. The ensuing flood of buying would restore prosperity.

Letters about it poured in. Long Beach's old folks, solvent or insolvent, were pleased to hear that they could save the nation by renouncing work for a basic livelihood of $5 a day, $10 for couples.

---

* The sources of Townsend's ideas remain matter largely of surmise. McWilliams (*Southern California Country,* 299) mentions the contemporary pension scheme of a Technocracy-minded Seattle dentist, C. Stewart McCord; Schlesinger (*Politics of Upheaval,* 32) says there is no evidence of any connection. Holtzman (*Townsend Movement,* 25) adduces the National Old Age Pension Plan of Los Angeles chiropodist J. E. Pope, who was gathering in many 10-cent memberships when exposed as a habitual criminal. Far the unlikeliest but also the most amusing possibility is that somehow Townsend saw in the slickly high-ticket magazine *Vanity Fair* (August, 1931) a piece spoofing Depression panaceas by Bruce Barton (of Batten, Barton, Durstine & Osborn, one of the ranking Madison Avenue advertising agencies). It proposed to retire every adult American at the age of forty-five on a pension of half his average yearly earnings at time of retirement. That would create "a special automatic class of Consumers.... The Farm Problem would disappear because farmers too would retire at forty-five. And one third of all present farms would be necessary for additional golf courses...."

Indeed, the tail of the scheme was soon wagging the dog. Mom and Pop couldn't wait to get their hands on that monthly check; yes, it would be nice if that incidentally took care of the Depression, too. Townsend abandoned the shreds of practice that had been his sole support and turned to promoting this genie climbing out of his bottle. To help him, he recruited a younger real estate man for whom he had once worked, Robert E. Clements. There is small reason to doubt that Townsend's motives throughout were primarily altruistic. His personal economic advantage, though welcome, was probably secondary. He did get more and more impressed with himself, but that might well happen to a previously obscure oldster so rapidly become folk hero of a million or so contemporaries. The Co-Founder, however, as Clements was known, was all too probably in it for pickings. He had no objections, of course, if the consequences of his able selling of snake oil actually did benefit the old folks and the economy.

The thronging believers were organized to circulate petitions to Congressmen demanding immediate action. The stipend was raised to $200 because, Townsend gravely explained, economics experts had set $2,400 as the critical yearly amount that, spent by 8,000,000 oldsters, would restore prosperity. The other explanation for it was that any less amount would "not permit the enjoyment of enough of the spiritual, educational and artistic features of life to bring out the really valuable traits of human character and make the most of our citizenship." [113] In August, 1934, while Sinclair was scaring the wits out of the Los Angeles *Times* and San Francisco's Market Street, the circus grew a second ring—the Townsend Clubs, 1,200 formed by the end of the year, 2,000 more by June, 1935. They spread coast to coast; least in the South, where few whites of any age wished to see elderly blacks get $200 a month, most in California II, of course, which remained the central nebula of a rather lopsided galaxy. After Merriam endorsed Townsendism, Townsend denounced Sinclair and EPIC as irresponsible deceivers and sinisterly Socialistic. The rest of the nation looked on agape. What with Long, Coughlin, Technocracy and the Communist Party, America could not complain of dearth of visionary nonsense and gullible wishful thinkers. But even so the national witches' brew was more dilute than this concentration of dim-witted fantasies in the part of the country where, as Frank Lloyd Wright once said, it seemed that the map had been tilted so all the low-grade people slid into the southwestern corner.

The Townsend Club members' pledge began: "The Townsend Plan WILL succeed. I therefore pledge my allegiance to its principles, to its founder, Dr. Francis E. Townsend. . . ." Following their small-town WASP traditions, they often held meetings in churches, and it was notable that their regional leaders, satraps under the Co-Founders, were mostly preachers by trade. Chicago's extraordinary Mayor Thompson, one of the alarmingly many politicians who cozied up to Townsendism, called it "the most Christ-like plan that has been conceived since the Crucifixion." [114] So it was altogether fitting that the songs they sang lustily were familiar, pertinent hymns from back home in Decatur: "Bringing in the Sheaves," "Then There Will Be Glory for Me" and their own exultant lyrics to tunes of traditional prestige:

> Onward pension soldiers,
> Marching as to war,
> With the plan of Townsend
> Going on before....

and:

> Mine eyes have caught the vision of our Dr. Townsend's plan,
> Which is sweeping o'er the nation, only as a good thing can....[115]

Their secular war cries grew more oldster-centered as time passed: "Youth for Work—Age for Leisure!" and "Honor Thy Father and Thy Mother!" They staged picnics, dances, church-basement sociables of the back-home-in-Iowa kind, whereby the movement acquired a secondary utility as occasion for interactions that insecure old folks needed. The Townsend publications often recorded marriages between Townsendites who had met and decided to go down the valley together in consequence of the movement. Logically its magazine carried many an advertisement of drugstores and mail-order nostrums to mitigate the physical shortcomings of age. The *Townsend Weekly,* private property of the Co-Founders, did so well from them that when Clements left in 1936, his share cost Townsend $50,000. One must not assume, however, that Townsendites were all elderly. One in five was middle-aged or less. The attractions seem to have been, first, that a cure for the Depression would benefit all age-groups; secondly, that to take 8,000,000-odd persons out of the actual or potential labor force would open up a considerable number of jobs for others. Add the thought that Grandpop and Grandmom really didn't need $400 a month between them,* so some of it might drip down in cash or kind

---

* Today, when Social Security payments to retired couples run well over $400 a month, it is strange to read critics objecting to Townsendism's 2 × $200 as more than adequate for many couples. This book mentions dollar data as little as possible because it is difficult to state them without gravely distorting differences in purchasing power between the 1930s and 1970s. But for an exception: Take it here that $400 in 1935 was—very roughly—equivalent to say $1,200–$1,300 now.

on favored grandchildren or, for that matter, middle-aged children. That would be illegal but likely enough.

The detail that makes one want to weep and swear is that as Townsend fever spread, furniture and department stores, automobile and real estate agencies in California II had to get used to shabbily dressed but smilingly excited old folks picking out the living-room suite or Dodge sedan they would acquire the moment Dr. Townsend got Congress to see the light. For was it not written in his printed gospel that the plan entailed increased demand for not only "beans and corn meal ... but [also] ... bath tubs, pianos and perfumes, overalls and satin gloves, electric refrigerators and automobiles"? [116] Lewis W. Douglas, FDR's first Director of the Budget and affluent politician from Arizona, said of it all: "... no more cruel hoax has ever been attempted on the American people." [117]

Some of the politicians in Congress and elsewhere who truckled to Townsend were probably remembering how the Anti-Saloon League had blackjacked the nation into Prohibition twenty years earlier and noting that Townsend & Clements' tactics and strategy were very similar. The ASL had conquered by organizing minority blocs of voters pledged to vote, regardless of party, for whichever candidate in a given election promised to vote Dry in Congress or state legislature and, more to the point, against any candidate who didn't. In states or districts where the two national parties were at all closely matched, only a few thousand such ironbound votes could and often did make a disastrous difference. So everybody knew what was implied when, in the mid-1930s, all Congressmen and Senators got questionnaire letters from Townsend's organization asking point-blank where their votes would go next time a bill establishing the Plan came up. Frank Kent estimated that thus the Townsendites held the balance of power in at least eight states, mostly Western. Among veteran politicians who considered themselves statesmen and yet found it advisable to butter up Townsendism was William E. Borah, the self-righteous senior Senator from Idaho. It is subtly interesting that whereas FDR could for a while stomach pretty close contact with Long and Coughlin, presumably to bolster Democratic power, he snubbed Townsend when he sought an interview. Apparently a mistake, this turned out well. The old gentlemen's consequent resentment led to that ill-starred alliance with Coughlin, Lemke and Gerald L. K. Smith. The snubbing from the voters that the National Union Party received started Townsendism downhill, and by the end of the decade it was just another clot of California II cranks.

It had always been even easier than EPIC to discredit. Pencil and paper showed that to pay $2,400 a year to the 8,000,000 who would probably apply would turn over some 40 percent of the national income to at most 7 percent of the population, or, as Nicholas Roosevelt, diplomat-journalist cousin of FDR, put it, it would equal the massed incomes of everybody in the United States who paid federal income tax. Lippmann best discredited the other aspect of the plan: "Dr. Townsend wishes to remove from productive labor a paltry 8,000,000 persons. When the depression was going strong, 16,000,000 persons had been removed from productive labor. It did not make us prosperous.... [Townsend] holds that if there were fewer persons working and if those who do not work spend more, the country would be richer ... then ... why not ... $10,000 pensions for persons over thirty? ... If Dr. Townsend's medicine were a good remedy, the more people the country could find to support in idleness, the better off it would be." [118]

"Dr. Townsend himself is not so significant as the importunate credulity he reveals in the American nation," wrote Raymond Gram Swing, liberal radio and magazine commentator at the time. He rightly saw that a good part of that was trauma from the Depression: "Six years ago, during good times, he could not have obtained 25,000 signatures for his plan." [119] Yet minor significances persisted after World War II made the Depression history. However flimsy or morbid, such movements usually leave residues. Long's noisome career left Louisiana with better roads and so on. EPIC showed politics the way to Madison Avenue. Townsend, Holtzman soundly points out, made "older people ... [see] themselves as a common-interest group ... a new group in the population," [120] a counterbalance for the Younger Generation of the Jazz Age that reconstituted as Youth in the radicalisms of the 1930s. That had more than a little to do with today's "retirement colonies" and glamorous-grandma advertisements. Townsendism also to some extent helped shape the New Deal's Social Security laws toward at least token old-age pensions. But nobody can ever know what would have happened had Grandpop and Grandmom been turned loose with all that cash. The only people over sixty to whom the plan brought ample regular income were Dr. and Mrs. Francis E. Townsend, drawing $250 a week (and expenses) at the height of the doings. And about the only difference it made for them was that now his clothes were noticeably of better quality.

In a column headed "California, Here It Comes" Pegler glumly expressed the mid-1930s version of chronic wonder at the Golden State's ideological capers:

> ... this region contains a very disproportionate element of used-up people who trooped in from everywhere, couldn't maintain themselves, and finally became a terrible problem. The cause is something fit to

rend your heart; but the effect has been crazy as a dream. Because they do live and they do vote, and ... they want to vote themselves rich, vote themselves young. ... [Society should] establish beautiful reservations for old people in southern California ... instead they are left to scratch for themselves and to be played for chumps by dumb or wicked Mahatmas who promise them everything and, of course, have to pay them off in regrets. [121]

In some ways Sinclair and Townsend might well seem dumb but wicked only inadvertently. What Pegler probably had in mind at the time was the contemporary Utopian movement competing with EPIC and Townsendism. For whereas the thimbleriggers climbed on board EPIC and Townsendism only after they were under way, the Utopian Society was promoter-spawned to begin with under circumstances strongly suggesting undiluted opportunism.

Actually the Utopians were first in the field, born in the feverish summer of 1933 months before Sinclair registered as a Democrat and Townsend wrote to the newspaper. Its three fathers were all jobless: one a self-styled promoter, the second a bond salesman, the third a former stock salesman for the Julian Petroleum Company bubble, the bursting of which in 1927 had been to California what Florida's real estate crash of 1926 was as dress rehearsal for Depression. Their first plan was not too promising: to form another of the lodge type of secret fraternal order with emphasis on insurance advantages. It would have the usual rigmarole ritual, regalia, secret grips, passwords and see that, while alive, the right worshipful brother or sister got social life at regular lodge meetings and, when dead, a decent burial. The recruiting method was the innovation: Each of an original group of ten members would in turn form another group and so on in galloping chain-letter-style progression. Even if it took a month each time to recruit ten, that process, if unchecked, would have signed up every soul in California in six months.

Though the snowball reached no such diameter, the device was useful. But what really blasted the scheme into the stratosphere was injection of the Plenty-for-All psychology then so pervasive. The chosen name, the Utopian Society, proclaimed Sir Thomas More as one ancestor. Others were the Plato of *The Republic* and Bellamy of the perennially fecund *Looking Backward.* There is internal evidence that somebody had seen Mrs. Martin's *Prohibiting Poverty.* Strikingly like her cooperative commonwealth, Utopia was to be a completely production-for-use economy, generously educating all "minors" from birth to age twenty-five, working everybody between twenty-five and forty-five at agreeable tasks with short hours that supplied everything needful and retiring them after forty-five to live the Good Life ad lib.

Something for Youth, even more for their elders, no real need for sweat in between—the appeal was that clear and simple.

The promoter trinity had so little money they could not hire a hall. The first meetings were held in private houses. But the initiation fee was $3, dues 10 cents a month. As members flocked in—the rate of gain was presently 5,000 a week—cash became gratifyingly plentiful, and Utopia could afford to hold its mystic initiatory rites in a 7,000-seat auditorium. Within a year it could afford the Hollywood Bowl for a public propaganda meeting, and there was small reason to doubt the official estimates of 600,000 members paying dues.

The feature of initiation was a dramatization of Plenty-for-All economics that Creel likened to a medieval morality play. It also bore a suspicious resemblance to the holy shows that the Reverend Aimee Semple McPherson staged to promulgate her Four Square Gospel in her Angelus Temple in Los Angeles, though Sister would never have put up with the Utopians' collectivist ideas. Their curtain rose on a counter piled with loaves of bread, behind it a "fat, oily creature exuding avarice from every pore. [Enter] a mob of women and children dripping rags and begging him to save them from starvation." [128] But they have no money, so the Food Merchant rejects them, shouting that all he cares about is profit. Next the Clothes Merchant, presiding over shelves piled with garments; he brutally rejects the needy on the same grounds. Then the Moneylender. He will supply money, but only if the suppliants let him load them with chains signifying interest. Soon Food Merchant and Clothes Merchant enter, also ragged and in chains, for they too have fallen thrall to the predatory Moneylender.... Blackout, and then a spotlight picking out a luxuriantly whiskered Hermit Reason, who promises to strike off the chains and lead them all to "the Land of Plenty where everybody produces what he uses and uses what he produces." [122] Now the neophytes were ready to learn the grips and secret signs.

On the night when Carey McWilliams attended such an initiation the sample neophytes were a small businessman, a woman physician, the manager of a lumberyard, a marine engineer, a carpenter, a barber and two muncipal clerks. To him the membership seemed "overwhelmingly ... white-collar lower middle-class," the same stratum, unusually thick in California II, to which EPIC simultaneously appealed. In fact, the Utopians probably did the Republicans an inadvertent favor by siphoning off funds and energy that Sinclair might otherwise have had. The consonance between the two was so close that when EPIC came apart after defeat, so did the Utopian Society because, in McWilliams' view, "The promoters ... never did seem to know just what to do with ... the phenomenal enthusiasm they had aroused." [123]

For the moment that left exploitation of California II's appetite for wild swings to Townsendism. But the field was too rich for monopoly to go unflawed. A fast-talking young man, Robert Noble, who had been a minor EPIC missionary, was now doing news commentary specializing on political corruption for KMTR-Los Angeles. He considered Professor Irving Fisher, august father of such monetary radicalisms as "the commodity dollar," his mentor in economics but was likely aware of Townsendism too when he laid before his radio audience a scheme for fixing everything by paying everybody over the age of fifty $25 every Monday. The instant popularity that ensued was his undoing. He sought help handling it from Willis and Lawrence Allen, minor specialists in ballyhoo. They saw vast opportunities in his Payroll Guarantee Association, as Noble called his scheme. Local politicians resenting his growingly bitter attacks supplied the Allens with a police captain who engineered a corporate *coup de main* that deprived Noble of both his radio program and his brainchild. The Allens moved implacably into both. Noble went spinning into space. When he returned a few years later, it was to make himself so intemperate in opposition to World War II that the federal authorities got him convicted of sedition and the state authorities ditto for violation of the State Subversive Organization Registration law. A young man born to trouble.

Meanwhile, the Allens were flourishing with two new slogans for their hijacked movement. The first, "Thirty Dollars Every Thursday!," raised the sights and ran trippingly off the tongue; the second, "Ham and Eggs!," * was even more successful. Its speakers prefaced their spiels with a shout of "Ham and Eggs!" like a Nazi's "Heil Hitler!" and back from thousands of throats resounded: "Ham and Eggs!" Mass meetings, pressure on politicians, sociables for the elderly, huge folksy get-togethers in parks on Memorial Day and the Fourth of July—the familiar pattern. Control of KMTR allowed the Allens effectively to ride the airwaves with screechings about predatory bankers and feverish begging for contributions to the great cause. Inevitably Downey and to some extent Olson got into this act too. For its first eighteen months the movement had no discernible program, just hysterical success in growth and noise. Eventually a local disciple of Father Divine provided the germ of a fantastic expansion of the

---

* This seems to have originated in one of the Allens' hired spellbinders telling an audience that when he and his boys were through promoting Thirty Dollars Every Thursday the notion would be as familiar to all Americans as ham and eggs. Subliminally its success may reflect yearning for a time when old folks could afford ham and eggs whenever they chose—as at that time many certainly could not. But it is fruitless to try to account for it in any intelligible way. This was, after all, California II.

perishable-scrip idea: All unemployed over sixty to receive every Thursday thirty $1 "state warrants" that, to remain valid, had to have a 2-cent tax-stamp stuck to it each week it remained unspent. That is, unless the holder spent it within a week of getting it, it would gradually lose value until in fifty weeks it was worthless. Such warrants would be legal tender for all state taxes. Their basic financing would consist of a 3 percent gross income tax on all persons, corporations and so on.

By mid-1938 Ham and Eggs was taking in $750,000 a year from the faithful. Much of it stuck to the Allens' fingers. They secured more than 750,000 signatures on a petition to put Thirty Dollars Every Thursday on the ballot as an "initiative" measure—legislation proposed and directly voted on by the people. Some 2,500,000 Californians voted on this proposal. Some 43 percent, better than two out of five, actually voted yes. The next year the Ham and Eggers, more numerous than ever and better skilled in ballyhoo and arm twisting, pulled out all stops. By August they had the state in much the same state of delirium that EPIC had achieved and—a newly sinister touch—the revised proposal to be voted on gave the administrator of the scheme something like dictator's powers over the whole state government. This time it was not only conservatives and reactionaries who closed ranks. Wonderingly Robert Glass Cleland, that very level-headed historian of California, describes how "Harry Chandler [of the reactionary Los Angeles *Times*] and Upton Sinclair saw eye to eye; Carey McWilliams and William Randolph Hearst stood in the same group. ...."[124] Sinclair, usually so ready to believe others' nonsense, took to radio to denounce Ham and Eggs on the undeniable grounds that "it would not work ... [would prove] a cruel hoax"[124] on those hoping to benefit and—watch this one whiz past—destroy small business.

The Allens timed their agitation to peak in August, when, they thought they had reason to believe, Governor Olson, presumed strong friend of tottering Townsendism and the defunct Utopians, would set a special election for the initiative. Actually he set it for November. That gave the eclectic opposition time to bring its guns to bear while Ham and Eggs slipped down from the peak of momentum. This time only 1 in 3 of almost 3,000,000 votes said yes. Ham and Eggs went into the garbage. Not even fetching in Gerald L. K. Smith to inject anti-Semitic pepper halted the decline. But even that cannot be ascribed to an excess of common sense; rather to Olson's finesse—if no worse term applies—and to the distractions and new jobs consequent on the approach of World War II. It was still amazingly true that 993,000 adult Californians—about the equivalent of the entire population of Cleveland, Ohio, at the time—had still voted for Ham and Eggs after a year of responsible public education to think it over in. In the land of the Doasyoulikes one lies under shady trees all day while little roast pigs run about within reach squealing, "Eat me, eat me!"

The Ham and Eggs try for a dictatorship was only one of several ways in which California heightened the fashionable fear lest America go Fascist that Communist propaganda found so helpful. The Associated Farmers' pick-handle response to labor organization among migrants; the crude blackjacking of EPIC; so much specially resourceless despair among the upper-blue- and lower-white-collar strata who in Europe were most vulnerable to Black- and Brownshirtisms; the local tradition of freewheeling, *ad hoc* political movements temporarily taking over and elbowing aside the friable existing parties—such symptoms were likely alarm signals supplementing epidemic looniness. The most lurid expression of this uneasiness came toward the end of the decade in Nathanael West's *The Day of the Locust* (1939). Its witless, sadistically prurient crowd gathered outside a movie premiere at Kahn's Persian Palace Theater in Hollywood tear themselves apart in a pointless riot that completes the artist hero's notion of his great painting-to-be of "The Burning of Los Angeles," celebrating those "who come to California to die; the cultists of all sorts, economic as well as religious ... who can only be stirred by the promise of miracles and then only to violence. A super 'Dr. Know-All Pierce-All' had made the necessary promise and they were marching behind his banner in a great united front of screwballs and screwboxes to purify the land. No longer bored, they sang and danced joyously in the light of the red flames." [125]

West's further description of the projected masterpiece could be a typical ideology mural of the school of Rivera-cum-Federal Art Project. Its point here is that, as Richard Gehman suggested in 1950, West used "Hollywood as microcosm ... [had like] other writers since ... discovered that everything that is wrong with the United States is to be found there in rare purity.... The lesson is clear: the life [Americans generally] are living ... is the kind best suited to kindle authoritarianism and wild mob rule ... it should have been evident that [West] was a reflector as well as a prophet, but ... nobody seemed particularly frightened ... or even much interested." [126]

This contention, that California is America handily distilled down into epitome, is indeed familiar and, as Gehman implies, no particular contribution of West's.* Maybe thanks more to European observers

---

* Gehman also expressed the long since fashionable opinion that this is "the best book to come out of Hollywood." (*Locust,* intro., xix.) A tenable evaluation though, in different and very possibly superior ways, Harry Leon

than to natives, though common among them, too, it has become a cliché in a limited way. Some of its validity, such as it is, comes of the Californian innovations permeating the rest of America, some long ago, some since World War II: allowing the automobile to smother public transportation; the shopping center; the shelterless gas pump; the neon slum of grotesque gimmicks that some now profess to admire; "patio living"; the ubiquitous swimming pool; pink axle grease for "French" dressing, but on the plus side consider also the acceptable practice of serving salad as first course. Beyond that the observation is not even visibly sound. I recall a pair of California-born and -reared sisters making their first trip east in the 1930s who complained about the stuffily luxuriant greenery of the Pennsylvania countryside. They were homesick for a sparsely vegetated landscape that stayed a proper tobacco brown ten months of the year.

The cliché may have originated in the European observer's perceiving that Los Angeles County was what the movies and the *Babbitt* kind of book had told him America would be like. Here are wheels within wheels. Nobody sought consciously or unconsciously to imitate George F. Babbitt. But the immense cultural effect of the movies on what America wore and did with its leisure and libido had long since been infecting the rest of the nation with what Hollywood thought America was like. Clark Gable wore no undershirt in *It Happened One Night;* from Key West to Eastport to Seattle sales of undershirts fell off. Marlene Dietrich reaps publicity from her liking for wearing slacks? Slacks become and remain a fluctuating but never extinct part of American women's wardrobes. Very well, why not? Only the trouble was that movie backgrounds and modes of behavior have also been influential, and those creating them, the controlling minds of Hollywood and the second echelon that implement their orders have always been, as Gilbert Seldes pointed out, "nearly all of them ...

Wilson's *Merton of the Movies* and Budd Schulberg's *What Makes Sammy Run?* are also in there. West's work does try for important, not to say pretentious, values, sometimes not unsuccessfully. But from a literary point of view it may be most notable as a leading example of a kind of novel now widely produced and almost always by writers who, like West, served in Hollywood's author stables—written as if turned into conventional narrative from a shooting script to be published in paperback or an old-time fan magazine. His text is compact but not terse. The characters' actions are on-set business described for guidance of director and actors. The dialogue is sound-track style. The run of narrative seems lumpy and skimpy to the reader of the printed page but would translate well into film footage. Another well-known example would be James Norman Hall's *Lost Island*. This often comes of the writer's having sale of movie rights in mind. In some cases it may be due to long immersion in scriptwriting.

[men] with no great knowledge of the people in the world round them." [127]

For lamentable consequences see a cluster of movies released in the decade after World War II: *The Best Years of Our Lives, A Letter to Three Wives, What Happened to Harry*. Harry's Vermont and Vermonters were as much like the real things as Oscar Hammerstein II's *Oklahoma!* was like the land the Okies came from; maybe the other two reflected life among the middle-income brackets in Riverside, California ... and it is probably just to attribute those shortcomings to the encapsulation of the movie industry within 100 miles of Hollywood and Vine. But how was the innocent European to know? Particularly when even so conscientious and shrewd an observer as Leo Rosten tells him, carrying it one involution farther, that "The aberrations of our [American] culture are simply more vivid, more conspicuous, and more dramatic in Hollywood [narrowing it down from California, even down from California II] than in New Bedford or Palo Alto." [128]

A curious consequence from the equation "California = America" was to set Hollywood's upper-income stratum—writers, actors, director-producers in diminishing incidence—to playing Party-lining games in the late 1930s. Like West, most of them were migrants from Back East, hence likelier than long-term residents to be dismayed by the at-first unfamiliar local vagaries. Doubtless it heightened their uneasiness to be half-incredulously drawing high salaries and living easy lives to which they had not been accustomed as newspaper reporters, Broadway press agents, slick-magazine fiction cookers, struggling novelists or playwrights, stage juveniles and ingenues often "at liberty," and all the while it was difficult for any but the most callous not to be aware of the Okies' and the old folks' plight. Those thus newly affluent who let the studio heads shake them down for the anti-EPIC war chest had special cause to feel troubled. As the decade lengthened, these same studio heads hired from Back East committed Party-liners such as Lawson, Donald Ogden Stewart, Dashiell Hammett prone to become dutiful foci of Party-lining in the heavy-sugar ghettos of Beverly Hills. Now if it was true that this sordid, hysterical, inhumane California II was, as so many impressive persons averred, the essential America, that made it far easier to despise and yearn violently to purge the whole system that produced it. The highly understandable anti-Fascist impulse also furthered what was primarily misanthropy sweetened with modish clichés and bad financial conscience. Ah, those long, lazy talks about come-the-Revolution around the electric-lighted pool!

The immediate dividend for the Party was the heavy support in sympathetic publicity as well as money that Hollywood's radicalized stratum gave the Loyalists in the Spanish Civil War—of which more later. The size and weight of this were overplayed after World War II by HUAC as it made headlines pillorying writers, actors, directors *et al.* who had been either card-carrying members or ardent fellow travelers. In many such cases the propaganda demands of a war in alliance with the USSR had beguiled enthusiasts into the illusion that discretion was pointless, the honeymoon had such momentum that it would never end. But to refer to exaggeration does not mean that the infiltration had not been real. It was very much so and on a scale that would never have been tolerated had it been aimed at benefiting Fascism.

The Fascistic element in America's can of worms of the 1930s had its major propaganda triumph, however. It exploited the prestige of Charles A. Lindbergh, Jr., as leading edge of the isolationism that worked so much to the Nazis' advantage. They could not plume themselves too much on it. It was American in origin, Midwestern in a tradition already powerful long before anybody but Hitler's company commander in World War I had ever heard of him. But from Berlin it could doubtless be made to look like a clever leapfrogging across the Jew-dominated Eastern Seaboard and the Slav- and black-infested industrial centers of the Old Northwest into the purer air of the indrawing, Nordic-strong subculture west of Chicago. This region, not so readily defined as California II, had deep-rooted functions as the nation's breadbasket and butcher shop. Another of its special traits—a chronic reluctance to look beyond its own confines—is illustrated by the strange things that happened to Lindbergh.

Recounting this story is a depressing task. It involved so much undeserved personal agony and consequent understandable bitterness. It is one of those stories, like the mutiny on the *Bounty* and Joan of Arc's career, apparently created by a good but cruelly brutal novelist or playwright working not in words but flesh and blood, with real, not rubber, daggers, careless how grievously one or another episode in his scenario tore and maimed a participant or two.

The great aviator's father, Swedish-born Charles A. Lindbergh, was a burly, good-looking, self-made Minnesota small-town lawyer and Populist (= Non-Partisan League) politician who had several terms in the US House of Representatives. He hated banks, specially large Eastern banks that monopolized the money supply and crucified the farmer on a cross of mortgage credit that had to be repaid; railroads that took first bite out of what the farmer got for his wheat regardless of the going price; manufacturers who set arbitrary prices for the machinery, apparel and fertilizer that the farmer had to have while prices of what he raised fluctuated. Adrenaline-fueled heat like that was what made his movement a force to reckon with in his country just before and for a good while after World War I. For a great many Scandinavian, German and Bohemian farmers felt the same way.

So, for that matter, did many of the region's equally put-upon WASP farmers. But this was at bottom a first- or second-generation immigrant's party. The WASPs' background lacked two of the others' emotional patterns: The former Scandinavian peasant or his New World-born son usually retained some of the peasant's special mistrust of townward institutions. Nor was this mere economic wariness, as among farmers named Smith. It also carried a sense of immutable social caste that took a few generations to slough off. One of the most significant talking points of a Norwegian leader advising his country-men to go to America 100 years ago was that in the new country a farmer entering a shop in town *needn't take off his hat unless he felt like it.* Another weighty reason why such peasants uprooted themselves was that to do so relieved them of the old country's military conscription that took young men away from home at ages when they were most useful. Hatred of that and of the potential war implied was pandemic. Any time government might start a war that meant not only depriving the household of the boy's services but doing so permanently by getting him killed. So government, any government on the national level, was sinister. This was pacifism but not of principle—a pacifism of recalcitrance.

Few of Congressman Lindbergh's constituents can have been sur-prised, then, by his bitter following of the antiwar line from 1914 on through World War I. Europe's catastrophic ordeal was just what, in his view, persons of good sense hoped to stay away from. And his other ideas fitted in: He postulated a distant big-city "inner circle ... of money sharks" [129] conspiring to tempt Americans to travel in foreign ships that German submarines would sink, thus inflaming public opinion and tricking America into an alien war to ensure fat profits for Wall Street from sales of munitions and floating of war loans. He denounced the Red Cross as basically a tool for entrenching America in the European economy after the war. Doubtless he really believed all to be gospel truth. The book in which he set forth these and other ideas of comparable tenor Uncle Sam suppressed not because its content was transparently paranoid—though it was—but because it damaged the war effort, which it probably did to whatever extent it exerted influence.

In 1902 his second wife, a strong-minded WASP schoolteacher, had borne him a son who grew up as handsome as his father but in a James Stewartish rather than the sire's Clark Gableish way. It was not an ideal marriage. The lady lived apart from her spouse as much as she could, coming to Washington with the boy only just enough to keep up an impression that the gentleman from Minnesota's home life was conventionally harmonious. Her crankish abstention from tea and coffee, cola drinks (and tobacco and alcohol, of course, not respectable for women where she came from) rubbed off on Charles, Jr.; he had tried them all, he told people later, disliked them and thought himself better off physically without them. Imperturbably he kept to those abstentions throughout his early career among raffish barnstorming fliers; as for girls, he wouldn't go to movies supposed to be at all sexy. His father's influence was probably more diffuse but real in the long run. A born mechanic, the adolescent boy took charge of the family Model T and, driving the Congressman to many a political meeting, heard a great deal very emphatically stated about international bankers, foreign entanglements and vested interests.

Like Frank Lloyd Wright, who later blowsily endorsed his isolationism, * young Charles soon left the University of Wisconsin for more interesting things—mainly flying, just then taking on widely among civilians after great expansion in World War I. Exulting in his mechanical genius, perfect reflexes and 200-proof courage, "Slim" Lindbergh was an air cadet, barnstormed, flew airmail. . . . In the late spring of 1927 he made his blazingly famous solo flight across the Atlantic, continent to continent, west to east. Furor, not to say apotheosis, ensued, and why not? The lone barnstormer getting ahead of more elaborate rivals; the Sunday hiker's commissary of lunchroom sandwiches; the engagingly diffident landing at Le Bourget. . . . The whole world already knew his name and had been hanging on the radio ever since he had been signaled making the coast of Ireland on course; the tall, relaxed good looks. . . . This Paul Gallico story illustrated by Norman Rockwell was a timely coup for Uncle Sam's public relations, then badly corroded by international bickerings about war debts and the capers of American tourists high on devaluated currencies. Indeed, the consequent relaxation of strain between France and the United States is often credited with making straight the way for consummation of the Kellogg-Briand Treaty.

---

* ". . . a square American. I sent him the following telegram: 'We knew you could fly straight, but now when everything is equivocation and cowardice you not only think straight but you dare speak straight.' . . . And this goes for his brave little wife." (Frank Lloyd Wright, *Autobiography*, 500.) In view of the modern use of "square" this is an amusing and accurate double entendre.

Fetched home in triumph in USS *Memphis,* Lindbergh was ticker-taped in New York City, launched into a highly lucrative career as consultant pathfinder for Pan American Airways and presently married Anne, daughter of Dwight Morrow, the statesmanlike Morgan partner then US ambassador to Mexico. One cannot know how Charles A. Lindbergh, Sr., would have taken this connection with the banking house that for him and millions like him meant predatory fat-cattery. But it is certain that marriage to this book-intelligent, gently reared, shy and generously loyal heiress gave the young hero just the helpmeet he needed. After arranging that, however, fairy godmother flew away. Luck ran out. One man had already predicted it. On that evening when everybody was talking about the great flight, the headlines thick with LUCKY LINDY, I was in the same room with that great federal judge Julian W. Mack. He listened to all the gurglings and said, "The best thing that could happen to that young man is that he tries to fly back and doesn't make it."

How cruelly the luck had run out was not altogether evident until the gratuitous, ingeniously brutal kidnapping-murder of the Lindberghs' first child. But this was connected with the story-so-far. A certain kind of disturbed personality yearns to make a mark on the very famous. Add wealth to the bait; it promises a kidnapper immense gain to compensate for his insignificance and signify his revenge on the fortunate. In those terms the crime to some extent resulted not too indirectly from the universal adulation of Lindbergh, a stimulus maybe sharpened (in the criminal's view) by the most famous marriage of the day. Blame the press, too. It was almost five years since the Paris flight, but reporters and photographers had never lost their greediness after the last detail about the Lindberghs. That partly reflected how much the public continued to care about them; the rest was misbegotten enterprise among managing editors, then the whole Fourth Estate's reaction of he-can't-do-that-to-us when Lindbergh showed growing distaste for publicity. America, wrote Pegler, had been fumbling toward making the couple a sort of equivalent of Britain's royal family, but the Lone Eagle "declined the nomination in the manner of a man in a white suit slapping down a clumsy but affectionate dog with mud on its paws." [130]

It seemed he couldn't grasp the terms on which he had come to fame and fortune. He had immense prestige in his chosen world of flying, a private fortune steadily growing through in-on-the-ground-floor investments and lavish pay from Pan American, an affluent, well-connected wife and consequent easy access to people of power and sometimes cultivation. But he missed the significance of the fact that the very name of his famous plane, *The Spirit of St. Louis,* had been a publicity gag to secure him the money to build it. Grumpily at first, then exasperatedly, he balked at paying in spoiled privacy and smiling docility the debt the press thought he owed it for making a professionally respected but not too popular civilian flier into a world-renowned hero. Just as air resistance was essential to a plane's getting airborne, so publicity was *sine qua non* of what had happened to him. It was the core of his job as Pan Am's ambassador-at-large and symbol of technical integrity. Another Scandinavian, Greta Garbo, could make complete rejection of press interview and flashbulb one of the best publicity gags of all time. But Lindbergh was obliged to be photographed shaking hands with this statesman, making inspection tours with that industrialist, being decorated at a banquet by the white-tied chief of state.... It would probably have helped little if P. T. Barnum, Ivy Ledbetter Lee and Dr. John B. Watson had all explained to him that since he couldn't be as consistently inaccessible as Garbo, he couldn't go on eating his cake without paying for it. The lone-wolf stubbornness, like his father's, that had supported his great feat of 1927 would have kept him from assimilating any such advice.

When the ladder broke and the baby died, Lindbergh's relations with the press were already badly strained. During the miserable sequelae culminating in the trial the boys showed him rather more consideration than their guild traditions required. But for him as target it was necessarily a vastly embittering ordeal and poor preparation for further strains. The blowup came when news cameramen seeking unauthorized pictures forced off the road an automobile containing the new Lindbergh baby. The Lindberghs went into outraged self-exile, sailing incognito in an obscure freighter to England, where, they hoped, the press would behave better. And so it did. But presently they sought even more reliable seclusion on a tiny island off the coast of Britanny recommended by Dr. Alexis Carrel, distinguished member of the Rockefeller Institute (now Rockefeller University) in New York City.

Carrel was a shaping force in Lindbergh's later career. This stubby French martinet had won a Nobel Prize in 1912 for surgical innovations important in transplanting organs and was famous in the popular press for having kept a chicken's heart tissue alive *in vitro* for twenty-five years. Lindbergh and he made fast friends while the younger man was taking his mind off his woes by designing pumps for artificial hearts in Carrel's laboratory. They collaborated on a technical book on such devices—a tribute to Lindbergh, for Carrel was not the man to let another sign with him unless he was vastly impressed.

Indeed, Carrel thought himself not only a great medical scientist, which he was, but also a great philosophico-biological thinker capable of telling a sick world how to pull itself together. His best-seller, *Man the Unknown* (1935), did so even while questioning whether the degenerating human race would have the brains and stamina to take his advice. Most of the text was a readable and authoritative saunter through contemporary physiology-cum-psychology-cum-genetics, but every now and then a few pages bloomed into socioracist dogma smelling strongly of Nietzsche and Spengler: "Man is the hardiest of all animals, and the white races, builders of our civilization, the hardiest of all races. . . . The descendant of a great race, if he is not degenerate, is endowed with natural immunity to fatigue and fear . . . looks upon himself as destined to fight, to love, to think and to conquer. His action on his environment is as essentially simple as the leap of a wild animal upon its prey. . . . The stupid . . . have no right to an education . . . the democratic principle has contributed to the collapse of civilization in opposing the development of an elite." [131] His topical references often have the reactionary tingle: "The passion for conquest . . . led . . . Mussolini to the building up of a great nation. . . . The response of the women to . . . industrial civilization has been . . . decisive. The birth rate has at once fallen . . . not a new thing. . . . It has already been observed in past civilizations . . . a classical symptom. . . . We know its significance." Delphically and ominously he says no more about *that*. [132]

Carrel was not tall. He came to the scientific conclusion that "Men of genius are not tall. Mussolini is of medium size, and Napoleon was short." And as he gathered speed, the personal nature of his gospel grew clearer. What the world most needed was the guardianship of "a thinking center," including "a few individuals [likened to the US Supreme Court] . . . trained in the knowledge of man. . . . It should perpetuate itself automatically . . . acquire enough knowledge to prevent the organic and mental deterioration of civilized nations . . . free from political intrigues and cheap publicity." Molière again! Not musicians this time or Technocratic engineers, but godlike medical researchers—there is a good deal of Plato-and-water here, too. Then Carrel proposes creation of a second-echelon elite of the most promising specimens rearing their young in isolated Spartanoid communes with "rules of conduct . . . like [medieval] monastic orders . . . orders of chivalry . . . corporations of artisans . . . all submitted to strict physiological and mental discipline. . . . [133]

That may give you and me the shudders or the giggles. But it was pretty respectfully received in the mid-1930s when people were still desperate about what to do with the nation. In any case it was heady stuff for Congressman Lindbergh's son fresh from the ordeal to which his egalitarian, mongrelized, city-dominated, herd-cultured country had subjected him. Further to fit him to be a transmission belt for the Nazis, the Lindberghs' stay in England introduced them through Harold Nicolson, a seasoned diplomat who knew the best people (and had done Dwight Morrow's official biography) to Britons high in government or close to those who were finding this handsome, reticent hero and his quiet wife actually presentable. Suppose Lindbergh wished to discuss something weighty with the permanent secretary of a government department or a key Member of Parliament, he knew the right people to arrange it. And in the latter phases of his self-appointed mission Joseph P. Kennedy, then isolationist-minded US ambassador to Britain, was a great help.

In 1938 Colonel Truman Smith, air attaché of the US embassy in Berlin, interested in the powerful air force that, defying the decayed Versailles Treaty, the Nazis were building, persuaded Field Marshal Hermann Göring to invite Lindbergh to Germany to have a look. Smith's formal purpose was to enable Lindbergh to see and report to Washington on things that might open up specially for so eminent a guest. Yet there may have been more to it. Smith admired the new Luftwaffe and its creators and maybe, doubtless subliminally, yearned for sympathy for his quasi-partisan faith that it was irresistible. Lindbergh hobnobbed teetotally with Göring and his staff, was shown through huge, beehive-busy manufactories of airframes and motors, flew some of the latest Luftwaffe planes, was given production figures as fat as Göring and returned to Britain in the frame of mind best suiting the Nazis' needs.

That is, as trailblazer for aviation, he was delighted with what he had seen, while as American and well-treated resident of England and France at a time when knowledgeable people thought a new world war imminent, he was aghast at what he assumed would be the impact of the Luftwaffe if war came. His reports to Washington are said to have been highly useful. Doubtless they were, for, though lacking combat experience, he knew a great deal about planes and flying. He seems greatly to have overestimated potential production; logical again, for he knew relatively little about industrial matters. But the important thing was that he began to tell high-placed Britons and Frenchmen that to fight Hitler's Germany spearheaded by the planes and pilots he had seen would spell disaster. Soon he arranged close looks at British, French and USSR military aviation and came away doubly alarmed. Then a second trip to Germany more than confirmed his impressions. Gradually he increased the number of his high-echelon contacts in Paris and London, and his warnings grew more fervent. It may well be that the successive British-French decisions to let Hitler have his head were at least partly, possibly crucially, influenced by this sincere young man's assurances that Göring's great weapon outweighed anything that France and England together could summon up in the air in the foreseeable future.

In spite of a consciously cultivated reluctance he was also under the influence of growing admiration for Germany-as-force. Telling himself that of course he disliked Nazis, he nevertheless felt in the Germans he met "a sense of decency and value ... in many ways far ahead of our own" and considered Germany and Italy "the two most virile countries in Europe today." [134] Crossing in a German liner next spring (1938): "I can't help liking the Germans. They are like our own people." Later that year: "The Germans are a great people ... their welfare is inseparable from that of Europe." In his talk with David Lloyd George it bothers him that the nippy old veteran "Said the Nazi system was just as bad as the Russian system." Early in 1939: ". . . of all the European countries I found the most freedom in Germany." In London he visits first a Communist street meeting, then one of Sir Oswald Mosley's Nazistic Blackshirts and thinks their tone of "a much higher quality.... It always seems that the Fascist group is better than the Communist group." For summary of the blend of this Teutophilia with his father's isolationism: "We should be working with [the Germans] and not constantly crossing swords. If we fight our countries will only lose their best men.... It must not happen." [135]

And once Congressman Lindbergh's son set down an opinion he stuck to it like a Victorian maiden to her virtue. In 1940, when the Luftwaffe failed to live up to his predictions in the Battle of Britain, he managed almost altogether to look the other way. As Leonard Mosley's recent biography of him notes, he showed none of the exultation so keen a flier might have felt at the spectacle of British pilots' devotion and skill so gloriously proving themselves in the air. Their amazing, hard-earned victory was not in the script he had written. Nor does he seem ever to have suspected that those orderly, showily efficient, air-minded Germans had either deliberately or opportunistically used him in the highest quarters as cross between Cassandra and the Trojan Horse. It is difficult not to agree with the New York *Times'* review of Mosley's book: "The kindest interpretation of Lindbergh's activities [in this pre-World War II phase] is that he was an extraordinarily witless dupe of his Nazi hosts." [136]

In early spring, 1939, Britain's promise to support Poland in case

Germany attacked it made him so uneasy that though he kept telling people the odds were against war that year, he moved his household back to the America that had treated him and his so barbarically. He accepted a commission as colonel in the US Air Force and went on temporary active duty in technical surveys for its high command—for which he was eminently well suited. The curious thing was that at once this well-meaning but ill-qualified military and diplomatic expert—he had never been in a war, never commanded a platoon, never been on the inside of a diplomatic staff—was respectfully consulted by anxious persons of protoisolationist flavor: former President Hoover, William Castle (former Undersecretary of State), US Senators William S. Borah, Gerald Nye, Harry F. Byrd. He kept saying that war, though possible, was still unlikely because Britain and France knew they were too weak to risk it under any circumstances. In late summer came the Hitler-Stalin pact, soon Germany and the USSR walked into Poland— and in spite of Lindbergh's advice, Britain and France went to war about it. Within two weeks he had appointed himself to keep America out of what, in his view, had had no business happening. If none had dared beard the Nazis, no war would now be tempting.

He made a conspicuous speech over all radio networks warning that this was no affair of America's, skip it at all costs. Superficially it might have been just another example of the nation's fatuously paying attention to Henry Ford's ideas on education because he was a great maker of automobiles, worshipfully listening to Albert Einstein on international problems because he was the most momentous scientific theorist of his day, electing a worthy young man US Senator because he was an able astronaut, reading Shirley MacLaine's account of the People's Republic of China. But one may surmise that this busybodiness came at least partly of the same thing that had probably deepened his respect for the Luftwaffe—dread of a war that might involve America. Call it a welling up of his father's bitter, corn-fed revulsion from anything threatening to breach the migrant peasant's New World sanctuary.

Now that the threat was actual, his status as hero enabled him openly to apply public prophylaxis against what had been on his mind—again subliminally if you like—all along. He had not kept war from igniting. But he could follow the amorphous promptings of his hormones and phobias into an isolationist crusade that would have dazzled his father. Never mind that marriage into the House of Morgan; the boy was a chip off the old block. Overcoming his chronic diffidence, he was making speeches from platforms as well as before microphones in studios, publishing articles, consulting with powerful colleagues.... Go traipsing overseas to help against the Germans? Wasn't America well enough protected from even the Luftwaffe by the width of the Atlantic and economically self-sufficient enough to ignore Europe's bloodbaths? Let Uncle Sam cultivate his garden, the Western Hemisphere, scrub Pacific commitments beyond Hawaii and Alaska, keep Western civilization snug and safe from sea to shining sea no matter what Europeans or Asians chose to do!

That cyclone-cellar psychology, so suitable to the Midwestern provenance of Lindbergh's group, was tinged with racism in his first magazine piece, "Aviation, Geography and Race," written for the *Reader's Digest* at the same time as his maiden radio speech: "Western nations are again at war ... in which the White race is bound to lose ... which may easily lead our civilization through more Dark Ages if it survives at all." Wars end with "the prostration of one contender, while the other can still stagger ... all about the wolves of lesser stature abide [sic] their time to spring on both. ... Asia presses toward us on the Russian border. ... [Let us] turn from our quarrel and build our White ramparts again to guard our heritage from Mongol and Persian and Moor." A quick peace could combine against Asian threats "an English fleet, a German air force, a French army [at the time real experts as well as Lindbergh thought the French Army reliably formidable], an American nation, standing together. ..." [137] *
A few months later readers of the staid *Atlantic Monthly* learned from another Lindbergh piece (duly reprinted in the *Digest* for maximum readership) that this new war was essentially "a conflict between differing concepts of right ... the longer [it] goes on, the weaker our family of nations will be, and the more it will add to the conquests of Russia and Japan." [138] There was much Carrel in that, and a whiff of the Third Reich. Such doctrine immediately got him called Fifth Columnist, of course, and abused for having accepted a civilian decoration from Göring three years previously.

His sincerity and stubbornness would probably have kept him battling single-handedly. But already a dozen or so US senators—Pat McCarran of Nevada, Champ Clark of Missouri, D. Worth Clark of Idaho, Henrik Shipstead and Ernest Lundeen of Minnesota, Burton K. Wheeler of Montana, Arthur Vandenberg of Michigan, all significantly from west of Ohio—were sounding the traditional isolationist alarm, and reciprocity between them and this magnetic volunteer was close. These were the shifting junta that let Viereck use their franks and

---

* Note that America's contribution to this defense of the West was to be merely benevolent encouragement to those doing the resisting.

speeches and wrote for the now German-owned *Scribner's Commentator*. Lindbergh was quite cozy with its editors. Whether he ever knew where the money came from is uncertain; in any case here were the Germans using him again. For it he wrote "Impregnable America," and other issues carried an account of his fan mail sounding as if done by a Hollywood press agent and "A Westerner Reacts [oh, so favorably!] to Lindbergh" by Verne Marshall, editor of the Pulitzer Prize-winning Cedar Rapids (Iowa) *Gazette* and soon to be leader of the Keep America Out of War Organization. Beyond Senators there were "Can America Fight in Europe?" by Colonel Robert R. McCormick, pompously corrosive rajah of the chronically isolationist Chicago *Tribune,* "An American Foreign Policy" by Henry Ford and "The American Quality" by Frank Lloyd Wright, telling how to build "an impregnable free nation" by getting rid of "fashion-mongers," the movie star system, "wise crackers," military strategists, installment buying and "the private money-power of London and New York." [139]

A growing sense of solidarity among such men soon led to formal organization. Marshall's KAOW movement was founded specifically to counter the candidly interventionist Fight for Freedom movement and the rather more gingerly Committee to Defend America by Aiding the Allies set up in May, 1940, by William Allen White, the nationally renowned, congenitally liberal and yet Republican editor of the Emporia, Kansas, *Gazette.* Marshall's co-chairman was Hamilton Fish, Jr., reactionary Congressman from FDR's district in New York State. Both were too brash and vituperative to earn the confidence of the disparate personalities and shades of opinion gravitating toward the isolationist attitude. Solider help came in midsummer, 1940, with the America First movement.

John P. Diggins has well described it as "an expedient alliance of liberal isolationists, Republican reactionaries, genuine patriots, and pro-Nazi supporters." [140] All but the last would probably have agreed in the error well diagnosed by Selig Adler: "In 1918, Americans had been led to believe that war would settle everything ... in their disillusionment they fell into the reverse fallacy of believing that war settles nothing." [141] Under its first name, Defend America First,[*] it was born at Yale, begotten by law student R. Douglas Stuart, heir of the Quaker Oats fortune, who had been an ardent New Dealer but

---

[*] "America First," as "America First, Inc.," had been used in 1934 as an agency "to give the New Deal an X-ray exposure" with a lawyers' auxiliary "to restore the Constitution to its full powers" under the leadership of James True, a minor Shirtist. It was highly evanescent. (New York *Times,* September 10, 1934.)

had trouble following FDR into his developing policy of all-aid-short-of-war. He organized fellow students, including Kingman Brewster, Jr., now president of Yale, and Sargent Shriver, John P. Kennedy's conspicuous son-in-law, to have second, third and fourth thoughts about interventionism. This attracted General Robert E. Wood, chairman of the board of Sears, Roebuck & Company—which hardly needs identification—who took it and Stuart off campus, launched it nationally and blew a necessarily widely heard bugle blast for all good men to rally round and keep America out of unnecessary overseas adventures.

Members of the founding committee flocking to the colors were mostly Chicago industrialists presumably sensitive to the sentiments of their Midwestern cronies and customers plus their own indrawings: Philip T. Swift, John Cudahy, Jay C. Hormel gave it a strong odor of meat-packing. For wider appeal its avowed supporters at one time or another included Sears Roebuck's Lessing Rosenwald; John T. Flynn, liberal economist-journalist; Sinclair Lewis; Janet Ayer Fairbank, Chicago novelist versed in Democratic politics; George N. Peek, chief of the New Deal's defunct Agricultural Adjustment Administration and big man in the farm implement industry; Eddie Rickenbacker, World War I combat ace and big man in commercial aviation; Mrs. John P. Marquand, an old friend of Anne Lindbergh's; Amos Pinchot, chronic friend of offbeat causes whether occult, radical or restrictive; Norman Thomas, perennial symbol of Socialist suspiciousness; Chester Bowles and William Benton, originally partners in a very important advertising agency and, though following divergent careers, agreeing with Bruce Barton, another prince of Madison Avenue, that America First had something there; Kathleen Norris, queen of serial stories for women's magazines; Ruth Hanna McCormick of the Chicago *Tribune*-International Harvester clan; Lillian Gish, queen of the silent screen, speaking winningly at America First rallies in Los Angeles; Alice Longworth, Theodore Roosevelt's astringent daughter, a professional great lady. . . . The number of women is notable. A generation earlier neither women nor the leaders of America First would have bothered. In view of what Mrs. Charles Sabin (chaperone of Repeal), Dorothy Thompson, Eleanor Roosevelt and Anna Louise Strong had been doing, these women seemed bent on showing that the other sex could also be effectively reactionary.

Lindbergh's contact with this peevishly eclectic group had begun in a conference with Wood and Stuart in the office of Harry Bennett, Henry Ford's chief thug and toady. The Lone Eagle had a strong stomach when he needed it. The campaign against lend-lease and the destroyers-for-bases deal included most of the US Senators previously listed, mostly with America First backing, plus Henry Cabot Lodge and David I. Walsh, both of Massachusetts, presumably aware of the hard-core Irish opposition to helping Britain. It is amusing now that Nye, cooperating pretty freely with America First, found himself in grave trouble with his Norwegian constituents as soon as—not a day before—the Nazis attacked Norway. But all those headliners paled once Lindbergh gave up the too flashy KAOW group and enlisted with America First. For its last six months, says Wayne S. Cole, a sympathetic biographer expert on these matters, he was the organization's most popular and controversial speaker.

By then he was consciously looking to his father's * overheated career. In his first speech for America First appropriately made in Minneapolis, he said, "The conditions which exist in Germany today will seem moderate in comparison with those which will result from a prolongation of this war. Men and women of Minnesota, I say to you what my father said a quarter of a century ago: the future of democracy depends on our ability to govern our own country. . . . What happens in Europe is of little importance compared with what happens in our own land." [142] A little later he told his diary: "I think the greatest satisfaction I have had at any of these meetings is the applause I received when I spoke of my father. . . . People are beginning to appreciate his wisdom and his courage." [143] His growingly emphatic speeches were customarily prefaced by a reading of a poem sent him by an admirer. It began: "Lindy's pa saw it all from afar, / Said, 'Son, don't take up a gun.' " [144]

His wife's loyalty was a fine thing in this couple's notably reciprocal lives. To do her share while flying with him on often hazardous surveying flights, she became a competent navigator. Hence her first two books, subduedly lyrical and enjoying great commercial success. Now, as Lindbergh's new career as self-chosen younger statesman called on him for set speeches and signed articles, her skilled hand pointed up and polished their texts, † and as pressures rose, her well-

---

* On this point Cole (Charles A. Lindbergh, 19) says ambiguously: "One might have supposed that young Lindbergh was consciously following in his father's footsteps. . . . He insisted . . . that his father had no direct influence. . . . He did not share his father's radicalism. . . ." One must allow, however, for the only secondary significance of the particular targets of the paranoid-tending temperament. The basic thing is the impulse toward hypersuspiciousness, fear of "they"-type of conspiracy, fascination with strong-hand social solutions, which can be worked out in dozens of contexts of different idiom.

† Cole (Charles A. Lindbergh, 74) says that though Lindbergh drafted "all his own noninterventionist speeches and articles . . . Anne . . . read that first address carefully in advance and had suggested improvements; she did so with

deserved ready access to editors enabled her to back up her man with ardent writings of her own where they helped most.

Midway in the confusing Phony War phase of World War II the *Reader's Digest*, with the widest readership of any American magazine, ran her "Prayer for Peace," reproaching Americans for acting like "Spectators at a gladiatorial contest [wanting] more action, more attacks" instead of using American leverage to "put an end to a war which has scarcely begun." The purpose was not so much humanitarian, however, as strategic. Yes, indeed, "[certain] things done in Nazi Germany ... were ... like a blow in the face ... [but] ... the suppression of liberty [has] been seen over and over again in ... revolution ... our own country was built by ... force and aggression ... broken promises to the Indians ... how else did we acquire ... our Southwest? Is Hitler the colossal lone adventurer? ... Or ... the embittered spirit of a strong and deeply humiliated people? ... Against a strong and united Europe—even against a strong Germany— the hordes of Russia are no menace. But against a divided Europe, bled by wars and prostrated by devastation...." [145] The same song her husband had sung a few months earlier and kept on singing even after Carrel, who had lent some of the music, if not the words, panicked and renounced his previous judgment that "if he had to choose between fascism and communism, he would take fascism every time." [146] One should also note that at this same time the lady also did much to help the Quakers' efforts to arrange food relief for the Europe that the Nazis had in their sights.

In October, 1940, she published *The Wave of the Future: A Confession of Faith*, a hardcover pamphlet written while the Battle of Britain was still on. The *Reader's Digest* featured it in slightly condensed form. Meanwhile, the USSR's bungling assault on Finland and the Nazis' dismaying successes in Norway, the Low Countries and France had blasted the Phony War apart. *The Wave* was a casuistic variation on Alexander Pope's "Whatever is, is right" or rather: "Whatever succeeds in coming to be is right." It began with cultivated references to Boëthius and Chekhov, then spoke kindly of those seeing the new hot war as a struggle between Right and Wrong: "... are persecution, aggression, war and theft sins or are they not? ... They *are*.... But there are other sins ... blindness, selfishness, irrespon-

---

most of his speeches and articles." Unless I have lost my nose for personal writing styles, many passages in most of Lindbergh's articles, beginning with that in the Atlantic in 1940, represent influence from his wife almost amounting to collaboration.

sibility, smugness, lethargy and resistance to change ... which we 'democracies' ... are guilty of.... To resist change is to sin against life itself." How much wiser to regard the war as "an expression of one of those great mutations of history.... Something, one feels, is pushing through the crust of custom.... I believe that it is, in its essence, good; but ... because we are slow to change it must force its way ... violently.... The Forces of the Past are fighting against the Forces of the Future.... Germany and Russia have discovered how to use new social and economic forces.... The evils we deplore in their systems are ... scum on the wave of the future.... [It] is coming and there is no fighting it ... in America ... it should be possible to meet the wave of the future in comparative harmony and peace." [147] Instead of futile gestures with destroyers-for-bases and peacetime draft registration and so on.

The respect with which Anne Morrow Lindbergh's unmistakable integrity had been consistently recognized kept the reaction among help-the-anti-Nazis people from being severe. At the time, of course, the Communists and fellow travelers, who might have been expected to scream the shrillest against such equating of the significances of the Third Reich and the October Revolution, were dutifully soft-pedaling anti-Fascist sentiment because of the quasi-alliance of the Hitler-Stalin pact. Among others Irwin Edman, widely influential professor at Columbia, struck about the representative note in a conspicuous review: "Mrs. Lindbergh writes better than her husband but her soothing words are still in the language of appeasement." [148] Not until the Fourth of July, the following year, was emotionally pertinent antidote applied in a radio script from Stephen Vincent Benét, a more considerable poet:

A TOTALITARIAN VOICE, PERSUASIVE:
My worthy American listeners,
I am giving you one more chance.
Don't you know that we are completely invincible, don't you?
Won't you just admit we are the wave of the future, won't you?
You are a very nice, mongrel, disgusting people—
But naturally you need new leadership....
Now be sensible—give up this corrupt and stupid nonsense of democracy
And you can have the crumbs from our table and a trusty's job in our world-jail.[149]

Mosley calls *The Wave* "a strange amalgam of faux naïveté and sentimentality, cloudy, imprecise and illogical." [150] All true, yet one feels validity in the patent joy, evident in buoyant rhythms and felicitous phrasings, that this nimble casuist took in helping her husband's crusade. Her widowed mother and her sisters and most of her family friends were all out for Britain. But somehow they kept up cordial relations with Lindbergh, and vice versa, while he plodded on from meeting to meeting, conference to conference, deeper into it every step but grimly pleased so to be. In April, 1941, FDR publicly likened America Firsters to the Copperheads of Civil War times. Furious, Lindbergh resigned his active-inactive commission. That can hardly have displeased FDR and gave the Lone Eagle more freedom for maneuver than he had been taking. "The pressure for war is high and mounting," he told his diary on May 1. "The people are opposed to it but the Administration is hell-bent on war. Most of the Jewish interests ... are behind war, and they control a huge part of our press and radio and most of our motion pictures. There are also the 'intellectuals' ... 'Anglophiles' ... British agents ... allowed free rein [one such was Aubrey Morgan, his wife's brother-in-law, chief of the British Information Service in New York City], the national financial interests. ..." [151]

This motif was not newly acquired. In 1938 he had been inadvisedly receptive to German palaver about the Jews as responsible for Germany's collapse after World War I and manipulation of the consequent disastrous inflation to acquire fine houses and automobiles and the use of the prettiest girls. The following year he was agreeing portentously with Castle and Fulton Lewis, Jr., Mutual's reactionary radio commentator, about the "Jewish influence in our press, radio and motion pictures." [152] Now in July, 1941, he brought down on himself and America First unnecessary opprobrium by going public with it. He told a large audience in Des Moines, Iowa, that the three forces inveigling America into war were the White House, the British and the Jews. If any of those relaxed pressure, he said, the situation might yet be saved; let America look to it. But if all three kept it up, there was no stopping their conspiracy "to prepare the United States for war under the guise of American defense ... to involve us ... step by step, without our realization ... to create a series of incidents ... to force us into actual conflict." [153] That moved masterfully from probable fact to fair likelihood to melodramatic suspicion. His father's only objection would have been that he left out those "international financial interests." Maybe he assumed that "Jews" said it all.

It split America First wide open. Norman Thomas and Henry M. MacCracken, liberal, gullible president of Vassar, announced they would no longer speak at America First meetings. The Chicago *Tribune* called it "an impropriety"; even the Hearst press deplored it as "intemperate and intolerant." [154] Flynn was utterly dismayed. Wood suggested that America First had better adjourn *sine die* to await the end of the war. It had already been having enough trouble fending off the embraces of Shirtists and crypto-Bundists, embarrassing what really did consider itself a responsible, statesmanly movement. "It was not always easy," says Adler, ". . . to be certain if the wearer of an America First button was a simon-pure isolationist, a man who believed that F. D. R. was planning the destruction of the republic, a fifth-column Bundist, a member of a lunatic-fringe hate-group, or a devout Coughlinite." [155] The Communists' sporadic efforts to cuddle up to America First had also been irksome; that stopped abruptly when Hitler attacked the USSR only a few days before Lindbergh's disastrous speech. But all such considerations were losing weight now that he had tossed the monkey wrench into the right place. "America First had fallen into wide disrepute before the organization sank from sight with the battleships destroyed at Pearl Harbor," [156] Adler concludes. On that memorable December 7, 1941, Lindbergh telephoned General Wood, whose surly comment was: "Well, he got us in by the back door."[157]

Lindbergh doggedly shut his mouth, worked awhile for Henry Ford on the new Willow Run bomber plant, then signed up with the US Air Force as civilian consultant and did outstanding service checking up on operations and equipment in the Pacific Theater. Several times, civilian or not, his testing of pursuit planes took him into very creditable performance in dogfights with the enemy. Until his recent death he remained secluded, interested in the ecological problems that had long been on his wife's mind. A parallel to Coughlin? To some extent; but life did not give the Lone Eagle a square shake. What it did do to him was far more of a waste than what the parish priest of Royal Oak did to himself.

Before taking leave of Lindbergh and Carrel, have a sniff at their peripheral relations with another score for the Nazis, not important but symptomatic of what the 1930s did to American common sense.

Twenty years hence a candidate for a PhD reading Raymond Chandler for his dissertation on the sociology of the whodunit will come on a minor character in *Farewell, My Lovely* identified as an adherent of Moral Re-Armament. Exploration will bring him to the pudgy, oozily articulate figure of Dr. (of Divinity) Frank N. D.

Buchman. His gospel, originally for postadolescents, then adapted for prosperous adults (in years anyway) was making waves in the late 1930s by prescribing his formula of "absolute honesty, absolute purity, absolute love, absolute unselfishness" as the practical prophylaxis against such things as the Moscow purges and the Nazis' seizures of Austria and Czechoslovakia. This Era of Wild Swings, it is already clear, teemed with implausible prophets and proposals. But FB, as admirers called him, was special in that his following consisted almost altogether of persons with safe-deposit boxes, college educations and two automobiles as well as conservative inclinations.

Lindbergh knew much about him. Late in 1939 his close friend James Newton, of the high command of FB's Moral Re-Armament, got the two together at dinner; Lindbergh's finding was "a certain magnetism and openness ... sincere and honest." [158] Carrel knew who he was. When they celebrated FB's sixty-first birthday that year, congratulatory telegrams came from Secretary of State Cordell Hull, former President Hoover, Dr. Alexis Carrel. ... Three years earlier, when the Oxford Group, as FB's following was known before Moral Re-Armament was born, gathered 2,000 strong at Stockbridge, Massachusetts, those getting on their hind legs to confess their spiritual debt to him included Alice Elizabeth Morris, debutante, describing what happened to her as "the thing for which the younger generation [has] been searching; God needs people who will give their lives to bring America under his control"; J. E. W. Duys, Socialist member of the Netherlands' Parliament—awkward initials for a man who ended up collaborating with the Nazis; Lord John Addington, younger son of a British peer; the Baroness de Watteville-Breckheim—the Oxford Group liked names with handles to them—who told the faithful that "the real security of the nation is in the moral and spiritual quality of its citizens." Carl Vrooman, former Assistant Secretary of Agriculture, promised that Buchmanism would substitute "stewardship for greed ... produce enough wealth to satisfy the legitimate needs of all classes." To represent the other-than-affluent classes appeared a Greenwich Village butcher predicting stabilization of the economy by Buchman-style "policy dictated by God and carried out by those who feel a real commitment to Him"; Chief Um-Pa-Tuth, a real Red Indian whose witness for FB consisted mostly of complaints about the poor quality of education at the Indian institute at Carlisle, Pennsylvania; and a Scottish former Communist with the notable name of James Watt. He said the Party had expelled him for "betraying the working class by getting religion." More in charitable sorrow than in anger he explained that the comrades could not understand how the

Oxford Group "bridged the gulf that separates master from man, class from class and nation from nation." [159]

In token of international harmony-to-be the platform displayed massed national flags centered on those of the United States, Britain and Canada, the hotbeds of Buchmanism. Among the others the Nazi swastika was unavoidably conspicuous. So nice it's there, the faithful said, see how FB brings nations together! At the time he was planning a European foray. As preliminary he sought an interview with FDR— which he did not get—on the interesting grounds that Hitler had offered to receive him and it would be awkward to have to admit—in "absolute honesty"—that he had never met America's head of state.* Maybe arrangements with the Nazis had come of FB's long-standing acquaintance with the mother of Ernest "Putzi" Hanfstaengl, the jolly Harvard-educated, piano-playing expert in hands-across-the-sea active in liaison for Hitler in the late 1930s. Whether Buchman really met Hitler is unknown, but Germany must have treated him cordially. He came back late in the explosive summer of 1936—Spain was erupting, the AFL had just expelled the CIO, the presidential campaign was gathering acerbity—and contributed to the hullabaloo an interview in the New York *World-Telegram* that his followers were still trying to explain when he died twenty-five years later.

"I thank Heaven for a man like Adolf Hitler," he told the astonished reporter, "who built a front line of defence [*sic*] against Communism. My barber in London told me Hitler saved all Europe from Communism. . . . I don't condone everything the Nazis do. Anti-Semitism? Bad, naturally. . . . But think what it would mean to the world if Hitler surrendered to the control of God. Or Mussolini. Or any dictator. Through such a man God could control a nation overnight and solve every last, bewildering problem. . . . God is a perpetual broadcasting station and all you have to do is tune in. . . . Spain has taught us what godless Communism will bring. . . . Human problems aren't economic, they're moral, and . . . could be solved within a God-controlled democracy, or perhaps I should say a theocracy, and . . . through a God-controlled Fascist dictatorship . . . in a God-controlled nation, capital and labor would discuss their problems peacefully and reach God-controlled solutions . . . business would be owned by individuals . . . but the owners would be God-controlled. . . ." [160] Say, a worldwide NRA with God instead of Hugh Johnson in charge. . . .

---

* For this and many other bits I am much indebted to Tom Driberg, *The Mystery of Moral Re-Armament* (1965). Driberg had no use at all for Buchman, but he is a most trustworthy digger out of facts.

Denunciations naturally ensued, but the stauncher Buchmanites paid no heed. They already knew how FB consulted God every morning in his "quiet time"—Oxford Groupers thus received Guidance (always capitalized) daily—and so doubtless had good authority for thus saying what seemed extravagantly fatuous. And the implication that Communism was worse than anything Fascists did was in a loyal Buchmanite's view sound doctrine. Dutifully the faithful followed FB in the metamorphosis that within a couple of years created Moral Re-Armament out of the Oxford Group. Lindbergh several times complained to his diary that no matter how patiently his friend Newton explained it, he was unclear just what MRA's glorified solution for the world's troubles might be: "They all believe in truth and good will and are against sin ... apparently feel that the problems of mankind can be settled by good will. ... I can't believe [they are] the answer but they may be a sign pointing in the right general direction." [161] Yes, indeed—the general direction of elite authoritarianism à la Carrel.

He was not the first thus puzzled and yet temperamentally drawn. The thing had begun early in the Jazz Age in Britain's Oxbridge universities * as Buchman's one-man campaign to clean up the morals, particularly the erotic lapses, of undergraduates. He relied on personal exhortation followed by gang confessions and mutual support in sinning no more, emphasizing the "quiet time" and adherence to the rule of "absolute honesty ..." and so on. Lewd fellows of the baser sort called it "a Salvation Army for the well-to-do," and undeniably its more prominent adherents usually carried a whiff of heavy sugar cooking. Buchman brought it to his native America with such success on Ivy League campuses—and such overheating of the neophytes—that President John Grier Hibben of Princeton ordered him off the premises. Gradually he turned away from undergraduates toward their well-heeled elders and their anxieties about the 1930s. The new doctrine was that, as Lord John told the faithful, the remedy for the world's horrors and shortcomings was for everybody to turn Buchmanite and let God work "through ordinary men and women like you and me ... [carrying] out His plan." [159]

So Buchmanite agapes were no longer held in campus YMCAs or the rumpus rooms of fat-cat undergraduates' parents' country places but, as in the one Edmund Wilson attended *c.* 1934, in such gaudy, public and prestige-rich places as the rococo grand ballroom of the

* His calling the movement "Oxford Group" naturally infuriated many an Oxonian. This account of its first phase is necessarily too scanty. For much more see my *Great Times,* 371-74.

Plaza Hotel in New York City. Wilson thought these middle-aged men in black ties and middle-aged ladies in long dresses "infinitely sad and insipid. . . . If they were a little more definitely neurotic, they would be going to psychoanalysts. If they were sillier they would be nudists. . . . But it has been the triumph of Buchman to put patent-leather shoes on the Christ of the missions." [162] FB steadily developed the international aspect of his mission with busy travels into the Far East as well as Europe to widen his acquaintance among susceptible people-who-mattered or sounded as if they did. His traveling expenses were provided for by the generous checks that, he said, always miraculously turned up in his mail when need arose.

In 1938 inspiration! He seized on the headlines' timely obsession with "rearmament" to reorient the Oxford Group into a worldwide remedy for domestic and international conflicts, Communism and, though by now incidentally, sin. "Moral Re-Armament" would be the new name and redefined purpose of organized Guidance. By making everybody, particularly important persons, into God-guided messengers of Grace, MRA would purge the world of violence among other bad habits. "Guidance or Guns" was the slogan of its World Assembly held in Switzerland in September, 1938, just before the doings at Munich that made the whole thing look, if possible, sillier than ever. Until World War II came and the issue of intervention shredded American tempers, MRA in the person of FB and his logorrheic staff, usually good-looking, always elegantly turned out, kept up its preposterous momentum and found enough retired admirals, offbeat legislators, deviant parsons and—most indispensably—women beneficiaries of large trust funds to keep its reactionary, smirkingly articulate pot simmering.

Few had the effrontery to identify "paranoid symptoms" [163] in MRA as did Dr. Harry C. Steinmetz before the annual meeting of the American Psychological Association in 1939. Thirty-three of the nation's forty-eight state governors signed a statement that "MRA is our most urgent need," [164] statesmanly indeed in midsummer, 1939, when unemployment was still high and Europe on the verge of explosion. Their names were read out at a great MRA luncheon in Hollywood where Louis B. Mayer, dean of the movie industry, and Will H. Hays, its slippery front man-spokesman, praised FB and his handiwork to the skies as preliminary for a great MRA meeting that evening in the Hollywood Bowl. The crowning jewel of this occasion was, however, FB's meeting with Mae West. She wore a pink negligee when posing with him for the news cameras. After he briefed her for half an hour, she told the press, "I owe all my success to the kind of thinking MRA is," and FB replied, "You are a splendid character, Miss West. You have done wonderful work, too." Whereupon she advised him to look up W. C. Fields because "Moral Rearmament is just the thing he needs. Give it to him in a bottle and he'll go for it." [165]

THEY DIDN'T JUST STAND THERE

MEN MIGHT AS WELL BE IMPRISONED, AS EXCLUDED FROM
THE MEANS OF EARNING THEIR BREAD.

—John Stuart Mill,
On Liberty

The particular hit in *Americana,* an unusually astringent revue
produced in New York City in mid-October, 1932, was "Brother, Can
You Spare a Dime?" The bare title gives tone and content. Single-
mindedly heart-rending, it was put devastatingly across by "a band of
bread-line tatterdemalions," who, said Brooks Atkinson, "expressed the
spirit of these times with more heartbreaking anguish than any of the
prose bards of the day." [1] Until then the salient theatrical use of the
Depression had been the "Posterity Is Just Around the Corner"
number in *Of Thee I Sing* making a jaunty joke of the exasperating
cliché so widely attributed to President Hoover. In vaudeville Depression jokes had multiplied, but then came a fairly effective movement
to bar them.* Now overnight "Brother . . ." was on all radios, wailed

---

* *Fortune,* January, 1932. One of the most heartless gags was in the Marx
Brothers' *Horse Feathers* movie released in 1932: A panhandler braces Harpo
for "a dime for a cup of coffee." Harpo reaches grinningly into his all-purpose
overcoat and hands him a steaming cup of coffee, which is peevishly rejected.
A better than average Depression joke: "Who was that lady I seen you with
last night at the sidewalk café?" "That was no lady, that was my wife. That
was no sidewalk café, that was our furniture." That must have been cooked up
after legal beer returned in the spring of 1933, when New York City bloomed
with tables outside restaurants with bars. Most of them soon disappeared
under harassment from soot and the authorities.

out by plump tenors in small nightclubs, having broken the dam by realistically exploiting the panhandler, the symbol of the ongoing catastrophe most familiar to those still able to cope economically—still a huge majority but dwindling.

By then street-corner apple sellers were fewer. Hoovervilles usually grew on the other side of town beyond the dump or under the bridge and were soon out of sight as automobile or train sped past. But here on the sidewalk all over town was this poor sheepish victim of he didn't know what, too cheerless to talk above a whisper, foul from enforced squalor, numb with fear of a world no longer affording him a place. The song rubbed one's nose in him. It was probably 1930 when I met him on the north side of Washington Square. Times were not exactly bright with me just then. But I was doing this and that, netting maybe $800 a year, and at worst I knew where a roof and dead-emergency loans were available, and I had four or five dollar bills in my pocket, and he looked miserably harassed, so I gave him a dollar before he asked for it. He took my hand in both of his and bowed over it as if he were about to kiss it. But that wasn't it. When I got it back, it was wet with a few tears.

Correction of the stereotypes and clichés that posterity attaches to the Great Depression need not imply that none was justifiable. Yes, Virginia, by the first anniversary of the Great Crash there were many evictions, long breadlines, newspapers lining out-at-elbows coats, fathers deserting families out of frustration, spreading clusters of shacks of salvage lumber, flattened tin cans and cast-off automobile tops. They looked no worse and were often better shelter than the rickety housing to which Dixie relegated sharecroppers and fieldhands good times and bad. But in the waste areas near Chicago and Detroit the winds off the wintry lake were keener than anything in Alabama's nasty enough January weather, and in summer the nearby dumps smelled worse than anything but the privies back on the home farm. "Hooverville" was unfair, of course. So was "Hoovercart" for the horse-drawn vehicle made of the rear assembly of a derelict Model T fitted with shafts; "Hoover hogs" * for the armadillos that hard-up Texans found nourishing and tasty; "Hoover Pullmans" for the empty boxcars in which the unemployed drifted pessimistically from town to

* The New York *Times* (May 26, 1975) had a story about the annual armadillo festival in Victoria, Texas (for the Texans, not the armadillos) that derived "Hoover hog" from Hoover's having allegedly advised Texans to eat armadillos as emergency ration in the Depression. Local inquiry leads me to believe that Hoover didn't even know 'dillos were edible, let alone ever recommended them. This seems to be just another and interesting example of how the primitive impulse to personify misfortune kept picking on Hoover.

town. Yet the man in the White House was, after all, standard-bearer of a political party that took credit for the glories of the New Era and chose him on that basis. When the ball dress turned into rags, neither he nor his party could justifiably resent having to take much of the blame.

A grimly conspicuous segment of victims of the Depression was the aimless, gradually degenerating young folks hitchhiking or riding freight cars from nowhere to nowhere. By 1932 most estimates numbered them around 200,000. They were not totally new. The wide, loose-jointed United States was already used to considerable numbers of adolescent boys and young men taking regardlessly to drifting because they felt restless, or because their deviant dispositions clashed with their families' staid ways, or because of a "broken home," or because home was in hard luck and could no longer feed the marginal mouth—a situation as old as Grimm's fairy tales. Several of those motives might combine. Usually many such young migrants got wandering out of their systems and came back to settle down. Others joined the rootless bindlestiff-merchant seaman stratum that vibrated in and out of Skid Row. The unluckiest or least stable hardened into hopeless drifters, eddying among the hobo jungles on the fringes of towns. Over the years benevolent agencies—the Salvation Army, the Travelers Aid, miscellaneous welfare agencies—formed loose coast-to-coast agreements to feed, shelter, bathe and counsel itinerant young-sters and ship them home again on "charity tickets" that railroads supplied very cheap. It was worth their while. Professional vagrants were already enough nuisance in freightyards and trackside bushes without fresh recruits to swell their ranks.

In the 1920s the spread of automobiles and consequent hitchhiking had so encouraged footlooseness among youngsters that Hallgren thought the bulk of these 200,000-odd vagrants represented merely "the restless spirit of the [pre-Depression] era"[2] persisting. Morris Markey got the same impression motoring across Missouri in 1931: "The roads are full of boys and girls seeing something of the world. . . . They drift slowly, working a few weeks and pushing. . . . 'Seeing the world and looking for a good time,' most of them will say. . . .'"[3] But on the West Coast the picture was no longer hippie-ish but bleak; Markey was astonished by "the number of people . . . hurrying along [without] any destination. They simply find it easier to fill their bellies by begging, and petty thieving, and sporadic labor . . . walking or in cars, flowing along. . . ."[4] As the 1930s sagged, the nation's load of such misfits not only grew heavier but was changing character. Particularly in the Southwest railroads acquired so many new riders of blind baggage and the rods—tenfold in a few years, the St. Louis-San

Francisco reported—that management finally threw up its hands and told the shacks and yard detectives to let 'em ride, no more savaging or arrests. It got so there were more passengers on a given freight train than on the transcontinental limited on the next track. The Missouri Pacific had 269 deaths on its property from unskilled trespassers trying to board or get off its trains in the first seven months of 1935, and that was after the peak of it.

Earlier most of the freeloaders were young, heedless and often bewildered. The swamped welfare agencies of the towns they dropped off in could supply little more than bread, beans, coffee and a flop for a maximum twenty-four hours, then on your way by thumb or side-door Pullman and don't come back, you hear? This, *Fortune* reported as of late 1932, "put a premium on the vagrant's vagrancy. Since each city will ... offer him no more than one meal and a night's lodging he is impelled to continue. If desperate he may say to himself—Move or Starve; if adventurous—Move or Eat. The result is the same." [5] The US Children's Bureau reported discouragedly that "the excitement and camaraderie of the road" tended to turn rootless kids into "seasoned transients" [6] increasingly difficult to resocialize.

Few places were as harsh as Atlanta, Georgia, which fed and lodged the footloose for thirty days—in jail or on a chain gang. Miami, Florida, gave kids the loan of bathing suits and use of the beach for a day before trucking them to the county line and heading them north with a warning. Deming, New Mexico, assessed each employed citizen a small percentage of his weekly pay to feed them. Los Angeles, more solicitous than most, tried to find healthy youngsters some sort of work or head them homeward—only in many cases the kid carried a letter from Mom or Pop saying this is Junior Mackay from Springfield, couldn't feed him no longer, so he has our leave to go shift for his self. It struck many as yet more morbid that girls were showing up in ever-larger numbers among the boys. They usually wore overalls to reduce visibility but not enough to prevent high incidence of VD. Surveys among social agencies involved showed that job hunting was usually what had drawn them away from home to begin with at ages beginning at sixteen or seventeen, because there was no prospect of support at home; sometimes even houseroom was lacking. As state laws tried to crack down on hitchhiking, they came to rely mostly on truck drivers whose big boxes offered plenty of room for concealment. The end of the line—often by way of successive small-town jails—was the hobo jungle. On a given night 6 percent of the jungles' denizens were women.

Malnutrition-based diseases were rife. So was the problem of sodomy-minded professional vagrants corrupting boys as well as girls in the trackside jungles. These national stepchildren were often likened to the *besprizornyi,* the gangs of Revolution-dislocated children and adolescents that infested the USSR in the 1920s and gave the Kremlin so tough a problem in rehabilitation. But as the US Children's Bureau fair-mindedly said, these young American drifters seldom clotted in snarling packs, and so far as their plight was new, it came not of violent Revolution (nor yet of the schizoid roots-phobia of the hippies of the 1960s) but of the creeping strains of Depression. In 1932 the only specific remedy the bureau could suggest was community services to keep them at home in the first place. And that, of course, was only one of a dozen doors that should never have been left unlocked.

As catchword-label for the New Era's unexpected litter of hard times, conservative publicists used the economist's bloodless term "depression," less destructive to morale than the elder "panic." Soon, however, sinister connotations from psychiatry and meteorology took over. In revulsion against euphoria America was acting as if in the down phase of a manic-depressive state or as if gasping in the results of a low economic barometer. Britain did better with "slump," France with *la crise.* Both at least applied impermanence. "Depression" might well never end.

Proper statistics, particularly for unemployment, are not available, so one cannot know whether previous panics and ensuing hardships were of the same order of severity—most notably the great panic of 1873 with its prolonged privation and violence. Alvin Johnson, able up-from-the-grass-roots economist, saw the panic of 1893, part of his own experience, as still a down phase of "the [1873] depression, which had afflicted the country since the early seventies, advancing or receding like a glacier, but as a rule advancing.... Hundreds of thousands ... had given up all hope of regular employment. ..." [7] But the pathology of the Depression of the 1930s was special because in the interval the physiological balance of American society had changed. *C.* 1870 families dependent on payrolls, blue or white collar, were only a growing minority; farm families were in the majority. And since the tradition of the largely self-feeding and -fueling farm was still strong, a good many suddenly jobless Americans had a resource to fall back on stabler than the local charity or hastily improvised state relief afforded the unemployed in 1930. The wage-committed house-hold, probably rather hand to mouth in good times, often unwisely entangled in time payments, in distress the moment the job lapsed, was the dominant, no longer the minority, case. Failure to grasp the scale and significance of this was one of the understandable, if deplorable, reasons why elder political and business leaders felt too little impulse to Do Something as the problems of unemployment and hyperliquidation grew. W. W. Businessman or his father had been through previous crises and, fighting the last war like the proverbial generals, thought chiefly in terms of how those previous panics had come unbidden and then gone in the not exactly good but anyway better-behaved old days.

And in any case the bosses still ate well and lived warm, so whatever Do-Something they felt was somewhat abstract. Things were far more poignant and concrete for the poorly padded individual. In a heartbreaking number of cases singly or in groups, Depression-harried Americans did their damnedest to Do Something to keep their own and, if possible, their neighbors' chins above water. Maybe the purest, if least constructive, form of it was the son's or daughter's turning vagrant to take a load off a family in hard luck. As Depression cruelly exploited Lord Bacon's "hostages to fortune," the adult breadwinner's emotions were corrosively grim. Hunger, cold and time on the hands were humiliating enough for a single man accustomed to self-support. For a husband unable longer to feed and clothe the woman who had married him for better or worse, and their children, that situation could be totally shattering.

Daniel Willard, president of the important Baltimore & Ohio Railroad, one of the best liked of the nation's management nobility, told a congressional committee that if he were jobless, he'd steal before he'd go hungry. There was astonishingly little of that version of Do-Something. Only the migrant kids did any substantial raiding of bakery trucks and, following the professional vagrants' lead, clothes lines and chicken houses. The bulk of industrial unemployed confined themselves to applying for what private or public relief was available and sentencing themselves for as long as courage held up to walking the streets from one NO HELP WANTED sign to another. The one thing widely agreed on about the Depression was that it infested the whole country, so there was small reason for a laid-off man to move his folks elsewhere. But in the most depressed farming areas—particularly the special situations of the cotton-crippled South and the famous Dust Bowl of the Great Plains—there was a chemical trace of sense in a pathetically purposeful self-uprooting and striking out for something that could hardly help being better. In some ways the most striking example of spontaneous Doing Something was the celebrated mass migration of the Okies.

World War I's greediness for wheat had led to much plowing up of Great Plains grassland for dry farming—a method that produced fairly well into the 1920s because rainfall persisted at average or better expectation in that off-and-on semiarid region. Then coincident with

Depression came droughts, the effects of which showed heedless mankind what bad medicine it was to plow that country. "I know this land. . . . Never was much good 'cept for grazin'. Never should a broke her up," [8] says the only character with ecological good sense in John Steinbeck's *The Grapes of Wrath*, the best-selling novel of 1939 that supplied today's legends about the Okies. The catastrophe that the headlines called the Dust Bowl was not, however, in spite of radicals' scoldings, all the fault of greed heedlessly plowing where God had set His mind against it. Scientists now know that long before the white man's plow came, long before the browsing buffalo and the fire-setting Indian arrived, climatic variations—less rain, more wind—had produced extreme Dust Bowl episodes on the Great Plains. It was just that by removing the turf that alone protected the soil, the dry farmer was tempting Nature to behave even worse than usual next time around.

So in the already calamitous early 1930s, as the skies refused to rain and the winds blew hard and then harder, from the Texas Panhandle up into eastern North Dakota the surface of the land rose up in dark, stifling clouds and went elsewhere. Like blizzarding snow, it banked against houses, made dikes of fences, buried automobiles, sifted into cracks around windows. But the worst was the stripping of topsoil from the fields and the obliteration of plantings. The land was not ruined for good. Water, time and the New Deal's ably applied remedies eventually restored it to its present fickle fertility. Only that was years in the future. Big operators could afford to wait. The "suitcase farmer"—the outsider hiring help and tractors to work leased land, no lasting stake in the country—could get out licking his wounds. But the smaller farmer settled on that land because his pop had filed in the land rush, now saddled with a family and a mortgage, was as badly off as if his land had suddenly changed into so many acres of the Sahara Desert.

Things were already bad enough. The mortgage acknowledged that all through the 1920s low prices for wheat and cotton made the going rough. Larger, more efficient farm machinery had simultaneously been reducing wage work available from big operators consolidating small farms. Being "tractored out" as the foreclosed farm was merged into a huge operation dislocated many a family yet to be "dusted out." The sea-of-dust landscape not only ruled out crop planting but starved livestock too. Credit at the store gave out. Hundreds of thousands managed somehow to hang on until the New Deal's help began after 1933. Their grandchildren are still there. Other hundreds of thousands got out while they still could raise gasoline money. The demographic hole they left is striking. In the 1930s the nation's rural population, even though dwindling relative to urban, rose slightly as a whole. But in the Dakotas, Nebraska, Kansas, Oklahoma—where the drought was driest and the winds stronger and the term "Dust Bowl" was born—rural population was lower at the end of the decade than at its beginning. Suppose an element of self-selection in those emigrating in contrast with those staying put, and there are several interpretations: The emigrants had more inner Do-Something than their neighbors or, looked at unfavorably, lacked the stamina to stick it out; or the farsighted had already been on the verge of pulling up stakes when drought and dust came along to clinch the matter. Anyway, lock, stock and barrel; old woman, kids, dog and cat; skillet, guitar, mantelpiece clock, radio, sewing machine and cardboard suitcases—just like in that movie—they loaded persons and plunder into the old Ford and headed West.

Their circumstances might well be as straitened as *Grapes* said, for they were leaving situations lean to begin with and worsened by several years of hard times. The USSR eagerly imported prints of the *Grapes* movie to show the shortcomings of American capitalism. The showings backfired because Russian audiences were less impressed by the Joads' plight than by the fact that they owned an automobile, for even the equivalent of a Ford jalopy was beyond the reach of the common man over there. Actually in the previous decade even the outcast and starveling Mexicans who preceded the Joads in California's fields and orchards had been using rattletrap cars to follow the crops in. In this context the ironist should also note that the "tractoring out" that probably caused half the dislocation in *Grapes*—great hell-snorting monsters driven by cold-blooded hirelings ruthlessly straight across foreclosed smallholdings, obliterating boundaries, annihilating the pitifully small dwellings—was the same process of consolidating individual farms for the most efficient use of agricultural machinery that, as part of the sacred Five-Year Plan, many of Steinbeck's readers had been applauding. The chief difference lay in mortality consequent on this dislocation. In the Dust Bowl no substantial evidence of higher death rate. In the Ukraine several millions dead of starvation or hardships involved in forced deportation.

The Coast's generic label for refugees from the Dust Bowl was "Okies" because though they came from all up and down the Great Plains about two out of five were from Oklahoma. A Farm Security Administration survey showed the typical Okie family to be man and wife about thirty years old with two or three children—unlike the nine Joads of *Grapes,* though still many mouths to feed on the scanty, sporadic wages of the Promised Land. They were westward bound not because of any Berkeleyan visions of the Course of Empire, so dear to mural painters and pseudofolk poets, but because they, like the rest of the nation, had been siren-sung by boosters' propaganda, particularly that of California II. Oregon and Washington State got a good many, too, but even as early as 1933 it was estimated that half the nation's homeless, job-seeking "gasoline gypsies" were in Southern California. According to Steinbeck and others, unscrupulous agencies for California truck and fruit farmers had flooded the Dust Bowl with handbills promising well-paid, steady, clean work, come one come all, in order to attract many times more hands than were needed in order to keep wages low. Certainly such a dodge was not inconsistent with the group ethical standards of the Okies' prospective employers. Even their apologists admitted that some of it had been done. Only how much was never responsibly determined, and if the scale had been important, radical investigators would have had it all down, chapter and verse, whereas there is practically nothing about it in, for significant example, Carey McWilliams' authoritative *Factories in the Fields.* No such sharp practice was needed. Movies and folk talk derived from Chamber of Commerce ballyhoo had long since taught Americans about the orange-surfeited, sunshine-drunk, snow-free, bathing-beauty-infested Land of the Doasyoulikes 1,500 miles westward. The Okies' version of the old I-ain't-gonna-be-treated-thisaway blues had the added line: "I'm goin' where the orange blossoms blow...." [9] *

In one way the Okies' swarming to the Coast was propitiously timely. In the early 1930s measures taken by the Mexican and United States governments sharply reduced the supply of migratory, seasonal Chicano field labor that over the years had succeeded the Japanese, who had succeeded the Chinese, as crucial part of California's fruit, vegetable and cotton growing. A great deal of it was and is nasty "stoop labor," the sort that nobody with a tolerable alternative would conceivably do, and squalid and insecure to boot. An illuminating crosslight comes from Carey McWilliams' analysis of wage policies involved: "Since many crops have the same maturity dates, employers must draw from the same pool ... competition ... might become ruinous if uniform [wage] rates did not prevail. High wages, in many

---

* No doubt the Okies sang that often enough to justify the Lomaxes in calling it "the blues of the *Grapes of Wrath* people." (*Penguin Book of American Folk Songs,* 140.) But a *Fortune* reporter spending some months undercover in Okie camps in 1935 found the songs he heard oftenest were mostly from Tin Pan Alley; he mentioned "Anybody Seen My Gal?", "The Trail of the Lonesome Pine," "Twelfth Street Rag"; for folk items, "Comin' Round the Mountain" and "Red River Valley." Note how out of date the Tin Pan Alley items were. Apparently in the Dust Bowl it took a long time for a hit to pall.

California crops, have a tendency to reduce the supply of labor, since the work is so thoroughly undesirable that workers will pick for a short time and then quit." [10] California enterprise was not healthy anyway. Hard times, meaning disorganized price structures and dwindling ratio of demand–production had struck the Coast ahead of most of the country, thanks to deflating oil booms and real estate rackets. So here were 300,000 newcomers—give or take 50,000—pouring in between 1931 and 1935, more each year, "looking for the land of promise," said R. L. Duffus, at a time when it "was not able . . . to keep any promises." [11] Their prospective employers were in an harassedly penny-pinching mood, and the best the Okies could hope for was cutthroat competition for merely seasonal, widely scattered migrant jobs at scandalously low pay while living in squalid company shacks or foul, informal campsites.

The effect on both them and California's agricultural community was naturally dismal. After their precarious westward pilgrimage—here Steinbeck is trustworthy—they were ragged, dirty, broke and understandably peevish. Seeking work for a few weeks or months where there was little to be had made them dirtier, more ragged and ferally resentful of the lies they had wishfully swallowed. Such newcomers, whom unsympathetic eyes readily saw as swarmingly subhuman, inevitably brought out the worst in California's traditional vigilante-minded, law-in-an-ax-helve, power-jealous economic leaders. To make sure frictions would do their worst, the Communist Party, seizing on this situation to create fertile dissensions, led new *ad hoc* unions in "drives"—meaning strikes, riots, mobs, dead and crippled pickets and so on—to organize the Okies. For the atmosphere see *In Dubious Battle* (1936), out and away Steinbeck's best novel, deliberate propaganda, yet validly candid about Communist motives and methods. Los Angeles County grew so alarmed that it sent its own police illegally to the distant border passes to turn back "unemployables" among the Okies flooding into the press agents' paradise. These checkpoints were soon withdrawn, leaving the job to the state's pest-control agents, but the emotions that so flagrant a caper represented continued to grope for expression in lawmen's bullyings and beatings of migrant labor.

Not that the morass on which the Okies floundered was completely inhumane. Public health authorities and in time such New Deal agencies as the Farm Security and Resettlement administrations strove to alleviate their lot and afford them reliable information about work opportunities. Commonsense discount of the miseries and atrocities adduced in *Grapes* would be about 50 percent. To judge from the results secured in 1975 by a New York *Times* man asking today's survivors of the movement still living in the San Joaquin Valley how they've done and what it was like, that discount should be higher still. Here, too, crude vital statistics are a corrective guide. Several hundred thousand generic Okies entered California in the decade 1931–40, and many encountered great misery. Yet the state's death rate (population increasing, meanwhile, from 5,600,000 to 6,900,000) stayed pretty stable—rather lower than New England's, which was normal expectation, rather higher than the nation's as a whole, which was also normal, usually ascribed to the large number of old folks annually entering California and presently dying. That looks as if there were something in the protests of California's powers-that-were that Steinbeck exaggerated; as if once the situation was grasped, much was done to give many Okies health care and emergency nourishment.* Had things been as bad as propaganda made them sound, the state's death rate should have been noticeably affected. Nevertheless, even if it weren't directly lethal, the Okies had found poignant, creeping misery for no greater fault than being born in the wrong place and believing what they heard. And there is one minor demographic fact not to be omitted: In 1936–37, the years when the sequelae of malnourished maternity would have come home to roost, California's index of infant deaths, which had been steadily dropping, jerked definitely up again.

A man from Mars might sniff poetic justice in all this. The decades of ballyhoo meant to attract tourists with money and elderly couples susceptible to real estate swindles ended attracting hordes of virtual paupers whose plight tempted many Native Sons of the Golden West to act like the lugs they were. For earthlings the irony is marred by some sense, however remote now, of the hordes' plight. Presently irony of a higher order came in. By Pearl Harbor time a good many Okies had got work in defense industries, which boomed the whole Coast; that enabled them to accumulate assets to stabilize their positions. Others took advantage of the generally reviving economy to strike economic roots where they had been working. Nowadays in consequence many of the employers bitterly battling Cesar Chavez's union for field labor, successors of the Okie migrants, came west as Okie youngsters forty years ago. These once scrawny, starveling kids have sons and daughters in college, shiny hardtops and air-conditioned ranch houses—and the back of the hand to "squat labor" and "fruit bums." For such as these the Land of Promise came through after all.

---

* For such protest at its best see Frank J. Taylor, "Labor on Wheels," *Country Gentleman,* July, 1938, and "California's Grapes of Wrath," *Forum,* November, 1939, reprinted in *Reader's Digest,* November, 1939. For antidote, tendentious but deserving careful attention, see Chapter XVII of Carey McWilliams, *Factories in the Field* (1939).

Also in the Golden State certain Depression-harassed persons recalled where its name came from and took to the hills to seek gold in the same streambeds that drew the forty-niners there eighty years previously. In some Rocky Mountain states the bureaus or schools of mines gave courses in gold panning and sold students the necessary equipment at cost. They added little to the world's gold reserve but between what old-timers had missed and what had washed down in the gravel since their day, perseverance with shovel and sluice box could net enough to keep a family alive, and there was always the odd chance of a big nugget. The New Deal's sharp increase in the dollar value of gold in 1934 encouraged such "fossicking," usually confined to Chinese patiently working the tailings over. Once allow the absurdity of gold's being valuable because all agree it is, and this was another beautifully simple instance of the individual Do-Something reaction. Close behind, though less dependent on luck, was the bootleg coal industry in eastern Pennsylvania, where the law looked the other way while unemployed miners dug anthracite out of company-owned hillsides and took it to market, no questions asked, in spavined secondhand trucks.

The strangest individual reaction—and economically glorious—was that of Charles B. Darrow of Germantown, Pennsylvania, whom the Depression made rich by stimulating him into, so to speak, mining his own memories of better days. A middle-aged heating engineer, he had fallen on hard times in 1930 like so many others. Odd electrical repair jobs, dog walking and so on barely kept him and his wife one breathless jump ahead of the relief office. In the intervals of dreary pavement pounding he tried to invent toys that might catch public favor. None did. He sometimes fell into reverie about the weekends and vacations that had been so enjoyable when the Darrows went to Atlantic City. One evening he sketched on an oilcloth table cover a diagram for a cutthroat sort of super-Parchesi scored with stage money, based on the street names of Atlantic City—Baltic Avenue, Boardwalk and so on—and, as it developed in evenings of experimental play, wheeling and dealing in mock real estate. It was a great time killer, for it took some hours to play out, and so amused many of the Darrows' neighbors that he was kept busy making sets for them, then for Philadelphia department stores. Eventually Parker Brothers, high among American game publishers, took it on, even though it defied all their professional preconceptions: Successful board games were supposed to have simple rules and not take long. Within a few months the firm's struggle to keep up with the demand was "like trying to cap six oil gushers at once." [12]

The presumption about such runaway game successes, like the Mah-Jongg that the 1920s borrowed from China, is that they will be immensely profitable for a few years and then burn out. Monopoly went on and on to become almost as deeply embedded as bridge in American social life and spread overseas in versions in fourteen languages. There is an annual world championship Monopoly tournament the award for which is the Charles B. Darrow Cup. Its contestants are adults, but Parker Brothers now believes it is the game's immense popularity among children that keeps it onward and upward. Only not in the USSR. There it is anathema because it reeks of capitalism, which it certainly does. Nevertheless, at the United States trade exhibit in Moscow, the one at which Vice President Richard M. Nixon had his celebrated brush with Nikita M. Khrushchev, six successive sets of Monopoly were stolen from the recreational display.

Other plucky victims groped for a way out through organizing. The base might be mere consumer-mindedness or a yearning toward the vague glories of the Cooperative Commonwealth. Sometimes the presumably incompatible individual and collective impulses blended into curious shapes. The germ was often barter, the most elementary transaction, spontaneous result of A's awareness that B has what he needs and C over there has something else everybody needs. Here, too, the Coast was conspicuous. In Los Angeles County, about the time the Okies began flocking in, some of the local unemployed made deals with vegetable growers for whom slumping prices made it unprofitable to gather crops. The jobless harvested on shares and hauled their quota away in trucks lent by kindly warehousemen to divide among themselves or swap with unemployed tradesmen for laundry, house repair, mending or whatever. Gradually the group widened until an Unemployed Citizens League had two borrowed fishing boats supplying 200 pounds of fish a day, a crew unloading and sorting bottles in a dairy in exchange for surplus milk for members, another sweeping out a produce market in exchange for 300 pounds of surplus fruit and vegetables a day. Members going out on repair and maintenance jobs paid in 50 cents an hour to the league's treasury to keep up, among other things, three bunkhouses giving a night's shelter and free breakfast to all comers. These were good people. Other cash from collecting salvage newspapers and cutting cordwood was earmarked for fresh meat. Each member—1,700 of them at the peak in 1934–35—worked sixty hours a month at whatever was needed and received as much as was available, share and share alike, of what he needed.

About the same time up the Coast in Seattle teachers in the collectivist-minded Seattle Labor College organized white-collar victims of hard times for indoctrination in radical theory while working a prescribed sixteen hours a week in multiple-swap programs giving most ingredients of a basic living. Fuel came from member gangs sent out in borrowed trucks "to cut firewood on stumped-over land. . . . Vegetables and fruit were contributed by friendly farmers . . . fishermen [members] brought their catch . . . provision dealers contributed goods left over at the end of the day; packing houses gave meat, sometimes free, sometimes in return for work . . . furniture and machinery were lent . . . tailor shops and cobbling shops . . . were added. . . . Barber shops, and even one beauty-parlor to keep up the appearance of the girls . . . looking for work . . . an unemployed pharmacist dispensed simple remedies contributed by wholesale drug firms. . . . A carload of wheat was contributed . . . a bakery got under way . . . abandoned coal mines were worked . . . with the owners' permission . . . automobile mechanics . . . in a vacant garage [worked on] cars belonging to members or borrowed from friends. . . ."[13] Cooperating landlords gave living quarters rent-free in return for repairs and redecorating done by members. At its height this improvisation fed and managed the labor of 50,000 men, women and children, making up about 13,000 families served by twenty-two branch commissaries—all without any money nexus. Nobody paid for anything received; nobody was paid for anything done.

Salt Lake City's Natural Development Association, however, used a private medium of exchange, harking back, it was thought, to the pioneer days when Mormon scrip lubricated the encapsulated economy of the Kingdom of the Saints. This revived a device not uncommon when normal currency breaks down or employer monopolizes his employees' purchases. Expressed in dollars and cents, it was accepted by local stores and cleared through local banks—clear demonstration that stage money is as good as any if people want it that way. It all began with a carload of potatoes turned over to a group of unemployed. Eventually it borrowed from Depression-damped owners a shoe factory, an oil refinery and several canneries and offered services from carpenters, dentists, doctors and other experts paid with the scrip that member clients got in exchange for their own services on cooperating farms, in workshops or wherever. To prevent hoarding and keep circulation lively, all scrip was torn up as spent. Basic necessities went to members "according to their needs, regardless of position, station or birth," and on the job "Each member must contribute to the organization more than he withdraws."[14] In Dayton, Ohio, a Council of Social Agencies midwifed a similar cluster of production Units that operated a shoe factory and a bakery and raised rabbits for meat. Admirers of these and sister developments estimated that at the bottom of the Depression 1,000,000-odd Americans were involved in them in twenty states, mostly west of Pittsburgh. Say 1 American in 100. The difference between them and Sinclair and his EPIC was that these people made it go before trying to make an institution of it.

Obviously it was occasion for timely thought. Seattle seemed to confirm Technocracy's hope that an economy would work without a price system. Salt Lake verged toward Marx's "To each according to his needs...." Less specifically but cogently much of this "self-help" activity implied that when times were tough enough, society had a right to take over the means of production shut down because private enterprise's system of distribution was out of kilter and man them with those whom private enterprise could no longer afford to hire. Did this presage a crisis-born, spontaneously American collectivism innocent of overweening Technocracy or Communism but deep-rooted in the rule-of-thumb practicality of Production for Use? "We think this is the end of the capitalist system," a zealous self-helper told a reporter late in 1932, "and our league is ready to lead the way into a new area. But if ... there is another period of improvement before the end ... we want ... our members conscious ... that even if they are re-employed there is no security for them under the present system." [15] Dayton's self-helpers were so confident of a significant future that they organized a Production Unit for recent high school graduates finding that "the jobs in industry and business for which they spent years in training do not exist.... [They] are being made to see this movement not merely as a stopgap for the period of the depression but as an entirely new way of living." [16] Less dogmatically Frank D. Graham,* professor of economics at Princeton, no radical either, proposed a continuing national program of swap-minded, self-helpful enterprises to take up slack in hard times and retire into skeleton standby in good—just in case. Thus, to arrange for the unemployed almost to support themselves would greatly lower the load on charity- and tax-financed agencies.

Whether wishfully ideological, as in Dayton, or just using whatever came to hand, as in fossicking, here certainly was the American's vaunted self-reliance. Maybe that was why America's Communists bitterly opposed all such developments. Communism's "Unemployed Councils" in industrial centers preferred to stage "hunger marches" to draw the police into killing a few demonstrators, as was neatly managed in Detroit. For good Party members it was immoral to try to

---

* Not to be confused with Frank P. Graham, president of the University of North Carolina, later US Senator, doughty New Dealer.

keep up the morale of the jobless by modifying the System. That blurred the iniquities that suited Communist purposes. From other points of view, other flaws are evident. Salt Lake's carload of free potatoes was symbolic. To one or another extent self-help projects were parasitic on the crippled old economy, depended too much on contributed commodities and borrowed facilities. To become a going concern, not just a stopgap improvisation, self-help had to own, not merely wangle use of, land and buildings; to make, not merely salvage, trucks and sewing machines. Nor could its catch-as-catch-can recruiting create the balance of skills necessary to produce all goods and services while getting the most out of each pair of hands. Once everybody's shoes were resoled, too many cobblers would have to be put to cutting firewood. Who could weld the crack in the salvaged commissary stove? Rational remedy for such problems led straight to economy-wide, conscription-minded Technocratic schemes, in any case into things that most individual self-helpers did not have in mind and would be distressed by.

Close scrutiny sometimes brought out also a disquieting invidiousness in self-help's emotional foundations. It sometimes sounded as if it were bent primarily on sparing the Depression-harassed white-collar man the ignominy of having to mingle with those for whom resort to breadlines and Skid Row now and again was well within normal expectation. Hallgren noted uneasily that the bulk of self-helpers were not proletarians at heart but lower middle class. Even radical-minded Seattle's scheme disclaimed interest in the marginally unemployable and concentrated on "citizens who work hard, raise families, buy homes and pay taxes ... now caught in the wreckage ... homes and savings gone, facing in terror and bewilderment a future which seems hopeless." [17] The goal was like a tourist third class distinguished from outright steerage not so much in quality of food or berth as in the company one kept while doing things out of one's usual white-collar line. Cleaning out the privy on the borrowed truck farm was not quite so self-erodingly smelly when one was aware that the other fellow with a shovel had been a teller in a bank forced to close its doors. That sort of feeling sometimes surfaced later in other kinds of relief programs—an almost-explicit assumption that unemployment and the consequent erosion of self-respect somehow impinged harder on bank tellers and shipping clerks than on those who had always been pick swingers.

America's black community had already set a pre-Depression precedent for cooperative self-help. Father Major M. J. Divine's "Heavens" not only flourished long before Salt Lake or Seattle dreamed of such projects, but also outlasted them. Doubtless they arose so early and lasted so late because the nation's blacks suffered from chronic hard times before and after as well as during the Depression. This movement had several morbid aspects. But two things could be said for it: It kept many a hard-up black's chin above water, belly full and habits steady, for teetotalism and celibacy were imposed. And it avoided the ethical-ethnic mistake, often so tempting for spellbinding black leaders, of trading on blacks' thoroughly understandable but largely self-defeating dread of and hatred for whites. Indeed, some of Father Divine's black detractors accused him of insidiously aiming at amalgamation of blacks and whites.

He was a very stubby (five feet two inches), medium-colored, mustached, middle-aged black of high charisma—a word he would certainly have delighted in had he known it, but fashionable jargon had not yet borrowed it from theology. He had once been George Baker, scraping a living in Baltimore either at waterfront odd jobs or mowing lawns and clipping hedges—take your pick of legends. Such data were not available from Father himself. He denied any memory of what he had been before he was suddenly born again in 1900 at the corner of Seventh Avenue and 134th Street in Harlem; can you remember things happening before you were born? Maybe he hailed from rural Alabama. Maybe it was in Savannah, Georgia, that he began groping toward a career as preacher to storefront congregations, eventually basing his followers' belief that he was God on I Corinthians 3:16: "Know ye not that ye are the temple of God, and that the spirit of God dwelleth in you?"

By 1915 he and a few followers were established in an apartment in Brooklyn's small but influential enclave of blacks. This collective household combined dictatorship with cooperative economics. Father secured paying jobs, usually menial, for his flock. On payday they gave him all their wages, and he supplied them with a complete living—food, clothes, lodging and the nightly ecstasy of exhortation and singing. Medical service was not included, for he deplored doctoring, instead dabbled in faith healing and taught, like the usual self-created deity, that those genuinely believing in him would never get sick, let alone die. His commission, so to speak, as employment agent and community manager consisted of as good a living as most blacks had ever known and the emotional rewards of consent to his delusions of grandeur.

The temporary slump of 1919–20 brought him more job-needy adherents than the Brooklyn apartment would hold even three or four to the room—sexes duly segregated. For $2,500, paying $700 cash down from a thick roll of bills, he bought them a commodious house in Sayville, Long Island. It was available to blacks because its owner wanted to spite his next-door neighbor. The source of the cash remained hazy, for the Reverend J. Devine, as he called himself during the transaction, persuaded his flock that his will alone produced all the good things they needed. The worldly assumed that this and other large sums he got up on occasion were shrewdly husbanded residue from his devotees' wages less the cost of maintaining them. Soon a few crackpot whites got wind of him—in Sayville he became simply, candidly "Father Divine"—and came to see, believe and join up. One was a former New Thoughter—"mental scientist"— another a "mystic lecturer," a third a Boston automobile dealer who failing to find peace in Unity, Mental Science and such, discovered what he needed in Sayville, gave Father a secondhand Cadillac and became his secretary. With divine farsightedness Father drew no color bar.

At first Sayville regarded him not unfavorably. The domestic help that he recruited for local summer cottages and nearby fat-cat estates proved unusually reliable and efficient. But their evening corroborees in praise of Father, all singing, shouting, dancing and Pentecostal-style trances and glossolalia, were pretty noisy and grew more so as their numbers swelled during the 1920s. Hard times added more. In 1931 mounting complaints to the police about the nuisance that their "Heaven," as they called the establishment, had become brought Father into court, charged with the usual misdoings. The judge sentenced him to a year in jail and a $500 fine. Five days later the judge dropped dead of a sudden heart attack.

Father never said flat out that this was his doing, just as he never quite said, in outsiders' hearing anyway, that he was God. Only if his flock wanted to put up banners inscribed "Father Divine is God," they were privileged thus to state their opinion. Certainly in both contexts they had a right to put two and two together. The dead judge was Father's title clear to mansions in the skies. It was mere anticlimax when an appellate court reversed the court of first instance. Subsequently Father went several rounds with the law. But among his adherents was an able black lawyer, the faithful proved to be admirably obfuscating on the witness stand and the serenely suave confidence of Father's own courtroom presence was brilliant defense in itself. The law never laid a glove on him. The way he told it, he owned nothing, his people owned nothing, all connected with them and him were of divine origin and neither secular government nor backsliding renegade suing for recovery of his contributions should be allowed to obstruct the ineffable joy of praising Father's name.

The spread of his reputation among the 200,000 blacks then in Harlem led to a branch "Heaven" there. The influx of neophytes in the 1930s led to proliferation of Heavens there and elaboration of the nomenclature and organization that now was drawing attention from the white press, hence coast-to-coast fame. A highly compelling detail was the stick-to-the-ribs provender that went with Father's holiness. At the bottom of the Depression each Heaven was serving hard-up Harlemites, come one, come all, a daily dinner of chicken, spareribs, sausage meat, pig's feet, lamb stew, liver and bacon, rice, hominy, boiled or fried potatoes, several kinds of greens, stewed fruit, cake—all blessed by Father himself or by proxy. "Angels"—believers giving Father their earnings—dined free. "Children"—outsiders from among whom Angels were recruited—paid 15 cents if they had it, nothing if they were up against it. The low price was practical partly because the Depression had brought food costs somewhat down, partly because Father's staff cleverly prowled New York City's wholesale markets for quantity bargains in low grade but still edible and nourishing foodstuffs. An economist might say merely that the Angels were wise thus to pool their scanty purchasing power for cooperative buying and cooking. The average partaker at one of Father's groaning boards saw it as an inscrutable miracle of the loaves-and-fishes sort.

The supernatural flavor was deepened by the orgiastic doings that went with the feast. This or that Angel would rise and whoop or babble praise of Father's love or confess the lurid details of the sin or penury from which he had redeemed his lamb while the rest moaned and shouted the "Peace, it's wonderful!" that was the cult's chief slogan. They sang "Father, I surrender, I surrender all to you...."

> Father, I love you, I do
> Because you saved me when ev'rything failed me....[18]

or to the tune of "Casey Jones":

> Father Divine! he is my father!
> Father Divine is walking in the land!
> Got the world in a jug
> And the stopper in his hand! [19]

Naomi Mitchison, radical British novelist who visited such a feast in 1933, admired the accompanying music from "a superb orchestra of violins and trombones, the rhythm held or syncopated by a tambourine-waving maenad in a scarlet beret." [20] It usually induced the symptoms of religious ecstasy so common among Westerners "feeling the power" whether Harlem blacks, Southern poor whites or certain exhibitionistic Episcopalians—whirling dances, volleys of handclapping, "the jerks," "the flops"... and all the while the tiny brown man sat at the head of a huge U-shape table eating, poker-faced, until he finally rose and launched into one of his vertiginously logorrheic discourses, maybe beginning, "God's presence is real and tangibleated! It has been tangibleated and it can be retangibleated!" [21] A word that Father worked over was probably never the same again. His rhetoric, said V. F. Calverton, the radical critic, was "distorted and agglutinative ... scarcely more than mystical mumbo-jumbo ... twisted, gnarled, humpbacked words ... consummate incoherency...." [22] Thus: "The Person will reflect in you and the Inspirator will demonstrate in you. You will observe the demonstration of the Impersonal, the Demonstrator and the Inspirator—the one who is inspiring you, reflecting and impressing in your personality and in your individuality.... But you must not bind yourself from your thoughts to the mortal versionated point of view as you might observe it...." [22] Obscure and clotty, true; but it probably sounded good on top of a square meal and is by no means more obscure than a great deal of early Christian theological speculation that DDs still have to take very seriously.

The cult's word-happiness was also striking in the names that Angels chose, like monastics taking their vows. Biblical references mixed with shreds of Tin Pan Alley and New Thought as Father's followers called one another in token regeneration Loveliness Rest, Martha Blue Heaven, Peaceful Magdalene, Truthful Baby, Blessed Thomas, Queen Esther, Continual Thank You Father, Miss Angel Gabriel.... My particular favorite is Frank Incense. It did not necessarily follow that Frank was a man or Peaceful Magdalene a woman. There is no sexual distinction in the beyond, so there was none in these symbolic labels. Angel women fanned down into Manhattan as come-by-the-day houseworkers in jobs Father found for them directly or indirectly. Employers troubled by having to call a grave, self-possessed black woman Beautiful Smile Love were reconciled as they learned that, unlike some of her unredeemed sisters, she always came when she said she would, did a generous day's work, stayed honest and sober—at $10 a week, the minimum that Father set. The new Social Security Act (1935) did not cover domestic help, so these women's refusal to admit their previous names made no trouble with the federal bureaucracy. But there was some—eventually resolved in the Angels' favor—when during Father's forays into politics they tried to register to vote as Tree of Life, Serious Ezekiel....

Further anticipating self-help—and recalling the blacks' disastrous Marcus Garvey movement of the early 1920s—Father went into cash-earning businesses. Beginning with sending otherwise useless Angels out to earn dimes by shining shoes, he presently studded Harlem with Father Divine-labeled restaurants, grocery stores, beauty parlors, barbershops, pushcarts selling "Peace Father Fresh Vegetables"—all profits to the support of the Heavens, for none of the peddlers, barbers or whatever was paid more than basic livelihood in kind. His Angel John Matthew, asked in court who owned the secondhand truck in which he fetched bootleg coal from Pennsylvania for the Father Divine Peace Mission Coal Company, said nobody owned it; Father "blessed" him with it for that purpose. In 1935 he paralleled the Back-to-the-Land phase of self-help (to be gone into later) and impressed the press as well as his flock by putting down $7,000 cash on purchase of an august Hudson Valley estate,* soon adding to it a nearby bankrupt hotel and several other house-and-land parcels. On them he settled numbers of the faithful to feed themselves and send surplus produce to the Heavens in town. More Heavens appeared in Jersey City and Newark, New Jersey, Bridgeport, Connecticut, Baltimore, Detroit, Chicago; developed footholds in Britain, Canada, Australia, Switzerland; and, though never getting a good start in Dixie, inevitably leaped the width of the continent to take root in, of course, California II.

His vicar apostolic there was Faithful Mary, a brand snatched from the alcoholic burning, or so she said, in Newark. Her missionary work was almost as effective among whites as blacks, which gave a special character to the Coast branch. Not even after she apostasized and tried to set up a competing cult did it altogether burn out. But the core of the new religion naturally stayed in Harlem, the blacks' cultural capital, where by 1933 Father's hold was so firm that even Fiorello H. La Guardia, that independent-minded politician, found it advisable to show up at a Father Divine rally in Harlem. The already ecstatic crowd, distracted by Father's doing a buck-and-wing on the platform, paid scant attention to this deferential visitor. But he made his way down front and saluted Father bravely: "Peace, Father Divine! ... No matter what you want I will support you! ... I came here tonight to ask Father's help and counsel...." [23] A great moment, but maybe Father relished even more his Easter Parade that spring when, riding in a blue open Rolls-Royce with a white policeman on one running board and a black one on the other, he led 5,000-odd Angels through Harlem. Easter the following year saw him riding over the parade in a specially decorated airplane.

His following was only one of many segments of Harlem, of course.

---

* The seller was Howland Spencer, later conspicuous in Shirtist movements in Florida. His motive in selling is said to have been partly to annoy FDR, whose Hyde Park country place was within sight of the new Heaven. (Harold Lavine, *Fifth Column in America*, 52.) If so, the purpose failed, for Father's subsistence colonies kept very low profiles.

STORMY WEATHER / 309

Its movie audience frequently laughed and jeered when he was in the newsreel. Established black leaders often followed the Reverend Adam Clayton Powell, Junior, dashing incumbent of the Abyssinian Baptist Church, who denounced Father in the *Amsterdam News,* Harlem's chief newspaper, as "the colossal farce of the twentieth century." [24] Similarly ten years earlier Garvey had been disowned by A. Philip Randolph, statesmanly chief of the Pullman porters' union, and W. E. B. Du Bois, mainstay of the National Association for the Advancement of Colored People. As Father's tribe increased and his emotional temperature rose to match, he followed Garvey by slipping into unquestionable megalomania. He was claiming 20,000,000 followers and telling audiences he was "The great Universal Mind ... the cosmic forces of Nature work in perfect agreement with me...." [25] He had long shown the eagerness for money as well as power that to a Messiah's enemies looks like cynicism but to insiders means only that all things work together for good in them that love the Lord. In Sayville he had denounced all forms of insurance, moving his new converts to cash in their burial insurance and give him the proceeds, at the same time that he carried heavy fire insurance on the Heaven building. But unlike Garvey, whose temperament took him deep into persecution mania, Father remained bland, faintly smiling, secure in a sort of innocence that enabled him simultaneously to turn his flock out to swell Communist-organized parades—they marched carrying stuffed white doves—and to oppose all labor unions, sometimes even sending some of his people out as strikebreakers.

The teaching that he could never die held up well for ten years after World War II. In 1965 he succumbed to what doctors described as arteriosclerosis complicated by diabetes. They said he was over one hundred years old. Nobody really knew, but he was probably pushing ninety. They buried him in a $500 silk suit. It was explained that he had long since imbued his white Canadian second wife, Mother Divine, with an ample quota of his divine spirit, so in effect he hadn't died at all but lived on to his own greater glory in her tall, buxom, impressive person....

Yes, most of this followed patterns that paranoids have carved out among the credulous and emotionally vulnerable of all colors hundreds of times in history. In minor details, such as Father's fierce resistance to medical care and indifference toward what happened when a woman became Precious Rubies and entered a Heaven, abandoning her children, his influence was noxious. Yet the police in Harlem came to regard him as a constructive influence, infecting Angels with values such as those in the testimony of one: "I worked as a chambermaid at a hotel and not a day passed but what I'd steal something, but now I've paid the hotel for everything I stole and now

I wouldn't read a newspaper that someone else was holding in the subway, because I feel that it would be stealing." [26] Part of becoming an Angel might be turning oneself in for previously undetected petty crime, taking a jail sentence and serving it out in expiation while Father's staff kept little gifts and letters coming along to keep the spirits up. A citizens' committee appointed by a Newark judge to evaluate Father's social consequences respectfully described his "restraining effect" [26] on crime and his substantial service in keeping many of the needy fed and encouraged. And in any case he did create "the most successful communal movement ever developed in the United States" [27]—E. David Cronon's description. New version of the old proverb: *Quos Deus vult nutrire....*

The *Reader's Digest* of February, 1933, on the stands in the blackest days just before FDR took over, carried a few pages about self-help projects. They struck the camera eye of King Vidor, one of Hollywood's most fertile directors (*The Big Parade, Hallelujah, The Crowd* and so on), and moved him to write a movie script based on the need of the nation's unemployed for self-respecting, self-supporting functions to perform. Unable to find other backing for *Our Daily Bread,* his admirable title for his story, Vidor financed and produced it himself—a poignant index of how near it was to his heart.

It showed a nice young city couple, husband out of work because of the Depression, using their last dollar to buy a chicken so they can invite to dinner Her prosperous uncle, who might have a job for Him. No job in prospect, but the old boy has just foreclosed a mortgage on a farm, and he likes the chicken well enough to let Him and Her use the place for shelter and subsistence until they can do better. On it they develop an all-for-one-and-one-for-all collective (with Salt-Lakeish, Seattleish overtones), as in the *Digest* piece, of work-hungry, decent victims of hard times—a carpenter, a stonemason, a tailor, a violinist, an undertaker. One recruit proves to be an escaped convict so keen on the project that he lets them turn him in and collect the reward on his head to finance needed improvements—an episode said to have been suggested by Charlie Chaplin, who also got booking facilities for the picture from United Artists, of which he was a founder. For a while there a serpent in the shape of a slithery blonde threatens the movie's Eden, but then an exacting crisis that forces all hands and the cat frantically to dig an irrigation ditch to save the crop from drought also saves Him from Her—and gives the thing a rousing climax of significantly triumphant collective effort.

The setting was an abandoned golf course on the outskirts of Los Angeles—a proper symbol of its time. Most upper-level reviewers applauded what they took to be an effort to bring to the American screen an equivalent of the USSR's use of movies in social education and by corollary a breach of Hollywood's traditional reluctance—never a flat taboo but tacit policy seldom flawed—to rub the customers' noses in the shortcomings of their society. The Hearst papers denounced *Our Daily Bread* as subversive. For ironic antidote the Russians, who showed it and gave it a second prize in a film festival at Moscow, told Vidor that it would have won first had it not been capitalist propaganda. The box office's verdict was equivocal. Vidor and his friendly backers lost nothing but made little. Much would have to happen inside and outside the movie industry before a cognate effort, *The Grapes of Wrath,* would make a resounding success in 1940.

The comment that now seems to stand up best was in a tirade of Edmund Wilson's against Hollywood as of 1937: "The vultures of the Coast get them all. A director like King Vidor, who has serious aspirations, ends by turning out the worst kind of monstrosity, the bad serious picture." [28] One should not, however, miss the meaning of what the hero of *Our Daily Bread* says in the last reel: "There's nothing for people to worry about so long as they got the land." That is a monstrously sanguine sentiment from a man fresh from shattering worry about drought, which is only one of the several potential threats to well-being that always hang over those committed to living off the land. Take it here not as a psychiatric datum but as Vidor's recognition of the contemporary cult of Back-to-the-Land that lent momentum to self-help in the early 1930s. It has been noted in Father Divine's arrangements. It was strong in the local self-help cooperatives outside Dayton, in which local agencies settled likely member families on tracts of a few acres. The hope it fostered was that between intensive farming, primarily for family subsistence, and seasonal cash earnings from industry, a cluster of such ventures could become a permanent community and show the way out for important numbers of unemployed. FDR's first inaugural address dwelt on that in a fashion that had considerable effect on several interested New Deal Programs.

Back-to-the-Land had a strikingly mixed ancestry. It included Prince Pyotr Alexeyevich Kropotkin, bearded, genial prophet of anarchism; Henry George, prophet of the single tax, the native American radical theory that jostled so many of our forebears into one or another social heresy; Henry Ford, most cantankerous of cracker-barrel mavericks. Kropotkin seems to have been first to suggest that instead of letting industrial workers cluster in festering slums around large factories, society should break factories up into small, coordinated units scattered through the countryside as nuclei of communities of small-holding, subsistence farmers who also worked in the factories part time or seasonally. This was part of the anarchists' persistent vision of an economy of semiautonomous, loosely symbiotic communes; it cropped up again in Loeb's version of Technocracy. But hygiene and morals too got stirred in. The Back-to-the-Lander assumed that the part-time farm family would be healthier because of all that fresh air, fresher, more nourishing food and salutary seasonal rotation of kind of work. And cash wages would free them from the farmer's ever-nagging, soul-warping, fertility-destroying problem of the cash crop to pay for taxes, hardware and clothes. Such notions seem to have infected Henry Ford at several removes from their sources—enough to purge them of anarchistic taint. Or he could have worked them out for himself from memories of his farmboy youth. Anyway, he actually set up a pilot-plant system of the sort—small factories on restored mill sites, making small parts for his assembly lines with local labor released seasonally for subsistence farming.

That was the bucolic, best-of-both-worlds fork of what we may call the settlement-house road Back-to-the-Land. Well before World War I it was recommended by Bolton Hall, a labor-minded, single-taxer, Irish-American lawyer in New York City. He had been impressed by the success of local slum dwellers when encouraged to raise garden truck in vacant lots. In view of the exercise, improved morale and better nourishment that they got from a few packets of seeds and a hoe, why not move them out to the countryside to acquire a minimum cottage and an acre or two grouped with other such refugees so that necessary transportation and schools would be feasible? The prototypes were the several rather tenuous such colonies set up by adventurous single taxers in suburban situations in Massachusetts, New Jersey, Delaware, California, of course, and—for reasons I cannot yet determine—the Gulf Coast of Alabama.* There was also the Fellowship Farm project of certain sanguine Socialists near Hingham, Massachusetts,

The distressing unemployment consequent on the panic of 1907—no such tidal wave as that of 1873 or 1929 but rough on those losing jobs—was what brought into the Back-to-the-Land movement another single-taxer, a Hungarian-American advertising consultant, William Borsodi. In New York City's Union Square one miserably snowy night he saw a long line of men, "hands stuffed deep in pockets, while they shivered and shivered, nose, cheeks and lips blue and purple from the

* This Fairhope, Alabama, single-tax colony was also and very naturally, the site of Marietta Johnson's-much discussed go-as-you-please Progressive Education school (John and Evelyn Dewey, *Schools of Tomorrow*, 22–39).

cold," waiting hours in hopes of earning a dollar or so shoveling snow next morning. Already aware of Hall's ideas, Borsodi wrote to him, asking "why all these people should not live on your three-acre farm, even in a large dry goods box rather than ... swell the ranks of the objects of charity.... In all countries and climates I have found that all people would benefit by ... keeping close to the land ... thousands of those now in the hospitals, lunatic asylums and penitentiaries or .. in abject poverty ... could have kept in healthy condition had they gone back to the land in good time." [29] A romantic Antaeus complex if you like; certainly not a responsible social theory. Yet pedantic jokes or mistrust of amateur sociology need not discredit the man's civilized pity for those poor devils in Union Square.

Already, however, Hall was shifting away from welfare-mindedness and part-time subsistence toward individualism and intensive, market-dependent cash crops. He wrote books about Back-to-the-Land entitled not *Candide's Cooperatives* but *Three Acres and Liberty* and *A Little Land and a Living* (both as of 1908). He dwelt on the example of Denmark's full-time farmers able to fertilize, sweat and coddle livelihood out of small parcels of land that American farmers would think too small for schoolyards. Brashly he laid it down that "[On one acre] any dunce can raise onions ... three hundred bushels ... make at least as big wages [as in a slum-surrounded factory].... The city man who has brains enough to conduct a shop ... is a good enough financier to meet his monthly bills, knows enough to make money out of the soil. The same attention to details ... [in] an orchard ... vegetable farm ... fruit farm ... will bring far greater profits." His rallying chant for Back-to-the-Landers was:

> Get three acres and live by it.
> Get a spade and try it.
> And get out of debt.
> Get off the back of the workers.
> Get out of the power of the shirkers.
> Get up and Get! [30]

Fellow zealots from among horticulturists applauded him. Presently the War Gardens of World War I showed that sometimes inexperienced tilling of a patch of ground really would produce tasty and inexpensive nourishment. But not until after the Armistice did Borsodi's engineer son, Ralph, supercharge the movement by lending it a frank intellectual snobbishness and an ascetic flavor going well with his lean, hawk-profiled, Savonarola-istic appearance. Early in the 1920s he added to his father's Back-to-the-Landism a dollop of Production for Use, then the promising but inchoate war cry of the militant consumer-movement-to-be. After hard work with a slide rule Borsodi convinced himself—probably without grueling difficulty—that in spite of the real efficiencies of mass production, many consumers' goods could be made at home more economically than they could be bought from retailers. True, he said, the Campbell Soup Company's mass-processed can of tomatoes of acceptable quality cost it much less than the housewife's Mason jar of tomatoes that she had grown and canned herself, if you figured in the theoretical cash value of her time. But the costs of selling and distribution between the Campbell plant and the grocery store in Springfield were so high that it would actually pay her—in ascertainable dollar-and-cents terms—to roll her own from tomato patch to cellar shelf.

Gamely, acting on that belief, Borsodi, his wife and children forsook Manhattan for Rockland County, New York, handily near the city but not yet seriously fouled up by real estate development. They bought seven acres with a decaying small house, successfully remodeled it and cleared and cultivated the land. Then they bought a larger tract nearby and, using newly acquired skills and confidence, started again from bare beginnings. Their new house, using the ideas of Ernest Flagg, a progressive Manhattan architect, combined concrete with stone picked up on the site and was built on a concrete slab with no cellar, then a novelty. Soon they had satisfactory production of vegetables, fruit, eggs and fat capons from a flock of sturdy Rhode Island Reds. The cow they bought gave so much milk—not the usual problem—that they sold her and got a couple of doe goats, the kids born to which proved tasty on the dinner table. The more highly bred doe they named Isadora Duncan. When they found the local idyllic Little Red Schoolhouse full of bullying and perversions, they taught their children at home. Two hours a day of undistracted tutoring kept them well able to pass the examinations that the local school board let them take in lieu of attending. Beyond that, as an admiring piece in the *New Republic* pointed out, the little Borsodis' wide range of domestic chores was exactly "the sort of thing that the most fashionable and expensive [Progressive] ultra-modern experimental schools in New York City go to no end of trouble to reproduce." [31]

They didn't quite go to the length of boiling down their own salt Indian-fashion from the nearby tidewater Hudson. But they wove their own woolen suitings and blankets because they thought that to do so was emotionally healthy as well as cash-sparing. Weaving was, Borsodi pointed out, much used as occupational therapy in mental institutions: "[We have] taken the looms out of our homes ... transformed them to factories ... the absence of the creative work they used to furnish is producing an ever increasing number of neurotic men and women ...

an endless number of 'problem' children." [32] With sewing machine and purchased paper patterns they ran up clothes better made than store hand-me-downs. Machine and patterns were mass-produced, true; so were the washing machine, the pump that kept up pressure in the pipes, the electric mill that ground grain for unbleached flour more nourishing than bleached stuff from Minneapolis. But they made a nice distinction between mass-produced equipment to make things with and mass-produced consumer goods. They were candidly in-debted to several crucial technological improvements new at the time—pressure cookers, for instance, that expedited home canning and improved its quality, too; septic tank systems superseding the outdoor privy in situations lacking sewers; extension of electric power to rural areas, already spottily anticipating the New Deal's Rural Electrification program. Borsodi's authority in the semisubsistence movement grew to where he was made chief consultant of Dayton's hopeful experiment in municipally financed and encouraged "homesteading" projects following his example.

It troubled purists that all those electric gadgets—Borsodi's setup required thirty-odd electric motors—kept the homestead dependent on the power company with its inescapable monthly bills. In his case his engineering assignments, pursued sometimes in the city, sometimes at home, supplied cash for wattage, taxes, gasoline and the considerable number of other things that mass production made more advan-tageously than individual hands could. Any homesteader who really tried, he came to believe, could find some part-time equivalent. As missionary for homesteading—a role he relished from the beginning—he brushed aside doubters' objection that many lacked the requisite knack with tools and green things: "Any intelligent man who can study textbooks and follow instructions can learn enough of ... these crafts for life upon the land and so acquire a new delight in life because he has heightened his mastery of his environment." Stoutly he insisted that for "the average man and woman ... investment in a homestead equipped with sufficient domestic machinery [yields] larger returns per dollar ... than investment in insurance, in mortgages, in stocks and bonds." [33]

The go-thou-and-do-likewise book that laid it all down in 1929, *This Ugly Civilization,* he very properly dedicated to his wife, Myrtle Mae, for the "Courage, Initiative and Resourcefulness [that] made this adventure possible." Indeed; for the third potential flaw that he too lightly dismissed was the intending homesteader's poor chance of finding such a helpmeet-chatelaine-forewoman-seamstress-webster-gov-erness-horticulturist-field-hand-dairymaid-nurse-cook-laundress. It is dauntingly apparent that Myrtle Mae, who even stewed up her own floor wax, never lacked for occupational therapy. The growing offspring were always available, too. Obviously Borsodi was a tower of strength in all departments. But her formidably versatile, super-humanly capable part in it all was a striking example of the power of ideas on a doughtily healthy woman.

Clearly, if sometimes indirectly, they borrowed much from artsy-craftiness, no longer for mere aesthetic satisfaction but now in nutritional, thermal, hygienic earnest. Add a dash of Thoreau's cabin with the bean patch in the clearing stirring a certain kind of temperament to "arise now and go to Innisfree." Rather gingerly Borsodi also added a drop of the then-respected example of Gandhi's anti-imperialist cotton spinning. But his invidious, growingly frank elitism was probably what enabled him to reach the inspirational hegemony of Back-to-the-Land. The human raw material he sought to appeal to was no longer slum dwellers needing good done them but cultivated white-collar couples considering themselves pluckily worthy of the Good Life Creative.

Admirer of Nietzsche, Borsodi headed each chapter of *This Ugly Civilization* with an arrogant text from *Thus Spake Zarathustra,* for his too was a gospel of many called and few chosen. He analyzed America: 97 percent numb slugs fit only for assembly-line jobs; 2 percent "quality-minded" predatory exploiters, of whom John D. Rockefeller, Sr., was archetype; 1 percent "quality-minded," of whom Charles W. Eliot, president emeritus of Harvard was archetype. These last constituted "an aristocracy of superior persons ... [who] cannot be selected by examinations ... or the demagoguery necessary in ... some form of election ... recognized merely because they are superior." [34] For, like Technocracy's omnipotent Planning engineers, this enthusiast reformer was bent on recasting social values in the admirable images of Ralph and Myrtle Mae Borsodi. Yet again, Molière!

Those quality-minded were to answer Borsodi's call to free them-selves of quantity-mindedness and its parasitic exponents, get the best of both worlds by using the handy machines that mass production makes so well to foster the joys of husbandry and handicraft: "First, for their own sakes—that they and their posterity shall be comfortable; and then for mankind's sake—that their pattern of living may the sooner be imitated," [35] for these homesteaders were to think of themselves as, like Christ's early converts, the leaven in the lump that would eventually redeem the whole. Borsodi promised that "the quality-minded rulers of mankind ... [will] become dependent on *and subservient to* [Borsodians] (italics mine) ... for the first time ... businessmen, politicians and soldiers ... [will have] to treat with artists, scientists, teachers, doctors and professional men generally on a substantially equal basis ... armies and navies [will] go to the scrap heap ... Government be restricted to the barest minimum ... for the restraint of stupid and vicious individuals...." [36]

When published a few months before the Great Crash, *Ugly* seemed like just another symptom of the day's mistrust of Big Business' merchandising methods and the new vogue of consumer interests. But the strains of the 1930s gave it wider pertinence. Many of the kind of bright young people Borsodi hoped for were newly straitened by Depression and, being bright, likely to try to do something clever about it. Understandably they clutched at this flattering potential solution, no less because the implied austerities contrasted enticingly with the vulgar fat-cattery of the recent New Era. By 1933 *Ugly* was republished with an introduction by Harry Elmer Barnes, popular liberal polemicist, calling it "one of the most challenging books of recent years ... the only way out for many of those staggered by the insecurities of modern industrialism." [37] Soon after it Borsodi published his less Nietzchean but still edgy *Flight from the City*—in the context of 1933 a most significant title. Plenty of those artists, scientists, teachers and such duly vibrated to his recalling how, when the Borsodis lived in a rented apartment, "our lives were barren of real beauty ... which comes from contact with nature and from the growth of the soil, from flowers and fruits, from gardens and trees, from birds and animals...." [38]

So the early half of the 1930s saw thousands of couples, usually young, often as yet childless, doing what John Erskine, astringent Columbia professor and writer of best-selling spoofs on classic legends, called "buying up of deserted farms and converting them into a refuge from something or other." [39] They made a runaway success of a supplementary book, *Five Acres and Independence* (1934). Its author, M. G. Kains, was a professional horticulturist-journalist reared on an old-timey farm that had taught him "fruit and vegetable gardening, poultry and bee-keeping, horse and cow care ... canning and pickling, soap and candle-making," and he tried honestly to warn rash yearners that the intensive farmer was inexorably committed to "hard manual work from dawn to dark—and then by lantern-light." But three pages later he too was infectiously remarking that a period of depression always means "tacit acknowledgment [from] city dwellers that 'the farm is the safest place to live'... when ... his savings melt away [the wage earner] begins to appreciate the advantages of a home which does not gobble up his hard-earned money but produces much of its up-keep, especially ... food for his family ... ," whereas the urban rent payer gives his children only "a narrowing, uneducative, imitative, more or less selfish and purposeless existence . . . tainted air, restricted sunshine and lack of exercise. . . ." 40

After that no cautions about what kind of land to look for and what not to do with it could dampen certain temperaments' urge to lay their burdens on splendid old Mother Earth—given, of course, a certain cash nexus with the world that made wheel hoes, kilowatts and paper. Ample choice of acreage was available. Persistent decline in traditional farming had left many farms—the soil half worn out or eroded away, but the buildings still in recognizable shape—going cheap within easy distance of Boston, New York City (in Connecticut and New Jersey as well as the Borsodis' Rockland County), Philadelphia (notably in Bucks County), Baltimore, San Francisco (notably in Marin County) and doubtless a dozen other such situations of which I was not directly aware. It was usually the old farmhouse of freestone, brick or frame-and-clapboard, tumbledown but with good proportions and heavy Currier & Ives connotations, or the noble old barn with most of the shingles still actually in place, or just the quaint little fallen-in springhouse that caused a young wife in a dirndl skirt to say to her pipe-smoking husband, "Oh, yes, this . . . *this* is it, isn't it?" And for a surprising number of them the venture did not entail gradual disaster. Chances were best, of course, when cash income was high enough to reduce the subsistence factor far below what Borsodi envisaged.

The dominance of ideas over ecology in such circles enabled them to give low priority to favorable climate and soil; otherwise, they would not have so often chosen New England's stony fields and short growing season. Indeed Scott Nearing, the old firehorse radical whose first successful homesteading was done in Vermont, the next in Maine, insisted that New England was specially suited to the Good Life Creative because of stimulating scenery and prevalence of woods for fuel, yes, but even more because "soft climates probably produce soft people and certainly produce parasitic people." 41 That meteorological dogma may puzzle anthropologists aware of the tough Ashanti of West Africa and the hard-bitten Maori of northern New Zealand, a climate far milder than anything north of Mason's & Dixon's line. But it will trouble none aware of the strong flavor, seldom realized, of asceticism in the white-collar homesteader's yearnings.

Nearing's case demands attention and not least because it still persists up there on the bleak Maine coast, a museum specimen in full bloom. In 1932 he and his wife saw American society as "gripped by depression and unemployment, falling a prey to fascism" and rejecting "our pacifism, our vegetarianism and our collectivism." 42 So they bought a parcel of run-down land in Vermont for $300 down, $300 to pay. On it they built a chaletlike dwelling of local materials and with a minimum of local paid help. With lavish and assiduous use of compost they created a garden fertile and large enough to supply most of their food, learned to boil down sap from the sugar maples on the land for cash crop, supplemented that with fees for lectures at colleges and city forums interested in Nearing's always pungent, flauntingly leftist notions, usually so individualistic that the Communists finally expelled him not long before he took to the hills. With heroic, utterly earnest and well-planned hard work they made a go of it for nineteen years. Then the influx of outsiders and growth of their maple sugar business to irksome size made them uncomfortable. They sold the place for ten times what it cost them and bought an even less promising site near Harborside, Maine, to begin again on. At the time Nearing was sixty-eight years old.

They have made that go, too, and are still there past Nearing's ninetieth birthday. According to their recent account a year-round average of four hours a day of what they call "bread labor" * indoors and out keeps them fed, sheltered and warmed. Clothes, taxes and supplementary provender, such as peanut butter, margarine, raisins, brown sugar and honey, are paid for by Nearing's lectures, usually concentrated in winter, and sale of his books on this version of the Good Life and his experiences as a go-as-you-please radical. They keep hearty on their diet of 50 percent fruit and fruit juices; 50 percent vegetables including nuts, for other carbohydrates, fats (including vegetable oils) and the small proportion of protein afforded chiefly by grains, peas and beans. Their success with such a regimen is the more striking because it is hampered by eccentric doctrines that make the Borsodis sound like rank Sybarites. Rigid vegetarianism deprives them of not only meat but also nutritionally useful milk, poultry, eggs and the fish in the adjacent ocean. Not only hygienic but moral, it carries the principle of not exploiting animals, of respecting life †—or at least that is the emotional pretext—so rigorously far that the Nearings renounce most of the effective measures against crop-destroying animals and insects and won't even use animal manures on

---

* Apparently this does not mean that each day's stint is only four hours of bread labor; rather that this a year-round average. Long trips in winter, when they do no work at all at home, compensate for full days of bread labor when taking advantage of short growing season.

† A vegetarianism thus refusing to take life in order to nourish oneself betrays its absurdity as a moral attitude. Since man is an animal and, like all animals, directly or indirectly parasitical on plant life, he cannot nourish himself at all without destroying life. The nuts on which the Nearings live are each a living thing designed to sprout and create a new individual nut tree. A carrot is bursting with potential for second-year development of flower and life-carrying seed. A leaf of spinach is utterly alive when cut.

their vegetable garden.* When life can be maintained under such clogs on husbandry, one understands better how the peasants of the Dark Ages managed to survive—those who were, as Nearing must be, tough as whang leather.

That is the positive part. The negative, sometimes obtrusive in the 1930s, was a feeling that come the Revolution—which, for Borsodi's elite, was not a dread prospect—those who knew how to maintain themselves under their own vine and figtree would be better insulated from the popping of a socially constructive hell and afterward might lead reconstruction along Seattleish-anarchist lines. Apropos, the late Paul Goodman noted in 1970 "how very many young people . . . have decided to try subsistence farming and natural foods for nearly the same reasons as the Nearings. . . . Most . . . imagine that they thought it up out of their own heads, just as they imagine they invented pacifism. . . ." 43

All that is a necessarily fragmentary account of a thing that, though directly touching only a few tens of thousands, had clinically interesting consequences. Thus, the health-food-organic-gardening syndrome was there, though not to bloom until after World War II. And as slightly better times came in the latter 1930s, another snobbishness supplemented Borsodi's. Upper-bracket couples fraternizing with the Borsodian elite learned of the Good Life Bucolic and imitated such invigorating plain living and high thinking—superficially. The liberal but prospering young lawyer with a good apartment on Murray Hill valued as complement a renovated saltbox on twenty stony acres well up the Housatonic Valley. As he prospered further, it spread to those with incomes in six figures. Never doubt the historic truth in the bit in the J. P. Marquand novel about the Connecticut barn elegantly converted into a cultivated fat-cat dwelling—its hayloft full of fireproofed hay.

The colonizing sort of Back-to-the-Landism even cropped up marginally in the distressful story of the Bonus Army. The thousands of middle-aging men and hundreds of their women and children in the crowd scenes of that scenario were clingingly hopeful, baffled, hungry people, who on the whole behaved better than anybody had any right to expect under the circumstances. It is an ungrateful task to have to pin their fumbly version of the Do-Something, self-help impulse down on the corkboard. Nothing they did was half as fumbly as the handling they got—the unhappiest example of the Hoover administra-

---

* The only precedent for this that I know of was a similar renunciation of animal manures at Bronson Alcott's Fruitlands in the 1840s.

tion's clumsiness in its last year. Actually responsible hindsight sees the whole mess as mostly fumbling on both sides, not callous brutality or a Red-hot threat of chaos as in the conflicting legends evoked by mentioning the episode.

Where veterans of an extensive war can vote, particularly where conscription is resorted to, the duty of society specially to favor them is not exactly taken for granted but usually acted on as if it were. In 1923 veterans' organizations had forced on the federal government "adjusted compensation certificates"—a device for assuaging the veterans' natural grievance over the low pay they had got in uniform while civilians at home were getting high pay in war industries. Roughly the arrangement provided free paid-up life insurance policies maturing in 1945 with cash value upwards of $1,000 varying with length of service and time overseas, on which a veteran could borrow before maturity in amounts increasing yearly. As unemployment and frustration peaked, Depression-plagued veterans sought to make this eventual "bonus"—their shorthand term for this cryptoasset—a means of self-help. Let's have the cash now, they said, when God knows we need it, instead of thirteen years hence, when many of us will already be dead. We can use it to keep the mortgage from foreclosure or the little store from going bust or at worst to keep shirts on our backs till things improve—and incidentally, most of what we do with the money will give the economy a needed shot in the arm. US Representative Wright Patman of Texas, a veteran himself, building a career on hypersensitivity to peevish resentments down among the grass roots, sponsored a bill for immediate cash payment with a special new issue of unsecured (= "greenback") federal currency.

Several small bonus-hungry groups tried to support the bill by a "march on Washington." This roused memories of Coxey's Army, the thousands of loosely organized protesters against hard times who converged on Washington in 1893, plus thousands more from the trans-Mississippi region who never got there but attracted much notice anyway. It may have reflected some awareness of *Fascismo*'s March on Rome in 1922—an association that, with some reason, led some to smell an American Fascism in these veterans' doings. Among organizations threatening such a gesture was the Workers' Ex-Servicemen's League, a minor Communist Front. But Earl Browder, Stalin's American viceroy, preferred to concentrate on more widely based "hunger marches" in industrial centers. Though later the Party saw it had missed an important opportunity and tried hard to steal the Bonus Army's thunder, it succeeded only in getting it annihilated. The cleavage between their hundreds and the other bedraggled thousands stayed deep. Reds the Bonus Army were not. They felt little hope of social change and not much more of solidarity with other victims of the Depression. Throughout their feckless history they regarded themselves as specially deserving special cases entitled to special help from special arrangements to give them their special just dues.

The premonitory handfuls "marching on Washington" did little more than pester Congressmen for a day or two and go home again. In the spring of 1932, however, great things seemed to be shaping up for a movement set off by a nucleus of bonus seekers in Portland, Oregon, who worked out a new approach—march on Washington, OK, then stay there till Uncle Sam did right by them. Among their leaders the one reaching and staying at the top was Walter W. Waters, a former medic sergeant whose job in a local cannery had disappeared, leaving him with savings soon exhausted and a wife and two children on his hands. He was rather a drifter, blaming "the unsettling effect of the war on me" [44] for his inability to stay long in any kind of job in the booming 1920s. Garage mechanic, automobile salesman, baker's helper. . . . Then he left his native Idaho, changed his name and spent several years deliberately cut off from his folks as migrant worker in Washington State. He told people he had been assistant superintendent of that cannery when actually he had been just another pair of hands on the payroll.

Consonantly the 20,000-odd veterans who several times upheld him as leader give a group impression of greater-than-average instability. Certainly they were no representative cross section of the millions of veterans extant at the time. Waters' amateur analysis of the data in their membership applications for his Bonus Expeditionary Force shows disproportionately few from large cities; relatively high incidence of WASP names, low of Poles, Italians, Jews. They were high in unemployed industrial workers and included a large number of small businessmen bitterly conscious of having been their own bosses and penalized for it by insolvency. In view of the character of Mussolini's and Hitler's early followings, this makes it the stranger that, in spite of threatening hints, no substantial Fascism came out of the BEF. Few were members of either the American Legion or the Veterans of Foreign Wars, which may mean they were not temperamentally "joiners." Another significance may lie in Waters' observation that "Most of the men were married and had left their families behind . . . [in] an overwhelming number of instances . . . strained family relations . . . had led to bitter permanent separation between man and wife." [45]

That reads like too many months of strain on tempers as work proved unattainable or bankruptcy came nearer. Yet, other things being equal, it can hardly have been the cream of the unemployed breadwinners of Portland or Kalamazoo or Binghamton or Corpus

Christi who thus left wives to cope at home while they hoboed off to make Congress see the light. Their own leader described them as spotlight seekers: "Any camera ... within a hundred feet of the camps attracted a rush of men ... they straightened their shoulders and strutted a bit...." [46] A reporter for the Washington *Star* saw them as "an army of starving bewilderment ... a flight from reality ... from hunger ... the cries of starving children ... [and] worn, querulous women ... the harsh rebuffs of prospective employers." [47] Roger Daniels' recent invaluable study refers their behavior to the Do-Something that has been concerning us: "the essentially optimistic nature of the average American ... [impelling] him upon what was clearly a pointless pilgrimage ... mindless activism that insisted it was better to do something even if it turned out wrong." [48] And E. B. White, twitchily sensitive voice of the *New Yorker,* a veteran himself, though believing that as "bonus-grabbers" they were in a poor cause, saw them as "more than just a lobby ... [rather] the expression of men's desire to huddle together when their courage is gone. Going to Washington meant a change of scene, a temporary escape from the aimlessness of idleness, and they jumped at the chance." [49]

On the official level the Legion denied the BEF support. On the state and local levels, however, Legion posts sometimes informally gave supplies or small cash sums. The VFW, smaller and often more aggressive than the Legion, gave official endorsement as well as supplies. It is a tribute to its somewhat flawed leaders that with so little support the BEF managed as well as it did. The Portland nucleus half wangled, half bluffed the Union Pacific and other pertinent railroads into letting the boys ride empty boxcars as far as St. Louis. In towns en route between trains they forbade individual panhandling in favor of formal solicitation with four veterans led by a drummer marching along with explanatory placards, holding out hats for contributions. In East St. Louis, where they mistakenly hoped to find the Baltimore & Ohio as obliging as the Union Pacific, resistance was strong, the National Guard was called out, but after a few days of touch-and-go the governor of Illinois got rid of the problem by lending it trucks and automobiles to take it to the Indiana line. Indiana, Ohio, Pennsylvania followed his equivocal example.

Meanwhile, their predicament in East St. Louis had drawn national attention. Thenceforward the Bonus March, as Daniels * has said, ranked among the news stories of 1932, right along with the Depression, the Lindbergh kidnapping, the upcoming election and the

* This section relies much on his *The Bonus March* (1971), but it must not be held responsible for all my interpretations.

Culbertson-Lens-Jacoby bridge match. This was indispensable promotion for the BEF idea. Until then few were aware of the Portland nucleus and its dramatic purpose. Now all America was aware of them and their counterparts in most states—fewest in Dixie for some reason—hastily organizing and setting out for Washington in boxcars or jalopies. In a few weeks about 10,000 of them were milling about in the nation's capital uncertain how to expedite the Patman bill and what to do with themselves on very slim resources until they figured it out.

The timid commissioners governing the District of Columbia under federal suzerainty were baffled by the problem they presented. Fortunately it developed its own hero stopgap. The superintendent of the District police was a tall, spare, levelheaded, original-minded retired West Pointer, Pelham D. Glassford, once colonel of the 103d Field Artillery in the AEF, then its youngest brigadier general, now Sunday painter and popular man-about-town. Personally—though he said nothing pro or con till all was over—he disapproved of the BEF. But the issue it represented was up to Congress and indirectly the White House. Glassford set himself to get the BEF a square shake with neither help nor hindrance from authority. While Congress dithered and the White House anxiously augmented its security force, this civilized soldier rode wherever he felt needed on his favorite mount, a large blue motorcycle, helping Waters keep the boys behaving so well there would be no excuse for cracking down on them. It was even he who suggested the name "Bonus Expeditionary Force" in nostalgic reference to the AEF. Its members were soon so thoroughly persuaded of his good faith and goodwill that they elected him their secretary-treasurer.

When the commissioners advised Glassford to use his policemen to evict these unwelcome reminders of the nation's woes from the District, he demanded written orders. None was forthcoming. When they threatened to get the White House to fire him, he said he'd like nothing better. Privately he besought Congress' leaders to bring the Patman bill to a vote to settle matters before his and Waters' balancing act came apart. Neither Congress nor White House did anything useful. Glassford found billets for the swelling BEF in condemned and partly demolished buildings in downtown Washington—they named the complex nearest the Capitol Camp Glassford—and encouraged the overflow to create a huge Hooverville on empty public land on the far side of the Anacostia River. This Camp Marks—named for the kindly, helpful police captain of the nearest station house—was within sight of the Capitol but separated from the city proper by a drawbridge that could be raised in emergencies. From the

National Guard Glassford borrowed field kitchens and tents to supplement the shacks the boys put together with the usual salvage lumber and flattened tin cans. Sightseers included Camp Marks in their summer vacation tours of Washington. Among its sights were a mock graveyard with carefully tended and flower-bedecked graves marked "Hoover" and "Mellon" and a real grave for Joe Angelo, holder of a Distinguished Service Cross, buried alive six feet down with a partner charging visitors a quarter for the privilege of chatting with him through a speaking tube. As Camp Marks took on an air of quasi-permanence, wives and children, making the trip God knows how, began to trickle in.

With Glassford's support Waters and staff kept the lid on well. The BEF had its own MPs, dug latrines, kept street panhandling down, issued chow share and share alike, banned liquor, set up athletic programs, eventually stiffened discipline with close-order drill. When the commissioners, borrowing a dodge from California's tactics against Communist-led strikers' camps, warned Glassford that the BEF's settlements should be destroyed as hazards to the city's health, he told them the sanitary conditions complained of "do not offer one-half the menace ... that is offered by ... a dozen alleys I can show you in Washington" [50] about which nobody ever did anything. Sensibly he also provided against the day when the BEF would be evicted by creating an emergency refugee camp just over the District line in Maryland. Its site was a thirty-acre tract lent by its owner, John H. Bartlett, former Republican governor of New Hampshire, member of one of President Hoover's advisory commissions. Already adept at staging benefits and tapping affluent friends for eating money for the BEF, Glassford now worked local benevolence for surplus lumber and other supplies that a picked crew from the BEF turned into rough barracks and so on at Camp Bartlett. He added farming tools and began to envisage the place as a pilot plant for self-help subsistence colonies, whence down-and-out veterans could carry back to their home states husbandry and organization for a national chain. He said that in view of the BEF's "demonstrated discipline ... loyalty ... ability to take care of themselves ... provide extemporized shelter ... subsist on the most simple and inexpensive food ... ," [51] Uncle Sam might well settle them on federal lands or those the states were acquiring through tax delinquency. It all began to sound like a vast expansion of *Our Daily Bread* with Gary Cooper playing Glassford.

The House eventually passed the Patman bill. Many who voted for it were cynically aware that the Senate was most unlikely to do so, and in any case President Hoover was sure to veto it. The BEF continued to roam the corridors of Congress' office buildings, buttonhole Senators, gather in desultory knots on the Capitol grounds. But they were the only people in Washington unaware they were flogging a dead horse. As the weather heated up—Washington summers are what Tom Paine meant by "times that try men's souls"—and prospects dimmed, their situation degenerated to match. The boys grumbled about the contrast between their frowsy, threadbare mufti and Waters' shiny boots and paramilitary riding breeches, between their sordid quarters and Waters' bedroom in a house borrowed from a friend of Glassford's. Control over panhandling was slipping. The public's benevolent sympathy persisted, but its contributions of cash and comestibles were dwindling.

While Glassford held his breath, the Senate rejected the Patman bill by an ostentatiously lopsided vote in the teeth of thousands of BEF massed on the Capitol grounds. Hoping they would take this resounding no for an answer, President Hoover proposed and Congress voted $100,000 for rail fare and eating money en route for BEF men going home. Over the next few weeks some 5,000 accepted the offer; some 2,000 more left at their own cost. The Red Cross, which had stayed aloof from the BEF itself, paid the way for 500-odd wives and children going along. But something like 10,000 remained. Presumably those departing included men whose reasons for coming had been nearer rational, however ill advised, and those staying were more of the escape-from-reality sort, doubtless with a higher average level of inclination toward turbulence.

Their stated reason for staying was to force Congress to reconsider the cash-payment bill before its late-summer adjournment; a few glib legislators had mentioned that possibility. Presently Congress stifled that by adjourning without any such action. The boys stayed on to agitate for a special session to reconsider, they said. For many—2,000 to 5,000, Waters thought—the more cogent reason was that they had nothing like homes to return to and with local relief agencies so swamped in Walla Walla, Carbondale and Freehold, few would eat as well there as on the precarious rations of Camp Marks. A few hundred others who were not veterans but had managed to evade the BEF's slackening precautions against imposters could not qualify for transportation orders. And doubtless these comradely weeks of demonstrations, lumber hunting, shack building, softball games, interminable bull sessions about hard times and shavetails and top kicks had come to seem better than life with Depression-harried families. In spite of efforts to discourage them, the more loyal wives and children were still trickling in. At the peak, before the major exodus, the count had been 700-odd wives, 400 children; several babies were born in BEF camps.

One wife told Bartlett that times were really tough at home, and she was better off in Camp Marks than she had been there for a year.

Sinister signs multiplied. A fanatic unemployed roofer from Los Angeles, Royal R. Robertson, brought in some 4,000 "Death Marchers" pledged to picket the Capitol until the veterans got their dues. Mrs. Evelyn Walsh McLean, owner of the Hope Diamond, whose glittering eccentricities were the joy of Washington's society columns, sent the Death Marchers a thousand sandwiches to keep their energy up. Waters, by now representing himself as an ex-Socialist, was not only shouting, "Billions for bankers ... nothing for the poor!" [52] but toying with a scheme for a permanent third political party of veterans, wearing and calling themselves Khaki Shirts. Father Coughlin sent $5,000 to the BEF on strict conditions that none of it go to any veteran suspected of Redness. Smedley D. "Old Gimlet-Eye" Butler, US Marine general whose noisy career as clean-sweeping head of Philadelphia's police had endeared him to the wrong kind of people, came to make the BEF snarling speeches about sticking it out till the White House caved in; they were the salt of the earth, he said, and deserved to have the nation by the tail. Add the stultifying effects of the weather, and those portents alone account for the commissioners' decision in late July to swallow hard and order Glassford to clear the BEF out by stages.

Yet the real credit for bringing this order about probably goes to the small but dutifully militant group of Communist-led Reds in the BEF. Their importance, Daniels says, "cannot be gauged by numbers alone. They were important because they were feared and ... these fears ... [were] used as a pretext for action." [53] The White House had been seeking something to discredit the BEF in the eyes of a nation rather inclined to sympathy. Spell it Camp Marx, and its embarrassing presence would be more safely got rid of. The Reds' effort to raise their visibility came at just the right time. The contrast between their attitude and the BEF's was evident even in their songs: The BEF's favorite was: "My bonus lies over the ocean, / My bonus lies over the sea.... O, bring back my bonus to me!" The Reds' revision of a traditional number went to the tune of "Over There": "All you there! All you there!/ Pay the bonus, pay the bonus, all you there!/ For the Yanks are starving, the Yanks are starving...." [54]

The Communists' Workers' Ex-Servicemen's League—its acronym, WESL, allowed its detractors to call its members Weasels, of course—and its alter ego, the Central Rank-and-File Committee, so hated Glassford that it took great pleasure in trying to poison the temperate atmosphere he created. The previous winter his easygoing, commonsense handling of the Communists' Hunger March on Washington had frustrated its hopes of tempting the authorities to use violence. Now his skill in keeping pressures down and channels open confirmed its conviction that he was cynically sabotaging the veterans' real interests by double-dealing friendliness. Worse, the Reds were beholden to him. They were Johnny-come-latelies, turning up in some numbers under a smug Party stalwart from Detroit, John Pace, only after the spread of the BEF had shown Browder was wrong, the bonus issue might make the Party a good stalking-horse. When they entered the BEF camps, they were hooted at, held by BEF MPs for trial in kangaroo courts, at best haled off to the District line and told not to come back, at worst flogged beforehand. Glassford intervened, laying down the doctrine that Reds had as much right as any to harangue veterans. Further to reduce friction, he assigned Pace's hard-nosed little group separate quarters in disused buildings well away from the others. His eventual reward for that was to have Communists throw him down and tear off his superintendent's badge when their hopes for violence were finally consummated.

Waters called Pace's boys "the best and truest allies the [Hoover] administration had" [55] in supplying reasons for cracking down. During the previous two weeks the WESLs had twice picketed the White House in force and got Pace arrested. That widened alerts for federal troops in nearby installations. Late in July the commissioners finally gave in to the administration's growing belief that the BEF was falling under Red control and definitely ordered Glassford to go ahead with eviction, starting at Camp Glassford. The pretext would be that the demolition crews wanted to get on with their work on the occupied buildings, and since Congress was adjourned, the BEF no longer had valid use for them.

Stalling as long as he could to give the BEF ample warning and himself time to plan, Glassford eventually set the first eviction in motion. The hundreds of veterans involved included a stiffening of tough oilfield boys from Texas, but apparently the police and the US Treasury agents whom they backed up were working things out peaceably when trucks began to arrive, some carrying groups from Camp Marks, but others—here was the detonator—carrying Pace's trouble-seeking Reds. The rubble-strewn site was rich in handy brickbats. Glassford's police, after several days of overtime duty, were half out on their feet. The ensuing shindy, spearheaded by Communists, was temporarily smothered but not before word of it got to the White House and caused issuance of an already cocked and primed order to the alerted Army units to get into motion, the District police were unable to handle things. A few minutes later, as if to justify this step after the fact, the shindy began again, and two veterans stopped police bullets. Both died.*

Late in the afternoon the Army moved in: 300 infantry with fixed bayonets, 200 cavalry with unsheathed sabers, five tanks. The command was assumed by Chief of Staff Douglas MacArthur, then known as a brilliant young chief of staff of the Rainbow Division in World War I. To posterity the military talent deployed sounds excessive. MacArthur's liaison with the police was Major Dwight D. Eisenhower. Commander of the cavalry was Major George S. Patton whose life, as it happened, had been saved in France by the same Joe Angelo who was buried alive at Camp Marks. The force MacArthur required is usually called unduly numerous by those insisting that the ensuing "Battle of Washington" was a fiendish massacre. But his objective was wider than the White House order, which merely called for sweeping the Camp Glassford and other outlying bodies of BEF across the Anacostia and then waiting for further instructions. MacArthur took the bit in his teeth, drove on into Camp Marks, dispersed the BEF root and branch and demolished or burned—who first set the fires is still in dispute—their pitiful shacks. At Camp Bartlett, planned as their city of refuge, resident veterans, alerted by the glow in the sky over Camp Marks, spontaneously demobilized themselves when a cavalry patrol came reconnoitering.

MacArthur's 600-odd regulars was a force hardly out of line with this icily headstrong egocentric's self-assigned mission of breaking up a potential mob of 10,000-odd all trained to arms, many combat veterans. They did it without firing a shot, using only tear gas, the sight of bayonets and shiny sabers and the trampling of horses. The two veterans dead of police bullets were the only fatalities. But there were necessarily many minor injuries and much screaming, and the rearing horses and burning shacks made powerful newsreels and newspaper photographs. Later the Reds played up the funeral procession taking the two corpses to Arlington National Cemetery. A newborn Camp Marks baby allegedly dead from inhaling tear gas took his place with the legendary babies spitted on German bayonets in World War I. (The poor little thing did die in hospital but of natural causes.) All over the nation went the impression, persisting today, that President Hoover as ruthlessly called out the regulars to shoot down the Bonus Army in the streets of Washington as if he had been the czar ordering the Cossacks into a demonstration in St.

---

* Just who was directly responsible for the White House order has never been determined. The above is necessarily a telescoped account. For responsible presentation of the data, see Daniels, *The Bonus March.*

Petersburg. Had public exasperation reached such heights that people wanted to believe him capable of such atrocity? That must remain surmise, for his time had no reliable POPs.

The Communists profited little from their opportunism, even though MacArthur's insubordination heightened the impact of the episode. The obvious beneficiaries were the Democrats in the approaching election. By then, however, Hoover's candidacy was hopeless anyway. The press in general took it that once the White House was mousetrapped between the BEF's persistence and the Reds' provocateurs, eviction was the only course. *Time* brashly and justifiably blamed the whole mess not so much on Hoover or the Communists as on Patman, Senator Elmer Thomas of Oklahoma and other legislators who had kept feeding the BEF "false hopes and promises" [56] and so kept them in Washington. *Collier's* provided a fair epitaph for the BEF a few weeks later; it was "assembled in folly and dispersed in anger and stupidity." [57]

The next spring there was a replay largely at Communist instance, though most of the participants were not Reds. FDR played it like a master, as he was. The 3,000-odd who showed up were billeted in a nearby Army camp and well fed. Mrs. Roosevelt was sent out to shake their hands and make them a settlement house sort of speech. A delegation had twenty minutes with FDR and, though he was firm against the bonus, came away respectful. And when he offered them a chance to enter an *ad hoc* adult branch of the newly formed Civilian Conservation Corps, six-sevenths of them accepted and were shipped out, and the remaining 400 were sent home at government expense. It was already New Deal times, and as the new CCC showed, Do-Something had become Uncle Sam's new chief concern.

The Communist Party had hardly bothered to disguise its attempt to use the first Bonus Army to make bourgeois government look vicious. In the early 1930s that was unusual. The Party was then programmed for "boring from within," infiltrating existing organizations of promise in order gradually to turn them into foci of dissatisfaction, social corrosion, violence where possible ... for much of which the climate of hit-or-miss Do-Something was favorable. As the 1930s decade passed its halfway pole, the programming was complicated by adding the Popular Front concept, meaning semiopen collaboration of the Party with liberal-to-radical factors. Liberals inclined to welcome this as showing that the Party was entering on a new, constructive phase of candor and cooperative behavior. But it never meant that clandestine subversion was abandoned. Indeed, it can be regarded as a mere occasional supplement to persistent boring-from-within sometimes so devious that whether or not Party influence was directly involved can still be doubted by those who would prefer it not to have been. An instructively twisty example was the effort to deflect the American consumer movement, a promising branch of Do-Something, into Party-lining. It can serve as miniature model of a good many things going on at the time.

In the early 1930s a new form of consumerism was making great progress. Its focus was Consumers' Research,* a self-supporting minor institution using independent-minded technology to advise its subscriber members against the misrepresentation, snob appeal and deliberately flimsy-made products reflecting industry's alliance with advertising. Its birth auspices had been liberal, mildly settlement-housey but not cranky, its tone incisive but not shrill. One of its most popular book offspring was, for instance, Mary Catherine Phillips' *Skin Deep*, a commonsense exposure of the 90 percent of nonsense and 1 to 2 percent of danger that women get for what they spend on allegedly cosmetic items. It was just as severe on the vegetarianism that often goes along with liberal inclination. CR's monthly bulletins and annual compendia of "Recommended" and "Non-Recommended" brands of canned stuff, razor blades, electric fans, socks and so on became gospel for a growing number of alert, largely white-collar, mostly college-educated disciples. F. J. Schlink, the quick-minded engineer who, along with Stuart Chase, founded CR, and Miss Phillips (who became Mrs. Schlink) had it paying its own way on subscriptions in an old stone factory building in the country town of Washington, New Jersey. Its canny thriftiness and skepticism about Big Business appealed to Depression-honed minds. Prospects for growth of membership and of awareness of the virtues and vices of the American standard of living were good. Among the stimulating innovations that the thoughtful discussed over bathtub-gin-and-ginger-ale as 1932 became 1933, CR made much more sense than Technocracy, Back-to-the-Land (though CR had a touch of that), the Five-Year Plan, *Fascismo* and Social Credit all put together.

Inevitably its growth irked Madison Avenue. It was not good medicine for Space & Billings to have even 50,000 Americans and their wives gossiping disturbingly among their acquaintance about the phoniness of claims for toothpaste, most makers' guarantees and the fallacy of Aunt Agatha's traditional belief that "you get what you pay for." As the consequent rattle of sniper fire from the advertising industry got under the skins of CR's staff, their pronouncements took on a more nervous stridency. This waspish tone heightened when

* For details on CR's early history see my *Great Times,* 509–14.

Arthur Kallet, a young, like-minded engineer less pragmatic and rather more radical than Schlink, joined up. In 1933 he and Schlink collaborated on *100,000,000 Guinea Pigs,* a book on the reluctance of government to protect its citizens from health hazards in consumption goods. It sold 250,000 copies and left behind it much prematurely gray hair—which one dared not dye because the book emphatically alerted one to the poisons used in commercial hair dyes. Page 4 told how a man aware of the amount of potassium chlorate in Pebeco toothpaste had committed suicide by eating half a tube of it. Page 19 identified ingredients in every item in Mrs. Jones' grocery order (Kellogg's All-Bran, Crisco, dried apricots, white bread, cider, canned salmon, milk) as long-run causes of obscure gastric and renal ailments and deaths occurring five to ten years earlier than necessary. Add popular home remedies, cosmetics, the hamburger of commerce: ". . . about as safe as getting your meat out of a garbage can standing in the hot sun" [58] and too often doused with chemicals to mask incipient putrefaction.

Page 193 came down hard on the moral: "While the profit motive continues to dominate all manufacture and distribution, the exploitation of the consumer through . . . misrepresentation can be taken for granted; economic fraud can be controlled perhaps slightly better than it is now, but it cannot possibly be wiped out . . . the effort . . . must be made . . . if need be, squarely against . . . the trend of business enterprise." [59] That was tougher than CR's previous position, stated as late as 1932: CR "holds no brief for any particular kind of economic conduct or social or political order . . . only the belief that consumers have as much right to increase the purchasing power of their dollars as have business enterprisers." [60] It was, in fact, an almost open call for the economy of "Production for Use, not profit" that underlay most of the panaceas, Technocracy and Communism included, then vying for public favor. Note, too, that in the early New Deal the tempers of the consumer-minded grew short because efforts to get consumer interests fairly represented in the National Recovery Administration failed and because Congress was smothering the "Tugwell Bill" (so called for Rexford G. Tugwell of FDR's Brain Trust) meant to strengthen Uncle Sam's hand in controlling irresponsible merchandising of food, drugs and cosmetics.

To take over little CR with its useful reputation for clean-hitting reliability would give Party-liners access to the minds and hearts of thousands who, on the whole, assayed higher than most Americans in the urge to Do Something and lower in emotional commitment to the existent social system. Kallet's qualifications as bridge for such a Trojan Horse were described after the consequent schism by a reliable magazine interviewer: "Kallet will tell anyone that he dislikes our economic system ... feels it is doomed ... hopes the Russian experiment will succeed so well that we shall be compelled to adopt it ... denies that he is a member of the Communist party and so does many a man whose name is right there on the rolls," [61] a hint strengthened by the fact that at the time Kallet was using the *New Masses,* the Party's acknowledged publication as medium to attack CR in.

His earlier mordant influence within CR was reinforced by the enlistment of a tireless couple, Mr. and Mrs. J. B. Matthews, whose Party-lining was hardly a secret. After some years as a Fundamentalist missionary Matthews became an ardent Socialist, chief of the Fellowship of Reconciliation, an aggressively pacifist group with religious and radical overtones, and chairman of the Party-lining League Against War and Fascism. While working for CR, he collaborated with R. H. Shallcross on *Partners in Plunder* (1935), a book that slashingly depicted Big Business as determined to foist Fascism on America and the New Deal as a sneaky accessory shedding crocodile tears over the "Forgotten Man." That was the Party line about the New Deal at the time. For constructive contrast the book played up the USSR's abandonment of profit-mindedness and its two significant consequences: immense social and economic vigor released within Russia, and outside it, slander heaped by disguised reactionaries on the Five-Year Plan and its implications. In those days chances of Party-liners' being able to take over and make the consumer movement a seedbed of class-war emotions were better because such liberals as CR's founders had not yet grasped how casuistic and ruthless the Party could be. It would have felt reactionary—an unpardonable attitude—to suspect one's close associates of setting one up for hijacking. Yet by then Kallet was Party-liner enough openly to sign the call that created the League of American Writers—a flagrant Party front formed by seventy-five Party members and fellow travelers.

Popular as CR was with readers of the *New Republic* and the *Survey-Graphic,* small jarrings had occurred. CR sometimes cast doubt on the cult of milk as perfect food. This irked those habitually urging public health agencies to give slum dwellers milk and more milk. Eminent radicals kept nudging at CR to go beyond price and testable quality into making the labor conditions under which goods were made a third criterion of acceptability—a legacy from the Consumers' Leagues formed before World War I. Schlink declined on the grounds that such considerations could not be intelligibly tested. But it was labor union organization, the great cause of the latter 1930s, that set off the intramural fireworks that split CR wide open. The chief pyrotechnician was Susan Jenkins, a CR proofreader, former editor of a pulp magazine, *Telling Tales,* later on the staff of the Communists' *Daily Worker.* Now she organized some of her 80-odd co-workers into a local of the Communist-inspired Office Workers' Union. When rival co-workers brought in a rival AFL affiliate, she and her faction took it over. Management discharged several union leaders; they demanded reinstatement; arbitration was offered, refused, withdrawn, a strike was called, a third of the payroll passed the picket line, tempers sizzled all around, the National Labor Relations Board, newly created arm of the new Wagner Act, was appealed to. Here came demands that a union stalwart replace Mrs. Schlink and Matthews—he had now backslid from Party-lining—among the directors. That confirmed Schlink's suspicion that the purpose was "to capture Consumers Research . . . to political purpose . . . [make it] a communist-controlled organization." [62] In view of what the Party was up to elsewhere at the time, he was probably right.

The American Civil Liberties Union, then Party-infiltrated, supported the strikers. So did a committee of eminent CR members, telling themselves that they hoped to mediate settlement. They succeeded only in enabling Kallet to lead an ideology-based schism that took the strikers and thousands of subscribers away to found a rival Consumers' Union (CU) with headquarters in Mount Vernon, New York, where it still prospers. CU was pledged to do everything CR did, plus dabbling in labor agitation and politics. Accordingly its bulletins denounced Fascism and advocated boycotting goods from Nazi Germany. Its manifesto proclaimed: "All the technical information in the world will not give enough food or enough clothes to the textile workers families living on $11 a week." [63] Its advertisements in labor union periodicals offered discounts on group subscriptions from union locals. It sent free to union editors a regular column, "Your Dollar," rich in realistic advice on good buys and bad. By 1940 CU had rather more subscribers than CR (75,000 to 60,000), but the blue-collar appeal had fizzled. The majority of its list consisted of teachers, engineers, civil service people; only one-third had manufacturing or merchandising jobs. That such campaigns were futile Schlink already knew. Several years previously he had tried it with small success. The hourly-wage group proved more interested in more dollars than in how to get the most for them.

The NLRB made no serious effort to enforce on Schlink its order to "bargain collectively in good faith" as the Wagner Act required. Once the decks were clear of Kallet's strikers, CR filled away on its previous course somewhat wiser for its brush with ideology but saddled among liberals with an undeserved reputation for black reactionaryism. In

1939 Matthews, by then research adviser to the Dies Committee, a sort of St. Paul in reverse, described CU as Party-dominated. In a strict sense that was probably untrue. What was true was that it probably would never have come into being had not certain Party-liners, whether or not assigned to that duty from on high, considered CR worth moving in on. Six years after the split a student of consumerism wrote ruefully that "the two leading testing agencies now serving the public are more or less captive—Consumers' Union to the labor movement; Consumers' Research, politely speaking, to a highly theoretical and no longer realistic conception of 'free enterprise.' Why could we not have had one bona fide organization pursuing the true, undefiled end of testing consumer goods?" [64]

Why not indeed? Because in the 1930s the Party's untiring efforts to extend its leverage in the interests of the USSR's policies consistently cast it in the role of spoiler.

The testing-agency schism persists today. CR, still piloted by the Schlinks, issues from the same old stone building regular advice to 100,000-odd subscribers. Newsstand sales of its *Consumers' Bulletin* do not, however, compare with the 2,000,000-odd to which CU has built its monthly *Consumer Reports.*

THE LITTLE RED FOXES

IN THE HEAT OF BATTLE, THE REBEL IS EXALTED BY A
WHOLE-HEARTED TENSION WHICH IS EASILY MISTAKEN FOR A
TASTE OF THE FREEDOM WHICH IS TO COME.

—WALTER LIPPMANN,
A Preface to Morals

It was noted that the Party's leverage on the Bonus Army was
disproportionate to the number of its adherents in the ranks. Such
discrepancies would persist in America's sociocultural life for at least
the next thirty years. This was no merit-acquiring compliment to the
promotional skills of the second- and third-rate persons who managed
the Party's American schemings. It was rather the doing of two other
forces, often synergistic: one, the long, long shadow cast on the
imaginations of many other peoples as well as Americans by the
momentous adventure on which Russia embarked in November, 1917;
the other, the fascination, which sometimes seemed as bird-and-snaky
as it did elective-affinity, that the USSR exerted on many self-
consciously literate and receptive persons, also in a negative, revulsionary way on many too dull and ignorant to know they were so. Great
segments and fragments of that still persist. Today's context may be
the People's Republic of China, but it means the same old thing.
Gradually swelling in the interval between the Armistice of 1918 and
the lowering of the Iron Curtain, it has already cropped up in this
book now and again. Henceforward it will appear even more often,
bobbing up for many pages sometimes, then submerging for a while,
then back up for another romp on the surface like a suddenly
uninhibited Loch Ness Monster. This is the doing of the cultural facts,

not mine. The Party's American career was astonishingly pervasive and as social pathology not to be missed.

When social workers and journalists discussed the adolescent vagrants of the early 1930s in terms of the USSR's *besprizornyi,* they were following a well-established fashion. Toward the end of the New Era such people's awareness of developments in the USSR was enrichening their minds with that and other words: *valuta, tovarich, kulak, piatiletka, komsomol....* In his *Exile's Return* (1930) Malcolm Cowley embodied this early result of the Depression. Open-minded, still rather young, his critical instincts and stereotypes reliably consonant with his significant contemporaries, he was fresh home from Montparnasse waving farewell to Ibsen and exulting because the new tutelary spirit of the once Lost Generation was Karl Marx. He took seriously, as other critics have since, however mistakenly, the observation by F. Scott Fitzgerald that a salient trait of the nihilistic or hedonistic Jazz Age was to be antipathetic to society's organized traps for the soul. Now suddenly he saw and testified raptly: "All the ivory towers were vacant." [1] Indeed, many of the previous diem carpers were already calling themselves Communists in innocent disregard of whether or not the Party had vouchsafed them a Party card.

His accounting for it suitably partook of economic determinism. Depression dried up the various forms of money-from-home—allowances from Pop, fellowships from foundations, subsidies from fat-cat admirers, in some cases payments from American publishers or magazine editors—that had supported the self-exiled cream of American creativity in Europe. Now they had to come home, and their dismay was not alleviated by the confusions they found on landing in God's country with its severe case of jitters. The tremors fissuring the sleek world they had taken for granted and patronizingly despised at once rubbed their noses in politics and made them feel "an all-consuming need for affirmations" [1] that, Cowley and they agreed, Communism might well assuage. Their scorn of Morgan, Babbitt (George F., yes, but Irving, too, among those who had heard of him) and the Old Lady in Dubuque had prepared them to take the next step and yearn for violent overthrow of the system that had spawned such monsters. One merely substituted *écrasez* in the old bohemian war cry of *épatez le bourgeois* and learned to pronounce it *bourzhui,* Russian-style.

One must credit Cowley with duly modifying this diagnosis, as he pointed out that since nothing like that had happened in consequence of the panics of 1873 or 1893, one could not postulate the hard-and-fast equation: Hard Times = Writers & Artists to the Barricades!, and

Depression or not, not all American writers and artists went broke after the Crash. Indeed for some lucky enough to be already handling the right subject matter, like John Dos Passos and Erskine Caldwell, their undeniably sincere convictions meshed lucratively with the new vogue. But he did not give due weight to the fact that there had long been strong anticipations of this shift to the left* among cultivated Americans. Cowley himself was in a position to know that it merely picked up and intensified a thing beginning before World War I and only partly obscured by Eliot, Fitzgerald and Hemingway in the half dozen years between the Great Red Scare and the grim execution of Sacco and Vanzetti.

In 1912-13 an addictive Radical-Chic had spread far and wide from Mabel Dodge Luhan's yeasty salon on Lower Fifth Avenue. In 1919-20 a swirling semimillennial cult of an imminent world revolution consequent on Bolshevik success in Russia flooded both Montparnasse and Greenwich Village; among its minor symptoms Fitzgerald's early "May Day," a story giving little hint of how proudly apolitical he soon would be. On these foundations, dug deep into emotional habits and automatic reaction to buzzwords, reared the significant revulsion against the System and in favor of those hoping to smash it that was set off among most such persons when the law electrocuted the radicals' martyr-saints in Charlestown Prison.† That was summer, 1927, two full years before Wall Street crashed and hard times forced so many self-exiles back where they came from.

The revulsion was the stronger because during the interval (1920-27) the social and emotional importance of Russia's ordeal had secured the USSR the best kind of propagandists—volunteers. "The Russian magnet," says Theodore Draper, scholarly connoisseur of American Communism, "attracted a small group of Americans . . . forerunners of a new type in American journalism—foreign correspondents turned political missionaries."[2] Early among them were John Reed, Albert Rhys Williams, Anna Louise Strong (at one time or another all three of them were directly on the Kremlin's payroll), Steffens, Louise Bryant (Reed's handsome widow, presently mistress of Eugene O'Neill, then married to William C. Bullitt, newspaperman and eventually first US ambassador to the USSR), whose *Mirrors of Moscow* set the tone as well as any in calling Russia's Communists "the knights errant of

---

* This is one of the few uses of the left/right dichotomy in this text. For definition of its use in this book and the dozen or so other terms unfortunately necessary in discussing the 1930s, see the Appendix.

† All this at much greater length in *Great Times* (1974).

the twentieth century ... their slogan of 'internationalism' is but revival of that old, old banner of 'Brotherhood.' " [3] * Not only in America's newspapers and magazines but also in impressive books published by old-line as well as radically inclined houses these hero-worshiping Fourth Estaters became the nation's rose-colored windows on the USSR.

Miss Strong's candid autobiography, *I Change Worlds* (1935), makes her case particularly illuminating. Endowed with a high IQ, daughter of a pacifist parson, she, like the Reeds, grew up in the energetically radical Northwest. Out there she organized cooperatives and wrote for radical papers. Meeting Steffens, she confided to him how she longed to immerse herself in the revolutionary new-world-a-forming in the USSR. He said, "Why don't you?" So she did, infiltrating by way of a job with the American Friends' (Quaker) relief organization in Poland, then in the USSR. Soon she was Moscow correspondent for the International News Service and selling capable articles on Germany and Russia to Norman Hapgood, editor of *Hearst's International* magazine: † "Do the Jews Rule Russia?", "What Makes Lenin Great?" She was more and more drawn to the Communist magnet as, of course, consciously or unconsciously, she had long hoped to be. When the *International* vanished in a merger, she decided to become "leading specialist on the Soviet Union for miscellaneous publications." [4] This entailed no objectivity, for she was a high priestess of "advocacy journalism" years before the phrase was invented. Consciously, consistently, her writings and lectures kept the USSR's best foot forward, making the capitalist public pay her to be flack for the Kremlin, just as Child was simultaneously doing for *Fascismo*. No

---

* She often sounded as if writing soap opera: "Lenin adores his wife and speaks of her with enthusiasm. The first time that I told him I wanted to meet her, he said: 'Yes, you must do that, because you will like her, she is so intelligent.' ... She invited me to take tea with her in her apartment and I was very glad to go, since I wanted to see for myself how the Lenins lived." (*Mirrors of Moscow*, 20.) Or: "One day last winter I interviewed Litvinov while he was eating his lunch, and he said ... he wished he could ... get away for a few days to visit his family [then in Denmark, he in Moscow]. His wife had just had a baby. 'Boy or girl?' I asked.... 'The telegram didn't say,' he said, 'and God knows when I'll have a chance to run over, and find out.' " (*Ibid.*, 200–1.)

† INS was, of course, also part of the Hearst empire. Ten years later, when Hearst and his properties had gone hysterically anti-Bolshevik, none of them would have had any truck with her. But Hapgood was of liberal bent, and in the early 1920s Hearst's persisting sulkiness about World War I still got him some acceptance among antiestablishment people.

mention of German sponsorship for Lenin's return to Moscow, the USSR was allowing "absolute freedom of religion"; [5] and since she was as fervently anti-French as pro-USSR, some of her partisan predictions swung wildly. In 1923, for instance, "Very soon ... there will be no more Germany. Clemenceau willed it. Poincaré brings it to pass. Big Business and Landed Interests, in Germany herself, help in the murder of their motherland, for private gain." [6]

"My job," she wrote, looking back, "became a game between editors and myself; it amused me to see how much I could 'put over.' ... I sold one [editor] articles because he wanted 'travel' or 'women'; to another because he was anti-British ... on Asia.... Some helped me to 'put it over' on owners...." [7] She seldom broke into the mass circulation magazines, but for the rest of the 1920s her by-line was familiar in *Harper's,* the *Atlantic,* the *Independent, Current History—* read by the cultivated but not necessarily as yet radically committed, the very ones whose attitudes mattered in gaining growing acceptance of the validity of the USSR. Her annual lecture tours aimed at the same public supported this influence. After years of such devotion she was given the mind-blowing, soul-wrenching job of creating the Moscow *News,* the USSR's English-language paper. The consequent ordeal by ideology, bureaucracy and casuistry proved her a Red immortal, rewarded by a personal interview on the paper's policy with Stalin Himself: "His eyes were grave, giving rest and reassurance...." After his esoteric Marxist casuistry resolved her difficulty with esoteric Marxist strategy: "It seemed that work might [now] be forever clear and joyous, if only sometimes one might go to him with questions.... other hours in my life ... when I have adored great men ... all died out. I cannot recapture their feeling. But ... even today I can feel the atmosphere of that meeting." [8] Not my will but Thy Dialectic be done! Further to understand this strange but not correspondingly rare case— particularly how strong her stomach proved in the USSR of mass famines and purges—savor what she told a Nazi Party public relations man in Berlin in 1933: "The world is telling atrocity stories about you. I'm not interested in atrocities. Every regime puts down its enemies as ruthlessly as it has to." [9]

Claims like hers were staked out more distinctly because Moscow's censors operated as if in wartime; indeed, much of what seems puzzling about the USSR falls into place when one recalls that the Bolshevik dictatorship was a side effect of war, had to fight several wars to survive, remained convinced that war with non-Communist powers was imminent, conceived of its own growth within its own boundaries as war on hostile classes—and consistently used warlike metaphors as propaganda devices. That being the prevailing mood long after the wars were over, the Kremlin naturally supplied accreditation, travel facilities, interviews, living quarters and, most crucially, entrance visas and residence permits to foreign correspondents with a readiness proportionate to their sympathy with its purposes and doings and willingness not only to file discreet or favorable cables—less trouble for censors—but also to write "constructive" (= on the whole admiring) articles and books when they got outside the USSR. Any American wire service or newspaper wanting coverage from within Russia had to accept such facts of life. Not to do so risked deportation for one's man in Moscow and difficulties in arranging a replacement. Much the same sort of minimum footsie was also being played by the American press in Italy at the same time, of course.

The only alternative was to post correspondents in the crummy rumor factories of the Baltic states, where reporters had many of the same handicaps as those now trying to make out events in Saigon by laying the ear to the ground in Bangkok and Hong Kong. The quality of this near-and-yet-so-far work was no better for the hunger of many Western publishers for rumors extravagantly derogatory to Bolshevism. Their use of almost or entirely groundless concoctions considerably fouled up US-USSR relations, for the Kremlin naturally assumed that everything the American press printed had Washington's approval at least indirectly. But such fantasies had little effect on those Miss Strong was gunning for. They were unlikely to read such papers to begin with, let alone believe anything in their columns even when, as sometimes happened, one of those grotesque rumors from Riga proved to be true.

Chief among Miss Strong's rivals—a dubious term, their gnawing purposes were identical—was Maurice Hindus, brought to America at the age of fifteen by his Russian-Jewish immigrant parents. A hard-earned American education led into a foothold in magazine journalism gained by writings about the Doukhobors—Russian religious fanatics settled in Canada's wheat country, famous for stripping naked for mass demonstrations whenever they felt put upon. In 1925 he visited his boyhood home in White Russia, sold pieces about it to nonradical magazines, such as the *Century* and *Asia,* and gathered them into a book, *Broken Earth.* Its preface was supplied by Glenn Frank, recently editor of the *Century,* incumbent president of the University of Wisconsin. It extolled Hindus' objectivity in describing matters and issues previously obscured by radical or reactionary prejudices.

True, Hindus did put in his former peasant fellow villagers' complaints about the new regime's bureaucratic rigidity and premonitions of the farm collectivization soon to tear up the new roots they had struck in the soil since the Revolution. But the gist of his book was that the Russian peasant, the eternal *muzhik,* was as bestial as ever—violent, dirty, drunken, selfish, shortsighted, reactionary, lecherous and light-fingered—indeed, the worse now for having largely lost his religion, such as it had been. Implied conclusion: anything the Kremlin did to him would be an improvement. In this *muzhik*-encumbered countryside the only nucleus of civilization was the *sovkhoz,* the government's demonstration farm on a former nobleman's estate, which the peasants shamelessly raided for feed, pasture and hardware. Somehow out of such unpromising raw material, Hindus promised, would "crystallize . . . a new type of politico-economic state . . . a blend of the collectivism of the city proletarian and the individualism of the peasant . . . nationwide cooperative enterprise with the state as general manager." [10]

That sounded enticingly like the Cooperative Commonwealth that American elder radicals had long preached without being specific about what it would be like. Two years later John Dewey, a chief keeper of the nation's liberal conscience, a sturdily open-minded philosopher-educationist, visited the USSR and returned agreeing that the consumers' and workers' cooperative-to-be would shape Russia's future. He also endorsed Hindus as valuably objective in an introduction to *Humanity Uprooted,* the book arising from a second nostalgic foray into the old home. This time Hindus traveled far and wide in the USSR under the lubricant auspices of its government, which, it was clear, *Broken Earth* had pleased. The odd misgivings now included concerned the possibly coarsening effect of the USSR's permissiveness about Sex and uneasiness lest the Kremlin's internal propaganda lead to a new nationalism mingling old-timey chauvinism with class hatred. Meanwhile, Stalin had abolished the New Economic Policy that allowed much minor individual enterprise and ruthlessly taken the opposite tack—no more paltering with capitalist values! Ho for collectivized farming and heavy industry and the famous Five-Year Plan! So *Humanity Uprooted* was even more severe on the brutish recalcitrance of the *muzhik*—a creature as foul as he was indisputably expendable—and showed the Young Communists leading the New Russia to be selflessly glorious, however heavy-handed, Hindus' own preface contradicted Dewey's endorsement with a warning that he (Hindus) had renounced objectivity: "Life in Russia is so violent an experience, so painful a trial, and to him who bursts with the new faith, so glorious an ecstacy, that one cannot remain simply passive." [11]

Weeks before the Great Crash marked the end of capitalism's vulgar party, *Humanity Uprooted* was selling like circus popcorn. In 1931 Hindus lit a third candle to his waxing faith, *Red Bread.* During the ensuing decade his further articles and books matched in fervor the rising popularity of the USSR among the cultivated. His prewar Russian roots gave him special standing among the new crop of American writers and lecturers specializing in pseudojudicious pan-egyrics of the USSR as a surgeon specializes in, say, plastic or orthopedic work: Louis Fischer, Moscow correspondent of the *Nation;* Walter Duranty, British ditto for the New York *Times;* Julian Bryan, master of the Reddish travelogue; H. W. L. Dana, specialist in the USSR's candidly propagandistic theater; Sherwood Eddy, whose standing as a world leader of the YMCA gave him ready access to Main Street; the less corny Jerome Davis, ordained sociologist of the Yale Theological School. . . . Clergymen reared in the Social Gospel movement of pre-World War I days often partook of this heady cup. Just as some reformers saw cooperative retailing as the eventual end product of Russia's convulsions, so did the Reverend Hopley Porter frequently predict that in God's good time the USSR would bring forth a new and highly edifying kind of economically humane religion. Hear Francis A. Henson of the National Religion and Labor Foundation in *The New Russia,* a symposium written by a group visiting the USSR under Jerome Davis' wing in 1932: "The Russians under the present regime have been called 'a society of adolescents.' . . . Who was it . . . said that only persons who become like little children could enter the new world?" Foot of the class, Brother Henson; what He said was "enter the kingdom of heaven." [12] Other clergy more directly and certainly more consciously hero-worshiping the USSR were the Reverend William B. Spofford of the Church League for Industrial Democracy; the Reverend Harry F. Ward of Union Theological Seminary and the Methodist Federation for Social Service; certain strategically placed leaders in the Federal Council of Churches. . . .

Whether or not outright partisans, such articulate witnesses all fostered the rising fashion of regarding "the Soviet experiment," as one called it, with a smugly tolerant sympathy. Yes, yes, Communism in its Russian present or future might not fit America's needs. But none could deny it was fascinating to see the Russians building themselves a logical new world. The creators of the Five-Year Plan and the Dnieproges Dam—or was it Dniepestroy?—were so full of hopes and energy, so stimulating a contrast with capitalism's muddled despair. How thrilling to live in such crucial and constructive times! In that spirit they mass-produced resounding statements about matters on which these few-weeks or few-months pilgrims had no business whatever pronouncing. Thus, Professor Henry C. Krowl of the City College of New York, another of Davis' symposium party, quelling ugly rumors that in the USSR speech was not as free as it might be:

"... if one's loyalty is beyond suspicion, there is no curb on criticism or ridicule." [13] Or Theodore Dreiser, who like most such sociological rubberneckers, knew only a few hastily acquired words of Russian and depended entirely on government-supplied interpreters: "... never had I seen more genuine optimism, even enthusiasm, on the part of both worker and peasant." He was also astonished by "absence of all sense of petty politics ... of any subsidiary group or clique ... each individual that I talked to impressed me as ... wholly concerned with the welfare and practice of clean and flashing principles ... for the welfare and advancement ... of all the peoples of the earth." [14] Or Harold Clurman, reporting as of the spring of 1935, year of the mass arrests after the assassination of Kirov: "The deepest impression I carried away ... was the sense of a *sane* people ... tempered by suffering and struggle into hard common sense, patience, tolerance and determination ... no unreasonable fanaticism, no frustration ... no conflict between the ideal and the real...." [15]

But the game was not left to these second-echelon climbers on the bandwagon. In 1931 Steffens' wildly best-selling *Autobiography* persuaded many waverers to follow him into fascinated thralldom. His young British wife, Ella Winter, earned high marks for *Red Virtue,* a lyrical account of the Soviets' permissive handling of the problems of women as workers/mothers/lovers that delighted feminist elements unaware that by the time it was published the Kremlin was reneging on most of what she praised.* This phase of the rising tide peaked in 1932 with *New Russia's Primer,* an expanded pamphlet on the wonders of the Five-Year Plan written by a nimble-minded Soviet engineer and ably translated by George S. Counts,† an habitually Reddish professor of education at Teachers College-Columbia University. Frankly and effectively it borrowed from Chase's Planning-minded writings, invidiously juxtaposing the USSR's applying logic to production/consumption with America's failing to do so and promised the Russian masses the world with a little Red fence around it within two decades, including not only Plenty-for-All and a classless society but also completely electrified railroads, fleets of electric-powered trucks and

---

* I have never been able to decide whether the following passage from *Red Virtue* shows that Miss Winter would swallow anything or rather that she thought her readers would: "The measures the enemies of the [Bolshevik] regime will stoop to are a model of fertile inventiveness. Two years ago, when queues before the shops were leading reporters and observers to conclude that the new state was breaking down and could not manage retail distribution, bands of people attached themselves to the queues to make them longer still, for the sole purpose of producing a more unfavorable effect." (p. 74.)

† Counts gave generous credit to his collaborator in translation, one of his assistants at the International Institute, Nucia P. Lodge.

automobiles, major kilowatt production from windmills—that must have been the windiest aspect of the Five-Year Plan. Gilbert Seldes said *New Russia's Primer* was as much "a bold attack on America" as " 'an excellent piece of propaganda for Russia.' " [16] Admirably observed; but for our purposes in dealing with America's recent past, its most striking aspect was Counts' notion of its proper audience. He explained that though it was "written for [Russian] children from twelve to fourteen years of age" to explain "the nature of a planned economy and ... social planning," he did not expect American children to use it. Instead, he meant it to "acquaint [American] adults with a phase of the Russian experiment ... the greatest social experiment in history." [17]

Gradually an opposition—part libertarian, part common sense—complaining that the emperor was rather lightly clad, formed independent of the banalities of the chronic Red baiters. In 1932 e. e. cummings, the immensely talented lower-case poet, whose standing as hater of militarism, conformity and fat-cats was unimpeachable, went pilgrim to Moscow, returned shuddering and said so elaborately in an impudent book, *Eimi,* that greatly distressed little groups of serious thinkers. Will Durant, former lecturer at anarchist and Socialist institutions, whose *The Story of Philosophy* was a best-selling major means of adult education in the 1920s, went to Russia the same year, saying, "I am afraid Communism in Russia cannot succeed but I hope to God it does," but came out dismayed, saying, in a book called *The Tragedy of Russia,* that there "as elsewhere Capital takes its return first and struggles with the worker for the larger share. [The USSR] is one monstrous and united capitalist, a vast and inescapable corporation which controls all workers and all life, and can do no wrong." [18] William H. Chamberlin, Moscow correspondent of the *Christian Science Monitor,* respected by most of his competitor colleagues for the integrity of his footwork, came home to put many things repugnant to the faithful into his *Russia's Iron Age.* All the while Old Guard Socialists, mistrusting the tendency of a majority of their comrades to palter with Bolshevism, had been making it clear that their kind of Marxist had no more use for Lenin or Stalin than for Mussolini. But the shift toward the Red end of the spectrum had too much momentum.

Some of its components were funny; some not. The one known Communist venture into whimsicality came about when a few new Party members choosing their "Party names" put "Franklin D. Roosevelt" or "Barbara Hutton" [19] (the harried and much-married Woolworth heiress) or some other such absurdity on their Party cards. I recall a party for a Soviet novelist, whose great book nobody present had yet read; we all sat dumbly around him, like children sizing up a new teacher, while in the background the host, well known for liaison between the two worlds, wrung his hands because the only Russian-speaking guest had not arrived. The calm thoroughness with which Miss Strong, lunching at an eminent millionaire banker's, explained the advantages and disadvantages of various ways to liquidate peasants while Mrs. Banker expressed herself as delighted with the ruthless intelligence of it all. The colorless ease with which Raymond Robins, humanitarian great man of American relief in Russia, confidant of several of the USSR's leaders, dean of sub-Red Sovietophilia in America, just back from Moscow in 1934, privately assured a group of fellow houseguests that the USSR finally had a logical and beneficent economy 'going and was showing a consistent humaneness toward criminals and that in a personal interview Stalin had explained to him the reason for the great famine in the Ukraine: It was just a matter of practicality; when recalcitrant peasants died like flies, it saved the government powder and shot and did not clog the railroads with wholesale deportations.

Cowley's speculations about the causes of the boom in Soviets Preferred barely mentioned the enthusiasm roused by the Five-Year Plan. That was unfair to what was the USSR's finest public relations gag even before Counts' stroke of luck with *New Russia's Primer*. This *Piatiletka,* as the knowing usually called it, was probably meant chiefly for internal effect as *reassurance—*Big Brother has it all worked out; as *spur—*better do it all in synchronization as fast as possible, else all will fall through, as *excuse—*disregard of human lives and needs is temporarily unavoidable, after the magic Five Years plenty of pie in the sky. The eventual result—a lopsided, fragmentary economy, millions starved to death or otherwise destroyed along the way, smothering of the advances toward educational, aesthetic and personal freedoms that the Revolution had tried fumblingly to make—was not widely appreciated for years. At the time it could not be because of the cloud of dubious statistics and changes of schedule that the Kremlin cast over it.* But from the beginning, early in 1929, an outside world, half-guessing that the Bolshevik regime was aborting— as the backward-looking NEP seemed to hint—found the brash

---

* Duranty (*I Write as I Please,* 282) properly pointed out that some of the causes of the lopsidedness were beyond the Kremlin's control, so no reproach to its planners and administrators. The Depression drastically lowered the world prices of the wheat, oil and so on that the USSR exported while it still had to pay pre-Depression contract prices for machinery ordered before 1930. The military threats arising at the same time from the Japanese and the Nazis

symmetry of the *Piatiletka* instantly momentous. It was thrown down like an ace of trumps, as if leading from unsuspected strength. In 1931 it was more impressive still because of the international economic hemorrhages that President Hoover blamed for the intensifying hard times in America. This bold confidence that Planning could turn an industrially backward nation unable even to feed itself into an industrially potent antagonist of the West founded on rationalized factory farms offered shining contrast with the downhill flounderings of private enterprise.

The relation of the *Piatiletka* to the wordy cult of Planning in the early 1930s has been gone into. In that context one of its side effects was inadvertent—it helped prepare America for the New Deal's National Recovery Administration. More lastingly "Five-Year Plan" became, as the *Columbia Encyclopedia* truly says, "a household word throughout the world." Durant marveled at the "magnificent machine of propaganda ... formed to turn tractors into dramas, pigiron into poetry, statistics into literature ... not only did Russia believe that [it] would put [itself] industrially abreast of western Europe ... every sentimental and rebellious soul in every continent believed it too." [20]

Year after year the Hinduses, Strongs *et al.* kept telling their nicely widening public that oh, yes, they do order these things better in Russia; I'm just back from another glorious visit into the future-that-works and the *Piatiletka* is rolling toward a magnificent consummation. The innocent wonder of it is that they did it so spontaneously as well as incessantly. The circumspect American correspondent in Moscow may occasionally have acknowledged to himself that even when on a lecture tour at home, he had better leave unmentioned the thronging indirect evidence that famine had been deliberately used as a tool in the collectivization program. Authors of best-sellers on the USSR may sometimes have felt lucky that their temperaments had drawn them into so rich a field. But in the vast majority of cases it probably was luck, not opportunism, and incidental. Of most of the writers mentioned here and dozens more, profiting more or less from cultivated persons' yearning to hear or read heartening things about the USSR, one can only say, duly wondering, never mind the handsome pickings, it would be erroneous as well as cynical to deny

---

made it advisable to "graft upon the original plan a fresh network of war factories and their subsidiary supply factories, which for strategic reasons must be placed ... two hundred miles west and eight hundred miles east of the Ural Mountains ... the [consequent] strain to an already overworked transportation system and a dwindling food supply was almost intolerable."

that their hearts were genuinely in it. Having one's heart in this or that is not, of course, as the volunteer propagandists for *Fascismo* also showed, the same as having one's heart in the right place. And to take the cardiological metaphor farther, Cowley's Reddening writers and artists were like that appropriately Russian demon-deity, Koschkei the Deathless, whose heart was not inside him but thousands of miles away, no longer just 3,000 miles away in Paris but 5,000 miles away in Moscow. Many of those people had an inextinguishable *nostalgie de l'outre-mer.*

When the *Piatiletka* was only a few months in circulation, but still well before Wall Street laid that egg, the USSR unlimbered another economic device with marked public relations effect in America. In 1927, as part of the celebration of the tenth anniversary of the October Revolution, the newly founded VOKS—an arm of the USSR's government to promote cultural relations with other nations—had invited 1,000 or so foreigners of presumably sympathetic stripe, mostly Americans, to come as guests. In their footsteps the existing trickle of Sovietophile tourists widened. This seeking of the Red Star hanging over the Kremlin brought the USSR's degenerating railroads and disintegrating hotels foreign money—*valuta*—badly needed to pay for imports of capitalist-made machinery and other exotics necessary to the *Piatiletka.* Within the USSR any stray franc, pound, mark or most particularly dollar had uniquely high economic significance. Suppose more and more tourists, tens of thousands instead of mere hundreds, each valuta-laden.... In 1929 a Soviet government tourist agency called Intourist opened offices in some of capitalism's great cities, New York included. It specialized in paid-in-advance group tours steered around the USSR by Intourist's own guides. Thus, it was simpler to control the strangers' movements. The ideological explanation came from John Rothschild, whose Open Road travel agency sold such tours under the auspices of the International Labor Defense, a Communist front: "The Russians like to deal with people—each other or visitors—in groups, and groups have the right of way in the Soviet Union today." [21] Occasionally a deviant of marked sympathies who insisted on booking solo was allowed to. But he was still tied to Intourist, for only through it could he or any other visitor obtain lodging, guides, interpreters, meals or transportation as he sought out the sights that Intourist let him see.

Both in Russia or abroad Intourist offices were sluggish, glum and inefficient. But as sympathetic curiosity about the *Piatiletka* rose, Intourist's bookings grew anyway. By the summer of 1935 it claimed to have about 30,000 making the pilgrimage—which, on a moderate estimate, pumped some $2,000,000 into the valuta-craving USSR's bloodstream. A few years earlier France or Britain would rightly have thought that small potatoes as tourist spending. But times were tough, and the New Deal's devaluation of the dollar had sharply raised the cost of Americans' trips to Western Europe, whereas the USSR, its ruble already wildly overvalued officially, could use the dollar's difficulties as opportunity for Intourist to advertise: "Travel Dollars Have Not Shrunk in the Soviet Union." [22] The schoolteacher or middle-aged widow no longer able to afford a month in France or Italy with American Express could still afford to go see Intourist's Rembrandts in the Hermitage, Red Square and the scenic wonders of the Georgian Military Highway.

That appeal to conventional tourist values was, however, a sideshow. The main point was direct contact with this immense, aggressively fascinating thing that everybody was talking about. The dust jacket of Intourist's $2.50 guidebook quoted George Bernard Shaw and Ray Long, quondam editor of Hearst's *Cosmopolitan,* that "Russia is the most interesting country in the world" and the Manchester *Guardian* that its "different ... political, economic and social organization furnishes the strong attraction of novelty for the restless wanderer who wishes to escape the beaten path." The text opened with "Every state is an organization of the ruling class" [23] and proceeded into 175 more pages of Leninist Marxism before relaxing into information about cities, museums and so on—nine-tenths of which Intourist's clients would probably never see because they would most definitely *not* be allowed to stray from the beaten path.

The *Nation*'s annual spring department, "The Intelligent Traveler," concentrated on announcements of conducted tours to the USSR on the obvious assumption that intelligent travelers would naturally be flocking thither. Some were captained by Party-lining university faculty such as Counts, Ward, Jerome Davis; some by Russian émigrés who had made their peace with the Kremlin, such as Countess Irina Skariatina, who had been lecturing acceptably on "The New Russia" for ten years before she returned to have a look at it; some by journalists who had earned a welcome in Moscow, such as Fischer, Bryan, Miss Strong.... The few tour captains who were not committed Sovietophiles took care to behave as if they were. Many were sponsored by the Communist fronts springing up as harbingers of the Popular Front of the later 1930s: the Russian-American Institute, the League for Industrial Democracy, the America-Russian Chamber of Commerce.... Specially toothsome was the University of Moscow's summer school package of four weeks of lectures and seminars on the USSR state (in English) followed by two weeks of sightseeing. The committee sponsoring its first year (1934) as the Anglo-American Institute included the presidents of New York University, the University of North Carolina, the University of Chicago, Smith College, Oberlin College, and other resplendent names, usually with some degree of entanglement, such as John Dewey, Counts, Hallie Flanagan, Vassar's renowned leader of dramatics.

The Indians squired about by the tour chiefs were well defined by Eugene Lyons when his stomach would no longer stand sincere Party-lining as the UP Man in Moscow: ". . . amateur sociologists, bubbly school teachers, liberal ministers, earnest probers, socialite thrill hunters and miscellaneous neurotics." [24] Durant listed: "thin virgins seeking a new religion, school-teachers flirting breathlessly with heresy, and professors anxious to approve of everything." [25] The strong academic flavor implied was still there among the hundreds of American tourists I encountered there in the summer of 1935. My tour was led by two Ivy League professors of Slavic studies and a sociologist from California II who had studied in Russia before the Revolution. It included several college students, a freshwater professor of economics, several Midwestern high school teachers, an elderly member of a Midwestern school board who had been making anti-USSR speeches and thought he would go see what he was denouncing—the only intelligent impulse he manifested—and an elderly widow from Kansas who had yearned to visit the Kremlin ever since she saw a picture of it in her school geography.

We crossed the Atlantic with 200-odd registrants for the University of Moscow summer school, mostly students but with a sprinkling of young and middle-aged fellow travelers and a few Communist Party members as sheepdogs and briefing officers. As the ship cast off, they massed forward and sang "The Internationale" and a song about "A Chain Gang Down in Georgia" to the tune of "A Rainbow Round My Shoulder." Unattached notables among us in third class were a somberly clever black Communist going to Moscow for retread because he disagreed with Party policy among blacks; a standoffish young Ivy Leaguer-Communist revered by the run of the summer schoolers because he was noted for successfully boring from within farmers' groups; another Ivy Leaguer of the same vintage who had once worked six months in a Leningrad foundry and now made a career of writhing dances accompanied by his own Whitmanesque poetry about the emotional joys of labor under the dictatorship of the proletariat. Glowingly he advised us not just to stand there when visiting a Russian factory but to grab shovel or hammer and demonstrate solidarity with the workers by pitching in.*

---

* This section concentrates on American pilgrims because they were a majority among outsiders visiting the USSR in the 1930s, and in any case this book is about America. For comparable observation of British counterparts see

Most such definitely Red pilgrims were well equipped with shibboleths, stereotypes and elementary data. Many of the mere moths following the Red flame were strangely ignorant. Intourist guides we chatted with told us of one lady who asked whether a certain statue represented Lenin or Peter the Great. Another wanted to know where Karl Marx was now living in Moscow. The economist in our party inquired whether Trotsky had been allowed back into Russia since the Revolution. Too few knew enough about Western counterparts of what we were shown—factory farm, assembly plant, hydroelectric plant, candy factory, rehabilitation center for prostitutes and so on—to appreciate scale or gauge efficiency and lacked the background to correct the guides' seldom-failing assurance that capitalism could show nothing like a linotype machine. They didn't even blink when the guide, steering us into a Park of Culture and Rest, said that since American parks were reserved for the rich, it would surprise us to see workers' children playing in this one. On a huge wheat farm the guide, who had spent several years in New England, told us that American farms, which consisted of only small fields encumbered with stones, couldn't compare.

That true-believing habit of mind practically guaranteed that the net propaganda effect of fetching in eager visitors would be favorable, no matter how ill fed, shabby and feckless the workers' paradise actually looked. In this department our 1935 summer schoolers, whose predecessors in 1934 had vastly enjoyed themselves, passed a severe test. They arrived in Moscow blissfully anticipating the opening session—and the whole thing was called off. At first there was no explanation at all. Then something lame about how the professors in charge had been ordered away on emergency duty for the state and no adequate replacements were available. (Informal surmise among correspondents at the bar of the Metropole Hotel linked it with the ferment of shootings and deportations still going on in consequence of the Kirov affair.) No offer to refund paid-in-advance tuition, board and lodging, but the frustrated students could, if they wished, do enough sightseeing travel to work off the unexpended balance.

The result was Orwellian. With only minimum grumbling the bulk of these mesmerized zealots, most of whom had made sacrifices to get up the cost of the trip-plus-study, some of whom could ill afford the waste of academic time, all of whom would have screamed bloody murder had any bourgeois institution done anything a tenth as

---

Godfrey Blunden, *A Room on the Route* (1947), and Malcolm Muggeridge, *Winter in Moscow* (1934). Both the writers did a stretch as correspondent in Moscow. The latter is better handled but somewhat flawed by a peevish anti-Semitism. Edmund Wilson, *Travels in Two Democracies,* also has some useful bits.

flagrant, trickled off meekly in small groups to see what they could of the object of their affections. Here and there in the next few weeks we other pilgrims encountered them still dutifully starry-eyed, though often thinner, for many of them scorned to observe the recommended dietary precautions against "Russky complaint"—known elsewhere as "Montezuma's revenge" or "Gyppy tummy" or "African quickstep." For their loyalty to everything USSR-sponsored, their resentment of comment on the shortcomings of this hard-pressed economy, extended even to what one ingested. The *New Masses* denounced me with bell, book and candle because I put in print such vicious lies as that Soviet brandy, though harmless and effective, stung like an adder and that in Moscow that hot summer the butter tasted like "something between tarragon vinegar and underripe cheese." [26]

It had been clear after a few days in Russia that no sloppiness or harshness would shake the sympathetic pilgrim's faith in the USSR's future as he chose to envision it. Tales of deliberate famine could not distress our chipper little sociologist, for he was as confident as the Reverend Mr. Porter that out of the Kremlin would eventually be born a merciful, nonsuperstitious religion to replace the Christianity it hated. Our mathematician vacationing from an industrial laboratory relied on Gosplan for a rosy Technocratic future, never mind how creakily and spottily Planning was obviously working out. Our high school principal never doubted that, no matter how sternly Communism refused legal status to political opposition, in due time the USSR would develop a liberal-democratic, multiparty system. And for that matter, our reactionary school board member stuck to it that sooner or later they'd have to get back to private ownership of the means of production.

Home they came, trailing fragmentary observations and half-baked conclusions, innocently unaware that they still knew little more about the USSR than when they had left home. In a Park of Culture and Rest in Moscow we stopped to watch holidaying workers listening to a map-and-pointer lecture on the Ethiopian War. Courteously they made way for us. The guide explained we didn't need to come nearer because we understood no Russian. One of the workers said, and I think the guide enjoyed translating faithfully, "In that case why did they bother to come all the way here to begin with?" In Rostov we had a more emphatic reaction. At a street corner our excursion bus returning us from some factory or other blocked the way of a local pedestrian. He ran his eye over us, disheveled but still looking well fed on what Intourist gave second-class visitors, and his lip curled. *"Turisti!"* he said. "Phooey!" And defying all the teachings of the new Soviet hygiene, he spat in the gutter.

The head start that Miss Strong, Hindus *et al.* gave the Great Redward Swing of the early 1930s was supplemented by the striking success on American screens of the USSR's propaganda movies. Late in 1926—again in the brash middle of the New Era—Amkino, a new agency for casting the Revolution's celluloid pearls before capitalist swine, brought to New York City's Biltmore Theater, no garish movie palace but a top-ranking legitimate house, S. M. Eisenstein's first world-famous movie, *Armored Cruiser Potemkin,* about a premonitory mutiny in the Imperial Russian Navy in 1905. Its masterful camera work and cutting made that monumental flight of steps in Odessa as famous as Van Gogh's Provençal bridges and drew deserved hosannas from watchfully arty critics. Eighteen months later American showings of Vsevolod Pudovkin's *The End of St. Petersburg* and Eisenstein's second salvo, *Ten Days That Shook the World,* showed that *Potemkin* * was no flash in the pan. The USSR had managed to breed young directors who, studying the previous work of California II and Germany, fired by Marxist zeal and spontaneous talent, transcended their dreary purpose of propaganda-by-the-screen and splattered tendentious footage about with an authority and originality well worth acquaintance, no matter what the message.

Ideally they and the numerous other USSR-made movies that followed them into the Western world should have been shown in working class neighborhoods as how-to-do-it for the potentially revolutionary proletariat. Actually they remained largely esoteric attractions for the cultivated. They earned *valuta,* however, and in any case the self-consciously arty moviegoer to whom they most appealed was often the same potential Redward Swinger in whom, for better or worse, lay the USSR's best hopes of strategically placed sympathy. In 1927, say, a typical subscriber to the *Nation* who had just read *Humanity Uprooted* and been drawn to USSR-made movies by the critics' promises of rare aesthetic treats came away not only gratified in that respect but also nudged farther toward ranking the October Revolution with the Emancipation Proclamation and the founding of Hull House as sacred-cow events. The stuffy Briton then reviewing movies for the New York *Times* was not alone in noticing that the presumably art-minded audience of *Potemkin* wildly applauded such crude bits as a subtitle "Down with the Czar!" and a shot of a Navy officer being thrown overboard.

The best such movies were usually shown in a cozily angular "art cinema," serving free coffee in a lounge hung with black-and-whites by Rockwell Kent, not in the frowsy former burlesque house on Union

---

* Often billed as *The Battleship Potemkin;* this comes of the popular delusion that "battleship" and "man-of-war" are synonymous.

Square—Elia Kazan recalled it as "a firetrap ... an ancient, narrow, cavernous box" [27]—that showed run-of-mine USSR movies to the few genuine proletarians bothering to come there. The distinction lay not so much in content, which could hardly be more flat-footed than that of Eisenstein's best, as in wooden technique that sometimes made them even worse than run-of-mine Hollywood. After seeing one of these stodgy items in Moscow at this period, Edmund Wilson wrote: "... almost with a shock one realizes that it is possible for a Russian film to be dull." [28] He would have felt less shock had he patronized that Union Square place as often as I had to get the feel of the scanty audiences and the witless fare they relished. The best production I ever saw there was an admirably humorous animated cartoon celebrating the staying power of the USSR's bedbugs and showing how to get rid of them. The Kremlin was lucky to have Eisenstein, Pudovkin *et al.* to sugarcoat the simplistic blatancies of Leninist Stalinism. Fascism had no such talents at disposal. So far as American screens showed between World Wars, no Italian movie industry existed. The few Nazi-made movies sneaking into Yorkville were shoddy technically and watery as propaganda. The sole exception was Leni Riefenstahl's ecstatic filming of the Nazi-sponsored Olympics.

Neither Miss Strong nor Miss Bryant before her could be suspected of the objectivity that doctrinaires then, as now, denied validity in either reporting or comment. Even Miss Thompson and Mrs. Roosevelt felt the nonobjective pull of collectivism to which the settlement house mind is necessarily and sometimes constructively subject. Mrs. Roosevelt's consequent embarrassments with Party-lining Youth are to be treated later. Note here that one can plead in defense that in neglecting the journalist's traditional nagging duty to try not only for nothing but the truth but even the whole truth, she was merely the amateur following professional examples. The Sheeans, Thompsons and Peglers had renounced that quest of the unattainable will-of-the-wisp, pursuit of which is nevertheless so healthy.

Among their excuses might well have been the plea that while their talents were developing, the Red version of collectivism-humanitarianism was invading stage and fiction in terms so beguiling that deliberate advocacy seemed professionally liberating as well as the social duty of anybody writing for print. "[Alexander] Woollcott's friends," Wolcott Gibbs observed in the *New Yorker*, "who had had no political convictions to speak of in 1920, began to think rather intensely and presently occupied conflicting positions ranging all the way from mild liberalism to the ultimate hammer and sickle." [29] In that climate the novelist or playwright could not, even if he wished to, wall off his conscience and artistic integrity from the social repercussions of his writing, for obviously no published writing could lack them. Say a stenographer took out of the library even so apparently neutral a best-seller as *Anthony Adverse*. The several dimes it cost her might have bought her the *New Masses*. Its content, however peevish now and then, failed to depict the past as the significant welter of class villainies that it really had been. She should be reading Upton Sinclair. It also lost her precious hours in which she might have been indoctrinated in the class struggle and set to organizing the office she worked in. "Art is a class weapon," was the motto of the Party-front John Reed Clubs for writers. Indeed, printed pages, stage, movies were either such weapons or worse than nothing—opiates for victims of capitalist exploitation. Had not the Sacco-Vanzetti case and the post-Crash breadlines shown any and all intelligent, sensitive, decent writers and actors where their moral bread and butter lay?

This ringing summons was reinforced by writers' awareness that for several decades Reddish-to-Red government hating had been fashionable among their literary-scholarly-intellectual counterparts in Europe. The Party's practical purpose—to enlist writers' prestige and skills in concocting free, high-grade propaganda for the Revolution (and the synonymous USSR)—did not mar the genuine, if casuistic, sincerity of the adherents and publications singing the song of *le-bourgeois-à-la-lanterne*. For writers not yet arrived it was gratifying thus to be sought out for the role of the rejected stone being made head of the corner. For those already arrived it was a stimulating distraction from the flabby clubwomen who welcomed them during lecture tours. Those of the Lost Generation had been expected deliberately to withdraw from the impertinent culture around their roots. That was an emotionally precarious, socioculturally malnourished situation. Now they were flatteringly urged to join the beckoning mainstream of history, become part and parcel not of that parochial, bourgeois, doomed Babbitt Warren but of the cosmopolitan intellectual fellowship of Marx, Lenin, Trotsky *(strike that!)*, Maxim Gorky, Anatole France, Romain Rolland, André Malraux, Palme Dutt, Dreiser (off and on), Mao Tse-tung, presently Paul Robeson.... How soul-satisfying to throw back one's head and sing in unison with other dedicated wise men: "The *inter*national Sohohov*yet* / Shall *be* the *hu*man *race!*" In 1930 Dos Passos suggested that the cause needed a PR director "like Ivy Lee [dean of the American PR industry] to familiarize the public with the idea of communism and induce people at least to remain neutral toward communist agitation instead of clapping all the Communists in jail." [30] Actually no such agent was needed. As the swelling tide of Moscow-bound writers was already showing, as the Party's Popular

Front would show a few years later, Madison Avenue had little to teach.

The Party's trust in the Sacco-Vanzetti case * and the Depression as bait was well founded. The events leading up to that electrocution did much to flaw the indifference to social trauma then attributed, usually in exaggerated terms, to the Jazz Age. That prepared the way for what happened when such a writer as Cowley, having quit America for the Left Bank as the New Era was really beginning to glitter, now returned to a country fouled up with unemployment and hunger and floundering in frustration and backbiting. The typical reaction was further revulsion from the moneymen's polity, alarm for one's own welfare, pity for the dislocated, hurried grasping for remedies—all of which impulses trained revolutionaries and even astute reformers well know how to exploit. Not all the susceptible filed into the same doctrinaire barracks, of course. Differences in timing, place or temperament took this handful into Technocracy, that gaggle into Social Credit, many no farther than the settlement-house premises of the New Deal. Some ended up shilling for such reactionary juntas of the late 1930s as the America First Committee. But the largest group were writers who looked on the guiding light when it was Red and felt no need to blink.

Orrick Johns, an editor of the *New Masses,* the Communists' literary flagship, called its office "the center of the leftwing literary movement." [31] As samples of talent consistently contributing he cited Joseph Freeman, James T. Farrell, Edward Dahlberg, Josephine Herbst, Nathan Asch, Alfred Kreymborg, Maxwell Bodenheim. By early 1935 Waldo Frank, Kenneth Burke, Cowley had been attracted through the American Writers' Congress, an early and highly successful Party front. Discussing it thirty years later, Granville Hicks, a zealous literary Party member who fell off when Stalin rounded the curve of his treaty with Hitler, said, "Sometimes ... I just can't imagine how I could have been damn fool enough to support the Communist party. In other moods ... it seems to me that was exactly the thing I had to do in that particular time." [32] One or another stratum of the Party's Parnassus soon included Edmund Wilson, Dorothy Parker, Donald Ogden Stewart, Sherwood Anderson, Carl Sandburg among names firmly established then, still known. Among adherents beginning to make themselves felt were Erskine Caldwell, Dashiell Hammett, Nathanael West, Ruth McKenney, John Steinbeck. For some of these "workers and peasants of Manhattan," [33] as Lillian Symes obliquely called them, their deepening Redness proved a help in getting

* For an account of this factor see my *Great Times,* 267–72.

published, securing reviews in good places and word-of mouth publicity at the right gatherings. Yet it is probably safe to say of all those
listed above and many of the smaller fry that, handy as it was, this
consideration had no part in their espousal of the hospitably polyg-
amous Party. Their emotional bents would have taken them there
anyway had their Redness not been expedient. Indeed, many of them
were probably acting from at least a firm illusion of generous motives.
They thought they were risking a good deal by thus acting on their
anger about the plight of the Gastonia strikers and their conviction
that social decency demanded violently remaking the world along lines
that Marx recommended, or would have if he hadn't always fought
shy of specifics. Their cult was so deadly serious and earnest that when
cummings' *Eimi* proved full of ideological *lèse majesté,* some of his
best friends stopped speaking to him.

Degree of formal commitment matters little here. There was little
sense in the congressional committees' later question: "Are you now or
have you ever been a member of the Communist Party?" A good
number of those mentioned above really had Party cards and were
presumably prepared to submit to full Party discipline with "Party
names," undercover identities, message drops and the rest of the
paraphernalia to make them feel like younger brothers of the can-
onized Old Bolsheviks. Orrick Johns' pride in having carried a card
was probably typical: "... a serious step.... For four years ... I no
longer had a personal life.... I was the servant of ... a semi-legal
cause, under the control of my superior at all times ... dedicated to a
poverty ration.... Not one of us ever went to bed at night without
expecting to be raided and arrested [he never was] ... the solidarity
which unites even a small band of serious and loyal people, threatened
by violence ... was ... an education I would not have missed at any
cost." [34] But since the special usefulness to the cause of many of these
writers, actors, painters and so on whom it recruited consisted of being
attention-drawing window displays, most of them were never asked
thus to play for keeps. The much larger group never formally enrolled
may have yearned for the emotional benison of a card signifying full
acceptance but meekly agreed with the decision of the "dreaded D.O.,
or district organizer" [34] that they were more useful (and doubtless less
bother) as mere fellow travelers. Many of those were among the
dauntless intellectuals signing the manifesto of 1932 declaring for
William Z. Foster, the Communist Party candidate for the presidency,
that caused so much stir.

Obviously there was no doubt about the status of Mike Gold, the
New Masses' perdurable hatchet man who earned the post with *Jews
Without Money,* an able propaganda novel about the East Side ghetto

(1929): "My parents . . . wanted me to go on to high school. . . . Even then I could sense that education is a luxury reserved for the well-to-do. . . . Momma! Momma! . . . I believe in the poor because I have known you. The world must be made gracious for the poor! . . . My mother had that dark proletarian instinct which distrusts all that is connected with money-making. No one can go through the shame and humiliation of the job hunt without being marked for life. . . . There can be no freedom in the world while men must beg for jobs." [35] Everybody knew that "Robert Forsythe," regular book reviewer of the *New Masses,* was actually Kyle Crichton, on the masthead of *Collier's,* the slick weekly. Beyond such cases, however, things were so Byzantine that for a writer openly to label himself Communist might mean that he never had been a card carrier—just a sympathizer too ill informed to know that genuine comrades seldom admitted membership, whereas a Sovietophile liberal denying he was a Communist, threatening to sue anybody who called him one, might well have held a Party card ever since Limbo University had dispensed with his services in 1928.

Nor was going pilgrim to Moscow a reliable earmark. In some unmistakable cases that meant advanced training for a minor leader, in others a summons to the woodshed. But its primary use was to widen and deepen the apparatus: Class A = tight cadre of real Party members; Class B = clique of well-coordinated fellow travelers, many of them bucking for membership; Class C = loosely controlled fellow travelers shading off into mere ardent sympathizers relied on to read the Party press, contribute regularly to Party causes, turn out for mass meetings and never forget that any cocktail or dinner party was the time for all good men (circumspectly) to come to the aid of the Party. Those strata cut across the world of writers just as they did across the worlds of Red-minded labor organizers and federal employees. "The American intellectual," said the hero of *The Hucksters,* ". . . considers himself a leftish liberal . . . [is] trapped in ideologies. . . . He always feels compelled to accept . . . or reject [any political act or idea] on the basis of Soviet interests." [36] For they were identical with the Party's and vice versa. That was the emotional reflex, leading to a sort of supranational patriotism identified with the USSR's policies and demands, that, to considerable public astonishment, betrayed so many able young Americans and others into becoming infiltrating traitors.

Edmund Wilson, indubitable intellectual, made his pilgrimage in 1935. In Leningrad he saw a statue of Lenin that wafted him into a rhapsody epitomizing what took him and so many of his kind to invite their souls there: ". . . right hand and arm outstretched and in the eyes [*of a statue!*] a look both piercing and genial, at once as if he were giving back to labor what it had made and inviting it to share for the first time in its heritage of human culture, and as if he were opening out to humanity as a whole a future of which for the first time they were to recognize themselves the masters, with the power to create without fear whatever they had minds to imagine." [37] No artistic artifact had been so eloquent since Walter Pater's Mona Lisa. But such talk has the relative coldness of expository statement. As literary Redness deepened in hue and more writers took up the class struggle, they often wrote "the proletarian novel"—a thing as fashionable as "the problem play" had been twenty years earlier. It was seldom written by proletarians. Its subject matter was seldom limited to the proletariat. Proletarians whom it depicted seldom much resembled real ones. Nor did "novel" apply to many consequent items in any but a most charitable sense. Indeed, the average level of quality was rather below that of the watery prototypes previously supplied by Upton Sinclair.

The standard-bearer was, of course, Dos Passos' *USA* trilogy published in 1931–34, the period when recruiting of writers was at its height. But its misanthropy and simplistic view of social forces cannot be blamed on the post-Depression boom in radicalism. Dos Passos had been writing that way, though in less elaborate forms, since the end of World War I. *USA* was actually the culminating item in the dribble of Postwar Disillusion. What pertinence it had to the new dispensation of Hoovervilles and Planning was flawed when, in consequence of some months in war-tortured Spain, its author lost his Red moorings and drifted off to leeward into growingly reactionary sympathies. It was the young sprouts, not of the Lost Generation but of one that insisted on trying to orient itself, who presently furnished the significantly worst (Caldwell) and misguidedly best (Steinbeck) of the crop.

Caldwell's proletariat was genuine—the sharecropper/millhand stratum of the South, the duplex subculture in which, one of Lardner's wry-mouthed ballplayers said, the girls got all excited when they saw a man with shoes on. Caldwell had known it as son of a hand-to-mouth preacher in a Calvinist splinter sect who—take it on the word of Ralph McGill, great editor of the Atlanta *Constitution*—was authentically saintlike. Apparently the doctrine of original sin helped the old gentleman accept the results in the cotton and tobacco areas of heredity, malaria, hookworm, malnutrition, former black slavery, current sharecropping, soil-mining agriculture, runaway textile mills, differential freight rates, snuff dipping and Dixie's myriad forms of hell-snorting religion. These same data seem to have struck the son as funny in a way that made him a harbinger of what is now called black humor. He owed the favor that book buyers accorded *Tobacco Road* and *God's Little Acre* largely to the shock-amusement value of middle-aged she-preachers marrying halfwits for stud purposes; senescent fathers lip-lickingly appraising their daughters' "rising beauties"; wife attacking her millhand-husband with a hairbrush because it annoys her to find him whiling away the time between her sister's legs.

Caldwell's handling of these materials, as terse as a movie treatment, relied on dialogue that, though it got better as he went along, was at its worst in his earliest, most popular work. Ten years previously—suppose it had got by the less permissive courts of 1922—*Tobacco Road*'s consequences would hardly have reached beyond the Broadway stage adaptation that ran longer than *Abie's Irish Rose,* (Not until the end of the decade was that stain on the American audience's reputation washed away by the even longer run of *Life With Father,* in which Howard Lindsay and Russel Crouse brilliantly adapted to the stage Clarence Day's sketches of his redheaded family and gave Lindsay and his deftly winsome wife, Dorothy Stickney, their roles of a lifetime.) Though Caldwell's early narrative often sounded like a clumsy translation from something Russian,* some of it was good unclean fun. And this worthy child of his time invented, or perfected, the technique of ideology inlay that qualified so many works of fiction of the day as proletarian novels.

In *Tobacco Road* every thirty pages or so Jeeter Lester interrupts his tribe's wallowings and twitchings to soliloquize about tilling the soil and the socioeconomic forces that keep him from doing so; then, after maybe a page of it, they all go back to gnawing on turnips or one another. The husband who gets whacked is at home that afternoon because the local mill is on strike; as strike leader he sometimes fires off a hundred words about the millowners' reluctance to let their labor force be unionized or how niggardly it is of the Red Cross to distribute to the strikers the flour and sugar that Washington sends as early Depression relief. Caldwell seldom bothers to weave such interpolations in with his raunchy anecdotes. That may be as well, for the two tones are wildly inconsistent, as though John Cleland had stuck passages from *Baxter's Saint's Everlasting Rest* into Fanny Hill's reminiscences. Similarly the Communist-led hunger march glued on the end of James T. Farrell's Studs Lonigan trilogy has no more to do

---

* Thus from *Tobacco Road:* "Dude went to the pine stump and sat down to watch the red wood-ants crawl over the stomach and breasts of his sister. . . . The grandmother fell on her knees and clutched [the turnips] hungrily against her stomach while she munched the vegetable with her toothless gums. . . . His reason for hating rats was because of an incident that had happened when his father died while Jeeter was a young man."

with the preceding thousands of pages about the rancidity of Chicago's lace-curtain Irish than the finale with the girls grouped around Columbia, waving Old Glory, had to do with the burlesque show preceding it.

The other method was to permeate the novel with class-conscious values. The solidest examples, anyway the woodenest, were the stories that, in his Red phase, Whittaker Chambers wrote for the Communist press. Sometimes, however, the end product was far better. Steinbeck's first success came of the deft sentimentality of *Tortilla Flat.* There his genial taste for mavericks and innocent little prostitutes wearing the regulation heart of gold on the sleeve enabled him to celebrate the quaintly charitable virtues of assorted vagabonds, Anglo or Chicano. (The other old reliable is the mental institution with everybody inside saner and nicer than everybody outside.) In the mid-1930s, however, the newly modish class struggle stirred some iron into Steinbeck's cosmos. Now his already-promising skills had something to chew on.

Whoever recruited him should have had the Order of Lenin, for out of it came *In Dubious Battle,* an entry in the Proletarian Novel Sweep actually worth reading for its own sake. It made drama, not blueprint, of the struggle of the half-undercover Party to organize the migrant harvesters of the West Coast—cultural and often actual cousins of the Tobacco Roaders whom Caldwell patronizingly caricatured. Steinbeck's versions had three dimensions and organic juices; when you clubbed these refugees from private enterprise, they did bleed. Nor were the experienced or apprentice Communist organizers whose casuistic courage stiffens the book mere symbols of righteous class hatred but individuals sweating out the strains as the Party's demands haul on their personalities. "Mac," one of them is told by the sympathizer MD in the strikers' camp, "you're the craziest mess of cruelty and hausfrau sentimentality ... I ever saw." [38] Yet raw Red doctrine is implicit in most of what happens as well as in explicit statement. Here is Communism's natural history from the inside out by one who indubitably knew, for not the least notable thing about it is the commonsense evidence it affords, superfluous but valuable, that the Party was the backbone of California's migrant labor troubles.

Its successor, *The Grapes of Wrath,* was, of course, superlatively conspicuous. It shifted the focus from the Communist organizers to showing how their Okie raw material for the Revolution got to California. Its grotesque final episode, originated by Guy de Maupassant fifty years previously but still likely to attract notice in America in 1939, has the newly delivered girl mother of a dead baby suckling a starving vagrant. Other episodes—the truck driver and the hitchhiker working out disclosure of the latter's stretch in the penitentiary; the

countergirl and the candy-hungry Okie children at the roadside diner—
are able variations on the theme, sound when not overplayed, of
common-folks-can-be-mighty-decent. But this context has to go further
into contrasting them invidiously with the kind of uncommon folks
who have money, power or both and so must be, by definition, vicious
as well as stuffy. The big shiny cars whisking by on the highway to
California contain "Languid, heat-raddled ladies. . . . Lines of weariness around the eyes, lines of discontent down from the mouth . . . the
mouths panting, the eyes sullen, disliking wind and earth. . . . Beside
them, little pot-bellied men . . . with puzzled, worried eyes . . . hungry
for security and yet sensing its disappearance . . . [hoping to] reassure
themselves that business is noble and not the ritualized thievery they
know it is. . . . " [39] That is just a Bob Minor cartoon from the *New
Masses.* Then there was bald gurgle of the *Our Daily Bread* sort in the
decent harmony of the New Deal's camp cooperatively controlled by
the migrants' own kangaroo courts and *viva voce* voting, contrasted
with the local reactionaries' sneaky effort to discredit and destroy the
place. The interpolated essays on how America acquired California
and how the banks moved in and so on are about as temperate as a
hotshot district attorney's summing up at a headlined murder trial.
And the stated moral is: " . . . when property accumulates in too few
hands it is taken away . . . when a majority of the people are hungry
and cold they will take by force what they need." [40]

Yet Steinbeck also neglected the Party-line duty to blame everything
on private enterprise. As previously noted, *Grapes* at least implicitly
admits that drought and catastrophic wind erosion were not capitalism's fault. And the occasion of that suckle-the-starving bit at the end
is a flood emergency that would never have occurred had not the
climate of California, sometimes as prodigally irresponsible as mankind, applied too much rain to a vulnerable topography—and Steinbeck's account of it makes this clear. In the orthodox Communist view
such matters impertinent to the class struggle are distractingly cryp-
toheretical and should never have been brought up. It follows that
Steinbeck was no Malraux—hardly news. It may show further,
however, that in spite of his orthodoxy in *Battle,* he harbored an
independence too deep within him for the Party to smother it. That is
consistent with his distinction as the only American writer winning the
Nobel Prize whose work is discernibly related to the actual terms of
the Nobel bequest—"the [writer] who shall have produced in the field
of literature the most distinguished work of an idealistic tendency." [41]

In step with the novelists certain playwrights and ancillary directors,
actors and producers of appropriate temperament were persuaded by

the Sacco-Vanzetti complex, the Depression and the rise of Fascism that it was their duty to make the stage a Party-lining weapon. Precedent was there in the plays of a group called the New Playwrights—Dos Passos, Lawson, Elmer Rice, Paul Sifton *et al.*—who in the later 1920s used the stage to heighten radical feeling, often borrowing the fluid, austerely mounted, symbol-heavy methods of Europe's "expressionist" school of theater. Their angel was Otto Kahn, multimillionaire partner in Kuhn, Loeb & Company, epitome of capitalist power banking. He would have done well to ponder certain passages in Sifton's *The Belt*, produced in October, 1927, just two years before the Great Crash. It denounced Henry Ford's production line as destroyer of human beings and dwelt on the social irresponsibility of his prolonged shutdown to retool for Model A, and its hero shouted with sharp economic foresight, "Something's going to break pretty soon and I want to be ready. ... Maybe tomorrow. ... I ... made you guys sore by asking ... where'd you get off when the bubble bust and people got so oversold on every damn thing under the sun that they couldn't pay any more first instalments [*sic*]. ... " [42] But that market tip was overlaid by the finale, an expressionistic riot that, in another kind of prophecy, dismantled the assembly line while "The Internationale" was rendered by the whole strength of the company.

This footlighted radicalism had several interrelated targets: *modern industry* as dehumanizer; the nation's *armed forces* because they abetted the munitions industry in fomenting war and were a potential curb on attempted revolution; *war* because it enabled predatory capitalism to enslave colonial markets; *banks,* such as Kahn's, because they enabled predatory capitalism to enslave farmers and create monopolies grinding the faces of the poor; *universities* because they truckled to reactionary wealth, discouraged radical ideas and often provided military training; *the church* because much of it preached distracting "pie in the sky" and seldom denounced predatory capitalism as un-Christian. That series of positions varies widely in relative validity, say from 90 percent to 10 percent. Within that range sort them out as you like. But all derive from the oversimple, immature, *post hoc* notions of human behavior common among Marxists and axiomatic among radicals by dint of incessant repetition. It was such a deep satisfaction to call J. P. Morgan a murderer and robber.

At the very bottom of the Depression, seven weeks before FDR was inaugurated, while his decision not to collaborate with the lame-duck Hoover administration kept things at dead center, Elmer Rice tied it all up in one bundle in the seethingly indignant *We, the People:* Factory foreman's daughter-schoolteacher's pay is months in arrears because hard times have bankrupted the city. She can't marry her white-collar boyfriend because the bank he works for can't or won't give him a raise. The mortgage on his widowed mother's farm is about to be foreclosed. Her son-in-law might keep it going in spite of sagging farm prices, but he is a drunk shattered by World War I and her younger son has just enlisted in the US Marines out of economic despair. He gets killed advancing imperialism in Haiti. Foreman gets laid off, so his son has to give up study at State U. Industrial big shots nominate for the presidency the distinguished president of State U who has just discharged two radical professors for making speeches that annoy the powerful and for encouraging the campus newspaper to resist ROTC. Foreman's unemployed son steals coal to keep the family warm, goes to penitentiary, comes out revolution-minded and shacks up with radical freshman girl whose Polish immigrant father died of tuberculosis brought on by low pay and sweatshop work. During a riotous demonstration of the jobless foreman is killed by company guards, son is arrested for allegedly killing a guard—it's actually a frame-up based on a pistol the police steal from his room—and is sentenced to hang. He becomes an international *cause célèbre*. The finale is a mass meeting presided over by the discharged faculty members, a high-minded country parson who stood up for the foreclosed widow, the frustrated schoolteacher-sister of the convicted man, and his Polish girlfriend, now pregnant by him, of course, for Rice wasn't letting anybody off anything. Haranguing the audience, whom the production incorporated as if they were sympathizers attending a real protest meeting, she played up her interesting condition:

" . . . millions . . . ask for bread and peace and they are given only starvation and war . . . if they protest they are shot down and sent to prison. So that a few people can have a thousand times what they need, millions must live in darkness and hunger. I shall not be silent . . . my lover was not silent . . . he must die . . . when my child is born, I shall teach it to protest too . . . we shall go on, the poor and oppressed . . . until we strike off our chains . . . win for ourselves the right to live!" The younger professor spells out the Sacco-Vanzetti motif: " . . . when you murder . . . judicially, in an access of frenzy and fear. . . . You proclaim to the world that America has forsaken justice for lynch-law, democracy for class-rule." The parson asserts that "men of liberal political opinions were rigorously excluded from the jury . . . the judge is the son of the proprietor of a group of influential newspapers which, stridently demanded . . . conviction . . . constant emphasis was laid upon [his] social and political philosophy . . . he was tried for his opinions, rather than for the crime with which he was charged. . . . " [43]

In Western culture few plays had laid it on thicker since *Uncle Tom's Cabin* and *Ten Nights in a Barroom*. It was like a clipsheet of episodes for the radical-minded plays appearing the rest of the decade under various auspices. Some of those call-to-the-barricades dramas came from the Group Theatre—an organization formed in 1930, chiefly remembered now as cradle of Lee Strasberg's "The Method" school of actor training. In its day the Group was a striking effort among like-minded actors, directors, playwrights to create a theater transcending the aims of the commercial theater—to develop, in the pretentious terms set down by Harold Clurman, one of its three director mainstays: "a vehicle of human being ... [plays] to make men more truly alive." 44 Its forebears were the American Laboratory Theatre, a sort of histrionic academy of the late 1920s presided over by veterans of the illustrious Moscow Art Theater, under whom Clurman, Strasberg and others in the Group had studied, and the Theatre Guild, the commercial but high-minded organization, another child of the 1920s, that produced what it took to be and sometimes were important plays, usually from Europe, for a subscription audience.

In 1929 the Guild set some of its young apprentices—Clurman, a sharp young woman, Cheryl Crawford, and J. Edward Bromberg of the American Laboratory—to creating the Guild Studio, a junior unit to give subscribers promising talent in second-string productions on Sundays. Their first, *Red Rust,* was New York City's introduction to the new work issuing from the USSR's brilliant, state-dominated theater. The Guild Studio chose it before the Great Crash, but appropriately, in view of its inevitable propaganda content, it was January, 1930, when the New Era was already down by the head and sinking fast, before its curtain rose. Clurman has since insisted, "The choice of a Soviet play represented no ideological bias on anyone's part," and professed to have been surprised when it brought great numbers of "Soviet sympathizers [showing] themselves for the first time on Broadway" 45 and applauding wildly when "The Internationale" was sung as curtain raiser. Within a few days the Guild Studio (learning fast? or playing the next card?) held a symposium on *Red Rust* that drew a standing-room-only crowd to the large Martin Beck Theater. Joyously they heckled the sole speaker invited to deplore the production, no other than shopworn George Sylvester Viereck, then in his between-wars doldrums. Raptly they welcomed H. W. L. Dana, tireless, prolix, zealous in the great cause, and Hallie Flanagan, chief of Vassar's Experimental Theatre, later national director of the New Deal's Federal Theatre, who had come back bubbling exultantly from her pilgrimage to Moscow.

Late that year the Theatre Guild itself had a moderate success with

Roar China!, a formidable, USSR-created spectacle dramatizing capitalist bullying of Far Eastern societies. The Guild Studio was presently disbanded with the dynamic result that its staff and a number of its actors combined with others from the American Laboratory to produce on their own as the Group Theatre. Semi-cooperative, smugly dedicated, bulging with underexperienced but sparkling talent, self-consciously hardworking, always able somehow to raise minimum money to stage what it wished to do, some of it even from the proverbially crass Shubert theater-owning interest—the Group was in many ways a heartening phenomenon for the eight or nine years of its vicissitudinous history.

Its work was not exclusively a call to revolution like that of the New Playwrights or the later Theater Union. Its first venture, fairly successful, too, was Paul Green's *The House of Connelly,* an item in the rising literature of dat ol' decadent Dixie. Its most profitable one was Sidney Kingsley's *Men in White,* all about the complicated life of the MD and ancestor of all the radio and TV serials about same. But the note that *Red Rust* struck kept reverberating. Clurman and others tried to make this seem nondeliberate; they just did "the best dramatic material available." * But Jay Williams' recent *Stage Left* rates the Group as one of "the three leading prospectors in the field of socially conscious drama." [46] Some of the results were worth while in their own right like *In Dubious Battle.* The Siftons' *1931* was a genuinely poignant expressionistic fable following an extravert warehouseman down the labyrinth of unemployment into the depths of despair, ending with the usual riot accompanied by snatches of "The Internationale." Almost impossible to stage, it failed, but its glow kept up the Group's taste for daydreams of revolution. The next year they did better with Lawson's *Success Story,* a hard breather about the corruption inherent in capitalist values, and early in 1935 better still with Clifford Odets' *Awake and Sing,* about the revolution-encouraging potential of Jewish home life in the Bronx. From the stockpile this drew the veteran of World War I bitter about his missing leg, which demonstrates that war is unnecessary, and the tired old Marxist telling the resentful young hero, "Boychick, wake up! ... take the world in your two hands and make it like new. Go out and fight so life shouldn't be printed on dollar bills!" [47] But Odets, long an actor with

---

* This quotes Alexander Kirkland, a fine Group actor. Clurman's own attitude, he said, was that of D. H. Lawrence: "The essential function of art is moral ... a passionate, implicit morality, not didactic ... which changes the blood ... first. The mind follows later. ... " (*The Fervent Years,* 176.) That, of course, is an admirable description of the most effective propaganda methods.

the Group, had already lifted it to its peak of ideological hankering and the masterpiece of the decade's radical theater: *Waiting for Lefty.*

This one-acter was worked out on a bare stage—a growingly tense meeting of a taxi drivers' union deliberating whether to strike against utterly unscrupulous employers. The audience was asked to think of itself as rank-and-file union members. The proceedings were interspersed with sparse episodes illustrating the woes and injustices of the hackie's predicament. Finks try to sidetrack the strike; blunders are sketched in; nothing can really be done until the arrival of their inexplicably delayed leader, Lefty. Finally down the aisle and up on the stage rushes a wild-eyed messenger: No use waiting any longer for Lefty; the owners' goons have killed him. Facing the audience, the messenger shouts, "What's the answer?" and plants in the house, then the whole audience, so infectious is the staging, roar back at him, 'Strike! Strike!" It would have raised the hair on the back of the neck of a stone-dead codfish. At the time it was a sort of adrenal sacrament for audiences, most of whom came craving it. "It was the birth cry of the thirties," Clurman wrote. "Our youth had found its voice ... 'Strike!' ... not alone for a few extra pennies of wages ... [but] for greater dignity, strike for a bolder humanity, strike for the full stature of man. ... " [48]

Coupled with Odets' short anti-Fascist tract *Till The Day I Die,* *Lefty* was a little gold mine, both financial and ideological, for radical groups and causes in the neighborhood of New York City. Radical-minded amateurs produced that double bill in thirty-odd cities coast to coast. Several cities, led by Boston, used its profanity as a pretext to ban it; actually, of course, for being exactly what the local police thought it was—a resounding incitement not to mere riot but to a shapeless, hence less controllable cult of exasperated revolution.

Odets went on to write other effective, less corrosive plays and had several stints in Hollywood that plowed him up apparently as much through a sense of his own shortcomings as through the movies' sleazy values. In the later 1930s federal subsidy enabled the doctrinaire theater of which he was chief ornament to go epidemic. In tone and method the result resembled official propaganda for a popular war. Everything after *Lefty,* however—even the WPA's Living Newspapers and Orson Welles' *The Cradle Will Rock*—was anticlimax. *Lefty* was one of those once-in-a-lifetime triumphs like a hole in one, 200-proof hokum, pure hormone-rousing stagecraft as voluptuously mindless as a lynch mob, as dedicated as a nihilistic assassin, as spontaneously fluid as an orgasm. It stands halfway in time between *The Green Pastures* and *Our Town* as one of the three dramatic peaks of its remarkable— to put it mildly—decade. All three were making the most of the essential staginess of the stage. Hence probably their superlative quality.

The impressive list of writers adopting the Party line need not obscure others: those whose adherence vacillated or eroded and those who had little or nothing to do with it. Of the first kind Hemingway, swaggering alongside and then, born maverick, standing off and on, is one illuminating case. Few such publicly took the position that most vexed their quondam allies—the grim view that Communism and Fascism were King Log and King Stork and that sound instincts, moral or aesthetic, would give neither the time of day. And neither the backslidings of some as time brought disconcerting developments nor the inability of others to get religion at all necessarily implies genuine social gumption. In some such cases insensibility, in others congenital aloofness, may be the reason. Which applies in a given case is hard to determine.

One sometimes wonders—it may not hold water very well—whether the quality of American writing in the 1930s may not have varied inversely with degree of involvement in the class struggle. Some of the evidence would be the constellation of talents then coming up in the *New Yorker,* when it was refining the smart-aleck flavor of its first few years into a style and approach all its own, versatile and yet consistent. In that amniotic fluid flourished White, James Thurber, Joseph Mitchell, Wolcott Gibbs, S. J. Perelman. White's "The Wall," Gibbs' story of the dead cow and the freight car float in New York Harbor have some of the finest qualities American writing showed at any time after 1900. Now most of the magazine's consistent contributors were to one or another extent radical-to-Red-inclined. Some were later identified as card carriers. But, maybe because such nimble writers valued their tools too much to let anybody use them to build barricades, they never got the hammer and sickle mixed up with the typewriter. So far as the reader could tell, they usually confined themselves to writing as well as they could about things swimming up from their private cerebellums—which leaves little to say about them except that the best of them did it invaluably well.

This full institutional bloom did not last much beyond the decade, for its rather narcissistic virtues carried within themselves the seed of degeneration, thank you, Herr Marx. There soon was a *"New Yorker* style" unmistakable, if hard to define, that, for neophytes, tended to become a straitjacket, supple and clean·but a straitjacket for all that. Gradually the feel of the contents, which had been amusingly ironic on several levels, turned peevishly wistful, dominated by what Corey Ford, a steady contributor in the early days, called "self-analytic and pastel stories [such as those of] Sally Benson, Thyra Samter Winslow, Robert Coates, John Cheever. ... " [49] If, as W. A. Swanberg said, *Time* soon came to sound as if written by a single impudent man, most of the *New Yorker*'s nondepartmental things came to sound as if written by a single (in both senses) lady cousin of Katherine Mansfield. Another hazard was neurosis flogging, stock-in-trade of the first team. White was principal carrier of that symptomatic cultivated peevishness aforesaid. "The Wall" would fit as well into a textbook in elementary psychiatry as into a course on writing English. Thurber's best-known stories concern a schizoid's multiple fantasies and the illusions of a mentally retarded scrubwoman. Neurosis imbues every fiber of what Wilfred Sheed calls Perelman's "dark and guilty imagination," a harbinger, one now sees, of J. D. Salinger and Donald Barthelme.

Sheed also dwelt more strongly, however, on the "freakish mastery of language [making Perelman] a writer who has to be read seriously ... [who] did for American humor what Joyce and Proust did for the novel ... carried it to the point where it could survive only by being something else." [50] And beyond that consideration, which is a little solemn for the subject, there for a few years when Ogden Nash, Phyllis McGinley and White were keeping rhymed wit alive, and Fadiman's book reviews were taking William Faulkner and Mabel Dodge Luhan over the jumps, and the Profiles were shooting fast ones close to celebrities who had been crowding the plate and the cartoons were teaching international journalism concision in caption and intelligence in drawing ... all that in the middle of what is conventionally and not erroneously thought of as the most dismal period in American history. John Leonard, looking back in 1975, found this irritating. For him that *New Yorker* was "a smarty-pants parish tipsheet that dreamed its way through the Thirties as though there were no Depression and no Fascism." He applauded its post-World War II change into "a journal that altered our experience instead of just posturing in front of it," [51] beginning, presumably, with John Hershey's watershed account of Hiroshima. The moral to this anomaly may be that *Zeitgeister* are unreliable because afflicted with tunnel vision.

Certain others thus showed the 1930s that one could both flourish and be true to one's writing potential without borrowing plumage from the Party-liners. A highly gratifying example was Thornton Wilder. His early reputation came from three novels of the latter 1920s that deftly skirted preciosity: *The Cabala* (1926) about a Henry James-flavored Rome; *The Bridge of San Luis Rey* (1927) about a romantic

Spanish Colonial Peru; and *The Woman of Andros* (1930) about a retired Greek hetaera of classic times of such serene cultivation that she might have been Pallas Athene no better than she should be. All were admirably written. Publication of *The Woman* in the first year of the Depression brought down on Wilder a scathing review from the Communists' Mike Gold, abusing her creator as "Prophet of the Genteel Christ" callously snubbing the American scene and its intensifying class struggle. This caused seething talk and contributed heavily to Wilder's being relegated by many to what Cowley recently called "the world of middle-brow authors not worth talking about." [52]

In 1934 his *Heaven's My Destination* showed that he could continue on his own course steady-as-she-goes while shifting to America for material. Its picaresque hero was a Midwestern textbook salesman prowling the grass roots like a Don Quixote trying to be Mahatma Gandhi. The backgrounds smelled as genuine as chile parlor or high school gym; the characters' talk was as chewily terse as Hemingway hoped to be, almost as funny-wry (without condescension) as Lardner. And doubtless to Gold's further exasperation, Wilder was still snubbing the class struggle in favor of more subjective struggles and more private vicissitudes. He occasionally lent his name among dozens of others to Party-front causes, but they all sounded as unimpeachable as the League Against Man-Eating Sharks, and his doing so meant little more than goodwill and lack of briefing—as in many other such signatures.

In 1938 he rubbed his recalcitrance in, inadvertently again, by exhibiting it on the stage with a success that seems headed for perpetual motion. They say *Our Town* is still played somewhere in the world every night of every year. Spain's intestine agony was nearing its wracking crisis, the Party-liners were shouting dogmatically and impressively that it was now or never, the choice is Fascist or Communist, pick your fancy before the ball stops rolling! So Wilder, who had been tinkering with plays for some time, invaded Broadway with two hours of ostensible nostalgia about the nation's small-town innocence, which the previous generation's taste for Spoon River, Illinois, and Winesburg, Ohio, and Gopher Prairie, Minnesota, had presumably demonstrated never to have existed. Yet the staging of this intellectual heresy was the highest power yet of a radical simplicity that made the strip-to-essentials-comrades productions of the Federal Theatre look cluttered. *Our Town* had no scenery at all and few props beyond chairs and stepladders. Much of the action was worked in by offstage noises and a narrator leaning against one side of the proscenium arch. With matching simplicity the script too stayed within the scant outlines of lives lived by people-as-persons. At a time when wisenheimer misanthropy was *de rigueur* these were nice people, as nice as they were straightforward, so nice they by no means deserved the fading after death postulated in the culminating graveyard scene. Halfway through *Our Town* a curmudgeon might still have been glibly impolite about Wilder as Gold's faddling optimist. The bleak diminuendo of that finale spoils it. "He chills the living," said John Mason Brown's review, "by removing his dead even from compassion." [53]

The austerity with which the dread of the void here takes over from genial pity significantly troubled Mrs. Roosevelt. She told readers of "My Day" that she found *Our Town* "interesting ... original ... but I did not have a pleasant evening." She girlishly liked being amused, she allowed, she dutifully liked being stirred, but this play was depressing "beyond words," and that she disliked. With arch chivalry Atkinson of the New York *Times* took her to task. She had printed her high opinion of *Pins and Needles,* the vastly amusing revue of Federal Theatre-style skits and satirical Garment Center numbers put on by the amazing amateurs of the International Ladies Garment Workers Union, but had muffed the swelling aesthetic buoyancy of what he thought "one of the finest dramas written in the last decade ... a distinguished work of art." [54] Though he carried it no farther, he may have touched the key to her uneasiness. What she missed in *Our Town* was what the settlement house mind (or what Lilienthal had called her "social service point of view" [55]) had taught her to value. Atkinson should have pointed out that one of the best songs in *Pins and Needles* was "Sing Me a Song of Social Significance."

His superlatives were not misapplied. Indeed, there was no reason not to call *Our Town* out and out finest of its decade. It had so notably an up-from-the-spinal-cord feeling for what the theater is and what to do with it. Then, in 1942, Wilder's "infallible sense of the theater," [56] as Alan Schneider of Washington's Arena Stage recently called it, enabled him to top *Our Town* with *The Skin of Our Teeth,* a seethingly impudent tribute to mankind's visceral assets. Here, too, the content flouted fashion, but this time the tone was disrespectfully astringent, not elegiac. Pearl Harbor had struck, the Nazis were trampling the soul out of Europe, the Hitler-Stalin pact had pulled the rug from under intelligible Party-lining ... and here Wilder bobbed up behind the footlights of a showshop with the effrontery of illogic, saying in effect, "You think you got troubles? Better men than you have survived worse and will again. Who's better than you? Human beings, that's who. Like you, tougher, foolisher, nastier, randier, smarter, more durable than anybody." Nor were there assuaging hints of the inspirational lecturer or the football coach between halves. All the way he was jeering—genially at times, but jeering.

Clurman, pillar of the Group Theatre sort of thing, whose cup of tea *Skin* was unlikely to be, called it "the most memorable play of the war years." [57] Here, too, upward revision of an originally handsome statement is indicated. I'd rather he had said that the stone that Mike Gold rejected had written the most brilliantly theatrical script that ever came from an American playwright; in that respect it is a monument of the same order as *Macbeth* and *Cyrano de Bergerac.* And in view of that description, it would be wrong to discuss "what it has to say" like a Victorian preacher quoting Longfellow or one of today's academic critics looking to D. H. Lawrence for "meaning." The point of *Skin* is its form—or blithely flagrant lack of it. If the Ibsen of *Peer Gynt* had worked with the Ferenc Molnar of *Liliom* and *The Play's the Thing,* the Kaufman and Ryskind of *Strike Up the Band* and the Vsevolod Meyerhold of *Roar China,* something like this might have resulted. Schneider made it "Woody Allen or Mel Brooks plus Aristotle," [56] but that misses the multilevel counterpoint. Not in terms of ideas but of purely theatrical interweavings these stage jugglings have the spontaneity of a jazz jam session. The very scenery got into the action.

Those aware that Dashiell Hammett went to a federal prison for refusing to identify as Communists persons he had worked with on Party-front committees may be surprised to find him here among eminent writers little affected by Party criteria. Yet chronologically that is sound. It was in the depths of the Depression that he emerged from the sludgy Grub Street of the pulp magazines * with several

---

* This book should probably go at some length into the rise and fall of the pulps. The rise took place largely between 1900 and 1930, however, and the fall, owing partly to hard times, partly to the competition of radio, partly to that of "comic books," was just a matter of undramatic dwindling. For the rest, many readers will recall them as providing melodramatic, often paranoid-flavored, often of special interest flavor (for those interested in railroads or World War I or flying or whatever), often cheap-sexy entertainment for a sizable public, mostly male. The best that can be said for them was that their quality averaged higher than that of the comic books, though it would stand comparison with little else. Nostalgic admirers point out that among writers cutting their teeth on pulp stories were not only Hammett but MacKinlay Kantor, Philip Wylie, T. S. Stribling, Ray Bradbury, but those were occasional tyros; the bulk of the stuff came from steady practitioners of no further promise. A recent anthology giving a somewhat too impressive cross section of the genre contains the following all-too-representative sample of the sexy variety, date 1931: "The wisp of unimportant drape added a touch of mystery, but absolutely no disguise to the lively pink contours of her pinkly pert person. She threw her arms around Ferdinand and began to writhe and tremble in his embrace. ... Anisia sat down on a low divan, crossing her legs with an all-revealing sweep. ... And almost immediately she was a throbbing,

novel-size detective stories distinguished for being just about the only examples of the genre since Edgar Allan Poe with unmistakable literary worth. His high quality cannot have owed much to formal education. After one year of high school* he went drifting at odd jobs and then worked for several years as private detective for the great Pinkerton agency in California. How many detective stories come thus from genuine, experienced detectives? Recent compilations of Hammett's pulp stories show from what shoddy beginnings he grew into his very fine narrative style, with a growing sense of certain kinds of character. For another rarity, almost always even the early flounderings of a writer destined to real talent will show streaks of sporadic verbal pay dirt. Hammett's very seldom did. Yet his stuff was enough better than the run of the trade's hacks could do to earn him an intraindustry reputation. Maybe that was what stirred him into trying novel length—a piece of good judgment, for something about the consequent elbowroom, maybe the scope it allowed for changes of pace and study of walk-on parts, released the writer that lay latent in him. Most of his later works *(The Thin Man* is an exception) read lucid, buoyant and verbally well integrated. The able hack drew breath and took off as though he had decided to start writing the way it was said Hemingway did. Or say that his new virtues had much in common with Stephen Crane's. Dorothy Parker, while doing her "Constant Reader" reviews in the *New Yorker,* saw this clearly: Hammett, she said, " ... is so hard boiled you could roll him around on the White House lawn ... a good, hell-bent, cold-hearted writer, with a clear eye for the ways of hard women and fine ear for the words of hard men, and his books are exciting and powerful ... anybody who doesn't read him misses much of modern America." [58]

His break away from *Black Mask* magazine brought no sloughing off, however, of the claptrap and the often-pathological emotions that made his work sell. The world in which his private eyes trampled through other people's sordid problems for pay remained rank with pulp-magazine wise-guy misanthropy. Nine out of ten characters were petty or overweening monsters. Even juicy women included for box-office value tended to grow into she-monsters of cruelty or greed or opportunism. The protagonist detective was usually alone in cleaving

---

panting, wanting bundle of mobile femininity in his arms. .... They writhed in a hurricane of undisciplined liberty. ... " This is from "Hot Rompers" by Russ West in *Parisienne Life.*

* It must mean something about higher education that several of America's best novelists of the 1930s never went to college: Hemingway, O'Hara, Hammett, Saroyan. A long-standing tradition, of course. Neither did Melville, Howells or Mark Twain.

to his own skewed but firm notions of right and wrong. That is nicely spelled out in his best (and first) novel, *Red Harvest,* where the Continental Op, hired by the capitalist tyrant of a Western mining town to ferret out those who killed his son, goes ahead with the job even after the client calls him off for fear his findings will be noisomely awkward. His technique is to play Apple of Discord, cynically setting all the goons in town by the ears so cleverly that they all kill each other off. Toward the end bodies are lying around like splintered timbers after a mine disaster. The client, old, sick and frustrated, is left alone.

It would be grisly comic if only it weren't evident throughout that the author stacks the cards that way because he hates everybody but himself and thee—and thee can be pretty loathsome sometimes. As complement his sadistic relish in what the Op's dupes do to one another is exceeded only by that in *The Glass Key* (1931), the hero of which, like all Hammett's heroes, is as implausibly indestructible by either violence or alcohol as he is misanthropic. Pitted bloody but unbowed against the noisome, people-infested darkness, they are the universe's sole traces of self-respecting bowels and mother wit—a high intensification of the paranoid twitchings so often pervading detective stories. Some years later Raymond Chandler played the same snarling tunes in Los Angeles County instead of Hammett's Bay Area. As a recent critic has said, Hammett "fixed the aura of paranoia in literate forms." [59] *

That self-aggrandizing, egocentric bent, inseparable from Hammett the writer, may have partaken in the process that turned Hammett the person solid Red † in the mid-1930s about the time he stopped writing for print and went to work in Hollywood. His novels had only minor traces of a potential fellow-traveling orientation. In *Red Harvest* he led with a burly, candid Wobbly agitator apparently destined to swing much weight in the town's reactionary atmosphere and then, as politics and racketeering took center stage, forgot all about him. Even in

* The terms "paranoia," "paranoid" and so on have been miserably abused of late. It is very difficult now to use them responsibly, for as things are, to say "paranoid" can mean merely that the referent person or attitude responds vigorously to strains. In this passage Michaels overplays his terminology, of course. But keep it in mind that "paranoid" means more or less "exhibiting traits of probably pathological significance that may lead into overt psychosis" and the term is still useful.

† For unsatisfactory discussion whether or not he was actually a card-carrying Communist, see Lillian Hellman's introduction to *The Big Knockover* (Vintage Books, 1966); also in *Scoundrel Time,* 45: "I am fairly sure that Hammett joined the Communist Party in 1937 or 1938."

1933–34 *The Thin Man* carried only flickers of reference to Technocracy and "Come the revolution. ... " But his inner climate was consonant with those carrying the Marxist torch out of hatred for the powerful and contempt for the weak who put up with malefactors of great wealth—the Veblenish sort of thing that envisaged a tiny elite fraction using its knowingness to make the world a decent place. That was good Lenin. James Wechsler recalls how, when Hammett was assigned by the publisher to sift the contents of *PM,* Marshall Field's harshly liberal tabloid, for material affecting the then fashionable Popular Front psychology, "he [Hammett] could never bring himself to tolerate anything that the *Daily Worker* might have labelled 'red-baiting' ... his effort to impersonate objectivity was unconvincing." [60] Thus, Hammett's bitter narcissism could readily evolve into the definite Party-lining then trying to infiltrate Hollywood.

Strong as the Reds' gravitational pull was, however, misanthropy did not always shift writers toward that end of the spectrum. John O'Hara's case is instructive. Once he got beyond short sketches reading as though he were star of a good college course in "creative writing" keen on Dorothy Parker and Ring Lardner, he took to painting his fellow-man as a suppurating wart of highly nauseating qualities. Even those in the subcountry-club stratum of his Gibbsville, Pennsylvania, with which the author was not really concerned, had to recommend them "their illegitimate babies, their incest, their marital bestiality, their cruelty to animals, their horrible treatment of their children...." [61] Now and again a few of them, like a few of the stumbly monsters in the upper stratum, too, manifested discernibly creditable traits. But no suspicion that a few righteous men might actually be found in either Sodom or Gomorrah ever suggested to O'Hara that a well-managed revolution might give righteousness a reasonable chance to flourish. This contrasts with the case of Farrell, whose Irish Chicago was, as has been noted, a festering mass of viciousness, who was yet driven eventually into hope that somehow a revolutionary Hercules could empty even that social cesspool.

Did that mean a relative difference in temperamental resistance to intellectual fashion? Actually one feels that O'Hara can hardly have wanted the cesspool cleaned out. He was too zealous a snob about Ivy League clothes and which fork to use to have welcomed that. Or say that any such hope as Farrell's, however superficial or fleeting, would have hampered O'Hara by flawing the gorgeously satisfactory hatred of things (mankind included) that he anchored his universe on. To proffer him a revolution or any other possibly ameliorating device was to suggest to Pharaoh that a genie improve the landscape by causing the new royal pyramid to vanish.

Novels so bleak and black seldom go to the public heart unless (like

The Jungle) they carry an absorbing ideological sauce, yet several of O'Hara's were great best-sellers. Offhand that looks as if for once primarily literary virtues—vigorous narrative, subtle interactions, the much admired (if often necessarily dreary) accuracy of their talk—were reaping due reward. On second glance, however, it is likelier that the reading public's enjoyment of *Appointment in Samarra* (1934) and *Butterfield 8* (1935) came of sadistic relish in the characters' vividly handled brutalities and the prodigal viciousness of their sex lives. One had always wondered just what did go on behind the half-timber front of that five-bedroom Tudor manor house on Greencrest Drive. Well, this Mr. O'Hara borrowed Asmodeus' horns and took off that many-gabled roof so we could peer inside, and my dear, you have no idea! Remember this was in the primitive 1930s, when, though the courts had let down a number of bars, they had not yet made bonfires of the whole fence.

The point was made in reverse toward the end of the decade when O'Hara took time off from upper-bracket monsters to shape for the *New Yorker* his sketches of *Pal Joey,* a light-footed blackguard of devilishly scrawny charm as corrosive and real as that of, say, Jimmy Walker, New York City's Jazz Age mayor. His love life was that of a tomcat with the ethical standards of a cardsharp, though, maybe because of the *New Yorker*'s notions of printability, few details were given. And though it caused comment in its magazine installments, *Pal Joey* was no great item with the bookbuying public that had so cottoned to *Samarra* and pseudo-Starr Faithful's adventures on Park Avenue. It helped not at all that for the first time O'Hara's fine ear for human manipulation of talk in the self-revealing first person, sensitive nose for human depravity and zealous misanthropy had finally fused into genuine creation. Joey did not go to town until Richard Rodgers and Lorenz Hart, reigning princes of musical stage wit, used it for that very rare thing, an adaptation making something deftly new out of a tempting original without either spoiling its tone or flawing its materials. As it turned out, however, this was only temporary cause for rejoicing. *Pal Joey* was the last as well as the nippiest among Rodgers & Hart's collaborations, and O'Hara, after thus showing what his talent could do when given its head, that he could write like a drill team of exasperated yellowjackets, reverted to his previous fascination with the glumly sordid and unresilient.

WHAT THEY SAID ABOUT DIXIE

CATO DID NOT RIDE THROUGH CARTHAGE ON THE TRAIN
AND BLAME ITS CONDITION ON THE CARTHAGINIANS.
—JONATHAN DANIELS,
A Southerner Discovers the South

Such innocence of radical intent did not, however, necessarily mean lack of social effect, even of aid and comfort to radical doings. This applies particularly to the South and its rise into rivaling California II as the radicals' favorite whipping-boy region. Thus, while Caldwell played a large part in it, very probably deliberately, William Faulkner bulked equally large in the matter, though his immunity to siren songs of social significance was about as high as O'Hara's.

He exemplifies the vagaries of this discussion because his recalcitrance cannot be offhandedly set down to naïveté or the elementary misanthropy that so stubbornly shielded O'Hara. Yet neither can gumption have played much part. Maybe Faulkner followed his own bent across, not with, the current of his time so doggedly because he shared with Wilder an unusual stiffness of backbone. As his literary impulse gained momentum in response to adverse comment, a consequent hypertrophy of his writing oddnesses was probably bad for his work. But it did develop into what at least looked like a heartening case of a tub standing on its own by-God bottom. Fadiman, who stuck to it for years that either he was diametrically wrong or Faulkner was overrated, nevertheless found this quality remarkable as early as 1930: " ... the author of *As I Lay Dying* ... [is] untouched by the platitudes of the day. His cosmos is awry, but it is his own, self-created. Genuine idiosyncrasy is rare among our younger novelists." [1]

Though Faulkner had to wait long for syllabus and lecture to canonize and embalm him, the timing of his case shows how risky it is to generalize about a literary—or any other kind of—epoch. In one way he might be, as the calendar implies, a holdover from the Lost Generation sticking to an anachronistic last regardless. Not exactly one of its classic members, however. In World War I he did get into the Royal Canadian Flying Corps in spite of his diminutive size—in middle age he looked like a handsome French general seen through the wrong end of a telescope—but he never got overseas. He had a season of neo-Bohemianism and tinkered with poetry in the 1920s but not in Montparnasse, not even in Greenwich Village, only in New Orleans, No. Five road company. (Nos. Two, Three and Four were Chicago, Carmel, Taos.) Like many another Lost Generationer, he was badly scarred by drink, but John Barleycorn's ravages were by no means confined to practitioners of the arts in that or any other time. As for other symptoms of what the clichés teach us to expect of writers born in the last decade of the 1800s, there are fewer demurrers. Like Fitzgerald and Hemingway, he was innocently anti-Semitic. He was warped by admiring emulation of *Ulysses*. And being a Southerner, he was sentenced always to thrash about in the interrelated kinds of trauma consequent on black slavery and the Civil War.

Every few years since Henry Grady coined the phrase, another Southerner thus afflicted comes up with a prescription for a "New South" healed of the economic shortfalls and cultural lags of the Old. Faulkner's differed from journalists' or politicians' blueprints in being no sanguine remodeling, rather a suicidal transmutation of New and Old gnawing each other's vitals like angry weasels playing yang and yin. This had romantic support, however, from the Southern Agrarian group centered in Nashville, Tennessee: Allen Tate, John Crowe Ransom, Robert Penn Warren *et al.* As the 1930s began, they were advising Dixie (in prose better than the advice) to look away from the North's crass industrialism, which had got the nation into such a mess, and re-create the self-respecting old days.* Slow shrewd talk on the gallery after supper, dogs asleep under it, sprightly womenfolk, plain vittles but plenty of them, gentleman's-word-his-bond, mutual respect between responsible Big House and a reliable local yeomanry; the blacks ... there things tended to blur, and the Jeeter Lesters were seldom mentioned. But there was comfort in it, even though its

---

* It is notable that the symposium kickoff of the Southern Agrarians was entitled *I'll Take My Stand*—a tag from "Dixie," which was written by a show-business Irishman for a minstrel show produced by Northerners and performed by largely Northern white men synthetically blacked up to look like Dixie's blacks.

proponents were intelligent enough to know that no such Dixie had ever been dominant. Faulkner's formative years probably also felt influences blowing from less erudite quarters. In the same years when Faulkner was maturing his method, Margaret Mitchell, the determined amateur, was tossing off page after page of *Gone with the Wind,* spicing up the usual magnolias, juleps and scalawags with Scarlett O'Hara's opportunistic feminism. A little later weighed in *So Red the Rose,* a best-seller celebrating the ineffable graciousness of befo'-de-wah Natchez written not by some nostalgic gray-haired gentlewoman polishing grandfather's dueling pistols but by Stark Young, a figure respected in Manhattan's radical circles as dramatic critic of the *New Republic.*

Of these innovating variations on the foolish elder formulas Faulkner's version was certainly most drastic. He cast his downgoing patrician Sartoris family as the dwindling element of Light in a pessimistic Manichaean world. The Dark was the upcoming red-neck Snopes clan, prehensile as Yankees and slimy as only the South's genetically tainted trash could be. These motifs, too, had precedents. In their novels of Reconstruction published when Faulkner was still in short pants, Thomas Nelson Page and the Reverend Dr. Thomas Dixon, Jr., had made great play with villainous scalawags. Faulkner's contribution was to make these stock situations glow in the hellfires of his own demon-ridden temperament. The people of Königsberg, legend says, had trouble associating the universe-shattering teachings of Immanuel Kant with the spidery, frail little man who took his daily constitutional on their city walls. Faulkner's tiny, charmingly diffident person fitted just as oddly with the three-ring witches' Sabbath that he stewed up from the staid delusions of the magnolimaniacs and the Agrarians. Kant's thinking was better, true. Otherwise the likeness extends even to the obscurity of style that each imposed on himself.

Faulkner's was a new South indeed. His data doubtless welled up from half-hushed, highly flavored, oblique gossip heard on the twilit gallery or pieced together in pauses between elliptical anecdotes swapped among sharecroppers squatted in the dust on the shady side of the crossroads store. Caldwell probably used such sources, too. But whereas he diagrammed and reduced such materials to the scale of privy-wall art captioned "Workers of the world, unite!" Faulkner projected them larger than life on a gigantic screen. Not all erotic: He also relished imbeciles' dribblings, torture of animals by sadistic toddlers, the exact details of when and what drunkards throw up and how it feels to do so, and the raw-head-and-bloody-bones results of men fighting naked battles royal. He made little use of excretion or homosexuality. Set that last down to residual fastidiousness, not to

Bible-ridden Yoknapatawpha County's never having heard of the patriarch Lot's neighbors. But without that wide range of erotics Faulkner might never have gained the eminence that led to a Nobel Prize. His splashiness with rape and incest made Caldwell's seem mere paltering. "Mr. Faulkner has pushed his horrors so far in ... *Sanctuary* and *As I Lay Dying*," wrote Donald Davidson rather reluctantly, "that ... one feels inclined to accuse him of being either a literary sadist or a harlequin." [2] Good parody is useful here in showing just what one is talking about; let me exhibit Corey Ford's "Popeye the Pooh:" "Popeye walked at the rear with both guns levelled, his face pale and indistinct like the underside of an old dead haddock. Before them a child's foot protruded out of the quicksand. It twitched feebly once or twice, and then the mud swallowed it and belched politely. ... " [3]

Yet Faulkner probably was not, as Caldwell may have been, willing to exploit guffaws and lip lickings. Had he been so, he would, like Caldwell, probably have written with bald clarity, a quality seldom found in what is now considered his most important work. He took early advantage of the then-newish doctrine that novelist as well as poet not only may but should ask the reader to do most of the work. His intent may have been so intimately to immerse the reader in hormone-heavy stimuli, with his antennae kept at concert pitch during sentences running unbroken for a page and a half, that he would fully feel the fictional doings—rape, say, or drowning or drunkenness—under consideration. It was an arduous task, however, nor was it lightened when the crowding, breathless data filtered through what passed for the consciousness of an idiot or had to be read in the crosslights from several preceding passages, just as torrential, treating the same incoherent events through several voices. Under such strains the attention often burned out like the mistreated clutch of an automobile, and the style drifted into facile rhapsody tending toward lame iambic pentameter—a sure sign of weakness in English prose and a reminder that before the grand design of Yoknapatawpha County possessed him, Faulkner had hoped to be a poet.

Between content and manner the effect was much too often hysterical or ridiculous. A blend of Edvard Munch with George Grosz was demanding enough without asking one to glimpse the results by flashes of lightning while standing under a Niagara Falls of logorrhea. Yet what came through was often so startling and the writer was obviously so desperately in earnest that though he still lacked a wide sympathetic public, reviewers kept an eye on him. In time—maybe predictably—he was taken up in Britain and France, where, in addition to their literary originalities, these compost heaps of ordinary and fratricidal murder, lynching, assorted psychoses, mental retardations, arson, land piracy, mayhem, incest and moonshining were interesting supplements to the works of Caldwell, Sinclair Lewis and Upton Sinclair as accounts of life in America. As has happened so often, this European *réclame* encouraged American critics to take Faulkner seriously and then more seriously. By the mid-1940s, when, for good or ill, his major work was done, persistence had paid off. A consensus crowned him with a wreath of Miss Emily's roses and candidates for PhDs began to comb *The Bear* for cryptosymbols.

Thomas Wolfe, whose literary advent more or less coincided with Faulkner's—both *Look Homeward, Angel* and *Sartoris,* first of the Yoknapatawpha saga, were published in 1929—managed almost as completely to snub the class struggle. About all he did about it was to be rude about the Sacco-Vanzetti cult. In his case the reason probably was that his writing cosmos was highly autobiographical, and in Asheville, North Carolina, where he was reared without ever growing up, Karl Marx was little known. Wolfe's was no cotton-perverted South utilized as pervasive chief character in fiction in the manner of Caldwell and Faulkner too. This was the hill country with fewer blacks, social strata among whites less distinct, yeasty religions and feckless economic tossings and turnings. He viewed it and its people with high disfavor, true. But Asheville had no cause to take that to heart. His opinion of New York City or Cambridge, Massachusetts, was no higher. As his novels grew defiantly interminable and his shadow to seem (to him) coterminous with the whole United States—physically at least he was very large—it grew clear that no mere regional label sufficed, whereas Caldwell and Faulkner, like Page and Dixon before them, persisted in cultivating the juicy garden that sprouted them.

So, though Wolfe may be called a Southern novelist, he had only a minor share in the side effects of the literature of Dixie in the 1930s. One was mainly literary: By the end of World War II Caldwell and Faulkner had done more than all the lawyers and complaisant courts to erode reticence about violence and erotics in American writing. The other was folklore-cultural: They two had begotten a whole school of Southern writers depicting the region in terms that made it the always available locus of the growing national habit of cultural Pharisaism.

For reasons, if any, too subtle for pursuing here, the writers who took up and best sustained this note in the next generation were women. Not that Southern women had not already outshone Southern men in fiction. Ellen Glasgow and Katherine Anne Porter could write rings around any trousered novelist ever born below Mason's & Dixon's line—the one possible exception consisted of James Agee's *A*

Death in the Family, which was not published as a whole until the 1950s. But this is a matter of parietal inflammation. By the end of the 1930s Lillian Hellman's *The Little Foxes* had indelibly fixed a new group portrait of those living behind tall white pillars as foaled out of harpies by vampires, and Carson McCullers' *The Heart Is a Lonely Hunter* had peopled a standard small town with enough maimed monsters to suggest that she had summoned up Hieronymus Bosch lest she be called a Southern Sherwood Anderson. The suspicion is unjust no doubt. Randall Jarrell said of T. S. Eliot that he'd have written *The Wasteland* about the Garden of Eden, and the corrosive emanations from Miss McCullers' tortured psyche would probably have made her turn the Abbey of Thélème into a snake pit. Use certain filters and lenses and Watertown, New York, and Sheridan, Wyoming, will obligingly resemble Spoon River, Illinois. Miss McCullers' substantial references to Fascism and the presence of a radical labor agitator are banally appropriate in a book written in 1938. But the writer's appetite for grotesques is so much stronger than her modish groping toward radicalism that even her agitator is 60 percent monster.

Fairness also calls for saying that the consequent misanthropy is as gamy as Faulkner's, if more comprehensible. The extraliterary trouble with this sort of thing is, however, that readers are innocently likely to take the specific for the general, to rely on the described background and the antics of the cast as sound sociological observation. Indeed such things as *The Little Foxes* may feel as if done in hopes they will be mistaken for general validity. Be that as it may, Dixie has suffered from such naïveté. "Put a slut in a book about the South," Jonathan Daniels wrote *c.* 1937, " ... and ... non-Southerners will accept it as a panoramic photograph of Dixie.... It is not so much that literature confuses, as that the easily confused are able to read." [4] Nor is that risk limited to the dimwitted. Many among well-informed and self-consciously discerning Americans drew large elements of their notions of the South from *God's Little Acre* and *The Sound and the Fury,* just as their parents had drawn other kinds of mind-clogging from *Red Rock* and *The Clansman.*

The change was no overnight affair. In 1931 the Group Theatre insisted that Paul Green end *The House of Connelly,* about a slatternly old plantation and its blithering owners, not with the murder of the plucky poor white heroine by the black she-trolls who have played Chorus throughout, but by letting the girl live for a chins-up, new-day curtain. Five years later no such even faint hopes for Dixie would have been likely to occur to such a group. For as the 1930s evolved, people were happy to take the Faulkner-Caldwell South at face value. A Depression-harried nation needed a regional scapegoat-laughingstock, a general horrible example to match the individual scapegoats skipping to the high hills ... Hoover, Mellon, Insull. ...

Justice again, harsh this time: In many aspects and to considerable extents what they said about Dixie was sooth. She actually was the stronghold of Fundamentalist religion based on cheap mass ecstasy, bigotry, starvation of the mind and a theology of obscurantist faith. The notorious Scopes trial had been a local Chamber of Commerce promotion stunt that disappointed its backers; but that was not widely known, and the ignorance that led so many Southern legislators to vote for such "monkey laws" was all too real. Lynching, a frontier institution once rather widely spread, had almost disappeared—except in the South, where it helped W. J. Cash, subtlest critic of the region, with his thesis that in spite of skyscrapers and radios in many cabins, Dixie was still living on or near the frontier, or, as H. C. Brearley said, it was "that part of the United States lying below the Smith & Wesson line." 5 Worse, whereas the lynching of Colonel Sherburne's time was more or less color-blind, shooting or hanging both blacks and whites as situations seemed to require, after its retreat into the South it applied largely to blacks as a growingly sadistic way of "keeping them in their place"—meaning primarily, though not exclusively, away from white women, which lent erotic overtones to the torture that often went with lynch law. The Northern intellectual's notion that just to stir up excitement in the courthouse square on a warm Saturday evening, one bored red-neck said to another, "Let's go lynch a nigger," was exaggerated. But there is evidence enough that the visceral twitchings that went with lynching were important. Grisly souvenirs were taken— ears, genitalia, fingers—and memories were cherished.

Add that the Ku Klux Klan of the 1920s had first oozed to the surface in Georgia, then done well all over the Old Confederacy and scored its greatest gains outside Dixie in the Border States of 1861 and such Southern-flavored states as Indiana and Kansas. Nor could the big-city minds that steered national public opinion forget that since 1900 the South had led the battle for Prohibition and then fought hardest to maintain it and that even after Repeal not only did Mississippi, probably the most deeply Southern state, persist in its own bone-dry laws but other Southern states kept up statewide or local clogs on the Demon Rum—no-drinks-sold-in-public, local option in Magnolia County or state liquor stores so far apart and hard to find that the motoring Yankee could die of thirst before finding supplies. Being aware of the facts of moonshining, he resented the likelihood that the wooded hills along the highway were probably awash with strange-tasting but potable booze in Mason jars—if one only knew the ropes!

So many of the region's little ways seemed to bring out the Pharisee in such Yankees. Yet it was notorious that, grim and inhumane though penal institutions were elsewhere, Dixie alone kept up chain gangs. And in 1931, as luck would have it, her nose was elaborately rubbed in that noisome archaism by a best-selling book, Robert Elliott Burns' *I Am a Fugitive from a Georgia Chain Gang,* about a white convict's experience with the system's sweatboxes, cowhides, manacles, brutal working and living conditions. Movingly lurid, probably little exaggerated, it made one wonder what, if things were that bad for white losers, could chain gangs for black Georgians be like? Soon a blistering movie version told the same tale to the vast movie audience and established the permanent Hollywood stereotype of the Southern policeman-trooper-deputy-prison guard in a cowhand-model Stetson, sleepily vicious and all hard tallow in face and backside. The type existed.

Yankees might reflect further that however corrupt politics were in Philadelphia or Sioux City, at least there were two political parties to ride herd on each other and lend more or less meaning to elections as well as primaries and that no discriminatory laws or taxes kept certain proscribed social classes from voting at all.* This picture of Dixie as a social swamp overhung by grotesqueries grew even darker when, in the same winter that *Fugitive* was so popular, Huey Pierce Long broke into the national scene as junior Senator from Louisiana.

Mostly he was the brightest and toughest of Faulkner's Snopeses, outdoing the others in predatory getting-up-in-the-world. His folks were prosperous relative to the upcountry region he was born in, about as cotton-poor and hookwormy as the Snopeses' country the other side of the Mississippi, but it was only a two-generation, we're-as-good-as-them prosperity, nothing emotionally secure about it. The neighborhood's one distinctive trait was a small streak of radicalism. Populists had won local elections; Huey's father was one of them. The local cotton buyer who worked on the boy's ambitions actually called himself a Socialist. The account of the old fellow's attitudes in T. Harry Williams' indispensable biography of Long tells much about the cracker-barrel radical of eighty years ago: "He was vociferously against war, the Bible, Wall Street, bankers, corsets and high heels ... intoxicating liquors, strict discipline in prisons, the microbe theory, algebra ... he was convinced that most of the big international

---

* Even in 1940 Cash (*Mind of the South,* 250) still noted that poll taxes, the best device for keeping blacks and poor whites from voting, were being retained as pretty effective in many Southern jurisdictions.

bankers were Jews ... working together to further the power of world Jewry. ... " [6]

Hence maybe the boy's persistent wrath over the plight of the South's neglected common man. It seems to have fused, as often happens, with his insatiable ambition into a career beginning with improving things for others and ending in loudmouthed megalomania edged with reptilian cunning. The one thing probably genuine about Long, making it a mistake to see him as merely the highest power of the Theodore G. Bilbo or J. Thomas Heflin type, was that he really yearned to get upcountry Louisiana out of the mud. Hence he did more than any of his more decorous, if usually almost as corrupt, predecessors at Baton Rouge to put roads, bridges, schoolbooks, hospital care and so forth within its reach, and took the poll tax off its back to boot. Doubtless Mussolini too, veteran Socialist, had such benevolent impulses and, when he drained the Pontine marshes, took lively satisfaction in freeing their miserable inhabitants from the age-old curse of malaria.

In 1931, however, the nation knew little of these gains and much more about their social cost. The press was paying growing attention to Long's virtual dictatorship partly because it was alarming in its own right, partly because he was successfully raising hell with not only his political peers but also the powerful national oil companies with vast properties in Louisiana. For a while it was all going on in a single state that had always been outside the main drift even of the South, let alone America. Its strong dash of Central America and candid lack even of a wish to pay lip service to the copybook virtues gave it unique flavor. But now here was this loudly dressed, blabbermouthed, impudent medicine-show spieler dealing himself as wildest of wild cards into the US Senate in the already disastrous worst year of the Depression.

He called himself the Kingfish after that character in the *Amos & Andy* radio show. The buffoonery that he had learned as itinerant salesman of groceries and nostrums in his youth now got him headlines. Filibustering in the Senate, for instance, he filled the time not by reading from dull books but by such amusing devices as disquisitions on mixing his favorite drink, the Ramos gin fizz. The headlines went sour in the summer of 1933, when, a guest at a show-business benefit party on Long Island, he drank too much—he was a dirty drinker—and did something in the washroom that got him a bloody cut on his forehead.* But early the next year, long since

---

* Available details are in Williams, *Huey Long,* 680-84. Whatever actually happened, it is clear that Long looked bad as he tried to lie himself out of some kind of disreputable behavior.

broken off with FDR and the New Deal, he appealed openly to the nation's Neglected Man over the administration's head with his Share-Our-Wealth movement, promising free education for all the educable, "adequate" pensions for the elderly and so on and on—in developing alliance, as previously noted, with Father Coughlin. He was ominously effective over the radio, in the same league as Coughlin and FDR, both back home in Louisiana and nationally as the first US Senator regularly to use the air to lay his ideas before his countrymen. As Share-Our-Wealth warmed up, he hired a ghost and authored what may still stand as the most impudent document in American political history, *My First Year in the White House.* It named the prominent Americans to whom President Long would give posts in the Cabinet, which they accepted, and sketched the conversations in which he gave them their orders for the campaign to make Every Man a King. Thus Senator James Couzens of Michigan, once Henry Ford's chief henchman, now a valuably independent-minded legislator, was to be Secretary of the Treasury and meekly reform the nation's banks along lines laid down by Father Coughlin. It promised to solve the Dust Bowl problem by setting the US Corps of Engineers to creating huge reservoirs in the Rockies "up near the headwaters of each [Great Plains] river . . . the dust storm areas of the west . . . couldn't very well get rain when even the mountains were dry . . . these . . . reservoirs will supply a source of rain, in addition to permitting the construction of thousands of irrigation projects." [7] The problem of how water in a reservoir was to be got into the atmosphere to become rain was blithely disregarded. So was that of where to recruit the faculty to teach all the courses that the nation's universities would have to set up when, as the book went out of its way firmly to promise, "every youth [will be] in the colleges of professional or vocational education and training, regardless of the ability of parents to pay . . . " [8]—and *without delay,* within that first year.

The book had to be published posthumously, thank heaven. It has been noted that Upton Sinclair borrowed the idea for his EPIC campaign with almost equally grotesque content. More to our purpose here is the way Long as Southerner, his intensely Southern kind of speech on the radio persistently rubbing it in, contributed to the ill repute of the South and Southerners as such. For it was unhappily true that this consummate vulgarian, this self-aggrandizing charlatan, this half-cynical, half-megalomanic, yet sentimental swindler, dangerous as a cancer quack and capable of shouting Fire! in a crowded theater if it would get his picture rescuing somebody into the papers, was the South's most conspicuous contribution to history since Woodrow Wilson.

The Pharisaical Yankee could also feel invidiously better because his community paid at least some lip service to racial equality, and occasionally it might even mean something, whereas once the US Supreme Court gave Jim Crow the keys of the kingdom with that separate-but-equal ruling, he had gradually installed those white/black schools, waiting rooms, railroad cars, drinking fountains and so and on, measures more discriminatory than the slaveholding South had found necessary for its considerable population of free blacks. It was troublingly evident that even when Dixie tried to slough off archaisms, the effect could be almost as dismal as the Southern Agrarians said. Most versions of the "New South" recommended imitating the Yankees' industrialism to keep the cream of the South's resources at home to benefit those who owned them. That usually meant that a Northern textile company was persuaded by labor trouble and rising costs at home and the blandishments of Southern governments to take up offers of free factory sites and tax exemptions and move southward into efficient new mills manned by poor whites hungry for cash wages, eager to work for much less than New England's veteran millhands. Dixie's promoters shouted, "Unlimited Natural Resources ... Cheap Anglo-Saxon Labor." [9] As added attraction, these hillbillies, like many of their Okie-Arky cousins gone to California, were too ignorant and too independent-minded readily to listen to labor organizers.

Hence a strikingly multiplex example of what New York City's garment unions called the runaway shop. Maybe fifty years from now it will be seen to have been constructive. What it meant in the short run was blisteringly well described in the early Depression by Benton, whose Missouri rearing and taste for footloose prowling enabled him to pick up the feeling of a county seat in the hilly end of Alabama better than any Yankee sociologist, however pliant, well meaning and professionally competent. It was a several-level intelligence that saw the South's upcountry thus:

... the great textile mills, built under promise of cheap, non-unionized labor ... have lured the people of the hills into wage slavery ... and encouraged, along with some better things, a disreputable urbanity. The lure of cash money ... has come to the shiftless as well as to those who could fall in with the rigid patterns of industry and work for wages. The textile towns, like the coal towns, have their shack patches of cunning, misery and embittered revolt. Miserable hillbillies descending on the great mills find themselves temperamentally unfitted for the long monotonous hours of work or for subjection to foremen. ... They do not, however, return to their corn patches ... but hang about, digging their subsistence out of the fields of vice which abound in newly congregated populations ... to the lower reaches of the mill town ...

the workless hillbilly drifts with his women and his ignorant emulations
... a tough social problem, not only for the sheriffs and bosses, but for
intelligent millworkers who would develop some sort of social solidarity
among the "havenots." ...

To this incisive sketch of the effects of deliberate dislocation the
artist, who had seen much of such big cities as Chicago, New York
City and Paris, added shock:

The industrial South is a great land for riotous whoredom. The loudmouthed, Bible-quoting morality of its public citizens is a thin layer ...
over a lot of sexual filth. Nowhere in the country have I had so many
obscenely gestured invitations as in the South. Nowhere is fornication so
completely in accord with the evil implications of the word. Even with
the respectable young ... sex is a snickering indulgence ... a domain of
stink and foul association ... in the lower reaches of society [it is]
frequently monstrous. I am not a touchy person but the sexual ribaldries
of the South are too much for me. They are not Rabelaisian but dirty.

He was severe on the landowners whose sharecroppers got little for
their toil but "a bitter subsistence and a dose of pellegra." [10] Curious
that he failed to add hookworm. In his time the part played by that
enteric parasite in keeping the poor white sallow, lazy and feckless had
been known for some while, yet the simple preventive measures—
always wear shoes, defecate only in a privy or equivalent—were still
widely neglected. (To some extent the neglect was self-sustaining; in
the sharecropper's terms shoes were wildly expensive, so he left them
off in warmer weather, when the risk of infection through the soles of
bare feet was higher, and the debility caused by hookworm discouraged the effort needed to dig latrines.) Of these two ailments with
social consequences pellagra, however, was worse. Not only did its
diarrheic symptoms lead to general malnourishment, but severe cases
often developed a special psychosis conspicuous among admissions to
Southern asylums. Maybe it had as large a hand as malaria and
hookworm in dooming poor whites, sharecroppers and millhands alike,
to be what Will Alexander Percy, a cultivated observer from the
landowning stratum, still called c. 1940, "the most unprepossessing
[breed] on the face of the ill-populated earth." [11]
    The institutional psychiatrists getting nowhere against these psycho-
ses should have known about Thomas Dabney, the antebellum
Mississippi planter who, when his slaves had "black tongue"—one of
the symptoms of pellagra—fed them red meat for a few days and

usually obtained recovery. But its etiology remained unknown until, some sixty years ago, Dr. Joseph Goldberger, a US Public Health Service epidemiologist, working from such hints as that it plagued millworkers eating only cornmeal and fatback from the company store, showed that it was a deficiency disease caused by lack of niacin (part of the B complex of vitamins), present in red meat, eggs, some vegetables, but woefully low in both corn and fat pork. Presumably the pre-white Indians so heavily dependent on corn got enough niacin from game and beans to prevent pellagra,* whereas the millhand or sharecropper was out of the habit of planting a garden, had small opportunity to go hunting and was culturally committed to Dixie's "hog and hominy." In demonstration pellagra tended to fall off as the Depression sent jobless millhands back to the land, forced to plant gardens again or starve. Gradual use of Goldberger's discovery through "enrichment" of cereals, notably the cornmeal the South is so fond of, with added niacin, has practically eliminated pellagra in America. This dietetic cure of what psychotherapy had failed on for decades was one of the first fertile hints that biochemistry could be a crucial tool in psychiatry. In 1929, however, when Benton was exploring, pellagra was at its peak—and another reason for Northerners to regard the South as all social decay and degeneracy, much as Faulkner, Caldwell & Co. depicted it.

Thirty years ago, Ellen Glasgow, an authentic Southerner, august and astringent, wondered whether all those nasty things would have happened to Temple Drake had not Cindy Lou of Magnolia Hall previously been so ethereally, unapproachably *intacta:*

> I have refused to be carried away by the present grotesque revival in Southern fiction . . . a remote logical result of our earlier . . . sentimental fallacy. The sense of horror is . . . a . . . legitimate literary *motif.* . . . One may admit that the Southern States may have more than an equal share of degeneracy and deterioration, but the multitude of half-wits, and whole idiots, and nymphomaniacs, and paranoiacs, and rakehells in general that populate the modern literary South should flourish nowhere but in the weird pages of melodrama. There is no harm in the fashion . . . until it poses as realism.[12]

* Cash (*Mind of the South,* 206) made the error, excusable thirty years ago, of calling pellegra "nearly peculiar to the South." Later research has shown that it tends to crop up wherever the local diet becomes overdependent on corn—in northern Italy, in southern France, in Egypt. See review of Daphne A. Roe, *A Plague of Corn,* in *Scientific American,* March, 1975.

But that is just what unwary readers and those in need of something to despise had been egging it on to do—as if one took the antics of the House of Atreus to represent normal home life in Mycenaean Greece.

A likely side effect of the myth was a bleeding away of the South's store of intelligent people northward or westward. Britain's recent term for such a trend is "brain drain." It was not Faulkners or Caldwells who set it going. Southern stuffiness about ideas had begun before their times, as those with leanings toward, say, Darwinism or racial equality "found it convenient to ... seek posts in the North where their heterodoxies might be less conspicuous. One cannot deny," wrote Willard Thorpe, a learned and sympathetic student of Dixie, "that for this reason, among others, the South has been steadily drained of intellectual leadership." [13] Other causes for this could have been mere uneasiness of marked talent and broad-shouldered minds needing breathing room—and often, of course, attracted by more dollars. After 1900 the same sort of northward trend, presumably with even stronger motives, did the same cultural damage to Dixie's black population. (The few white Northerners reversing the process tended to be subalterns of banks or large industries sent South to handle the firm's interests in New Orleans or Atlanta, and keep their mouths shut, or the less likely preferring an instructorship at Magnolia State to unemployment.)

Such movements occur elsewhere. Shaws and Bonapartes have often left neglected Irelands and desiccated Corsicas to reap status and money in the suzerain nation. Nor was the South the only American region to lose promising children because their elder brothers were bad-mouthing the land that bore them. All regions of America feel the gravitational pull of the Big Town. The ambitious youngster in one or another Decaturville, c. 1922, though half aware that *Main Street* chose out and heightened only the most deplorable aspects of the town, might nevertheless decide after reading it that he would never have the scope he deserved in such a place. But the connotations with which Miss Glasgow's "grotesque revival" burdened the South were far more dispiriting than those hung on Gopher Prairie. It may affect fairly robust spirits to learn that most of their literate countrymen think of them as waist-deep in quicksand somewhere between Sodom and Gomorrah.

It should follow that the South's brain drain was more severe than California's, the Old Northwest's or New England's. Informal observation of journalism hints as much. Men like Julian Harris (editor of the Columbus [Georgia] *Enquirer-Sun,* son of the author of *Uncle Remus*); Virginius Dabney of the Richmond *Times-Despatch;* Ralph McGill of the Atlanta *Constitution;* Hodding Carter of the Greenville (Mississippi) *Delta Democrat-Times* were among fine newspapermen sticking it out where they came from and giving Dixie something of the responsible press that she so needed. But for every one such the North probably acquired a dozen highly promising specimens gone North for fresh air. To widen the findings, I recently ran a rough amateur check of a dozen pages in *Who's Who in America.* Among the first 113 cases (Southern origin, came North; or non-Southern origin, went South), 70 Southerners had made their careers outside the South, while only 43 Northerners or Westerners had made the change of scene in reverse. The high proportion of academics among those whom *Who's Who* includes may make this a particularly significant brain drain. And consider that this was as of the early 1970s; doubtless the thing was even more disproportionate forty years ago before Northern industry cut so wide a swath below the Ohio River.

One must assume that this diaspora imposed on the bright Southern PhD and the highly promising Southern junior executive choosing to migrate a degree of cultural strain beyond that usually resulting from region shifting. For manners still differ from one side of Mason's & Dixon's line to the other. (Ignore the Northerner-distorted enclaves of the Florida peninsula and the area around the District of Columbia.) Indeed, at first many a Southerner destined to make it big in New York City or Boston must feel that these Yankees have no manners at all, nor, according to his standards, does Chicago or San Francisco behave much better. Conversely, the Northerner in Dixie still often marvels at the courtesy he gets from drugstore cashier, diner waitress, motel manager as well as the banker, editor, managing director or dean of faculty to whom he is personally recommended. He may rightly suspect that what seems to him generalized friendliness is mere custom. It nevertheless is a delightful contrast to be greeted by a convincing "Good mawnin'!" and sent on one's way with "Come back and see us!" or "Yawl hurry back." *

It may even occur to him that this geniality-as-folkway could mean there is more to the Southern Character—whatever that may be—than fashionable stereotypes allow for, else it would not have persisted in Magnolia County while tending to disappear in equivalent contexts in the Old Northwest and Upper New England. Could it have come of mere relative isolation from the notorious exasperations of modern life? Or of relative lack of frictions among half a dozen contrasting ethnic elements? The other side of the coin, the Southerner's bewilder-

---

* Within the last five or six years a welcome pandemic of using "Have a nice day!" as farewell has somewhat softened this in the Northeastern Quadrant.

ment at the way he is treated up North, appears in two passages in Percy's semiautobiographical *Lanterns on the Levee* (1941). Seventy years ago he came home from his first year at Harvard Law School, and the most patrician * elderly lady in the college town of Sewanee, Tennessee, asked him, "Will, up North there, did you meet anybody who was a ... gentleman?" and when he said yes, she demurred: "I'm certain you'll find you are mistaken." [14] He also tells of his New Orleans classmate in Cambridge who, when a Boston Brahmin student deliberately chose, as the breed often did, not to show common civility, knocked him kicking right there on the duckboards. John A. Rice, Carolina farmboy of the same generation, later chief founder of liberal-radical Black Mountain College, similarly resented the same blank insolence and took the same countermeasure. That version of Southern violence has arguable points.

Anyway, the new writers had the South's reputation and the Depression touching bottom at about the same time. So when the New Deal began its physiotherapy, Dixie, notoriously the most ailing area, got a generous share of attention. Hence, as Virgil might have written, hence the Tennessee Valley Authority and the lofty Norris Dam, making the South the region where the New Deal looked its best.

What would soon be TVA country—specifically where the Tennessee Valley cuts across the southeastern corner of Tennessee and then the northern end of Alabama—had already done much to make the South look bad by staging the Scopes "monkey trial." Now it did it again in other but quite damaging terms with another world-notorious attention getter—the case of the Scottsboro (Alabama) Boys. Nowadays they would be called the Scottsboro Nine.

The area had a high proportion of poor whites, a low one of blacks, for it was never big plantation country. In the Southern nature of things that meant particularly virulent antiblack feeling as the poor whites wrought to keep themselves reminded there was somebody they could feel superior to and hate because they might get uppity. Gradual local industrialization on an irregular front in the region had set up special economic and emotional strains. In 1931 the epidemic strains of hard times were also present but not necessary to what happened. Depression got into the act only in the particular circumstances of the bedraggled cast of characters.

* Percy apparently was unaware of or maybe chose not to pick up the ironic fact that the lady, though "born and bred in one of the great houses of Natchez," was daughter of General John A. Quitman—filibuster, soldier, Southern hero, right enough, but for all that born and reared in upstate New York and then coming South as a sort of protocarpetbagger.

Depression-style, a freight train on the Southern Railway westbound from Chattanooga, Tennessee, to Memphis, Tennessee, had on board a dozen or so young white vagrants. Two were young women in men's overalls and women's winter coats. They were occasional millhands whom the editor of the Montgomery (Alabama) *Advertiser* called "hookwormy Magdalenes" [15] when, toward the end of the story, it was clear what havoc to Southern self-esteem their testimony had wrought. At a way stop a comparable group of young black vagrants boarded. Interracial fighting began. The blacks forced most of the whites off the train except two boys and the two girls. Word of this violence was wired ahead to another way stop, where local authorities took the blacks off the train. The girls, Victoria Price and Ruby Bates, presumably seeking a diversion from the possibility of their being jailed as the vagrants they were, proclaimed that between the fights and the arrests the blacks had gang-raped them. All were taken to Scottsboro, the county seat, a sleepy town of about 2,000 people with several third-rate textile mills.

In this inflammatory emergency Scottsboro behaved at least slightly better than might have been expected of such a place. An immediate mass lynching would have surprised nobody, least of all the black boys, shiftless-looking products of malnutrition, ignorance and caste onus. Instead, the authorities safely sequestered them from the gathering mob and even went to the conscientious length of having the girls examined by two doctors. Their eventual testimony under oath was that neither showed either physical or emotional trauma from having been violently raped less than an hour earlier and that though semen was found in both vaginas, its condition under the microscope made it likely that it had been deposited much earlier, say during the preceding night when, it developed, the girls had been with white boyfriends in a hobo jungle. At this access of rationality, however, Scottsboro balked. The local position was that, as a judge would expound it later in the same case, no white woman, however low-down, would admit rape by a black unless such degradation had actually occurred—so her word to that effect was not to be rebutted. The nine boys, regardless of age (twenty to thirteen), mental condition (at least four were mental defectives) and perfunctory defense by an alcoholic, court-appointed lawyer, were tried, convicted and sentenced—eight to the electric chair, the youngest to life imprisonment.

Scenario by Erskine Caldwell? It looked even more like it when, just as Caldwell would have written it, class struggle now entered the story. The broad grounds of Communist policy on blacks were, of course, that capitalist-associated racism was deliberate and that its victims would be more readily organized for mass violence leading to revolution if their plight were consistently exacerbated, so the more noise the Party made about cases like this, and the longer their ordeal could be strung out, the more constructively bitter would be the reaction of America's blacks generally. The case also offered the Party a chance to repeat its brilliant use of the Sacco-Vanzetti case to make propaganda and collect money on both sides of the Atlantic. Then oceans of publicity had cast Communism as guardian angel of victims of capitalism wherever found. Millions of dollars contributed to help Sacco and Vanzetti had been diverted into the Party war chest, and just to make sure they stayed martyrs, hence useful generation after generation, they had been gratifyingly electrocuted in the end.

So the Party rode ostentatiously hard to the rescue. The pace was sharp anyway because unless action came soon, the Boys would be executed and their usefulness lapse. Further, the Party had to get control of them before the National Association for the Advancement of Colored People, proper watchdog over blacks' interests, got into effective motion. Its trouble was reliance on slow and sluggish reports from local representatives, and for the time being it was impossible to move fast. The Party soon had the Boys signing papers to entrust their destinies to the International Labor Defense, the Communist front that handled such matters; its executive secretary happened to be a black, William L. Patterson. For the next few years a sideshow of the Scottsboro case would be the periodic efforts of the NAACP to pry the ILD's grip loose. At times the ILD even asked the NAACP for help, chiefly financial. Then the ILD's insistence on dominance would break up the alliance again ... and again ... and again. ...*

Cynical as the ILD was, however, its dog-in-the-saddle policies coincided with the Boys' interests for some time. The counsel that it hired lost appeals to the Alabama Supreme Court, of course, but went to the US Supreme Court and won requirement of new trials on the grounds that in the first instance the defendants had not had proper counsel. It all took eighteen months. The Boys spent them in sluggish misery behind bars in the same Birmingham jail that was so feelingly celebrated in the blues song. The ILD used the time to ballyhoo their plight. In big industrial centers Party-lining "workers' theaters" staged grim dramatic sketches about the case, a genre that culminated in the Theatre Guild's *They Shall Not Die* on Broadway. Its author, John Wexley, had written *The Last Mile,* a sensationally effective visit to the

---

* The details are well spelled out in Dan T. Carter's *Scottsboro* (1969) a solid piece of even-handed research on which this section gratefully depends; see also Walter White, "The Negro and the Communists," *Harper's,* December, 1931.

death house of a major penitentiary, which qualified him to make propaganda capital of the Boys' predicament. Its distinguished cast included Ruth Gordon as the Ruby Bates character under another name and Claude Rains as the defense lawyer.

Within two weeks of the ILD's putting its brand on the Boys, Communist mobs, mostly young, were smashing the windows of US consulates in Dresden, Berlin, Leipzig, Geneva; the bottle thrown in Dresden contained slips of paper: "Down with American murder and Imperialism. ... An end to the bloody lynching of our Negro co-workers." [16] In Havana a similar mob with "Yankee Imperialism" banners attacked a branch of the National City Bank. Mrs. Ada Wright, mother of two Boys, was sent touring Europe parroting Communist slogans at mass meetings. In America she and several other mothers of Boys were trouped coast to coast so pervasively that at least two responsible observers close to the situation but not to the ILD suspected that some of these alleged "Scottsboro mothers" were ringers—nine boys could never have had so many mothers. Morris Ernst, hardheaded liberal lawyer also close to the situation, estimated that such tactics probably raised $1,000,000 for the ILD. The Reverend Dr. Allan K. Chalmers, pastor of New York City's Broadway Taberna-cle Church and coordinator of later campaigns to free the Boys, estimated that everything the ILD did for them couldn't have cost more than $60,000. Since embezzlement for private gain was never a problem for American Communists, the balance, whatever it actually was, must have gone to the Party's war chest for other purposes. Those occasions when the ILD promised to mend its manners if the NAACP would help pay its bills probably meant it had siphoned off funds prematurely.

The ILD also played poor when doing the Boys the crucial favor of securing them the best man to defend them in the new trials after the US Supreme Court decision. Samuel S. Leibowitz was a fortyish New York City lawyer up from the ghetto by his own bootstraps, whose uncanny successes in getting acquittals for seemingly hopeless criminal defendants had him ranked with Clarence Darrow—unlike whom he went on to become a much respected criminal court judge. Since he was a nonradical registered Democrat and hardly needed publicity, least of all the kind consequent on being retained by Reds, he probably took the case because it challenged his talents—maybe also because his Jewish values somewhat sharpened his sensitivity to caste-based issues. When the ILD said they couldn't pay him a fee, he said he'd not only waive that, but pay his own personal expenses. During the next several years of shuttling back and forth to Alabama and the District of Columbia, he did just that. He also refused to accept—but waived making a point of it—the ILD's pious denials that it was a Communist front.

That might have warned them that except for his determination to keep the Boys out of the electric chair, Leibowitz might be the wrong man for their purposes. Anyway, once he got to Alabama and had his first sniff at local jurisprudence, he was outragedly set on doing all that ingenuity could toward acquittal. That set him at cross purposes with the ILD and the Party. They wanted maximum prolongation of appeals and new trials for optimum exposure of Dixie's recalcitrance to culminate at long, long last, as in the Sacco-Vanzetti case, with nine martyrdoms.* Leibowitz wanted to exploit every conceivable angle that would right the wrong done the Boys. In the process he did more than any white man of his day to get blacks, North as well as South, better treatment from courts. As Quentin Reynolds' account said, he made Alabama "take cognizance of all the United States Constitution," [17] not just the parts suiting Dixie's notions.

In his first time around Leibowitz shattered Victoria Price's repeated testimony by putting on the stand one of the white vagrants who had been on the train—he swore no rape had occurred—and by giving due emphasis to the testimony of one of the examining doctors that the condition of the semen found was inconsistent with its having been so recently deposited. Then came Ruby Bates. Meanwhile, the ILD had wafted her to New York City, where she confessed to the Reverend Harry Emerson Fosdick, famous liberal minister of the Rockefellers' Riverside Church, that her story had been pure perjury. He advised her to recant, and now she did so on the stand under oath. The new judge, abler and fairer than the first, impressively charged the jury to avoid hatred and prejudice. But this was, the jury obviously felt, no time for tampering with white supremacy. They convicted. The death sentence was mandatory.

Leibowitz appealed. Before the appellate court could act, the judge astounded everybody by reversing one of his rulings and granting Leibowitz's routine motion to set the verdict aside on grounds that Victoria Price's testimony was unacceptable. His reason for doing so was a secret for years. Then it came out that the second doctor had come to him privately and said he didn't dare testify again because of local feeling where he was practicing, but he had no medical doubt that the story of the rape was false. The ensuing third trial, under a third judge rather worse than the first, ended in another conviction. The Alabama Supreme Court upheld it. Leibowitz appealed to the US

* This is surmise, of course; I don't think anybody reasonably well acquainted with Party tactics at the time will think it implausible.

Supreme Court on grounds that among other irregularities, the list of veniremen had been tampered with to make it look as if blacks had been included, when actually they had not. He had already been using exclusion of blacks from jury lists as legal ammunition.

Meanwhile, the meddling ILD had seen fit to send two lawyers to bribe Victoria Price to change her testimony. She pretended to consider it, went to the local police about it, was told to play along— and here it was in the papers that the tampering lawyers were under arrest for attempted bribery. This exhausted Leibowitz's fraying patience with Communist shenanigans. He severed his connection with the ILD in a blistering statement: "I knew nothing of ... the two men from the International Labor Defense ... attempting to bribe Victoria Price ... [that was] a foul blow to the Scottsboro defendants. The Communists have raised large sums ... by the exploitation of this case. ... I gave my services free. I do not propose to have myself or my clients used any longer to provide funds for their parades to City Hall." [18] To keep his hands on the Boys' fates, he helped form a new Scottsboro Defense Committee representing the NAACP, a newly formed Alabama Scottsboro Committee, the American Civil Liberties Union—and on Tuesday and sometimes Thursday the ILD. The rest of the time they were trying to persuade as many of the Boys as possible to repudiate Leibowitz—some did, some didn't—and holding mass meetings in Harlem to "fight Sam Leibowitz." [18] And just to make sure the Boys' interests were best served, the ILD's national secretary kept warning all readers of the Communist press that fairness and justice for them could not possibly be looked for from the capitalist-spawned federal courts.

On April 1, 1935—the traditional meaning of the date received no notice in the Court's ruling—the US Supreme Court upheld Leibowitz's appeal. Alabama had to start all over again. Doggedly it did so, and Haywood Patterson, the most conspicuous Boy, on trial for the fourth time, was again convicted. But by now rising pressures on Southern public opinion were coming from endogenous non-Communist forces that gradually, as inconspicuously as possible, began to effect and lubricate a gradual hauling in of horns. Presently charges against four of the Boys were dismissed. The convictions of the remaining five were variously juggled into life sentences or less. After a while paroles went to all but Patterson. Eventually he escaped from prison and hid with relatives in Detroit. But he had the bad judgment to let a sympathetic writer ghost for him an autobiography, publication of which forced the Federal Bureau of Investigation to come around. He was arrested leaving the Detroit office of the Civil Rights Congress, the Party front that had succeeded the ILD. The Reverend

Dr. Chalmers strongly implied that since to the Party Patterson was "a more valuable asset in jail than out," [19] it was the CRC that turned him in. Michigan refused to extradite him to Alabama. In 1950 he was arrested again for killing a black man in a brawl in a Detroit bar, convicted of manslaughter and two years later died in jail.

A dismal story from beginning to end. But it had one gleam of silver. When they were forming a jury for Patterson's last trial, the panel of veniremen included *twelve blacks*. None was empaneled, but it was the first time since Reconstruction that any such thing had happened thereabouts. Somewhat later an Arkansas jury that sent a black to the electric chair for killing his wife included *a black juror*. Now in the late 1970s every time a black face appears in a Southern jury box, every time a Northern prosecutor takes care to have blacks in a jury trying a black, it is a monument to the hellish persistence of the lanky "Jew lawyer from New York buttin' in where he don't belong."

WHERE ANGELS FEARED TO TREAD

MORE MATTER WITH LESS ART.

—WILLIAM SHAKESPEARE,
Hamlet

FDR (and his speech writers) owed "New Deal" to the title of a *New Republic* article by Stuart Chase on the need for Planning as a way out of the Depression. For Democrats in 1932 the phrase handily fused Theodore Roosevelt's Square Deal with Woodrow Wilson's New Freedom. Both then still carried attractive overtones of the sort of constructive thought about public matters that had gone on before the New Era betrayed America to its worse self. And its mild flavor of shirt-sleeved cardplaying neutralized some of the self-righteousness that the elder slogans had carried in 1904 and 1912 respectively.

Soon FDR's kind of Democrats were using "New Deal" as recommending stamp on any measure in the extremely wide range of things the White House embarked on. Not long afterward the Chicago *Tribune*'s kind of Republicans tried to make it a brand of sociological shame. Some New Deal improvisations and attitudes stuck. Others, for good or ill, petered out, sometimes significantly. But before sidling into this thorny thicket, observe that in both categories it often happened that, whatever the first intent of a given project or measure, opportunists of one or another stripe often tried to seize on and develop it far beyond anything originally contemplated. Thus, Big Business sought to use the National Recovery Adminstration to draw what teeth remained in antitrust laws. The new consumer movement tried to conjure up within NRA a badly needed vigilant Big Brother for the consumer.

For a while zealots in the cooperative movement rode high on the backs of certain parts of the Resettlement Administration. Such maneuvers had unsavory precedents—for instance, the corporation lawyers' success in making "due process of law" into unintended shelter for entrenched wealth against social control, or the South's perversion of "separate but equal" into a situation flatly contradicting itself. But good causes usually need all the help they can get. In view of how legal and administrative shenanigans can further bad causes, there is no good answer to Rowland Hill's "Why should the devil have all the good tunes?"

The Federal Theatre Project (henceforth FTP) was a good example of attempts to hatch unanticipated eggs in New Deal nests. It was one of four sister projects collectively known as Federal One, the cultural department of the Works Progress Administration (WPA), giving relief employment to showfolk, writers, musicians and painters and sculptors. Government subsidy then being rare in American aesthetic endeavors, its ancestry must be described to account for its existing at all: Early in the New Deal it was decided to shift the federal share in relief for the unemployed from simple handouts usually administered by the states—Hoover's hesitant method—to direct federal hiring of the jobless at minimum local wages to do local chores—building or improving schools, airports, roads, sewer systems. . . . Those not physically up to such work or lacking needed skills were put to clerical work or cleaning up parks and playgrounds. The purpose of this Civil Works Administration (CWA) was to keep up the self-respect of the unemployed by the feeling they were doing something to earn their eating money; in the terms of the day, to avoid "pauperizing" them. Another word frequently used was "boondoggling"—borrowed from the Boy Scouts, it was said, by the mean-minded to describe the marginally necessary or frankly unnecessary chores to which relief administrators resorted in order to keep up the illusion of utility—leaf raking was the established reference.

The chief designer-builder-manager of CWA was a man on whom FDR had already relied in forming New York State's proto-New Deal—Harry Hopkins, a sensitive, yet ruthlessly able veteran of New York City's private social agencies. The several influences that led CWA into patronizing the arts for their practitioners' good may mean that some such idea was latent in those involved in the program, for instance, FDR himself. In May, 1933, he had a letter from George Biddle, a member of a practically ducal Philadelphia family, brother of the Francis Biddle who would soon be a creative New Deal lawyer, and a painter of acknowledged importance, Paris-trained and all. He wrote to "Dear Franklin"—they had been elder/younger friends at

Groton and Harvard—that his administration would do well to follow the example of the radical government of Mexico in encouraging young artists to "work at plumbers' wages ... to express on the walls of the government buildings ... social ideals.... The younger artists of America are conscious as they have never been before of the social revolution that our country and civilization are going through; and they would be eager to express these ideas in a permanent art form." [1] FDR replied sympathetically, and after much backing and filling, with help from important new dealers such as Frances Perkins, Rexford G. Tugwell, Jerome N. Frank *et al.,* Biddle had the satisfaction of seeing Hopkins turn over a few of CWA's hundreds of millions to a bureau of the US Treasury to be used to pay artists to paint murals on federal real estate. The painters recruited were not all relief cases as such. But as that able and renowned painter John Sloan said, "Artists have always been in a depression. It's just that other people have joined us now." [2] And the ice was broken. Relief and Art had been blended in what proved to be a heady mixture.

Soon Aubrey Williams, Hopkins' lieutenant, had a letter from Gutzon Borglum, not yet graduated from Stone Mountain to Mount Rushmore, congratulating the CWA for thus beginning to organize "the latent talent whose belly has been [long] empty and who carries a double hunger, unexpressed, creative longing, fitted and anxious to be a part in the great comeback," maybe by filling the nation's school-rooms with "color and design, fairy tales and history, home life ... coax the soul of America back to interest in life." [3] Williams gave it to Hopkins, whom it strongly affected, already prepared as he was by Biddle's campaign. His sensitivity to what hard times did to artists probably went back to 1929, when he had been helping the staff of New York City's Association for Improving the Condition of the Poor assign work-relief jobs created by Red Cross funds. He had noticed men carrying violin cases standing in line for pick-and-shovel jobs and, struck by the thought that fiddlers' hands were probably disastrously vulnerable to such work, saw to it that the lightest jobs went to them. Between that and Biddle's and Borglum's suggestions it need have surprised none that among Hopkins' innovations for the CWA was a policy of asking out-of-work singers, musicians, dancers to earn their relief money in government-organized variety shows for schools, settlement houses, churches. Eventually CWA was sending out marionette shows and even a Gilbert & Sullivan troupe. For actual performance before audiences is the best way to keep voices and reflexes free from rust.

Thus to its first purpose—nonpauperizing help for victims of Depression—the New Deal now added that of preserving showfolks' skills.

There was ample need. For fifteen years movies and radio had undermined live show business. Rep shows and road companies were foundering, minor theaters resorting to movies, vaudeville tending to dwindle, local stock companies getting nervous and pit-orchestra musicians consequently finding jobs scarcer. Then the Great Crash cut down the public's spending money. By 1933–34 free CWA shows were the first live entertainment that many neighborhoods had seen in years. And their obvious enjoyment suggested to certain eager minds in high places that such entertainment might be good for a nation down in the dumps. Mightn't government even consider using the live stage to supply such therapeutic stimulus as a permanent public service?

While these hints of usurping purposes groped toward the light, in 1935 the new Works Progress Administration took over from the hastily improvised CWA. It was given about $4 billion with which to pay minimum living wages to employable persons recruited from relief rolls for work "within their skills and trade" [4] as opposed to the higgledy-piggledy of previous work-relief programs. Emphasis remained on minor construction jobs. But there was enough elasticity to allow Hopkins to summon Hallie Flanagan of the Experimental Theatre of Vassar—"A vivacious little lady with an Irish wit and reddish hair, indomitable will and ambition, great administrative and artistic ability . . ." [5] says one capable and respectful observer. Even in heels she stood barely five feet, but this game was management—organizing, finagling, cajoling, scolding, decision making—not basketball, and Hopkins had chosen the right person to mortise show business into the new WPA.

CWA had done a little for showfolks, he told her, but that was "all relief . . . does it have to be that way? . . . didn't you spend a lot of time making a survey . . . of the way foreign governments run theatres?" [6] Enter modestly Purpose No. 3, already hinted at by Biddle and Borglum—why not move on from mere rescue of artists and their skills into positively, permanently employing them? Nor was Hopkins thus ambitious for the stage alone. He took Mrs. Flanagan to a gathering of the eagles at the house of Henry Alsberg, Socialist-minded foreign correspondent and stage-minded intellectual, soon to be national director of the WPA Writers' Project (FWP). There Holger Cahill, expert on "primitive" American art, soon to be national director of the WPA Artists' Project (FAP), assured them that "government subsidy was the next logical step in the development of American art [as] functioning part of our national life." [7] Soon, as such things go, a Federal Music Project (FMP) was added under Dr. Nicolai Sokoloff, former conductor of the Cleveland Symphony Orchestra. From WPA's billions $27,000,000 was set aside for this four-square Federal One—less than 1 percent, true, but since $9 in every $10 was to go directly into paychecks, here was an unprecedented godsend to thousands of hard-up sculptors, writers, painters, instrumentalists, dancers, jugglers, actors and so forth.

Government as angel of stage arts was just the stuff for Mrs. Flanagan. She was a pillar of the self-consciously cultivated, noncommercial—"amateur" is unfair to the best of it—movement that had been infiltrating college curricula up from settlement houses, campus, dramatic clubs and local Little Theaters of the previous decades. Its exponents spoke impressively of "the drama" as sociocultural focus of classic Greece. In the writings of Kenneth Macgowan, Norris Houghton and the contributions (Mrs. Flanagan's included) to Edith Isaacs' *Theatre Arts* magazine, a remarkable piece of editing, it envisaged a national theater of regional nuclei developing local plays and players in town halls as well as big city playhouses. Deploring the overcommercial values of Broadway, it dwelt on Dublin's Abbey Theatre and the Provincetown Playhouse and now in the early 1930s on the new Russian theater so imaginatively staging what the Kremlin thought it well for workers and peasants to see. And being chronically short of money—for directors' salaries, costumes, scenery, electricity, lighting equipment and so on—it was itchily aware that in the USSR, as in Sophocles' Greece and most of modern Europe, government subsidized the kinds of shows that the culture took most seriously.

Mrs. Flanagan had heard the call as student at Grinnell College (Grinnell, Iowa), where she and Hopkins had been contemporaries. It was one of the small private Midwestern colleges (like Carleton in Minnesota, Kenyon in Ohio) managing to develop respectable academic standards as well as respectable alumni. Among other concerns, Grinnell was theater-minded. Hallie Flanagan's nimble pursuit of Thespis and his crew through the grove of Academe got her invited to Harvard to stage-manage the plays turned out there in George Pierce Baker's famous playwriting course. Then she had a year on a Guggenheim fellowship, observing the new theatrical doings in Scandinavia, Germany and particularly the USSR. Then Vassar asked her to coordinate studies in acting, set design, stage lighting and so on into an Experimental Theatre. Its notably energetic productions, some using home-cooked scripts, exploited the innovations that Mrs. Flanagan had observed overseas and drew respectful attention from the New York City press. Alistair Cooke told his British readers that "almost any routine production [at Vassar] makes half the productions of the West End or Broadway look like the village concert."[8] For writing, acting and stage managing Mrs. Flanagan attracted some of the brightest girls in a student body swaybacked with brains and energy, and enough male recruits from nearby Poughkeepsie and not-too-far-away Yale. President MacCracken, chronically stagestruck, took time off from his duties to play Enobarbus in *Antony and Cleopatra* and the professor protagonist of Alexander Afinogenov's *Fear* (a problem play from the USSR). He told Mrs. Flanagan that when presenting diplomas at commencement, he could "tell ... which girls are drama majors ... not by any theatrical bearing or appearance [but] because in their eyes I see an awareness of the moment." [9]

At the time FDR was on Vassar's governing board and a near neighbor at his Hyde Park estate, and my account of his wife has failed if the reader does not assume that she was, as a sympathetic authority says, "the official mother of the [federal] arts projects." [10] Thus, it was she who asked MacCracken to give Mrs. Flanagan leave of absence to create the Federal Theatre. Certain passages in Mrs. Flanagan's book on her work at Vassar even have the same cadence and ring of content as "My Day": "[In Moscow] I was impressed by ... a long and learned play on transmuting oil into rubber. After the last act the entire audience of several thousand youths rose to take a pledge to go without sugar in their tea ... to save money to help the government equip laboratories for such experiments." [11] Or why she decided to do Euripides' *Hippolytus* in the original Greek: "... not all our students would know Greek, but they could learn it. The audience wouldn't all know Greek, but you don't need to know Greek to understand it. Plays would be better if we didn't understand them so well—just had a powerful emotional sense of what they meant." [12] That last is better understood when one is aware that the lady making it had come to a richly subtle understanding of the USSR's theater, traditional as well as "constructivist"-modern, from only a few months of witnessing its productions with only a few words of Russian to bless herself with.

Her account of FTP vaunts, as if indisputable, its suddenly acknowledged, though long incumbent, Purpose No. 4: "... for the first time the preservation of the skills of the worker, and hence the *preservation of his self-respect* [italics mine] became important." [13] Thus, to slip self-respect into the equation blurs distinctions among kinds of skill. Rust from disuse is a genuine hazard for acrobats, singers, dancers, musicians, possibly even graphic artists. Among writers and dramatic actors the case is otherwise. A writer with a newly fattened bank account may stay away from his desk for months and write all the better for it when he next applies seat of pants to seat of chair. An actor who has been "at liberty" for a year will read a part for a casting director as well as ever. It follows that while the FMP orchestras with which Uncle Sam kept musicians active in their craft did mean genuine skill protecting, Federal One's writing and dramatic work did not.

Since salvage of skills was not involved, there was no reason why an actor should not have been asked to do any honest work the community suggested in exchange for an emergency livelihood—if he was physically up to it. If to do so impaired his self-respect, he was out of step with a venerable American tradition—the assumption that, as in W. S. Gilbert's prophecy of an equalitarian aristocracy: "The Noble Lord who rules the State, / The Noble Lord who scrubs the grate ... / The Lord High Bishop Orthodox,/ The Lord High Coachman on the box,/ They all shall equal be!" The American college student has long taken any licit job, however arduous or menial, without losing a sliver of his self-respect. The hard-up youngster bent on writing or painting feels it no disgrace to support himself by five days a week of car washing. It ill became the admirably equalitarian New Deal thus to countenance the white-collar man's invidious reluctance to get his hands dirty—a thing already hinted at in the communal self-help projects. It cropped up in the Writers' Project too. "Every community," wrote Katharine Kellock, Alsberg's right hand, "had some unemployed people of education, to whom it owed a debt it wanted to pay with a saving of their pride ... formerly prominent or influential citizens for whom it wanted to do face-saving ..." [14] and so tucked them in among the FWP writers to do the equivalent of leaf raking. In American terms there was more social health in the Depression-broke businessmen whom Frank Walker found in Montana "digging ditches and laying sewer pipe [for CWA] ... wearing their regular business suits because they couldn't afford overalls ..." but to his surprise and admiration "happy to be working and proud of what they were doing." [15]

One need not labor the point. It is made here only to show how subtly blending of new purposes with the originals can reshape social programs. Almost at once Mrs. Flanagan, avid as the Fisherman's Wife in the folktale, was going farther still. She meant to use this willingness of government to provide stage work for actors to bestow on show business the blessings that Biddle and Borglum sought for their arts—public subsidy for the Theatre-as-such long hoped for by those interested in the Higher Things. Mrs. Roosevelt, in fact, advanced as one reason why Mrs. Flanagan should have the FTP job that "the time has come when America [may] consider the theatre, as it [is] considered abroad, a part of education." [16] Similarly Mrs. Flanagan saw FTP as enabling "the worker in the theatre ... [to create and reach] a much wider audience" than private enterprise afforded, "to extend the boundaries of theatre-going, to create a vigorous new audience ..." and—here Purpose No. 5 suddenly cantilevers out from the leading edge of opportunism—"experiment with ideas ... the plays we do should be informed by the consciousness of the art and economics of 1935." [17] Not necessarily unworthy purposes, but far from the intent of Congress in appropriating funds for WPA.* In some respects the social net effect was, however, more palatable than the opportunism of those reshaping Federal One's function nearer to their hearts' desire. For even at worst—and the worst could be pretty bad—Federal One did keep above water the chins of thousands of hard-luck cases, many frightened because through no fault of their own they could not extract a living from their chosen cultural craft.

Actual professionals were scarce among the top echelon of this organization to rescue their kind. Eva Le Gallienne, that fine actress and able manager, Hopkins' first choice to command FTP, declined when she learned it did not mean subsidy for a repertory theater under her command. Most of the dozen regional directors whom Mrs. Flanagan chose were, like herself, prominent in campus drama departments or directors of well-established "community playhouses"— meaning big-time Little Theaters. One was editor of a serious magazine. Only three were Broadway figures. Of those Elmer Rice soon resigned because he smelled censorship in Washington's refusal to let the first Living Newspaper field impersonations of Mussolini and Haile Selassie. The other two resigned within a year. So did almost all their non-Broadway colleagues, unwilling further to cope with local versions of the same thronging difficulties that the formidable Mrs. Flanagan, in the national context, chewed up and spit out. The talent recruited, particularly in outlying areas where showfolk were necessarily scarce, included many hungry youngsters who had done little or no acting but welcomed a chance to try it at public expense. The director of FTP's Negro Theatre in Harlem—an outstanding unit—estimated that a third of those originally enrolled as performers "had never acted, danced or been on a stage or a concert platform in their lives." [18] But the bulk of the beneficiaries were real professionals, if usually rather obscure, and

---

* This issue came dimly into the open in 1941 when a Library of Congress-sponsored committee was assaying the value of Federal One. John Steinbeck asked whether it had been "feeding artists or creating artistic expression?" Archibald MacLeish said, "What you people did in WPA was completely hypocritical.... You kept telling yourself you were actually giving people a job, but you were really more interested in your program." To which Florence Kerr replied, "You must admit it was one of the higher forms of hypocrisy." Mangione, *The Dream and the Deal* (1972), 347.

the administrative ability of those running the unwieldy show was nearer adequate than there was reason to expect. For nearly four years, lurching through shifts in policy, cutbacks in financing, sniping from Party-lining groups and congressional committees, the FTP worked.

As things shook down, out of its national headquarters spouted streams of scripts—established items, fresh-baked items, operettas, plays for children, plays for Easter and Christmas, plays for Catholic, Jewish, German, French, Hispanic audiences, plays propagandizing against war and syphilis, and for public electric power, archaic warhorses such as *The Old Homestead, After Dark, A Texas Steer* and good-natured recent Broadway hits such as *The Whole Town's Talking, The Wisdom Tooth, You and I*. Out of each regional office troupes took these and other vehicles to derelict city theaters, schools, long-disused county seat "opera houses," sometimes working under canvas, often alfresco in a park. In their satirical *I'd Rather Be Right* (1937) Kaufman and Hart had the seedy leading man of an FTP tab show explain apologetically: "Whenever we see three people together, we're supposed to do a show. . . . it's pretty hard to go anywhere these days without tripping over the Federal Theatre." Motorized units of vaudevillians went round CCC camps, old folks' homes, orphan asylums, juvenile reformatories. Headquarters often deplored the corny material that these small-time hoofers, monologists, contraltos and jugglers employed but soon understood that it was all right; these audiences were just as corny and lapped it up. Other FTP pensioners went from one CCC camp to another, helping the boys put on their own shows. Psychiatrists at New York City's Bellevue Hospital got help from FTP in developing the then new technique of therapeutic staging of patients' emotional tangles.

Admission ranged from nothing for minor efforts to 55 cents top for FTP showpieces in Broadway or Chicago Loop houses. In view of such modest charges George Bernard Shaw and Eugene O'Neill gave FTP the run of their works at a flat royalty of $50 a night. The semimonopolistic Shubert chain of big-city theaters, Octopus of Broadway, lent a hand on the shrewdly crass grounds that FTP shows might rent some Depression-darkened houses and these four-bit productions, the best of which did SRO business for months, might create a habit of theatergoing in people who, as things picked up, might pay Broadway prices. That was about the extent of help from the chiefs of conventional live show business. John Golden, eminent producer, professed fear lest the low quality of FTP shows complete the ruin of the industry by turning people against theater generally. Mrs. Flanagan secured a good legitimate house in Brooklyn wherein her actors would try out scripts that Broadway producers thought promising but hesitated to risk tryout money on. Little came of it. Brock Pemberton, another leader among producers, said the kind of actor who had to go on relief wouldn't have the professional style to bring out the merits of a script to begin with.

Among FTP's demonstrations that Pemberton was wrong and that helping minor troupers was worthwhile were two triumphs of flashy, gimmicky showmanship staged by all-black companies under white direction: First up in Harlem an all-black *Macbeth* tricked out in voodoo doings and later in Chicago an all-black *The Mikado* prospered greatly there and on Broadway, also spinning off the Broadway production of *The Hot Mikado*. New York City's early showpiece was T. S. Eliot's *Murder in the Cathedral*, rights to which Mrs. Flanagan could secure because Eliot had liked her staging of *Sweeney Agonistes* at Vassar. But her hopes for FTP also included original scripts proclaiming social needs. Her most brilliant bit of management was to steer Sinclair Lewis' *It Can't Happen Here* past the author's temperament into a workable stage version and present it in twenty-seven cities simultaneously to celebrate the first anniversary of FTP. Its authors turned out two different plays about Abraham Lincoln and one about John Brown, all well received.* A melodramatic conventional treatment of the black revolution in Haiti, complete with a French heroine who learns her father is a former slave, was well done by the Harlem unit. Presumably for balance a wooden but respectful original play about Jefferson Davis was produced at the instance of the Daughters of the Confederacy. None seem to have broken out of the ruck of average pseudohistorical stuff. But Mrs. Flanagan's cultural ambitions, shared with many of her colleagues and performers, took her into written-to-order vehicles handling living persons and events as immediate as tomorrow. And in this context balance got short shrift.

She did sometimes warn her staff against taking political sides. The implicit reason was that FTP, financed by public moneys forcibly extracted from taxpayers of various political shades, could not safely claim the right to sound off that clearly belonged to theatricals privately financed. She chose in practice to take that risk for FTP,

---

* Estimates of the quality of FTP's stagings are all based on secondhand data because, the reader must be warned, I saw none of its productions. By 1935 growing deafness had combined with mumbly actors and the poor acoustics of most theaters to discourage me from seeing any but a very few shows—among those pertinent here only *Waiting for Lefty* and *Pins and Needles,* both of which I greatly admired. Here I am concerned chiefly with content, however, and that an experienced reader can derive from scripts supplemented where indicated by reviews, autobiographies and such.

however, and the further risk of filling almost all such insistently timely productions with what anti-New Dealers suspected of being hostile propaganda. One good reason for their doing so was that it often was exactly that. Atkinson, a warm admirer of FTP, nevertheless described its Living Newspaper show *Power* as "[coming] out impartially against the electric light and power industry and for the TVA, practically defying the Supreme Court ... the most indignant and militant proletarian drama of the season ... staged with government funds." [19] When Harry Hopkins saw it, he said, "People will say it's propaganda. Well, what of it? It's propaganda to educate the consumer. ..." [20]

Mrs. Flanagan's tongue was more slippery. Much of the time she maintained that FTP was "interested solely in ... the best possible plays." But she also mentioned "a series of anti-war plays [obviously propagandistic]" as deliberate part of her "national plan." [21] In both its author's and FTP's intentions *It Can't Happen Here* was outright anti-Fascist propaganda, nor could it conceivably be included as "one of the best possible plays." Speaking to the national Theatre Council in mid-FTP career, she announced, "The theatre, when it's good, is always dangerous." [22] That left little room for *Macbeth, The Beaux' Stratagem, Ruddigore, Liliom* or *The Emperor Jones* but helps explain why she was as eager as any to see FTP produce Marc Blitzstein's *The Cradle Will Rock*, brilliant free-form theater that was propaganda for Party-lining labor as undiluted as the pro-Nazi propaganda in *Mein Kampf.*

There had already been storms about the Living Newspapers, which, like *Cradle,* were technically as well as ideologically radical. The dramaturgic ancestors were: First, the stripped-down stage techniques, relying on lighting, multilevel stages, turntables and sparse detail, of European expressionism and constructivism. The associations here were highly radical, as the New Playwrights showed. Secondly, the satiric musical theater of the late 1920s and early 1930s dominated by Kaufman and collaborators: *Strike Up the Band,* a piercingly amusing pacifist tract with a great score from George Gershwin; *Of Thee I Sing,* which swiftly snipped sharp-edged paper clowns out of the extensive tissues of the American political process; its sequel, *Let 'Em Eat Cake; I'd Rather Be Right,* set in Central Park with George M. Cohan playing FDR—every time he does something, the US Supreme Court pops up from behind a rock and calls it unconstitutional. Thirdly, *The March of Time,* which had accustomed the public to faking on radio or screen, by the acting out of actual events in synthetic versions as oversimplified as those two-reel historical epics shot by Biograph in 1911. But what probably tied it all together for

Mrs. Flanagan were the Living Newspapers developed by the "Blue Blouse" troupes in the USSR, dramatizing for workers' clubs, schools and such the economic gospel for the edification of the masses.

"Newspaper" implied timeliness. *The March of Time,* exploiting flexible movies and even more flexible radio, could be almost as timely as the commercial newsreel. But the FTP Living Newspaper, one purpose of which was to give walk-on and crowd roles to scores of relief-roll actors, took much writing and prolonged rehearsal. That restricted its content to broad handling of ongoing phenomena, meaning it was a series of sociological pamphlets-behind-footlights. Misnomer though the name was, however, the series was sponsored by the New York City Newspaper Guild, then at the height of its Party-lining phase. Its writing staff was organized nominally newspaper-style with managing editor, city editor, reporters, copyreaders. The first effort of this gratuitous charade, *Ethiopia,* aborted because in the process of flaying *Fascismo,* it put *Il Duce* on the stage in person. The nonjournalistic occasion for the venture was that FTP had fallen heir to a stranded troupe of genuine West African dancers and singers, who, it was thought, would make admirable ethnic atmosphere for the courtyard of Haile Selassie's palace.* Actually the first Living Newspaper to hit the stands, so to speak, was *Triple-A Plowed Under,* a snarlingly vivacious setting forth of the American farmer's plight in relation to the Depression and the US Supreme Court's invalidation of the New Deal's Agricultural Adjustment Act. As counterforce the play recommended the Farmer-Labor Alliance then shaping up in the wheat regions much applauded (and half-openly promoted) by the Communists as part of their new Popular Front policy. Similarly the next Living Newspaper, *Injunction Granted,* violently attacked the use of courts to hamper labor organization. Its makers reinforced the original script with material so intemperate that even Mrs. Flanagan took alarm and put on her impartial-responsibility hat: "I will not have the Federal Theatre used politically ... to further the ends of the Democratic Party, the Republican Party or the Communist Party," [23] she announced.

---

* For all their much talked-up "research" the Living Newspapermen seem to have been too weak on Africa to know that West Africans and the Ethiopians whom *Il Duce* was brutalizing had little more in common than Finns and Sicilians—both Europeans. Eventually these Africans were the core of the voodoo doings in that all-black *Macbeth.* Houseman's *Run-through* (352–53) has a grisly-whimsical bit about them: Percy Hammond, then play reviewer of the New York *Herald-Tribune,* gave that *Macbeth* a scathing review. The reputed witch doctor who led the African troupe resented it and put on an all-night closed session of esoteric dances and such in the theater. The next day, says Houseman, Hammond was hospitalized with pneumonia and in a few days was dead.

She was respectfully pleased with *Spirochete,* a Living Newspaper from Chicago's FTP, supporting Dr. Parran's momentously frank campaign against syphilis. But she was sniffy about *Highlights of 1935,* a newsreellike Living Newspaper because it had "no point of view ... just strung together" evocative reenactment bits about the trial of Bruno Hauptmann for the murder of the Lindbergh baby, the first transatlantic air service in flying boats. ... In her and her supporters' view the best Living Newspaper was *One-Third of a Nation,* a crackling dramatization of American housing problems and the corollary need for publicly subsidized dwellings for the lower-income brackets—a high-priority New Deal concern. She told HUAC in 1939, "I certainly would not sit here and say it was not a propaganda play." [24]

This was the apple of her eye, fruit of the Federal Summer Theatre, a long "workshop"—as her world was already calling such powwows—at Vassar financed by the Rockefeller Foundation, to which she summoned forty-odd of the FTP's writers, directors and designers to immerse themselves in Living Newspaper techniques. The consequent Vassar version was played against a fixed background of loomingly huge depictions of artifacts connoting the miseries of the slums, "the leaky faucet, the leprous garbage can, the rotten fire escape. ..." [25] The later New York City version used actual morbidities gleaned from Manhattan's alleys, tenement hallways, rooftops. Among the script's virtues were hints that predatory landlords were not exclusively and altogether to blame for slums, and amusing byplay between the protagonist—a sort of John Q. Public-Everyman—and his friend the Loud Speaker, a bullhorn with a quirky personality and good lines to match, who coached him on the problems involved.

It is unlikely that Mrs. Flanagan was ever actually advised to keep on saying, "I will not have the Federal Theatre used politically," while making Living Newspapers the show-business arm of the New Deal's public relations. In such contexts the explicit is seldom needed. The forces of darkness were so strong and unscrupulous that temperaments like hers could be counted on spontaneously to stretch a point for settlement-house values and a good deal of crypto-Party-lining. Thus, the nation-blanketing productions of *It Can't Happen Here* coincided with the hottest phase of the presidential campaign of 1936. This timing caused remark. And few seem to have noticed that somehow, in being adapted to the federal stage, Lewis' story had lost its sporadic reprehensions of the USSR's high-handed dictatorship.

This betokened, though maybe not resulting directly from, another effort to steer Federal One's projects into Party-lining. By "boring from within," the Communists hoped to get the use of Federal One both to secure livelihoods for the comrades and their satellites and to spread protorevolutionary ideas. The agency was a union of WPA labor called the Workers' Alliance originally set up by Socialists but soon taken over by Communists using familiar, usually successful tactics. A sister union in New York City, the City Projects Committee, represented WPA's lower-echelon office staff. Their infiltration was effective. Mrs. Flanagan soon learned that WA's leaders knew about changes in policy and cuts in appropriations days or weeks before she did. Their strikes against layoffs were impressively observed. Party members or fellow travelers securing influential posts as directors, writers or researchers kept pushing to imbue FTP productions with ideas and emotions that, though not exclusively Marxist, would create the kind of steaming social compost in which Communism hoped to sprout and flourish.

As this built up, the FTP seemed to unsympathetic observers to go beyond mere fealty to its New Deal overlords into more mordant ideological capers. Inevitably it and its feisty directress were charged with being Communist or next thing to it. Never budging, she denied any knowledge that the WA-CPC was a Party front, even though the handbills they circulated in FTP offices and on the sidewalk between acts at FTP theaters carried recruiting coupons for the Young Communist League. She denied that the bulk of the "theater-party" ticket sales that were the backbone of FTP audiences went to organizations to some extent identified with Party-lining. When a member of HUAC asked her on the stand whether the *New Masses* wasn't alleged to be a Communist publication, she snapped back, "*Alleged* to be," [26] which was about like saying that the *Congressional Record* was alleged to be a publication of the US Congress. She was better off denying that she herself was a Communist, for she very probably was not. But she let the finale of *Triple-A Plowed Under* recommend by name two important undercover Communists as spokesmen champions of the American farmer with no hint that, as she should have known if she didn't, they were among the Party's keenest fishermen in the troubled waters of the wheat belt. She let Earl Browder, titular chief of the Party in America, be respectfully impersonated on stage in *Power* on the same footing as several US Senators.

She could easily have prevented such needless asking for trouble had she wished to, for by her own admission she considered "directors of a government theatre ... necessarily censors ... on questions of public taste and policy ... motivated by the general principles of a theatre as vigorous and varied as possible." [27] She approved of the Chicago FTP's aborting a show about the Townsend Plan—which lacked FDR's approval—because she said, FTP should "neither satirize

... nor sponsor Townsend." [28] But it was her superiors in Washington, not she, who withdrew FTP sponsorship at the last minute from *The Cradle Will Rock* presumably because its blistering anticapitalist content—after all, it was Bertolt Brecht, the momentous German Party-lining playwright, who had urged Blitzstein to write it—was too hot to handle on taxpayers' money. Brecht's godfathering of *Cradle* probably was deliberate manipulation of a susceptible artist in the interests of the Party. As for Mrs. Flanagan, however, one need not postulate direct tampering to account for her indiscretions favoring the Party's purposes. She merely shared the fondness of such people in her time for the rosy glow emanating from things associated with the USSR.

She had long manifested typical stigmata. To judge from her gurgly account of her trip to the USSR in 1927, she felt no more queasy about the Kremlin's heavy hand than most pilgrims in that decennial season. At Vassar she staged the *Masse Mensch* of Ernst Toller, peer of Brecht among Party-lining German playwrights, and two overt propaganda items, *We Demand* and *Miners on Strike* from the Party-lining Workers' Theatre in New York City, and was billed as coauthor of *Can You Hear Their Voices?*, Vassar's stage adaptation of a *New Masses* story by Whittaker Chambers about the catastrophic drought of 1930–31. Neither Chambers, who worked from a newspaper clipping, nor Mrs. Flanagan had ever been near the drought area, but the script described in high-impact detail how for lack of milk to feed it a farmer's wife killed her baby while the relief supplies from the Red Cross were denied local people by bureaucratic error and the heartlessness of the local Scrooge. For happy ending undercover-Communist leader of the farmers faces arrest for fomenting looting and sends his adolescent sons off to Party headquarters to "make a better world for kids to live in." "... none of us [at Vassar at the time] considered it radical," [29] Mrs. Flanagan wrote in ingenuous retrospect. Its production style was much like that of the later Living Newspapers. Its content not unnaturally got it very widely played through the 1930s by Party-lining theater groups.

In 1934 Mrs. Flanagan was a contributing editor of *New Theatre,* magazine of the League of Workers' Theatres, printed in Moscow, on the same masthead as several conspicuous fellow travelers and Communist Kyle Crichton; the league was American arm of the International Union of Revolutionary Theatres, headquarters in Moscow. In 1939 she told HUAC, "No, I've never been connected with workers' theatres." [30] Nobody laughed. But the world she lived for laughed its cultivated head off when, apropos of a reference to "Marlowesque madness" [31] in an article of hers, a member of HUAC asked her whether this Marlowe was a Communist. Such opponents were pushovers. Gilbert Seldes had uttered a word of caution about such management as hers in 1936; that proved unnecessary, but at the time few could be sure of that. He wrote that he personally didn't object to the "intellectual-proletarian overtone" in Federal One's theatrical doings but thought it a pity that it "has somewhat alienated the body of citizens who still feel they have a stake in the present form of society, the people of the middle class who are so hastily abandoned by radicals that they become an easy prey for demagogues and fascists." [32]

He could have added that it was a pity that Mrs. Flanagan's impulsive plungings made FTP the Achilles' heel of Federal One. Maybe lasting support from Washington for the arts could never have been built on emergency relief. Even now not too many Congressmen are really comfortable with the idea. Forty years ago! After hearty praise for what Federal One did in its first few years, *Fortune* flat-footedly stated that, whatever the hopes of "well meaning but uninformed people" for seeing it made permanent, "the more intelligent officials connected with [it] are strongly opposed ... it would inevitably produce the arthritic rigidity everywhere associated with governmental control of the arts." [33] Of the three other sister projects, FMP, doing little but form scratch orchestras to give concerts where such things were scarce and music lessons to those previously unable to afford them, had the lowest profile. FAP had headline-making trouble with Party-liners and mural painters' fondness for class-conscious symbols but nothing that stung like *Cradle*. Party-liners sometimes came close to taking over big-city FWP projects, but what actually got printed was so closely watched on high that little got beyond a flavor of settlement-house-cum-folk-festival. For that matter, among FTP's 800-odd productions only a few dozen had corrosive overtones. But most of those originated in New York City and got very wide attention. As it grew unmistakable that Mrs. Flanagan wanted her Living Newspapers (which FTP troupes took over much of the country) to tub-thump for the New Deal and that though she might often prefer to keep Party-liners out of the act, she was incapable of insisting on it, her shortcomings—if you like, her intellectual habits—gave FTP an unnecessarily bad name in powerful places. The US House of Representatives laughed out of countenance Representative William I. Sirovich's bill to create a permanent Federal One. In 1939, after four years of anomalous, ambiguous vigor, the lights were doused on all FTP marquees.

Well before then cuts in funds, local apathy and lack of professionals outside the largest cities were smothering the dream of creative, noncommercial, low-admission regional theaters richening culture coast to coast with everything from marionette shows to local-born drama of social significance. Only New York City, Chicago and Los Angeles maintained momentum. The South was mostly flaccid; the Old Northwest outside Chicago hard to get moving. In Minnesota, for instance, FTP was so fragile that it could not survive the row that broke out when a vaudeville troupe sent to a CCC camp included a former fan dancer. But the original purpose of relieving the needy by paying them to do their own thing was better served. About 9,000 out-of-work show people had drawn some economic and maybe psychological help from FTP. Of those about 2,500 somehow got back to work in commercial activity. Thus, Arthur Miller was an FTP reliefer at $22.77 a week for a year while writing radio scripts on the side. When he sold one, he went permanently off relief, doing a series of historical broadcasts for Du Pont. The several black troupes' successes probably widened blacks' access to professional theatrical work as well as encouraged all-black theater as such. FTP (and other branches of Federal One) worked with Paul Green and the academic Carolina Playmakers to put on a dramatic pageant about the Lost Colony on Roanoke Island. It became a permanent tourist attraction and launched Green on a new career as specialist in such localized, pseudohistorical gropings after the past—the sort of suitable-for-the-whole-family fare that a more tactful FTP would have kept expanding.

Green was already an established playwright, of course. FTP turned up little new talent, but there were Bil and Cora Baird, who met and married as FTP reliefers; at the time he was an acrobat in its extravaganza *Horse Eats Hat*. John Kriza had his first good chance in an FTP ballet in Chicago. And what happened when Washington pulled the rug from under *The Cradle Will Rock* not only gave the American theater an exhilarating legend but also arranged Orson Welles' first blast-off toward becoming show business' anticipation of Muhammad Ali.

Not that FTP discovered Orson Welles. He had already done that himself. Well before he could vote, he was renowned among radio people for his variety of voices: as the Shadow—"The Shadow kno-o-o-ws!"—and for *The March of Time* as Field Marshal von Hindenburg or Sir Basil Zaharoff or, for a choice of emperors, Hirohito or Haile Selassie. ... His friend John Houseman and he midwifed for FTP that all-black *Macbeth* and later a memorable staging of *The Tragical History of Dr. Faustus,* Welles in the title role, a black playing Mephistopheles against gaunt expressionist sets and frenetic decorations that, by all accounts, could have come from a P. T. Barnum version of *The Cabinet of Dr. Caligari.* In spite of the creative confectionery, however, what young Alfred Kazin remembered best was the way Welles' face "swelled and brooded over the empty stage like an inflated goblin's." [34] Welles was not the man to let any kind of fireworks, even his own virtuosity in stagecraft, upstage him.

The Cradle Will Rock was Blitzstein's view of the current head-on collision between the Committee for Industrial Organization and the American steel industry. At the time the CIO was relying heavily on Communist help, so this was no polemic "documentary" giving a bill of particulars of the bosses' sins à la Elmer Rice, but an incitement to riot as limber as a medieval mystery, with characters of cognate paper-doll flatness. Personifying the forces of darkness were Reverend Salvation, Editor Daily, President Prexy, Professor Trixie, Mr. Mister (the dominant plutocrat). Its first sponsor was the Party-lining Actors' Repertory Company, which had won its spurs with Green's folksily pacifist *Johnny Johnson*. When Actors' Repertory's money ran out, Welles and Houseman, who knew the piece from private hearings, persuaded Mrs. Flanagan that they should do it for FTP. Its musical brilliance, loose but terse script and bitter, rousing protorevolutionary shrillness made her easy to persuade.

For three months Welles and Houseman rehearsed it in the small but elegant Maxine Elliott's Theater, relishing its lean stylishness, honing cast and content keener and keener. Thus, word-of-mouth, the lifeblood of show business, had plenty of time to stew up attention-calling gossip about this anticapitalist, pro-working-stiff hymn of hate. In repercussion the eve of dress rehearsal brought from Washington, bypassing Mrs. Flanagan, orders to postpone the opening into mid-summer. That, all assumed, meant scrap it. Frantic consultations on some kind of salvage suggested doing it without FTP sponsorship. But theater, scenery, lights, costumes, props, orchestral instruments all were WPA property and once postponement was official, taboo. Further, Actors' Equity, the actors' professional union, forbade them to set foot on any stage thus dehallowed.

In the end the cobwebby old tradition of the-show-must-go-on, maybe reinforced by reluctance to see all that 200-proof propaganda go to waste, proved too strong for bureaucratic sabotage. At the last minute Welles and Houseman secured use of a frowsy theater a mile uptown and sent up there a rented piano and, by taxi, subway and on foot, the cast and the loyal first-night audience, which consisted largely of a Party-lining theater party. The only available spotlight picked out Blitzstein and the piano on an empty stage. The performers dispersed in the dusty boxes and among the audience. As, in place of orchestra, Blitzstein worked through the score—his piano handling of it was already famous—the performers, dutifully never going near the stage, rose in their places on cue and went through the whole show all the more juicily, no doubt, because of the excitement of those preceding few hours of crisis.

It was the run-through of the century. Piercingly, janglingly, streaking in from a dozen different directions within those dingy four walls, the score told how "There's something so damned low about the rich" and about "Frame-ups, shakedowns, lockouts, sellouts ... toiling, ailing, dying, piled-up bodies. ..." The audience, radical-minded enough to begin with, tipsy with vicarious revolutionary fervor, meltingly inclined through admiration for the company's pluck, nearly tore the house down when, in the finale, the protagonist labor leader, Larry Foreman, cornered Mr. Mister with a driving proclamation predicting "a storm that's going to last until the final wind blows ... and when the wind blows ... The Cradle Will Rock!" It was *Waiting for Lefty* all over again, only, by all accounts, more so. It took an hour to get the audience calmed down enough to leave. That cost an extra $20 rent and well worth it. Management and performers had had an orgastically perfect evening of self-righteous passion and release. Heywood Broun called it "the best play of the present season ... because it shouts and sings that this earth can be made to glow and glisten if working men and women will only decide forthwith to kindle flame by rubbing together souls and shoulders." [35] For two weeks—that was the FTP limit on time off for relief clients—*Cradle* played in that dislocated, run-through fashion to packed houses in a *succès d'estime* that, as Houseman wrote years later, "made [us] reputations such as we could not possibly have secured elsewhere." [36]

After some backing and filling Welles and Houseman shook the evanescent dust of FTP from their buskins and, operating as the Mercury Theater, independently produced items that had been on the FTP agenda when the storm broke—*Heartbreak House* (Welles as Captain Shotover), George Büchner's durably flashy *Danton's Death* (Welles as Danton). ... How much the Party-lining support meant became clear when the audiences at *Danton* suddenly shrank drastically—because the Party had decided that the breach between Danton and Robespierre was too like a parallel with Trotsky/Stalin unfavorable to Stalin. The Mercury was safer with its anti-Fascist masterpiece *Julius Caesar,* done with practically no scenery, the mob in seedy, shirt-coat-and-pants American street attire, Roman soldiers in World War I uniforms belted Fascist-style, Caesar got up to look like Mussolini, Welles as, of course, the antidotally idealistic, doomed Brutus. An admirer called it one of "those electrifying revisions of classics which read a modern meaning into the ancient words." [37] Hell was bubbling across the Atlantic and though the parallel between Rome's troubles in 44 B.C. and the Western world's in 1937 was gimmicky nonsense, the energy of the production and the audience's already high sensitivity to Fascism made the gimmick seem imaginative.

The Mercury Theatre presently petered out. Welles' Martian spaceship wafted him to Hollywood and *Citizen Kane*. Such a baby volcano was bound to make a broad, deep mark somehow. But it is a strange thought that it probably would not have happened this zigzag way had those violin cases not gone to Harry Hopkins' heart—and through him to Mrs. Flanagan's head.

The Federal Writers' Project, second most conspicuous arm of Federal One, left so cordial a memory that one of its high-ranking alumni, Professor Jerre Mangione of the University of Pennsylvania, recently suggested reviving it to help the new crops of young writers through the 1970s. Its sweet flavor had several causes: It supplied libraries with a body of useful reference works that, because tangible and legible, is more readily appreciated than the evanescent capers of the Living Newspapers and is, God knows, superior to most of FAP's murals and conscientious landscapes. The roll of budding talents it nourished physically and maybe in some cases artistically—Saul Bellow, Ralph Ellison, John Cheever, Loren Eiseley, Nelson Algren, Richard Wright, Willard Motley, Chester Himes, Kenneth Rexroth *et al.*—is more impressive than anything either FTP or FAP could muster. And its chief, Henry Alsberg, contrasted favorably with Mrs. Flanagan at least as administrator. Though he too hankered after showing government how pleasant and proper it is to be patron of the arts, writing included, he concentrated more than she on keeping individual chins above water and getting Uncle Sam a widely acceptable return for some of his money. To that end Alsberg held FWP pretty closely to organized journalism—not primarily creative,* not social comment

---

* This hardly means that Alsberg was indifferent to the importance of creative writing (God help the phrase, but there is none better). On the quiet he allowed ten writers in the New York City project to work at home whenever they liked on condition of reporting in once a week with evidence of something accomplished—a basis much the same as that afforded many painters by FAP. Some so favored were already established: Maxwell Bodenheim, Harry Kemp, Claude McKay; some, like Richard Wright, unmistakably promising (Mangione, *The Dream and the Deal,* 245). Apropos of Alsberg's then unfashionable lukewarmness to Party-liners, note that at the time he was nevertheless giving special breaks to at least four known Communists if you add in his appointment of Orrick Johns to head the New

but legwork, compilation, research and pull-it-all-together to produce detailed description of all parts and many aspects of America done informal-guidebook style. Then, though of admittedly Socialist background, Alsberg had spent much time in relief work in the early USSR, knew Communism from the underside better than culture tourists like Mrs. Flanagan possibly could and did not share her reflex cordiality toward Party-lining hopefuls. So, no matter how close the Party-liners came to taking over certain important FWP branches, Alsberg retained enough control at the top editorial level to keep the copy that went to the printer fairly clear of the sort of radical gospel shouting that *Cradle* and the Living Newspapers represented.

How management as hit-or-miss as Alsberg's ever got so much to the printer is a puzzle, the more so because his human material assayed highest in inexperience and lowest in professional character of any of Federal One's projects. Mangione described it as "largely ... workers with little or no writing experience ... almost any person on relief who could write English might be eligible." [38] A headquarters questionnaire sent to FWP supervisors in 1938 (thirty-five replies) showed that of 1,700-odd FWP employees on writing, reporting or research, only 83 had had a book published by a bona fide firm, 399 had managed to get paid for something printed in a newspaper or magazine, but 139 had to be classed as "beginning writers with promise" [never a word published], and 213 wouldn't answer even that assumption. On the newspaper side some 400 had held some sort of copy-connected job for at least a year; 159 mentioned "a little" newspaper work, but the usefulness of many such was impaired by heavy drinking. FDR and his wife asked Alsberg to find a FWP berth for a cultivated, hard-up family friend, explaining that their candidate had "a drinking problem" that made responsibility inadvisable. Alsberg replied: "... if we made it a rule not to hire writers given to drink, we probably would not have a Writers' Project." [39]

This huge admixture of (to put it politely) subprofessionals was partly his own doing. In an early memorandum he invited applications from "young college men and women who want to write, probably can write, but lack the opportunity." [40] This is a nonprofit version of the familiar advertisement headline HOW DO YOU KNOW YOU CAN'T WRITE? and nonsense in any case, since any youngster who can scrounge pencils, paper and occasional access to a typewriter can

---

York City project. A fair-minded man. The reader should, however, also be referred to Harold Rosenberg's review of *Dream (New Yorker,* January 20, 1973)—a view of FWP that takes as flaws much of what seem to me virtues, written by a man who was one of the project's writers and somewhat involved in its internal politics.

"write" if his urge to do so is strong enough. In they poured by hundreds, seldom scrupling to represent themselves as destitute enough to qualify for relief—prerequisite for any WPA job. Bitterly the Authors' Guild protested against this necessity for faking—or admitting—pauper status, and also what George Creel of the Authors' League, parent of the guild, called "the stupid arrangement by which each state has been given a certain amount of money regardless of whether [it] has writers or not ... writers are largely grouped in various centers ... in New York the quota is utterly inadequate to take care of the professional writers ... desperately in need of work." [41] That is, if funds were to be used as intended—to get eating money to the needy—Arkansas had to field as many writers-on-relief as Connecticut. They weren't there. Hence cases like those in North Dakota where a twenty-year-old girl ambiguously self-qualified as a "news writer" managed a staff of sixty, including nobody who could be called a writer but some "barely literate" and "some bright young kids who could not find jobs elsewhere." [42] In most such cases, however, learning-by-doing eventually got local data flowing into a growingly competent writing-editorial staff; their copy went to headquarters in Washington, where it was plowed through and sent back for revision ... *da capo, da capo* ... at long last a respectably useful and informative state guide emerged, maybe also some pamphlet monographs on particular towns or areas or aspects of the state's culture or history.

The administrative excuse for the FWP's disproportionate number of enrolled Communists and fellow travelers was good as far as it went: Seeking to keep WPA from becoming a Democratic political tool, Republicans in Congress had stipulated that no effort be made to ascertain any applicant's political views. This not only was pointless—most WPA employees were at least bright enough to credit FDR's party with that godsend paycheck—but cleared the way for any Party-liner, young or getting on, hungry or just looking for an unexacting livelihood to enable him to concentrate on Party concerns. The result was that in San Francisco 10 percent plus of FWP employees were openly acknowledged Communists leading whole cadres of Party-liners. Boston was much the same way. In New York City the post of FWP director went to Orrick Johns, a conspicuous, one-legged, drunken, womanizing Communist writer who had persuaded Alsberg that his background in Red labor organizing on the Coast would enable him better to keep the FWP's thronging comrade writers under control. Maybe he could have curbed his many fellow Stalinists on the payroll, but the minority of Trotskyites proved so turbulent that Johns had to go. Things remained very open indeed. FWP's Party-liners presented a birthday copy of a book of Earl Browder's to an elderly comrade colleague; gratefully he asked them all to autograph it for him and collected on its title page and endpapers more than 100 signatures to such telltale sentiments as "Revolutionary greetings! ... Yours for a Soviet America! ...." There was Red-faced explaining to do when the old gentleman turned his book over to HUAC. In Boston Conrad Aiken wrote for the Massachusetts guide a section on "Literature" emphasizing Yankee individualism instead of the orthodox Marxist view of literature as class weapon. His Party-lining colleagues protested so formidably that the state FWP director, no Marxist either, had to print next to it an antidotal, Party-lining piece on "Literary Groups and Movements."

The other excuse for big-city FWP becoming a Party meal-ticket was wider and probably sounder. In the intellectual climate of the time, the heyday of Popular Front-Spanish Civil War feeling, any program employing a representative sample of either recognized or aspirant writers would assay high in Party-lining. Mangione gives pertinent vignettes: In 1934 the Party-lining pickets of the Writers' Union demanded relief for writers from the CWA with placards: CHILDREN NEED BOOKS/WRITERS NEED BREAD. Among them was scholar-translator Samuel Putnam, fresh home from Montparnasse, who said he turned Communist because of his young son: "When he grows up, I want his respect. I don't want him asking why I was never a Communist." [43] FWP reliefers flocked to the raise-funds-for-Spain parties given by affluent sympathizers in Upper East Side penthouses and Greenwich Village brownstones. The guest of honor would be a writer refugee from Germany or Spain or a clutch of conscientiously restless youngsters just enlisted in the Abraham Lincoln Brigade ... no, Tom Wolfe did not invent Radical-Chic; he did wittily name it. To the attractions of idealism, much drink and luxurious free lunch was added the opportunity to draw wisdom from established writer guests—Granville Hicks, Odets, Cowley. ...

From the point of view of the indigent writer, the Party-liners' relation to FWP, once it was set up, was damagingly paradoxical. What with Alsberg's half-exasperated, half-permissive policies and the pressures applied by the Writers' Union, the League of American Writers and the Workers' Alliance, Uncle Sam actually was subsidizing the rank and file of the Party's literary wing. Enough Party-liners had supervisory jobs practically to guarantee that any college graduate at loose ends and newly converted to Stalinist Marxism could be got onto the relief rolls and then the FWP payroll in a matter of weeks. In San Francisco Party-lining administrators gave the faithful the afternoon or day off whenever Party affairs summoned them. The pay, usually

$21.66 a week, was enough to live on healthily from 1935 to 1939 particularly when He and She, separately enrolled as deservingly creative paupers, shacked up together, with enough left over for frequent small contributions to Spain and Party dues for the elect.

In view of these great advantages, one would have expected the Party to cherish its golden goose. It is understandable that the dominant Stalinists could not keep the Trotskyites from the intestine intrigues, backbitings and occasional fistfights in the office that made FWP look bad. But the Party was unwise in risking cutoffs or reductions of FWP funds by flaunting its usurped powers under Congress' nose. Yet it even stirred up its satellite unions to strike in protest against lowered appropriations, set up picket lines, stage sitdowns taking over the FWP offices, hold top administrators hostage. FTP and FAP saw some of this; FWP the most.

Such strikes are now so familiar that the underlying lunacy* no longer troubles the public mind. Students' strikes, relief recipients' strikes—when the only thing accomplished by downing tools in the lecture hall or the FWP office was to save the university wear and tear on the lecture hall and the government a day's pay for all concerned. In the usual terms of economic conflict in which the theory and practice of strikes were born, that is. Down in the next layer of class conflict, however, the Party's purpose, maybe only instinctive, can be glimpsed. True, Federal One was valuable as meal ticket for the comrades and consequently bait for recruits. But Alsberg's watchfulness at high levels was thwarting another purpose—to turn out exacerbating propaganda in print at Uncle Sam's expense. Worse, this ongoing program of eating money for needy writers Party-lining or not, was inconsistent with the Party's picture of Uncle Sam as crypto-Fascist, pseudodemocratic, hypocritical and incurably sordid. It looked civilized, even generous. The Party could not afford to let anybody think thus of capitalism. And its tacticians knew as well by instinct as by training that there is nothing like a strike, particularly when women are mixed with policemen using nightsticks, to get the adrenaline pumping and the class hatred rising to bursting point.

When Federal One was on trial for its life before HUAC in 1939, Alsberg, succeeding Mrs. Flanagan on the stand, was a propitious, low-keyed contrast to her bristling swordplay. He made it unag-

---

* Recall the old story of the village dimwit-ne'er-do-well to whom the kindly town fathers gave a bare living wage to do nothing but keep the cannon on the village green nicely polished. One day he came home and told his wife he had quit the job. "What will we do now?" she asked. "Oh, we'll do fine," he said. "We've saved up enough to buy a cannon and go in business for ourselves."

gressively clear that though he liked radical ideas, he had small use for
Communists and their unscrupulous works. Freely he granted that in
some instances high-level vigilance had failed to keep unnecessarily
corrosive bits out of FWP copy, but his very doing so illuminated how
well careful fumigation had worked on the whole. Candidly he
described Party-lining ructions in New York City and then the steps
taken to clear that mess up. To the vast annoyance of the faithful, who
wanted martyrs and clear challenges to the committee, its chairman
complimented Alsberg on his frankness and helpfulness. An even
more effective part of his defense was a shelved library truck loaded
with the impressive number of FWP's solid publications, including
many of the extremely well-received state guides. And economy-
minded legislators were struck by the eagerness with which some of
the nation's ranking commercial publishers had agreed to market those
guides—a tribute to their quality that saved Uncle $1,000,000-odd in
printing costs.

So when WPA abolished Federal One later in the year, FWP fared
better than FTP. Whereas the Federal Theatre was summarily
knocked in the head, with Mrs. Flanagan returning to Vassar trailing
not ill-deserved glory,* the Writers' Projects with unfinished business
were turned over to appropriate states to manage with minor federal
help. In 1941 publication of the last of the forty-eight state guides
(Oklahoma) brought a burst of recognition of the lasting importance
of FWP's work. Ralph Thompson had set the keynote in a resounding
piece in the New York *Times* in 1938: ". . . when we of this generation
are all dust and ashes, the American Guide series will be still very
much in evidence. And . . . in use; our children will be thankful for it,
and their children and their children's children . . . one of the most
valuable series of books ever issued in the United States." [44] FWP's
special-topic items also included several admirable contributions to
Americana: *These Are Our Lives,* edited by W. T. Couch of the
University of North Carolina, interviews with Southerners of assorted
social strata that Charles Beard called "More powerful than anything I
have read in fiction"; [45] *Gumbo Ya-Ya,* piloted by Lyle Saxon and
Robert Taillant deep into Creole folklore and Deep South black
culture; and under the guidance of expert B. A. Botkin other
adventures into folklore, resulting in *A Treasury of American Folklore*
(1944), *New England Folklore* (1947), *Southern Folklore* (1949). Acquaintance with such scalps at FWP's belt makes one sulkily grudge
the many other valuable contributions it might have made had so

---

* Vassar's present campus theater is named the Hallie Flanagan Davis
Powerhouse Theatre. "Powerhouse" because the building used to house the
campus power plant—but what a case of *ben trovato!*

much of its nervous energy not had to be wasted keeping the Party liners from completely taking over.

Some deplored the label "Federal Art Project" on the logical ground that it misleadingly implied that only graphic and plastic artists produced art, whereas in general usage writers, dancers, actors, instrumentalists, singers, composers had long been "artists" and the results of their activities could be lumped as "art" in a highly flattering sense. Few paid heed to such carping, least of all the painters, sculptors *et al.* for whom Federal One's paychecks represented the first approach to economic health they had ever known in their professional lives. But in its several phases, FAP included, Federal Art did show distinctive features: It was first to get substantially airborne and left behind a more extensive body of daily visible end product than any of its sister projects. "Extensive" is doubly the word, for much of that residue consisted of 2,500-odd murals decorating public places very high and very wide, though by no means always handsome. By Pearl Harbor time one could hardly buy a postage stamp or visit a federal office without encountering in lobby or stairway a well-meaning example of Federal Art, and although many such have now vanished through normal attrition or official neglect followed by painting over, many still survive.

And many are obviously offspring of the mural-mindedness that the early 1930s owed to those impressive Mexican artists discussed earlier. Biddle, as warm a candidate as any for the title of Godfather of Federal Art, was then fresh from discipular hobnobbing with Rivera, Orozco, Siqueiros *y Cia.* in Mexico City and himself breaking in as muralist with huge canvas pseudomurals for the Agricultural Building at the Century of Progress. The hullabaloo about the Mexicans at Pomona, Detroit, Dartmouth and Radio City was still filling the air, and the consequent associations between mural painting and radical content were, though adventitious, persuasive with him and many artists of his time. In stirring up FDR about the Depression as opportunity for government-subsidized art, Biddle said later, he consciously wished to see young American painters Depression-moved to "face life and realize [the artist's] social and political power" and create "the picture of democratic justice and spiritual beauty." [46] A recent critic writes patronizingly of "those remote days when it was still felt that political comment could give art relevance." [47] That has it by the wrong end. Harold Rosenberg did better a little later: "Left-wing theorists [were educating] artists to see themselves as the cultural representatives of the masses ... endowed thereby with ... a say as to how governmental institutions, and even privately endowed ones, should be run." [48] The attractiveness lay in the prospect that the artist, theretofore a sort of tolerated, amenity-creating stepchild, could become personally a force, the Pied Piper of social justice.

To put into practice this Marxist view of art as sociological weapon, Biddle, encouraged by "Dear Franklin," got a sponsoring panel of like-minded artists (Henry Varnum Poor, Maurice Sterne, Boardman Robinson, Thomas Hart Benton [who later withdrew], Reginald Marsh, John Steuart Curry) to draw up and get into the right hands in Washington a manifesto, "A Revival of Mural Painting," that bade government turn loose on "public wall space ... social-minded creative artists of the first rank ... to express the social ideals of the government and people [with] as complete freedom as possible." It also gave government leave to "assign mural subjects and veto any expression of opinion which it considers embarrassing" [49]—the right that some of these same artists had vehemently denied when the Rockefellers exercised it on the Rivera mural they paid for. Nor was it made clear how painters—nice fellows often, good craftsmen, at their best culturally invaluable—were qualified any more than first violinists or county agents to express the people's social ideals.

The scheme jelled into a Public Works Art Program through which the procurement arm of the US Treasury commissioned established artists to decorate the blank interiors of federal and other public buildings. In new buildings they were paid 1 percent of construction costs. Among artists thus obliging were Reginald Marsh, painting the history of New York City in the rotunda of the US Customs House; Poor doing economics allegories in the stairwells of the US Treasury Building; Biddle ornamenting the Department of Justice Building— each working as an individual. Elsewhere projects went to groups of local artists of promise, A doing this panel, B the next and so on, often with greater consistency than might have been expected.

Some of that was consistency of tone—of the dreary woodenness with which assignment to paint a picture on a wall too often afflicts painters. They seem to find it as hard to eschew platitudinously symbolic objects and persons as for commencement speakers not to share the wisdom of their ripe experience with those charming young people out front. Whether the content of a given mural is Edwin Abbey's love of a fictitious medieval chivalry or Orozco's of an idyllic pre-Columbian Mexico, the blahness is the same. To this PWAP murals tended to add a special common quality—the clichés of method and composition that the Mexicans had fetched in and that, even though one had never been in Mexico City or Detroit, were readily come at in elaborate photographs widely reproduced in art magazines and books. The Mexican influence could be so strong that in face and build PWAP painters' Midwestern farmers and Yankee seamen actually looked like Rivera's oppressed peons. The same imitativeness—this also held good of much that the later FAP turned out—grouped human figures in clumps like bunches of flowers and painted them as if they were waxworks partly melted down. The occasional landscape backgrounds were puffily semiabstract. One's inexplicable and probably unworthy first-glimpse impression was that this had been done for an amusement park and, no matter how grim or momentous the social message with which the artist was in labor, carried its own built-in banality.

What minor San Francisco artists painted inside the Coit Tower was fairly representative: shipping in the Bay; industrial workers; unemployed miners and a placer dredge; power lines and oil wells; a dairy very modern as to the staff's white coats, very archaic as to their milking by hand; a slaughterhouse, hogs to hams; a hulking farmer by a disk harrow, a cowhand with a lariat; net fishing, a surveyor and a reservoir dam—and in a corner a small panel with a hammer and sickle and another: "Workers of the World, Unite!" The clothes on all these figures are loopily wrinkled as if soaking wet; all are posed precariously but with a stiff permanence as if sired by the Tin Woodman. Or take the mural in the post office at Winnemucca, Nevada, showing a bunch of whiteface steers apparently carved by an old-time maker of ships' figureheads wrangled by cowhands with blank faces and shirts and pants of pastel-colored plastic. It's no worse than the mural about Old John Brown in the post office at Torrington, Connecticut.*

Ben Shahn, one of the soundest artists ever to draw a federal paycheck, looked back over Federal Art ten years ago and found it at least culturally valuable because it "begot an enlightened public art for today ... [and] the first widespread indigenous art movement that the country has known. ... Government ... accepted all attitudes in art, all schools ... provided an un-judged, un-censored fellowship to hundreds of artists. ... " He also liked its having left "a heritage of depression symbolism exceeding that of any other phase of our existence. ... The once emptied Utrillo-inspired street ... was now wont to contain an eviction scene ... the breadline, the unemployed.

* All this emphasis on subject matter and representation may and maybe should annoy readers preferring to take paintings, as they should, as aesthetic entities regardless of the stylistic traditions, spheres of reference and ostensible ideas that they employ. The chief concerns of this book, however, are with such superficial qualities as inter- and intracultural data. Anyway, were I to go into the aesthetic merits of the Federal Art I have seen, I would do too much complaining about the hardships of having to look at so many flabby paintings in order to acquaint myself with what their perpetrators thought they were doing.

... Dust storms, western migrations ... the burning of western wheat found their way into art as middle-class prosperity had never done. Labor gained a ... place of eminence in art." Yet he also honestly admitted, "In quality, the average, through sheer weight of numbers, had to be low." [50] Biddle, too, conceded that PWAP "rarely [got its commissioned artists' best work]" and that FAP, the successor, "rarely expects to obtain great art" [51]—meaning, I suppose "expected rarely to get it," which was just as well. And Francis V. O'Connor, today's expert on these matters, says " ... it must be admitted that American mural art [in the 1930s] never reached a peak of human and artistic intensity comparable to that of the Mexican creations which inspired it." [52]

As chief of FAP, which afforded relief for 4,000-odd artists as supplement rival to PWAP, Holger Cahill almost welcomed the lack of brilliance encountered. What he sought, he said, was "not the solitary genius"—a romantic obsession of Victorian times—but a sound general movement, "art as a vital functional part of any cultural scheme. Art is not a matter of rare occasional masterpieces ... [but] a great reservoir ... created in many forms, both major and minor." [53] Biddle's explanation was: " ... if one creates a cultural background, art will follow." [54] Accordingly FAP encouraged individual easel painting pretty much go-as-you-please so long as evidence of work was presented. Many of the 50,000-odd paintings resulting were hung in federal offices; on retirement or dismissal the incumbent often took home with him that genuine oil painting of the old icehouse at Pawaddagummick or of Omaha's Hooverville, and nobody ever missed it. Others went to schools, hospitals, libraries. Many of the more creditable examples of what one did with brushes and pigments were organized into exhibits taken into art-starved communities that, it was hoped, and sometimes justifiably, would value what they had been missing. *Fortune* called it a "most arresting and disturbing" discovery of FAP's "that art teachers in American schools ... had very frequently never themselves seen an original painting in their lives." [55] As partial remedy for such aesthetic malnutrition FAP gradually set up 600-odd local art centers in settlement houses, schools, churches to expose susceptible persons to cultivated visual values. FAP artists played an indispensable part in Dr. Lauretta Bender's early experiment at New York City's Bellevue Hospital with using picture making as key to the emotional disturbances of children and then adults. And Cahill's favorite scheme, handsomely carried out, was an Index of American Design, done by artists sent out to track down and photograph or draw the irreplaceable artifacts of America's past and rapidly changing present.

Otherwise FAP more or less paralleled FWP. The developing talents that it fed at a time when they needed it included Jackson Pollock, Willem de Kooning, Jack Levine. It, too, was plagued by a fellow-traveling Artists' Union and a Party-lining Artists' Congress that dutifully put on sit-in strikes, picket lines and so forth in hopes of turning FAP into a Party meal ticket. Rosenberg recalls, "Although [said congress] pretended to speak for America's professional artists, it was a political unit in a network of homogeneous [Red] fronts ... it collapsed after the attack on Finland by the Soviet Union as an ally of Nazi Germany." Its other *raison d'être,* he went on, was the Depression-fostered idea of art's being "a trade, whose practitioners were out of work" on the same basis as stereotypers or die casters. This fitted, of course, with "the Leninist conception of the artist as cultural worker." [56] So organized artists *c.* 1936 duly bedeviled FAP supervisors who tried to keep raw radicalism out of the end product, held mass meetings to cheer the CIO, endorse the Farmer-Labor Party (then high in Communist good graces) and Party-lining US Representative Vito Marcantonio. Some federal-paid muralists even secured an AFL charter in the Brotherhood of Painters, Paperhangers and Decorators.

The Federal Music Project could not be expected altogether to escape those ordeals. When retrenchment of funds forced discharge of some thousands of Federal One beneficiaries, the organized protests from them and allies included musicians staging a fairly serious hunger strike in New York City, a sitdown in the concert hall that FMP used on West Fifty-ninth Street, and a concert given at the Lincoln Memorial by 100 musicians wearing their pink slips as badges. On the whole, however, neither FAP's Cahill nor FMP's Sokoloff had such hot potatoes to handle as fell to Mrs. Flanagan's rather heedless lot or Alsberg's more canny one. Certainly one must credit Cahill's arm of Federal One with probably doing as much as MOMA to acquaint George F. Babbitt's nieces and nephews with dimensions of art transcending those of the famous Leyendecker covers on the *Saturday Evening Post.* Even if most of the supra-Leyendecker ideas thus spread were cant, not all were, and some could be stimulating to potential talent. Add that FAP's exhibits and centers also certainly had something to do with the proliferation of Sunday painters that, much to the benefit of their own souls and the profits of art-supply stores, began in the 1930s and flourishes today. If that be the underlying "great reservoir of art" that Cahill had in mind, make the most of it.

In one way FAP fell short of FTP and FWP. It failed to give black talent much forward nudge, whereas the able research-and-writing of FTP's Florida and District of Columbia black units, plus the leg up afforded Ellison, Wright, Motley *et al.* considerably furthered acceptance of the black writer. And those all-black productions of established pieces written for whites to some extent shook the tradition that the black actor's scope was limited to specifically black roles in black backgrounds as in *The Emperor Jones* and *Porgy.* The 1930s needed that hint, for the decade had begun with *The Green Pastures*—a vastly and in some ways disastrously successful example of black actors, making the most of white customers' enjoyment of seeing the black world staged as a cross-cultural romp.

For two generations black spirituals and the blacks, notably the Hall-Johnson Choir, Paul Robeson, Roland Hayes, who sang them in whites' concert halls had suggested certain black potentialities. In musical shows like *Shuffle Along* genuine blacks had done some of the white theater's things better than most professional whites could. The catalytic effect of West African artifacts on avant-garde Western art (they had little to do with American blacks, but such matters confuse easily) was impressing cultivated whites. At best, however, the whole attitude enhanced by *The Green Pastures* was that of the culture tourist extolling the primitive spontaneity of black chorines and the primitive grief expressed in "Deep River." At worst it expanded the unhealthy old values of the minstrel's show's artificial blacks and the synthetic ones of *Amos & Andy.* What *The Green Pastures* did was to take the unpleasant old comic situation of the black only half getting the hang of white ways and make it insidiously charming.

Looking back on this show is instructive about how the black's position in America has changed in fifty years. The parentage of *The Green Pastures* was lily-white. In 1928 Roark Bradford, newspaperman from Tennessee, published *Ol' Man Adam an' His Chillun,* a sheaf of engaging retellings, as if by a Deep South grandson of Uncle Remus, of the Bible stories: Adam and Eve, Noah, Miz Potiphar, Ole King Pharaoh the magic buff.... The spelling skillfully indicated the slurrings and vowel shifts of Deep South black speech; de Lawd says, "Ain't nobody kin cut my chillun's heads off an' not yar from me." That device was expected then, in nonblack contexts too. Milt Gross' *Nize Baby* similarly retold nursery tales as of New York City's Jewish enclaves, and nobody minded, whereas recent writings about blacks, Jews, Italo-Americans and so on rely gingerly and not always successfully on mere rhythm and word order to give ethnic body to dialogue. Yet—this may be news to those remembering *The Green Pastures* on stage or screen—the biblical characters of whom Bradford's richly faithful black idiom told in terms of cotton, mules and crossroads churches are all Southern whites and shown as such in the ink-sketch illustrations. Balaam is an overalled, cowlicked, fair-haired cracker; Noah, a brass-buttoned white steamboat captain; "de Lawd," a frock-coated, black-brimmed, Big House planter. The only black is "Nigger Deemus," the segregated, fifth-wheel Disciple who gets only cold corn bread when the others, the white Disciples, feast on fried chicken and ham.

The bitterness of that corn bread is only one reason why the New York *Times'* Brooks Atkinson should not have called Bradford's book "hardly more than sophisticated travesty." [57] It has many small ironies as well as cross-cultural burlesque. It sold fairly well, but glory began when Rollin Kirby, famous political cartoonist of the New York *World,* recommended it to Marc Connelly, a remarkable Broadway playwright and member of the Algonquin Round Table group of mutually admiring wits. His great inspiration—all wrong one now sees, but masterly showmanship in 1929—was to transform Bradford's cast of Old Testament whites as blacks would conceive them into a black Adam,* a black Noah, a black Moses, even black angels and a black "de Lawd."

This bore no relation to the sporadic efforts of black militants to preach a black God, sell Bibles with pictures of a black Jesus and persuade blacks to buy black dolls for their children. Instead, it was Connelly's expert way of exploiting the tradition that blacks were typically, sometimes wistfully, sometimes outlandishly entertaining. The tone was set in the delightful early bit when de Lawd, on a walking tour of inspection of the world He has created, comes on a clump of cute-as-a-bug's-ear little blacks got up as flowers. "How you flowers makin' out?" He asks, and gets a piping little answer in chorus: "We OK, Lawd!" Richard Harrison, the elderly black elocutionist who played that role serenely and superbly straight, "passing miracles" in dignified confidence, was himself a histrionic miracle, yet Paul T. Nolan, a recent student of Connelly, rightly says that "in spite of the fact that the Lawd was played by a Negro actor, his character is based in part on ... the 'Good White Man' [the paternalistic Bourbon plantation owner] good to his niggers," [58] white by definition. It was a significant touch that the Canadian-born Harrison, descendant of pre-Civil War runaways, contained so many white genes that he had to wear brown makeup to look dark enough for the part.

The first ensemble scene was a masterpiece from Robert Edmond Jones—a glistening heaven as background for a black folks' fish fry all folksy-chuckly with de Lawd graciously mingling with his subject angels and a golden-winged Gabriel frustrated because he is not allowed to blow his horn just once—exactly what, the charmed

---

* Fifty years ago the likelihood that *Homo sapiens* originated in Africa had not yet been impressively stated. There is no reason to guess that Connelly's black Adam was thus suggested.

audiences told themselves, the lyrically simple blacks (only they said "Negroes" back then as the right word among persons of goodwill) would dream up for the supernal hosts of heaven enjoying themselves. Pharaoh's throne room travestied the meeting hall of the black benevolent-society-lodge tradition hung with the banners of the "Sublime Order of the Princes of the House of Pharaoh" and the "Mystic Brothers of the Egyptian Home Guard Ladies Auxiliary No. 1." Countervailing seriousness came from interpolations of the superb spiritual singing of the Hall-Johnson Choir. Gradually Connelly worked in the traditional parallel between the Jews' troubles in Egypt and the blacks' in Dixie * and then took wing into a faintly Gnostic view of the New Testament's God of Mercy with an offstage Crucifixion as climax. But it was the first two-thirds of the show, before Connelly diluted it with pretentiousness, that made *The Green Pastures* what Atkinson considered "a masterpiece . . . compassionate comedy without precedent." [59] In the then still flippant *New Yorker* Robert Benchley wrote: "I cried because it was so good." [60]

And so it was, wonderful theater, glowingly memorable, deserving its two-year run on Broadway, coast-to-coast triumphs on the road and many European productions—the Swedes did it in terms of the peasantry of Dalecarlia, which seems to be Sweden's Ozarks. Only Britain was deprived of it; somebody in the lord chamberlain's office ruled it blasphemous to field any actor, black or white, in the role of God. So London's stage never heard what Broun valued as "almost the finest single line in modern drama" [61]—Gabriel's sonorous "Make way for de Lawd God Jehovah!" as de Lawd's entrance cue at the fish fry. Yet some who already knew Bradford's book had reason to wonder, on thinking it over a few days, whether $3 bills might not be the appropriate admission fee. That came of turning whites into blacks.† When it was revived in 1951, it did not do well, and there were mutters from thoughtful blacks about its perpetuating "outmoded stereotypes." [62] By 1963 Howard Taubman thought he had good reason to write that whereas he had thought it "total enchantment" in 1930, he now found it "uncontrovertibly and offensively condescending." [63] Meanwhile, that black *Macbeth*, however hoked up with anomalous juju, and the black actor playing Mephistopheles in the FTP-Orson Welles *Faustus* had infected the public mind, however

---

* Taken to *The Green Pastures* not long after seeing Al Jolson in *The Jazz Singer,* the small daughter of a distinguished Jewish judge said that she didn't know whether it was queerer to see a Jew playing a black or blacks playing Jews.

† In fairness to Connelly, there is no reason to believe that Bradford objected to this change, and he was certainly aware of it almost from the beginning of Connelly's work on the adaptation.

equivocally, with the possibility that there might be black actors who didn't need material specifically written at their blackness. That was improvement of a sort in a field where any at all was rare and welcome.

Why any improvement in the situation of American blacks was so notable is readily illustrated. In that same year in the great New York Hospital, then down on West Sixteenth Street, doctors, secretaries, laboratory workers, all assistants, ate lunch in the same dining room— except for one highly qualified research technician. He had his meal with the elevator operators and sweeper-outers because his skin, like theirs, was black. The Furness-Withy shipping line was then advertising "Red Headed Picaninnies" as one of the picturesque tourist attractions of the West Indian island of Montserrat. * The *Ladies' Home Journal* unhesitatingly printed the White House housekeeper's description of the incumbent doorman as "the biggest, blackest and most amiable darky in Washington." [64] The failure of Marcus Garvey's misguided effort to organize blacks for self-respect and economic independence, extravagantly covered in the nation's press, had unfortunately deepened Americans' previous poor opinion of blacks' stability and common sense. Daily *Amos & Andy* contributed to the same end for millions of Americans who had never heard of Garvey because they read only the sport pages and the comic strips— the sport pages that as yet admitted blacks to the headlines only in track and field and boxing, the comics occasionally depicting blacks as comically subhuman and nothing more. Then came further damage from the whites' taking Father Divine as primarily funny, whereas though Father himself might be so, the insecurity, hunger and ignorance that sent blacks flocking to him were not. As late as 1939 the Daughters of the American Revolution refused to let the great black singer Marian Anderson give a concert in their auditorium, appropriately called Constitution Hall, in Washington. In an admirable gesture Mrs. Roosevelt, whose patrician family tree was of the sort the DAR most valued, made front-page headlines by resigning from the organization and arranging for the singer to do her concert on the steps of—happy thought!—the Lincoln Memorial. But the high-chinned Daughters stuck to their guns maybe as much because of bred-in-the-bone racism as of their already-savage reprehension of That Man's conspicuously subversive wife.

---

* This genetic anomaly said to persist among the blacks of Montserrat is traditionally ascribed to the large number of Irish exiles colonized there in the late 1600s. Several sources mention it. I saw no redheads there in 1938. Maybe by then the strain, being recessive, had pinched out.

Yet some good was faintly stirring in Nazareth. A Gallup Poll reported 67 percent of Americans approving of Mrs. Roosevelt's action. Even 45 percent of Southerners did so, and many disapproving said it was "making a fuss about it," not the notion of a black singing on DAR premises, that disturbed them. Since 1900 the annual rate of lynching had dropped about 80 percent, and although the ratio of blacks to whites thus socially murdered was rising, even in the South the annual toll of blacks was getting steadily lower. This significant decrease survived the sinister strains of Depression, which heightened job jealousy.

It was also encouraging that in 1932 the Century of Progress thought it advisable to proclaim Jim Crow barred from the grounds—a policy probably owing to the weight swung by Chicago's black vote but, for all that, hygienic in tendency.* Local black organizations could make much of the curious but actually rather meaningless fact that the first non-Indian settler on the site of Chicago was a stray black from the French West Indies, Jean Baptiste Point du Sable; there was a reconstruction of what his log cabin was probably like. But, as Nigger Deemus would have warned, this official order was too good to be altogether true. Blacks paying admission were welcome. At the Ford exhibit of assembling Model As, a black mechanic represented Ford's policy of giving blacks a square shake. But a duly scheduled "Negro Day" was fouled up by local black politicians' rivalries, and there was good reason to deplore as "patronizing" the "Old Plantation" concession and the "Darkest Africa" show that carried on the old world's fair tradition by exhibiting genuine West Africans dancing, singing and drumming in airy allegedly native costumes. And in spite of the Urban League's exhibit of what it was doing to get blacks into the economic mainstream—all true as far as it went—Chicago's blacks found that, barring a few security and clerical jobs, all the Century of Progress offered them as employment in those hard times was shoeshining and acting as attendants in washrooms and model homes.

Frictions heated up when the financial success of 1933 persuaded management to revive ACOP for spring, 1934. Though local relief rolls were top-heavy with last-hired-and-first-fired blacks, the consequent refurbishing and repainting jobs went largely to whites. But there was still time for the NAACP to work on the Illinois legislature about the Pabst Brewing Company's refusal to serve blacks at its food-and-drink concessions, with local authorities looking the other way. The legisla-

* This discussion owes much to August Meier and Elliott H. Radwick, "Negro Protest at the Chicago World's Fair, 1933–1934," *Journal of the Illinois State Historical Society,* Summer, 1966.

tive act keeping ACOP in business another year carried an NAACP-inspired rider with teeth enough to justify the Chicago *Defender,* largest of the city's black newspapers, in telling its public the bars were down, go to the fair and eat anywhere you can afford to. With only slight difficulties that advice proved up. That made the ACOP grounds just about the only community in the United States where that equality of footing for blacks substantially existed. From the black point of view that put a little meaning in a Century of *Progress.*

That an improvement so small should have been gratifying! Such social abuse of blacks had, of course, long since struck the Communists as suiting their tactics of exploiting weak spots in bourgeois society. From that not only Federal One and the Bonus Army but also the labor movement would suffer greatly in the 1930s. Claude McKay, Jamaica-born black writer who did his zealous duty as Party member until his intellectual honesty got the better of him, described the purpose as "radically to exploit the Negro's grievances. Therefore [Communists] use their influence to destroy any movement which might make for any practical amelioration of the Negro's problems." [65] This was deliberate, not such incidental spoiling as was manifested in the Scottsboro case. It was clever, but maybe there was a contrary influence in the stars, for by and large it usually went sour among American blacks. In the Black State agitation of the late 1920s, for instance, the Party proclaimed the blacks' right to "national self-determination" and demanded "an independent Negro state and government in the South" [66] in the Black Belt, where black population was then concentrated. Doubtless this sounded good in the Kremlin, which was then encouraging separate ethnic states of the USSR with built-in straitjackets, as democratic-looking window dressing. But it attracted few American blacks. They knew American realities and possibilities better than the Kremlin did. Communist doings following instructions from overseas often thus suffered from *a priori* dogmatism. All that came of the Black State was supply of a propaganda plank for the new-forming Black Muslims who, though they never let the Party gain a foothold among them, saw no reason not to appropriate any ready-made delusion appealing to their deviant psyches.

Then there was the scheme to take to Moscow enough black American sympathizers to act in a movie about the horrors of black life in America written by a German comrade and produced in the USSR by Russian comrades. In such hands it would probably have been memorably absurd, and it is almost a pity that it was never shot. But among them its sponsors fumbled the project to pieces, and those American blacks who got home again brought along considerable disillusion with the workers' paradise. That fiasco attracted small attention. The same was true of James L. Ford, the black orator and fairly able party hack whom the Party ran for Vice President in 1932. But in the Depression decade it did manage to find one ace—and played it very well, too, thanks to the man's dogged sincerity—in the towering person of Paul Robeson. He made up for many miscues. After World War II he denied under oath that he had ever been a Party member. It may well have been true. But, as with other top-ranking fellow travelers, his subservience to Party ends kept him as useful as if he had carried a card.

As a boy his father had run away from slavery and become a well-considered minister of a black church in Princeton, then of one in Somerville, New Jersey. Son Paul, one of two blacks in the local high school, made high grades, played all games and went to nearby Rutgers College on a scholarship. Tall, rangy, powerfully quick of mind and movement, he twice made All-American; Walter Camp, arbiter of All-American football, called him "the greatest defensive end that ever trod a gridiron." [67] His color often got him special roughing up, but he was just as rugged in spirit as in body. He also starred in baseball, track and basketball at a time when even in the North blacks were extremely rare on varsity squads. He made Phi Beta Kappa. He led the college debating team; his magnificent bass-baritone voice and soberly alert good looks were as effective as his alert brain. With summer jobs in resort hotels and oddments in winter he worked his way through Columbia Law School and acquired contacts in Harlem's black show business and the fringe where it overlapped with white show people.

His wife, a stimulating comrade for him, persuaded him to dabble in the theater. He played a black slave chief in a lurid, pretentious thing called *Taboo* that drew the attention of Mrs. Patrick Campbell. Under the title of *Voodoo* she took it and Robeson to London. Robeson's interpolated song in it was supplemented by more and more spirituals and black work songs until it became more of a concert than a play. This was the baptism of fire for the singing voice that became one of the great entertainment phenomena of its time. Robeson's training had not gone much beyond joining in hymns in his father's church. But he seemed to know just what to do with the instrument back of his Adam's apple to make it sound like the last trump scored for angels. When he sang "Deep River" and "Water Boy," there never was any better singing of anything anywhere, not because these were black songs and he was black but because his integrity matched his superb physical and vocal endowment.

Returning to New York City, he acquired more stage experience as the long-suffering black married to the neurotic white girl in O'Neill's

All God's Chillun Got Wings and then launched on a notable career of concerts interspersed with acting. His impresario was Lawrence Brown, an able black musician who knew absolute talent when he saw it. Extensively in America, even more extensively in Britain, they took spirituals and work songs up and down the land with brilliant success. Understandably liking the relative lack of racial discrimination in Britain, Robeson centered his life there. London afforded him a great success as the terror-ridden black dictator in *The Emperor Jones,* as the black roustabout singing "Ole Man River" in *Show-Boat,* but even there he could not get real release from the specialness of being black. His greatest role in London was ... Othello. The roles British movie makers gave him were also black, of course—the West African hero chief of *Sanders of the River;* in *Song of Freedom* a black London longshoreman who, after great success singing, learns that one of his ancestors was king of an African island and goes there with much misbegotten palaver about "the call of the African heritage." His only American movie, made by independents, was an ill-advised expansion of *The Emperor Jones.* When Moscow invited him in 1934, it was to play Toussaint l'Ouverture in a Soviet version of John Vandercook's *Black Majesty* planned by Eisenstein.

It was never shot. But this visit to the USSR made him a permanent, eager, consistent Party-liner. In Britain he had come to know the keen iconoclasts among Labour's leftists whose analyses of class and caste were unsettling. In Nazi Germany on the way to Moscow he encountered menacing hostility. In the USSR he was wide open, ready to take at face value what the Russians probably poured over him—that the USSR's cordiality toward him showed that pure respect for great artists was part of the People's Revolution; that Western racism was only class repression masked as color prejudice and one of the stirrups that kept capitalism in the saddle. It is so easy to understand the emotional magnetism that such talk exerted on a black man of great talent and stature who had been rubbed raw by discrimination.

For the rest of his days Robeson was the Party's loyal tool. He sang at Party-lining front meetings and benefits wherever found. He sang for the Loyalists in Spain and at the great welcome-home when the survivors of the British elements in the International Brigades came back. When Stalin and Hitler went to bed together in 1939, his stomach was strong enough to take him through any amount of singing and speaking at the Party's "peace"—meaning isolationist— rallies in America. Then, when Hitler attacked the USSR and opposing Nazis was again orthodox, he assiduously trouped his native land in bond-selling rallies and USO shows. The year after Pearl

Harbor he joined Patterson to found the Party-front Abraham Lincoln School in Chicago as magnet for black proselytes. In 1948 he was a founder of the Progressive Party that, under Communist influence, ran Henry Wallace for President. And when the Cold War was well under way, he told a Party-lining audience in Paris that it was "unthinkable that American Negroes will go to war on behalf of those who have oppressed us for generations against a country [the USSR] which in one generation has raised our people to the full dignity of mankind." [68]

If that meant anything, it meant that Robeson was encouraging his fellow American blacks to refuse to fight Russians if the Cold War turned hot. The vindictive consequences that naturally enveloped him are beyond the scope of this book. But note here that none of them made him falter. He stubbornly remained the pellucidly sincere believer ready to be exploited as a formidably impressive front man. One would like to be able to kick the Party's pilots who thus took advantage of his vulnerability. Never were integrity and the will to believe more unscrupulously abused. The wonder, however, is not that so worthy a man should have been so flimflammed as that myriads of other blacks were not thus recruited. For on the whole they proved insusceptible. One must postulate an immense fund of common sense among American blacks. Therein they contrast sharply with the many American intellectuals—again a deplorably loose word but there is no better—who, under far less emotional pressure, went Party-lining.

OZYMANDIAS IN WASHINGTON

I HOLD THAT MAN IS IN THE RIGHT WHO IS MOST CLOSELY IN
LEAGUE WITH THE FUTURE.
—HENRIK IBSEN TO GEORG BRANDES

FDR's famous Hundred Days, beginning early in March, 1933, set
in motion several real or apparent innovations meant to turn the
despondent and ailing nation around and head it toward convales-
cence. Those therapeutic measures were ill or well conceived depending on who was talking then and later on the concrete results. As
general practitioners are aware, however, even more than psychiatrists,
the magic ingredient without which remedies often fail is the bedside
manner. In FDR's practice it was the fireside manner. Its empirical
function is to persuade the patient that he may actually get well and
that clever persons are doing impressive things to that end. But
meanwhile, half-inadvertently the new regime had smoothed its own
way by another bedside ploy supplementing the major approach—
focusing the patient's attention on his most easily corrected symptom
and convincing him, by showing improvement there, that a positive
trend is forming, that, in the words of the song the Democrats
borrowed from Tin Pan Alley for the campaign of 1932, "Happy Days
Are Here Again!" For that purpose the New Deal found the
impending rescission of federal Prohibition very handy. About the first
thing the new Congress did was to amend the still-effective Volstead
Act to legalize beer of 3.2 percent alcoholic content as earnest of
sweeping change in prospect. To keep the medical metaphor going, it
was as though a new doctor had put the sufferer on enough whiskey

per diem to prevent his thinking he was *in extremis* while the internal medicine department sought out ways to treat the ailments that were actually wearing him down.

Understandably, probably correctly, the nation credited FDR and the New Deal with that overdue and stimulating—in a small way economically, a large way biochemically—correction of a great error in social judgment. Yet to a considerable extent it was merely a matter of slightly speeding up change in moral climate. Only five years earlier Americans had still been so far from grasping their lesson that Alfred E. Smith's frank enmity for Prohibition probably had as much as his religion to do with his defeat in the presidential election. Late in 1931 Clarence Darrow, the great, cynical defender of liberal attitudes and foe of copybook morality, was staunchly repeating what he had been saying for years, that even though "Many, many of those who gave their voices and votes [for Prohibition] which has brought chaos and disillusion to the land have now changed their minds ... there is no hope for the repeal of the 18th amendment." [1] Two years later the old man could, and probably did, buy legal booze in any large city his eventful practice took him to.

The Depression probably had much to do with the shift of public opinion against the experiment-noble-in-purpose that by New Year's Day, 1933, had made Repeal just as thinkable as it had been unthinkable in Coolidge's time. Since 1918, true, an Association Against the Prohibition Amendment founded by William H. Slayton, Baltimore shipping man and former US Navy officer, who was high in the Navy League and knew powerful people, had been sniping away. Andrew Sinclair, well-grounded British student of America, calls its methods no more scrupulous than the old Anti-Saloon League's, which is harsh but doubtless justifiable. Year after year that and other such agitations looked more futile. But at first obscurely, then more openly, the accumulating disasters of Prohibition were stirring up many of the same stratum as those industrialists and merchants who had so effectively supported the Drys' breakthrough a generation earlier. Some of the Du Ponts, for instance, and eventually with them, writing checks and speaking out loud, Edward S. Harkness, Nicholas F. Brady, Arthur Curtiss James, among moneymen of note; the presidents of the Metropolitan Life Insurance Company, Western Union, the Pennsylvania Railroad, R. H. Macy & Company; Charles H. Sabin of the Guaranty Trust Company. As a portent all in himself, John D. Rockefeller, Jr., consistent subsidizer of the Drys, came out for Repeal in 1932. It was the most popular move such magnates could have made at a time when their prestige was so low. There also appeared the Crusaders, a sort of Jaycee skirmishers, young men pledged to vote for any candidate, however grubby otherwise, who chose to profess and act on candidly Wet sentiments—turning the old Anti-Saloon League's tactics against Prohibition.

The most cogent portent, however, probably was an editorial in the *Ladies' Home Journal,* which up to then had been utterly and outspokenly Dry,* saying late in 1932 that "bootlegging must be eliminated even if Prohibition has to be repealed." [2] That underwrote in the name of middle-income housewives a revolution on the distaff side that had begun in May, 1929,† months before the Great Crash, when Sabin's wife, flouting the wide belief that Prohibition was impregnable, had set up a Women's Organization for National Prohibition Reform. She began with 17 members; fifty-four months later she had about 1,500,000. This reddish-haired and charmingly able lady, born with a silver saltspoon in her mouth—her father was Morton's ("When It Rains It Pours") salt—was deep in Washington and Manhattan society and also in Republican politics. In her wildfire agitation both contexts were important. Here for the first time women, made free of public life by the Nineteenth Amendment in 1920, really did pull the weight they had been promising.

Maybe it had something to do with Prohibition and the speakeasy's having made them free of the barstool. Certainly in 1929 it was not the shocking anomaly it would have been in Mrs. Sabin's girlhood that her kind of affluent, capable, usually decorous women should go to bat for the Demon Rum. Shades not so much of old Carry Nation as of Frances Willard and Jane Addams! When Repeal came, William Allan Neilson, president of Smith College, felt obliged to remind his girls of the crude attitudes toward drinking that Prohibition had fostered and challenge them to show that they could be trusted with the stuff and that it could add to the beauty of life. *C.* 1910 it would

---

* The magazine's position in mid-1929 had smacked of despair but not of surrender. It was then scolding "apparently self respecting men and women [who] ... have been making millionaires out of gangsters. ... The prohibition tangle will never be solved by putting the bootleggers in jail ... [but] when the customers stop buying. Happily an influential portion of our population is beginning to recognize that fact. Social leaders are sending out word to their dinner guests: 'If you must have a cocktail, get it before you come; we are not serving liquor any more.' " (July, 1929.)

† Not that this was the first effort to enlist women for the Demon Rum. In 1920 the young AAPA sponsored a Molly Pitcher Club to fight Dryness in New York State. In 1926 another such effort took the candid name of Women's Committee for the Repeal of the Eighteenth Amendment. It made little stir, though it did survive to throw a party at New York City's Ritz-Carlton to celebrate Repeal. (New York *Times,* December 12; December 18, 1933.)

have been thought no more unfitting for him to advise them how to comb their whiskers, and such talk would have brought parents flocking to get their daughters out of so corrupting an environment.

At their peak, coast to coast, Mrs. Sabin's forces consisted of 25 percent housewives; 40 percent women in the professions and business, clerical help included; 20 percent in industrial jobs. Their best motto was: "We Are the Temperance Party Now!," for it was newly fashionable to assume—on no assignable grounds, just with winsome hope—that once the drinker had legal booze again, he would handle it better this time. They invaded local radio programs, lectured before women's clubs—Mrs. Sabin was heard in thirty-one states in a single year—organized luncheons for the press to report, set up propaganda booths at county fairs, in short used the WCTU's own tactics against it. Among their motives may well have been 1920s-ish impatience with the WCTU's notion of womanly attitudes. They could and did, said *Vanity Fair,* give the lie to the WCTU's claim to "represent the women of America. ... It merely represents ... the more parochial, hysterical and self-righteous element. The Sabines ... represent as many women ... a cultured, charming and temperate body of women, who do not propose to let the country be ruined or their children debauched in the name of American womanhood." They also reflected the widespread dread of organized crime and distaste for the hip flask and the tipsy prom trotter. But basically, like their counterparts on the Dry side in the 1870s, they showed a redoubtable pride in being able, once they made up their minds, to show men how to do it. Particularly as lobbyists in Washington they wrought havoc with women's special weapons, using social blandishments and sex appeal as WCTU types never could have done. "Young, pretty and intelligent women are not so numerous in political society ... the drys have nothing to offer as a counter attraction. ... No one would care to sit next to a member of the W.C.T.U. at dinner or to cultivate the Anti-Saloon League for social graces.... Senate and Congress permit themselves to be captured ... by [this] ruthless and bewitching group who have done more in two years to make Repeal possible than the men of America have done in a decade." [3]

At the same time their speeches and printed materials went into the economic points suited to Depression-racked times to give Repeal extra forensic strength. To legalize liquor, they and other Wets insisted, would widen the farmer's market for the cereals needed for beer and whiskey; create hundreds of thousands of jobs in newly licit breweries, distilleries and ancillary fields like glass, transport and sales; restore to federal and other treasuries the hundreds of millions in excise taxes that Prohibition had cut off; save government the huge expense of futile efforts at enforcement. Some of that carried more than met the eye. At least some moneymen promoting Repeal probably hoped that restoring liquor excise would lower the bite on high-bracket income taxes. And labor's growing support of Repeal, though hardly forgetful of unemployment, also came of resentment over the boss' being able to drink as much as ever at home or in a relatively expensive speakeasy while disappearance of really cheap beer and the corner saloon tended to force the workingman into unwilling abstinence. In any case, sound as some of these debater's points were, they may have been mere forensic masks for a generalized impatience with what was now so clearly seen to have been an emotional mistake.

In 1931 the federal-sponsored Wickersham Commission, nominally studying law enforcement in general but concentrating on Prohibition, released a voluminous report that, no matter how its members and the White House tried to draw its sting, left no further doubt in reasonable minds that Prohibition was a farcical imposition. As its implications sank in, actuality began to confirm Corey Ford's statement a few months earlier that a revulsion from Prohibition had so spread that anybody still supporting it was thought self-condemned as "a fool or a fanatic ... or if he is not an honest imbecile, then he is swayed by ulterior motives of political expediency or greed." [4] It was noted that the Congress of 1930 (the House now Democratic by a very narrow margin, the Senate still precariously Republican) spent far more time on Prohibition and what if anything to do about it than on the Depression and what to do about that. The Dry cause even fared badly at the Republican convention in mid-1932. It tried to hedge in deference to President Hoover's stubborn commitment to the Drys' sinking ship but nevertheless promised a Repeal amendment to give the nation an opportunity for reconsideration—a concession of vast significance. The Democrats' convention abandoned wonted gingerliness about the Dry-minded South and plumped outright for Repeal. That made the reinstatement of John Barleycorn apparently highest on the party's priorities, a handy vote catcher in many constituencies. Their presidential candidate's stand was noticeably less firm, which, in view of the difference between a national and a state-level candidacy, Daniel Boorstin called "a shrewd reluctance" [5] on FDR's part.

Both parties piously stipulated safeguards against "the return of the saloon"—its disrepute had been a principal cause of the victory of Prohibition in the first place. If that meant anything at all, it meant binding Uncle Sam to outlaw selling by the drink. The prevailing weariness with federal enforcement made that about as likely as revival of the federal fugitive slave laws. Nothing of the sort was done.

After the election of 1932 politicians were so eager to be associated with Repeal that they couldn't wait for the new administration to act. It was not the new Congress but the lame ducks of the election of 1930 who passed and sent to the Senate the new Amendment (Twenty-first) canceling the Eighteenth and saying nothing, implicit or explicit, about the saloon. The New York State Assembly ratified it with a roaring ovation for Mrs. Sabin as, chin up and triumphant, she tripped winsomely down the aisle. The vote was 150–0.

Formal Repeal was not complete until Utah's convention ratified on December 5, 1933, waiting until then to make sure of being the magic thirty-sixth to do so. But the obvious Wetness of the state convention delegates elected in November made the result foregone. Curiously, however, the only community to jump the gun on the situation was New Orleans, where the speakeasies took down their window shades to bloom openly forth and the press was full of pictures of barkeeps pouring Sazeracs. Elsewhere John Barleycorn's rise from the dead waited dutifully until word of Utah's action came over the wires—and failed to set off any huge wingding. The party might have been rowdier had it occurred during the Great Bull Market. In late 1933 dollars were scarce and the mere privilege of buying a legal drink in one's own country—a novelty for all under the age of thirty-four— apparently sufficed for most. Along Broadway, where, if anywhere, things would be happening, a few enterprising hotels gagged up their regular supper dances—at the Park Central, for instance, a black-garbed figure of Prohibition walked a plank into the swimming pool. But the apathetic crowd in Times Square disappointed the news photographers. Their exhortations—"Look happy! Show some enthusiasm!"—were largely fruitless. What seemed most to impress celebrants was the unwonted potency of manhattans and martinis made with genuine liquor for a change.

The many speakeasies going legitimate continued to welcome women patrons. Thus keeping the feminine factor in the newly forming equations was salubrious in the opinion of Bernard De Voto. In speakeasies, he recalled fifteen years after Repeal, "the presence of women enforced quiet behavior and good manners. When Repeal came we had the sense to apply the lesson and a good bar today is indistinguishable from a good speakeasy of 1930." [6] That may be overstated—or the witness was extremely choosy about his speak-easies—yet doubtless to some degree women's patronage did keep many joints from reverting to the frowsiness and raffishness of the Railroad Avenue saloons that had given drinking a bad name. When disbanding her troops, Mrs. Sabin exhorted them to convert drinking into a "temperate, decent and respectable social custom" in "forty-eight states that are now in effect forty-eight laboratories wherein experiments in liquor-control will be carried out for years to come." [7] The *Ladies' Home Journal* too was urging "such measures by the various states as will actually promote temperance, effectively prevent the return of the saloon and bring the liquor traffic into the open." [8]

That was the sanguine way to regard the ensuing crazy quilt of liquor laws persisting from pre-Prohibition days or hastily passed in anticipation of Repeal or cobbled up as its effects began to be felt. Some municipalities forbade women to stand at the bar, apparently feeling that drinking is another of those things ladies should do best sitting down. Others, hoping to keep the genie fresh out of the bottle from playing as rough as he once had, forbade bars altogether. Still others required what was thought to be the emollient influence of minimum restaurant service—hence "barngrill," New York State's post-Repeal term for a gin mill. Or forbade serving drinks even in transient dining and club cars on Sunday which often caused hardship from unexpected drought among those riding the Broadway Limited to Chicago for Monday-morning appointments. All such measures aimed to promote moderation and decorum; none was notably effective but lasted because any alternatives suggested wouldn't do much better. Sweet reason has always had about as vexing a time with booze as with Sex.

Among dubious ingenuities certain states revived the discredited old device of state monopoly of retail package liquor, with its tendency toward corrupt ties with distributors and narrow range of brands and kinds stocked and its great risk of being impossible to get rid of because it means jobs for too many deserving nephews. With that often went a ban, borrowed from certain Canadian provinces, on sale-by-the-drink—hence much bottle tilting in hotel bedrooms and proliferation of nominally private "locker clubs" that came close to reproducing the presumably defunct speakeasy. A few states, Virginia included, allowed only beer and wine in public. What would the ghost of William Byrd II have said had he come back and his favorite Williamsburg tavern, all spruced up again by the Rockefellers, refused him a bowl of rum punch? A few others, Mississippi most stubbornly, retained full state Prohibition while doing little to stanch the flow of bottled goods impeccably legal just over the state line and duly carrying federal revenue stamps.* True, the Twenty-first Amendment had made importation into Dry areas illegal. But nobody even tried to prod Uncle Sam into enforcing it. The only noticeable effect was that

* Just to keep things straight: Mississippi some years ago threw in the sponge, and Virginia now allows hard liquor by the drink under certain circumstances.

since imported fifths and pints paid no state tax in Dry Mississippi, good whiskey cost less there for a while than anywhere else in the country.

Adjustment to legal open bars with ample stocks of genuine Old Younameit had some grotesque results. The first evening of Repeal, one heard, rookie barmen, instructed that those huge inhalers were the proper thing to serve brandy in, filled them to the brim with cognac and charged only the listed price for an ounce. Inexperienced restaurateurs laying in good wines let them stand upright in warm rooms and spoiled them. The spring of 1934 brought a self-conscious wave of drinks alfresco at sidewalk tables—ah, the dear Café de la Paix!—but over the years little has come of that pleasant promise. In the South the post-Repeal loss of jobs by the hard-bitten youngsters who had run the moonshine down out of the hills in high-powered touring cars led them to found and develop the new grass-roots sport of stock-car racing. Even more morbid were the effects of Repeal on the martini cocktail.

That came of inexperienced persons' misinterpretation of the term "dry" as applied to alcoholic beverages. The story is tortuous but must be clarified here and now. Wherever the martini was born—Old San Francisco's claim looks better than most—it began as two parts gin, one part *sweet* vermouth (drop of orange bitters or bit of orange peel optional), probably an iced stepping up of Britain's traditional "gin-and-It." A very good preprandial item, too—call it Martini No. 1. Then somebody tried dry vermouth in the same proportion and secured a flavor even less banal than that of No. 1—so call this version Martini No. 2. It deserved and gained immense popularity. In between was the "Perfect" cocktail—two parts gin, one-half part dry vermouth, one-half part sweet, also quite palatable, try it some time. Logically enough No. 2 became known as the dry martini because it contained dry instead of sweet vermouth. With Repeal the return of properly flavored materials revived particularly the dry martini, by divine right king of cocktails, whereas No. 1 and the Perfect languished neglected in old bartenders' guides. At the same time gabby novices, hoping to sound knowing about wines, were spreading the impression that the quality of dryness is essential to all acceptable table wines, hence the term became firmly associated with prestige and connoisseurship. Dry martinis being smart, obviously drier martinis would be smarter. * And somebody

* I know no satisfactory accounting for the name "martini" for this cocktail. So far in the text my chief authority is the late George Rector, son of the founder of Rector's, Broadway's outstanding lobster palace *c.* 1900, who was in a position to gather authentic lore from his father's bartenders. Albert Stevens Crockett, *The Old Waldorf-Astoria Bar Book,* 59, more or less confirms

somewhere—these disastrous errors can seldom be pinpointed—reaching for a stronger kick in his martini, which is no goose milk even in the original proportions, made it 3-1, using as excuse that thus it was "drier." Didn't it say "dry gin" on the label?

Actually this change had the reverse effect. Dry gins were then and still are perceptibly sweeter than dry vermouth. Hence the more gin, the less dry the cocktail, but also the stronger the kick, which is, no doubt, why Madison Avenue pursued this heightening, if ever more fallacious, dryness in martinis. It went to 4-1, 5-1, where the needle stuck awhile, then on up to 6-1, 8-1. A passage in Elliott Roosevelt's book about his parents details the process by which FDR's offspring successively talked him into gradually shifting his formula from the original 2-1: "My gosh, father.... Everybody makes them five-to-one nowadays ... "[9] and so on to the 7-1 mark. Eventually jokes about just letting the shadow of the vermouth bottle fall on the stirrer became no joke at all, and practically straight gin with a dash of ice water became the expense-account American's aperitif of choice. There are worse drinks. But gin and water sound so inelegant that few of its devotees can admit what happened. Of late, however, advertisers have been sneaking toward a new candor in recommending "the Italian martini" (gin on the rocks with two drops of anisette), "the naked martini" (gin on the rocks), and a striking piece of name-confusing sleight of hand: "Discover the English gin so temptingly dry and crisp, many consider it by itself the perfect Martini."[10] Shades of Sairey Gamp!

So Repeal greatly damaged the martini, which, as boon to mankind, outranks such other American contributions as the Colt's revolver and the airplane. That was more than made up for by Repeal's enabling native wines to crawl out from under the crudenesses that Prohibition had entailed. Leon D. Adams' authoritative *The Wines of America* (1973) attributes their good quality today to this accidental opportunity to "[start] anew. The American wine industry reborn ... in 1933, chose the scientific approach.... Rejecting the traditions, cobwebbed cellars and primitive methods that hinder wine progress in much of Europe, it

---

Rector, though it gives a lower proportion of gin in No. 1 and reduces Rector's "Perfect" to one-third gin, one-third dry vermouth, one-third sweet, with lemon peel as a permitted variant on orange peel. For other corroboration see, for instance, the advertisement of El-Bart gin in *Life,* April 11, 1915, and this stipulation from a passenger instructing a barman in a transatlantic liner in Sinclair Lewis' *Dodsworth,* set early in the 1920s: " ... half Booth gin and half French vermouth ... no Italian vermouth, remember, no Italian vermouth." (p. 48.)

utilized the new research in viticulture and enology ... [and] removed the guesswork from wine-making." [11]

His point is undeniable. Yet by most accounts California's best red table wines and New York State's champagnes could look Europe not too diffidently in the eye even before Prohibition. Back then, true, the viticulture of both areas relied too coarsely on imitation ports and sherries with high alcoholic contents and low prices that made them the wino's delight; that also plagued them for years after Repeal, for the high-yield-per-acre grapes used in such "fortified" * wines are not suitable for table wines of subtler appeal and lower alcoholic content. Yet seventy years ago there had been an encouraging trend toward planting the kind of grape needed for table wines—interrupted when Prohibition swung the whole industry downhill. For under the Volstead Act, which permitted generous amounts of wine making for one's own consumption, vineyardists learned to coin money with high-yield, thick-skin grapes that shipped well fresh or worked up into the "wine bricks" and juice sold as concentrates or in kegs that the ferment-in-small-lots buyer wanted. The law assumed he was an Italian or Hungarian supplying his family what they had always had. Much oftener, of course, he was supplying "red ink" to speakeasy restaurants. With so wide a market it was little wonder that vineyards of high quality were often torn up for replanting with high-yield varieties, and feverish expansion led to trouble, as infiltrating gangsters lowered the quality of management. Repeal enabled distillers to go ahead into an eager market. Brewers, though also often gangster-plagued, had immediate optimum markets and ample raw materials available. But in 1933, when the new day dawned, good American wine was years behind where it had left off twenty years earlier and the discerning wine drinker was a rare bird indeed in the new potential wine market.

At first hopes that Repeal would eventuate in a growingly wine-minded public buying rewarding American vintages were dim. Amer-

---

* California wine makers today deplore the term "fortified" because it seems to imply that the kick of such wines is their chief virtue. Actually it means merely that small doses of brandy or other distilled liquor are added to sherry, port, Madeira and so on as preservative and flavor emphasizer both in their ancestor countries (Spain, Portugal, Madeira) and wherever they are imitated. So far, though American sherries, mostly from New York State and California, are at best cheerful aperitifs, I know of none of quality altogether matching the originals—as nowadays American table wines do. In my experience American ports are deplorable. American brandies are at best potable but better suited for highballs than for the postprandial sipping that makes good cognac and Armagnac so rewarding. At that, however, the same could be said of Spanish, Portuguese and German brandies.

ican viticulture seemed even more than ever committed to the wino's cheap jag. Yet a few signs lightened the gloom. Throughout Prohibition the University of California had kept up a cadre of oenologists who could now encourage planting of quality grapes and supply trained young winemakers (counterparts of brewmasters) to handle them. Certain veteran pre-Prohibition winemakers were still available, and particularly in California I, source of some excellent American wines before Prohibition, some old-timers remembered the great stuff that had once come from the Napa, Sonoma and Livermore countries and warmly supported the university's work. In New York State, too, vine-improvement operations got back into action. Whatever resulted had to come slowly. New-planted vineyards take four or five years to come into rewarding bearing. What sound wines came from the few quality vines surviving were mostly soaked up by knowledgeable local people, and the rest of America knew little of them. And meanwhile, the attention of Americans hoping to learn wine wisdom was captured by European imports. The American industry contributed to this by keeping up the widespread pre-Prohibition mistake of borrowing for its products the names of Europe's famous wine regions—California "burgundy," New York State "sauternes." A potential customer who had learned to like good genuine burgundy trying a coarse California red pretending to resemble it might decide never again to waste time or money on American wines.

Years passed; the new plantings came into bearing; the young winemakers gained experience. By 1939 a substantial body of sound drinking existed. The nation at large learned of this through a canny and expertly but not snobbishly wine-minded American, the late Frank M. Schoonmaker. After earning a name as writer on eating and drinking, he became a trustworthy wine importer. For novice buyers, and knowing ones, too, "A Frank Schoonmaker Selection" was a welcome guide. Now he began choosing from California, New York State and Ohio under that aegis and, to make sure his choices stood on their own merits, got the vineyardists to *drop those customary imitative names.* He revived a once-sporadic, always-commendable practice of using, instead of the derivative "burgundy," the name of the variety of grape used—among the reds Cabernet, Zinfandel, Pinot Noir; among whites Chardonnay, Gray Riesling. They sounded exotically fascinating, and when inquisitive buyers with palates unclogged by snobbery tried them, they came back for more.

Such "varietal" labeling spread and is now customary for a given house's superior wines in both California and New York State. In fact, a good rough rule in buying American wines is: If it carries a French regional name, look in the next bin for a varietal that, though probably rather higher priced, will be worth it. By now so many

Americans guide themselves by these native varietals that some French exporters, going against all French practice, ship us their Bordeaux labeled "Cabernet" to appeal to American eyes. There, ladies and gentlemen, is a switch. The validity of varietal labeling is heightened when one learns that though genetically the grape going into this California Pinot Noir is the same as that in this red burgundy, the first cannot and need not have precisely the same drinking qualities. It may be better or worse; but in California that grape has become a biochemical entity in its own right, its wine is usually sound, if properly handled, and in the best examples, allowed properly to age, can be idiosyncratically remarkable. Of late years price snobbery—for once a constructive thing—has appeared, with some California Cabernet Sauvignons fetching $140 to $150 a case, some whites over $100. That removes the last barrier from acceptance among certain kinds of buyer.

Maybe rising quality and quantity would eventually have got American wines their hearing anyway. But without Schoonmaker it would have taken longer. The positive trickle he set going slowed after Pearl Harbor, of course, but picked up lively after V-J Day partly, many winemen believe, because of the many returning servicemen who had learned in the European Theater that wine with a meal was a great pleasure. In every ensuing year America's consumption of its own wines has risen, so has production and—a specially welcome sign—in 1968 our consumption of table wines finally exceeded that of fortifieds. There—as in so many fields since 1900 and this time most constructively—California has shown the nation the way. It not only drinks more wine per capita than any other state, but also knows more about what it is drinking, so drinks more table wine per capita than any other. It slightly startles the Easterner—not the Californian—when, if he orders a half bottle of Chenin Blanc with his lunch in an utterly unpretentious California roadside eatery, the waitress brings it chilled down to just the right point and pours him out that ritual half ounce and waits for his approval.

Both one's olfactories and statistics draw a distinct line between California (or say the West Coast, for Oregon and Washington are getting promisingly into the act) as wine country and the rest of the nation. The reason is doubtless partly soil but mostly climate.*

---

* This is apart from what one used to hear: that California winemakers did not date vintages because the climate was so consistently perfect for vines that one year's pressing varied very little from last year's and so on. As vintage dating grows commoner out there, one hears less of that rationalization. A good thing, too, for the date at least enables the buyer to gauge how long the reds have been aged—and they used to sell many of them too young to be at their best. With whites the issue is, of course, not so pressing.

California's wine vineyards have always been dominated by the European wine grape, *Vitis vinifera,* brought in numerous varieties by Spaniards first, then French, Swiss, Hungarian, German and eventually Italian immigrants with vineyard skills. *Vinifera* vines are very difficult—and correspondingly costly—to grow in America except on the Pacific slope. The important wine industry of New York State and its minor competitors in Ohio, Michigan, Missouri *et al.* rely chiefly on domesticated varieties of the extravagantly vigorous, wild native American 'grape, particularly *Vitis labrusca,* that the Indians found here thousands of years ago but did little with.

Labrusca thrives in the rigorous climate of even the Finger Lakes and southern Ontario wine areas, where *vinifera* can survive only if expensively coddled. The most familiar version of *labrusca* is the blue Concord grape sold for table use and producing the bottled grape juice of commerce and the sweet Jewish sacramental wines. Generations of earnest gene juggling have created almost as many varieties of *labrusca* as Europe derived from *vinifera,* but all to some extent carry the species' crucial trait—virtue or vice, depending on taste—a pungent flavor overtone that those who like it call "grapy" and those who don't "foxy." To the excellent sparkling white wines that New York State calls champagne it lends a little tang that most open-minded drinkers enjoy. Those reared to it really miss it in *vinifera* wines. Many California retailers stock several distinctly foxy Finger Lakes wines for New Yorkers migrated westward who still think wine should taste like that. My own view of it has been softened by analogy with the Greek retsina (slightly dosed with resin) wines that startle non-Greeks but can be got used to and are most lovingly embedded in Greek culture. I once suggested that to a man who knows much about wine. He approved and said he had found retsinas went best with native Greek dishes, so why not try a moderately foxy Niagara or Moore's Diamond with wild turkey or lye hominy? That is a chance the Indians missed. A generation ago Philip Wagner, a great man in American oenology, wrote that *labrusca*-tinged wines are "not only capable of, but cannot avoid, standing on their unique qualities ... every wine lover who is also a patriot must find profound satisfaction in the knowledge that we have certain wines whose unique and charming qualities cannot be duplicated else where." [12] The best of them, given this inbred eccentricity, are superb examples of sound winemaking, at which New York State's best wineries are acknowledged masters.

For complicated reasons involving vine diseases French oenologists began generations ago trying to marry the inbred resistances of North American grapes with the subtle biochemistries of the *vinifera* strain. Attempts thus to borrow the sturdiness of *labrusca* were baffled by the refusal of its foxiness to be bred out. They turned to species native to

Appalachia and Texas that, patiently juggled, led into promising foxiness-free hybrids. In spite of heavy prejudice against them in the strongly traditionalist French wine industry, it now makes inconspicuous but substantial use of them. The point here, however, is that among the American traits that they retained was ability to flourish about like *labrusca* varieties in the eastern United States. They were available when Repeal turned America's wine potential loose. So, happily, were the patience and feel for wine of Philip Wagner, who has, more than anybody else, made it a strong likelihood that through these French hybrids Americans may acquire a third major regional wine tradition.

Wagner was then a rising newspaperman—later managing editor of the Baltimore *Sun*—and one of the thousands whom Prohibition had set developing amateur skills in legal, after-hours winemaking. He had been getting encouragingly palatable results with grapes bought from surviving high-quality California vineyards that were available if one looked hard for them and paid a little more. He was sorely troubled when with Repeal California began at once to keep all such grapes for its own reviving wineries, which shut off his supply. Incurably wine-minded, he knew of the French hybrids and fetched some over to try in Maryland. They did well, and he handled their grapes solicitously. Various whites, reds, experiments with rosés; this one sounds promising, let's send for it too. . . . While his newspaper career matured, and so did his wife's as a psychiatric social worker, they were developing on the side a small vineyard and winery in the country northwest of Baltimore.

Few hobbies burgeoned more gratifyingly. Wagner's retirement a few years ago gave him none of the usual problems about what to do with all that empty time. His Boordy Vineyard in Riderwood, Maryland, is now nucleus of a French-hybrid-based wine operation with branches in Washington State and New York State. His Riderwood nursery sells more and more French-hybrid vines to winemakers in most states of the Union. And that is only one facet of the hybrid-creating game. In California, particularly at the University of California in Davis, hybridizing experts have long played with other genetic ingredients and come up with original varieties, some admirably palatable, that Bacchus never dreamed of. Wagner's special significance lies, of course, in the rash of small wineries that his vines encourage in the exacting climates between the Missouri River and the Eastern Seaboard. Their virtues might lead to a phasing out of *labrusca* in New York State. In any case it all means more and better wine drinking and healthy rivalries coast to coast.

* * *

It would be farfetched to represent the present American wine industry as an outward and visible sign of the New Deal's riding to the rescue forty years ago. Its association with Repeal, it has already been pointed out, was partly chronological. Repeal's time had come, and the politicians scrambling for and achieving power at that juncture got the credit for it and, to some extent, for its eventual, indirect consequences. Today's scenery and atmosphere supply plenty of other monuments to the New Deal, dead or alive, still important or fallen out of public consciousness, physical or moral, of unquestionable pertinence. Thus, one of the most eloquent memorials to its social ideals still exists in the Resettlement Administration's Greenbelt towns. Not one American in a hundred probably knows where they are; not one in five has ever heard of them. So the tone is necessarily elegiac. But it is gratifying to report that all three of them survive today with an ongoing health that is nothing like as dismal as the sight of Ozymandias' vast and trunkless legs of stone; it is only the original hopeful significance that is missing.

Resettlement was set up in 1935 as part of the "Second New Deal," the post-honeymoon, now-we-really-have-to-be-about-our-business phase that succeeded the US Supreme Court's extinguishing the flickering light of the National Recovery Administration. Its purpose was to rehabilitate impoverished farm families by good advice and production-enhancing loans or by helping them move from hopelessly lean acres to more rewarding land. The tracts thus abandoned would, it was hoped, be reforested or otherwise rescued from further abuse. The ideal project would be, say, to persuade pellagra-stricken hillbillies worse off every year in an eroding cove in the Ozarks to let themselves be reestablished in some part of the West newly irrigated by the Public Works Administration, while the Civilian Conservation Corps under supervision by the Forestry Service planted the denuded slopes with trees. Looked at one way, the Okie-Arky migration was a sort of spontaneous Resettlement demonstrating why such help was needed.

Pilot of Resettlement was Undersecretary of Agriculture Rexford G. Tugwell, a specially cogent Brain Truster who had a hand first and last in several of the New Deal's liveliest schemes. He was a renowned exponent at Columbia of the unorthodox economics taught just before World War I at the University of Pennsylvania's Wharton School of Finance by Simon Patten and Scott Nearing. In NRA days he had been closely identified with the strong food-drug-and-cosmetics "Tugwell Bill" that outraged Madison Avenue and the powerful nostrum industry and got him called many, many undeserved names ranging from "impractical professor" to "Rex the Red" and sometimes downright "Communist." That he was not, though he did show that curiously squeamish insistence on giving Party-liners better than the benefit of the doubt that characterized his intellectual stratum.

Among such people's stigmata, not invariable but of high incidence, was a fondness for the "Garden City" movement, partly because it promised to alleviate the socially warping consequences of big industrial towns, partly because its aesthetic ideals appealed to persons of constructive imagination. (Frank Lloyd Wright's Broadacre City was one of scores of tendentious variations on this theme.) The British had started it well before World War I with organically planned new settlements with up-to-date water systems, sewerage, utilities, health and educational services and so on shielded from creeping urban blights and sprawl by circumambient "green belts" of farm- and parkland dedicated in perpetuity to chlorophyll and its corollary amenities. In the New Deal personal tastes were as weighty as in any other manipulative institution. Hopkins' fascination with show business and FDR's country squire fascination with trees had marked consequences, sometimes constructive. Tugwell's "greatest interest," according to a recent student of his career, the thing "closest to his heart" was "the well developed ideology of the garden city movement." [13] It followed, if not altogether logically, that his Resettlement Administration would go adventuring after greenbelt towns. The stated purpose of thus diverting funds and energy from direct rehabilitation of needy dirt farmers was not only to benefit city dwellers resettled in greenbelt situations but also to provide neighboring farmers with local markets for produce and more stimulating cultural contacts. It is altogether fitting and proper that the archives room in the public library in Greenbelt, Maryland, is called the Tugwell Room. Note, too, that the pattern is familiar. Here was purpose-usurping again, another laying of alien eggs in unwary nests. And as sometimes happens—only don't count on it—the consequences were not at all bad.

Fragmentary uses of the Garden City idea had already appeared on Long Island in Garden City and Forest Hills and in the street plans of housing developments built during World War I in Bridgeport, Connecticut, and Camden, New Jersey. But the first two soon went middle-income white-collar, and after the Armistice the others dropped out of sight. Revival of the idea began in 1923 with the Regional Planning Association, a little group of serious thinkers in New York City who met frequently for lunch or dinner to dream up ways to keep modern conditions from smothering mankind's best interests. Sometimes they and their wives had think-tank country weekends enlivened by earnest folk singing and square dancing taught them by Benton MacKaye, founder of the Appalachian Trail and the Wilderness Society. This foray into the Virginia reel and "Careless

Love" was an early manifestation of what would prove a highly enjoyable part of the New Deal syndrome. In the persons of Frederick L. Ackerman and Stuart Chase—whose breadth of interests keeps him cropping up in this book—the RPA overlapped with the original Technocrats. The key spirits were Lewis Mumford, already deep in incisive study of the effect of technology on man; Clarence S. Stein, a planner-architect already Garden City-minded whom Mumford called "the foremost exponent in his generation of urban statesmanship,"; [14] and A. M. Bing, a Manhattan owner-administrator of real estate of considerable wealth and imagination enough to take the RPA's hopes seriously.

In 1924 Bing financed and Stein had a major hand in designing a consequence of the RPA's symposia—Sunnyside, across the East River from Manhattan on what had been underutilized railroad property. Its two- and three-grouped row houses and low apartment buildings were scaled for installment sale to lower-to-moderate-income families. City Hall forbade change in the rigid gridiron street plan laid out years earlier, so dead ends and circle-back secondary streets could not be used to reduce noise and traffic hazards. But one of the basic Garden City ideas did appear—the dwellings all faced away from the street onto wide inner courts rich in trees, shrubs and grass for common enjoyment. Kitchens, delivery doors and other utility details faced on the street.

Sunnyside sold well, not least because a sprinkling of the intellectual-minded were attracted by its idealistic tone, bought for themselves and talked the thing up among susceptible acquaintances. This encouraged Bing to try a far more comprehensive application of RPA ideas on a site giving them adequate scope. He bought a tract of farmland in New Jersey where the then-building George Washington Bridge would stimulate real estate values. On it Stein and colleagues put a model suburb, Radburn, including much of what British garden cities had learned and adding heightened safeguards against an aspect of town living that had meanwhile got out of hand—the automobile's noise, smells (with respiratory hazards for both people and plants) and danger of accidents to pets, children and grown-ups alike. Facing Radburn's dwellings inward considerably reduced such hazards to begin with. Speeds were lowered by keeping purely residential streets narrow, often dead-ended and irregularly curved. Cleverly routed footpaths and underpasses separated pedestrians from traffic-heavy streets. The inner gardens were all run together in what amounted to ribbon parks winding among the dwellings. "A town to live in—today and tomorrow," an admirer wrote as of 1929. "A town for the motor age ... turned outside in—without any backdoors ... where roads and

parks fit in together like the fingers of your right and left hands. A
town in which children need never dodge trucks on their way to
school ... newer than the garden cities and the first major innovation
in town-planning since they were built." [15]

It was all true and promising, too. Only then the Depression struck.
Bing's financial arrangements, premised on sales to a steady stream of
economically stable buyers, grew shakier daily while his installment
payments from Sunnyside slacked off amid much heartache, backbiting and hardship. As Bing's fortunes sank—it was too bad, what
happened to him for being that rare thing, a really enlightened real
estate man—Radburn had to remain only half built. Even in truncated
form, however, its virtues were so striking that it caused much
comment in the right quarters. When the New Deal-Resettlement-
Tugwell complex decided to show how to combat urban congestion
and decay, Stein's half-demonstrated principles naturally became
foundations of the scheme, and Stein and some of his colleagues from
RPA were chief consultants of the newly created Suburban Resettlement Division.

"Today," said the official statement of purpose (rather optimistically
for 1935), "the construction industry seems to be coming back to life.
There is real danger that the next wave of building may serve only to
increase the Nation's litter of badly planned—and often badly built—
houses. [Suburban Resettlement projected towns] are intended to show
... how both city workers and farmers can be provided with low
rental homes equipped with all the facilities for healthful and decent
living. For both private builders and public housing authorities these
projects may serve as invaluable examples." [16] Overall planning was
hasty but good. Large open tracts were bought not far from congested
cities at bargain prices per acre, reflecting the depressed, not to say
suicidal, state of agriculture. On each would be built a "demonstration
of suburban planning" [16] combining the best features of British garden
cities with Radburn's automobile-taming tricks and, of course, wisely
using existent woods, streams, elevations. The architecture would be
sturdily simple partly for economy, partly to allow much use of semi-
and unskilled labor in general work relief. Rents would be low enough
for poorly paid, rent-ridden city families, blue- as well as white-collar.

Once the first Greenbelt town was in being as pilot plant, others
modified to match its experience would rise in other parts of the given
tract with plenty of greenbelt room between. The outlying farmer thus
bought out would be encouraged to lease the old place back and keep
it producing, but with less emphasis on staple crops and more on
dairying and garden truck for the new market created by the new
settlement. Farms worst suited for tillage would become parks. The

farmers' families would have good town schools, churches, movies, sports fields, social doings only a mile or so away. In a healthy group symbiosis the town kids would have green fields and woods to explore, animals to learn about, summer jobs to keep them in shape and in touch with the good earth. "Rurban living" [17] was the label for it coined by J. S. Lansill and Wallace Richards, enthusiastic director and executive-in-charge of the kickoff example.

Details and spirit represented the worthiest aspects of the New Deal and its guiding personalities. Sites for four pilot towns were soon worked out. Maybe because "greenbelt" sounded so wholesome and quaint—greenbelt, greenwood, dancing on the green all in a ring-O!—that reference became the capitalized generic label, the Greenbelt Program, and in addition to Greenbelt, Maryland, there were Greenhills, north of Cincinnati, Ohio; Greenbrook, northwest of New Brunswick, New Jersey; Greendale, south of Milwaukee, Wisconsin.* The anti-New Deal press called the lot Tugwell Towns in mistrust of their chief sponsor. Greenbrook was an error in siting. Local hostility kept its elegant blueprint from translation into concrete block and cooperative shops, and only the name now survives for the neighborhood where it was to be. Choice of the Greenbelt site reflected the nearness of the developing Agricultural Research Center at Beltsville, Maryland, on which Resettlement counted for tenants and jobs. It might today have been awkward that two of the three were built on the edge of the South. But in 1935 inclusion of blacks was highly improbable. Greenbelt's being only a few miles from Virginia, Greenhills only a few from Kentucky, made it inconceivable. Greenbelt's excuse was that new federal public housing in northeastern Washington would take care of blacks' needs. So far as I can learn Greenhills never found an excuse necessary.

First and last about 9,700 men chosen from among the jobless, where possible, earned pay for swarming over the future Greenbelt's 3,300 acres, grading, clearing and damming the local swamp into a site for a lake, installing sewers, blacktopping pathways and streets in curiously curving patterns, preparing foundations for row houses and three-family apartments facing inward on garden blocks of several acres. Some of cinder block, others of frame-and-brick, their exteriors

---

* Note that though one purpose of such projects was to slough off the typical real estate promoter's values, these names sound just like commercial subdivisions with some of the same disregard for topography. Subdividers seldom thought twice about calling the flattest piece of land in the area something like Kenilworth Heights, nor did it trouble Resettlement that there was nothing like a dale on the site of Greendale. Greenhills was at least in rolling country.

were austere for economy, but fortunately by the mid-1930s the fashionableness of the International Style enabled forward lookers to find such austerity admirable. Sound use of glass brick and Resettlement-designed furniture of sturdy simplicity were modish, too. The houses' proportions were not bad. Forty years later they are good, half-masked foils for the greenery grown up round them, and over the years the basic construction has held up well. At the time, of course, they stood out bald and dreary on raw dirt in September, 1937, when the first inhabitants moved in. But they were shelter in a shelter-short time and place. More than 9,000 families applied to be among Uncle Sam's first resident guinea pigs—as tenants, not time purchasers. For Bing's sad experience at Sunnyside had contrasted eloquently with what happened in Chatham Village, a Stein-inspired garden town outside Pittsburgh that, handled strictly on a for-rent basis, rode out the Depression safely.

With only 885 dwelling units available from the first round of building, Resettlement could and did pick and choose to give Greenbelt optimum chance to succeed. In view of the purpose of social and physical betterment for lower strata among city dwellers, incomes over $2,200 (for families of six) and under $800 (for singles) were not eligible; at the time 65 percent of urban Americans with jobs earned $1,500 or less. Rents varied to match from $18 to $41 a month, around the 20-percent-of-income level that sociology said was economic. In the selection young married couples with a child or two were favored, doubtless on the principle that they would adjust more flexibly to this novel environment. To further like-mindedness, hence neighborly harmony, applicants deemed susceptible to Greenbelt-style ideas were also favored.* Another objective was a mix corresponding to the District of Columbia's payrolls—70 percent government, 30 percent nongovernment—and to its religious groupings—30 percent Catholic, 7 percent Jewish, balance Protestant, all sharing in use of the community center for religious services.

For the original purpose—to show how to rescue industrial labor trapped in decaying inner cities—these ratios robbed Greenbelt of much of its point, for most government employees were by definition salaried, career, white-collar. Nor did Resettlement try to attract to the area industries widening the blue-collar stratum, even though the Baltimore & Ohio, offering sidings for new factories, ran only a few

---

* At Greendale one of the chief family selectors was very musical and convinced that community music making would help greatly to bring about good interactions such as model towns needed. He now cheerfully admits that he did all he could to get the inside track for any applicant family including one or more members who could play a musical instrument.

hundred yards beyond the Greenbelt margin. Yet it may be unfair to dwell on that. Because the New Deal was expanding federal payrolls, the District area badly needed new roofs. What more natural than that one hand should wash the other? As the national defense program grew toward the end of the decade—and pay scales rose to match—that $2,200 upper limit threatened to deprive Greenbelt of some of its best citizens. Rather than evict them for undue prosperity, Suburban Resettlement shifted to charging rent on a basis of ability-to-pay—and there was the program's first compromise with economic fact.

As a nest of the Good Life as Stein and the New Deal envisaged it, Greenbelt worked well from the beginning. Its manager-council form of government, first such in Maryland, was a much admired success partly, no doubt, because of the handpicked quality of the citizenry. Its eclectically Progressive elementary and high schools loosened up classroom atmosphere in a fashion that influenced other schools in the county. Its traffic patterns made gratifyingly good sense, and no dwelling was more than half a mile from schools and shops. Its surrounding belt of natural green nobly fulfilled the function Stein had in mind: It "shielded from external dangers and encroachments" as in medieval towns but not with "gray fortifications," instead with green playgrounds and woods and, for a while, crop- and pasturelands. But its greatest advantage, he said, was that, being permanently public, inalienable by sale, it "definitely limits the size of the community ... only so can [its] neighborly character be sustained ... [the] common interest of all be kept alive." [18] When Greenbeltery was under heavy attack for disproportionate cost, do-goodery, puerile restrictions, "creeping Socialism" and so on, it was curious that nobody used against it the most subversive idea it entailed—the notion, completely heretical then, still rejected among many, that a community may be the better off for refusing to keep growing.

Neighborliness was built not only into the site design but also into the tenants' temperaments, much to their benefit. One of their first collective projects was a mimeographed newspaper enhancing the new community's dynamic awareness of itself. Delivered free to each household, paid for by local advertising, it was a pioneer among shopping-news giveaways. Assiduously it chronicled the Boy Scouts, Girl Scouts, American Legion marching band, music club, Little Theater, camera club, mothers' club (managing a nursery school and revolving free sitter service), rifle club, athletic club. ... "Believe it or not," the paper presently commented, "a group of some thirty Greenbelters met ... last week for a social evening and they did not elect a group of officers and did not draw up a set of by-laws." [19] Those and other deliberately democratic, constructively comradely groups all persisted until the warping effects of World War II came on. Some of them are lively today. Obviously the interviewers choosing the right people for Greenbelt did their work well. As one of the original settlers said, he (and they) hoped to become part of "a classless society ... of persons of our own income status, where worth would be measured in terms of contribution to community welfare ... in a soil dedicated to democratic citizenship. ... " [20]

The name of the paper was the Greenbelt *Cooperator*—most appropriate, for the town took special pride in Cooperation, not only in the general all-together-now sense but also as designating the organized Cooperative Movement. Imported from Britain generations earlier, Cooperation sought to bypass the profit economy wholly or in part by organizing *producers*—farmers, sometimes industrial workers—to market their own products without paying tribute to middlemen and by remunerating participating members in proportion to the output of each, and *consumers* to pool their purchasing power in collectively owned retail outlets paying periodical "dividends" to participants in proportion to the total purchases of each. Imaginative labor leaders launched unions into Cooperation with varying success; anarchists liked its affinity with their hopes for brotherly production and distribution. Among consumers in the 1920s it was strong in the upper Midwest, specially in farm supplies and gasoline, and among city people in the lower Northeast, where the Eastern States Cooperative League thus purveyed groceries, general merchandise, restaurant service to some 13,000 members of its member co-ops.

That was a tiny segment of purchasing power relative to the huge public served by the great retail chains, and even though co-ops, being nonprofit concerns, were usually let off certain taxes, the dollars-and-cents savings were seldom substantial. But the notion of banding together to blunt the claws of rapacious profit seekers recommended Cooperation to the kinds of temperaments also susceptible to Technocracy and Planning, whether of industrial production or Garden Cities—that is, our old friend the settlement house mind, here in one of its best phases. The year before ground was broken for Greenbelt, E. A. Filene, Boston's philanthropic elder statesman of retailing, put some of his large fortune, created by competitive mercantile profits, into a Consumers' Distribution Corporation to finance co-ops and advise them on management. It was the most striking example of sheer paradoxical goodwill since Joseph Fels, the rich soap manufacturer, had put much energy and money into promoting the single tax panacea for the ills that capitalism had brought on the nation.

Nothing in the Greenbelt ideas as such necessarily led to Cooperation. But the kind of people who had so eagerly buckled greenbelts around Resettlement were likely to have a soft spot for it. So had the people they had chosen to live in their model town. Many of them already knew a form of it in the federal employees' credit unions— cooperative agencies lending to individual members out of funds secured by the pooled credit of the group. Resettlement had early asked Consumers' Distribution to finance a Greenbelt Cooperative Service to install and operate in the municipal shopping center not only an adequate grocery store but also a drugstore, barbershop (no tipping), beauty shop (ditto), variety store, tobacconist's, movie theater. Also organized as co-ops were the one-doctor medical service and its miniature twelve-bed hospital; the newspaper, of course; and the nursery school and credit union. In such a climate Cooperation so flourished that, probably much to Consumers' Distribution's surprise, the original $50,000 loan was paid off in six years. Greenbelters themselves soon took their shelter from the profit-hungry jungle "more or less . . . for granted," said the town's historian, "but to hundreds of visitors . . . it remains one of [Greenbelt's] chief . . . wonderments." [19] The flag Greenbelt flew for its first Fourth of July in 1938 naturally carried the device that was Cooperation's cult totem—a silhouetted green pine tree.* Never did an anomalous egg fare better in an alien nest.

Not everything worked out so well. The health service came apart in a few years as exception to the rule of success in Cooperation. Surface pollution and then the expense of lifeguards prevented use of the lake for swimming. But it looked charming, and the fishing was good after FDR came visiting and with his own hands dumped in appropriate species for stocking, so they stopped calling it "Wallie's Folly"—it had been Richards' pet project. Mrs. Roosevelt was, it goes without saying, a frequent visitor. A Greenbelt schoolboy whom she patted on the head vowed he'd never wash that spot the rest of his life. The hoped-for symbiosis between farm and town flagged maybe partly because local farmers were painfully aware how decades of tobacco-growing had depleted the fertility of those adjacent acres. But that left the more parkland for recreation and insulation. Less healthy was the planners' neglect to do anything permanently effective about mass transportation to and from the breadwinning jobs in Beltsville or the Navy Yard or in the paper-shuffling beehives of Washington proper. The unstable bus service led to uneconomic dependence on the private

* For accuracy: This was an adaptation. The official Cooperation symbol was *twinned* pine trees. That was why, when Greenbelt needed cooperative financing for the transition between public and private ownership after World War II, the agency in charge was named the Twin Pines Savings and Loan Association.

automobile—and the gradual discovery that the planners' parking-and-garage ratio of one car per household was utterly inadequate. That still plagues Greenbelt. The place is now free, however, of the early nuisance of sightseers driving out weekends to stroll around and gape. In the first months Greenbelters were likely to look up from eating Sunday dinner and see strangers pressing their noses to the windowpane as if the community were a zoo.

Much of the blame for that lay on the press for whooping up what it took to be the presumptuous half-bakedness of Tugwell Towns. Learning that some Greenbelters disliked the inward-facing dwellings because that meant displaying the family wash on the street instead of in the privacy of the conventional backyard,* reporters giggled in print over the housewife's reluctance thus to put her panties on public view. Another parietal problem produced this sample of fun with a sting in it: "Here every prospect pleases and not even man is vile.... The more abundant life flows almost as freely as if it were turned on with a faucet. But there is a serpent in this little Eden. When the chosen householders arrived at the City of Light they found the welcome mat down for themselves but not for their pets. All quadrupeds, including elephants and donkeys, were barred. Canaries and goldfish were permitted ... not cats and dogs. Forthwith there was a grand row in Utopia. ... " 21 That unnecessary rigidity was a fact, too, and in two successive referenda the dogs and cats lost out. But there was no basis for several other allegations of hyperdiscipline. It was not true, as the press insisted, that Greenbelters couldn't play radios after 9:30 P.M. and that a dormitory-type lights out at 11 P.M. was enforced by throwing the community's main switch. The most substantial derogation thus harped on was that the $13,000,000 cost of the whole project came to an uneconomically high figure per dwelling unit. But there were answers there too: Part of that admittedly large sum came from going out of the way to employ men who would otherwise have cost more on relief. And in any case, Greenbelt's housing, thanks to the very low cost of the acreage, came to much less per room than it was costing elsewhere to buy inner-city property, clear it and build public housing from scratch.

Within a creditably short time the place had shaken down well enough to have a movie made of it for finale to *The City,* produced by Pare Lorentz (then recently famous for *The Plow That Broke the Plains* and *The River),* score by Aaron Copland, script by Lewis Mumford crying woe, woe to Metropolis, the ogress devouring human-

---

* Forty years ago, remember, the withindoors electric- or gas-heated drier was no part of the average private household's equipment.

ity. Shown at New York City's World of Tomorrow Fair in 1939, it counteracted some of the press' misrepresentations. Greenbelt worked. So did its sister towns launched a few months later. Indeed, in some respects they did rather better. At both Greenhills and Greendale the farmers-townfolks symbiosis, fostered by skilled farm managers nursing the farm-lease part of the program, proved valuable for the first decade. Both towns relaxed soon about dogs. Both made the mistake of including many elms in shade tree plantings, so both had heavy damage from Dutch elm disease. In consequence Greendale is now rather short of trees. Greenhills replanted in good time and is now so rich with well-grown red oak, maple and so on that the inhabitants—calling them Greenhillbillies is frowned on—rate their town as handsomest of the three sisters.

Greendale has as counterasset the most engaging architecture. The municipal building is merely sub-Williamsburg. But the dwellings, designed by Jacob Crane and Elbert Peets,* happily combine the austerity of painted cinder block (often with brick pier corners) and elegantly proportioned peaked gables, tall chimneys and subtle window placement. After such serene charm it jars to come upon the town flagpole in front of the schoolhouse—its drum-shaped base a WPA-FAP sculpture, a sort of three-dimensional mural of thick-waisted, big-footed, ham-handed, coarse-profiled figures, presumably symbolizing the town's ingredients—Worker with apron and sledge, Teacher with books and a small girl at her knee, Youth (female) with tennis racket.... The WPA-FAP reliefs on the Greenbelt school are a *little* better.

Community doings also flourished in Greenhills and Greendale. This was specially notable in Greendale because its first citizens were 80 per cent blue-collar, mostly from the huge Allis-Chalmers plant nearby, and had relatively little experience with neighborhood all-together-now. Sociological studies showed that in their first year at Greendale their "social affiliations" [22] increased on an average of 100 percent. The white-collar minority that had had more previous experience in comradely activities increased theirs by some 600 percent. No wonder that the monthly luncheons at which the heads of Greendale's organizations went into local problems always numbered at least thirty. And Greendale alone has exerted demonstrable influence, as Resettlement hoped these towns would, on community planning in the vicinity. The subdivisions developed on adjoining land

---

* Early in the game Frank Lloyd Wright, then in his Usonian phase, came mousing around, but his ideas called for too much land per dwelling unit.

by a consortium of more or less enlightened Milwaukee business interests are disappointing as architecture, but their street plans do show lessons learned from Greendale, indeed improve on the example.

Both Greendale and Greenhills have found that turning the greenbelt over to county government for park purposes was wise. That was a necessary consequence of Uncle Sam's selling the three towns off to semiprivate or private ownership after World War II. Greenbelt's greenbelt went down the drain awhile ago when a six-lane monster of a limited access highway cut part of the municipality adrift. Adding up the score on the whole program is not simple. Each town now includes some blacks of comfortable income level; no strains reported, which is certainly social gain. Certain original fundamentals persist: These communities are still self-respectingly well run and maintained and have fewer troubles than most suburbs with crime, practically none with traffic. Some all-togetherness survives, even though most of today's residents entered these insulated enclaves after Uncle Sam divested himself of them. The additions, some rather elaborate, that those buying the original houses have gone in for amount to a gradual upgrading—aluminum siding over the old concrete block or asbestos shingle, for instance; attached garages; in Greendale two adjacent single dwellings turned into one by bridging the gap. And in Greenbelt the original 80/20 ratio of blue–white collar has reversed to the present 75/25 white–blue.

Either situation would answer the relative homogeneity that Resettlement preferred in the beginning. By now, however, that trait, so marked in Tugwell Towns then and now, is frowned on by theorists believing that social health requires a stimulating mixture of income levels and ethnic groups. Until theory changes again—give it another fifteen years—the sister Greenbelts must view one another with sociological suspicion. Failure of a second generation of Greenbelt towns to rise on the periphery has also disappointed the founders' hopes. That came partly of diversion of Washington's attention toward the end of the 1930s, partly of the effect of Pearl Harbor, which threw the whole design of Greenbelt, for instance, out of kilter with 1,000 hastily built units of housing for defense workers.

A recent student of Greenbeltery, Joseph L. Arnold, properly regrets that it had to remain "a road not taken." [23] With better luck it could have done more to cure the rodent ulcers of city slums, wean developers from cookie-cutter subdivisions and foster Cooperation as a gadfly healthy for the profit economy. It may be a pity that Greenbelt, Greenhills and Greendale survive only as living relics of long ago. Much likably ingenuous ingenuity went into them. Stroll along

Greenbelt's lake, listen hard—that's the gurgle and plop as a grinning FDR pours in fingerlings to stock Wallie's Folly.

Mumford once expressed regret that Greenbeltery was not applied to that "great project in socialized planning," the Tennessee Valley Authority. When the TVA was born, however, the Resettlement Administration was still two years from birth, and though the TVA's model bedroom town, Norris (near Knoxville, Tennessee), included some Garden City features, there was as yet no pervasive Greenbelt gospel to infect sister plans. True, one might call the TVA itself a huge Resettlement scheme. But it had a dozen other significant aspects, all giving its midwives plenty to do without borrowing some trouble. The best introduction to TVA may be through seeing it as a masterpiece of alien egg laying.

The Tennessee River's constituent tributaries—the Little Tennessee, the Clinch, the Holston, the French Broad—are major streams in their own right. Among them they drain the heaviest rainfall accorded any watershed in the eastern United States. The Tennessee gathers it all into what Stuart Chase called "one of the lordliest and wildest rivers of this continent," [24] sluices it westward almost to the Mississippi, then northward to join the Ohio. Its raindrops fall on parts of seven states, in no case one of a given state's most prosperous sections as of 1930. The Tennessee's usefulness for water transport was impaired some 200 miles from its mouth by the Muscle Shoals, impassable except at times of very high water. In the upstream mass of tangled mountains that the tributaries drain and in the rolling country of the lower reaches the climate encourages sheet erosion of topsoil as well as gullying of slopes. For six generations the Tennessee Valley's people had been impoverishing their environment by unwise farming methods—plowing steep hillsides for corn, clearing woods for firewood and timber without reforesting, mining the fertility of the occasional rich bottoms without replacing nutrients. They weren't stupid; it was just that they knew no other way to use land. In the upper country they ran to the self-respecting hillbilly type, elsewhere down to the demoralized sharecropper stereotype. Here and there coal and iron mining varied the economic pattern, or textile mills exploited the understandable local thirst for cash wages. Regional income was less than half the national average per capita.

Off and on Knoxville, virtual capital of the upper country, and Chattanooga and smaller towns along the Tennessee were devastated by floods, and then topsoil-muddy water raged on downstream to augment floods on the Ohio and the Mississippi. Except for desultory fishing and minor barge and steamboat traffic on the lower river, the

Tennessee had long been worse than useless—it was a social liability. Until Dayton and Scottsboro came to fame, each in its own ignominious way, the one place in the Valley that could count on headlines was Muscle Shoals. There within a few miles the riverbed dropped ninety feet. A dam-and-powerhouse would create 600,000-odd horsepower for conversion into electricity. Not that that backward corner of northern Alabama and western Tennessee offered a market for any such potential wattage. But World War I made acute the need for nitrates to go into fertilizers as well as explosives. To create nitrates from the free nitrogen in the air requires great quantities of electricity. Here, it seemed, was the job Muscle Shoals had been created for. Hugh Cooper, already famous as builder of the great Keokuk Dam on the upper Mississippi, later of the Dniepestroy Dam for the USSR, was assigned by the War Department to harness the Tennessee to power two nitrate plants, one using an ill-understood German process, the other a familiar one. While the dam was a-building coal-fired steam plants would oblige.

The war stopped in 1918 before the Wilson Dam, as it was fittingly named, was finished. Appropriations to complete it fluctuated as Washington blew hot and cold. Its purpose became fragmented. With coal-generated power the German-process plant was mishandled; after a trial run the other went on standby. Only two of a dozen dynamos installed—there was room for sixteen—went on line. The Army sold the power to the unenterprising Alabama Power Company. In the mid-1920s none of it seemed commensurate with the grand spectacle of the Tennessee River, of the same order as the Rhone or the Danube, hurtling over the Wilson Dam with energy enough to industrialize a small kingdom.

Well before the dam was finished (1925), its presence *in posse* stirred up disputes. Many advised Uncle Sam to sell the whole ill-begotten shooting match to the highest bidder and take a shocking loss as further penalty for having got sucked into Europe's discreditable squabbles. Liberals, however, saw this white elephant as a socially valuable windfall. Government should use it as a bridge into the power business, thus learning from the inside about costs and potential consumption in order better to cope with the second-deal artists of the great private electricity combines. It was assumed—not without reason—that what with the power companies' devious bookkeeping, complicated structure and unerring sense of who could be had for how much, government's regulatory agencies needed all the savvy they could muster. Here and there municipal power companies not only serviced their communities well enough but also served as economic lenses—"yardstick," the liberals said—through which to study private enterprise in the same context. Why not let Uncle Sam make Muscle Shoals his own huge yardstick, particularly since it was already in being?

For the rapid rise in use of electricity since, say, 1910 had resulted in the mere words "power company" smelling bad in many noses. Even where electric light had completely taken over, the consumer-voter's electric bill was only 2 to 3 percent of his budget. But as high-tension lines and sporadic rate reduction (à la Insull) spread current to rapid transit, farms and factories and the small-motor appliances grew more ingenious and popular, it was gradually realized, maybe more viscerally than intellectually, that "power" had two meanings. Here was a private operation to which government accorded eminent domain and area monopoly reaching out for exclusive supply of the energy that ran trains and streetcars, powered factory machinery, lit the same factories plus churches, courthouses, schools, hospitals, dwellings, hoped soon to cook the city's food and heat its rooms.

Thanks to coal- and oil-fired locomotives, boilers and cellar furnaces, there was still room for maneuver. But the trend was clear. Certain temperaments grew uneasy every time Insull or one of his less consumer-minded rivals ran in a new generating plant, whether coal or water powered it. For its output increased the whole industry's potential *power* in the most generalized sense over the whole economy and each person in it. The hand hovering over the powerhouse switch began to look dismayingly like the hand that ruled the world. And now here were fast talkers proposing that big government, the federal government, should neglect a windfall opportunity to show big power how electricity could and should be used to serve not primarily for profit, though still on a paying basis, to correct the tendency of power companies to regard "electricity only as a commodity to be sold, not as a developmental or social force" while neglecting "the low-rate, high-use theory of marketing"[25]—as a hearty proponent of TVA defined the issue. The dispute was the hotter because the chief power seller in the Muscle Shoals area was the Alabama Power Company, owned by British and Canadian investors and noted for "swollen and padded rate bases"[26] and reluctance to follow Insull's example of electrifying outlying neighborhoods. Indeed those living within sight of the Wilson Dam paid Alabama Power 6 cents per kwh—for which the US Army charged the company only 1/5 cent.

In 1922 Henry Ford, wrongheaded master of grandstand plays, got into the act. The previous year his personal newspaper, the Dearborn (Michigan) *Independent,* had launched against Jews a sizzlingly irresponsible campaign. It had disastrously backfired. Now, maybe because Ford felt that his public image needed the healing effects of a change of subject, he made a headline-creating offer to take Muscle Shoals off Uncle Sam's hands. He would lease the Wilson Dam installation at an annual rent of 4 percent of what it would cost to complete it and pay part of its upkeep; pay $5,000,000 outright for the nitrate plants and other oddments that had cost $85,000,000 to build—even their scrap value was figured at $8,000,000. In consideration of all that, for the glory of Henry Ford and the sake of public support, he would guarantee a yearly 110,000 tons of nitrate for fertilizer to be sold to farmers well under going prices—at least 50 percent under, his henchmen were whispering in the right ears—while keeping the nitrate-making facilities poised and ready for military emergencies.

It was well aimed. The mud-scorning Model T and Ford's pose as the ingenious farmboy who still ate grass roots for breakfast even after making billions in the teeth of city-slicker bankers had made him the idol of farmers. Now, as the New York *Times* said, "The mere rumour [*sic*] that he was to take over Muscle Shoals persuaded many a farmer, especially in the South [where nitrogenous fertilizers were indispensable to cotton growing on land nearing exhaustion], that a new day was to dawn." [27] For other tastes, anyway to please himself, he added fancy touches about reforming the international gold standard and drawing the claws of international bankers (= Jews, of course) by retiring paper currency with the huge profits that a Ford-operated Muscle Shoals would certainly roll up. The nation, he said, had fought World War I to free itself from militarism fostered by "the international money power." Now his scheme would "free American industry and American agriculture from the same money power" [28] as well as create a flourishing megalopolis seventy-five miles long, like an urban comet with Muscle Shoals for head, where breadwinners would combine part-time or seasonal factory work with small-acreage farming nearby. Nobody, Ford least of all, knew how he would get the bugs out of the nitrate systems or market the surplus power from the 850,000 horsepower that he said Muscle Shoals would produce. Cloakroom talk mentioned new factories to make small parts for Detroit, electricity-hungry plants making aluminum from bauxite. It sounded great, particularly to cotton farmers. And to the real estate brokers of Florence, Alabama, and other nearby towns who went into speculative orbit buying outlying farms to lay out as subdivisions—an atmosphere faithfully and disrespectfully recorded in some of T. S. Stribling's novels.

But it sounded outrageous to Senator George W. Norris of Nebraska. This cherub-faced maverick with a black bow tie had stood out against entering World War I and the League of Nations as stoutly as he had once led the Progressive fight to free the US House of Representatives from the grip of Speaker Joseph G. "Uncle Joe" Cannon. Norris was a chronic foe of "the interests" in any guise. The only reason why it still said "(Rep.)" after his name in the newspapers, where it often appeared, was that the deviant Republicans of Nebraska kept voting for him. Gifford Pinchot, Theodore Roosevelt's prophet of conservationism, now Republican governor of Pennsylvania, doughtily backed Norris against the facile enthusiasm roused by Ford's proposal. It was, he said, "seven parts waterpower, one part fertilizer." [29] With him were both Senators from Ford's home state of Michigan, Arthur Vandenberg (Rep.) and James Couzens (Rep.), once Ford's right hand in the automobile industry, now making a career in politics the more successfully independent because he had the millions with which Ford had bought him out. By late 1924 this curious group had Ford fought to a standstill. He withdrew his offer and reverted to Jew baiting. Consequent collapse of real estate in the neighborhood of Muscle Shoals led to a bitter local joke: This was "the only place in the world where you can shoot quail from paved sidewalks." [30]

After this defensive victory Norris went on the offensive. With help from the sizable Democratic minorities in Congress, who instinctively identified their Republican rivals with willingness to see Muscle Shoals sold down the river, he proposed laws requiring Uncle Sam himself to use the installation—specifically, borrowing Ford's gimmick, to make cheap fertilizer for farmer-voters. In view of how Norris, other Progressives and many Democrats felt about power companies, it was hardly incidental that a Muscle Shoals in full spate would generate slathers of surplus power for Uncle Sam to sell at exemplarily low rates to a widening consuming public right in the Alabama Power Company's territory. (To some extent Norris was borrowing from exotic experience; he had closely studied Canadian hydroelectric projects created by provincial governments to supply power at use-encouraging low rates.) Such a bill passed in 1928. President Coolidge pocket-vetoed it. Another passed in 1931. President Hoover vetoed it on the orthodox grounds that government had no business competing with private industry. Norris kept the potentialities simmering. In 1933, two months before inauguration, he took FDR to visit Muscle Shoals. Three months later the Tennessee Valley Authority was born.

Norris' stubborn devotion had hit the jackpot. The legislation secured would not merely make Progressive-style use of Muscle Shoals because the dam and so on already existed and it would be a shame practically to give it away to "the interests" for any such song as Ford sang. Instead, the TVA would make the national white elephant into the core of an unprecedented, gigantic, multiplex plan to rehabilitate the whole run-down Tennessee Valley. FDR's message to Congress spelled it out lyrically: Muscle Shoals was "but a small part of the potential usefulness of the entire Tennessee River.... [Beyond] mere power development ... flood control, soil erosion, afforestation, elimination from agricultural use of marginal lands, and distribution and diversification of industry ... national planning for a complete river watershed involving many States and the future lives and welfare of millions...." [31]

Yes, the pilot plant would get into fertilizer, oh, sure. But also into a dozen more dams to help the Wilson Dam check the headstrong river's floods and create a channel for major barge traffic all the way to Knoxville. And reforestation to minimize flooding and erosion. And always and forever electricity by myriads of kilowatts. All those dams coordinated in a fashion that private companies would find difficult—and probably illegal—would harness the river's vigor to bring new industry (and jobs) and domestic efficiency to some 2,000,000 people, a good many of whom were still in the kerosene-lamp stage. Even before those dividends came in, many would get jobs building dams, ancillary roads, housing and so on. This was, among so many other things, the ideal work-relief program. And for its agin-the-interests sponsor its peculiar beauty lay in promising the long-hoped-for yardstick to beat—in both senses—the power magnates with.

Plenty-for-all. In 1930, after long agitation about damsites and a nine-foot channel to Knoxville, the US Army Corps of Engineers had got leave to build a supplementary dam upstream from the Shoals. The Tennessee Electric Power Company was building another. In 1912 a federal commission had roughly sketched such objectives. But the ingredients now agitated in the shaker were far more numerous than ever before. It was no accident that FDR had a chief hand in the formula. Being governor of New York State had familiarized him with governmental power developments in the St. Lawrence basin. His administration had made unusually sensible use of the unemployed in conservation work, particularly the reforesting about which the Squire of Hyde Park had long been zealous. Here was an early major example of how much the New Deal owed to the luggage that That Man in the White House, brought along from the Executive Mansion in Albany.

The TVA bill passed the Senate by a 3-1 vote, the House by 2-1. The public corporation set up was a political freak independent of federal departments or agencies normally concerned with forestry, farming, waterpower or whatnot. It was to deal as a sort of *ad hoc* regional government with the seven state and myriad local governments in its territory. And it was particularly forbidden to let logrolling or political pull affect anything it did. The very able and dedicated people who manned this notable ship actually made that clause stick. This puzzled and then annoyed elected patronage mongers like Senator Kenneth McKellar of Tennessee, appointed ones like James A. Farley, FDR's Postmaster General (and political bottle holder) and empire builders like Harold Ickes, his Secretary of the Interior. Senator Alben Barkley of Kentucky, a TVA state, admitted with rueful approval that in his experience TVA was so tough about political influence that a recommendation from any politician was not only fruitless, but a distinct handicap to getting a job with them—a thing none ever said about any other New Deal agency. Some political veterans came to like this eccentricity because once they knew they couldn't get around it, it saved them the frictions that often go with the power of patronage—making one friend may create several enemies. Eventually it had serious consequences for the nation. Not for the TVA, however, and meanwhile, its success widened the spreading impression that this TVA thing was a good deal of a miracle.

Legally, too, it was a curiosity. Whether the electricity-producing aspect was the chief consideration was never settled in many attentive minds. FDR was irked because "the damned newspapers have made it out that TVA is simply a power agency.... We aren't just providing navigation and flood control and power. We are reclaiming land and human beings." [32] TVA Chairman Arthur E. Morgan protested in the *Atlantic Monthly* that the agency's "flood control and navigation are not 'a masquerade.' Though the entrance of the government into the power industry was prominent in the minds of members of Congress ... [TVA can be] a great advance in the planned and orderly development of a great river system." [33] Improvement of navigation, afforestation, support of farming and industry, promotion of national defense were already accepted federal functions. A constructive casuistry could, of course, get the nitrate projects in under defense, for, as Ford had suggested, explosives and fertilizer might again be as crucial as they had been in 1916, when Muscle Shoals was first blueprinted. But nobody could scotch the surmise that Ford—and Norris—and all other "interests" and politicians promoting optimum development of the Tennessee Valley by taming its river would never have got anywhere had not its head of water promised so massive an accretion of kwh. The power magnates had to challenge the constitutionality of Uncle Sam's thus using tax-backed financing to compete with them in the energy market. And when the US Supreme Court rejected their protest, the reason was that it managed to find the established purposes of flood control, irrigation and so on adequate pretexts for government's selling a by-product of those activities—electrical energy. That was the most momentous by-product since mankind learned that alcohol is the residue from the multiplication of yeasts.* Few now regret that decision. But the pretexts are notable cases of egg laying. It was a far cry from the buoys and dredges of conventional navigation improvement to the TVA's eventual coal-fired and nuclear generating plants. It makes a knotty problem: In such a situation which factor was cowbird and which was the usurped nest?

In 1932, before his victory was won, Norris had denounced others' use of this subterfuge in the disputes about Muscle Shoals: "... every bid [from private interests] ... had somewhere ... beautifully concealed ... a joker ... the object ... was to get possession of the power facilities ... the fertilizer proposition was only a blind." [34] What Norris did, with the best intentions, was to filch that joker from the hand of the "interests" for the public to take tricks with. Within a year of passage of the TVA act the TVA's agronomists decided that nitrates were the wrong approach to rehabilitating the Valley's agriculture. Nitrate fertilizers tempted farmers to go on concentrating on erosion-causing cotton or corn, whereas a change to *phosphate* fertilizers combined with antierosion measures would promote shifts into hay, livestock, dairying—anything to get away from the plow—and begin to heal the Valley's wounds. For phosphates encouraged planting of clover, alfalfa, lespedeza for cover crop—all "leguminous" plants the roots of which carry nitrogen-fixing bacteria that naturally enrich the soil with nitrogen. Every pound of phosphate thus used put three pounds of such nitrogen into the land. And as it happened, the Valley contained large, underexploited deposits of phosphate-rich rock. So TVA's chemical engineers converted Muscle Shoals' ill-starred nitrate plants to manufacture economically compact phosphate fertilizer and under TVA's guidance, field-workers from the seven states' agricultural colleges trained local farmers to make it the base of an agricultural new day.

An admirable program indispensable in the agency's purposes. Note, however, that it left no vestige of the nitrate-fertilizer program that had sweetened the idea with Southern legislators or of the original reason for the Wilson Dam, which was, you recall, to make nitrates for national defense. In neither was there any hint of navigation, flood

* Several years after the US Supreme Court's decision, Pritchett, *The Tennessee Valley Authority* (1943), p. 33: "To most people the T.V.A. has seemed primarily a power project. The constitutional contention that power was only a by-product of a plan for rendering the Tennessee River navigable and controlling floods has seemed to them a peculiarly fictitious legal fiction. And yet it is true that the government's concern for an overall development of the river ... has been genuine."

control, afforestation or contour plowing, let alone water-skiing on dam-created lakes or the square dancing that clear-eyed young TVA personnel eagerly learned and promoted as suitable to their new fiddle-and-sunbonnet environment. Note further how—at this point the irony bites its own tail—it turned out that the TVA, giant successor to narrow-purposed Muscle Shoals, was indispensable to national defense after all. The vast quantity of new electric power coming on line in the late 1930s proved essential to the huge new industrial developments, particularly in aluminum, chemicals and boatbuilding, that made the Valley an arsenal of democracy in World War II. Not to mention that TVA kilowatts were and are the breath of life to the Oak Ridge installation crucial to the atom bomb that ended the war.

Yet, however tortuous its origins, the TVA's course was straightforward once it was launched. Chairman of its executive organ was Arthur E. Morgan, self-trained expert in flood control who had become president of Antioch College (Yellow Springs, Ohio) and was closely identified with its famous program of alternating semesters of actual work in the outside world with semesters of study on campus. One of his coadjutors was Harcourt A. Morgan, eminent agricultural biologist and president of the University of Tennessee. The other was David E. Lilienthal, a youngish Wisconsin lawyer deep in the state's Progressive ideas of government, which, like New York's, were proto-New Deal. All were men of stature. Lilienthal particularly proved to be one of the ablest of his or any other American generation. For this job it was good preparation that he grew up in small towns in northern Indiana and went to college at freshwater DePauw University, an utterly Hoosier, primly Methodist institution. Soon after the US Supreme Court came down on TVA's side, Wendell Willkie, president of Commonwealth & Southern, the holding company chiefly affected, negotiated its sale to TVA for $44,728,300. Willkie too was a Hoosier—Ickes sneered at him as "the barefoot boy from Wall Street"—and as Lilienthal handed him the check for that amount and the photographers aimed their cameras, he said, "Dave, this is a lot of money for a couple of Indiana boys to be handling." [35]

The TVA's triumvirate had intramural difficulties, but all understood from the beginning how intimately its purposes, whether spelled out in the law or owlishly implicit, were interrelated. Begin with flood control—that is, dams to hold water back when too much is coming downstream and sluices to release it when the river falls below normal level. Reservoirs above dams gradually go useless as silt in the water from up above makes them shallower and shallower. Hence TVA's seeking to persuade farmers to do things to check sheet erosion. Further to prevent silting up, it had to create major forests on the hills instead of the spotty second growth, a tenth of which burned yearly and left blackened, exposed soil to wash down into the streams. Then dam control of floods opened the possibility of consistent depth of water under the keels of towboats and barges. TVA built locks to lift or lower them bypassing the dams and gave the nation the economic blessing of a nine-foot channel year round—the Tennessee has no ice problems—to carry coal, oil, automobiles, metallic ores, steel preassemblies far more cheaply than rail or highway can. And now for doubling back to agriculture, the barges on this "unbroken stairway of navigable lakes" [36] bring in from the Old Northwest the cereal feeds needed by the cattle and poultry industries replacing soil-eroding corn and cotton. Also modern dairying and poultry raising depend on electricity for pumping water, heating, lighting, grinding feed, milking machinery, refrigeration. So the dynamos set between reservoir and downstream must provide power to new industry created by the need to revise the Valley's landscape to make it practical to build the dams to keep the river from running away with the land's fertility, instead re-forming that river into a docile highway for transporting things that the Valley wouldn't need or be able to buy had not the dams been built in the first place to establish flood control—or anyway, that was what the law started out with.

The head swims as the spiral of cause and effect gains speed. Take the tree part of it. Before TVA most persons in the Valley knew no reason to take trees seriously except as fuel, building material, environment for squirrel shooting and coon hunting. In the first phase of erosion control the TVA relied heavily and gratefully on the Civilian Conservation Corps, the arm of the New Deal that turned jobless young men on to outdoor work of long-term values. For TVA they planted millions on millions of tree seedlings where they would do the most good. Gradually local farmers caught on as they listened to TVA foresters' suggestions that a planting of pines up the mountain yonder would make sense: We supply seedlings; you put them in the right place the right way and protect your land. It took doing. A TVA veteran recently told me how amazed his grandfather was when they advised planting black locust on a particular slope. The old man had spent much of his life grubbing up volunteer black locust as a pest. He was unaware that the species is a good erosion checker and shares with clover and so on that nitrogen-fixing function of the bacteria on its roots.

In time the Valley's people developed such sound tree-mindedness that individual farmers had a major hand in putting the total of some 600,000,000 trees to work healing the land. Black walnut and pine, favorites of the early years of clothing those slopes in a hurry, took on fine. TVA now emphasizes classic hardwoods—white and Northern red oak, tulip poplar, black cherry. Its nurserymen develop specially thrifty strains of such species to restore the Valley's forests to the original glory. Already all over the upper Valley are great stretches of cool, tall, deep-shady forest, marketable timber where, fifty years ago, it was all gullies and gaunt, abandoned slopes. Engineers say that thanks to such plantings, plus crop reform, silting up of reservoirs will be no problem for 200 to 300 years. Timber, pulp and other wood products now rank fourth in the list of job-creating industries in the Valley. Every year the acreage of healthy forest widens.

At first TVA suffered from the occupational hazard of the missionary and the settlement worker—the solicitous insistence that this is how it should be done, believe us, we know. "The Utopians entered upon the scene," a Yankee journalist wrote during the first year, "... came down from Washington ... to tell the Tennessee Valley people all about themselves and their colorful, promising future ... bent upon saving the benighted heathen ... singing a gospel of reform ... [speaking] glowingly of introducing basket-weaving and other manual arts into the little homes ... folk lore and folk songs and folk dances ... [told local people] they would be taught the uses of electric refrigerators, modern cooking stoves, heaters, vacuum cleaners ... as though they were the untutored inhabitants of some island colony...." [37] It was true enough that a fair number of the Valley people had yet to grasp the purpose of modern plumbing, let alone vacuum cleaners. But the missionary attitude was ill adapted to those as sot in their ways as East Tennesseans. They had, after all, persisted stubbornly in voting Republican for generations right in the middle of the Solid South. (This often vexed Washington politicians; why didn't a Democratic administration loyally concentrate these millions of dollars and thousands of jobs in the *lower* Valley, where folks always voted Democratic?)

Wisely TVA shifted the emphasis to: We supply the opportunity. You roll your own. Primary credit for this goes to Lilienthal, who understood better than many of FDR's leading lieutenants that in many contexts *suaviter in modo* was the procedure of choice. Presently he succeeded Chairman Morgan in top command and became the Cavour of the Tennessee Valley, where, incidentally, it did him no harm in local eyes that he had a good eye for a fine saddle horse. Were the United States method of choosing Presidents rational, he could and probably should have been the first Jewish tenant of the White House. When Mrs. Roosevelt, troubled about the hitches in her own disastrous rehabilitation schemes, asked him how the TVA "gets these people to consent to such programs," he told her of "grass roots methods ... demonstration and learning by doing and example. And [the advantage of] being close to the problem ... we are a regional, not a Washington outfit." He told his diary that he hoped she "got it and ... will pass it along to a member of the household who, God save the mark, can stand some education along the same line." [38] He had been spending much time and energy keeping FDR from allowing Ickes to take over TVA for his Department of the Interior.

The demonstrations that Lilienthal recommended were sagaciously kept low key. Thus to persuade the cotton-or-corn, two-mules-and-a-plow farmer to try new things, hifalutin showplaces would have been tactless. Instead, TVA offered a given neighborhood's best-thought-of farmer ample supply of the new phosphate fertilizers for the mere cost of transportation—giving it free would have been poor psychology—on condition that he try cattle, forage crops and so on and, as he got the hang of it, let the neighbors come and see how it worked. It was the consequent thousands of such TVA-inspired but essentially private experiments that brought the Valley its healing farm revolution. By now some 1,500,000 acres are in such soil-protecting operation. On the same principle, as transmission lines began to march across the countryside from the new damsite powerhouses, TVA stayed low pressure about distribution of electricity. One way was to stage county-seat demonstrations of electric stoves, water heaters, pumps, refrigerators and so on and tell onlookers from unelectrified communities, well, it's up to you, if you want efficient conveniences like these, you'll have to organize a local nonprofit electrical cooperative, and then we can bring in the power. The necessary pylons and miles of wire may irk today's sensitivities, but, a Valley-reared Congressman recently told an interviewer, "If my mother were alive, you'd have a hard time convincing her those lines are ugly. She thought they were beautiful. They changed her life." [39]

Encouragement of electrical co-ops and small new municipally owned distributions systems worked so well that the private power companies suddenly began to string wires all over landscapes that they had previously neglected and woo new customers formerly thought too poor and too widely scattered to be worth having. One of the reasons why Commonwealth & Southern capitulated was that such Johnny-come-lately tactics didn't work well. It was also notable that in a few years electric rates in Valley cities with private power, such as Chattanooga, went down twice as fast as in the rest of the country, whereas previously Chattanooga rates had stayed close to the national average, and that as rates went down, average household use of electricity in town almost doubled. Valley households now use twenty-five times as much electricity as in 1933, when few but urban situations—only 3 Valley farms in 100—had it available. Now the bulk of its farms use it to light the barn as well as the house, milk the cows, cool the milk, grind the feed, pump the water, grind the tools, wash the clothes, store the garden truck. I recently talked with a dairyman south of Florence, Alabama, one of TVA's first demonstration farmers. He rents large acreage from his neighbors who spend most of their time on nearby TVA-powered factory jobs, hence can use only ten or a dozen acres of their family farms in spare-time husbandry of a few beef cattle or for raising custom-harvested corn. Thus has come to practical realization Henry Ford's pet scheme of the 1920s, which he himself hardly got off the ground in experiments he made in Michigan.

Elsewhere in America the Rural Electrification Administration, beginning to follow TVA's lead in 1936, accomplished much of that sort of thing. Here in the Valley credit goes solidly to Senator Norris' versatile, organically complicated brainchild. Almost automatically the first dam that TVA built on its own, the towering sweep of concrete taming the Clinch River, one of the great sights of the Southeast, was named for Norris. So was the nearby town where the construction force was quartered. It was built from scratch with some Radburnish features and fleshed out with a library, basketball courts, movie theater, hall for weekly square dances, free adult classes in arithmetic, handicrafts and so on—a new sort of environment for so many men (and families) down from the hills. At first the construction engineers were unhappy about TVA's policy requiring them to recruit local labor. "... too light [in physique] ... not used to working in crews," [40] veteran foremen said. To their surprise these greenhorns caught on fast and, once Norris was finished, went on building dams up and down the Valley like so many hillbilly beavers. As they moved out, TVA's administrative and field staffs moved in with their families, and Norris became a permanent municipality.

Jonathan Daniels, able newspaperman and son of Woodrow Wilson's newspaperman-Secretary of the Navy, felt uneasy in Norris in 1939; it was oppressively domesticated, too blandly cooperative. The looping street patterns might be safer for dogs and children but bewildered outsiders trying to find So-and-so's house—an insuperable disadvantage of such arrangements in Tugwell Towns, too. And the place was so artificially new that it even lacked a graveyard. He'd never been able to like company towns anyway, he said. Each for its own shortcomings—Kannapolis, North Carolina; Kohler, Wisconsin; Norris, Tennessee *—stuck in his craw. One can share that feeling, yet

---

* Norris ceased to be a company town after World War II, when the TVA sold it into private holdings. Now many of its residents are connected with the AEC operation at nearby Oak Ridge. Maybe for that reason it retains much of the prophylactic serenity that Daniels noted.

wish he had gone on to say that at least Norris is preferable to Las Vegas, Nevada. Why the comparison? Because both were born to accommodate men building a great dam at about the same time—and what a difference in the end product! It was the intrusion of the Boulder Dam project's offices and its thousands of hard hats and attendant honky-tonks and wenches that gave that scrawny little town on the Union Pacific its first lurch toward its present lurid neon sprawl. Boulder Dam was sponsored by Calvin Coolidge and Herbert Hoover. It is unlikely that either had any such flashy, high-rolling side effect in mind.

High among fringe benefits from rehabilitating the Valley stands the enjoyment its people take in the "broad and lovely . . . Great Lakes of the South" [41] (Lilienthal's phrase) that the dams created. The sport fishing is fine—bass, crappies, walleyes—and a small commercial net-fishery catches carp and other "rough fish" for dogfood, an activity that few Congressmen can have had in mind when voting for TVA in 1933. Valley folks have taken energetically to sailing, powerboating and beach doings at lake resorts well sited and carefully supervised along the reservoirs' 9,000 miles of shoreline. Every year outsider vacationers throng in to do the same, and the millions of dollars they leave behind are another star in TVA's economic crown. Large or small, the side effects crop up wherever one looks. The temporary construction villages' libraries and bookmobile services became permanent community institutions after the work gangs moved on. Fifty years ago one in four of the Valley people suffered more or less from malaria, the mosquito-borne, soul-sapping ailment that helped pellagra and hookworm keep them lean and languid. Twenty years later it was hard to find a trace of malaria in Valley bloodstreams. Clever use of the new reservoirs was part of that. The malaria mosquito breeds only in very shallow water. Among the dirty tricks that TVA played on it—or her, for it's the bite of the female that spreads the disease—was raising the water level a few inches to cover previously dry shore, leave it there long enough for eggs to be laid and hatch, then suddenly drop the level, leaving the newborn larvae to dry out and die. That required quantities of dry-season water that would otherwise have created electricity. But TVA thought the loss of revenue well invested.

It also pumped surface water off wet bottomlands in mosquito season to check breeding and rented the dried-off areas to farmers to plant corn or sorghum on shares with TVA. The farmer harvested his share and left TVA's standing; then the land was flooded again to let the fall migrations of wild duck and wild geese feed happily on the grain. For in another side effect, afforestation and flood control have gone hand in hand with conservation-mindedness to make the Valley a far better place than it was for fur and feathers as well as fish. As for folks—as the everyday consequences of rehabilitation sank in, the Valley's people, who had previously been leaving home in throngs to seek a better life somewhere else even before the Depression, found it worthwhile to stay. Today incoming population about equals outgoing. The reason is clear—in 1933 average income was only one-half the national average; now it is three-fourths.

In sending the TVA scheme to Congress, before a shovelful of earth was turned, FDR candidly said, "If we are successful here, we can march on ... in a like development of other great national territory units within our borders." [42] At the time he probably had in mind the Columbia River and St. Lawrence River basins and expansion of the Boulder Dam project on the Colorado. Three years later, as TVA was already looking promising, Adolf A. Berle, probably the best mind in the early New Deal, assured Lilienthal that if things continued to go so well, "we would have to have many TVAs in many fields ... producing revenues and goods ... against which bonds could be issued to help with problems of the budget." [43] US Supreme Court Justice Louis D. Brandeis, no admirer of corporate bigness, private or governmental, had concluded that TVA-like projects all over the country could be "a prudent saving of the country's capital ... [providing] employment and at the same time [interfering] less with other normal private activities." [44] In 1937 FDR recommended seven little TVAs to expand these possibilities. Presently Governor Olson of California brought Lilienthal to the Coast to advise on a state-level TVA for the great Central Valley that would make more sense than letting San Francisco and Los Angeles dictate what to do with its rivers and boundary mountains. FDR thought of expanding it to create two great national authorities Southwest and Northwest coordinating and incorporating existing piecemeal installations. There was serious talk of a TVA type of authority for the Arkansas—a major river of which probably only a minority of Americans had ever even heard—and for the great Missouri from Montana to its junction with the Mississippi. And only three months before FDR died the *Wall Street Journal,* hardly an organ of wild-eyed enthusiasm, admitted that his proposals "for TVA's in every important watershed in the country [have] a certain logical foundation.... If TVA has been 'a good thing' for the Tennessee River region it should be a good thing for every other river region." [45]

Of all that, however, relatively little came to pass. The Columbia acquired the mighty and economically important Grand Coulee and Bonneville dams for flood control, power and irrigation. The Missouri was similarly harnessed at Fork Peck and elsewhere. Recently the Arkansas acquired a barge channel all the way up to Tulsa,

Oklahoma. But those are fragmentary by TVA standards of valley coordination and mostly the jogtrot work of the Corps of Engineers and the Department of the Interior. This stifling of the TVA idea may confidently be attributed to its having worked too invidiously well. It was hard for the Corps of Engineers, a bureaucracy as densely integrated as the dams it loves competently to build, to forgive the TVA for having taken over the Wilson Dam and its half-finished supplement upstream and then freezing the corps out of the rest of the huge development. It was just as hard for Interior to forgive Lilienthal for so successfully keeping the TVA out of Washington's stodgy hands. How many more of these regional changelings would come along to put empire builders' noses out of joint? Remember, too, how TVA had kept politicians' paws out of the trough—a deplorable precedent. Each of those three elements had had to sing small. And the inevitable consequence was a They-Shall-Not-Pass determination that it should not be allowed to happen again. Nor did it. TVA now stands un-emulated, a towering piece of history, vigorous but alone. And a road taken only once and then shunned is essentially another road-not-taken.

Flaws have developed, as they were bound to. TVA decided early to supplement hydroelectric power with coal-steam power plants because even with sound water storage, seasonal variations in rainfall could occasionally make it hard to keep wattage at a consistent level, and coal is plentiful in some of the mountains that the tributaries drain. As demand for power outstripped the hydroelectric capacity, more and more coal plants were built. In time waterpower, the thing that had made those engineers' slide rules tingle when taken near Muscle Shoals in 1910, was playing second fiddle. TVA is also projecting nuclear power plants, about $10 billion worth, to keep abreast of demand; its original investment through World War II (in uninflated, 1930ish dollars, of course) was about $700,000,000. How strange to see TVA, probably the most successful regional conservation project the nation ever saw, thus coming under the reprehension of conserva-tionists! For not only is nuclear energy anathema to them, but TVA's voracious appetite for coal has made it the Appalachian strip miners' largest customer. Nor does it seem to have done all it could—or at least what militant conservationists hope to force it soon to do—to see that its suppliers put the site back together once the power shovels and sidehill augers get the coal out.*

* TVA and others defend strip as opposed to deep mining of coal because it gets out more of the coal available at a site, produces less leakage of pollution into streams, is safer for miners and because better laws, better enforcement of existing laws and education of operators and their minor customers—the major

Conservationists also look askance at TVA's phosphate fertilizers, which may be unduly euphoricating the Valley's waters. And it has been a shock for policymakers reared in TVA's historic atmosphere to have to start persuading people to use less rather than the more electricity that has always been TVA's gospel. In the great days before energy shortages a good TVA man did nip-ups whenever he saw an electric bulb glowing where none had glowed before and the heavier use of electrical gadgets in a farmhouse, the better. But at least one of the developing anomalies had been in TVA's column of assets. In the 1930s its viewers-with-alarm savagely denounced it one of the most alarming examples of the New Deal's "creeping Socialism." Private enterprise would never be the same again in the country of Alexander Hamilton and William Graham Sumner. Certainly if, as the books say, Socialism is "public ownership of the means of production," TVA meant to be and became an attractive example in a strategic area of production—more clearly so than many other New Deal projects that also came under such suspicion. Here again the consequences stood reasonable expectation on its unprepared head. Some of the TVA's collective-minded subalterns were as dismayed as were certain reactionaries when power from its new dams was soon sold to large manufacturing companies. Thenceforward private enterprise, large and small, fed fat in the Valley on TVA's publicly produced kilowatts. The barge channel too led to some $2,000,000 in private investment in waterfront facilities for storage, loading and so on. By 1944 Stuart Chase thought it "the outstanding achievement of the Roosevelt administration." [46] And a few months later the New York *Times* observed with gratified wonder that "TVA has almost no enemies in its own territory. It is supported by chambers of commerce, by farmers' organizations and by men of widely differing political views ... a new sort of government agency ... of which Jefferson as well as Hamilton could consistently approve." [47]

Tugwell rated TVA as one of the two achievements "in the first New Deal days [that established FDR] in the regard of Americans as the fulfillment of their ideal in the president." [48] The other was the Civilian Conservation Corps—the CCC in the acronymic jargon that unsympathetic humorists called alphabet soup—"the Cs," as its recruits spoke of it among themselves. Indeed, it outdid the TVA in prompt acceptance. Whereas the notion of putting government into the power

---

ones already know most of the score—can heal a stripped area's wounds, indeed in some cases put it in better shape than it had originally. It is TVA's bad luck, however, to draw its coal from mountainous areas where putting the land back together is far harder than in more favorable areas.

business continued to dismay the Coolidge-minded, the Communists stood largely alone * in deploring this assignment of healthy single males between the ages of eighteen and twenty-five to healthy outdoor work at things needing doing. Among such things was afforestation—tree planting, the least exceptionable kind of conservation, proverbially honorific, carrying the worthy connotations of Arbor Day at school and "The groves were God's first temples. . . ." That was what the public chiefly associated with "the CCC boys." Correctly, too: Though they also worked on erosion-checking terraces, restoring historic sites, building recreation facilities and check dams, the bulk of their efforts beyond tree planting went into forest protection—creating firebreaks, clearing out fire hazards, building lookout towers, telephone lines and woods roads for fire fighters. It all meshed admirably with their single greatest accomplishment—planting a billion and a half tree seedlings in six years.

The association with FDR was also sound. His wife said it was the part of the early New Deal that gave him the keenest pleasure. As already noted, he had long been tree-minded both on his own estate and in New York State's affairs, and the CCC's potential as afforesting agency may have bulked as large among his emotions as its promise to help down-on-their-luck youngsters. Its name may have been the best clean double entendre of the century: It (a) set civilians to work at conservation and (b) did much to conserve those civilians for social usefulness. Both purposes were deservedly popular; in the context they were inseparable.

The CCC's work areas being so remote gave it a great advantage in public relations. "Only by questioning at country filling stations, by nosing up dirt roads, by guessing hazardously at rude forks can one stumble at last upon the more elusive [CCC camps]," [49] Frank Ernest Hill reported to the American Educational Association. For most of what it did took place away up in the hills or among the bushes out of sight of the general public, while the projects on which CWA and then WPA labor worked were often right in the middle of town with high visibility. Hence those peevish wisecracks about paying men to lean on shovels. Shovels were widely leaned on, true; but some of that meant legitimately needed breathers among those unaccustomed to pick-and-shovel work, and whatever the reason, the cracks came gracelessly from those who had never yet had to handle a shovel at all. It might well be that the CCC boys, being young, well screened for huskiness

---

* Socialist opposition came chiefly of uneasiness lest the CCC's quasi-military wage scales undermine those paid in union-dominated employment. See New York *Times,* May 27, 1936.

and seldom previously committed to less strenuous occupations, worked harder than most WPA men did. For example Company 896, 181 strong in 1934, put in about 17,000 man-hours in February weather, planting 25,000 pine and black locust seedlings, moving 200 cubic yards of earth out of drainage ditches, building 587 small dams, planting 13,200 feet of ditch banks with Bermuda grass sod and sloping 419,000 yards of same. But the beauty of it was that, work hard or not, they were not under the view of sidewalk superintendents inclined to suspect malingering to begin with.

Some of the credit for the CCC's persistent good press goes to an important academic philosopher. But then William James was a notoriously down-to-earth phenomenon. Among his preachments widely read in FDR's generation was a magazine piece, "The Moral Equivalent of War," telling well-meaning pacifists (of whom he was one in his own prickly way) that in some moods one could grasp the militarist's sense that the savageries of war were "a cheap price to pay for rescue from the only alternative supposed, of a world of clerks and teachers, of co-education and zo-ophily, of 'consumers' leagues' and 'associated charities,' of industrialism unlimited, and feminism un-abashed. No scorn, no hardiness, no valor any more! Fie upon such a cattleyard of a planet!" After which delicate tribute to the settlement-house mind: "Militarism is the great preserver of our ideas of hardihood and human life with no use for hardihood would be contemptible." He suggested harnessing these emotional verities by "a conscription of the whole youthful population to form for a certain number of years a part of the army enlisted against *Nature*.... The military ideals of hardihood and discipline would be wrought into the growing fibre of the people; no one would remain blind, as the luxurious classes now are blind, to man's relations to the globe he lives on.... To coal and iron mines, to freight trains, to fishing fleets in December, to dish-washing, clothes-washing and window-washing, to road-building and tunnel-making, to foundries and stoke-holes, and to the frames of skyscrapers, would our gilded youths be drafted off ... to get the childishness knocked out of them, and to come back into society with healthier sympathies and soberer ideas.... So far war has been the only force that can discipline a whole community.... But ... the martial type of character can be bred without war." [50]

The relationship is clear. Admirers of the CCC referred to James oftener than to the Swiss, Swedish and German precedents sprung up during post-World War I economic dislocation and pacifism. Not that the CCC took James as blueprint. Its "enrollees" were distinctly not "gilded youths" but almost all from social strata deep in hard times. The CCC did not conscript. All its rank and file were volunteers,

unmarried males of ages seventeen to twenty-five, usually got at
through social agencies telling of three square meals a day and the
opportunity to earn and send home to one's hard-up family $25 a
month. Nor did it ever include girls, even though James seemed to
suggest it, and feminist Eleanor Roosevelt once came out strongly for
putting the CCC boys' sisters to work in nurseries growing seedlings
for them to plant. James would probably have endorsed FDR's
decision to turn management of CCC camps over to the Army. So did
Eleanor. No other government agency, she faithfully explained to
those uneasy about that, had the necessary tents, clothes, mass
equipment and so on available. The overall supervisor, handling the
complicated relations between the CCC and the Forest Service, the
TVA, the Office of Education and other allied agencies, was a civilian,
Robert Fechner, borrowed from his job as head of the International
Association of Machinists. But it was two- and one-bar career
company officers who had to turn these hundreds of thousands of
unlicked, inexperienced two-legged cubs into a healthy work force—
and without much help from conventional Army discipline.

In 1937 a Gallup POP ascertained that some 75 percent of the
public thought regular military training in the CCC would be advisable, but it was never tried, for FDR was wisely determined that the
emphasis stay heavily on *civilian.* Nothing like Hitler's heel-clicking
"work battalions" distinguishable from troops in basic training only by
their drilling with highly polished shovels instead of rifles. So no
uniforms as such; the issue clothes were Army surplus fatigues and
informally worn. No drill beyond a prebreakfast lineup for roll call,
though here and there a camp commander might require enrollees to
stand at attention when being talked to. No saluting. No penalty for
going AWOL except automatic expulsion. That tended to weed out the
misfits and born-lazies. Within a few months this unsystematic system
processed some 300,000 enrollees at existing Army posts and shipped
them all over the country to the hardest kind of work in the
Hellangone Mountains or equivalent. The Secretary of War, Harry H.
Woodring, expressed pleased amazement at the way it had "recruited,
conditioned, equipped and mobilized more men than were enlisted in
the Spanish-American War and . . . so quietly and efficiently that few
. . . realized what was happening." [51] That it worked so well was a
tribute to the common sense of those captains and lieutenants
suddenly called on to improvise programs that they had not been
trained for.

Some trouble was bound to arise. In June, 1933, when the CCC was
just staggering to its feet, the *New Yorker* sent a staff man to Mitchell
Field on Long Island, where young fellows largely from families on

relief in the Bronx and Brooklyn were being processed. He learned that in the first few weeks of what was officially defined as "learning to live harmoniously in groups," 26 percent of the original 1,350 had gone AWOL and never come back in spite of free board and room, weekends off and very light daily maintenance chores—far lighter than tree planting was going to be. His first two interviewees had known gainful employment—the Jewish nineteen-year-old had once been a garment worker, the Italian-American a chauffeur. They were sunbathing and griping about the chow, the coffee, the nonappearance of the free cigarettes that rumor had promised: "But they can't make us do nothing we don't want to. We ain't in the Army." Most of them, a lieutenant said, had just reached working age when the Depression struck and had never held jobs: "They think loafing is the normal way to live." [52] Insubordination and fecklessness were cropping up, but, said the CO, when he thought how and where they had been recruited, the wonder was there hadn't been more than just one attempt to loot the PX and heavy trespassing damage to the flower beds of the Meadow Brook Club nearby. Camp Dix expelled forty-five enrollees who rebelled against the chow; later remaining malcontents were found trying to undermine post morale by twitting Army privates with the contrast between their pay and the CCC's—$30 a month vs. $18.50. But even so early the medical officer at Mitchell saw silver linings: "When they came here ... some ... were mighty near to being starved. We let them eat all they wanted the first few days.... [Now] they bathe twice a week, shave once a day, and look better and feel better. If they never plant a tree, the effort won't be wasted." [52] In spite of hard physical work, the average gain in weight in the enrollment period of six months was seven to eight pounds.

Shaking down was probably furthered by a policy of shipping big-city types far away to do their tree planting. Managers of mass labor, bond or free, have long known that willingness to stay on the job and work as directed is proportionate to how far away home is and how relatively strange the ambience. Sometimes discontent in a camp in the Adirondacks or Ozarks or Cascades boiled up in informal strikes. In a few such instances the CO expelling the leaders called them Communists, and though yelling Reds! was doubtless a tempting way out for the occasional incompetent camp commander, now and again there may have been something in it. For the Party declined to be deceived by the Fascistic New Deal's pious pretense of salvaging youth and conserving the environment. How sinister that Woodring boasted that the CCC had been formed without the people's realizing what was happening! Fascism was happening, that was what, deliberate preparation for reactionary military control of the whole country.

It could be assumed, of course, that the Party would denounce anything well calculated to ease the strains of Depression and incidentally put some $300,000,000 a year into the enrollees' needy families' pockets, as $25 of each boy's monthly stipend went home. Maybe the Party was also sulky over having failed to get optimum mileage out of the Bonus Army, and now here was something likely to make the officer cadres of the armed forces look good for a change— intolerable! This attitude was embodied in the anti-CCC play *The Young Go First,* by Arthur Vogel, a young Californian who had been in and out of the CCC and found sympathy for his dislike of it among the members of New York City's Party-lining Theatre of Action. This (alias the Workers' Laboratory Theatre) was one of the satellite producer groups the sponsors and staffs of which were more or less interchangeable with the Group Theatre and so on. The familiar names crop up: Elia Kazan, Lee Strasberg, Albert Maltz, Edward Dahlberg, John Howard Lawson. Vogel's script dealt with "tough city youngsters in a CCC camp. At first they find some enjoyment in the outdoor life and unusual circumstances but bad food, poor sanitation, and military discipline increase their resentment. They ... get up a petition to the camp commander, but this only gives them a reputation for trouble-making ... they are split up and sent to different camps to carry on their fight...." And it insisted that since "the camps [are] dominated by the army ... [they are] consequently a preparation for war." [53]

Another and certainly more representative set of data appeared in a WPA-FWP interview with a North Carolina enrollee. He had quit second grade when he was fourteen (think that over): "This is better clothes than I ever got at home ... they was so many of us we couldn't have much clothes ... summer time we just didn't wear no shoes and no shirts much...." He was eager to reenroll after his six months expired. "I git plenty to eat here. I didn't always at home, not the same kind ... we had plenty, such as it was, but it jist wasn't good like this, nor enough of it for the kind it was. I git to go more, git to see more. I'm learning too. I watch the others.... I have more clothes and can keep cleaner...." His chief concern was whether he was too old (at age twenty) to profit from the CCC's evening courses in reading and writing for illiterates. The others made fun of him because he couldn't "read the funnies nor nothing. I look at pictures in books in the recreation hall, so they won't laugh at me." [54]

If he stayed in the Cs, he probably did learn to read, for schooling of a baldly *ad hoc* sort soon evolved as a major function of the program, right after tree planting and conservation of human beings— if, indeed, the two could be distinguished. After some weeks of shakedown the Army asked the Forest Service to set up classes in forestry so the boys would understand what they were doing and why. (One such forester instructor lecturing an unprepossessing gang of big-city types about inconspicuous insect enemies of trees and asking at the end, "Now what is it that harms forests that you don't readily notice?" got the reply "The goddamn fucking bugs.") That went so well that the Army on its uncharted own launched on "general and vocational educational courses" with officers and civilian work supervisors teaching whatever they happened to know something about. Hill, by no means a militarist, surmised that such teaching "offered a welcome outlet for intelligent officers who enjoyed a field of effort somewhat different from their usual routine ... generals, welfare officers, C.C.C. officers and district commanders ... skeptical at first ... have gone farther in pushing education than [had been] dreamed or demanded." [55] The consequent catch-as-catch-can feeling proved an asset according to a retired colonel of my acquaintance who, as a young shavetail, commanded a CCC outfit early in the game. The boys, he said, took to learning all the better because the way it was done wasn't like what they thought of as school.

It had disciplinary as well as cultural uses, of course. The workweek was five eight-hour days, leaving much time to fill up if the boys were not to get uncontrollably restless. There were occasional movies, yes, eventually odd WPA-FTP troupes, but in the first years the latter did not exist. Saturday-night dances with girls invited in were practical only when a sizable town was nearby, which was not too often the case. (This may account for the fact that the VD rate among CCC enrollees was only a third of expectation among Army enlisted men.) The recreation hall seldom had more than Ping-Pong tables, a magazine rack and a scratch library of a few hundred books. Team sports available—softball, basketball—used up only part of the weekend in good weather, and bad weather ruled them out. Boys and officers too had reason to welcome classes as something to do. Within a year 40 percent of them were involved in something of the sort, and the US Office of Education was sending in a large staff of "educational advisers," meaning resident professional teachers.

A minor but highly important part was to rescue the 3 percent of enrollees who, whatever their previous contact with schoolrooms had or had not been, could neither write a letter nor read a newspaper. Within two years 50,000 such were workably literate. Some 300,000 more were "better grounded in elementary subjects...." [56] Beyond that the emphasis was on preparing for post-CCC jobs. In the same period more than 400,000 enrollees had left the Cs for regular employment—in many cases their first such experience—in an economy still sluggish from Depression. There was also conformity with directives "to develop pride and satisfaction in cooperative endeavor ... understanding of prevailing social and economic conditions ... appreciation of nature and country life" [57] and other rather windy but more or less attainable ends. Hill's informal survey of CCC schooling—two-thirds of the time nobody knew he was coming to check up—rated 5 percent of what he saw "really discouraging"; 15-25 percent "really fine"; the rest "distinctly stimulating." [58] How many other school systems would look as good as that? The US Education man in charge justifiably described it as "a great American folk-school movement" and hoped it would become "a recognized part of the American system of education." [59] And it was so much better at worst than bleak idleness and malnourishment in Greenpoint or Gila Gulch or Dirty Face Cove. If William James did (as he hoped to) find life after death, these frustrated drifters turned into horny-handed huskies full of high-grade proteins and mental and moral stimulus must have delighted him. It was not just what he meant but did show that America could take a hint and handle it well. A Forest Service information man truly said, "History may never record a more complete union of two tragic needs to produce such a totally beneficent result as ... the setting of the CCC to the task of restoring the nation's natural resources of forests, soils and waters." [60]

At the beginning of "the Second New Deal"—the more acrimonious, post-NRA phase—the CCC as youth salvager was supplemented by the more diffuse National Youth Administration. This met at least partly Mrs. Roosevelt's hope of helping girls, for it admitted both sexes; kept down the number of young people turning vagrant; cost less than the CCC in annual dollars per youngster, largely because it offered only part-time work; and usually, though not always, let the young client stay at home. At home or away, his meager paycheck channeled important totals to relief families on a basis encouraging self-respect. The residual effect—difficult to gauge but obviously considerable—resembled the CCC's. That is, it introduced 1,000,000 or so of the nation's young to work.

By the time the NYA came to bear, most of these "youth" *—the

---

* This collective noun was officially part of the NYA's title and—unfortunately, I think—unofficially part of the thinking of the 1930s. It smelled faintly of Germany's tallowy pre-Hitler *Jugendbewegung* and the Fascists' song "Giovenezza," in any case was a stratified abstraction likely to pervert meanings and fail to reflect actual situations. The literature was then full of "Today's youth believe.... Modern youth feel.... Youth hopes..." as if the central figure in a mural painting had issued a statement, when all that could conceivably be meant was that people who should have known better had encouraged postadolescents to make speeches and issue press releases. This still goes on.

limits were age sixteen to age twenty-four—had never known anything but the dispiriting job shortages of the Depression. Pop had long since lost his job, and it daunted a kid who had never held a job to find, when seeking one, that, even when an opening did exist, older applicants with some experience were always preferred. Matters were worse still where straitened school budgets, poor transportation and, in the tattered, stagnant South, one-crop farming had created a large second or third generation of half or whole illiterates with few and stunted skills or none at all. Black or white, all they knew was cotton chopping and picking and corn meal and fatback from the store. Through the NYA much of the nation learned how much of rural America teemed with farmboys with little idea how to farm and farmgirls who, though destined to early marriage, had small idea how to keep house, iron, sew or cook and preserve most foods—or do anything else suggesting potential employability to those with jobs at disposal. Nor was this hard on only the stultified individual. These were minus signs, not just economic zeros. "Destructive as enforced idleness may be at any age," said Betty and Ernest Lindley's survey of NYA in the late 1930s, "it is likely to be most devastating to youth. Older people usually have formed habits of work. If their work-habits and self-respect decay, they at least have less long to live than the oncoming generation. Youth who have not learned to work at all, much less how to do any particular kind of work, may be a dead weight on the nation for half a century...." [61]

Decentralized to let each state or region within a state determine its own needs, NYA fanned out with two shifting but typical objectives: to make potential workers out of feckless kids and to help actual or potential dropouts stay in high school or college. The second usually called for earn-your-way arrangements where Depression-strained budgets and local hard times had erased opportunities. The first meant wangling the local community into providing working quarters and materials for something it wanted—a swimming-pool-and-park, new school furniture, a town recreation center, a footbridge across a flood-prone stream between homes and schoolhouse, shelters and sand traps for the municipal golf course, book repair and minor clerical chores in the local library—and then training local boys and girls to create it. Or the municipality could utilize NYA boys' hands in minor maintenance or a local employer might sponsor training in welding or internal-combustion repair or the school board put girls to helping prepare school lunches or ... anything to expand a youngster's sense of personal capability with some developing skill to match that might lead into a better chance of finding a job. Any of it made more sense than the mere leaf raking of the early New Deal that put "boondoggle" into the public's mouth.

Here and there, of course, a slack or stupid NYA branch did little more than dole out small sums. At the other extreme certain NYA projects, particularly those for elder boys, followed the CCC into planting, erosion control, stream cleaning. The standard stint was forty-four hours a month concentrated in one week to save to-and-froing. Soon there also grew up resident centers with dormitory and eating facilities where part-time work outside and housekeeping chores withinside broke girls to normal domestic skills, sanitation, diet and social contacts or where black boys from the Deep South earned enough part-time to see them through basic farm education at a nearby school. All the while NYA was duly wary of stepping on organized labor's toes; the work its kids did never competed with going jobs. And against charges of mere youth coddling it gradually developed sound rebuttal—for instance, that in the year March 1, 1937, to March 1, 1938, while the average number on the rolls was 150,000-odd, 60,000-odd of them found jobs, graduating into the work force that so few of them had previously entered.

FDR and some others had high hopes that CCC and NYA would become permanent. In the short run the conscription that the defense program forced on the nation 1940, soaking up surplus young manpower, virtually extinguished them. Professor Duane Ravitch of Teachers College-Columbia University recently suggested reviving the CCC to clean up and civilize the cultural and physical mess smothering our big cities. How today's Youth would take to the privilege of working up a realistically dedicated sweat is uncertain. Anyway nothing of the sort is likely to happen. Like the pregnant examples of Greenbeltery and TVA, the demonstrated high potential of the CCC was let die on the vine. If you seek its monument, go into one of the forests the boys planted, draw a long clean breath and look around you.

Or next time you fly over the belt of America that slopes up from the Missouri to the Rockies, observe the rows of trees running as straight as surveyors could plot them along the northern and southern (sometimes eastern or western) boundaries of many of the huge fields below. Those are not just impromptu hedgerows betokening negligence along fences. Many are CCC work; all are as deliberate as they look. Trees again—and in a context reaching back certainly 700 or 800 years, probably many thousands more. This area south from the Canadian border into the Texas Panhandle has been set in its all too predictable ways for a long time.

Mile after mile of cropland richly green, homestead after homestead of house and barns smothered in trees. It is hard to believe that this was the Dust Bowl that forty years ago sent the Okies crippling westward. But this is what it was like those times on an 800-acre farm in northeastern South Dakota: Day after day the pitiless wind turned the landscape into "a sea of moving soils," [62] a "black blizzard" so stripping topsoil from the fields that only Russian thistles did not get uprooted and blown away. Cattle had no grass to eat, only dust; to keep them from starving, they were driven into pits and shot. Birds disappeared. The cottonwoods along the few streams mostly died. Sometimes the wind dropped, the dust settled, and bitterly hoping, a man might put in potatoes or wheat. Then here came the wind again, blowing the seed wheat rattling against the windowpanes, and the next morning potatoes set four inches deep lay exposed on the surface. Everything clear to the horizon was dust or sand in hummocks and long swirls of desolation. In his twenty-five years there William Mitchell, the farmer, had seen drought and dust storms, but nothing like this. All through the years he had done all he knew to minimize wind damage to his land—avoided overgrazing, planted crops in the strips that the county agent recommended, put in trees here and there. But now it was the sand and dust from less scrupulously managed farms scores and hundreds of miles to windward that were overwhelming him.

Too dry too long, too windy too long. It happens every twenty-five years or so. Recent reports hint that the Great Plains may soon become some such Dust Bowl again. Drought and wind had a menacing try at it in the 1950s but never quite matched the catastrophe of the 1930s. Agronomists hope that the difference lay in better soil-conserving, wind-taming measures more widely applied in the interval—conspicuous among them those rows of trees aforesaid. If a new Dust Bowl is cooking up, they can be counted on—those that are properly looked after, that is—greatly to reduce damage. Supplementary techniques now more widely practiced than before will also pull their weight. But it is a question whether all such dodges together can be effective beyond narrow limits. In this tempestuously temperamental part of the country much can be done to keep two- and four-legged creatures from unnecessarily tempting trouble. But major meteorological swings and unconscionable variations in rainfall and wind persistence are too likely periodically to devastate this off-and-on useful terrain, no matter what human brains think up. The short-term name for it might be Land of Every Twenty Years; only that takes no account of the probability that every century or two the area sees particular hell to pay, far worse than the Dust Bowl knew, during which the droughts themselves last twenty years.

The varying labels that white men put on the Dust Bowl-to-be show in which phase it was when they first observed it. Some described an area the size of all Scandinavia covered with grass as high as a man's shoulder, feeding millions of fat buffalo and the wolves and Indians that preyed on them; "The Great Plains" was the name for that. Others, however, crossing it a generation earlier or later, despairingly marked it "The Great American Desert," a desiccated, depressingly extensive topographical purgatory between the fertile Midwest and the fur- and timber-rich Rockies. Each label was justified in the year *x,* but inaccurate in the year *x* + *n.* The one thing all agreed on was treelessness. Only along watercourses and in a few patches in the hills on the western edge did this on-again-off-again region show sizable timber. That was why the incumbent Indians used buffalo "chips" (dried dung) for fuel. This lack of trees was taken as natural result of the climate's effects. The Indians' vague legendary bits about woods here and there in their forebears' time were obviously implausible. Until recently, that is, when archaeological botanists found widespread traces of impressive ancient forest in parts of the Great Plains always assumed to be fit for only natural open grassland. Here were huge burned stumps dating back to the time of the Crusades covered with thick layers of windblown soil deposited by the black blizzards that had devastated the adjacent lands long before the Okies' ancestors crossed the Atlantic. And for corroboratory demonstration that extensive stands of trees could indeed flourish thereabouts, experimental plantings made *c.* 1900 in western Nebraska are now healthy forest surviving the Dust Bowl and subsequent droughts.

Apparently much of this country could support trees under any but the once-in-a-long-while catastrophic conditions that burned off the ancient forest. Why weren't there more trees when, for instance, the Spaniards pushed up into the area 400 years ago? The educated guess refers to a long-past ecology in which, for a change, the guilty mammals are not white men. Buffalo and fires were the start of it. Buffalo are highly efficient grazing and browsing machines. Forests encroach on open country as their blown seed takes root beyond their shady margins. When the leading edge of seedlings is consistently browsed off by buffalo—or deer or neat cattle or sheep or goats—the forest cannot spread. Further, if the browsing animals have free access to the surface under the trees as their numbers rise, the impacting effect of their hooves gradually changes the forest floor into a surface unfavorable to trees, while the open country remains open and grassy—paradise for, say, buffalo. That process can account for the origin and spread of the "natural prairies" that so impressed the pioneers. Those strange areas of grassland in the big woods were larger and more numerous (in direct proportion to the population of buffalo) the farther west one went until here were the Great Plains, one vast prairie, and the millions on millions of buffalo that kept them that way.

Off and on lightning set fire to the dry prairie grass of autumn, and the flames, fanned by strong Great Plains winds, killed what open-grown seedlings had survived browsing. In one of those major droughts the forest would be so dry that the flames could drive right on in. The consequent forest fire would redeem a new area from trees, and the buffalo, exploiting the grass growing next spring among the blackened snags, suppressed seedlings from seeds blown in from unburned areas. After a few centuries of every-generation Dust Bowls, all traces of forest would be buried, waiting for exhumation by scientists in our time. As the adjacent Indians got horses from Spanish settlements and learned to exploit the buffalo-rich grasslands, they set deliberate fires, with no effort to control them, to harass enemies or drive buffalo into handy situations for slaughter or because they believed that burned-over ground grows richer grass, meaning bigger and better buffalo.

The Indian's part hardly fits today's sentimental picture of him as instinctively sound conservationist aware of the subtleties of ecological balance. Actually he was just doing his bit to manipulate land and flora and fauna to his immediate needs as regardless of the long-run effects on the environment as a beaver building a dam to make a pond to float his food supply. But at worst the Indian was a minor factor. The available evidence implies that if neither Indian nor buffalo had ever taken over the Great Plains, every two or three centuries one of those catastrophic prolonged droughts-cum-wind would probably have inflicted on this hapless part of the country a super-Dust Bowl that was nobody's fault. Then, as the cycle of merely normally severe every-generation trouble resumed, forest would start coming back.

Only the buffalo spoiled that. Just how much the deleterious influence of the white man as heedless farmer helped make the recurrent droughts worse than they need have been is uncertain. The equation contains too many wild cards. It may have been a good deal. As the intruding white man confined himself to running cattle on the grass that the buffalo had fed on, the long-established heavy sod protected the underlying soil fairly well from even pretty heavy winds. But when he plowed up the soil to plant cereals, eventual damage was inevitable. The treacherous part was that, given average or better rainfall, which can occur for six or seven years running, the area gives highly profitable crops of wheat and cotton, and moisture in the ground keeps erosion from being noticeable. So opportunistic or dislocated but hopeful men from Back East—anywhere east of Kansas City—plowed and, as long as the climate cooperated, prospered. When drought broke most of them, many went away. Then came World War

I's insatiable demand for food that turned into wheat farms millions of acres in the Great Plains that should never have been taken out of grazing, and this new generation of wheat farmers gradually persuaded themselves that in spite of dry spells, they could "average out" decade in and decade out. Until the early 1930s the weather treacherously kept their illusions alive. The awakening was all the ruder because the regional Dust Bowl drought coincided with the Depression. The sense of timing seemed to imply somebody up there with a vicious sense of humor.

So among the New Deal's early therapeutic projects was the Prairie States Forestry Project—the famous Shelterbelt Program, sending trees and shrubs to the rescue. Several agencies took a hand. The US Forest Service gentled thousands of farmers into individual plantings of state-supplied trees on their own. So did state-level propagandists. And without the CCC's vast pool of available arms, legs and foot-pounds the shelterbelt experiment could never have been tried on so vastly significant a scale.

It was not just tree planting because trees are a Good Thing. Precedents for the shelterbelt idea already existed, abroad as usual. In the 1700s Germans settled by the Russian government in windswept steppe country developed crosswind hedges of sizable trees to check erosion. In western Canada, cognate to America's Great Plains, similar shelterbelts had done well. Generations ago farmers from the Hudson to the Missouri learned that to plant Osage Orange hedges not only made lifetime fences but, as the plantings grew into stubby trees, somewhat protected crops to leeward. On the Great Plains, however, too few farmers were ecology-minded enough to recall such things. Too often their purpose was half-speculative. The local "suitcase farmer" came in on a short lease with fancy manpower-saving equipment, reaped good-weather bonanzas and left when the cycle turned adverse. Over the years some homesteaders, however, hoping to strike roots, learned that a belt of the right trees round the wind-harried house and barns was well worth planting. Such a windbreak, properly sited and maintained, usually on three sides, meant that in winter the house needed less fuel, cattle maintained weight on less feed and snow was less of a nuisance, while in summer the vegetable patch produced more and the whole place was a few degrees cooler. Awareness of that probably prepared the Dust Bowl farmer in deep distress but hoping to hang on to listen when the government man came suggesting applying the same principle to the fields, for a shelterbelt is just an extended windbreak for acreage. It doubtless also helped to explain that the neighbors for hundreds of miles to windward were trying the same thing, so that future droughts would bring less loose real estate swirling northward to enshroud and smother the farm again. In any case, the homestead windbreaks showed incontrovertibly that the indicated trees would flourish in this notoriously treeless land.

In came the Cs and additional labor from WPA making those east-to-west plantings of seedling trees and complementary shrubs. Species varied to match habit of growth resulted in strip plantings of three to seven rows, each of a different height, the whole eventually making a dense screen of branches and leaves toward forty feet high. Green ash, sycamore, honey locust, hackberry, cottonwood for rapid growth. For medium height Chinese elm or box elder, Russian olive widely favored for low-level wind stopping. As the deciduous trees heightened, red cedar's thick evergreen foliage filled in the lower level. By the early 1940s the Great Plains were striped with 18,500 miles of such shelterbelt as well as several thousand miles of added homestead windbreak. Naturally there were other worthwhile antierosion precautions also recommended and utilized. Farmers were immersed in tactful advice, which the bright ones took, about leaving stubble unplowed over winter to keep the soil from blowing; avoiding overgrazing, enemy of protective grass cover; plowing tricks to entrap drifting soil. Those accepting help in shelterbelt planting had to pledge to cultivate and foster the young trees for several years into a good start and to keep cattle from among them—for, as the buffalo showed, grazing beasts are death on woody flora.

Ten or fifteen years ago these shelterbelts came to maturity. Few knowledgeable observers doubt that they were and are magnificently worthwhile. Where well maintained, they have demonstrably not only minimized soil erosion but also better distributed winter snow to hold previous moisture in the ground; reduced windburn and "lodging" (toppling over) of grain crops; kept new-planted seed from blowing out of the ground; furnished wildlife, particularly songbirds and pheasants, with welcome refuge and provender. Up and down the whole area today state and federal agencies are talking up replanting and new plantings and selective cutting to keep shelterbelts in prime shape. The theory has seen changes. Certain tree species proved disappointing. The old five-to-seven-row belts of mixed species are now less in favor than one-to-two-row plantings of fewer species at shorter intervals across the field. Though less resistant to wind, this arrangement slows it down and never lets it pick up speed again.

The old style, however, well repaid care and makes a heartwarming sight. Correspondingly a neglected shelterbelt is a dismal one: gaps in the skyline where dead and dying mature trees should have been cut out; gaps in the lower level, wind whistling through, where cattle are allowed to browse.... Unfortunately the water needs and shade of a healthy shelterbelt tend to stunt the field crop for a rod or two into the field, and not all farmers want to believe the government man's assurance that this loss of product is more than made up for by higher yield in the other 98/100ths of area. That is one of the psychological quirks that tempt younger farmers out there either to suppress or to neglect existing shelterbelts. Another is sufficient-unto-the-day feckless-ness. It was their fathers, not they, who planted those seedlings in the black Dust Bowl days, frail hopes against cataclysm, and soon saw how much good they did. The sons can and do tell themselves that other soil-protecting methods add up to enough without the extra bother of wet-nursing trees. The weather in their time has held up fairly well. The black blizzards that Pop talks about were a long time ago. . . .

Farmers who neglect shelterbelts should be taken to see *The Plow That Broke the Plains* (1936), Pare Lorentz's documentary movie about that Dust Bowl of forty-odd years ago. If anything can, that will make believers of them.

That was the purpose for which the Resettlement Administration supplied Lorentz with only a few thousand dollars to make it—that is, to educate Resettlement's staff and Congress and the taxpaying public in the crimes against environment that wheat, cotton, greed, ignorance and negligence had committed out there. The quality of *Plow* was so high that, at Lorentz's own instance, Resettlement then set him making *The River* about the equivalent crimes that cotton, lumber, greed, ignorance and negligence had committed against the Mississippi basin. Having described the damage grimly well, both movies sought to go positive by showing the pertinent New Deal remedies—the CCC, for instance, the TVA and, rather dragged in by the heels, Green-beltery.

Aesthetically this was the New Deal's peak. Those two long-short strips of celluloid are widely considered among the best examples of documentary work ever screened. Prints of both are in heavy demand for campus courses in movie appreciation and moviemaking. It is hard to believe but true that before making *Plow* Lorentz had never written, directed or edited a movie in his life. His previous experience with the screen had been solely as fascinated spectator—ten years or so of reviewing movies for *Judge* (rival of *Life* when both were weekly humor magazines), *Vanity Fair,* slickly cultivated stablemate of *Vogue,* dead these forty years, and *McCall's,* a women's magazine far staider then than now. The wildly disparate natures of these publications did not keep Lorentz from giving them all his intense, emphatically expressed, highly individual reactions to what fed into the nation's projection booths. Coincidentally some of his positions were fashionable. Thus, in the late 1920s he agreed with those alarmed lest dialogue spoil the essence of movies as movie. With Morris Ernst he wrote *Censored* (1930), a book deploring legal censorship of the movies and the Hays Office's ectoplasmic resistance to it and calling for a more rational approach to unleash the medium's potentialities for "adult entertainment," then a modish doctrine far from what its basic phrase has now come to mean in the movie advertisements. Yet he was not addicted to what everybody else was saying. Just as briskly he disagreed with the adulatory cult of Greta Garbo * and uttered heresies about Chaplin's egocentric excursions into gluey pathos.

Such data are set down here not as history of opinion about movies but to show that young Mr. Lorentz did his own thinking and feeling in a manner to make waves. He got into newsmagazine work, then briefly had a syndicated Washington column enabling him to make acquaintances in or near the ganglia of the New Deal's nervous system. It must have been such people's sense of his impressiveness, his glowing potential merit, that got him assigned to do *Plow,* certainly no previous accomplishment as moviemaker. He knew so little about that that his technical crew complained his lack of technical jargon made his shooting script hard to work from. And not until all the footage was in the can did he get around to learning the techniques of the cutting room.

Still, he caught on dizzyingly fast. In spite of his uneasiness about the sound screen, he used it admirably in two different ways: A running off-screen commentary that he wrote himself in the semipoetic idiom then developing on radio was delivered with the indicated blend of mourning and reproach by Thomas Chalmers, a friend of his who had been a successful baritone in opera before turning successful dramatic actor. For a second sound dimension he called on what René Clair and Lubitsch had been doing with nostalgic or witty musical backgrounds as partner of screen action. For this he recruited another friend, Virgil Thomson, just then conspicuous for his score for Gertrude Stein's *Four Saints in Three Acts,* who stirred together a supermedley of association-heavy tunes. The way he skewed, foreshortened and juggled "Mademoiselle from Armentières," for instance, into a supplementary audible-emotional guide was maybe even more

* Miss Garbo's renown among people who mattered was one of the few instances of their agreeing with the mass public; for both strata she was, as Richard Watts, Jr., of the New York *Herald-Tribune* called her, "the ineffable one." His elder colleague, Percy Hammond, the paper's dramatic critic, tried but failed to redress the balance by writing that he could teach a seal to do anything she did.

disturbing than Chalmers' spoken words. In editing Lorentz used words-and-music as framework, tailoring the film to them, not, as was usual, the other way around. Visually *Plow* owed much to the Russians' evocative use of symbols: the luckless farmer's feet scuffing in the dust; the tractor junked among weeds. The footage of old-timey horse-drawn combines was pure Eisenstein, and all the better for it. The cutting might have been the work of King Vidor, still another friend of Lorentz's, who helped him secure the stock shots he needed. But whatever its technical ancestors, *Plow*'s heredity was all thoroughbred, and most harmoniously did this astonishing amateur groom them. The above also applies about as well to *The River,* Thomson's music and all. These two movies attained an artistic quality that—to be tactless—exceeded anything that the various federal graphic arts projects of the time ever did.

Reviewers turned handsprings over both movies as, one way or another, showings occurred. The step from completion to public view was vexingly costly. Hollywood disapproved of Uncle Sam's trying to exploit the screen audience and may well also have felt uneasy about the quasi-Populist tone of both items. So with the show of distracted negligence that it often found useful, it tried to smother Lorentz's little masterpieces. He fought back with noncommercial showings for the press and minor exhibitors and, though it cost him dear in time and his own money, pretty well won his game with *Plow.* The great break came when Arthur Mayer, maverick owner of New York City's Rialto Theater, booked it, advertised it as the picture on which "HOLLYWOOD SAYS THUMBS DOWN!" and presently ran it on the same bill as the roaringly successful *It Happened One Night.* By the time *The River* came along Lorentz's prestige was so high that major exhibitors thought only twice, not three times and out, about giving it houseroom. The eventual effect of all the pulling and hauling was to make these the most talked-about long shorts of the decade except *Three Little Pigs.* And apropos, Walt Disney, admiring Lorentz's work, went far out of his way to persuade those booking *Snow White and the Seven Dwarfs* to carry *The River* on the same bill.

All that whipped cream was crowned with a maraschino cherry when *The River,* entered at the Venice Film Festival in 1938 after deplorable fumbling and snarling, won first prize among documentaries over Leni Riefenstahl's *Olympiad.* Lorentz was, as W. L. White wrote in *Scribner's Magazine,* "one of the most influential young men in the nation." [63] The case has several striking details: Since he was working for the government, which charged no rental for such movies, he made nothing but his scanty salary out of either. Indeed, one of the things that made commercial exhibitors leery of *Plow* and *The River* was that they didn't have to pay for them; either they couldn't be any good or there was a gimmick somewhere.

Nor was that suspicion altogether groundless. They were obviously created to sell a bill of goods—to alert the public to environmental hazards and justify spending public money to diminish or avert them. Thus candidly dropped on the counter of public awareness, they rang clean and, all things considered, certainly in contrast with most institutional propaganda, pretty genuine. But demurrers must be filed. As public education in ecology they were flawed. They overstressed human responsibility for floods and dust storms and the potential effectiveness of remedial efforts. Early in making *Plow,* Lorentz had trouble with his technical crew, borrowed from a radical group called Frontier Films, because they wanted to make private greed the chief villain. Before launching on *The River,* he told an interviewer, "We are not going to argue that only man is vile ... we do want to show that if man will only adopt practices slowing down the flow of the river he will get the full benefit in fields free from erosion, in power, in clean water." [64] Admirably stated; only the net effect of both movies is nevertheless close to what he there renounced. *Plow* gives the viewer small reason to suspect that, as previously described, the Great Plains periodically go Dust Bowl and man can do little to help or hinder; or *River* that the Mississippi system was notoriously subject to hell-snorting floods and was sluicing horrendous quantities of topsoil into the Gulf of Mexico long before the white man's ax ever crossed the Atlantic. Chalmers' lugubrious voice intoned: "...a land of high winds and little rain ... this is a picturization of what we did with it.... In fifty years we turned most of [the Great Plains] into a dust bowl ... ruined, perhaps forever...."

These are, of course, the familiar, besetting sins of that basically valuable force, the conservationist. Too often his zeal to get minor, worthy measures taken obscures such major considerations as that instead of being a sacred *given* to alter which is sacrilege, the environment was appallingly different some thousands of years ago and will doubtless be so again in due time. For him the "balance of nature" is a sacred cow, not a useful biological fiction that never existed. Conservationists of collectivist bent are also given to use of sins against the environment to create social guilt feelings—"what *we* did with it!"—to discredit the current social system under which they occur, and assume that only private enterprise wreaks such havoc. They sulk if reminded that the USSR is making an awful mess of Lake Baikal and that the farming methods of the innocent inhabitants of Central Africa are a major, if maybe not chief, cause of the deplorable southward spread of the Sahara.

Then, still from a nonaesthetic point of view, *Plow* and *The River* necessarily suffer from being documentaries. The term is associated with evidence, with hard proof on paper, not hearsay, with certified responsibility of statement. So its connotations, borrowed by such movies (and TV equivalents), are deplorably deceptive. That is clear between the lines of the definition arrived at in 1948 by the World Union of Documentary: "... recording on celluloid any aspect of reality interpreted either by factual shooting or by sincere and justifiable reconstruction ... to appeal to either reason or emotion ... truthfully posing problems in ... economics, culture, and human relations." [65] Consider two recent statements in the New York *Times'* movie criticism: "... all movies are fiction, whether based on fact or not," [66] which is unimpeachable, of course, and "A documentary always has a point of view, sometimes called a bias, and there's nothing wrong with that as long as it is admitted." [67] Falseness is built in. The dust-harried, unshaved farmer looking up at the sky in *Plow* was a real farmer, not from Central Casting, and doubtless at the time was hoping for rain, but his pathetic behavior was all too probably suggested by the director. That grimy baby playing with the dust-clogged plow can hardly have got there by happy chance, and if it wasn't grimy enough, Mom was asked to apply a little more dust. *Grass, Nanook of the North, The River*—even the masterpieces of the genre cannot exorcise the thought that camera, cameraman and film editor, selecting, angling, changing sequence, rule out spontaneity and warp authenticity while seeking it. Add the illusion of immediacy, tempting the beholder to take the individual image as standing for a whole implied range of data. . . .

Still, if you stop thinking while the projector whirs, Lorentz's first two movies, the aesthetic fine flower of the New Deal, rank high among its worthy monuments.

In addition to things as solid as the Norris Dam, the New Deal created intangibles. Some turned out so well and are now so taken for granted that little needs saying about them except that—strange as it now seems—they did not exist fifty years ago. One such was the Federal Deposit Insurance Corporation as remedy for a widespread kind of Depression damage—the wiping out of individuals' money when the banks came tumbling down. The FDIC could not help those already hit. But once Uncle Sam in effect guaranteed individual accounts up to reasonable amounts the impulse to keep under the mattress whatever cash came one's way could reverse itself. It worked none the worse because it had never been seriously proposed before, though bank runs were as much part of America's business folklore as absconding cashiers resident in Nicaragua. And some side effects were benign. Bankers will never be the most popular fellows in the world. But the FDIC at least allowed hope of improving their public image because now the man in the street knew that no matter how foolish they might be with larger sums, his nest egg was thenceforth safe from their mistakes.

The other success in locking the stable door to keep the horse from being doped again was, of course, the Securities & Exchange Commission. In terms less simple than the FDIC's this new agency did to underwriters, brokers *et al.* what stock and commodity exchanges should long since have done on their own initiative—curbed the ebullience of salesmen, provided the small investor more reliable information about those potent pieces of paper and forbade the most flagrant kinds of thimblerigging such as pools and abuse of inside information. Say that the SEC was a monument under which to bury the memories of Raskob, Insull and the van Sweringens. In another sense it commemorates the high, if strikingly varied, talents of the three successive chairmen who steered it through the 1930s: Joseph P. Kennedy, formidable Wall Streeter obviously chosen on Charles Kingsley's principle that a gamekeeper is just a poacher turned inside out; then William O. Douglas, feistily brilliant professor of law, next stop the US Supreme Court; then Jerome N. Frank, fresh from the early travail of the New Deal, eventually a most distinguished federal judge. The consequent benefits, being repetitive, preventive and mostly behind the scenes, never struck the public imagination. But the occasional restiveness that moneymen evince when the SEC comes into play witnesses its unobtrusive effectiveness. The ghost of Jim Fisk returning to Wall Street would have every reason to say you'd never know the old place now.

Maybe the most striking intangible contrast between the New Era and now comes of the New Deal-effected change in American attitudes toward labor unions. This, too, is probably insufficiently realized. About the time my voice was changing, say sixty years ago, certain millions of Americans, such as backcountry Southern blacks and poor whites in the hills, had probably never even heard of labor unions, and to seven out of eight others the term's connotation was primarily sinister—not as vicious as that of "white slavery" or "Black Hand" but menacing all the same. (The residual eighth were those whose breadwinners or other relatives belonged to unions, maybe the more or less tolerable railroad brotherhoods, maybe the unspeakable Industrial Workers of the World.) "Walking delegate"—a long-obsolete term for the union organizer/business agent—meant a furtive outcast "usually represented in the press as an illiterate bully, interested only in his own prosperity." [68] Lewis Jacobs has noted the assumption in pre-World War I movies that "labor had no rights except those granted by an employer. Conflicts ... were always resolved by the patronizing generosity of the boss, who always forgave the 'lazy' or 'misled' workers." [69] And such movies were aimed not at upper-bracket audiences, as yet only edging into the habit of moviegoing, but at blue-collar neighborhoods where prounion sentiment would, if anywhere, be strong.

One's elders vaguely associated labor organization with tags of hearsay about Pennsylvania's murderous Molly Maguires (their memories kept green in the Sherlock Holmes story "The Valley of Fear," as well as by the Bourbon kings of Pennsylvania coal mining); the arson-prone railroad strikers of the late 1870s; the killings in the Homestead strike in 1893. . . . After 1900 the IWW's melodramatic violences in the Western mines deepened popular belief that unions actually preferred to stop at nothing. It was deeper still after John J. and James McNamara pleaded guilty to the dynamiting of the Los Angeles *Times* building that killed thirty-odd people. Organized labor had sunk immense emotional capital into depicting them as innocent victims of a boss-inspired frame-up. The damage to labor's cause was severe. It kept LA an open-shop town for the next generation and made "the McNamaras" a household word of the same order as "the James boys." Nor did it redress the balance—balance? in these contexts?— when in 1913 the Rockefellers' Colorado Fuel & Iron Company and the state of Colorado bungled and bullied coal miners into a minor civil war. Its culmination, the infamous "Ludlow massacre," killed a score or so, including women and children, in the pathetic tent colony into which evictions had forced them.

The law helped to keep the repute of unions low. Judges on various levels here and there disallowed what seemed to employers pushily labor-minded laws requiring the boss formally to state why a man was fired (to discourage blacklisting), forbidding payment in commodities or company scrip good only at the company store (to prevent gouging in real wages), to limit work hours, to recognize employees' right to organize. Other courts threw the book at labor organizers or strikers on charges of breach of the peace, coercion. . . . Such support from the bench enabled employers to lay about them with antiunion weapons, some traditional, some new, such as lockouts, strong-arm squads euphemistically called private police, industry-wide blacklists and the yellow-dog contract—the employee's signed agreement that as condition of employment he would not join a union.

The wonder was that against such measures any substantial labor organization could be effected. The long-defunct Knights of Labor had failed to organize workers industry-wide. But craft unionism, limited to the similarly skilled in vulnerable functions, gradually eventuated in a whole fistful of unions loosely tied together in the American Federation of Labor, pretty ably taking care of themselves in the building and needle trades, among longshoremen and teamsters, in specialty trades within show business and catering. Comparable craft unions outside the AFL were solid and powerful in railroads and printing. In those areas employers had willy-nilly to learn about union recognition and collective bargaining. Particularly in railroads and printing these lessons, though inevitably marred by wrangling and backbiting, proved valuable on both sides of the table. Elsewhere, however, the rise of craft unions had added another bad smell in the public's nostrils—the stench of corruption betraying the rank and file. Small to middle-sized employers forced to deal with craft union leaders who could shut down indispensable parts of the operation at will learned that when trouble threatened, a few hundred dollars under the table worked wonders. The walking delegate thus reasoned with not only would negotiate a "sweetheart contract" easy for the boss to live with, but would also jam it down the throats of any of his union members who wanted more. That readily turned into regular "strike insurance"—a new name for the old Scottish institution of blackmail. The building trades and the teamsters were particularly infested with such deals.

The union leader's image thus took on deplorable traits: prosperously well tailored, clandestinely greedy and expert in the strong-arm methods that kept him in power. Union constitutions and bylaws seldom adequately protected rank-and-file democracy and even where one-man-one-vote prevailed, lack of secret ballot and awareness of the headman's burly henchmen usually kept things under control. This must be stated carefully. Not all pre-New Deal unions were tainted by corruption. Many a union leader up from the ranks kept clean, retained his own and his employer antagonist's respect and lived legitimately on what the union paid him—which, as craft unions gained scope and complicated problems, could be considerable. But enough leaders were unscrupulous enough to foster the impression, welcome to an already antiunion public opinion, that unionism was mighty like a racket; that those walking delegates' fondness for the closed shop was actually hunger for power; and that once in the saddle, they sold their members down the river any time the price was right. For unimpeachable corroboration: Sidney Howard, radical-minded reporter soon to be a brilliant playwright, utterly sympathetic to labor, was investigating the labor-spy racket in the early 1920s and came out with the incidental finding: "... it is a fact [however impossible to estimate accurately] that a great number of union officials ... do accept employers' money ... in return for propaganda circulated and policy subverted ... strikes can be bought and sold, created and broken...." [70]

In both organizing and bargaining the strike was the union's chief tool. Where it remained solely an economic weapon, it had to be close to total to get results. For 100 years that had been recognized in the opprobrium visited on the "scab"—a British epithet originally meaning "mean, low, 'scurvy' fellow; a rascal, scoundrel" [71]—as America called the worker failing to join a strike. Very gradually during that time changing public opinion had modified the old common law presumption that collective, deliberate tool downing was an illegal "conspiracy." In 1929 Chief Justice William Howard Taft of the US Supreme Court, distinctly no radical, could lay it down that "A single employee [is] helpless in dealing with an employer.... Union [is] essential to give laborers opportunity to deal in equality with the employer ... to leave him in a body ... in order ... to make better terms.... The right to combine for such a purpose has in many years not been denied by any court." [72] No liberal weekly could have stated it better.

So emotionally and legally the strike as collective tactic was well established. But it seldom confined itself to terms of economic leverage and moral suasion. The boss often said in effect, OK, boys, quit if you don't like the pay; others aren't so grabby—and hired replacements where and how he could. In his view he had an inalienable right to hire whom he pleased just as the striker had the inalienable right to walk off the job if he pleased. The courts agreed. The striker saw it differently: He wasn't quitting; he was *striking*. Typical of the striker, wrote John A. Fitch of the New York School of Social Work *c.* 1935, "is the assumption that he continues ... attached to the industry or place of employment though not at work. Despite the legal contradiction involved, he thinks of the job as his own to be claimed again when the strike is settled. This tends ... to explain the bitter hostility toward strikebreakers." [73]

"Fink" was the epithet of choice for such traitors to their fellow workers. The strikers' weapon against finks was "picketing"—gathering to deny them entry to the plant to usurp strikers' jobs. That meant in ascending order name-calling; then mass obstruction of the gate passively to bar the way; then threats of violence; then fists, clubs, stones ... and sooner or later the police using clubs, firehose, in extreme cases firearms to enforce court injunctions ordering the strikers not to impede the strikebreakers' lawful access to their employment. "They say you got a right to strike but you can't picket," says one of the undercover Communist organizers in Steinbeck's *In Dubious Battle*. "...they know a strike won't work without picketin'. " [74] When, as often occurred, the finks were garrisoned in the factory day and night—a device presently turned against the boss in sitdown strikes—violence would flare up when management tried to run in food supplies or manufacturing raw materials.

Thus, what began as an economic weapon became intracultural war verging on the interclass warfare that the hovering Marxists represented to be inevitable under capitalism. The odds were with the boss. He could usually rely on help from police or state militia or, failing that, federal troops. For the law was so clearly on his side and would be until society saw fit to modify his presumptive right to hire, fire and do what he liked with his own property. In 1914 young Walter Lippmann stated the case for modification heatedly well: "Though I don't pretend for one moment that labor unions are far-seeing, intelligent or wise in their tactics, absolutism [among employers] does not work out any longer to civilized ends. Employers are not wise enough to govern their men with unlimited power, and not generous enough to be trusted with autocracy." [75] Not until the 1930s were substantial things done about that.

In simpler times strikebreakers were recruited by merely passing the word among the flophouses of Skid Row. But as both plants and management's apprehensions about unions grew large, many bosses depended on detective agencies for security guards and planted spies, and the next step was for the detective agency to recruit the strikebreakers as need arose and provide strong-arm squads to protect them. The effect as of a private army was heightened when local law enforcement agencies deputized the security men to give them powers of arrest and use of force to preserve the peace. Such private armies, one is told, were an outstanding case of only-in-America. The Old World's further developed labor folkways apparently had got beyond tolerating anything like the Pennsylvania mineowners' Coal & Iron Police of pre-World War I days.

Procurement and deployment of strikebreakers became a minor industry. The large or middle-sized detective agency had an "employment department" keeping on call numbers of semidrifters and minor thugs—a sizable minority of these standbys usually had police records—amenable to high pay on short notice. Local politicians might supply supplementary recruits. Other possibilities were heedless big-city blacks—sometimes the agencies' recruiters went down into Dixie to corral them—and footloose, indigent youngsters careless of the shame that even nonunion workers usually saw in strikebreaking. Among such neither general aptitudes nor specific skills were common, but that was beside the point. Substantial production during the strikebreakers' incumbency was seldom hoped for. The chief objective was giving an impression of business as usual to discourage the strikers. The presence of blacks unaware of the score lent a specially savage tone to situations nasty enough to begin with. The race riot in East St. Louis, Illinois, in 1917 came of local resentment of the local blacks' potential as strikebreakers. But that element was not essential to extreme violence. In 1922 in the nearby coal town of Herrin, Illinois, the striking miners hanged, shot or beat to death twenty-one white strikebreakers imported from Chicago who had surrendered after a siege of the mine premises on promise of safety. Five ringleaders were tried for it. A local jury acquitted them all.

The above model of industrial relations in your grandfather's time necessarily dwells on frictions. Keep it in mind that most of the time most wageworkers were neither on strike nor being betrayed by venal leaders. Indeed, most of them ran no such risk because they were not yet organized. But there was ample reason for Lippmann's harshness in describing labor-management relations in 1914—he could have said much the same in 1929—as below "even ... the level which we find in politics ... almost as little civil procedure ... as there was on the American frontier.... [Labor is] fighting for the beginnings of industrial self-government. If the world were wise that fight would be made easier.... But it is not wise ... the scab ... traitor to the economic foundations of democracy ... generates nine-tenths of the violence in labor disputes ... working men have to fight him ... as a nation has to fight a mutiny.... The clubbing of scabs is not a pretty thing, the importation of scabs is ... uglier ... there is no such thing as peaceful picketing ... we shall get, if strike-breakers and blind legislators and brutal policemen and prejudiced judges and visionless employers prevail, despair and hate and servile rebellion." [76]

As the 1930s began, leaders in the strikebreaking industry were the Pinkerton National Detective Agency, the William J. Burns Agency, the Thiel Detective Service Company. But coming up out of the ruck was Bergoff Brothers, later Bergoff Service Bureau. Unlike his competitors, who either never talked or stuck to windy nonsense about "industrial relations counsel," Pearl Bergoff, its bulletheaded, cold-eyed and pallid chief, was willing to discuss certain aspects of his doings. Maybe he hoped that the more people knew about what he so successfully did, the more fees would come his way. He said he had once been bodyguard of Stanford White, the flamboyant architect whom Harry K. Thaw murdered; then worked for William Travers Jerome, a famous corruption-fighting district attorney in New York City; then turned independent private eye, got into purveying security men, then strikebreakers.

His operation was not particularly original. Like the others, Bergoff

Service Bureau had a private arsenal of firearms, blackjacks, brass knuckles, billy clubs; rosters of husky, often police-trained company guards; teams of undercover specialists to go into industrial towns to counter union propaganda; other specialists in infiltrating unions, reporting on their members' projected tactics. But strikebreaking was the backbone of the business. Taxi drivers, whose takings were lean in the Depression, were admirably dollar-hungry recruits. Bergoff was proud of how swiftly his key-city branches deployed his forces. San Francisco's general strike of 1934 sent 100 Bergoff men shooting westward from Chicago by plane as well as train, another 100 from New York City. And he knew well how money slowed union activity down. "We have plenty of friends in the unions," he told a reporter for *Fortune*. "Let Mr. [William] Green [head of the AFL] think that over." [77] They gave him strike plans in advance, even on occasion strikebreakers. He boasted that on one occasion he had New York City longshoremen going by rail to break a strike in Boston while Boston longshoremen were being railed to New York City for the same purpose.

I was sent to see him once, listened for half an hour and never liked a man less. Only the archaic state of labor law—rather lack of a rounded body of labor law, leaving too much to outdated assumptions and precedent-heavy courts—could account for the flourishing of such a human fungus. Here, to reverse the proverb, "Bad law made hard cases." The only rights it recognized, as the US Commission on Industrial Relations said in 1912, were "the right of the employer to do business and the right of the strikebreaker to work." [78] By the 1920s new lesions came in alongside the expected ones. Thus, the Ford Motor Company, instead of retaining the services of such as Bergoff, recruited its own union-intimidating thugs and spies through the notorious Harry Bennett. Unions too hired professional plug-uglies to protect pickets and browbeat employers—whereby organized crime, the usual source of such skilled talent, gained a dangerous foothold in such fields as the New York City garment trades. For its campaign to take over the garment unions the Communist Party hired mercenary goons; getting it and them out of the hair of the Amalgamated Clothing Workers (men's suits) and the International Ladies Garment Workers' Union took a great deal of destructive doing; they remained well dug into the International Fur Workers.

As of the 1920s the best remedy for such fragmented turmoil seriously proposed was the Australian-New Zealand system of compulsory arbitration of labor disputes. Kansas had experimented with it until the courts frowned on it. New Zealand gave it up as a bad job in 1932. It implied wider recognition of unions than America had ever known. But it inevitably led to split-the-difference court decisions on wages, hours and so on that exasperated both sides and to great difficulties as to enforcement of unpopular findings. Anyway, the one thing that boss and union usually agreed on was reluctance to see infringement of the right to make one's own decisions and bury one's dead on one's own premises. In some industries both sides talked some and did a little about boss and union working together toward higher efficiency and stabler production. (In the chaotic garment trades, for instance, both sides sometimes admitted that the average union leader knew more than the average boss about how to run the business.) Some employers, sensing that labor organization was in the cards, set up "company unions" as lightning rods—management-sponsored but employee-administered goodwill machinery handling shop grievances, safety improvement, company picnics. Some company unions had recognizable virtues but not the crucial one of giving labor the feeling of collective power putting boss and workers on a fair, even footing.

That was the basket of snakes over America's arm as the Depression made the footing more treacherous than ever. Within ten years the New Deal had sharply reduced the number in the basket. But chronologically the first step was pre-New Deal. Early in 1932 Congress passed—and what's more, President Hoover signed—the Norris-La Guardia Act limiting use of court injunctions in labor disputes and making yellow-dog contracts unenforceable in federal courts. Fifteen months later the New Deal's most sweeping gesture, the National Industrial Recovery Act, became law, including the celebrated Section 7(a) that guaranteed labor the right to "organize and bargain collectively through representatives of their own choosing." In the confused jockeying that NIRA largely amounted to, a rush of employers to form company unions as nominal compliance reduced the potential effect of 7(a). But the ice had been broken all the same. Uncle Sam had consented to serve as law-wielding guardian of labor's special needs. When the US Supreme Court scuttled NIRA as unconstitutional, 7(a) was dissected out of the wreck, reincarnated in more specific form as the Wagner-Connery Act and made law in mid-1935. It not only protected labor's right to organize for bargaining, but forbade employers to indulge in such "unfair labor practices" as blacklisting, firing union leaders, forming company unions, refusing to bargain and set up a quasi-judicial National Labor Relations Board (a prototype had developed under NIRA) to rule on disputes about violations and supervise secret ballot elections enabling employees freely to choose among rival unions or even stay ununionized if they wished.

It had been argued that the spread of collective bargaining that the

Wagner Act would occasion would raise wages, hence expand purchasing power, hence mitigate hard times. That was just a debater's point. It was clear all around that the main purpose was more than to achieve tactical balance between boss and worker—it was to put the shoe on the other foot. Says a British study of American labor: "Although precedent could be found for many of [the Wagner Act's] provisions ... in the practice of wartime or in railway legislation [a field long subject to special federal handling] the novelty of the statute as a whole was its favorable treatment of the unions by comparison with the employers, for the unions suffered no restrictions whatever...." [79] Twenty years earlier exactly the reverse could have been said. No wonder they called the Wagner Act "Labor's Magna Carta"; only it should have been "Labor *Unions'* Magna Carta." The stage was set to make a union card as invariable an attribute of the American wage earner as his trousers. The following year Congress further weakened the boss' position by prohibiting transportation of strikebreakers across state lines. In 1937 the US Supreme Court pulled the rug from under resistance to the Wagner Act by upholding its constitutionality. To fill in intrastate gaps, states were passing "Little Wagner Acts" of their own and using laws regulating employment agencies to stamp out the strikebreaker industry. The National Labor Relations Board's early decisions, usually in favor of unions, were upheld when carried to the US Supreme Court.

The most striking effect of the Wagner Act, true to its purpose, was the proliferation of huge, national "industrial unions" of which only a few had formerly developed important size. For definition take Charles and Mary Beard: "based as to membership on the nature of the commodity [that the affected industry] produced, such as rubber, cement, or automobiles ... included all the workers in each plant who helped in its making, as distinguished from unions [of the type dominating the AFL] based on special operations, or crafts, and split up in each plant along craft lines" [80] The chief instrument was the Congress of Industrial Organizations.* Its chief begetter was John L. Lewis, head of the United Mine Workers, one of the AFL's anomalous industrial unions with a highly turbulent history. As a self-dramatizer with abilities as great as they were cantankerous Lewis ranked with Huey Long, Henry Ford and Frank Lloyd Wright. His shaggy eyebrows, massive body and rumbling, orotund eloquence were as striking as his obsessive concentration on the bitterly combative habits of the coal mines. His weakness—only it also contributed much to his

---

* Before the CIO seceded from the AFL in 1938, it was called the *"Committee* of Industrial Organization."

effectiveness—was to do things in personal terms. Confident that he had the personal clout to slough them off whenever it suited him, he encouraged the Communists to help his CIO with men, money and fanatic energy. When the sloughing off was tried, he proved to be only half-right, and the consequent internal convulsions almost wrecked the movement.* In the interval between the outbreak of World War II and Pearl Harbor his growing dislike of FDR plus his congenital self-righteousness made him a mindless isolationist. But without him the CIO would never have been born in such effective shape, if at all.

His outstanding lieutenants—more like Napoleon's ablest marshals— were the United Automobile Workers' Walter Reuther and the Steelworkers' Philip Murray. The minor steel companies and the major automobile companies, still cherishing hopes of frustrating the Wagner Act—or maybe they were just subrationally recalcitrant—fought frantically against unionization of their plants. The consequent violence, largely their fault, added the "Battle of the Overpass" at Ford's Detroit plant and the "Memorial Day Massacre" at the Republic Steel plant in South Chicago to labor folklore along with Homestead and Ludlow—handy ammunition for the CIO's ably handled propaganda. But its leadership made their own public relations mistake in at least countenancing a new ploy that appeared in the winter of 1936-37, "the sitdown strike." It had originated the previous summer in France, where, with strong Communist overtones, workers had struck not by walking out of the plant but by staying in it around the clock day after day and barring all others from making any use of it. The first American instance was a forty-four-day affair at the General Motors plant in Flint, Michigan. It was warmer than picketing and an economic weapon as effective as it was exasperating. Provisions came in from outside supporters, and the consequences of police efforts to prevent such abetting of pellucidly illegal behavior were dauntingly nasty; attempts at ejection were no more appetizing as the idea spread.

In the fields of rubber, steel, textiles, retail chains, wherever industrial unions wanted a foothold, sitdowns cropped up. All concerned were somewhat confused by the new technique: ". . . even labor leaders shrank from assuming official responsibility," the Beards noted,

---

* Morris Ernst, with excellent credentials as an outstanding liberal champion of constructive persons and causes, said (*A Love Affair with the Law,* 147): ". . . Lewis' naivete about Communists was difficult to explain. His chief counsel, whether a card holder or not, was a Communist and his great influence . . . was responsible for much of the direction and most of the troubles of the CIO. A managed party, such as that of the Communists, or those of local movements on the extreme right, can change history even though it has few members. . . ."

"...though they sometimes took advantage of it to press for negotiations and terms." [81] Yet to judge from the elaborate preparations that sometimes preceded a sitdown—arrangements for organized housekeeping, classroom courses and other time-killing devices as well as provisions—at least some minor leaders were deep in it. Radical minds began to speculate that out of sitdowns might come social and presently legal recognition of the worker's quasi-right to property in his job. Indeed, governors' and mayors' gingerliness about them did seem to hint at it. But far more likely was the prospect that if sitdowns persisted, reaction against this new manifestation of labor's ambitions would lead to destructive harshness. When sitdowns were new, 44 percent of a Gallup POP's sample said they were on the sitdowners' side, but a month later 67 percent were saying that sitdowns should be made illegal—as if indeed they already weren't—and two years later that proportion had risen to 75 percent. John T. Flynn wisely warned in the liberal *New Republic:* "...let labor pause in its huzzas to contemplate the possibility that presently we shall hear a long and now constitutional wail for national laws to deal with strikes and strikers and, above all, sitdown strikers." [82] Maybe because longer heads among labor leaders agreed, maybe because sitdowns were a fad burning out like miniature golf in 1930, the technique gradually died or was let die. But it had had a large share in furthering industrial unions and could readily revive if the going got rough again. Big Labor was lucky when, in 1939, the Supreme Court, laboring the obvious, took this very hot potato off its hands by declaring sitdowns illegal.

In the same period court decisions and shifts in union tactics were beginning to shape picketing into something that society could live with. The virtual disappearance of strikebreaking was what encouraged this. The minatory mob of massed strikers at the gate, garnished with women and children in case the boss' Cossacks were stupid enough to rough them up, was on its way out. What took its place was today's squad of placard-carrying pickets shouting that the plant is struck, no decent man crosses a picket line, while the police look wryly on, twirling, not swinging, the nightstick. Along with that went the boss' gradual acceptance of having to pay attention to the hands' organization, even sometimes positively exploring its positions. The relative scales were often reversed, too. The monolithic national industrial union was often dealing from strength with several large but not as well-coordinated opponents, as in the automobile business.

At least as Big Labor faced off with Big Business, both were a good deal more responsible than either had been when their compulsory wrestling match began forty years ago. A great advance on Bergoff,

Ludlow, Herrin and the McNamaras; a great feather in Senator Robert F. Wagner's cap; maybe the New Deal's finest, certainly its most extensive monument. One's grandfather would have looked at it all even more incredulously than at today's pornography industry as amazing evidence of how things have changed since his time. Forty years ago he might also have had to swallow the extraordinary spectacle of his promising son's going in for a career as economist or public relations man or some such for a labor union. For, as token of at least a temporary improvement in organized labor's social standing, so to speak, liberal-minded youngsters from the best colleges were not unlikely to consider that a suitable field for their brains and emotional commitments. Before the New Deal that would have been, if not exactly unthinkable, about as eccentric a choice as steeplejacking. What's more, some of them proved genuinely useful as well as enthusiastic.

Other consequences have been awkward. Periodic renegotiation of the contract usually sees the union demanding steep raises and settling, after due pulling and hauling, for raises using up most of the cash advantage from recent improvements in efficiency. Of late years the new contract often draws on the future, anticipating improvements-to-be. Frederick Winslow Taylor, father of modern efficiency, envisaged most of such savings being passed on to the consumer in lower prices, hence wider demand, hence higher standard of living. Nowadays between Big Labor and Big Business—which can usually raise prices to safeguard profits—the consumer no longer gets his share. That has been a factor—how important is for experts to say—in recent inflation. It will probably continue so to be. One bleak morning in the 1920s "Abe Martin," syndicated newspaper sage from Brown County, Indiana, said, "If capital and labor ever do git together, it'll be good night for the rest of us." [83]

FIRE UNDER THE ELMS

TIME IS A TAXIDERMIST—HE MAKES REBELS STUFFY.
—PETER VIERECK,
Shame and Glory of the Intellectuals

If shelterbelts eventually join the TVA, Greenbeltery and CCC forests as mere monuments to sound purposes sterilized by apathy, blame education. Not the county agents and Forest Service missionaries who carried the shelterbelt gospel. They weren't trained to be professional educators. True, those Army officers, no better trained for such social adjustment work, did far more with the CCC boys than any had a right to expect. But reflect that the boys, young and gristly, were more adaptable than Dust Bowl farmers, who may be assumed to have often shared with American farmers elsewhere a taste for land speculation (like their pioneering forebears) and lack of ecological foresight. Anyway, absence of professional educational skills can hardly have been critical. One of the few reasonably consistent things about the 1930s was the poor performance of professional teachers at all levels—from nursery school to PhD factories—in counseling the national mind. Actually that was not their legitimate purpose, of course, but neither they nor the nation would admit as much.

In itself the Depression was not as harsh on education as on certain other aspects of national life. Here and there it forced municipalities to withhold schoolteachers' salaries. But the bulk of them stayed nominally on the payroll—better than summary dismissal from private jobs—and eventually collected the arrears. It discouraged necessary as well as ostentatious building programs at all levels, cut down on contributions from alumni on which the privately endowed segment of higher education depended and inhibited expansion of teaching staffs. It increased strain on scholarship, student-loan and student-employ-ment resources just when they were dwindling. Nevertheless, though college enrollment fell off, in contrast with its striking rise in the 1920s, the diminution was proportionately less than in the national income that, one way or another, finances education.

Thus, it probably remained true that, as a very young Yale graduate, William Harlan Hale, averred in 1931: "... four fifths of the men now at college do not belong there." [1] At about the same time Morris Markey got the same impression from bull sessions with undergraduates at the University of Wisconsin. In 1936 Bernard De Voto derived the same ratio from eight years' teaching at North-western and Harvard. Apparently, even though Wall Street had laid that egg, many parents whose reasons for sending their spawn to college had always been the wrong ones could still afford to do so. The only difference was that the economic climate being dismal, they poor-mouthed about it verbally and by writing smaller figures on checks. In consequence one could at least credit the national disaster with one contribution to education—a great thing as far as it went—toppling Joe College from his hegemony over the campus subculture. He still infested fraternity and lecture. The fraternity system retained momentum. In spite of wishful predictions that the absurdly over-grown cult of football was about to shrink, it stayed viciously vigorous. But when Dean Christian Gauss of Princeton deemed it advisable to warn parents not to cut undergraduates' allowances too much lest "unnecessary privations" permanently embitter them, Joe's jig was obviously up. The consequent shifts in campus mores forced him to the extent that he persisted, to choose a low profile for reasons of fashion if not taste. By late 1931 the New York *Times* had sound reason to exult because Joe "has shed his coonskin coat ... given up his Fall houseparties and his automobile...." [2]

Also indirect was Alma Mater's contribution to the emergency—loan of academic brains to the New Deal. This was seldom a matter of the old lady's offering her best and brightest to the national cause. Good and bright they might be, but they were usually recruited at Wash-ington's, not her, instance, and often because they leaned toward heresies more or less repugnant to her board of trustees. The classic example was Tugwell, a yeastily imaginative economist at Columbia lacking experience as administrator of anything, least of all the cumbrously touchy machinery of government. A more promising case was that of Harcourt Morgan of the TVA, who, as president of the University of Tennessee, had at least served on the bridge of some sort of ship. Then there was Hallie Flanagan, zealously spicing the WPA's social service purposes with the aggressive ideologies of the Vassar campus *c.* 1930.

In spite of Tugwell's and Mrs. Flanagan's occasional wrongheadedness, all three proved adequately able. So did certain less conspicuous recruits from under the elms. The drawback was mostly a matter of public image. Those campus figures of high visibility enabled detractors of the New Deal to appeal to the long-standing American prejudice against learning/teachers/intellect—call it the Ichabod Crane complex. Hence pumped-up grumbling against "government by professors," those notoriously impractical visionaries, their judgment steered by theory instead of grass-roots savvy, likely to put out the clock and wind up the cat and so on and so forth. Not that this folk suspicion was wholly impertinent. Thus, George F. Warren of Cornell, a professor of farm management, not economics, derived from studying farm prices so great a respect for the quantity theory of money that he persuaded himself—and FDR—that juggling the value of gold was the way out of the Depression. The costly failure ensuing when the theory was tried out made "professor" more of a hissing and a byword than ever. The hissers forgot that several orthodox professors of economics had been among those loudly celebrating the New Era a few years earlier and that, as to the practical experience, the new-formed Committee for the Nation, heavily committed to the gold-juggling panacea, included such presumably canny nonacademicians as Frank A. Vanderlip, a most eminent retired banker, and Lessing Rosenwald and General Robert E. Wood of Sears, Roebuck. In any case, there were hardly enough professors in the New Deal to call for all that backbiting. It would have been more to the point to complain of "government by settlement house."

The 1930s saw notable efforts to convert Alma Mater from the traditional curricula and methods presumably more appropriate to the discredited New Era. One suspects cause-and-effect; only the extent of the relation is not clear, for much of it had roots preceding the Depression. For twenty years the prestige of the pedagogical shift known as Progressive Education had been growing hand over fist. No matter what happened to the economy, it would probably have got well into the elementary public school systems during the 1930s. In the 1920s it had bubbled into private secondary schools—not "prep schools" for the boys whose sisters went to "finishing schools," but tuition-charging day schools that impressed forward-looking parents. Discrepancies between the Progressive process and what Alma Mater professed to expect of freshmen came to disquiet both parties. Many of the products of Progressive handling were bright and adaptable enough to do very well in the Ivy League and the Northeast's

traditionally august women's colleges—Vassar, Smith, Bryn Mawr. . . .
But the strains of adaptation could be severe, and to the kind of
parents who had fancied Progressive ideas the conventional campus
seemed rigid, narrow, absurdly anachronistic. Lectures, textbooks,
quizzes, emphasis on required courses, instead of "projects," "round
tables," "workshops," field trips and wide freedom in choice of
subjects; large groups, hence less personal touch with preceptors;
emphasis on the documents and artifacts of the past instead of those
of the insistent and glowing present. Why give one's offspring a dozen
years of mind-stretching, soul-expanding Progressive experience and
then toss him into the arbitrary clutch of Procrustes University? Why
not create colleges to continue or at least not so traumatically to
reverse the Progressive process?

The motion was seconded by teachers in Progressive schools who, in
order to get such parents' young into the best-considered colleges, had
had to drop principle and drill them in languages and mathematics so
they could pass College Boards. Even before World War I a shipping
fortune left to encourage the arts in Portland, Oregon, had been used
to found Reed College along permissive lines with a continuation of
Progressive atmosphere in view. Its first president, William T. Foster, a
deviant Harvard economist, ruled out fraternities and intercollegiate
sports, which struck Oregon as radical to begin with,* and emphasized
go-as-you-please curriculum and informal relations between faculty
and students. In 1925 the previously undistinguished Rollins College in
Winter Park, Florida, brought in as president Hamilton Holt, a well-
thought-of publicist-journalist with a wide following among pacifists,
who revised curriculum and class system in a similar direction that
attracted numbers of Progressive-minded faculty. In Holt's hands the
scheme drew so much attention that he raised $2,000,000 in nice fresh
money from well-impressed persons of means.

Reed and Rollins were both coeducational. In 1928 Progressive

---

* Stewart H. Holbrook *(Far Corner,* 190–91) has celebrated the coincidence
of names that helped Reed College get a reputation for radicalism wilder than
it deserved: It so happened that the shipping magnate whom it was named
after had the same surname as another prosperous family in Portland whence
came John Reed, the conspicuous young Communist who played a chief role
in organizing the Party in America and was buried under the Kremlin wall as
a hero of the Revolution. "That neither John Reed nor any of his family had
any connection by blood or act with Reed College mattered not at all . . .
there are Oregonians who still believe that John Reed founded and supported
Reed College for the express purpose of training young commissars." And just
to make it worse heedless reactionaries also failed to distinguish between
William *T.* Foster, first president of Reed, and William *Z.* Foster, early
chieftain of the American Communist Party.

notions were much more sweepingly applied for women only in brand-new Sarah Lawrence College in affluently suburban Westchester County, New York. It threw out the medieval-flavored lecture system and renounced examinations, large classes, reliance on textbooks, required courses, required attendance, administration-fixed rules of behavior. Instead, it relied on small discussion groups, close sympathy between student and "don" (= faculty adviser), exploratory courses for freshmen to rouse interest in fields to pursue under one's own steam, frequent field trips, emphasis on original sources, zealous search for interrelations among disciplines, devout belief that the mind learned best when exploring matters relevant to one's ongoing experiences and then pushing sidewise and backward better to understand because one was eagerly interested; personal work in one or more of the creative arts—if that led to a career as dancer or painter, well and good, but in any case one's personality and range of interests would be enrichened.... Obviously, admittedly, this was transplanting the whole Progressive apparatus except the name from elementary/secondary to higher education. The basic purpose, Constance Warren, Sarah Lawrence's first president, implied after the first decade, was to coax lively young minds into learning how to educate themselves.

Also in 1928, a professor of government at Williams College, Robert D. Leigh, who had had three years at Reed, was chosen to set up another Progressive-minded girls' college at Bennington, Vermont. This pet scheme of a well-meaning, cultivated local clergyman did not burst from the Green Mountain State's forehead all alive-o till 1932. Note, however, that both these updated versions of Tennyson's *The Princess* were conceived (parthenogenetically, of course) well before the Great Crash presumably caused the nation to turn toward promising changes and against clogging elder ways.

The spirit of Bennington College was greatly admired in 1940 by a radical-minded magazine writer reporting on its formative years: "When a company of alert teachers get a hilltop, remodel a barn or two, gather a few eager students and set out upon a new ... cooperative search for truth, there is ground for celebration." Respectfully he cited the auspices of the quest: "Froebel and Pestalozzi had said many of the things which Bennington repeats...." [3] (He did not point out that those long-dead European high priests of Progressive Education based their theories and practices on experience with young children, not with the well-to-do's strapping daughters who were approaching voting age.) He also referred, properly enough, to such still-living heroes of the movement as John Dewey. Specifically Bennington chose its girls from among a throng of applicants as much for how bright they seemed in interviews as from their records at secondary schools. Turned loose on the hilltop campus with lovely views of distant mountains, for two years they explored intellectual and aesthetic interests with the carefully selected faculty as consultant Chirons—science, social studies, music, drama, painting, the dance.... It was the kind of place where one says "the dance," not "dancing"; not "Dancing is ..." but "Dance is...."

Sooner or later the eager browser circled more narrowly and gradually settled on one field to concentrate on in a "Senior Division" consisting of the latter two years. The one out of three who could not find such intellectual vocation was kindly but firmly sent into outer darkness at home or on a less demanding campus. In this respect the system was sound; it prevented much of the difficulty presented by Hale's four out of five college boys who didn't belong there. Two winter months were spent in fieldwork of the student's choosing in library or settlement house or studio or laboratory while the faculty caught up on their own interests and presumably recuperated from having to manipulate bright young spirits at the rate of an hour or more a week each. Courses consisted largely of "a running series of discussions each hanging on the last." [3] Regularly a student committee reported student opinions of the faculty's individual performances, pretty much no-holds-barred. No roll calls, no lights out, no out-into-the-snow expulsions. The few parietal rules about men on the premises, pet keeping, use of automobiles and so on were laid down by the students.

They took "a brisk joy in frog-dissection, Molière and the Industrial Revolution ... [were] eager to debate Roosevelt's foreign policy, James Joyce or the labor relations act ... all seem to have read the morning paper." [3] Given shrewd selection of girls likely to like that sort of thing, elimination of dawdlers and dabblers halfway through and the kind of faculty most susceptible to such approaches, hence likeliest loyally to pursue them, the omens were propitious. The abandonment of lectures was sheer gain to begin with. As alumni of the conventional campus are usually aware, nine-tenths of what any faculty member worth heeding had to say on the platform was already better available in print and in that form is far more intelligibly absorbed. The basic purpose of solicitous training for continuing self-education was admirable. Another avowed purpose—preparation for matured living, which led Sarah Lawrence to set up a course in preparation for marriage that most of the girls duly took—had at least an unimpeachable ring. (Vassar, too, was going in for that sort of thing under the impressive label of "euthenics.")

Yet certain difficulties were inevitable. President Warren's calling Sarah Lawrence a "laboratory college" implied that other colleges, coed as well, should go and do likewise, and she admitted awareness of the "problem of assembling a sufficiently large number of teachers to handle this new kind of education on a large scale . . . experience leads me to be hopeful." [4] That was lame. But no Progressive Educator ever yet found a better reply to the charge that if it is to be applied at all widely, Progressive Education requires absurdly more pedagogical geniuses than mankind is conceivably able to supply. In the post-Sacco-Vanzetti decade, besides, emphasis on building on the student's notions of "relevance"—overemphasis on which has been one of today's glaring errors—inevitably tended to the liberal-radical syndrome of attitudes. Molière and Joyce did not disappear from the potential agenda, but it was soon obvious that the Industrial Revolution and the Labor Relations Act were calamitously upstaging them. That cannot be blamed on permissiveness alone. At far less permissive Vassar the same ferments were working among the girls knocking themselves out for creative social significance in Mrs. Flanagan's program. These processes were more effervescent at Sarah Lawrence and Bennington, however, because most roads (except in laboratory sciences) led to the dissecting room with Western society as subject on the corkboard. "All the exploratory courses," President Warren wrote with pride, "raise problems of values and beliefs which lead toward many demands for . . . psychology, religion and social philosophy." [5]

Thus, such courses in literature might treat "the prevailing psychology and philosophy of various periods . . . Plato to [Harry Emerson] Fosdick." Or "Literature and Society" would take up " 'Women and the conventions of society,' 'war and peace,' 'culture of minority social groups.'. . ." Or "an English teacher with training in economics . . . decided that the problems of modern economics could be dramatized and made real . . . through the modern novel." [6] That sort of thing is commonplace now. Relatively new in Academe then, it conspicuously allowed ideas from settlement house to Marxist to flow in while the conventional societal assumptions a girl brought with her lost validity. It need have surprised none that in the late 1930s a survey of Bennington's effect on its alumnae found "a pronounced shift in political attitudes from conservative to progressivism . . . that tended to persist well after students left the college." [7] This disconcerted some of the upper-bracket families from which the great majority of Bennington and Sarah Lawrence girls came. Field trips to the New York Stock Exchange and then the Pennsylvania coal country—two days needed to cover that—tended to produce in her, a Sarah Lawrence student said, "intolerance for what seemed to [me] the hopeless conservatism of [my] family. . . . [I was] pretty obnoxious the first Christmas vacation." [8]

Yet since only one in ten Bennington alumnae reported such postcollege trauma one may assume what common sense suggests—that most parents sending their daughters to Sarah Lawrence or Bennington were more or less aware of and sympathetic to the place's ideological sensibilities. Compare the "red-diaper babies" of the 1960s. Those sympathies probably furthered the screening process that supplied these newborn women's colleges with the kinds of student who would take most readily to their tastes. Here Progressive Education was carrying into its pupils' early maturity what it had long vaunted as a chief end—to condition the rising generation to deem hankering after reshaping the world a key attribute of any civilized person. That was a contribution, probably empathetic, to the climate of the New Deal, not, however, necessarily a response to the Depression. For a generation that sort of thing had been fluctuating in the academic air, particularly on Northeastern campuses of higher-than-average student quality, typically on campuses in large cities, steadily intensifying since the execution of Sacco and Vanzetti in 1927.

As Bennington entered its second year a sort of super-Bennington was forming down toward the other end of the Appalachians. Its chief creator was John Andrew Rice, a middle-aged quondam Rhodes Scholar and classics teacher at Rollins. Blessed—or cursed—with a taste for drawing out young people's potentialities as the key to all things bright and beautiful, he was as pungently fond of teaching as of his own ideas and spoke his mind among both students and faculty with mischievous zeal. His students liked the way he chivied them over moral and intellectual hurdles as he played Socrates blended with H. L. Mencken. But in time President Holt and a majority of the faculty grew twitchy as Rice resoundingly deplored the chapel services as undignified, denounced undergraduate debates as encouraging sophistry, questioned the value of the college's athletic program of two supervised hours a day, attacked what he called the "feminization" of American college faculties and went swimming wearing only what on him, a pudgy man, struck many as inadequate shorts. Doubtless all that contributed to his dismissal. But when Holt told him he would not be on the faculty the following year, the grounds cited made Rice sound like Socrates indeed: His teaching, it was charged, tended to destroy "youthful ideals without inculcating anything constructive or commendable." [9]

Tentatively refusing the cup of hemlock, Rice appealed to the American Association of University Professors. The investigators whom they sent allowed that Rice had been indiscreet but upheld his right to speak his piece and found Holt in bad faith as to his academic tenure. Rice had strong support from several colleagues unhappy over the way the white-haired fat cats of Winter Park had been culturally and financially dominating Rollins. In the upshot most of these resigned along with Rice and determined to create elsewhere under his leadership a shining example of pure go-as-you-please higher education. With them as raw material came fifteen sympathetic students, including the president of the student body and the editor of the campus newspaper, who had also been finding Rollins stuffier than the catalogue implied.

One of them knew of a likely haven in the mountainous western tip of North Carolina—a church-flavored summer resort that could be rented cheap nine months of the year complete with beds, blankets, chairs, crockery and so on. Sympathizers, chiefly a Boston Brahmin who liked Rice's ideas, raised just enough money to float a beginning. Exactly what these Rollins rebels had in mind was no clearer for Rice's showing a trait common among movers and shakers: "In his role of gadfly," says Martin Duberman's recent study of Black Mountain, "Rice had often talked about what was wrong with education; but ... he felt far less clear about what [a school] should be than what it should not." [10] But he had sympathetic counsel from his brother-in-law, Frank Aydelotte, president of the Quakers' Swarthmore College; his rebel colleagues seethed with emotions popular among open-minded educationists; and within a couple of adventurous years, in spite of chronic lack of cash, Black Mountain College took shape—a shape owing its sometimes firm outlines to pride in being flexibly shapeless.

Visitors observing its simple style of living, lack of many usual college facilities and extremely high ratio of faculty to students—never over 1/3, often 1/2—often mentioned James A. Garfield's proverbial compliment to the then president of Williams College: "Give me a log hut, with only a simple bench, Mark Hopkins at one end and I at the other, and you may have all the buildings, apparatus and libraries without him." * The library was the pooled personal collections of faculty and students; the librarian was Rice's wife, who had had no training for the job but doggedly learned it and grew so loyal to Black Mountain that she stayed on long after Rice and the college split up. Though this or that science was taught whenever anybody versed in it was available and one or more students were interested, laboratory

---

* This is the full version from Bartlett. It usually appears in some such mutilated form as "Just Mark Hopkins on one end of a log and a boy on the other...." No, this was not the Mark Hopkins after whom the hotel in San Francisco is named. That one was one of the four gold rush supply merchants who built the Central Pacific Railroad.

facilities seldom got above the kitchen-sink level. Until a few ramshackle outbuildings were fitted up for married faculty, students and teachers alike lived in the great drafty barn of a hotel like mice in a packing case. The view of distant mountains was almost as good as Bennington's. Such parallels were not all accidental. Both institutions sprang from the same postulates about Education and the Good Life.

Thus, a teacher lectured if he liked, but lecture-minded academics were unlikely to be attracted thither, so the catch-as-catch-can discussion prevailed at Black Mountain. The new student sat in on different courses and gradually settled on a field to explore. After two years he was allowed to demonstrate in discussions and written papers that he knew enough about what he hoped to learn to warrant admitting him to a senior-level specialization—economics, history, biology, drama. . . . Students laid down what rules there were and enforced them in kangaroo courts. When the Board of Fellows (faculty) could not arrive at a decision on the Quaker principle of a community "sense of the meeting," the students were turned to for counsel. Their most rigid rule was to obey the DO NOT DISTURB sign on an individual's study door that probably meant work but might mean houghmagandy, for Black Mountain was, like Rollins, coeducational and, unlike Rollins, paid small heed to manifestations of primal urges. This naturally led to problems but not as many as might have been expected, for, as an alumnus told Duberman, Black Mountain students in the late 1930s were "much too serious about everything, including each other ... there was a certain Puritan quality. . . ." [11] The next most rigid rule was "Behave intelligently"—that is, discreetly enough not to heighten local people's suspicion of their new neighbors. North Carolina's hill people being illiberal in such contexts, there was bound to be gossip, mostly exaggerated, about nudism, free love and Communism up the mountain thar.*

For going beyond Bennington: Whereas most of Bennington's charming girls qualified for a degree, most Black Mountain students just drifted away after a few years. Whereas Bennington was merely eager about the creative arts, one of Rice's few clear beliefs was that they were the clue to mankind's highest goods, crucial ingredients of any brave new world that might be. "The center of the curriculum,"

---

* With the same advisable, albeit timid, restraint Black Mountain fought shy of admitting blacks as either students or faculty. Its leaders were aware of this being abstractly wrong but also felt that in view of the importance of the school as experiment, moral corner cutting of this sort was justifiable. Thus do serpents enter Eden. Not until after World War II did the school do anything in this way. The TVA took much the same sort of position, though Lilienthal was uneasy about it.

he wrote, "would be art. The integrity of the democratic man was the integrity of the artist." [12] So the place was stiff with courses in poetry writing, free-style dancing, ceramics, weaving, music—the scratch orchestra was pretty good—painting, theatricals. Nobody was forced to dabble in creativeness or reproached when his efforts fell short of Picasso or Martha Graham. But the unspoken assumption was that any actual acquaintance with creative skills, however clumsy the result, was socially and emotionally hygienic, never mind whether it led to professional competence. The purpose, Rice told an interviewer, was to develop people with "the artistic approach to life ... who will know and feel that life is essentially not competitive but cooperative everywhere.... Nearly every man is a bit of an artist...." [13]

The availability of graphic arts was increased by enlistment in the faculty of Josef Albers, exiled by Hitler's Nazis, Gropius' former colleague at the Bauhaus, practicing theoretician of an austere style of abstract painting; his wife, dancer and craftsman, taught alongside. As guiding spirit of Black Mountain Albers stood next to Rice. Third in the informal cadre was William Robert Wunsch, whose love for the theater convinced him that writing and acting plays had therapeutic as well as aesthetic virtues, releasing and making use of festering emotions, applying to performers what Aristotle surmised in audiences. The same principle, banal now, was behind the work the PWA-FTP and -FAP were doing with Bellevue in New York City. And in so trendy an institution Back-to-the-Landism had to crop up. Its particular exponent was Theodore Dreier, former teacher of mathematics at Rollins, who not only doubled as college bursar but also supervised the farm from which, he dutifully hoped, student labor would produce most of what the college ate. Rice, reared on a toil-cursed family farm in South Carolina, did not share this enthusiasm. Spitefully he recorded how some of his flock went on pilgrimage to New Jersey to sit at Borsodi's feet and came back sorrowing—while they were visiting that high priest of self-sufficiency, a conventional milk truck drove up and delivered the daily milk and butter. Field-work was no more compulsory than anything else at Black Mountain, just a matter of whether you felt like hoeing nine or more bean rows that afternoon. A hired farmer held the thing together, but it was also a credit to Dreier that one memorable year 60 percent of the college's sustenance came from the farm.

Faculty and students took all meals together, bused their own dishes together. Chronic propinquity was Black Mountain's trademark. It boasted that as much education took place over coffee cups as in classrooms. Elsewhere, Rice said, "education was part of the day and part of the man; in Black Mountain it was around the clock and all of the man ... no escape. Three meals together, passing in the hall, meeting in classes, meeting everywhere...." [14] It was held that emotional as well as pedagogical virtue resided in thus eroding privacy. "Community" as social description as well as abstract principle was a watchword and it remained a problem whether Black Mountain was a place where one learned first and was a social entity second, or vice versa. In Black Mountain's view, of course, the question was unintelligible.

In the third year among many other visitors was Louis Adamic, vivacious magazine journalist of Balkan antecedents and liberal-radical bent. By then twenty faculty were creatively blending with forty-eight students. He planned to stay a day or two; he remained for several delighted months. The article in *Harper's* that resulted not only gave a capable account of the place but dwelt on a facet of its aggressive sense of community that doubtless interested the anthropologists who drifted in and out of the faculty. Rice described this trait to Adamic as showing how a college can become "a sort of second womb from which young people are born to all-round human maturity." * Adamic's piece opened with: "A common saying in Black Mountain is that nearly every one who comes here has to go through hell [because of his] desperate attempt to preserve [his] superficial self. Scores of eyes focussed on you ... many mouths saying 'Don't think you fool us! We see through you!' ... turn the spirit inside out." The students called this "group influence.... [It] works from elevation to depression and back again ... one's thoughts about oneself are abrasive. One rubs down and down until one touches ... one's real self.... Black Mountain ... psychologically strips the individual." In supplement Wunsch's theatricals linked drama to this group influence to cast the arrogant in arrogant roles, the rich in plutocratic roles and so on, which "almost invariably leads to—painful ... but successful—corrective processes...." [13]

Adamic applauded Rice's hope that eventually colonies of adept students and faculty would found other Black Mountains in summer-resort buildings throughout the land, like St. Bernard's Clairvaux dotting Europe with Cistercian abbeys. That such a metastasis might not be benign could never occur to such minds. It probably puzzled Adamic when in the same issue of *Harper's* De Voto, who had seen

---

* As for the reliability of Adamic's account, Duberman *(Black Mountain, passim)* makes it clear that Rice read Adamic's final draft to the faculty and students and that though there were some objections to its depicting the place as more successful in achieving its ends than the facts warranted, there were none to its statement of those ends or description of the emotional concepts involved.

the article in galleys, opened heavy fire on it. He said Black
Mountain was no such scintillant novelty as Adamic thought it, only
a multiplex revival of certain weary old dreams of the cerebral-
flavored Good Life ... Brook Farm ... Helicon Hall.... As higher
education it was disqualified because in spite of Mark Hopkins and his
log, it lacked the libraries, laboratories and wide range of specialist
faculty without which the one in five college students worth bothering
with could never realize their potentials. And as second womb for fine
young spirits it was "downright dangerous ... like a sanitarium for
mental diseases run by optimistic amateurs who substitute for psychiatric training some mystical ideas and ... group practices that we
usually denounce when we find more conspicuous groups indulg-
ing.... [Such an atmosphere] can increase emotional instability and
maladjustment, and it can create them." [15] He drew a pejorative
parallel with Buchmanism. He might have added the hazings to which
boot camps, military academies and many preliterate societies subject
the young on reaching maturity, often with rites symbolizing the
rebirth that Rice, dissolving from Socrates to Mithra, had in mind. It
was still more alarming to read in Adamic that though Black
Mountain tried to screen out overly unstable applicants, "they take a
few neurotics, partly because they feel they can help them ... partly to
give the 'normal' people some training in living with difficult
persons." [13]

How well the screening worked is uncertain anyway. Fritz Moellendorff, a German psychoanalyst refugee who joined the Black Mountain faculty in 1935, told Duberman that the proportion of students
with "neurotic traits or whose neuroses were obvious" [16] was nothing
out of the way for the age-groups involved. But Albers said later,
"Lots ... couldn't make it in any other school. We were the real
wastebasket of the progressive schools." [17] As for faculty, Rice, even
more acid than usual after being deposed and exiled, described the
run of teachers yearning to come there as "the unhappy, the disillusioned, the misunderstood ... pretenders to art and other malcontents." [18] That, though in recognizable terms, may be harsher than the
reality warranted. It must be significant, however, that the community's high value on "group influence" tacitly assumed that everybody
arriving there was emotionally ailing and needed drastic restructur-
ing—as if a Magic Mountain were certain that anybody coming up
would be found afflicted with tuberculosis. Indeed, somebody lacking
previous knowledge might have mistaken it for a low-keyed psychiatric
institution. It had the usual isolation from normal pressures in
hygienic surroundings; any amount of occupational therapy in weaving, ceramics, farm chores; therapeutic use of psychodrama; an
intensive program of cooperative group therapy.... Duberman saw

analogies to several of today's avenues to acquiring merit, the blue-jeans commune, for instance, even if Black Mountain did get dressed up for Saturday evening. A flavor of Esalen is also noticeable. So far as I know, however, Black Mountain never dallied with drugs, just a certain amount of the local mountain dew.

Back to 1936: Rice's strictures did not appear for years. The *Reader's Digest* reprinted Adamic's article for its millions of readers without mentioning De Voto's blistering comments. This lordly publicity break brought a flood of queries from seekers of the Good Life and yearners after educational anarchy. Three years later they were still coming from "sailors . . . catching up on their reading . . . inmates of prisons. . . ." [19] Among further visitors thronging in, Rice approved only of John Dewey—"the only man I ever met fitted to live in a democracy" [19]—and Dewey's curmudgeon-millionaire friend Dr. Albert Barnes, king of Argyrol and splashy art collector. As for others, Rice noted, those keenest on comradely cooperation were also likeliest to leave their cars blocking the community driveway.

For a while there Black Mountain rivaled the CCC as the outstanding educational curiosity of the decade—rather a triumph for an institution that at its largest, after shifting to its own property on a nearby lake, seldom exceeded 100 in total. The CCC's forests are still there. But Black Mountain's empty shell, largely student-built to Spartan, Bauhauish plans,* now houses a summer camp, and the college is twenty years dead. World War II took away most of its male students. It was further harmed by Russophile and Anglophobe Eric Bentley, who joined its faculty in 1942 and seemed to enjoy throwing his intellectual weight about like a horse kicking a stall to pieces. The ensuing schism sent the disgruntled away in hopes—soon abortive—of founding one of those branch-Black Mountains. In such projects such fissions usually occur, for personal or structural reasons, every ten years or so. After the war Black Mountain had a frenetic spate of avant-garde composers, abstract painters, recondite poets and voluble photographers as if it were a far-out MacDowell Colony, only much less well financed. Then gradually, gustily, a slide toward extinction.

Its relative lack of consonance with its time is strange, for most of its faculty and students were of the sort given to social sensitivity. Yet in an age scorning ivory towers it neither sent many recruits to the picket lines or Spain nor supplied much of the abrasive literature of

---

* C. 1940 Gropius, who stayed in touch with Albers, drew plans for the new building needed at the lake site. They were much admired but needed more money and skill than Black Mountain could muster. Substitute plans by a young, modern-minded architect, A. Lawrence Kocher, were duly carried out with much use of student labor and local materials.

the Popular Front. The TVA, queen of the decade's social experiments, had its headquarters at Knoxville, less than 100 miles away. Not much farther the coal mines of eastern Kentucky were scene and occasion of deliberate student involvement in bitter conflict between labor and employer and among rival factions in labor. Black Mountain paid little heed to either. The metaphor of medieval monasticism recurs. Maybe subliminally its leading spirits hoped to hole up until better times, Dark Ages-style, or anyway stay somewhat above the battle while the barons and the Jacquerie had it out on the plains below.

The surmise that Black Mountain's withdrawal was somehow deliberate is strengthened by its sharp contrast with what then went on in more conventional colleges where presumably students were less encouraged to go ideological. However small or large the actual risk of revolution as the Depression peaked in the winter of 1932–33, many New Dealers feared it was real. That was important in determining what measures they took. Among presumed warnings of protorevolutionary strains were the Bonus Army, the Midwestern farmers' milk strikes and interference with foreclosure sales, the collectivist mood of the self-help projects and—by no means least regarded by those reading the wind from straws—a marked rise in radicalism on college campuses. True, Alma Mater's role in the nation's fitful fever was at least inadvertent. American colleges and universities varied widely in intellectual and moral climate, size and dependence on public opinion. But it is safe to say that as the 1930s dawned, 99 presidents or deans out of 100 would have felt chiefly bewilderment if assured that student agitators would soon be taking over the library steps to denounce the Reserve Officers Training Corps or protest dismissal of an instructor in economics for joining a Communist-led "hunger march" in the nearby big city.

"And high time, too," would have been the comment of impatient observers. Edward R. Murrow, fresh out of Oregon State and keeping up with his career of Big Man on Campus as president of the National Student Federation (organization of heads of student governments) rebuked its membership in 1931 for "political apathy and complacency." [20] "Why Don't Your Young Men Care?" was the title of a contemporary magazine piece from Harold Laski, British radical economist just then guest lecturing at Yale, who had made Harvard too hot to hold him in 1920 by championing the Boston police strike.*

---

* This does not mean that Harvard dismissed him for taking this stand. Many of its chiefs wanted to do just that, but President A. Lawrence Lowell

Among European university students, he admonished American readers, whom he frequently favored with his views of what ailed their country, "politics is ... the major nonacademic activity.... Everyone knows how great a part the student played in the emancipation of Russia...." [21] It exasperated him that of 500-odd American students he had known well not one made politics a career, whereas among his current British disciples at the University of London 60-odd were already active party workers. He was aware that here and there a campus "liberal club" had a tenuous existence and occasionally invited in a radical speaker. But America had nothing like the brilliant debates on live political issues in the Oxford Union and the close, master-and-apprentice personal ties between British politicians and promising undergraduates. Since he felt so strongly about it, somebody should have driven him over to Vassar to see Mrs. Flanagan's girls do *Can You Hear Their Voices?* in which a student tells her fat-cat Senator father: "Come out of the fog, old dear! I'm one of the country's educated women. I take a course in government and one in charities and corrections.... They've got more sense in Russia. When the farmers go on the rocks there ... they don't have to sit around for the Red Cross to dish them out charity. They've got something solidly back of them." [22] Further hope of a better time coming could have been had from Vassar's President MacCracken setting his brethren an unusual example: "For many years American college students have been censured for being wholly indifferent to the realities of the political world.... The introduction of ... political science in the college course has changed the students' academic reading.... Every college with well organized departments of economics, political science and history, must expect its students ... often to participate in the political movements of their day, just as every college which teaches music expects to have a glee club that amounts to something in the way of serious music." [23]

Laski's scorn vitiates MacCracken's assumption that the presence on campus of "well organized" studies in economics, government and so on would spur American students into political activity. For a generation, especially after the New Era began to glitter, departments of economics in the ranking universities had grown in size and scope, and undergraduates bent on postcommencement jobs in Big Business flocked into them. Those contemplating law school were likely to choose history or government. But seldom did their professors inculcate doctrines likely to radicalize, which was, of course, what both

---

refused to countenance it. Laski's resignation from the consequent unpleasant position was a voluntary and inconclusive solution.

Laski and MacCracken had in mind. There were few Simon Pattens and Thorstein Veblens precariously infecting student disciples with what seemed to most of their economist colleagues peevish heresies. An economics major could go all the way to a degree without even hearing of *The Theory of the Leisure Class* or laying eyes on a copy of *Capital.* During presidential elections conventional politics of the precinct-canvass, two-party sort might revive the campus Republican Club in hopes that a few students over voting age might take the trouble to register and vote. But there were few FDRs with family traditions moving them to do much more. In muckraking days a widespread, if sparse, movement to found Socialist clubs had sprouted under the elms. World War I crippled without quite extinguishing it. It was rather the settlement house, blending at its edge with and drawing susceptible volunteers from the local urban university, the Utopian aims of the Progressive elementary and secondary schools popping up here and there and the fluctuating pacifist movement that provided American campuses of the 1920s with coals live enough to respond when the Depression came and the opportunistic Communists blew on them.

In 1924, for instance, 400-odd college students from all over met under the auspices of something calling itself the Inter-Church World Movement in Indianapolis and unanimously pledged themselves "never, in any circumstances, to engage in war or any occupation furthering war." [24] A National Committee for the Limitation of Armaments was putting out a *New Student* periodical, striking notes sounding like ten years later: "Students hold within their careless, unmanicured fingers the preservation of our civilization. Our elders tremble at the casual way we grasp our inheritance. . . . [They turn] to youth . . . saying 'leave your shelter and seclusion and help us run the world.' " A later issue bragged: "The power of the future lies in our hands. We are almost the only section of the population which has the leisure and the opportunity to study the controversial questions of the day without bias and act accordingly." [25] That shapeless concept, Youth, left plenty of room for such group narcissism and windy generalization. In that same decade "the Younger Generation" was showing the same symptoms but with moral rather than sociopolitical connotations.

C. 1925, of course, not one American student in 100 was much aware of such palaver. Oliver La Farge (Harvard, 1924), speaking for his contemporaries just too young to have fought in World War I, told his elders that "between the horror of the next war and our disgust with the last, most of us have come not to think about war at all," [24] which fits my own impressions at the time. As the 1930s began, however, the encroachment of the Depression began to nudge certain kinds of students' attention toward activism at just the time when the Kremlin was hoping to rouse the Youth of the bourgeois nations to a class-conscious pacifism. The method was to represent Britain and the United States particularly as gathering to spring on the USSR before the inevitable success of the Five-Year Plan made it impregnable and the world revolution inevitable. Much of this fear was probably genuine, even though ill founded. It was hangover from the Allied interventions of ten years previously, deepened by the Communist dogma of ineradicable cobra-and-mongoose hostility between capitalism and collectivism. So Youth, the West's potential cannon fodder, was to be conditioned conspicuously to resist any and all military-flavored measures in the name of a generalized Peace—capitalized but distinctly not capitalistic. Indeed Peace could not be capitalistic, for in these terms it was the USSR's monopoly, whereas war was by definition capitalism's always latent, probably soon overt, violent imperialist aggression against the People's Cause.

Considerable groundwork had already been done by mostly well-meaning harbingers. For ten years or so isolationist politicians, revisionist publicists and eloquently disillusioned novelists dwelling on the discreditable aspects of World War I had created among literate Americans—those La Farge was talking about—a dominant mood of NEVER AGAIN as to overseas war. The more earnest students had absorbed much of it. It was not necessarily radical. Part of it partook of the xenophobia and agin-the-government impulses underlying certain kinds of reactionaryism—that of the Hearst newspapers, for instance. But it had ready affinity with the radical teachings that capitalism cooked up wars to gain profits from munitions making, that wars masked themselves behind patriotism or idealistic motives but were actually battles between industrialized Titan nations for trade with downtrodden colonies, that wars were things that nobody won but the workers always lost, their sons' lives included. These positions sometimes contradicted one another, but each had enough half-truth to appeal to Youth trained in the cynicism of Postwar Disillusion. "We came along at the peak of the intellectual revulsion against the first world war,"[26] said Eric Sevareid (University of Minnesota, 1935) of his fellow student militant pacifists. Stir in the national sense of insecurity from 1930 on, and this revulsionary pacifism was easily channeled into revolutionary feeling. Twenty years ago Wechsler was complaining about how soon people had forgotten "the sense of breakdown ... [that] swept ... American life ... [and] the absence of clear, affirmative and plausible alternatives to Marxism, the hesitancy of scholars and statesmen in the face of the Marxist critique ... the self-assurance of the communists proved contagious; the liberal loss of nerve repelled us." [27]

To exploit this opportunity, the Communist Party set up a National Student League * under close but, of course, clandestine control. This was necessary because antiwar sentiment could not be allowed to get too sweeping. The objective was to further the security of the USSR by undermining the fighting potential of capitalist nations. So the anathema was limited to the imperialist-aggressive kind of war assumed to be threatening it. To renounce all kinds of war, as conventional pacifism did, would condemn wars that a workers' democracy might have to fight to ward off capitalist threats. This doctrine was carefully spelled out at a Student Congress Against War held by the NSL at the University of Chicago, where the atmosphere had grown propitious, late in 1932 to denounce military training on American campuses. Naturally Party sponsorship was not acknowledged, but the steering committee was rich in card-carrying Party members as well as unblushingly prominent fellow travelers; the speakers included Earl Browder, chairman of the Party, Joseph Freeman of the staff of the *New Masses* and J. B. Matthews, then high in his Party-lining phase as specialist in organizing Peace Congresses. Donald Henderson, the Party's standard-bearer on the Columbia faculty, advised the delegates not only to oppose ROTC on their respective campuses but also to join any and all campus organizations "and seek to demoralize them from within." [28] Earlier Matthews' keynote speech was pontifically explicit about the error of indiscriminate pacifism and the moral beauties of a People's War. For window dressing the organizers had invited Jane Addams, Chicago's elder stateswoman, patron saint of America's settlement house movement and world-renowned leader of war-is-evil pacifism. Winningly and yet firmly she protested that this was all wrong, war was wrong, all war was wrong.... They didn't shout her down. They just ignored her.

Next year came a fine new weapon admirably suited to clogging the wheels of capitalism's war chariot, even though the Party did not invent it. The Oxford Union, the undergraduate debating society that Laski thought so highly of as training ground for precocious statesmen, debated the proposition that British Youth should renounce military service, specifically: "This House will not fight for King and Country in any war...." After pros and cons had been stated, brilliantly as usual, the customary vote among the undergraduate

* Not to be confused with the National Student Federation, an association of the heads of student governments of which Edward R. Murrow was leader 1929–32. It let itself be jockeyed into certain fellow-traveling positions but was never a Party front as such.

members carried the resolution by 275–153. This index of how deeply Postwar Disillusion had bitten into Britain's leaders-soon-to-be was an instant international sensation. Challenged and denounced, the union reconsidered, voted again—and the aye vote was higher still. In several minor British universities students followed suit. Across the Atlantic at Brown University the campus newspaper polled the student body and drew a thumping majority for what was now called the Oxford Pledge. The American Student Federation applied it to twenty-six representative American campuses and got an average response of 50/50.

Dexterously exploiting that ratio, the Party-lining NSL worked up "peace strikes"—daylong boycotts of classes—in order to hold antiwar demonstrations and take an American version of the Oxford Pledge: "I will not bear arms for flag or country." [29] Demurring and deploring did presidents and deans little good. The president of San Jose Teachers College, for instance, suspended two students leading such a "strike" and spoke up for moderation: "I'm not in favor of war.... I don't know of anyone who is ... a silly, disturbing, wasteful and unsatisfactory method of settling disputes.... I gladly pledge myself to use any influence I have [to avert wars]. However, I'm not going to ... state beforehand that I will not support my country if war should be declared." [30] The show went on regardless. The model was the "strike" that the NSL had staged at Columbia, its cradle, because the administration had expelled the editor of the campus paper for using it to promote student sallies into radicalism. Use of the term was a fine example of propagandist word twisting—the old trick of calling New Dealers "Communists" and riot-perplexed police "Cossacks." These campus capers bore small likeness to the labor union's generic strike exerting economic pressure and any physical intimidation that can be got away with. Class-cutting slogan-shouting students were merely depriving themselves of a proportionate fraction of the education that they or their parents had already paid for. But to call it a "strike" lent a dashing, antibourgeois, comrades-to-the-picket-line! flavor that incidentally showed to what an extent a probably small but yeasty number of undergraduates had come to identify emotionally with the Party. The height of it was probably at the City College of New York, where, Kazin remembered, half a literature class refused to read anything by H. G. Wells because he was a bourgeois liberal and "The arrogant stupidity of Communist instructors passed beyond anything I had ever known before." [31]

On many large campuses the NSL had a handy path to the sympathies of Youth through engineering collision between Peace and the ROTC. This calls for what the green Michelin guidebooks call *un peu d'histoire*. During the Civil War Congress sought to benefit farming and industry by the Morrill Act, which encouraged creation of state-supported "agricultural and mechanical colleges." The encouragement consisted of conditional grants of federal land as endowment. One condition—it was wartime—was military training for the future farmers and engineers. Some states attached such land-grant colleges to existing ones, such as Rutgers, or one then forming, such as Cornell. Others set up an A&M separate from an existing state university, as with Michigan State and the University of Michigan. Or the A&M college eventually became something broader, as in the University of Illinois.

All duly kept up some kind of uniformed drill, often rather perfunctory, under veteran instructors and student officers. In 1917 it was assumed that college boys with at least some knowledge of what "Squads right!" meant made competent officers sooner than those without. So land-grant military programs merged into officer-training programs on many sizable campuses. After the Armistice these improvisations became a permanent ROTC under US Army instructors that, it was hoped, would supply reserve officers enough for emergencies. On a voluntary basis as elective study ROTC got beyond land-grant campuses into many other conspicuous ones. In Joe College's day, particularly west of Pittsburgh, it infiltrated Limbo U's culture, holding periodic reviews, choosing pretty coed queens of military balls, working up a national fraternity called Scabbard & Blade—no reflection on the queens' virtue, few in ROTC knew much Latin—and adding cadet-officer rank to the ways of becoming a Big Man on Campus; Murrow, for instance, was cadet colonel at Oregon State as well as outstanding spellbinder in public speaking courses. ROTC probably earned its way in automatic selection from among at least nominally educated Youth those who would most readily take to soldiering in another war. The NSF recognized that advantage when it reversed its previous anti-ROTC position in 1933 because Hitler had come menacingly to power.

Meanwhile, however, Columbia's NSL, mother lodge of the Party-lining student movement, had hung the label "Jingo Day" on the annual ROTC review festival. The corps was an admirable target for solidarity-developing strike demonstrations and the creation of student martyrs by driving Prexy to expulsions. At the University of Maryland and Ohio State—land-grant situations—conscientious objectors refusing to drill were thus expelled. Twice the US Supreme Court upheld the compulsory feature of the land-grant system. At the University of Minnesota the editors of the campus paper got gloriously involved in protests against Jingo Day and student refusals to drill, which added the stinging issue of freedom of the student press to the cocktail of casuistry already brewing. The faculty contained an ardent disciple of Laski's, whose courses played up Marx, Lenin and Trotsky as well as Locke, Voltaire and Burke, whose undergraduate disciples' self-consciously turbulent Jacobin Club took over from the fraternity boys control of not only the paper but also the literary magazine, the law review and the student council.

Those Minnesota Jacobins also welcomed the Veterans of Future Wars—an undergraduate caper that had a strangely significant evolution. In late winter, 1935–36, Congress overrode FDR's veto of a bill giving World War I veterans most of what the Bonus Army had sought in 1932. Certain students of government at Princeton thought this a lamentable demonstration of a pressure group smothering common sense. They issued a manifesto: "Whereas ... this country will be engaged in war within the next thirty years ... we [the Veterans of Future Wars] therefore demand that the government ... pay a bonus of $1,000 to every male citizen between the ages of 18 and 36 ... the first of June, 1965 ... [since] it is customary to pay all bonuses before they are due ... we demand immediate cash payment ... for many will be killed and wounded in the next war ... they, the most deserving, will not otherwise get the full benefit of their country's gratitude. ..." [32]

It got into the papers and spread like the Monopoly game. In a matter of weeks 120-odd campuses had active chapters. The official salute was right hand extended palm up; the ladies' auxiliary was the Future Gold Star Mothers. Naturally furious, the American Legion and the Veterans of Foreign Wars called the boys rich men's sons and pacifist showoffs. The Princeton group demonstrated that their roster included a number of ROTC cadet volunteers and students working their way through. But the general campus climate of 1936 wouldn't let this neat piece of satirical comment go at that. The meaning of it began to shift from antipressure group to antiwar. Rutgers added an Association of Future War Propagandists; CCNY asked Washington for training in writing atrocity stories. Rensselaer Polytechnic formed the Profiteers of Future Wars. By April the Party-fomented Peace Marches of students here and there usually included contingents of Future Veterans indistinguishable from the NSL's other auxiliary groups. In the fall the Princeton founders officially called the whole thing off. But the lesson was clear: Let any lively idea, whether seriously or sardonically intended, hold still a few minutes, and somebody directly or indirectly Party-inspired would probably try to paint it Red.

Its growing momentum enabled the NSL to infiltrate and then to take over the Student League for Industrial Democracy (SLID), the

Socialists' campus arm, and create an entity called the American Youth Congress * that followed the Party line right into World War II, taking every curve and flipflop without losing stride. Under such auspices the Vassar girls went marching into Poughkeepsie, singing, "Little bomb, who made thee? / Who gave thee thy mission?" and thousands of students made a pilgrimage to Washington, marching on the White House, shouting "Abolish the ROTC!" and "Schools, not battleships!" and staging a liedown on Pennsylvania Avenue. FDR nevertheless cordially received a delegation of their leaders and saw to it that the two whom the police had arrested were freed. And all, or mostly, because the Kremlin had the wind up. The curious part is that the effect may have been to increase the likelihood that the USSR would be attacked. By then it was evident that the threat from Hitler and Mussolini was greater than from other Western nations. Between the Oxford Pledge and these semitolerated goings-on the Nazis and the *Fascisti* might conclude that they had relatively little to fear from Britain and the United States, hence could be as aggressive as suited them toward Russia.

The Party-liners' takeover of the bridge of Youth's ship eventually embarrassed many of these ardent young people's admirers, but it took a strangely long time. Mrs. Roosevelt was the classic case. Her commitment to Youth was, it hardly needs saying, generously total and, like many thousands of equally well-meaning people, she was incapable of skepticism about their vociferous demands for Peace—after all, who could be against it? She was never happier, never more sure that she was doing what Mlle. Souvestre would have wished her to, than when gathering Youth leaders at the New York City town house or the White House to discuss the problems of Youth in the modern world, the place of Youth in the future, the special contributions Youth could make to society. . . . She watched over the National Youth Congress like a cat with rather wayward kittens, pestered her husband about the latent militarism that, with others of like mind, she suspected in his favorite project, the CCC, and did much to get its educational aspect put into civilian hands.

* Strictly speaking, the AYC was the creation of an earnest young woman named Viola Ilma, who persuaded Anne Morgan, public-spirited daughter of the elder J. P. Morgan, that the country needed an overall organization of Youth movements. Thus financed, she called together representatives of dozens of well-meaning young people's groups, making the mistake of open-mindedly including the SLID and the NSL. Between them these two radical groups took over the whole show; then the NSL ousted the Socialists from leadership of the thing still called what Miss Ilma had dubbed it, the American Youth Congress. What Miss Morgan thought of the consequences of her sponsorship is not known.

By corollary organized Youth accepted her as a sort of den mother. She advised them on the drafting of the National Youth Act, their abortive effort at a sort of super-NYA; this she did in good faith without realizing that, as Joseph Lash, then in a position to know, would write later, the intent was not to get this patently impractical proposal made law but to "maintain young people in a state of belligerence and suspicion toward government and the older generation." [33] Whenever testy observers called the AYC a bunch of Reds, she came serenely to their defense. She made several close friends among their top echelon. When NSL-dominated City College of New York staged a mock legislature to express Red-minded doctrines, this self-constituted, earnest elder stateswoman was there graciously answering peevish questions and lending countenance. When the Party-steered World Youth Congress held its 1938 meeting at Vassar,* she was there again countenancing Party-lining themes that Lash describes as: "... youth [spoke] out for peace ... but the mood was militantly anti-fascist and anti-imperialist." [34] (They were playing the old game well—what decent person could be against peace and for Fascism and imperialism?) Now and again she privately expostulated with Party-lining Youth leaders for what struck even her as flagrant toeing to the Kremlin's mark. But in public she seldom did anything to mar the impression that she and they were hand in glove and she was willing to be used as front, like Will Hays/Hollywood, only without the handsome salary.

How dismaying it must have been when with the Hitler-Stalin pact of August, 1939, "the masquerade suddenly ended," as Wechsler said, and "one after the other, Youth Congress leaders who had been impersonating liberals abruptly revealed that they were committed to follow the Communist line no matter where it led." [35] As her protégés took up the new Party line—the democracies were as much to blame as the Fascists for the new war, FDR was imperialistically bent on getting the United States into it and so on—she did her best to avert her gaze. When HUAC summoned AYC leaders before it, she attended the hearing solicitously and at the noon break took half a dozen AYC stalwarts to lunch at the White House. In January, 1940,

---

* She did not, however, strike any note there as fatuous as did President MacCracken when defending Vassar and himself against the charge of countenancing a Party-dominated conclave: "Those who fear lest open-minded students should be captured by radical elements should bear in mind the counter possibility that the more radical elements, being treated with tolerance and good feeling, may become more tolerant of the democratic process. In my experience, the latter is more likely than the former." (*Vassar Alumnae Magazine,* June, 1938.)

another Youth "pilgrimage" culminated in a meeting on the White House lawn addressed by FDR during which his wife's interesting young friends booed him every time he said something inconsistent with the Party line. That seems to have given her some misgivings. She had more when she learned of the obstacles encountered within the AYC high command by dissidents trying to modify Party-lining. But it was early 1941, well after the USSR attacked Finland, at which the AYC blatantly rejoiced, before she managed to break with them. (Had she held out a few months longer, until Hitler attacked the USSR, all might have been sweetness and light again.) It was an amazing display of misplaced loyalty and the will not to believe. Lash writes from close knowledge of her and the AYC, "that ... she had attended their weddings, had lent them money, had given them gifts and helped them to raise the Youth Congress budget, and found it inconceivable that young people would repay friendship with personal deception...." No bitterness, however: "Although she refused to work with [AYC] leaders politically, she let them know that if they got into trouble personally, she was always willing to help them as individuals." [36]

It almost sounds like a case of that rare but existent thing, genuine Christian charity. But then again it may have had something of the doting aunt's inability *altogether* to write off the scapegrace nephew who has forged her signature and burned her house down. Either way, however backhandedly, it was one of her fine hours and far, far too good for the AYC boys who had so callously exploited her affection and goodwill. Their turn for kicking comes next after those who led Paul Robeson up the garden path.

How familiar much of it sounds! Careful selection of campus sore spots to raise hell about as training for more serious hell later. Student mobs massing under Alma Mater's gaze in front of the Columbia Library. Liedowns to protest military spending. Instead of the chant of "Hell, no, we won't go!," a song:

> No, Major, no, Major, we will not go!
> We'll wager, we'll wager, this ain't our show!
> Remember that we're not so green
> As the boys in seventeen.... [37]

Professor Henry J. Silverman of Michigan State University has traced a close identification of the Party-lining students of the 1930s with the university teachers whose student disciples went forth in the 1960s seeking "profound transformation of the existing political, economic and social system." [38] The chief difference he found between the generations was that the earlier militants were more closely under organized control than their recent successors. That, as Mrs. Roosevelt learned, poor woman, is probably true. The NSL-AYC leaders knew, though they carefully kept it from her, where they were going—straight to Moscow's doctrinaire Revolution. The Students for a Democratic Society, though driven by the same quasi-paranoid emotions, seem to have been far nearer nihilism—even taking pride in neither knowing nor caring what would happen after they took the clock apart.

SOME CORNER OF A FOREIGN FIELD

FOR THOUGH I UNDERSTAND SPAIN, I DO NOT UNDERSTAND
SPANISH.

—PHYLLIS McGINLEY,
"Public Journal"

The Jonathan Livingston Seagull of 1936 was Ferdinand the Bull, bovine protagonist of a fantasy written for children by Munro Leaf. Its 600-word story was simple. Though bred for fighting, Ferdinand never played rough with the other bull calves, instead sat under a tree and smelled the wild flowers. When they sought out the toughest young bull for a great bullfight, he was sure they'd never pick him. But just then a bee stung him, and his snortings and cavortings made him seem tough, so he was chosen. In the ring he just sat down and smelled the flowers the lady spectators wore in their hair, "so they had to take Ferdinand home. And for all I know he is sitting there still, under his favorite cork tree, smelling the flowers just quietly. He is very happy." "... political feelings became attached to this story," Lionel Trilling noted. "People chuckled over it as if it were ... folk-wisdom." [1] It became a runaway best-seller. For a while "Ferdinand" as a type of engaging innocence was part of the language. Was he one of several reasons why thirty years later the children of adolescents who had enjoyed him in the 1930s were likely to become "flower children"?

He fitted well into the synergistic mix of doctrinaire pacifism and cynical isolationism that suffused American opinion those days and had served the Party's purposes—so far. But in the following year events in Ferdinand's homeland would turn upside down the Party's tolerance of isolationism and insistence that Peace (in a dialectical sense) was as wonderful as Father Divine said. In July, 1936, General Francisco Franco y Bahamonde flew in a chartered plane from Spain's Canary Islands to Spanish Morocco. The consequent Civil War between Spain's reactionary elements and Spaniards hoping for something different and maybe better was soon to be the focus of the West's political emotions. ". . . 1936," Wilfred Sheed called "when the Spanish civil war started and the Communists decided peace wasn't so great after all." [2]

From within the Communist mind this was no change of gear. For the Insurgents' obvious heavy support first from Mussolini, soon from Hitler, almost immediately set the stage for the Party line's favorite doctrine of the essential cleavage between the Fascist and the non-Fascist world. Here in the western Mediterranean surfaced the dichotomy Red/Black, good/bad, them/us. And J. B. Matthews' doctrine for the Student Congress in Chicago was ready and waiting. Spain's legitimate, precariously but properly elected government was both authentic and conveniently leftist-leaning. Here was the clear case of a not only permissible but stirring People's War against Fascist aggression. The Fascist side was already getting help from Italy and Germany. It behooved decent elements in the world political picture— including, of course, international Communism and the USSR—to see that the other side, presumably liberal and democratic, got help enough to hold its ground. The USSR's floundering economy and governing class shaken by recent and ongoing purges could not do a great deal. It was up to international Communism in the Western capitalist states, particularly Britain, France and the United States, to provide the Loyalists * by sale or gift with the munitions and maybe men they would need—and the attendant risk of a situation escalating into world war was necessary. So the Party members and fellow-traveling faithful suddenly found themselves no longer shouting Peace! but All-out-for-Spain!

---

* Identifying labels for the contestants in the Spanish Civil War were confused at the time and are little better now. The American press often designated the government forces "Republicans" in the early stage because they were defending the Spanish Republic created when Alfonso XIII left the throne in 1931. As the Civil War went on, this term tended to disappear, even among sympathizers. "Loyalists," the most widely used later term, makes little sense either but, in view of the mixed pattern concerned, is at least better than "Reds"—their enemies' favorite label. *Time* early called Franco's forces "Whites"; William Carney of the New York *Times,* working on that side of the street, early used "Rebels." "Patriot" and "Nationalist" also appeared here and there. "Rightist" and "Leftist" would make more sense here than usual but it is probably better for this book to use "Loyalist" and "Insurgent" with full awareness that neither is very good.

Then and now the Spanish Civil War is called "dress rehearsal" for World War II. Agreed, provided the point is not overplayed. What is less often said is that in its external aspect it was a war of public relations, of propaganda—on our side of the Atlantic a war for the American mind. The Loyalists may be said to have won that external war on points but lost the internal one because they could not collect the prize of adequate support from the Western democracies. And for that a good deal of blame attaches to the residual pacifism-cum-isolationism that the Party had been cozying up to before Franco and his brother generals made their move. After all, only the year previously, Representative Louis Ludlow (Dem., Ind.) had got wide support for a constitutional amendment requiring a national referendum to validate declarations of war except in case of direct attack on the United States or its possessions. A nation with a large number of responsible people in that frame of mind about its government's trustworthiness in handling foreign affairs was not in a position to do either what made sense about this new Spanish situation or what the Party wanted it to do in the interests of international Communism.

Flabby hope of keeping the lid on the Spanish crisis created a Non-Intervention Committee in Geneva comprising the USSR, Germany, Italy, Britain, France—not the United States, which was thus put in a potentially interventionist position by isolationist gingerliness. Italy and Germany were already violating the committee's purposes and continued regardlessly to do so. The USSR, though lagging early, presently sent badly needed and sizable amounts of matériel and technical help. France played that game only in spasmodic driblets; Sheean attributed this less to the sinister leverage of French reactionaries than to Léon Blum's instinctive Socialist repugnance to anything to do with war. Britain helped the Loyalists hardly at all, though British public sentiment was probably more on that side than on the other. The same applied to the United States, where there were special factors. It is not necessarily true, as was widely held later, that the Loyalists could have stayed in power had they been properly supplied. Had heavy support from Britain and France brought on World War II in, say, 1937, when Britain's military resources were very low and France was quite as demoralized as it was in 1940, without a Pearl Harbor to bring America in, an Axis victory might have been disastrous to Spain and everywhere else. But it can be flatly said of the whole miserable business that the failure of the democracies to supplement the USSR's meager support of the Loyalists made extinction of the Republic certain.

In some degree American help for the Loyalists would have been intervention, of course. The 20–20 hindsight of American pacifists and

isolationists reacting to World War I had already equipped Uncle Sam
with instant remedies for such temptations to intervene as might arise.
The Neutrality Acts of 1935 and 1936 forbade substantial supply of
any belligerent beyond the Western Hemisphere. The obvious purpose
was to prevent development of the kind of emotional or economic
stake on one side or the other that, they said, sent "our boys" to
France in 1917.* For years, as we have seen, disillusion about World
War I had permeated the articulate strata of America. Then in 1934–
36, the years when Mussolini's attack on Ethiopia and Franco's
insurgency made it all threateningly pertinent, a headline-rich investigation of the munitions industry conducted by Senator Gerald P.
Nye of North Dakota vastly reinforced suspicion that the kings of
munitions and loans had inveigled Uncle Sam into that European
mess of 1914–18 first to line and then to protect their pockets. A best-
selling book, *Merchants of Death,* spelled it out for the same public
that simultaneously rejoiced in *Ferdinand.*

This lamentably simple view of history gets at best the Scots verdict
"not proven." That mattered little among Nye's isolationist-minded
constituents; or leaders of opinion unable to understand why FDR,
that well-considered liberal, opposed arbitrary ban on export of things
to kill people with; or radicals happy to see any stick beating the
capitalist dog. Though he grumbled that the Neutrality Act of 1935
was likely to "drag us into war instead of keeping us out," [3] FDR
signed it. In 1936 he signed a stiffer replacement. But it banned only
sales of arms and so on to "belligerents," so six months after Franco
struck, here was a joint resolution of House and Senate specifically
banning such exports to either of the opposing forces in Spain, neither
of which was under the circumstances technically a belligerent.
Legislators are as likely as pacifists and generals to fight a new war as
if it were the last one.

As the Kremlin woke to its opportunities, however, America's Party-
liners exploited the Loyalist cause in the same fashion as their
previous espousal of Sacco and Vanzetti and the Scottsboro Boys. The
Party's change of tactics in 1935 furthered this. A former policy of
boring-from-within bourgeois institutions was then, you recall, replaced by a so-called Popular Front lending Party support to the New
Deal, organization of industrial unions, consumer movements, any-

---

* The purport of the successive Neutrality Acts might seem to clear FDR *et
al.* of the charge of having failed the Loyalists; could they have been expected
to send help thus forbidden by statute? Yet there are, as none knew better
than FDR, more ways than one of skinning a cat. He could, for instance, have
permitted sale of arms to Mexico, which was ardently pro-Loyalist, for resale
to Madrid.

thing calculated to widen potential sympathy for international Communism (synonymous with the USSR in such contexts) in the impending battle to the death with the rising menace of international Fascism. Since that might go beyond mere economic-diplomatic juggling into major war, in which the USSR would need allies and munitions, previous paltering with idealist pacifism and antiarmament talk was now taboo. Much better if America increased its fighting potential and passed some of it on to the right side—anyway not the wrong one. And Spain's agony was handy for educating Americans in how to feel about this crisis. And it came just when the Party badly needed something to distract its external admirers from the stench of the Moscow trials. Already certain intellectuals were feeling ominously queasy about those slavering confessions. Better still, here was a nothing-to-lose program. If American public sentiment and consequently FDR's policies were swung behind the Loyalists, splendid; it would help take the burden off the USSR. If that failed, whatever pro-Loyalist sentiment was roused would be useful in the old protorevolutionary game of alienating Americans from their crypto-Fascist, capitalism-tainted, incurably bourgeois government.

Hitler's and Mussolini's similar game played with black instead of red pieces was incidentally helpful. Anybody judging Franco by the company he kept was bound to be revolted. But neither side of this polarizing tug-of-war wished world opinion to gather much as to the actual situation in Spain. That miserable country had long been skewed and confused by the presence of an illiterate and embittered peasantry; by the Roman Catholic Church deeply entrenched in its anachronistic economy and atavistic popular emotions; by fanatic sectionalism particularly strong in Catalonia and the Basque country, the two most industrialized areas; by anarcho-syndicalism in Catalonia incompatible with the country's more conventional array of squabbling Republican-to-varyingly-Marxist political parties; by a long-standing national habit of substituting church burning, firing squads, massacre, guerrilla skirmishing, riot and military coups for public discussion—a welter of social ailments that led even Herbert L. Matthews of the New York *Times,* ardent partisan of the Loyalists, eventually to admit, "The war was seen at the time as a confrontation of democracy, Fascism and Communism. This idea oversimplified and distorted the truth. The Civil War came out of uniquely Spanish circumstances and it was never anything but that to Spaniards." [4]

In the late 1930s it suited the purposes of both sides to persuade outsiders that this bloody tangle was a simple matter of good guys and bad guys and that to let the bad guys win would imperil good guys everywhere. The Party's hand had better cards and attracted the more articulate satellites and allies. The government that the Insurgents sought to overthrow was legitimately the result of democratic balloting. Their lack of broad popular base was clear in the fact that the core of their army was not Spaniards but the polyglot riffraff of the Spanish Foreign Legion imported from duty in Morocco and the Moorish regiments from the Moroccan colonial army who weren't even nominally Christians, let alone white. The disorders that immediately preceded and continued in the early days of the rebellion supplied the Insurgents' supporters with a convenient wealth of church burnings and miscellaneous slaughter of clergy, officials and known reactionaries by radicalized mobs. But the infamous progressive massacre that the Insurgents staged in the bullring after capturing Badajoz was excellent counterpropaganda and soon supplemented by further well-authenticated Insurgent atrocities that sounded all the worse for being staged by those sinister-sounding Moorish mercenaries. Maybe most significantly Pegler, Catholic-reared, by then in the black books of most American radicals, was so nauseated by continuing efforts to exploit among America's Catholics the heavy support Franco had from the Spanish hierarchy that the Scripps-Howard syndicate refused to print the blistering column he wrote about it. The radical *New Republic* published it for its probably astonished readers:

"In the early months of the fighting the atrocities seem to have been reciprocal. . . ." No longer, Pegler said; the Insurgents were obviously far outdoing the Loyalists, and instead of blaming the radical mobs for the early slaughter of priests and nuns, Spanish Catholics should blame their own clergy for long-standing failure to pay any heed to social needs and now for their conscienceless support of Insurgent heavyhandedness: "If I were a Spaniard who had seen Franco's missionary work among the children, I might see him in hell but never in church." [5]

As the war developed, American correspondents tended to turn up behind the Loyalist, not the Insurgent, lines. In itself that meant more words favorable or, thanks to censorship, not unfavorable to the Loyalist cause put on the wires. And though there were exceptions, on the whole even American correspondents without ties to radicalism, still seeking to be objective, tended to feel that violent, amateurish and presently Communist-ridden as the Loyalists might be, they were preferable to Franco's array of mercenaries, upcountry bigots, tunnel-visioned professional officers, white-collar petty bourgeois and many, many thousand "volunteers" from Italy and Germany. In certain cases such as Sheean's radical sympathies were half acknowledged. Martha Gellhorn, accredited from *Collier's,* soon to be the leggy heroine of Hemingway's pro-Loyalist *The Fifth Column,* proudly told the Party-front American Writers' Congress: "Instead of trying dramatically to scoop each other ... [American correspondents in Madrid] were working collectively ... daily endangering their lives, to cable the truth from Spain." [6] For her, of course, "the truth" was whatever made the Loyalist side look good. Hemingway, accredited from the North American Newspaper Alliance, left out of his cables much that he knew that was discreditable to the Loyalists: "[His] reputation for understatement was not earned by the things he wrote about the Spanish Civil War," [7] says Robert Rosenstone's *Crusade on the Left.* H.L. Matthews, swinging from admiration of Mussolini's troops in Ethiopia to a schoolboy crush on the Loyalists, well exemplified his notion that a correspondent's duty to himself and his reader was to get involved emotionally but refrain from including actual fictions. James Lardner, gone to Spain as a stringer for the New York *Herald-Tribune* at his own instance, was soon so taken by the Loyalists' cause that he enlisted in their Abraham Lincoln Brigade and was killed in one of their last skirmishes.

Phillip Knightley's recent study of war correspondents, *The First Casualty,* says this "failure ... to report the imperfect face of the Republican side does not seem to have been due, except in the case of professed propagandists, to ... duplicity, but to their preoccupation with the effect the war was having on them personally." [8] * Fair enough; but in most cases they might as well have been on the Loyalist payroll. Matters were even less responsible outside Spain. *Time,* then more dependent than now on newspaper accounts, despairingly printed a report from Paris that "the apparently innate tendency of the press to fake has been brought out sharply by the present Spanish war," naming as sinners the entire British press except the Manchester *Guardian,* the entire French except *Figaro* and *Le Temps* and then: "Each of the great international press services is faking in its Paris bureau and each says it has to do so to keep up with the 'colorful' competition." [9] It was also in Paris that Arthur Koestler, at the time an undercover Party member, was cooking up partly out of whole cloth for the Comintern a book called *Spanish Testament,* detailing numerous atrocities that had never happened at all. And Fletcher Pratt, waspish specialist in military matters, who had no use for either "the clerical high-binder Franco or ... the three left-wing elements [Loyalist] ... united in nothing but their opposition to him," [10] published an impressive professional analysis of how the New York *Times* copy-desk and makeup editors were, consciously or not,

---

* Though this is probably sound interpretation on this point, Knightley's approach to his subject is rather too bilious to allow his book to be much more than a clever case for the prosecution.

arranging for headlines and placement of stories to make the Loyalists look consistently good.

In spring, 1937, the Insurgents presented their detractors with an admirable hook to flay Franco on—the bombing of Guernica, the ancient Basque folk capital. Well before Pablo Picasso did that famous painting, Guernica had become the rhetorical equivalent of World War I's Louvain and *Lusitania,* of World War II's Rotterdam and Coventry. In his preface to his radio play *They Fly Through the Air...,* Norman Corwin wrote most puzzlingly: "I was among those disturbed by the rape and betrayal of the Spanish Republic ... into the hands of the loathsome Franco ... and the systematic bombing of Guernica.... [I] said relatively little about it at the time, for it was not yet fashionable to be anti-fascist...." [11] He must have led a sheltered life that spring. The testimony of Lillian Hellman, then in it up to the neck, was: "Never before and never since in my lifetime were liberals, radicals, intellectuals, and the educated middle class to come together in single, forceful alliance" [12] as they did about the Spanish Civil War as resistance to Fascism. Probably true enough, though—as Miss Hellman did not say—far from spontaneous. The Party had not been content to let sympathetic newspapermen and Nazi dive-bombers wage its propaganda war for it. Wherever a sympathetic group could be organized or an existing one manipulated, all over the world, the pressure was on. Philip Toynbee, then a Party member and Oxford undergraduate, said he was ordered from on high "to proliferate Spanish Defense Committees as a moth lays its eggs in a clothes cupboard." [13]

André Malraux, fresh from flying against Franco, famous for the Party-lining brilliance of *Man's Fate* and *Days of Wrath,* came to America to infuse radical-minded audiences with the glories of the Loyalist cause and—since propaganda works best *against* things—the iniquity of the Insurgents. He had to have interpolated translation, for his English was sketchy, but Kazin, who heard him, thought him "magnificently the writer as speaker ... the master of men's minds. His rhythms were so compelling that the audience swayed to them." [14] In Los Angeles, introduced by Ernest Toller, Party member and playwright exile from Germany, Malraux was just as effective at the Shrine Auditorium before a huge crowd of Hollywood celebrities of liberal-to-radical bent. Thenceforward, Clurman recalls, Hollywood's "community life was centered in the various parties given at the home of this or that writer, actor, or director, and at dinners or mass meetings to greet personalities active in the Loyalist cause ... the wave of enthusiasm struck starlets and top executives ... a grotesquely incongruous assortment ... Shirley Temple to Walter Wanger...." [15]

Manhattan was in the same throes. At a party in the gussied-up brownstone of Party-lining Muriel Draper, a conspicuous hostess and smart interior decorator, Ralph Bates, Party member and minor British novelist fresh from Spain, pumped numerous *Time* staffers full of orthodox hatred of Franco and orthodox adulation of the way Communist savvy and discipline were steering the Loyalists to victory. At a benefit Gypsy Rose Lee, the strapping stripteaser of whom Miss Hellman's "educated middle class" was likeliest to have heard because she wrote books, too, said, as she doffed the last integument, "And this is for Spain!" "Almost every writer, artist and professor in the country signed endless [pro-Loyalist] petitions," [16] Albert Halper recorded. The Party's array of propaganda-front organizations was, of course, carefully disguised behind labels that would not alarm "innocents." There was the American Committee for Loyalist Spain, the Medical Bureau for Aid to Spain, the North American Committee for Spanish Democracy, the Theatre Arts Committee for Democracy, a spinoff from the Group Theatre arranging "co-operation of actors and showfolk generally in the Spanish people's fight against Fascism." [16] Featured speaker at the Party-front American Writers' Congress that packed Carnegie Hall and turned away 100-odd more was Hemingway, just back from Spain. "It was magnificent," a believer recalled, "... as if everyone had taken him in their arms ... truly a companion ... in the fight against fascism." [17] The other principals were Donald Ogden Stewart, an outstanding Hollywood Party-liner, president of the Party-front League of American Writers, husband of Ella Winter, Party-lining widow of Lincoln Steffens; Earl Browder, chairman of the Communist Party in America; and Joris Ivens, acknowledged Dutch Party member who worked with Hemingway on *The Spanish Earth,* a propaganda documentary about the Loyalists. He showed part of it. Later Hemingway and he showed the complete print to the Roosevelts at the White House and to a big party at the Fredric Marches' in Hollywood, where it raised $20,000 for ambulances for Loyalist Spain.

Doubtless those ambulances took many poor devils of wounded men to hospitals financed by the Medical Bureau for Aid to Spain. To that extent and in that context the Party's war of words and dollars was unexceptionable. Since no charges to the contrary have cropped up, it is even probable that, unlike what went on in the Sacco-Vanzetti and Scottsboro cases, the bulk of the money thus raised in the name of Spain's ordeal actually was used for the purposes stated, not funneled off into the Party's general war chest. This is the likelier because such funds directly reduced the strain on the Kremlin of helping Spain. Its severity was such that supplies sent thither from Russia had to be paid for cash on the barrelhead in gold from Madrid's sizable reserve, whereas Hitler and Mussolini supplied the

Insurgents on credit, presumably with eventual economic privileges *quid pro quo.*

The Hollywood connection paid off steadily in contributions from liberal sympathizers as well as from the stiffer and growing group, never as large as alarmists feared but not negligible either, of high-salaried members of the movie colony, particularly writers, who had Party cards or were deep-dyed fellow travelers. Their nucleus was John Howard Lawson, perennial Party-lining playwright whose expressionist plays on radical themes won him renown in the 1920s and later. In writing the script of *Blockade,* he in effect borrowed Hollywood's production facilities to make a pro-Loyalist movie as blatant as if Madrid had paid for it;* the producer, Walter Wanger, was a cultivated big name and prominent sympathizer. Franco's secret agents are conspiring to bar a Loyalist port to a ship bringing food for the starving inhabitants. For a chancy while it looks as if Madeleine Carroll's lovely person will be sacrificed to foil them. But Henry Fonda, a progressive-minded Spanish farmer—his yen for tractors is early promise that he will come down on the decent (= Communist) side—rallies the peasantry to save the day. At one point he predicts that unless the world rescues Spain, bombing of London, Paris, New York City is sure to follow. Toward the end he steps out of character to lecture the audience head-on: "This isn't war. War is a thing between soldiers. This is murder ... of women and children...."

This pandemic among showfolk seemed to strike even Clurman as needing explanation. Rather patronizingly he attributed it to an innate gullibility: "Theatre folk are generally innocents; unpretentious, sentimental, credulous, enthusiastic...." [18] Kazin's Manhattan world then contained "So many editors and publishers ... fellow travelers ... complacently intellectual about Marxism [who] ... tended to miss the emotionalism of working-class commitment. The cool-looking types I met now at cocktail parties never seemed to find it odd to express the most 'revolutionary' opinions against the most luxurious backgrounds.... 'The future looks rosy,' I heard the *Collier's* editor, Kyle Crichton [who doubled as "Robert Forsythe," literary panjandrum of the *New Masses*], say at a writers' meeting for Spain...." [19]

Kazin, Hemingway, Malraux, Toller, Stewart, Koestler ... never was so literary a war! Among American pilgrims to Loyalist-held Spain were Dorothy Parker, Lillian Hellman, Dos Passos, Upton Sinclair,

---

* This was Hollywood's second treatment of the Spanish Civil War. The first, *Last Train from Madrid,* annoyed the New York *Times'* reviewer because it had "neither Loyalist nor Rebel [sympathies]." (New York *Times,* June 19, 1937.) Indeed its chief claim to distinction was in the production feat of getting it shot and released within eleven months of the beginning of the war.

Malcolm Cowley, Josephine Herbst—and they all wrote about it and got it printed where it would do the most good. The prize in that respect went to Miss Hellman, who must have been shaken when Hearst (for reasons I choose not even to speculate about) killed a column of Winchell's to make room for a piece of hers on war-torn Spain. It was chancy thus to expose writers to the realities of what Sheean called "the only just cause of first importance in our time." [20] A close look at Loyalist Spain, during which its Communist overlords shot a friend of his for getting out of line, was what started Dos Passos on the break with Party-lining that eventually took him well into the American reactionary camp. By 1939, for that matter, Hemingway was privately calling his pet war "a carnival of treachery and rottenness on both sides." [21] But such revulsions did not reach print in time to chill the elevation of "Spain" to the status of ubiquitous buzzword like "Belgium" in World War I. References to the moral meaning of the Spanish Civil War even cropped up in *After Many a Summer Dies the Swan* (1940) by Aldous Huxley, who was not as given to modish political reflexes as many of his fellow writers in California II. There was little even incidental demurrer * such as that of the cultivated Wall Streeter in S. N. Behrman's *No Time for Comedy* (1939) who, reproached for not being angry about it, replies, "The history of the human race is disgraceful.... Civil war is no new thing in Spain. They fought the Carlist wars for forty years. They kill each other because they want to—that is their pastime...." [22]

The richest early source of pro-Loyalist sentiment in America was Elliot Paul's immensely popular book *Life and Death of a Spanish Town.* Paul was a Montparnassian newspaperman expatriate risen to helping edit *transition,* a fashionably lower-case *avant-garde* magazine. Then he settled on Ibiza, smallest of Spain's Balearic Islands, now a Port of Missing Bohemians, of course, but in his time not yet overrun. Having made many friends among local shopkeepers, fishermen and peasants, he was understandably dismayed by the shattering effects, physical, emotional and social, of the Civil War on the minor village he lived in. The book he made of it all after he got out made juicy reading. His portraits of the characters grown up in this backwater isolated from the modern world were pretty good Steinbeck and by no means stultifyingly partisan. Paul knew and thought fairly well of some who went Insurgent, as well as many who went Loyalist, and of most of their women, who, poor souls, walled off by custom from

---

* F. Jay Taylor, *The United States and the Spanish Civil War* (123-24), makes the Hearst papers the chief exception to his statement that "Few papers and magazines of the secular press in the United States" manifested sympathy with the Insurgents.

knowing much about anything outside their kitchens, had no way of even trying to grasp what was going on. It genuinely helped outsiders understand when he "... began to appreciate how much damage the fascist *coup* had done to the island life, even supposing the Loyalists won.... Families, hitherto friendly and to whom political differences were of sixth- or seventh-rate importance, were now aligned in bitter feuds. 'It will be two hundred years before people here will be friendly again,' said Pedro.... I could not tell them that there were lean and terrible years ahead, that Spain, even if she could save herself from destruction or the ultimate degradation, would be crippled ... the flowering of all her hopes ... deferred." [23]

He had no doubt where the blame lay—on the priests, the economic overlords, the ridiculously numerous officer caste of the Army, the laggard democratic powers as well as the meddling Fascist powers. And long before he reached the intelligible despair expressed above, he had given potential Franco haters in America plenty of black-and-white values and overwritten stimulus: "Madrid? Oh, yes, there was Madrid, and I carry it like a photograph ... a ghostly bombardment continues day and night and what crumbles is the petrified meat of my heart. We are all Madrid, and we must all be shot to pieces, quarter by quarter, until the shells ... fall in the quarter of our self-respect, and then God knows what we shall do." He was somewhat lip-lickingly ghoulish about the projected doom of the girls of his village: "Their young bodies ... must be twisted out of shape to bear sons ... those who should lie with them are corpses, and the remaining ones ... are thieves and cravens.... German and Italian freebooters, bay-rum traitorous generals unworthy to be called Spaniards, leprous churchmen, fumbling, senile England, miserly, small-souled France. Come and take these girls!" [24]

Early in 1938 the Party-lining League of American Writers sent to 1,000-odd American writers * a request to answer and comment on the questions "Are you for or ... against Franco and Fascism? Are you for or ... against the legal government and the people of Republican Spain?" About 400 seem to have replied and were listed in a consequent pamphlet, *Writers Take Sides,* as 98 percent for the Loyalists, 1.75 percent neutral, with only one (elderly Gertrude Atherton, known for romantic novels about Old California) for Franco. Extracts or full statements from 195 were printed at some length. Among them one can easily identify 40-odd who were then Party members or 100 percent fellow travelers. The definition of

---

* *Writers Take Sides* does not give the source of the list. From the names of some who replied it can be deduced that it was far broader than the roster of the league's membership.

"writer" was broad enough to include Browder, Felix Frankfurter, Norman Thomas. (Maybe that was what moved cummings, who had already got ostracized for writing scornfully about the USSR, to return the letter unanswered in an envelope addressed "Donald Ogden Stewart / League of 'American' 'Writers.'...") But there were plenty of qualified professionals: Steinbeck, Hemingway, both Benéts, Dreiser, Wilder, William Carlos Williams.... Certain Red-hots professed to feel insulted by the mere asking of such questions. The fierier conformists vied in the shrillness of their variations on the Party line: Fascism was a world menace that had to be stopped in Spain lest it engulf everything. The Loyalists' was the "People's Cause," Franco a loathsome monster. Congress must at once repeal the embargo on arms to the Loyalists....

There was some nonconformity, however. The league's editors included some of it as window dressing. Half a dozen were allowed to state that they could not take sides either because the issues between the belligerents did not seem clear enough or because, as Channing Pollock, the veteran playwright, wrote, "I see very little difference between communism and fascism, and no choice whatever." [25] William McFee, novelist of the sea and notably respected book reviewer, said much the same thing at greater length. The lists of literary names sorted out by position-taken revealed that in all 20-odd of those questioned had demonstrated by at least backing away from the Party line that common sense had not altogether deserted writers.

Within sixteen months of the publication of *Writers Take Sides* the USSR and Nazi Germany ganged up on Poland, and there was devastation in those serried ranks of Party-lining writers as residual integrity finally moved dozens and scores of them to do themselves the intellectual and moral honor of apostasy. So maybe the most substantial literary result of American writers' clustering around Spain's festering ulcer was *For Whom the Bell Tolls,* and its debut was well after Franco won his game, too late to affect American feeling. Even had it come earlier, its propaganda effect might have been ambiguous. True, it stormed at Fascists and eagerly lingered on atrocities. But it was *both sides* that committed them, a lamentable admission. Further, though the hero was an American, another of Hemingway's romanticized alter egos, he was a lone cloak-and-dagger figure, not a member of the deservedly renowned International Brigades, with whom Hemingway was well acquainted. Indeed, he had just supplied a preface for *Men in the Ranks,* a fund-raising pamphlet for the Disabled Veterans of the Abraham Lincoln Battalion written by Joseph North, a Party stalwart who had been in Spain. The aspect of *For Whom*... pertinent here is that, now the shooting in Spain had died down, writers might again take a more professional interest in their work.* There had been too much reason for John M. Muste's comment on writings about Spain's troubles: "In the thirties . . . it was popular to believe that literature could be a weapon in the class war . . . these works show that . . . the result might be a weapon but it was not literature." [26] The most striking case was W. H. Auden's *Spain* (1937), its royalties earmarked for the Party-front Medical Aid for Spain. After a later look at it, Auden withdrew it and forbade inclusion of it in later collections of his work.

Thinking things over after World War II, in which he had had a hazardously active and informative part, John Mason Brown wrote: "[American] history knows no heroes braver, certainly none more imaginative than these young men who, for the sake of faraway freedom, fought in the Lincoln Battalion." [27] As to the bravery, granted; they were worthy fighting countrymen of those who died in the Alamo and stormed Missionary Ridge. One is less comfortable with the circumambient legend that their rush to defend what they believed to be freedom was originally their own idea. At the beginning of the Spanish Civil War several hundred young Americans did more or less that, severally and informally entering Spain to offer their services to the Loyalists and get swallowed up in the ongoing cataclysm. Not the boys of the Abraham Lincoln outfit. Theirs was not "a spontaneous immaculate conception," boasted the Communist Party's *Daily World* recently celebrating the thirty-eighth anniversary of the Lincolns. "It had its origin, inspiration and organizing somewhere. That was the Communist Party of the United States." [28]

---

* Dwight Macdonald was justified in calling *For Whom* . . . not a novel "but . . . a series of short stories . . . some excellent." *(Discriminations,* 279.) And the hero's final soliloquy seems to me to be the beginning of the process of maturing style liberation (from Gertrude Stein and his own phobias) that later enabled Hemingway to do *The Old Man and the Sea.* The whole is strangely marred, however, by efforts to keep the reader reminded that the hero and the rest of the cast are talking colloquial, sometimes rustic Spanish. Spanish words and phrases are stuck in, later translated when used again, and vice versa. Literal transplantings of syntax foul things up. Archaistic use of the English second-person singular gets so far out of hand that one character is allowed to say, "Thee would do well to go to bed now. Thou hast a long journey." Elsewhere the two usages are fused even closer: "Thee hadst." Absurdity got further, however, in the movie (1943), where the problem of conveying a sense of exotic talk was attacked by casting a Greek (Katina Paxinou) as the sibylline Pilar, and giving most of the other roles to actors of Slavic background, while Gary Cooper spoke straight United States, in accent, that is; to remind the audience he was speaking Spanish, he used such locutions as "How are you called?" instead of "What's your name?"

Apparently now it can be told, what many discerned forty years ago, that the International Brigades, of which the Lincolns were the dominant American unit, were a Party creation, the majority of its personnel Party members and Party control persisting throughout. Indeed, Cecil Eby, a conscientious student of these matters, has reason to call the Internationals "an autonomous army of the Comintern." [29]

The purpose was not so much to get manpower behind the Loyalists—that was the one thing they had enough of—as to reap in the outside world the propaganda value of trenchant demonstration that in spite of sulky bourgeois governments, the Western nations' mass hearts were against Franco and in favor of the Loyalists' "People's War." The scheme was first suggested by Maurice Thorez, head of France's Communist Party, taken up by Georgi Dmitrov, Bulgarian chief pilot of the Comintern and father of the Popular Front policy of 1935. Under him machinery for deliberate recruiting was set up wherever a Communist Party existed. Having long-run propaganda value in mind, he instructed those in charge to enlist as many non-Party men as possible: Socialists, liberals and what he called "Jewish Nationalists," so that "We can build the American Popular Front on the Spanish battlefields." [30]

Those kinds of sympathizers were duly enrolled, some so innocent as not to know the auspices. But by and large the major ingredient of the Internationals generally was actual Party members, acting on Party orders or gaining Party permission to show the *bourzhui* what social morality was, or fellow travelers eager to show loyalty. In the Continental contingents many were refugees from Nazi Germany, Fascist Italy, authoritarian Poland and Hungary, the socially snarly Balkans. Many such had known action in World War I as well as Party street fighting. Similar types among French, Belgian, Scandinavian, Cuban, Mexican radicals were also susceptible to the call of come-and-fight-Fascism, lend-a-hand-to-the-People's War and acquire merit in high places. Hugh Thomas' authoritative *The Spanish Civil War* * says that first and last some 60 percent of those whom the Internationals recruited were Communists to begin with and some 20 percent acquired membership in Spain. The topmost echelon of the Internationals was dominantly Central European or Balkan Communist professional henchmen given asylum with and working for the Comintern in the USSR before the trouble in Spain gave them a

---

* This section relies with grateful confidence on Thomas' admirable research, organization and clinical sense. Other works found indispensable: George Orwell, *Homage to Catalonia;* Alvah C. Bessie, *Men in Battle;* Robert Rosenstone, *Crusade on the Left;* Cecil Eby, *Between the Bullet and the Lie.*

sphere of activity under their Russian patrons' get-results-or-else orders.

Spain's Foreign Legion (= the Tercios), indispensable to the Insurgents, was a jumble of harshly disciplined misfits partly from Spain, partly men "shipwrecked from life" [31] from many nations. From a military point of view this worked well enough, as the Tercios' model, the French Foreign Legion, had long since shown. But the International Brigades soon learned that with their kind of personnel it was better to organize by nations in battalions named for departed heroes of some pertinence: Germans made up the Thaelmann Battalion, Frenchmen the Henri Barbusse Battalion, Italians the Garibaldi Battalion, Americans the Abraham Lincoln and George Washington battalions, Canadians (with a large admixture of Americans) the Mackenzie-Papineau Battalion and so on and on. A sort of Tower of Babel Battalion welcoming small contingents from any and all cultures to anti-Fascist discipline had to be hastily abandoned. Anybody thinking it incongruous to use Lincoln as totem for a Marxist fighting outfit should reflect about such a use of Washington, who, for all his civic and personal virtues, was a slaveowning, shareholding, land-grabbing speculator. To gibe at that is to be unaware of how imaginatively the Party of the late 1930s decorated its Popular Front slogan: "Communism is twentieth century Americanism." It also blithely borrowed Tom Paine, which made some sense; Thomas Jefferson, maybe a touch of sense; but also John Brown, Patrick Henry and Crispus Attucks—that made no more than Lincoln or Washington.*

The prestige-heavy name of Eugene Debs, homegrown tutelary hero of America's Socialists, was out of bounds; its bloom had already been taken off. Soon after Franco made his move Spain's ambassador in Washington suggested to Norman Thomas, chief of the dominant wing of American Socialism, that the Loyalist government would welcome American volunteers; doubtless he too understood the propaganda advantage. Here came plans for a Eugene Victor Debs Column 500 strong and $50,000 raised to equip and transport it. This was, of

---

* Who were these Party-chosen sponsors of International outfits: Ernst Thaelmann was Germany's outstanding Communist after World War I. Henri Barbusse, a chronic Communist, is remembered for his trend-setting antiwar novel, *Le Feu* (1915). William Lyon Mackenzie and Louis Joseph Papineau headed revolts in Upper Canada (now Ontario) and French Canada respectively against the colonial Canadian government in 1837. The Party tried to give the British battalion the name of Saklatvala, a conspicuous anticolonialist in India; it never took. They should have remembered Jack Cade or Oliver Cromwell—at least he would have fitted as well as Washington.

course, utterly inconsistent with the all-war-is-anathema pacifism that Socialists usually preached. The Reverend Dr. John Haynes Holmes, pastor of Manhattan's famous nondenominational Community Church, as eminent and cultivated a radical as Thomas himself, sounded off with the eloquence for which he was justly renowned:

"Times have changed since ... 1917 saw the Socialist Party refuse to support a war in which not a foreign but our own country was involved. By what right does any Socialist today profane the sacred name of Debs by using it to designate a regiment of soldiers enlisted for ... human slaughter? ... You and I, Norman ... stood fast when Belgians lifted cries as pitiful as those lifted by Spaniards today.... Are we to stand by idly when a new generation ... yields to the appeal for another fight ... to save democracy?" [32]

It was the more embarrassing because part of Thomas' new belligerency was a recent overeagerness to nudge his followers into playing Popular Front with their sworn enemies, the Communists. Mumblingly he told Holmes that times had changed and his ideas with them, and "in spite of some extremely pacifist utterances ... Debs said and did things which argued that he would have supported this Column." [32] After which deft exegesis—he had, after all, been a parson himself—he went on with the scheme much more openly than the Communists dared to with their International Brigades project, at least nominally clandestine from the beginning. Washington warned Thomas that federal law forbade Americans to fight in alien wars. He pointed out to both State and Justice that in World War I nothing much was done to check the export of volunteers for the French armed forces. His point was rejected, but something relaxed official vigilance to where, as long as it wasn't done in the street and frightened horses, isolationists and Catholics, the recruiting for Loyalist Spain was little hindered. By then, however, that helped only the Communist effort. The delay while things shook down had combined with lively residual pacifism of Holmes' kind to stifle the Debs Column. Young Socialists hell-bent on getting to Spain to fight Fascism found the best way was to enlist in the Kremlin-tainted Internationals—as a few did. It was an omen of how well Moscow eventually succeeded in taking over the prestige and strategic potential associated with outside intervention on the Loyalist side.

Hugh Thomas' estimates of actual numbers in the Internationals are as useful as any: 40,000 recruited over the two active years. What with casualties, desertions and sending home the disabled and sometimes others for propaganda or administrative work, the number under arms at one time probably never exceeded 18,000. French leftists, profiting by the common frontier, sent the most; then in descending order the

Germans and Austrians, Italians, Hungarians, Yugoslavs, Scandinavians. The English-speaking world sent 2,000-odd British, 1,000 Canadians, maybe 3,200 Americans. The rest scattered in from what is said to have been a total of thirty nations. The inner meaning of their being in Spain came out spontaneously when the first International unit to go into action, a mixed battalion of French, German, Polish, British and Belgians, marched through Madrid, and the Madrileños, making a sanguine and understandable mistake, shouted, *"Vivan los rusos!"* ("Hurrah for the Russians!") [33] *

The obvious American parallel, as Norman Thomas knew, was the Lafayette Escadrille, the unit of Francophile American fighter pilots whom the French government encouraged in 1915 because thus to dramatize American support was good propaganda. Indeed one of the Lincolns, David McKelvy White, son of a governor of Ohio, instructor in English at Brooklyn College, eventually repatriated to manage the Friends of the Abraham Lincoln Brigade in New York City, had had an uncle in the Lafayettes. Not parallel at all was the scratch handful of American fliers whom the Loyalists recruited early in the war to their and the recruits' mutual regret. The best known was Bert Acosta, who had been at the controls for Commander (later Admiral) Byrd in a famous pre-Lindbergh transatlantic flight. Later the best known was Harold "Whitey" Dahl, captured after bailing out behind the Insurgent lines and sentenced to the firing squad. His beautiful wife, who led an all-girl dance combo working minor night spots in both hemispheres, sent Franco a luscious photograph of herself and a plea for his life that reduced his sentence to life imprisonment and then release in 1940. Except for Ben Leider, a Brooklyn newspaperman who flew as a hobby and really hated Fascists, dying honorably in a dogfight in consequence, these were all mercenaries and professionals, frankly in it for the money, which was generous and included a $1,000 bonus for each Insurgent plane shot down. Within a few months all but Leider and Dahl (who couldn't) had quit the job and left Spain partly because of the obsolescent crates they had to fly, partly because soon the Russians came muscling into the Loyalist air force.

In further contrast with the Lafayettes of 1915, most of whom came from conservative, affluent WASP households, the Lincolns were mostly of first-generation immigrant parentage in what they would proudly have called proletarian circumstances. Eby mentions an early

* The USSR eventually admitted having sent more than 500 fighting men, mostly combat technicians packaged with the military hardware reaching Loyalist ports. If that many were officially admitted, it can be assumed that the actual total was three or four times as much. But few of those were enrolled in the Internationals.

machine-gun squad answering to Kavorkian, Simrak, Cuban, Tsermanges, Menendidis, Skepastiotis, Wagulevich, Tannenhaus; their sergeant, Bill Harvey, was born Horowitz. The Lincolns' leaders' "Party names," always used, usually had Old American connotations that, the Party apparently hoped, would give a deceptively WASPish sound; among the commissars, for instance, John Gates (once Sol Regenstreif) and Dave Doran (once Dransky). Steve Nelson (once Mesaroh), tough as any and ablest of them all, was sent specially from America to stiffen up the Lincolns' morale after bungling command and their own pluck and lack of experience got them cut to ribbons in their first battle. Edwin Rolfe, competent poet, editor of their house organ, was originally Fishback.

I know of no special effort to recruit blacks. They numbered 100-odd, made good fighting records as often as whites and were usefully conspicuous in the group photographs taken for propaganda use. One had quit the San Francisco PWA-FWP to join up, announcing, "I'm going to get myself one of those Moors." [34] Another said, "I wanted to go to Ethiopia to fight Mussolini.... [Spain] ain't Ethiopia but it will do." [35] Most black volunteers were probably moved by the same Party-line clichés as those inspiring the whites. And their public relations function was much the same. Mangione recalls the parties raising funds for Spain "in the luxurious apartments of wealthy radicals ... anti-fascist refugee writers [as guests of honor] ... [or] some young American ... about to ... join the Abraham Lincoln Battalion." [36] At gatherings of the Young Communist League, the Party-front League Against War and Fascism and so on girls conveyed to boys how heroic it would be to volunteer to fight for Spain. Those who took the hint and what might come with it came back, when they came back at all, shaken but closemouthed, one frequenter of such occasions recalls; he got the impression that they had been told to keep quiet or else. Eby suggests, however, that such reticence often meant that residual loyalty to what they fought for prevented admission of disillusion to outsiders. Doubtless both were present.

The typical Lincolns, however, were young Party members—notably younger than those in other International units—usually with some background in Party organizing. Students and seamen were the two most numerous categories. After cursory examination by a Party-lining doctor and careful interrogation by a panel of Party leaders lest stool pigeons or potential spies infiltrate the project, the recruit was told how to get a passport (illicit, since he had to conceal intent to enter Spain, a forbidden travel area once the Civil War began) and buy World War I surplus soldier clothes at a certain store. The Party paid his third-class passage to France. There a busy Party organization—

Louis Fischer, prominent magazine reporter expert on the USSR, was its chief munitions procurer—sent the new arrival south by rail. At first the border crossing was made by sea, later by smugglers' trails over the snowy Pyrenees. In Paris or later in Spain his passport was taken away for two probable reasons: Lack of it made him easier to control, and it could be doctored up and given to some Party member as false identification when crossing frontiers and encountering police.

Combat training was usually short and sketchy because weapons and knowledgeable instructors were scarce. Command was hampered by the old Red Army system of the "political commissar" as coordinate officer breathing down the nominal commander's neck and empowered to overrule him. That worked well when the commissar had as much force and savvy as Steve Nelson. But too few of the others were budding Trotskys, and the rank and file were often sour about these "comic stars," as they called them. The worst of it was that the Lincolns,* who lacked the stiffening of World War veterans that some International outfits had, were forced to acquire their fighting know-how the most dangerous way—as undertrained novices up against professional veterans. Eventually it made them formidable fighters. From the first such highly motivated volunteers were plucky. But meanwhile, it meant appalling casualties. Thomas puts their killed at 30 percent of those mustered in. Eby believes that the official figure of 1,500 killed out of 3,200 enlisted is too low. Add that in the Spanish kind of civil wars neither side is too solicitous about taking battlefield prisoners † and that the Insurgents tended to regard the Internationals as interlopers without belligerent rights.

It was significant of the outside world's low opinion of the Insurgent cause that so few outsider volunteers came its way. A small unit of reactionary French called the Jeanne d'Arc Bandera; a smaller one of White Russians snapping at the Kremlin's heels indirectly; a few hundred piously adventurous Catholics from the Irish Free State.

---

* This term is used throughout to mean American units in the Internationals. It usually includes those originally in the George Washington and Mackenzie-Papineau battalions. One reason is that with heavy casualties all three outfits eventually became so small that they were often consolidated as one battalion under the Lincoln totem. Another that the fund- and recruit-raising propaganda in America was usually in the name of the Abraham Lincoln Battalion, sometimes promoted to a Brigade.

† I do not mean that prisoners were never taken. On both sides practice obviously varied from command to command and time to time. The Italian "volunteers" on the Insurgent side took prisoners pretty freely with exchange in view. Toward the end the Insurgents took some hundreds of Internationalists prisoner on the Aragon front. Similarly in the crossing of the Ebro late in the war the Loyalists took a good many Insurgent prisoners.

Their presence makes one wonder where the Irish-Americans were. Nowhere, as to the Insurgents; the only such in the fight were on the Loyalist side, largely in the James Connolly * section of the Lincolns, mostly former Irish Republican Army guerrillas. Franco's Tercios probably contained a handful of American soldiers of fortune enlisted before the coup. For what the parallel is worth, and it may be meaningful, consider that in World War I, in spite of the valid ties of kinship and sentiment between German-Americans and their belligerent cousins, no counterpart of the Lafayettes went to fight for the Kaiser. In both cases such invidious apathy probably means that basic American sentiment was anti-German in 1914, anti-Fascist in 1936.

How then to account for the fact that regard for American Catholics' pro-Insurgent sentiment had so much to do with FDR's consistent refusal to lend the Loyalists even an indirect hand? High-strung liberals were soon muttering about overt pro-Fascism in high places in Washington. Lewis Mumford ascribed it to appeasement of Fascists in the Argentine, but that sort of thing was largely chatter at Aid-to-Spain cocktail parties. Probably the cards were stacked against intervention on the Loyalist side to begin with. The war began in a presidential election summer when a Democratic victory was not the sure thing it looked like after the landslide. Indignation among Catholic voters against anti-Franco measures might make a crucial difference in some big-electoral-vote states. The continuing Nye investigation kept strengthening the peevish isolationism behind those successive Neutrality Acts. And though if a choice had to be made, most Americans probably thought the Insurgents slightly more noisome of the two, there was plenty of room to deplore both. And the Vatican persisted in endorsing Franco, deliberately identifying the Church as a whole with the reactionary forces in Spain. By 1938 politicians seeking reelection might wonder how much ice that actually cut among voters in South Boston, Pawtucket and Hamtramck or any given Little Italy, but few cared to test the matter.†

Not until the war was practically over did FDR admit to Claude Bowers, home from his anxious stint as US ambassador to the Spanish Republic, of which he was candidly a partisan, that "we made a mistake in Spain." [37] One of the side effects of that mistake was to

---

* Irish Socialist conspicuous in the Rebellion of 1916; captured and executed by the British.

† Gallup POPS showed a good three out of ten Catholics pro-Loyalist and an even larger proportion not caring who won. The very high proportion of "No opinions" that Gallup obtained throughout the Spanish Civil War, even though pro-Loyalist sentiment gained somewhat as time passed, is the most interesting thing about these polls. (Gallup and Rae, *Pulse of Democracy,* 316.)

help the Kremlin grip on the Loyalist cause that eventuated in control even of anarchist Catalonia. In some ways the beefing up of the originally small Spanish Communist Party with outside talent straight from Moscow had constructive results. Bloodily imposed Communist discipline did much to change the Loyalists' rabble-in-arms into an organized fighting force able not only to die but also to strike back. That was one reason why the Hemingways and Matthews' took so dim a view of the anarchist enthusiasts who, for all their flashes of wild courage, kept fouling up plans and situations. But the Communist takeover was more than a mere victory for able leadership. The Loyalists' chief source of firearms, ammunition, tanks, planes and so on was the USSR. And it was Stalin's representatives in Spain who determined who got those supplies. In order to get the wherewithal to fight, Spanish commanders had to let the Communists call the military and disciplinary tunes. Had the United States let other-than-Russian ships fetch the Loyalists matériel paid for with gold from their reserve, the Kremlin's leverage would not have been so nearly irresistible. The founders of the American Youth Congress could have told Spain's Socialist and allied anti-Franco groups what was likely to happen once the Communist camel got his head into the tent. "... few politicians," Hugh Thomas says, "have successfully used a Communist party and not been later swallowed by it." [38]

The Lincolns' Party-member leadership can have felt small uneasiness about that. The non-Party, rank-and-file minority, who had presumably joined up with less rigid notions of how and why to fight for freedom, were in another position. But they were also in the middle of Spain without passports, having left home illegally, aware that surrender to the Insurgents might mean a bullet in the back of the neck, too foreign in speech and ways of doing to melt into the population. Besides, nobody likes to feel like a quitter, and little had happened to lead any of the Lincolns to change their original impression that killing Fascists was a good thing to do. Though the Internationals had wholesale desertions in their disastrous retreat in Aragon, the Lincolns eventually recovered enough coherence and spirit to behave most creditably in the Ebro offensive that was the Loyalist last hurrah.

After that petered out, the cause was down by the stern and sinking fast. As the Munich crisis neared, says Hugh Thomas' admirable summary, Stalin inclined toward "friendship with Hitler at the democracies' expense ... an end to Russian commitment in the Spanish War, and particularly of ... the International Brigades ... a majority of [whom] were now Spanish ... many ... from prison, work camps and disciplinary battalions.... Even the Lincoln Battalion comprised a three-to-one majority of Spaniards. . . . Negrin [the Spanish Loyalist chief] was able, without military risk, to propose . . . the withdrawal of all foreign volunteers in Republican Spain." [39] Muste thought this "a last desperate effort . . . to win sympathy and help from France, Great Britain and the United States." [40] The Lincolns marched in the Internationals' farewell parade in Barcelona. La Pasionaria, the Spanish Communists' blend of Joan of Arc and Madame Defarge, assured them that "for reasons of state . . . [we] are sending you back. . . . You can go proudly. . . . You are the heroic example of democracy's solidarity and universality" [41] and, though she neglected to say so, of the subservience of international Communism to the zigs and zags of the USSR's national policies. It had suited the Kremlin's book to muster the Internationals to help Spain. Now it suited to withdraw them, and that was that.

God knows they had earned the lady's praise. The way the Lincolns could get badly mauled and keep on going against the toughest men Franco could field was beyond praise. But while pulling out the old, timeworn stops of Party clichés, this she-catspaw of the Kremlin need not have so eloquently proclaimed that their dismissal, like their recruitment, was primarily a public relations stunt.

They said Yiddish was the Internationals' *lingua franca.* That may not have held good of their French and British volunteers, but it must have among the Americans. They probably ran well above 50 percent Jewish. That means, for one thing that will surprise nobody, that the proportion of young Jews in American Communism was high—an incontrovertible fact like the high incidence of Indians among New York City's structural steelworkers—and for another that anti-Semites' sneers about Jews' temperamental reluctance to fight had always been nonsense. It did not need the Six-Day War to show the world that Jewish fighting men were as good as any and better than most, worthy to wear the Maccabee tartan. Forty years ago the Abraham Lincolns had proved that far beyond the Near East's power to add or detract.

That was one of several ways in which the place of the Jewish segment in American culture was or should have been changing during the Depression decade. Changes were overdue. The Jews had been gaining visibility in a fashion unhappily handy for their sickest detractors. Actually the more outrageous anti-Semites were, though noisiest, less disturbing than others. They flaunted their own absurdity. The Elders of Zion, it seemed, were simultaneously using the international bankers' hold on capitalism to seize worldwide power and encouraging Communism to destroy capitalism. The charge that Jews controlled the press, industry and finance was hard to prosecute when everybody with the merest acquaintance with newspapers, banks and industrial concerns knew it was groundless. Yet there was a lingering flavor of plausibility because a disproportionate control did exist, however innocently, however divorced from Jewishness (whatever that may be), in certain other interrelated fields. By the end of the 1920s it was unmistakable that Jews clearly identifiable as such were in command of all three major broadcasting networks, all major movie-producing companies, the bulk of what was left of live show business, the bulk of garment manufacture, a conspicuously large part of general retailing. And in everything except radio—too young to have cultural traditions yet—that had been familiarly conspicuous for at least a generation.

Then, as the New Deal loomed high in public awareness, here were Jews conspicuous among its pillars: Lilienthal, for instance; Henry Morgenthau, Jr., FDR's Secretary of the Treasury; Felix Frankfurter, first the father confessor of the young liberal-to-radical lawyers (many of them Jewish, too) so numerous in the New Deal, then FDR's choice to succeed Louis D. Brandeis as the brilliant Jew on the US Supreme Court; Sidney Hillman, chief of the Amalgamated Clothing Workers, FDR's powerful consultant on labor; Benjamin V. Cohen, one of his best idea men. They were nothing like a majority in the topmost echelons but certainly much more numerous than Jews had ever been before in the American seats of the governmental mighty. It all came to a point in the raucous crackpots' growingly frank charge that FDR's surname had once been Rosenfeld and his provenance was clandestinely Jewish to match; hence his subversive fondness for Jewish lieutenants. Or maybe the queerest form of this new version of an old disease was the hysterical anti-Semitism shown by Milo Reno, head of the militant Farmers' Holiday Association, for he and his supporters were in orthodoxly liberal eyes protorevolutionary heroes theoretically immune to the Jew-baiting impulse. One would like to have been under the table that June day in 1933 when Reno told Henry Wallace and a Des Moines rabbi, "The Jews invented usury ... [and are] consequently responsible for the farmers' troubles." [42]

Even after Coughlin put his weight behind their delusions, however, such nonsense mongers were relatively impotent. Anti-Semitism eagerly enlisted to fight the New Deal but never succeeded in becoming a problem of the first order. For Jews—and for civic decency—the sticky problem was what Irving Howe's *World of Our Fathers* calls "social anti-Semitism ... that informal system of exclusion which made it possible for native Americans to keep at a minimum their social relations with Jews ... not a strategy for depriving Jews of their rights as citizens ... [just that] Jews were not to be received into that network of clubs, universities, schools, and places of recreation in which the American elite flourished ... once [Jews] moved onto the avenues leading toward assimilation they found many barriers on their path." [43]

Many in the wheat and cotton belts listened confusedly to Populists ranting about international Jewish bloodsuckers. But this other invidiousness was primarily an urban development, a large ingredient in which was relative numbers of Jews * in the given community. In the Midwestern small towns, for instance, the occasional Jewish family hardly met it at all. Lilienthal, no man to take things lying down, wrote of the "decency and tolerance" about Jews in county-seat Indiana where he was reared: "I recall no single instance of exclusion or hindrance because of my being a Jew. I was treated entirely on my own merits by the other boys ... in college [in Greencastle, Indiana] such a thing as social prejudice did not exist against me, either in fraternity or in campus political life." [44] From the Gentile side, Homer Croy's small hometown in northern Missouri had only one Jewish family. They owned the clothing store on the north side of the square. Their son, Moses Nusbaum, "was about like one of us. One day I heard somebody call him a 'sheeny.' I did not know what it meant." [45] In the hard-nosed coal-mining town of Ottumwa, Iowa, Edna Ferber as a little girl had "sheeny" shouted after her in the street but experienced nothing more of the sort in Appleton, Wisconsin. There even a sizable accumulation of Jewish families engaged chiefly in stock

---

* This discussion must get along without my illuminating it with an intelligible definition of who "Jews" are. It can be got at, not very satisfactorily, by reaching into farther and farther margins of association. Obviously a member of any synagogue, Orthodox or Reformed, is a Jew. So is anybody reared in any form of Jewish religion who, though no longer active in it, is not zealously devoted to any other. So, in most Americans' view, would be his children and grandchildren. But the religious test fails soon. Though Elizabeth Taylor was converted to Judaism, few would call her Jewish. Surnames are no guide. Too many Jewish families have Anglicized their names or changed them altogether without their progeny's ceasing to consider themselves Jewish, and of course, anybody who considers himself a Jew *is* a Jew—that is one of the few clear things about this. On the other hand, is the great-grandson of a Jew named Cohen who married a Gentile girl, whose offspring for the intervening generations all married Gentiles, a Jew because of his 100 percent Jewish name? Not even the Nuremberg laws would have maintained that. Yet a Cohen even now stands a poor chance of being elected into a really swanky country club. Leave it at: "A Jew is somebody who, whether he likes it or not, whatever he tries or does not bother to do about it, considers himself a Jew, or anyway has had some of the social problems attached to that status." For a looser and probably more helpful discussion see Glazer and Moynihan, *Beyond the Melting Pot* (2d edition), 142.

and feed dealing led to no noticeable strains. She noted that consequently, in contrast with big-city situations, "[Jewish] children did not stand spectacularly high in their studies ... probably because they had never experienced racial or religious oppression ... the persecuted Jew ... naturally tried to compensate for oppression ... the Jew left in peace for two hundred years ... would lose his aggressiveness, his tenacity and neurotic ambition.... If fools really want to destroy us, they need only let us alone. Incredibly adaptable, gregarious, imitative, we soon would be absorbed by the world about us." [46]

Applying such common sense to problems in acculturation would never do nowadays when ethnic fragmentation is fashionable. At that time (1960) she was speaking of elder situations more favorable than the vast majority of Jews present in America in the 1930s had ever met. Five generations ago the self-exiled German Jew landed in America with few resources but pluck, shrewdness and assiduity. Shown how to get credit with a wholesaler, he might go probing off into the Old Northwest or Dixie with a pack of notions and sundries on his back and an eye for promising situations. The renowned Yankee peddler then doing much the same thing usually graduated to a horse and wagon as he prospered but did not necessarily settle down. The Jew tended to find a spot that suited and go into fixed local retailing. Scores and hundreds of him—never really numerous—wound up like Croy's Nusbaums, serving a small community well and getting treated about like everybody else, not on principle—small towns are hardly more tolerant than large ones—but because it never occurred to anybody to do anything else.

It seems to have been best in the Old Northwest. The Dixie situation was mixed. There, Jonathan Daniels had reason to say in 1938, "... in most Southern towns, except where many Jews have recently come in, the direction of social prejudice at the Negro frees the Jews from prejudice altogether—or almost altogether." [47] Given the fact of less prejudice, one may question the cause; it may be rather another case of the rule of smaller minority = lowered hostility to it; there may have been some lightning-rod effect in the black presence but hardly enough to cover the situation. And there is another tone to W. J. Cash, a Southern newspaperman, too, and as well informed as Daniels, also rather more liberal, who wrote at the same time that even though Jews were relatively few down there, "the Jew, with his universal refusal to be assimilated, is everywhere the eternal Alien; and in the South, where any difference has always stood out with great vividness, he was especially so." [48] He may have had in mind the Populists' anti-Jewish ranting in the 1890s that sent Louisiana rednecks burning the stores of Jewish merchants to whom they owed money and their counterparts in Mississippi burning barns on their Jewish landlords' farms. (In calling the Jew "the eternal Alien," he was, of course, not thinking at all; Miss Ferber was a sounder sociologist.) In Asheville, North Carolina, which, as a health resort, had had more outside influence than most Southern towns, the boys in Thomas Wolfe's time, just before World War I, followed Jewish kids home yelling "Goose grease!" and gibberish supposed to be Yiddish. Wolfe particularly remembered little "furtive-faced . . . Isaac Lepinski . . . grinning with wide Kike constant derision." [49]

Here was by no means the only well-considered novelist of fifty years ago tossing off such epithets as "kike" with thoughtless relish. Dreiser was blatant in such matters. Returning to Manhattan after a long absence in the early 1920s, he complained that it had become "a Kyke's [sic] dream of a ghetto. The lost tribe has taken the island." Ten years later he suggested reducing the number of Jewish lawyers by 90 percent and maintained that thanks to their refusal to marry Gentiles, the Jews were likely to overrun America. "Hitler was right," he told a friend in 1934. ". . . The Jews . . . shouldn't live with the others. Let them have their own country." [50] Sinclair Lewis' *Dodsworth* dwelt on the dismaying ubiquity of Jews in Manhattan; the hero's lady love, a charming widow, describes the place as "Russian Jews in London clothes going to Italian restaurants with Greek waiters and African music! One hundred per cent mongrels!" [51]—words that might very well have come from the vivacious mistress of a high-ranking Nazi. To see such stuff in print is startling now. Back then even readers finding it distasteful would have recognized such talk as not exceptional. Well into Depression times an occasional cartoon of the big-beaked, gross-bodied, overdressed man or woman saying money-vulgar things would appear in the old (humorous) *Life,* even the *New Yorker.* And one of the latter's most popular features was Arthur Kober's sketches of Bella Gross, the Bronx working girl whose parents' mutilations of English were the cream of the humor: "Lettiss! A cow eats lettiss! A huss eats lettiss! It's just like a piece gress! Where does Mexie come to lettiss?" [52]

It was probably the noticeable clusters of German Jews in large cities that stirred xenophobia into creating Howe's "social anti-Semitism" within a generation of their arrival. The resort hotel, the college fraternity took measures. So did Wall Street. In the 1920s, though such redoubtable Jewish moneymen as Otto Kahn, Jacob Schiff, Bernard Baruch were well entrenched there, some 60 percent of brokerage houses employed no Jews at all, and the minority that did so sometimes made it clear that the purpose was nothing more liberal than to attract Jewish customers. In the white-tie department only a few unimpeachably wealthy Jews who had early changed their names into something that did not sound Jewish until you thought about it— August Belmont, for instance—were on the lists of Fifth Avenue hostesses. Just why Mrs. van Gramercy did not ask one to dine or what one missed by not belonging to the Stymie Country Club was hardly a grave issue except for the person snubbed. Possibly, almost but not probably, much of that would eventually have broken down— as was then happening to the once widely ostracized Irish. *C.* 1890, however, rolled in an overriding new factor—a second wave of Jewish immigration far larger than the first and far stranger in ways of doing, hence far more likely to perpetuate and heighten an already discreditable anti-Semitism.

For almost thirty years, until World War I, they kept coming in annual swarms, not from Germany and Austria but from rawer, cruder Eastern Europe—Russia, Poland, Austrian Galicia, Romania. They were fleeing persecution consisting of at best intolerable social and economic restrictions, at worst officially instigated massacre. Centuries of cultural isolation had focused their emotional lives on an Old Testament-rich religion that stressed racial exclusiveness as holy duty. Practically all were miserably poor, self-uprooted from rural slums that were inadequate preparation for big-city life in the New World. Yet it was largely into big cities—New York City first and foremost because nearly all of them landed there from the fetid steerages; secondarily into Boston, Philadelphia, Chicago—that they crowded. Able to afford nothing better, they crowded into the worst slums, displacing Italians and Irish and creating the nation's first ghettos, distinguishable from those of the Old World only because they were impromptu, not legally insisted on.

Some of their German coreligionists, disturbed by or aghast at their uncouth misery, made settlement-house-like efforts to help them learn the ropes. But the inevitable flavor of *de-haut-en-bas* irked the newcomers, and by and large they went their own desperately struggling way. Many went to work—the hours were unbelievably long, the wages grotesquely low—for the German Jews, who by then dominated the New York and Chicago garment trades. In that cutthroat industry the sweatshop was the condition of survival for employer as well as worker. Having found that economic niche, however dismal, they began a very gradual orientation and began to feel around for something a bit more rewarding, nervously exploring toward more elbowroom and higher economic rewards outside their self-encapsulated ghetto.

Within a generation or so that process made many among the immigrants' offspring, as well as some of the parents themselves, more and more noticeable. As rapid transit fanned out from Manhattan, colonies of unreconstructed Lower East Siders took their versions of sanitation, family life and religion into new enclaves in the Bronx and the Long Island boroughs. Their strange ways and clannishness roused the scorn of their Irish, German or whatever neighbors, who were almost equally clannish. In the 1920s the garment trades moved uptown into new-built skyscraper loft buildings in the middle of the island. Thenceforward every lunch hour saw milling multitudes of bushelmen, cutters, pressers, sewing-machine operators of both sexes clogging Seventh Avenue and talking sixteen to the dozen in mingled Yiddish and English in a vivid demonstration that one in five New Yorkers was a Jew. The American strive-and-succeed formula was also explored outside the garment trades. Ghastly overworked ghetto parents perceived that upward mobility by way of schooling existed here in terms the Old World never dreamed of. It fitted well with their ancestral cult of the rabbi and the Book, their view of the learned man as culture hero. As soon as the family income showed a chemical trace of surplus, one boy would be dedicated to high school and college as vestibule to becoming a doctor or lawyer—a prestige-rich, no-work-with-the-hands professional. His prospective higher cash income was only the minor reason for pushing him up there. The major one was the fact of "My son the doctor!"

The City College of New York, topmost rung in the municipal educational system, became almost solid Jewish. Private colleges in the area felt a rising tide of Jewish freshmen paying their way by heaven knew what family sacrifice eked out with on- or off-campus part-time jobs. It will take another century of research to determine whether, as some geneticists suspect, Jews really do average a touch higher in innate IQ than other Caucasoid groups. The notion is not *prima facie* absurd. In any case, however, the old rabbinical tradition could account for what WASP faculty, alumni and students saw as a disturbingly high incidence of Jews gathering in the best scholarships and high academic honors at Columbia, Harvard and so on, the basic locus of social acceptance. For not only did Jews have a cultural bent for study, but it never occurred to them to be diffident about it. They actually thought college was a place to learn in. This crude misapprehension made for another heightening of visibility in a crucial context. Hence these swarming Jewish students of the new crop met social reprehension of a stringency that the sons of German Jews—fewer, better assimilated, less hungry—had less often encountered. Affluent WASPs as well as college deans setting up quota systems for admitting/excluding Jews made no distinction between the two groups. They applied their new distaste for the sons of Eastern Jews to anybody and everybody carrying the label "Jew."

Side effects from this mordant element in the population were heightened by its half-accidental political geography. The states with the highest population of Jews—New York, California, Pennsylvania, Massachusetts, Maryland, New Jersey, Florida, Connecticut—all carried crucially large electoral votes; it was true in the 1930s as it still is that a presidential candidate carrying those eight by however narrow margins is 7/10± on his way to victory. And just as there was a distinct, if crumbling, "Irish vote," so there was by then a "Jewish vote" real enough to make politicians chary of saying or doing anything to wound Jewish sensibilities, which, in view of their past as whipping boys for bullies and bigots, were understandably tender. Strategically that was advantageous. Tactically it tended to deepen the popular impression that Jews were not only something set apart, hence suspect, but eager to use their differentness for self-serving ends.

Political considerations were still more awkward in that the rank and file of the nation's Marxist parties—the fumbly, retrograding, schism-riddled Socialists and the chronically opportunist Communists (whether Stalinist majority or tiny Trotskyite minority)—were mostly Jewish. WASPs like Norman Thomas and Earl Browder might be put forward to mask this ethnic fact; WASP liberals and other liberals of Old Immigration parentage might give protest votes to one or the other, but to little avail. The association American Marxist = odds-on Jewish was inevitable and as valid for the Communist Party in general as for the Abraham Lincolns. This had cultural roots: The Eastern Jews particularly had less reason than the Gentiles of their mother countries to feel affection or respect for the social systems that had abused them. Hence proposals, usually Marxist-inspired, to change such systems met far less resistance among American Jews, other things being equal, for merely going overseas does not change people's emotional proclivities. And even for those Russian and Polish Jews who were not specifically radical the 1917 Revolutions that shattered the czar's government, the instrument of the child conscription and pogroms that had driven them from home, came like a glowing fireball of exultant retribution. It followed—emotionally, if not logically—that any sequelae of that glory were sacrosanct whether occurring under Kerensky, Lenin or Stalin. Eventually the accumulating dismal facts about the USSR made that feeling harder to sustain. In many, however, it remained impregnable in persisting loyalty to the Communists' USSR. That enabled serious anti-Semites and their followings to equate Jewishness with Communism as if it were a matter of genetic corruption.

Note, further, that most of this went on in New York City, which, in the period since Eastern Jewish immigration had begun, had rounded out its hegemony of American culture. Though not quite to the same extent as in Paris or London, here unmistakably was the nation's center of power in finance, communications, fashion, the arts. Both the Communist Party and the American Telephone & Telegraph Company had their headquarters there. Directly or indirectly the bulk of what went on in America originated there or eventually sent tribute thither. And now this dominating ganglion was the world's largest Jewish settlement, the economic and demographic headquarters of the ethnic group that the Nazis' crackpot behavior was putting squarely into the international spotlight. Suppose Paris had become the chief settlement of the Basques ... but there is no good analogy. The Jews' double internal bracing from an exclusive religion as well as ethnic consciousness is, for reasons unique to their strange history, unique in the Western world. The point here is that by this concentration in New York City rather than Cincinnati—which was the elder German Jews' cultural capital—or San Francisco or Columbus, the Eastern Jews had guaranteed all American Jews still higher visibility.

Nobody has yet determined whether ethnic enclaves are basically chicken or basically egg. Is Hamtramck, Michigan, so solidly Polish because Polish-Americans, feeling put upon elsewhere, carved it out as protective place of their own? Or because Poles, as gregarious and xenophobic as others, positively preferred to keep non-Poles at arm's length? Some fringe effects of the Eastern Jews' experience in America seem to hint at the first alternative. Consider the history of "the Jewish Alps," the summer-resort enclave in the Catskills eventually spilling over the edges into nearby New England and Pennsylvania, now decaying, but by the 1930s flourishing as an extruded seasonal colony of New York's Jewish community.

In the 1890s a few Jewish immigrants of rural background had escaped from the Lower East Side, some for reasons of health, by settling on marginal farms up in the hills. Farming proved disappointing; they began to eke out by taking summer boarders from among ghetto acquaintances able to scrape up a few dollars for a cool vacation. As more such developed a little spare cash, any efforts they made to vacation elsewhere encountered the barriers that WASP summer places had already set up against German Jews. Besides, for the many still deeply orthodox Eastern Jews there was the dietary problem—what WASP-run summer hotel would bother with the ritual details of kosher cooking? So the discouraged Jewish farmers' little homesteads turned into gaunt frame-and-clapboard hotels with exclusively Jewish clientele institutionalizing this cultural bind—Gentiles preferred not to go where Jews were likely to be and Jews couldn't go where Gentiles did.

In time an area the size of the state of Rhode Island had as main industry some hundreds of more or less elaborate resort complexes of which the famous Grossinger's, lineal descendant of a rattletrap farmhouse, is the flagship. Presently came "camps" for a Boy-Meets-Girl clientele, equally Jewish, that inspired Arthur Kober's *Having Wonderful Time* (1937). About the same time the same causes—rising income, demand for seasonal recreation, exclusion from WASP resorts—made almost as much of a Jewish enclave out of Miami Beach, Florida. The same half-witted taboo made real estate agents * reluctant to show vacant apartments to persons named Cohen and advertise that this new subdivision was "restricted." Neither the cultural bad taste nor the legality of such ethnic bars would be seriously challenged until after World War II.

So, says a recent account, "every Jew in New York, it seemed, went to some hotel [in the Catskills] in the summer to escape the stifling heat of the city, meet (if single) a prospective mate, rock (if elderly) on the porch, eat huge kosher meals, take the fresh air, swim in a lake, engage in sports and calisthenics, dance and be entertained...." [53] The last word should be italicized. These resorts developed a tradition of entertainment for evenings and rainy days, not only dances and games but catch-as-catch-can vaudeville-cum-cabaret staged by talent hired for the purpose from among Broadway's beginners. What they got for knocking themselves out every day all summer was a few dollars a week, a stifling shoebox of a room up under the eaves and—a great point for many of them—plenty to eat three times a day. As competition among resorts grew, impromptu clowning and staging of skits filched from burlesque and big-time vaudeville routines led to a •new, if small, department of show business known as the Borscht Circuit with agents specializing in bookings to feed it, practically all Jewish. Growing elaboration culminated in tabloid troupes staging cut-down Broadway musicals, farces and even serious plays such as *Waiting for Lefty, Awake and Sing, Tobacco Road, Men in White....*

Just as the strawhat summer stock companies of the time gave apprentice opportunity to young dramatic actors with far more ambition than experience, so did the Borscht Circuit train feverishly energetic novices, practically all from the Eastern Jewish background, in the arts of catching and holding an audience. The roster of those coming to the top out of this annual scramble to the Catskills includes Eddie Cantor, Robert Alda, Dore Schary, Moss Hart, Elia Kazan,

---

* Probably true anecdote apropos: Morris Hillquit, eminent Socialist and prosperous lawyer, not notably "Jewish-looking," was leasing an apartment in a good Fifth Avenue building and about to sign the papers when the agent casually asked, "You aren't by chance Jewish, Mr. Hillquit?" "No," Hillquit said, "not by chance!" and tore up the lease.

John Garfield, Morrie Ryskind, Sid Caesar, Danny Kaye and dozens of others, plus nine out of ten of the stand-up comics who have been all over television since it was launched. And this was only one of several ways allowing such hopefuls to break into show business. The low-down vaudeville house's Amateur Night was another.

What would America's amusement world of the 1930s have been like without the offspring of those refugees from pogroms? It would have lacked the Marx Brothers, George Burns, Fannie Brice, Sophie Tucker, Lou Holtz, George Jessel, Bert Lahr, Al Jolson; most of Tin Pan Alley's songsmiths with Irving Berlin as Grand Master of the craft; and the most remarkable amateur show of all time, the ILGWU's semipolitical revue *Pins and Needles,* all its talent drawn from members of a union that a generation earlier had been fighting for its members' bare existence against sweatshop conditions. It is probably not true that Jews are more gifted than others in innate feel for the performing arts. But because they were concentrated in America's show-business capital, because there already was a presumption that they naturally gravitated toward footlights and because incisive young temperaments among them so badly needed a way out of the ghetto, it did look that way. "What made Sammy run," says Irving Howe, "was partly that his father and his father's father had been bound hand and foot." [54] It is a curious thought that America owed so much and such rich entertainment to the defunct Russian Crown's anti-Semitic policies.

By then Hitler's Brownshirts and not Russia's Black Hundreds were the leading exponents of anti-Semitism and obviously hoping to make it internationally fashionable. America should have been a likely seedbed. It had a great many conspicuous Jews and the largest admixture of first- and second-generation Germans to help spread the word—as the Bund tried to do. Yet some two years after Hitler came to power a *Fortune* study of the results in America found that though the older "longstanding prejudice"—meaning Howe's "social anti-Semitism"—persisted, no "deliberately incited, affirmative racial phobia" had gained any hold. "American organized anti-Semitism is a poor thing indeed," wrote some *Fortune* staffer. ". . . the great change from sheets to shirts has failed to save it." [55] Part of the evidence was one of Roper's POPs showing that 55 percent of Americans thought Germany would be worse off if it drove all its Jews out, only 14 percent thought that would make it better off and a whacking 31 percent declined to judge, which may imply that a vast number of Americans were healthily indifferent to whatever the Jewish problem might be. In view of the ferments then plaguing America, particularly Coughlin's protoparanoid toxins and indrawingly suspicious isolationism, those ratios are a credit to Americans' levelheadedness and to the persistent integrity of most Jews.

Among Little Groups of Serious Thinkers—always worth watching because they are usually influentially articulate, sometimes constructively so—the prestige of Jews, rather high to begin with because of their reputation for liberalism, had recently been reinforced by two new waves of immigration. LGOSTs had long been and continued to be fascinated by psychoanalysis.* The cult had had ebbings and flowings since being imported *c.* 1910 and suffered from schisms and vendettas, but its general momentum had not slackened—and a great majority of its missionaries had been Jews transplanted from Central Europe; soon they were reinforced by disciples, again mostly Jewish, acquired here. Indeed, in the 1930s a patient having his emotions probed in an accent that was not "Jewish"—actually German, Austrian or Hungarian—had some cause to wonder whether he was really getting the true, the blushful *Traümerei.* Hence an association between Jewishness and psychoanalysis as strong as that between Gypsies and fortune-telling. A layman should go no farther than surmising that the Jewish institution of the learned wise man-rabbi, whose view of human problems is always subtle and often stimulatingly topsy-turvy, may have had some predisposing influence.† The impressiveness of the oracle always contributes to its effectiveness, and vice versa.

When the emotional lives of so many well-placed Americans were thus anchored on Jewish-flavored holding ground, it was bound to add to the cultural stature of the Jewish segment of the population. Numbers of these exotic counselors had crossed the ocean before the Nazis took over. Some probably did so because they learned America was taking psychoanalysis more seriously than Europe did. Those coming later had a strong second motive—the Nazis deplored the psychoanalytic view of man and society, so that to be both a Jew and a psychoanalyst would involve double proscription. Thus, they became a sizable part of one of the most remarkable migrations in history. It was no great swarming—the number under consideration here is a matter of three figures. But the average level of distinction was

---

* I am aware that orthodox Freudians think that the term "psychoanalysis" should be used only for orthodox Freudian methods. Here, however, for lack of anything better, I have to use it more broadly to include all methods of psychotherapy involving basic reliance on the subliminal strata of the personality and prolonged exploration thereof.

† Glazer and Moynihan *(Beyond the Melting Pot,* 175) suggest that the high incidence of Jews among psychoanalysts *et al.* is due to the marked "secularization" of Western Jews consequent on their drifting away from the intellectual and emotional props of the old faith.

awesomely high and correspondingly impressed cultivated Americans already given to cultural hero worship of European intellectuals. Deservedly much of the consequent prestige rubbed off on the Jew generally, for a striking proportion of the whole movement was Jewish, a good 50 percent. Not Gropius or Thomas Mann, for instance, but Albert Einstein, John von Neumann, Edward Teller—to begin the roll call of the peerage of theoretical physicists. Indeed, Einstein took the fancy of a very wide public as the happy-looking little man with the exuberant hair who had turned the universe inside out in an inscrutably occult way just by fooling around with pencil and paper, and his Jewishness was as well realized as his importance.

Here was a beginning of a progressively pervasive sense that Jewishness was special, and for a change impressively so. Maybe this trend toward respect was a harking back to the feeling that some of our cultivated forebears had, George Eliot, for instance, about the Jew as mysterious bearer of higher truths. Anyway, America's gains from the impact of Hitler's poisonous effluvia probably amounted to even more than the cultural boon of Kurt Weill's music, even more than Uncle Sam's having available so much added scientific talent when the atomic bomb had to be quickly developed. For good or ill the Nazis' doctrines and deeds vastly heightened the "sense of group identity and group interests among New York Jews—a tradition common enough among them in any event," say Nathan Glazer and Daniel P. Moynihan. Nor did this dwindle after World War II. It has been leading edge of a consonant "enormous rise in feelings of ethnic identification" [56] affecting not only America's Jews but also its Poles, Italians, Chicanos ... and, in a rather different set of terms, its blacks. Here were the Jews leading a cultural trend again. And for a larger point: Thus, Hitler's cataclysmic effort to shape the German ethnic entity into the master race with the Jews as exemplary victim not only strengthened the Jews' ethnic structure but also set half a dozen other groups within America closing ranks and serving notice on WASPs and one another.

Current opinion applauds all that. The position is that it forces the nation to recognize what had long been getting clearer, that the Melting Pot was not doing its job, was at best only modifying the ways in which ethnic groups viewed themselves and their destinies. It ensures us cultural variety—the favorable way of saying heterogeneity. And in any case, since it is obviously here to stay, it must be lived with flexibly and graciously to prevent unnecessary frictions. Not a bad case, particularly the last. But it would certainly amaze Hitler.

THE POT AND THE CRADLE

MAY YOU LIVE IN INTERESTING TIMES!
                    —Ancient Chinese curse frequently cited by
                SIR DENIS BROGAN

Those following the sport of dowsing for historical watersheds may feel a strong pull when crossing the year 1937. Even in the spring of that year it was strong enough to set Henry F. Pringle, an able and prominent magazine journalist, uneasily noting that people were reviving the old patterns of flashy spending of the quick buck as if the Depression were finished. In 1938 a sharp downturn in economic indices reviving Depression-mindedness was, in those terms, bleakly reassuring. The end of distinctly hard times had to wait for World War II as exorcism. But for all that, Pringle's dowsing rod may have been responding to certain subtler realities, some trivial but leaving marks on the folkways. Thus, 1937 saw the first supermarket shopping carts, inspiration of Sylvan F. Goldman of Oklahoma City; women resisted them at first on the grounds that baby buggies gave them enough of that sort of machine. And highly apropos—and far more important—then began a rise in the birthrate seeming to hint that already in 1936 young copulators felt either newly careless of the future or newly confident about it. And, for a thing the scale and importance of which took a generation to weigh in, that was the year when the US Congress saw fit to take stringent measures about marijuana.

They meant to protect the nation from what they took to be a new threat to well-being. One effect, it is now widely agreed, was to foul up American culture with a previously nonexistent and maybe unnecessary set of social strains. It is not so widely agreed but discernible that another was to saddle the national mind with a calamitously fumbly debate. Blame for that lies on intellectual irresponsibility on both sides.

The first bad omen was Uncle Sam's getting the wind up prematurely and tempting what we now call "the media" to take bureaucratic handouts at face value and run with them. Preparations of *Cannabis sativa*—specific name of the plant causing it all, alias Indian hemp, now a household word and bone of contention as marijuana—had long been known in America. Its fibers make good cordage, and a great deal of it was grown in the lower Midwest in the mid-1800s. By 1900 there was minor uneasiness about the "hemp cigarettes" that the pimply kind of college boy sometimes smoked; he was not being rebel-minded, just droopily experimental, and in those days his elders looked slaunchways at any kind of cigarette. After World War I the rising cult of folk song among liberal campus types included self-conscious singing of not only the Basin Street-flavored snowbirds' anthem: "Have a little sniff on me, baby..." but also the Mexican number about "la cucaracha" refusing to go places without "marijuana que fumar," which spread awareness of the stuff in a vague but pruriently exotic-and-anti-Mrs. Grundy context. Today's cannabophile may think this juxtaposition unfortunate because it implies comparable orders of kick and risk in cocaine and marijuana. But fifty years ago there was no good reason not to believe anything derogatory that anybody wanted to say about little Mary Jane, alias "Merry Wonder," alias "Mary Warner" ... she had no friends.

The Mexican reference was valid. *Cannabis* as euphoric indulgence had deep roots in the cultures of India and Islam,* but it was principally out of Mexico's frowsy border towns into Texas and off ships from Mexican ports into New Orleans that it infiltrated to begin its Stateside career. In New Orleans "muggles" or "mootas," meaning marijuana cigarettes, became a minor institution among gringos as well as greasers in the same shiftless circles where cocaine also bulked large. When World War I closed the New Orleans red-light district that was the cradle of jazz, a diaspora of unemployed jazzmen went fanning outward to Chicago, Los Angeles, New York City. That may account for the persisting close association between jazz and "pot," "grass," "tea," "gage," "Indian hay," "weed"—whatever current or former cant name one chooses. Science doubts whether being high on pot makes any difference in the quality of a jazz combo's improvisings.

---

* One solemn authority attributes its penetration of Islamic cultures to Mohammed's denying his followers alcohol (Richard J. Bonnie and Charles S. Whitebread, *The Marijuana Conviction,* 1.)

But for at least two generations many have believed it does, which in practice comes to the same thing.

One may assume that as white musicians made themselves free of the mysteries of jazz and the folkways of the craft, they also took up marijuana. And concomitant with the spread of jazz after World War I went the personal cult of the jazzman, white or black, as subculture hero. So among scruffier showfolk, white or black, and their hangers-on, usually but not always young, it grew creepingly fashionable to imitate the habits as well as the showmanly sharp clothes of the jazz combo leader who was Pied Piper of the movement. One such habit might well be marijuana smoking. All but two states presently passed some sort of law against Mary Jane, but few were enforced, so she was readily available to anybody bothering to look her up.

She was the likelier to spread out from the world of jazz into related subcultures because the sleazier levels of show business had long dabbled in "dope." The Hollywood of silent days knew far too much about opium, morphine, heroin as well as cocaine. The old-time burlesque troupes from among whom Broadway often drew talent were known markets for cocaine. So was the blend of stay-up-late Park Avenue and nightclub Harlem so queasily commemorated by Carl Van Vechten in *Parties.* It was natural that under such auspices what was reputed to be an easily obtainable, inexpensive, readily ingested and genially effective euphoric—that is, a new, low-key "dope"—became a welcome supplement in the world of "high"-mindedness. By 1932 a Broadway revue, *Flying Colors,* had a little number, "Smokin' Reefers." The great Cab Calloway's jazz group celebrated "Marwanna" and "That Funny Reefer Man." Out on the Coast Raymond Chandler's unsavory characters were necessarily familiar with "jujus"—there is no limit to the number of Mary Jane's pet names. And when Nathanael West needed something fittingly sordid for the leading lady (if that is the word) of *The Day of the Locust* to show off with when libidinously drunk, he had her belting out the low-down song about the pothead as a "viper" dreaming of "a reefer five feet long. . . ." [1] *

Yet outside certain raffish circles it was little more than a toehold. A well-informed (white) biographer of Father Divine still thought it advisable in 1939 to explain to his general audience that reefers were "hemp leaves [made] into cigarettes" smoked with wet sheets over the windows to prevent telltale odors and "[lifting] you into the paradise

---

* This was just the first, of course, in a large body of such numbers. The Le Dain Report, p. 310, says, "The popular music industry has played a major role in encouraging drug use in general and cannabis in particular through the lyrics and other aspects of the records it has marketed. . . ."

of Mahomet . . . beautiful colors . . . beautiful women." [2] The commercial "tea pads" described by undercover police about this time in the La Guardia report were pretty well confined to Harlem, and the only area outside Harlem where reefers were readily bought was the showfolks' strip east and west of Broadway between Forty-second and Fifty-ninth streets. A veteran Los Angeles policeman told a reporter recently, "It used to be that only people in the poorest areas and rock musicians and actors and actresses in Hollywood used marijuana." [3] For in the late 1930s Mary Jane's reputation was, if anything, getting worse and worse. How she managed her subsequent social climbing is usually explained thus:

In 1931 the New Orleans police, facing a sharp rise in crime in a city where normal levels are bad enough, blamed it on growing use of marijuana, particularly among young hoodlums. State authorities and some social service workers concurred. The cue was picked up by Henry J. Anslinger, chief of the US Bureau of Narcotics and a veteran of the defunct federal agency for enforcing Prohibition. He decided to add marijuana to the bureau's list of taboo drugs. The implication usually is that he was an empire builder aware that to ride herd on reefers would add more money and men for his staff; this was most clearly hinted in Allen Ginsberg's essay on pot written under its influence in the mid-1960s. At that it makes a little more potential sense than David Solomon's suggestion that the liquor interests, fearful lest pot reduce sales of booze, put Anslinger up to it.

Anyway Anslinger put on a heavy publicity campaign, filling Washington papers particularly with antimarijuana scare material, making speeches before service clubs and over the radio about the sinister relation between the rise in "hemp intoxication" and juvenile crime. His high point in print was an article under his by-line in the huge-circulation *American* magazine: "Marijuana: Assassin * of Youth" ("No one knows, when he places a marijuana cigarette to his lips, whether he will become a philosopher, a joyous reveler in a musical heaven, a mad insensate, or a murderer . . ." [4]) and then seeing it picked up by the *Reader's Digest,* which was Bingo. The Communist *Daily Worker* was just as alarmed about it. In due time a stringent federal antimarijuana bill was drafted, and Anslinger had the time of

---

* A reference, of course, to the medieval legend about the Old Man of the Mountain, a Near Eastern sort of ogre who took young men into his outlaw band, filled them with hashish (concentrated form of pot), let them recover consciousness in a lovely garden garnished with voluptuous and willing women, and then told them that the way to get more of the same was to murder his enemies. Hence, says a romantic but probably sound etymology, "assassin" from "hashish."

his life testifying for it before the indicated House committee. He told them that Mary Jane was as likely as any opiate to go addictive, and under her baleful influence innocent youngsters brutally murdered their nearest and dearest, committed rape, mayhem, robbery with violence—even matrimony, as evidenced by a newspaper clipping put in evidence about a boy and girl in St. Louis who smoked marijuana and "lost their senses so completely that ... they eloped and were married." [5] Those escaping such explosive consequences sank into moral and physical debility. Schoolchildren were most numerous among her victims. He had only two good words for Mary Jane: She was not, as some Congressmen believed, the same as the cattle- and horse-destroying locoweed of the Southwest, and she did not lead into hard drugs: "The marihuana addict does not go in that direction. . . . The [average] age of the morphine and heroine addict is increasing . . . whereas the marihuana smoker is quite young." [6] Later he changed his mind about that, but at the moment this affinity between pot and Youth made it all sound more sinister than ever. Hollywood's Poverty Row had already cranked out a quickie, *Reefer Madness,* about marijuana's effect on high school hedonists. The copy on the lobby displays called the stuff "concentrated sin ... a weed from the devil's garden ... one moment of bliss—a lifetime of regrets. . . ."

The American Medical Association hastily sent its expert on narcotics law, both an MD and a lawyer, to suggest that Anslinger *et al.* were going farther than the evidence allowed; that neither the US Bureau of Prisons nor the US Children's Bureau had reason to believe that pot smoking was either on the increase or that, where it existed, it had much to do with either convicts' or children's problems; and that since most states already had marijuana laws, merely adding the stuff to the existing federal antinarcotics law would answer any useful purpose. Protest also came from the birdseed industry against the clause outlawing *Cannabis* seed as well as leaves to discourage illicit planting; the seed, it seemed was essential in commercial bird provender, particularly for pigeons, whose progeny didn't shape right without it, and canaries, who shirked singing unless they got plenty of it. After amendment to allow sale of seed sterilized to prevent germination, the committee ignored the AMA's position, and in due season the Marijuana Taxation Act of 1937, heavily penalizing importation, sale or possession, was the law of the land. It probably went farther than Anslinger had originally contemplated. Its outlawing of possession certainly exceeded anything federal Prohibition had done against alcohol.

Otherwise, says a legend now popular among sociologists of liberal bent, here was a close analogue to Prohibition reflecting Anslinger's past as enforcer of Dry laws—and eventually working out to dismayingly similar results. Or put it that it was the ladder by which Mary Jane did her social climbing. This open-minded position is: Marijuana is not addictive in the same sense as hard drugs are. Most of its users can take it or leave it alone, exploiting it only for occasional or regular euphoric relief from day-to-day strains, just as so many Americans use that other well-established euphoric, alcohol. Warning that pot predisposes to a hard-drug habit is as baseless as the old-time Dry's warning that smoking predisposes to alcoholism. Socially a marijuana "high" is no more dangerous than the effect of a couple of highballs. Physically it is probably less damaging. Maybe mankind would be better off had Mary Jane never entered the cultural frame. But human beings seem to have an emotional need to get "high" so nearly universal that it may well be normal. The Red Indian supplied it with tobacco in the West Indies, coca leaves in Peru, "sacred" mushrooms in Mexico, peyote in the Southwest; the Chinese with opium; the Polynesians with kava; the East Indians with ganja (a stronger preparation of *Cannabis*); the Mediterranean peoples with beer and wine; the primitive Germans with beer and mead; and, once the still came in, Western man generally with alcoholic spirits. And among them marijuana ranks among the least harmful in immediate dislocation and long-range consequences.

Until people got all in a sweat about it, it is held, what kept pot from wide acceptance was its scruffy reputation. Conversely what got it widely accepted was the mistake of banning it, which worked out here just as Prohibition worked out with alcohol. In spite of Anslinger's Marijuana Tax Act (slightly. modified now, but from the cannabophile point of view little improved), existing users stubbornly sabotaged enforcement and kept ample supplies available. And once again the attraction of forbidden fruit proved irresistible to Youth. Just as in Prohibition, the legal taboo became a laughingstock, a dead letter, a social calamity not so much because pot is so harmful as because the expense of enforcement is so great—as well as largely futile—and because the effect of such extensive law defying is morally morbid. How well it fits! In the 1920s killjoy stupidity rammed Prohibition down American throats and in no time, partly out of curiosity, partly to defy authority, partly to dramatize the distinction between themselves and their more docile predecessors, the kids took enthusiastically to drink. Won't the bluenoses ever learn?

Then the position reaches out for positive considerations. Canada's Le Dain Commission, studying our northern neighbors' problems with pot, similar to ours, was warmly tolerant about young folks' pot parties as means to "self-knowledge and self-integration . . . spiritual meanings

... related in some measure to the collapse of religious values ...
[enabling one] to glimpse another way of looking at things and of
relating to life and people." [7] The analogy with alcohol runs in here
too: The classic cult of Dionysus, god of wine, grew out of that
euphoria seeming to head toward transcendence that is a familiar
stage in drunkenness; the old teetotaler who drank a glass of gin by
mistake said he felt as if he were sitting on the meetinghouse roof and
every shingle were a Jew's harp. Why should not today's Youth,
deprived of the elder religious road to ineffable experience, be allowed
to get In Tune with the Infinite by this handy and minimally
dangerous biochemical gimmick?

It is reassuring to learn that those teenagers sitting on the steps
passing a roach from lip to lip are not the vacuous loafers they appear
to be, but a modern analogue to the early Christians' ecstatic sharing
of nearness to Christ in the love feast and true, the early Christians
probably were a pretty unprepossessing lot, too. Much of that is well
taken, but there are a few things wrong.* Its one firm element is that
marijuana is not physiologically addictive, but then neither is cocaine.
Few other confident statements about *Cannabis* are altogether reliable.
What with legal curbs on experiment, the difficulties built into such
research by having to rely on subjective impressions and self-selected
subjects, the whine and rasp of ax grinding on both sides of the
debate, an intelligible verdict is not yet possible. So the situation is a
welter of special pleadings and inconsistencies. The same expert,
whether physiologist or psychiatrist, says on page x that *Cannabis* is a
widely recognized, emotionally salutary euphoric operating through
biochemical channels, and on page y that the euphoric effect of pot
smoking depends largely on what the smoker has been led to expect
and where he is and with whom. Page a describes potheads as
immersed in a highly introverted state, exploring inner meanings as if
on a tourist-class LSD trip, little regarding others; page b says they
particularly value group encounter with the magic herb as in the love-
feast analogy above.

One authoritative study has pseudoanthropological description of
mankind's omnipresent urge to seek transcendence; then a few
chapters later the physician-author maintains that in a free, humane,
collectivist, peaceful society such as his cryptocollectivist temperament
obviously desires, this basic urge would never arise. Dr. Gabriel G.

---

* A good deal of the rest of the case for legalizing marijuana depends on
the "victimless crime" doctrine that also applies to the decriminalization of the
addictive opiates and the not-quite-so-hard drugs such as cocaine, mescaline,
LSD. I omit all that here because it is not needed to elucidate the issues under
discussion.

Nahas, eminent anesthesiologist, has described the 1970 report of the National Commission on Marihuana and Drug Addiction as reading "as if ... written by persons who had conflicting views of interpretations of observed data ... [set down] in sequence without transition on the same ream of paper." [8]

Now that pot has wriggled upward by a sort of capillary action from Burlesque Beach to group gropes to black-tie dinner parties, the open-minded recommend legalizing it even though science obviously does not know enough about it to pronounce its use reasonably safe. The longer it's outlawed, one is told, the more we damage the rebellious rising generation's social morals and the worse they think of their elders who guzzle martinis while warning Junior against Mary Jane as dangerous and degenerative. The principle seems to be that an innovative euphoric has the felon's right to be held innocent until proved guilty. The precedents are, however, unfortunate. In the 1930s medical authorities more or less nolle-prossed the inhaled tobacco cigarette because proof that it did major damage was lacking. Forty years later what we now know about lung cancer, heart trouble and the addictive nature of tobacco shows what a mistake that was. The old folks yammering about "coffin nails" and "the little white slaver" were right after all, if for the wrong reasons. Suppose that thirty years after we legalize *Cannabis,* suspicion about which is by no means groundless now, medicine allows itself to learn ... fill in any physiological catastrophe you like in twenty-five words. By then, of course, if society's experience with alcohol is any precedent, efforts to eliminate the stuff will be too late and fruitless. "Once young people decided they couldn't believe anything adults told them about marihuana, they stopped listening," says Dr. Donald Goodwin's recent *Is Alcoholism Hereditary?,* "and even if marihuana were conclusively shown to cause feeblemindedness, gum disease, and cancer, the marihuana generation might pay no heed." [9]

There the usefulness of analogy with Prohibition fades away. Its major flaw is chronological—it simply took too long to come about. The one thing on which practically all observers agree about this pharmacological bad joke—just whom the joke is on has yet to appear—is that pot did not really begin to move up out of, to put it politely, the demimonde until well into the 1950s and did not reach pandemic proportions until the 1960s, whereas Anslinger's law, presumed occasion for its getting airborne, went into effect in 1937. Consider that only a year or two after Prohibition arrived in 1918–19 the howls about hip flasks and Our Drinking Daughters were already deafening. Why this gap of toward twenty years? The ingenious dredge up this or that phenomenon that might have had a supplementary hand in persuading Dick and Jane to try grass: The list usually begins with World War II; jumps to the atom bomb; deplores the hedonism induced by permissive rearing; frowns at parents popping tranquilizers and soporifics; takes a poke at television (one well-qualified psychiatrist advances that one); glances at the Pill; tips the hat to Paul Goodman; adduces the euphoric trauma of rock music ... sunspots will be along any minute. But we are discussing the 1930s. Unless this was history's most remarkable example of sociological hanging fire, of *post hoc* delayed action, Mary Jane's rags-to-riches history cannot be blamed on Anslinger's misplaced zeal. It just took far, far too many days for the bread to return on the waters.*

The turnaround in the birthrate that made 1937 indubitably special was another example of sociological delayed action—and another hair shirt for the experts. One can see why at the time it began it caused no remark. Until the Bureau of the Census got the momentous data processed and published in the course of 1938—such things took longer before superhuman computers were available—there was no reason to suspect such a reversal of expectations. The reasonable assumption was that the nation's notoriously low birthrate, steadily declining for a generation, bottoming out in the mid-1930s, would never rise again and that demography could only postulate a stationary, maybe declining population as what America, along with other developed Western nations, had to contemplate. This was usually ascribed to an ill-understood tendency of industrialized societies to have fewer babies per fertile woman; to a widening use of newly efficient contraceptives and techniques promoted by the birth control movement; and sometimes to Youth's growing numbness toward the joys of saddling themselves with progeny. "They'd rather put their money in a new car than into a baby," † said a famous obstetrician. Headshakers never tired of quoting him.

The West's leading cultures seldom took this drying-up of human procreation as good news. To all but hot pacifists it sounded ominous that America and her potential allies would have fewer fighting men while such likely menaces as Japan and the USSR spawned more. For

---

* Obviously this section was written by a person who never smoked pot. Nor do I intend to. I had enough trouble twenty-odd years ago breaking my massive addiction (maybe part psychological but also, to judge from the severity of the withdrawal symptoms, part physiological) to three-pack-a-day cigarette smoking. In fifty years of fact writing I have, like most reporters, taken risks in pursuit of firsthand data. But no thanks, not that one.

† This and other quotations in this section lacking numbered references come from my "Baby Boom," *Ladies' Home Journal,* February, 1943; the general background owes much to the *How America Lives* series that I wrote monthly for the magazine 1939 into 1944.

economists it threatened the capitalist system, born concomitantly with rapidly growing population, maybe a function of it, with having to adjust to a receding tide. Who knew how severe the withdrawal pangs might be? For all but the most egalitarian societies it meant that, since efficient contraception in those days before the Pill and the IUD implied responsible forethought, lower birthrates would concentrate in the more responsible upper strata of society; or, less tactfully, that the more feckless strata would outbreed the rest more rapidly than ever. In Californian terms such considerations were stated in 1937 by Paul Popenoe, qualified expert-popularizer of eugenics and kindred concerns: "The family that sends a child to the State University averages two living children. The family that sends a child to the State Home for the Feeble Minded averages five living children. The family ... dependent on Los Angeles charity for more than five years ... beginning ... during boom times ... averages five living children." [10] Twenty years earlier Theodore Roosevelt had made "race suicide" part of the language. As experts grew more confident about the imminence of declining population, it sounded ever more dismal. Unemployment, international crises, crackpot movements, labor racketeering might come and go, but a shrinking citizenry was something to have the sociological night sweats about decade after decade.

Maybe the alleged inevitability was what moved Henry Pratt Fairchild, a prominent, pessimistic, WASP-minded student of such problems, to step out of character in 1938 and tell readers of *Harper's* that possibly things were not as bad as all that. Gamely encouraging backhanded hope, he discounted the military argument, saying the United States was "large enough, powerful enough, and technologically competent enough" to be safe anyway. He made fun of Hitler's and Mussolini's abortive efforts to bribe and cajole the women of Germany and Italy into breeding more cannon fodder. He feared, however, lest Americans, persuaded that shrinking population was inevitable, turn to all manner of ill-advised, often Fascist-like remedies. To head off panic, he called on his chronic faith in eugenics and his hope for wider utilization of newly effective contraceptives:

The birth rate ... [reached] 16.9 [per 1,000 population] in 1935, with no evidence of any tendency to recover.... The response to the accessibility of contraception ... showed that a great many people were having more children than they wanted.... If this is a socially detrimental state of affairs ... society [must] make moderate fertility sufficiently attractive so that married couples will deliberately plan to have enough children on the average [2.3 up to 2.6 per couple was the usual formula] to maintain a stationary population. It is no longer possible ... nor [sic] desirable ...

to rely for the maintenance of the population on unwanted babies ... the bulk of [such increase comes] from the least intelligent, the least foresighted, the poorest educated and the least self-controlled element of the population.[11]

The following year Frederick Osborn, anthropologist from the American Museum of Natural History, urged the New York Academy of Medicine to persuade physicians to direct new methods of control over conception to increased births among parents able to give their children a decent physical, moral and mental environment. Two months later P. K. Whelpton, a demographer with the Scripps Foundation for Population Research, pluckily met the economic aspect head-on. He denied that stationary or falling numbers would necessarily be calamitous. He suggested to the National Council of Social Work that once more and more people ceased to be the order of the day, society could cut down on making things to produce with (expansion of capital goods) and increase production of consumer goods. He even saw the *decrease* in numbers allowing abandonment of poorer mines, farmlands, forests, fisheries and so on and concentration on the more productive ones. That would increase production-per-man-hour—the crucial factor in the standard of living. He invited "big population people" [12] not exactly to change their minds but to bear with his heresies open-mindedly enough to' allow possible eventual effect on their thinking.* Meanwhile, of course, the best procedure was to give all strata optimum access to free, reliable contraception.

Osborn's purpose was double: openly to check the hazardous slide down to the point of shrinking numbers, and less candidly to reduce the dysgenic reproduction rate among two different groups—the socially incapable Jeeters and Jukeses and the underprivileged minorities, chiefly blacks and Chicanos, who, though doubtless potentially as eligible as others, were outbreeding those who, in spite of Depression, had managed to retain a stake in the country. During the winter of 1939–40 a few dozen earnest experts with good intentions were preparing a summary published in 1940 as *Foundations of American Population Policy* sponsored by the Committee on Population Studies

---

* It sounds as if he had been reading the heresies in John B. Watson's *Psychological Care of Infant and Child* (1928): "No mother has a right to have a child who cannot give it a room to itself for the first two years of infancy ... a *conditio sine qua non*. ... *Not more babies but better brought up babies* will be our slogan. The idea that our population must sustain itself and show an increase is an old fetish growing out of tribal warfare. Why should we care if the U.S. birthrate begins to decline ...? There are too many people in the world now. ..." (pp. 8–9.)

and Social Planning of the National Economic and Social Planning Association. All of that. Among its striking pronouncements: ". . . the only [American group] with a new reproduction rate high enough for permanent replacement is the population on relief. . . . Contemporary American society is inherently self-destructive in the sense that it does not provide conditions and motivations . . . adequate to assure the permanent self-replacement of the population on a voluntary basis." [13]

All that was still working from the prognostications accepted in the mid-1930s. Conscientiously people explored what to do about it. The Earl of Mansfield might have had a suggestion. He imported some storks to lend picturesqueness to the pinnacles of his castle in Scotland, and within the logical number of months the women roundabout experienced a striking number of pregnancies among the previously barren or long infertile. But in the States it was New Deal times, and the remedies proposed in *Foundations* had a New Deal flavor. Social services should create a sanguine, secure climate in which all segments of the population would want and have a reasonable number of children. That translated into free contraceptives and education in how to use them, sound schooling for all, decent housing subsidized where necessary, pre- and postnatal training for wives, unemployment insurance and, particularly important, converting the more literate and responsible wives to wanting the three babies that would ensure survival of their sort of values. It was a pilot-plant triumph for this approach that the birthrate in Greenbelt, where so much of that sort of thing was already lively, was four times as high as was normal for the Greenbelters' average incomes and ages (thirty-two years). The benevolent doctor in charge of Greenbelt's health service said, "The most efficient contraceptive device we know is economic insecurity." [14] A cozy sentiment—only the nation's highest birthrates occurred among rural blacks and sharecropping whites who couldn't even spell "economic insecurity," let alone hope ever to get shut of it. What he was seeing was probably an extreme example of the wave of largely deliberate baby having that, for no intelligible reason, had swelled up from among the American population some two years earlier without authority being in a position to notice.

Meanwhile, viewing-with-alarm, anachronistically regardless, swept on into the early 1940s. Manufacturers were advised to convert from baby buggies to wheelchairs. Grass would take over the playgrounds of elementary schools until they were torn down to make room for old folks' homes. Eventually tentative results of the 1940 Census began to supplement interim estimates of current births. Lo, a cloud no bigger than a baby's bottom—or call it a silver lining from a christening mug—rose on the demographers' horizon. The new figures showed plainly that for some three years, with sneaky lack of fanfare, the birthrate had been rising, starting in 1937. In 1938 it dipped a little, possibly reflecting the economic falloff that year,* but then rose buoyantly in 1940. By 1941 it had climbed back to the level of 1929, birth year of babies conceived in the culminating year of the New Era good times. If the man in the street had been looking, he would have taken this as the first significant reversal of the downward trend since the *Lusitania* sank.

There had been obscure hints of change in the reproductive weather. Retailers were noticing higher sales in the layette lines. Obstetricians' calendars were clogging up; beds in maternity wards had to be reserved farther ahead. But the bootee and bassinet buyers neglected to warn the population experts, letting them go right on deploring that coming falling-off in population. They did not resist the temptation to deny that anything significant was happening. Just a flash in the pan, they explained, one of those statistical bobbles in crude figures likely to mislead the layman but not scientific analysis of the number of live female births per fertile woman of childbearing age correlated with likelihood of marriage and corrected for prospective shifts in contraceptive methods—or words to that effect. ". . . only a ripple on a vastly receding tide," said Virgil D. Reed, acting director of the Bureau of the Census. ". . . a temporary boom," said Philip M. Hauser of the same bureau. "[Actually] the birth rate . . . is going steadily down." [15] In those days, as I reported after consulting eminent demographers for a magazine article on this don't-look-and-it-will-go-away baby boom: "Five years are no trend . . . not in the statisticians' high, thin, fatalistic atmosphere. The most hard-boiled . . . say they won't be impressed until the rise has lasted at least twenty years. . . . Others say that if [it] continues seven or eight years longer, it might play a real part in correcting the coming population-debacle." [9] Not until late 1941 did the bureau's chief of vital statistics admit: ". . . it now *appears* [italics mine] that the birth rate . . . is definitely increasing." [16] The late Louis I. Dublin, statistical chief of the Metropolitan Life Insurance Company, was among the few willing to allow that this five-year gain might conceivably lead to "a revivifying wave of progeny far into the nation's future."

As for why more babies were so tactlessly emerging—the experts did

---

* It may be absurd to do so, but to prevent confusion when one discusses relations between human emotions and the birthrate, it is as well to remind readers that it takes nine months from the gleam in father's eye to the birth of the consequences. Hence fluctuations in actual births are assumed to reflect fluctuations in the parents' behavior and intentions during the latter nine months of the preceding year.

not deny they existed, merely refused them significance—assumptions were to be diverse. The first factor usually adduced was the alleged tendency of the birthrate to follow the business cycle: More jobs = less resistance to the biological impulse to have that baby. This view had actually survived the contrary behavior of the birthrate of the 1920s, which had gone down, down through the good times of the New Era.* Indeed, ever since artificial birth control had gained some reliability, the better off married couples were, the fewer offspring they tended to have, and, as eugenists so lamented, the most children per family were born to those marrying on little or nothing and small hope of ever doing better.

No help there in accounting for the baby boom that began in 1937. When the curve climbed on up after Pearl Harbor, the experts turned to the alleged stimulating effect of war on birthrates. The bases for this theory were partly crass—a husband whose previously childless wife has a baby born or on the way stands less chance of having to go to fight—and partly superstition—a traditional, vague but picturesque notion that when a lot of killing is in prospect, Mother Nature, in her inscrutably wise old way, augments human fertility, particularly in boy babies. This alliance of poltroonery and supernal foresight sounds powerful but hardly applies to the problem. For the mysteriously numerous babies of 1937 were mostly conceived in 1936—five years before Pearl Harbor, four years before Congress enacted Selective Service, three years before Hitler went to war in Poland.

Certain small inner trends could be made out. More married couples in upper-income brackets were going on to have several children instead of one or two at most. The married, child-having members of Vassar's class of 1936, for instance, averaged a number of offspring markedly higher than alumnae of all American women's colleges. In the winter of 1937–38 a Gallup POP showed a strong majority of American women considering three or more children the ideal family size. The folksy, proto-soap-opera kind of newspaper comic strip was showing an epidemic of pregnancies among the characters. And the average age of primiparas—women having a first child—was dropping, which probably meant that the former tendency to enjoy several years of he-and-she-ing before considering "baby makes three" was eroding. It was also notable that a parallel rise in birthrate was occurring in Britain and several other non-Fascist

---

* In *Recent Social Changes* (William F. Ogburn, ed., 1929, p. 5) Warren S. Thompson had warned about this drop in the birthrate in the Jazz Age-New Era, "The generally supposed connection between prosperity and a high birthrate does not seem to hold. . . ."

European nations. Actually a commonsense case could be made for simple change in social fashion. The New Era-Jazz Age had been so sure that baby having was sentimentally old hat, emotionally unnecessary and, in view of all the pitfalls postulated by the new child psychology, a potential nuisance. The smart—in both senses—thing had been to skip it altogether or put it off until one arrived at solid economic security. Nor was this just Joe College and Betty Coed. In the 1920-30s styles quickly got into the bargain basements, ideas got around fast and more and more blue-collar wives—numbers of them Catholic—were dropping into the busy birth control clinics.

Now in 1936-37 the dedicated clinic staffs were having former clients from all social strata returning to say, "We've decided we want a baby now. Nothing's happened yet. How can we fix it so it will?" If they knew what had changed their minds, they couldn't describe it. But there was a supportive cliché cropping up widely: "Well, John and I decided it would be foolish to wait to have a family—we want our children while we're young, so we can enjoy them." That was the new thing to say—and act on—as "I want to live my own life without being tied down by babies" had been ten years earlier. Or a couple one knew who had seemed content with a good livelihood job, a Scotty dog, a convertible coupe, weekend jaunts and their own twosome evenings with the record player would cough diffidently, let people know they were expecting and, when surprise was evinced, waggle their hands and say, "Well, you can't put it off forever, can you?" Ten years earlier their counterparts would have felt: "Certainly, why not?"

The readiest way to account for that is to assume a revulsion from the egocentric individualism of the 1920s toward the irksome satisfactions of parenthood. But that is more description than explanation. It is possible that some change in social atmosphere rather too subtle for gross observation, maybe some side effect of the spirit of the New Deal, maybe just a quasi-mechanical reversal of fashionable attitudes, was replacing an apprehensive or cynical pessimism with a more sanguine view of things to come. Yet 1936 offered little to encourage optimism. On the economists' charts things were better, but not up to New Era standards. Millions were still unemployed; the relief problem was as badly snarled up as ever; a bitter presidential campaign was corroding what political goodwill the nation had left; Mussolini was mopping up his land piracy in Ethiopia; Spain exploded that summer; the first impressive attempt at a general strike in American history was followed by the first resort to the protorevolutionary sitdown strike. Maybe Progressive Education's harping on the charming creativeness of child shaping offered a new rationalization for the previously stifled maternal instinct, giving motherhood a new chance to be narcissistically modish. In 1941 the veteran head of a famous adoption agency, swamped with applications, saw hard times as influencing the change: "Not having a child was stylish. . . . [Then] the depression somehow made human relationships seem important again. People began to feel: 'We're not going to be left out of . . . living with a growing child.'" Said one of those trend-setting primiparas in a lower-middle-income bracket: "The only security I can count on is emotional security. Nobody knows what's going to happen, so I'm going to have a baby. Jim's crazy about the idea."

Hard times, better times, war times or, as in the old drinking song, any other reason why. In this context, too, a dash of sunspots may be added, not quite altogether as nonsense. In 1936, the year the baby boom began, Harlan T. Stetson, an eminent astronomer, suggested to readers of the *Scientific Monthly,* with all due tentativeness, that sunspot-associated variations in the ultraviolet content of sunlight might, directly through radiation, indirectly through effect on the vegetation we eat, obscurely affect "the sensitive ductless glands upon which our temperaments and moods seem to depend. . . . Perhaps some day we shall find that the psychology of the human race passes through periods of optimism and depression in some subtle way that depends upon changes in our terrestrial environment for which changes in the sun may be the ultimate origin." He adduced such well-known phenomena as the coincidence of tree growth-ring patterns with sunspot cycles and the inverse relation between them and the annual catch of rabbit pelts. Such a theory might well apply to the mystery of why baby having began to become fashionable, no matter just what was happening to sunspots in 1936, for: "The solar cycle of eleven years impressing itself upon some other natural cycle [Author: or several interlacing cycles] could result in a variation that has for its period neither that of the sun nor of the terrestrial phenomena under consideration but of a combination of both." [17] Suppose a small, indirect biochemical nudge of that sort combined with that well-known, if irregular, cycle, the human habit of getting tired of a given style of face or dress or attitude toward parenthood. . . . At least the American phase of the population explosion replacing the atom bomb as the prime threat to civilization thus *could* have come about because the minor star on which our earth depends is periodically afflicted with acne.

Pity that the demographers didn't think of sunspots as those inexplicable babies came weighing in. The application could obviously have been so vague as to suit any statistical pattern—up, down or sidewise. And it could have kept them from looking about as foolish as the financial wizards who so calamitously misread the New Era and the Great Crash.

Very early in 1937, as those inexplicable babies began to creep in unnoticed, certain conspicuous New Yorkers began to sell bonds for what they chose sanguinely to celebrate as the World of Tomorrow—motif of a New York City world's fair to be held in 1939. The pretext for that date—the 150th anniversary of the inauguration of George Washington, which had taken place down on Wall Street—was transparently slim. The real, well-understood purposes were to bring revenue into the Greater New York area and bolster current hopes that times really were getting better. When 1938 brought something of a renewed slump, a project that would provide so many construction jobs and sell so much building material looked better still. Unacknowledgedly the example of Chicago's recent Century of Progress was influential. By the time it was all built and operating the Big Town's version, however, would be twice as big and cost three times as much—comparisons that fitted the World of Tomorrow unfortunately well. Forty years later America would have twice as many people, and things would cost rather more than three times as much.

Room for a double-size world's fair within reach was available in a low-lying area on the shoulder of Long Island between the newish bedroom complexes of Jackson Heights and Corona and the venerable but already swallowed-up village of Flushing. Officially this was "the Flushing Meadows," unofficially "the Flushing dumps," a wasteland of hummocky, rat-infested garbage and debris always more or less on fire with the prevailingly westerly winds bringing the noisome smoke over the suburbs to eastward. Two years later several square miles were demurely landscaped, endowed with sizable bodies of ornamental water and hoked up with a remarkable conglomeration of exhibit buildings in one or another splashy version of International Style plagued by retrospective hankerings after Art Deco: "... a city of geometrical shapes ... of strip windows and ramps," Russell Lynes recalled, "... announced in indisputable terms that Modern of a sort was here to stay—at least for a while...." [18] Most of it looked flimsily gaunt in the steaming sunshine of a New York summer. (Probably the most imaginative exhibit was the Carrier "Cool Dog Stand" that advertised air conditioning by inviting visitors to shed their shoes and luxuriate ankle-deep in dry, cool, circulating air.) But after dark, when the most lavish colored lighting system ever seen outside the aurora borealis took over, it was an incredible show; magazine reporter Henry

F. Pringle said it made "the flare of Broadway seem but a candle in comparison." [19]

The dominating symbol, utilized on countless souvenir gadgets, was the Trylon (a 700-foot attenuated pyramid) standing beside the Perisphere (a vast globe) at the focus of the vistas. The combination looked like a problem in solid geometry. Its pertinence to the World of Tomorrow was clearer when one got inside the Perisphere and stood on a moving observation gallery overlooking Democracity—a miniaturized vision of the city-to-be created by Henry Dreyfuss, one of the nation's best-thought-of industrial designers. Model housing, model bus lines threading through it, model factories in model industrial parks—not a slum in it. That was poor prediction. So was the Railroads on Parade exhibit featuring elaborately comfortable passenger rolling stock. To leave no mistake about what was wrong there, La Guardia Airport opened late that same year not three miles away, and four-engine transports came roaring right over the Iron Horse's showcase; in the fair's season of 1940 the rails' other enemy, the National Highway Trucking Association, came in and built an exhibit nearby.

The prognostics were better—nowadays one almost wishes they hadn't been—in the General Motors' Futurama, a huge and elaborate vision of the nation completely committed to highway transportation by 1960. The effect on the visitor was as of flying at 1,000 feet over a summer countryside with grazing cattle, wide orchards, nicely contour-plowed or terraced fields, here and there barns and farmhouses with microscopic wash hanging on the line—all the fascination of miniaturization beautifully managed. And bulling through it all, fed by a network of minor roads, was a fourteen-lane superhighway, seven each way; outer lanes for lower speeds, inner for 75 and 100 mph; interchanges and exit access worked out in diverse-direction, long-sweeping ramps; not a traffic light anywhere, only traffic-control bridges every few miles giving drivers instructions by radio. On and on bypassing cities, surmounting a mountain massif with the aid of tunnels here, bridges there, out on a plain and a city beyond with a three-mile square airport and a Zeppelin hangar. On closer inspection the city was a doctrinaire triumph of glass-sheathed skyscrapers and multilevel traffic conduits. Except for a few details, such as the Zeppelin hangar, it really had the gist of today's interstate system combined with the maze of superhighways and streets in downtown Chicago. And utterly apropos, in August, 1940, well before the World of Tomorrow and the Futurama closed, the Pennsylvania Turnpike was officially opened. Most symbolically that momentous proto-superhighway from Harrisburg to the outskirts of Pittsburgh utilized the long-abandoned route and unfinished tunnels of an aborted railroad trunk line.

Stuart Chase—always in there thinking out loud, often cogently, sometimes not, when anything interesting came along—left the Futurama as pleased as any with its ingenuities and grateful for its implications in an idealized landscape that the nation could, if it wished to, get rid of "dumps, sludge piles, billboards, polluted streams, rusting roadside jalopies . . . open sewers, back-of-the-tracks housing, hot dog stands, tenant farmers' shacks. . . ." But he was unhappy about the megalomania of the highway cult at the core of it. Granted that the number of automobiles in use was bound vastly to increase and that in "populous sections in the East and on the Pacific coast" such gargantuan plans might be needed. But beyond that point "Who wants to drive at 100 miles an hour anyway? Who wants to drive hour after hour at 75? . . . where is the fun of hurtling across the land at such a rate? You can't see the country!" [20]

Admirable questions and what's more, asked in plenty of time. Never answered. By now, of course, the only response to: "Who wants to drive hour after hour at 75?" obviously is: "Apparently almost every American holding a driver's license." Among most visitors to the World of Tomorrow this Futurama seems to have been the most memorable exhibit of all, except maybe Billy Rose's spectacularly bathing-suited Aquacade. The consequent softening up of the public mind for such extravagant developments as the Los Angeles freeways and the interstate system may mark this as one of the most successful public relations efforts of the century. Only General Motors should have made the American construction industry pay half the bill.

Grover Whalen, the New York City businessman-politician whose morning coat and silk hat were usually the first tokens of hospitality vouchsafed visiting dignitaries, was the World of Tomorrow's front man and chief channel for predictions that 1,000,000 people would attend its opening day and at least 50,000,000 would go through its turnstiles that season. Actual visitors totaled some 600,000 the first day, 26,000,000 for the year. Disappointment also came to the New York restaurateurs and nightclub operators who had anticipated a heartening rise in the sucker trade; instead, they discernibly suffered from the competition of the fair's attractions, some quite good shows and many of them free, and of the various foreign restaurants operated as part of national exhibits—Italian, Swedish, French and so on. Indeed to compound the injury, Henri Soulé, presiding genius of the French entry, never went back to France when the fair closed, instead staying in New York City to create Le Pavillon, for years the best known high-ticket diner's paradise in the country; Ed Fitzgerald of WOR radio fame once referred to it as "Henri Soulé's bar and grill—all you can eat for $100."

One of the World of Tomorrow's other handicaps was negatively identified by New York City's scrappy mayor, Fiorello H. La Guardia, who told a Chicago audience that summer during a promotion trip that "Our Fair will not be remembered for a Hoochy-koochy dancer— and a fan means nothing to us." [21] That invidious invoking of the apocryphal Little Egypt of Chicago's Columbian Exposition of 1893 as well as of Sally Rand had its own reward. Miss Rand at the time was out in San Francisco in command of a troupe of girls wearing nothing but G-strings in an admission-charging gambol called Sally Rand's Dnude Ranch as attention attractor for the Golden Gate Exhibition competing with New York for the nation's summer vacationers; its *raison d'être* was given as celebrating the completion of the Golden Gate and Bay bridges. The World of Tomorrow made sporadic, desultory efforts to exploit the leer-and-giggle department but managed no breakthroughs. Gypsy Rose Lee was out there for a while with the old routine. A certain Rosita Royce got more or less into the papers by coming on wearing nothing but half a dozen pigeons trained to frequent strategic spots; sometimes she used only two large parrots. The headliner of a concession called "20,000 Legs Under the Sea" was the Bed of Venus, containing a girl with a silk sheet drawn modestly up to her navel and a few twigs scattered on her bared bosom. She told a reporter that she really did sleep through much of her daily stint. Certainly she was causing no such excitement as might have disturbed her slumbers.

Yet the chief trouble may have been the rising anxiety that made it sound so foolish when in the spring of 1940 Whalen announced that for its second year the keynote would shift from "The World of Tomorrow" to "Peace and Freedom." In that context certain omens had been bad to begin with. Though he persuaded sixty-odd nations to set up some sort of exhibit, conspicuously absent was Nazi Germany, not at all inclined to cooperate with the capital of world Jewry. Then the month before the fair opened the last vestiges of Czechoslovakia's independence were smothered. Before the fair closed for the winter, the Hitler-Stalin agreement had brought on the war that everybody had been hoping could be avoided. When the gates reopened the next spring, the Finnish, Polish, Norwegian and Dutch exhibits looked almost as forlorn as the Czechoslovakian. The Maritime Building's two great ship's prows made it as conspicuous as ever, but it was closed because for most civilized purposes so were the Atlantic sea-lanes. For the same reason the proud exhibit of the 10,000 vessels of the British merchant marine scattered all over the world on their lawful occasions was no longer on display. "Big Joe," the sixty-foot stainless-steel statue that crowned the USSR's pavilion, stuck it out, however; not until September, 1940, did they ship him home, whether to be reerected as symbol of Communist integrity uncorroded by bourgeois atmosphere or recycled into munitions of war was never stated.

A few weeks later the high point of the official closing-for-good consisted of sealing and burying the time capsule that the Westinghouse Electric Corporation had had on display throughout. It was—and still is, so far as anybody knows—ninety inches long, made of an alloy of nickel and silver. Its exact latitude and longitude to less than an inch were filed in trustworthy libraries throughout the world to help them find it in the stipulated year 6939, 5,000 years onward. Suppose anybody bothers then it will be found to contain a woman's hat, a fountain pen, cigarettes, copies of magazines and newspapers doubtless full of war news, mostly bad.... Meanwhile, there the capsule is, fifty feet down in the garbage below what soon became Flushing Meadows Park once demolition was finished. The brass plate marking its location is one of the few remaining relics of the World of Tomorrow. There will be none to tell those who open it that within 40 years, let alone 5,000, women's hats and fountain pens had become almost as obsolete as buggy whips and gas mantles. But by then such a consideration probably won't seem important. Any archaeologists worth their salt will be far more interested in the wealth of data on us and our times to be found in those millions of tons of garbage.

Though Pearl Harbor was still a year and more away, the new war was already skewing things here, stunting them there. Television was a clear case. For fifteen years such a device had been described as just around the corner. Indeed, experimental broadcasts had reached highly encouraging results, and by 1937 Little Orphan Annie's Daddy Warbucks was communicating by television with his Singapore office. But the first opportunity the nation in general had to stare at this fateful phenomenon was at the World of Tomorrow—living up to its theme all too well in this respect. NBC's appetite-whetting exhibit there showed first on a six-inch, then, in a gigantic leap, on a twelve-inch screen crude efforts at dramatic shows, baseball games and so on. By mid-1940 CBS, Dumont and the Don Lee network on the Coast were tentatively telecasting. But war lowered the boom. The component parts and production facilities needed to equip broadcasters and the public to exploit television were badly needed for defense programs. Television swallowed hard and went on ice until after V-J Day.

Yet war could also stimulate backhandedly. In the years during which the miracle of Flushing Meadows gestated and ran its course, today's pocket-size paperback book industry was born and reached wildly vigorous adolescence. It had forebears in the latter 1800s, when America's recalcitrance about international copyright had enabled American publishers freely to pirate the best transatlantic authors. In your grandfather's time, however, and up to the end of the 1920s, popular reprints of best-sellers, though plentiful, were cheap-paper hardcover affairs costing toward a dollar—much less than regular editions but with no such differential as to set off a landslide popular market. As the Depression led to hard times for books, too, imaginative publishers began nibbling at the notion of using the mass-circulation magazines' methods of printing and distribution to get really inexpensive—down to a quarter a copy, say—reprints into potential readers' hands. The result was what the late Freeman Lewis, who had a great deal to do with it all, defined as "From a marketing point of view ... neither books nor magazines but a hybrid product, a sort of 'bookazine.' " [22] It was a potential revolution in bookselling as far-reaching as the development of book clubs in the previous decade.

Early promising but presently abortive ventures came in 1937. In 1939 the proper avalanche began with the birth of Pocket Books, using high-speed magazine presses and magazine-wholesaling arrangements to get display racks of bright-covered paperbacks, largely fiction, into drugstores, dime stores, department stores, railroad stations and airports—in effect bypassing conventional bookstores and going straight to a vast subliterary public. Soon Britain's Penguin Books, an earlier parallel success across the water, came into America with a picked list of rather staider but likely titles. This innovation had its constructive aspects. Almost immediately it did the nation an aesthetic favor by smothering the already-floundering pulp magazines. And it did set in motion a widening of the reading habit of which America stood in need particularly now that radio was keeping spare-time attention away from books as such. Or, suppose it true that, as apologists for broadcasting maintain, it stimulates reading because its dramatizations of fiction and discussions of conspicuous books attract listeners to the originals, the low cost and wide availability of paperbacks give potential readers in lower-income brackets invaluable access to the books in question and then, as they learn to value reading, to books in general.

In 1941 Avon Books entered the new game. The goose was hanging very high when war-caused shortages of paper threatened to slow expansion. But what war took away with one mailed fist it eventually restored with the other through the long-run effect of the Armed

Services Editions—1,300-odd admirably chosen, specially manufactured paperback items distributed free (they cost 6 cents each to print, royalties waived) to servicemen. Some 125,000,000 of these handy off-duty time killers passed man to man until they fell apart. "Never before," said Frank L. Schick's study, "had so many books ... found such a large number of avid readers." [23] Publishers drew no direct profit. But the program contributed greatly to the skyrocketing success awaiting paperbacks after V-J Day. Thus, Fanny Butcher, the Chicago *Tribune*'s veteran observer of the book world, saw the GIs' experience with the Armed Services Editions breaking down "the feeling that reading a book was unmanly.... Automatically, painlessly books became a part of life for hundreds of thousands who had never owned or even borrowed anything except a textbook in school ... a taboo smashed with noble results." [24]

"THERE WILL BE NO TOMORROW"

The economic revival occasioned by war was an ironic silver lining. In the sixth year of FDR's efforts to get unemployment off the nation's back, success still lagged. True, times were better than when he took over but what with rising deficits, persisting scarcity of jobs and a nagging sense of running out of things to try, the net effect was flabby. In agreeing to cut up Poland as appetizer for greater things, Hitler and Stalin can have had no wish to buck up the sagging economy of capitalistic America. Yet that was precisely what they brought about. Beginning slowly, accelerating in the spring of 1940 as the Nazis' victories blazed up, FDR and Congress went into precautionary rearmament, providing not only jobs but fatter pay envelopes on a scale that New Deal measures had never reached. At the same grudging pace various administrative and legislative subterfuges and about-faces—cash-and-carry, destroyers-for-bases, lend-lease—drew the teeth of the Neutrality Laws and other barriers against "foreign entanglements" that so recently had seemed the height of responsible realism. Much of this entailed jobs making war-useful things for overseas. And late in 1940 the draft, the first such step ever taken in peacetime in the United States, was nibbling away at unemployment in a grimmer fashion. It was all lively before Pearl Harbor. The protorevisionists who were already suspecting FDR of hoping to jockey the Japanese into attacking in order to save his political skin forgot that it was unnecessary. Hitler and Stalin had already brought about prosperity for him, and it was highly unlikely that they had done it at his instance.

Through the above process Americans' emotions were changing to match, often rather ahead of governmental action. There was a long way to go. Sixteen months before the Nazis crushed into Poland a *Ladies' Home Journal* POP showed what fertile soil isolationism was working in. Women against fighting an overseas war again: 88 percent. Against ever fighting for economic interests abroad: 84 percent. Against lending money or sending supplies to belligerent countries: 87 percent. Almost one in three said they'd rather have a son go to jail as a pacifist than to war. As for whether the United States would be drawn into another general war, 56 percent said no, couldn't happen again—a classic example of wishful prognosis. To have included the ladies' husbands and boyfriends in the poll might have lowered some of those lopsided ratios but probably not critically. Contemporary Gallup POPs of both sexes were showing heavy majorities for pacifist or isolationist or anyway antibelligerency measures such as requiring national referenda before war could be declared or conscription imposed.

Once war came, however, 80 percent plus of Americans wanted the Allies to win and thought they would—another example of wishful judgment—and 62 percent were in favor of the "all aid short of war" policy already evident in FDR's doings. The "short of war" proviso was still all-important. During that winter, in spite of Finland's plight, it was still possible to believe it to be a Phony War, and feeling against potential direct involvement of the United States overseas stayed strong. But as Norway, the Low Countries and France went down and Britain, thanks to its pursuit pilots, just managed to keep chin out of water, the sledding for interventionists grew easier. "The American war spirit," says Selig Adler's *The Isolationist Impulse,* "was not whipped up by the sale of munitions, propaganda or financial investment [in the pattern that isolationists-cum-liberals attributed to World War I]; such militancy as existed prior to Pearl Harbor rose in response to Hitler's fierce lunges toward the nations bordering the Atlantic." [1]

A model for one version of the change conveniently exists in the case of Robert E. Sherwood, whose extremely successful plays often dealt with the revulsion from war and the cynicism about its causes he had derived from ample combat experience in World War I and the subsequent clichés of his time. In 1936 his postscript to *Idiot's Delight,* a play equally severe on Nazis and munitions makers, laid it down that "those who shrug and say 'War is inevitable' are false prophets ... the world is populated largely by decent people and decent people don't want war. Nor do they make war. They fight and die ... because they have been deluded by their exploiters." [2] When the Hitler-Stalin agreement burst on the world late in August, 1939, and so many previously loyal radicals, even many faithful Party-liners, jumped from the steamroller, Sherwood even tried stubbornly to see it as a matter of "Stalin ... playing his own shrewd game against Fascism." [3] But the next month a speech of Lindbergh's, which he took as evidence that "Hitler was already powerfully and persuasively represented in our midst," [4] so shook him that he called the Lone Eagle "a bootlicker of Adolf Hitler" [5] in a broadcast over Canadian radio. At the end of November the USSR's attack on Finland finished him off. He wrote *There Shall Be No Night* about the plight of a Finnish intellectual, which, Brooks Atkinson said, "reversed the boyish and amiable irresponsibility of *Idiot's Delight* ... [and] expressed a sense of public concern that was wholly admirable." [6] At the time Raymond Clapper called it "a rank, inflammatory job, pleading for intervention" but also "an incident of first rate national meaning" [7] likely deeply to influence public opinion. It did. And to make sure he kept doing so, Sherwood went zealously to work with interventionist groups that eventuated as the Fight for Freedom organization.

About the same time MacLeish, also a combat veteran of World War I, a writer of equal renown and probably greater mental balance, was going beyond reversing his stand. With unusual courage he most explicitly reproached those, himself included, who had trained their countrymen to feel the paralyzing, myopic bundle of emotions triggered by mention of Flanders Fields and the phrases "Merchants of Death" and "Oxford Pledge." For the *New Republic,* whose readers were exactly the persons most influentially affected, he deplored the stand taken by "the best and most sensitive writers of my generation ... Barbusse, Latzko, Dos Passos, Ford Madox Ford, Erich Maria Remarque and Richard Aldington ... not only against the hatefulness and cruelty of war.... [Their war books] were filled with passionate contempt for the statements of purpose ... on which the war was fought ... [and] drew the conclusion that not only the war and the war issues but all ... moral issues were false ... fraudulent ... intended to deceive ... this [was] what all of us who were in the war believed. But they ... have borne bitter and dangerous fruit ... the generation which read them ... was left defenseless ... educated ... to believe that all declarations, all beliefs are fraudulent, that nothing men can put into words is worth fighting for, and that there is a lowdown to everything.... [Their] books have done more to disarm democracy in the face of fascism than any other single influence. Some of them have devoted themselves to the fight against fascism.... I have no right to judge them.... I felt as they did and wrote, as far as I was able, as they were writing.... But ... what they wrote ... however true to them as a summary of their personal experience, was disastrous as education for a generation ... obliged to face the threat of fascism in its adult years." [8]

He might also have mentioned Hemingway who, a statesman-general even before he went to the Spanish Civil War, had been assuring his fan public in *Esquire* that the next war wouldn't break out for a while because "they never fight as long as money can be made without ... but [sooner or later] they fight," and a general European war will bring in America if "propaganda (think how the radio will be used for this), greed, and the desire to increase the impaired health of the state can bring us in," for inflation and war are "the refuge of political and economic opportunists." [9] Later he prescribed cash-and-carry for arms-needy belligerents: "Let the gentlemen of Europe fight and, if they pay cash, see how long it will last." [10] This was one form of what led Max Eastman to write a generation later: "The passion against war is almost as rabid as the military passion; it gangs men up and stampedes their minds in a similar way." [11] But when such figures as Sherwood and MacLeish found themselves morally obliged to change their minds out loud, it was going to take more than pontifical peevishness to reverse the growth of interventionist feeling. It was growing not so much among legislators, so many of whom were already out on a limb, as among voters. It was not so much policy thinking as visceral impulse well developed enough to contain America First when launched and go on to form the basis of wholehearted war against the Fascists when the Japanese obligingly triggered the situation.

The *Ladies' Home Journal* POP's women, in 1938 so cynically firm against mixing into Europe's brawls again—last time "We were just the goat for the Allies," [12] a Cleveland salesman's wife told the pollster—began to swallow hard in December, 1939, when their magazine published a letter from an Englishwoman contributor headlined MAY I HOLD YOUR HAND TILL I DIE? It told of the burst of air-raid precautions that war had brought. The children "have strong labels sewn to their clothes [carrying] names, ages and addresses. Why? The reasons won't bear writing down." And it told of the writer's small son, aware of what trying on gas masks implied, saying, "If there's an air-raid and I get hurt—may I hold your hand till I die? I didn't mind being put to sleep for my operation because you held my hand—so I won't mind dying, I expect." [13] The following fall, just when the Battle of Britain was simmering down, such women all over the country were making an explosive best-seller of *The White Cliffs of Dover,* a verse essay by Alice Duer Miller, an able writer of stage comedies and women's magazine fiction. Says its heroine, American widow of an Englishman killed in World War I, well, though still uneasily, embedded in English life:

> I am American bred.
> I have seen much to hate here—much to forgive;
> But in a world where England is finished and dead,
> I do not wish to live....

She describes the liberal-isolationists as standing:

> ...like the proverbial ostrich—head in sand—
> While youth passed resolutions not to fight,
> And statesmen muttered everything was right—
> Germany, a kindly, much ill treated nation—
> Russia was working out her own salvation....[14]

Lynn Fontanne, appropriately British-born and -reared and developed into a great lady of the stage in the American theater, read *White Cliffs* to a national audience over the air—just one of many, many examples of how radio would, as Hemingway predicted, be used to shape emotions about the war. (Isolationists were playing the emotional game in the other direction, of course. But no matter how often Lindbergh took to the national networks, his cause was failing to gain ground.) For a far wider audience Walter Winchell, persuaded that he was FDR's right hand in working up support for Britain, was using the air for shrill attacks on "Assolationists" as well as bearing down juicily on his long-standing conviction that Hitler was an abysmally corrupt homosexual. Elmer Davis, then radio's most impressive commentator voice, was a charter member of the group that became Fight for Freedom and while he conscientiously described the dismal succession of Nazi victories, left no doubt in hearers' minds where he thought the weight of American resources and sentiment should go. Even more effective was CBS' Edward R. Murrow, reporting bomb by bomb the pluck with which Britain was taking the worst the Luftwaffe could throw. He had a superb broadcasting voice—easy, deep but not pompous—and his style of using it was a great credit to a degree of Bachelor of Arts in Speech from Oregon State. The copy that exploited it was admirably terse and vivid, following:

"This ... *is London!*" He became the Sir Launcelot of broadcasting, intrepid, generous-minded, ungrudgingly looked up to by his colleagues in a fashion consistent with his having been not so long since president of the National Student Federation: "... a tall, thin man with a boyish grin," Eric Sevareid recalls, "extraordinary dark eyes ... alight and intense one moment and somber and lost the next. He seemed to possess that rare thing, an instinctive, intuitive recognition of truth." [15]

In the second year of World War II the truth—and it was one—that Murrow seemed to recognize and spread wherever the CBS radio network reached was that Britain's cause was civilization's and America had better get cracking before it was too late. He did it not by direct exhortation or reasoned exposition but by spontaneous, doubtless nondeliberate implication steaming up from what he was describing. Under such forces the spectrum of American sentiment was polarizing into two unequal divisions: a slowly growing majority not only hoping the Nazis would fail but becoming reconciled, if largely subliminally, to a degree of American involvement probably spelling war; and a static minority, sizable but frustrated, consisting of the isolationists grotesquely coupled with the Communists and their forlorn hope of fellow travelers and chronic aginners still managing to stomach the Hitler-Stalin pact.

The world never knew what that slowly skewing pattern would work itself into. For in the next six months two of history's most remarkable bad guesses wiped those terms off the blackboard. Hitler attacked the USSR. Reacting even faster than to the Hitler-Stalin pact, America's Communists immediately tore up their jaunty slogan "The Yanks Are Not Coming!" and, with an abject subservience to Stalin & Co.'s purposes that by then surprised nobody, whirled into noisy demands for all-out American intervention overseas. This relieved America First of the embarrassment of Communists as allies trying to be bedfellows. But their enjoyment of it was swallowed up when, only a few weeks later, Lindbergh made his anti-Jewish speech, and there went the ball game. And on December 7 what were left of the home team were showing various degrees of good grace in turning in their suits.

The switchboard of WOR-New York, flagship of the Mutual Network, was swamped with listeners complaining that an announcer kept breaking into their broadcasts with some wild talk about the Japanese attacking Hawaii. Five thousand miles to westward in Honolulu a local newspaperman in the traffic jam on King Street found himself stalled within arm's length of a key citizen whom he had often interviewed. The great man was red in the face and shaking his fist. "Young man!" he shouted. "The mainland papers are going to exaggerate the importance of this!"

Hardly. Fourteen months earlier FDR had received a letter signed by Albert Einstein. It described the Nazis' program to develop an atomic bomb. It suggested the high advisability of the United States' getting there first.

APPENDIX OF DEFINITIONS

The following definitions of ideological groups mentioned in the preceding text are based on those appended to the writer's previous *Great Times* and applying to the 1920s. They have been used as carefully as possible in the text, but it remains true, as the previous book noted, that they "have been so misused by propagandists and public scolds that accuracy in employing them is hardly possible."

ANARCHIST: Emotionally committed to the theory developed in Europe in the 1800s that governments are the crucial enemies of social justice and the way to it is by destruction of government and creation of voluntary cooperation. Anarchists vary widely in their notions of how much violence should be taken to bring this about.

BOLSHEVIK: (= "majority" in Russian) pertaining to the "majority" portion of the Russian Social Democrats (Marxist) who split away from the Menshevik (= "minority" in Russian) portion in 1903. On the whole the *Bolsheviki* were more militant and discipline-minded.

COLLECTIVIST: Temperamentally disposed to prefer cooperative to lone-hand enterprise and to believe that social justice is usually advanced in proportion to pooling of ownership of economic enterprises in public hands.

COMMUNIST: Formally enrolled member of the worldwide Communist parties. In certain non-Communist countries at certain times all or many Communists make a secret of membership. All are presumably under complete Party discipline as distinguished from the

FELLOW TRAVELER: A zealous proponent of Communist aims and ideas who for reasons of expediency or individual unsuitability is not formally enrolled but presumably follows Party directives received directly or indirectly deduced.

LIBERAL: The writer's private definition is: Disposed to consider the Preamble and Amendments the most important parts of the Constitution. In recent customary usage, however, it must mean something like: Temperamentally inclined to welcome changes promising wider social and economic responsibilities usually but not necessarily of a sort tending. toward collectivism *(q.v.)*; often also solicitous about maintaining individuals' rights and interests particularly when threatened by property rights.

PARTY-LINER: One consistently espousing the Communist Party's going attitudes, teachings, tactics and strategy, the consistency extending to abrupt changes of mind to match Party shifts. May be (1) a card-carrying, formally enrolled Communist; or (2) a fellow traveler *(q.v.)*; or (3) a zealous sympathizer emotionally committed to the Party's doings.

RADICAL: Should, of course, mean one inclined to get down to the roots of things to effect sweeping changes of whatever ideological flavor. Recent usage confines it to the admittedly collectivist liberal becoming impatient of gradualism. Radicals tend to go doctrinaire in either the anarchist *(q.v.)* or the Socialist *(q.v.)* direction.

REACTIONARY: Emotionally committed to a Good Old Days of free enterprise, unlimited opportunity and 100 percent Americanism that never existed in any such terms. Often goes with some form of racism, sometimes with religiosity. Shares certain psychopathological traits with extreme radicals. "Fascist" is often applied to the reactionary, but the two terms are not congruent, and the context of Fascism tends to remain awkwardly European.

RED: Emotionally committed to the Socialism of which a red flag is the traditional rallying symbol. Applies to a revolutionary, usually Marxist-flavored, frame of mind that includes much beyond specific Communism.

SOCIALIST: One who advocates public ownership and management of all—at the very least, the chief—means of economic production. How to bring this about—immediately or gradually, peacefully or violently, whether for moral or economic reasons or for both—depends on the kind of socialist. With a capital *S* means a member, avowed or secret, of an organized Socialist group. Since long before World War I Marxist Socialists have been the most conspicuous. They include Communists *(q.v.)*, of course, but only the Bolshevik *(q.v.)* segment of

Marxist Socialism is now properly called Communist; it has numerous splinters.

LEFT and RIGHT to mean opposite ends of a graduated political spectrum have been avoided wherever possible. These terms are imported from traditional European situations and, though not always meaningless this side of the water, usually oversimplify or distort an American context.

NOTES

Full information on the following references is given in the subsequent list of sources quoted; books only, periodicals self-explanatory.

I.

1. "The New School Murals of Thomas Hart Benton," no pagination.
2. Johnson, *Pioneer's Progress,* 329.
3. *Time,* October 31, 1929.
4. May, *The End of American Innocence,* 394.
5. Lippmann, *A Preface to Politics,* 89.
6. Lippmann, *Drift and Mastery,* 16–17.
7. Beard, ed., *America Faces the Future,* 7–8.
8. *Forum,* February, 1931.
9. Soule, *A Planned Society,* 21.
10. *Time,* November 11, 1929.
11. *Dictionary of American History,* "Panic of 1929."
12. *Time,* November 18, 1929.
13. *Fortune,* February, 1930.
14. Roy A. Wright, "Transportation," in Beard, ed., *Toward Civilization.*
15. O'Hara, *Appointment in Samarra,* 65.
16. Stegner, *The Uneasy Chair,* 92.
17. John T. Flynn, in Klein, ed., *Grand Deception,* 337–38.
18. Josephson, *The Money Lords,* 43.
19. *Ibid.,* 132.
20. Pegler, *'T Ain't Right,* 160–61.

II.

1. Saarinen, *The Possessors,* 366.
2. Emily Post, *Harper's Bazaar,* April, 1928.
3. Millay, *Three Plays,* 19.

4. Stevenson, "Virginibus Puerisque," I.
5. Mumford, *American Taste,* no pagination.
6. Hitchcock and Johnson, *International Style,* 42.
7. *Ibid.,* 15.
8. *Ibid.,* 13.
9. *New Yorker,* September 18, 1971.
10. Gropius, *Apollo in the Democracy,* 80.
11. New York *Times,* May 8, 1975.
12. Twombly, *Frank Lloyd Wright,* 302.
13. Hitchcock and Johnson, *International Style,* no pagination.
14. John Lloyd Wright, *My Father . . .,* 32.
15. Farr, *Frank Lloyd Wright,* 3.
16. Twombly, *Frank Lloyd Wright,* 276.
17. Frank Lloyd Wright, *An Autobiography,* 547–48.
18. *Ibid.,* 515.
19. Twombly, *Frank Lloyd Wright,* 33.
20. John Lloyd Wright, *My Father . . .,* 32.
21. Kaufmann and Raeburn, eds., *Frank Lloyd Wright: Writings . . .,* 232.
22. Lynes, *The Taste-Makers,* 247.
23. Blake, *Frank Lloyd Wright,* 112.
24. George Nelson, *Holiday,* July, 1961.
25. Blake, *Frank Lloyd Wright,* 109.
26. Kaufmann and Raeburn, eds., *Frank Lloyd Wright: Writings . . .,* 252.
27. Blake, *Frank Lloyd Wright,* 109.
28. Twombly, *Frank Lloyd Wright,* 132.
29. Frank Lloyd Wright, *An Autobiography,* 514–15.
30. Kaufmann and Raeburn, eds., *Frank Lloyd Wright: Writings . . .,* 269–70.
31. Frank Lloyd Wright, *An Autobiography,* 503.
32. Gropius, *Apollo . . .,* 30.
33. Farr, *Frank Lloyd Wright,* 276.
34. Mrs. Lloyd Lewis, personal communication.
35. Trilling, *The Middle of the Journey,* 208–9.
36. Owings, *The Spaces in Between,* 82.
37. Ted Morgan, *New York Times Magazine,* July 4, 1976.
38. Wells, *The World Set Free,* 258.
39. Chorley, *Williamsburg in Virginia,* 27.
40. [Colonial Williamsburg], *The First Twenty-Five Years,* no pagination.
41. Simonds, *Henry Ford and Greenfield Village,* 135.
42. Richards, *The Last Billionaire,* 112.
43. *Ibid.,* 187.
44. Stuart Chase, *Nation,* November 18, 1931.
45. Viereck, *Confessions of a Barbarian,* 126–27.
46. *New Yorker,* August 6, 1927.
47. Howard C. Warren, *Psychological Review,* March, 1933.
48. Hartman *et al., Nudist Society,* 257.
49. *Encyclopedia of Sexual Behavior,* 256.

50. Seldes, *The Seven Lively Arts,* 132.
51. Benton, *Artist in America,* 306–8.
52. Rembar, *The End of Obscenity,* 3.
53. *Ibid.,* 4.
54. *Ibid.,* 24.
55. *Ibid.,* 25.
56. Caldwell, *God's Little Acre,* no pagination.
57. Farrell, intro. *A World I Never Made,* xi.
58. Broun, *The Sun Field,* 141.
59. Dorothy Parker, *Esquire,* December, 1957.
60. New York *Times,* August 5, 1971.
61. New York *Times,* July 16, 1972.
62. *New York Times Magazine,* March 28, 1971.
63. Harry Leon Wilson, *Ruggles of Red Gap,* 161.
64. Parran, *Shadow on the Land,* 225.
65. *Ibid.,* 228.
66. *Fortune,* February, 1932.
67. Ringel, ed., *America as Americans See It,* 295.
68. Gallico, *Farewell to Sport,* 36.
69. *The Best of Life,* 287.
70. New York *Times,* January 7, 1974.
71. Rosalind G. Salzman, dissertation; at Pomona College.
72. Jorge Juan Crespo de la Serna, plaque; at Pomona College.
73. Carl B. Hess, *Dartmouth College Bulletin,* No. 12, 1934.
74. Rivera, *Portrait of America,* 13.
75. Detroit *Free Press,* August 26, 1932.
76. Detroit Institute of Arts brochure.
77. *Michigan Catholic,* January 12, 1933.
78. Detroit *News,* March 20, 1933.
79. *Ibid.*
80. Craven, *Modern Art,* 271.
81. Lippmann, *Drift and Mastery,* 110–11.
82. Boorstin, *The Americans,* 511–12.
83. New York *Times,* January 21, 1975.
84. Thomas Craven, *Scribner's,* October, 1937.
85. Craven, *Modern Art,* 344.
86. New York *Times,* September 5, 1971.
87. New York *Times,* January 21, 1975.
88. Bird, *The Invisible Scar,* 205.
89. Garwood, *Artist in Iowa,* 137.
90. New York *Times,* September 5, 1971.
91. *New York Times Magazine,* October 17, 1976.
92. Lipman, *Calder's Universe,* 40.
93. *Newsweek,* November 22, 1976.
94. New York *Times,* November 12, 1976.
95. Lipman, intro., *Calder's Universe,* no pagination.
96. *Ibid.,* 25.

97. *Ibid.,* 18.
98. *Ibid.,* 35.
99. *Life,* Vol. II, 1926; page unavailable because number cropped in run consulted.
100. *New Yorker,* June 9, 1928.
101. Dalton Trumbo, *North American Review,* December, 1933.
102. Fulton, *Motion Pictures,* 86.
103. Macgowan, *Behind the Screen,* 11.
104. *Life,* November 2, 1922.
105. New York *Times,* October 28, 1973.
106. New York *Times,* January 14, 1938.
107. New York *Herald Tribune,* November 14, 1940.
108. *Art News,* December 1, 1940.
109. Gallup, *The Sophisticated Poll Watcher's Guide,* 123.
110. Gallup and Rae, *The Pulse of Democracy,* 87.
111. New York *Times,* March 15, 1974.
112. New York *Times,* May 1, 1971.
113. American Institute of Public Opinion, *Questions Often Asked About Published Polls,* 7.
114. Gallup and Rae, *The Pulse of Democracy,* 5.
115. *Ibid.,* 133.
116. Nielsen, *Greater Prosperity Through Marketing Research,* no pagination.
117. Harmon, *The Great Radio Heroes,* 28 n.
118. Oboler, *Fourteen Radio Plays,* xv.
119. Seldes, *The Great Audience,* 113.
120. *Fortune,* September, 1932.
121. Thurber, *The Beast in Me . . .,* 191.
122. Higby, *Tune in Tomorrow . . .,* 123.
123. Landry, *Who, What, Why Is Radio?,* 57.
124. Wylie, *Radio Writing,* 180.
125. Higby, *Tune in Tomorrow . . .,* 133.
126. Edmondson and Rounds, *The Soaps,* 55.
127. Barnouw, *The Golden Web,* II, 97.
128. Thurber, *The Beast In Me . . .,* 260.
129. Harmon, *The Great Radio Heroes,* 246.
130. *Ibid.,* 115.
131. Gross, *I Looked and I Listened,* 72.
132. New York *Times,* February 21, 1972.
133. Bob Thomas, *Winchell,* 35.
134. Winchell, *Winchell Exclusive,* 323.
135. Weiner, *Let's Go to Press,* 12.
136. New York *Herald Tribune,* November 2, 1938.
137. Cantrill *et al., The Invasion from Mars,* 111 *et seq.*
138. Barnouw, *The Golden Web,* II, 138–39.
139. Wechsler, *The Age of Suspicion,* 215.
140. Seldes, *The Great Audience,* 147.
141. Barnouw, *The Golden Web,* II, 71.

142. Landry, *Who, What, Why Is Radio?,* 68.
143. Harmon, *The Great Radio Heroes,* 30.
144. Seldes, *The Great Audience,* 112.
145. John Houseman, *Run-Through,* 360.
146. MacLeish, *The Fall of the City,* foreword.
147. *Ibid.*
148. *Ibid.,* 30.
149. Carl Van Doren, preface to Corwin, *Thirteen by Corwin,* vii.
150. Oboler, *Fourteen Radio Plays,* 72–73.
151. Higby, *Tune in Tomorrow . . .,* 44–46.
152. Pegler, *The Dissenting Opinions of Mister . . .,* 1, 4.
153. Kramer, *Heywood Broun,* 102.
154. Broun, *Collected Edition of . . .,* 399.
155. Wecter, *The Age of the Great Depression,* 50.
156. Farr, *Fair Enough,* 119.
157. Pilat, *Pegler,* 133.
158. Pegler, *'T Ain't Right,* 87.
159. Farr, *Fair Enough,* 109–10.
160. Pilat, *Pegler,* 156.
161. Farr, *Fair Enough,* 128.
162. *Ibid.,* 119.
163. Pegler, *George Spelvin, American,* 30–33.
164. Farr, *Fair Enough,* 114.
165. Pegler, *George Spelvin American,* 178–81.
166. Ben Hecht, *A Child of the Century,* 386.
167. Pilat, *Pegler,* 24.
168. Rosenstone, *Crusade of the Left,* 214.
169. Sanders, *Dorothy Thompson,* 225.
170. *Ibid.,* 94–95.
171. Thompson, *I Saw Hitler,* 3.
172. Sanders, *Dorothy Thompson,* 199.
173. *New Yorker,* April 20, 1940.
174. Jack Alexander, *Saturday Evening Post,* May 25, 1940.
175. Sinclair Lewis, *It Can't Happen Here,* 432.
176. Eleanor Roosevelt, *If You Ask Me,* 102.
177. Lash, *Eleanor and Franklin,* 210–11.
178. *New Yorker,* April 5, 1930.
179. Eleanor Roosevelt, *If You Ask Me,* 81.
180. *Encyclopedia of Social Sciences* (1st ed.), "Social Settlements."
181. Eleanor Roosevelt, *If You Ask Me,* 81.
182. Tugwell, *The Light of Other Days,* 246–47.
183. Lilienthal, *The Journals of . . .,* I, 236.
184. Lash, *Eleanor and Franklin,* 306.
185. *Ibid.,* 307.
186. Eleanor Roosevelt, *It's Up to the Women,* 36.
187. Lash, *Eleanor and Franklin,* 554.
188. Eleanor Roosevelt, *If You Ask Me,* 41, 57.

189. *Ibid.,* 83.
190. *Ibid.,* 94.
191. *Ibid.,* 125.
192. Lash, *Eleanor and Franklin,* 426.
193. Eleanor Roosevelt, *If You Ask Me,* 154.

III.

1. Sandburg, *The People, Yes,* 42.
2. Jack Conroy, introduction to *Writers in Revolt,* x.
3. Clifford Odets, *Awake and Sing,* in Clurman, *Famous American Plays of the 1930s,* 46.
4. Gene Smith, *The Shattered Dream,* 66.
5. *Ibid.,* 81.
6. Couch, ed., *These Are Our Lives,* 185.
7. Eleanor Roosevelt, *If You Ask Me,* 27.
8. Fitzgerald, *The Last Tycoon,* in *Three Novels of . . .,* 5.
9. Frederick Lewis Allen, *Ladies' Home Journal,* November, 1932.
10. Benton, *Artist in America,* 259.
11. *Fortune,* January, 1932.
12. George Soule, *Harper's,* August, 1932.
13. Gardner Jackson, "The American Radical," in Ringel, ed., *America as Americans See It,* 187.
14. Edmund Wilson, *Travels in Two Democracies,* 188–89.
15. J. K. Galbraith, *Harper's,* November, 1960.
16. Herbert C. Hoover, "President Hoover's Plan," in Beard, ed., *America Faces the Future,* 387.
17. Richards, *The Last Billionaire,* vi.
18. New York *Times,* May 26, 1974.
19. Schlesinger, *The Crisis of the Old Order,* 240.
20. Hallgren, *Seeds of Revolt,* 30–31.
21. *Fortune,* September, 1922.
22. Ray Lyman Wilbur, *Woman's Home Companion,* June, 1922.
23. Hallgren, *Seeds of Revolt,* 30–31.

IV.

1. Schlesinger, *The Crisis of the Old Order,* 242.
2. *Ladies' Home Journal,* January, 1930.
3. *Ladies' Home Journal,* June, 1932.
4. *Ladies' Home Journal,* May, 1932.
5. *Ladies' Home Journal,* April, 1932.
6. Bernays, *Biography of an Idea,* 518.
7. New York *Times,* December 30, 1932.
8. Cy Caldwell, *New Outlook,* February, 1933.
9. Cummings, *Miscellany,* 143.
10. Kaplan, *Lincoln Steffens,* 117.

11. Milton Mayer, *Vanity Fair,* September, 1933.
12. Nathaniel A. Owings, personal communication.
13. William Gunn Shepherd, *Collier's,* September 17, 1932.
14. Delafield, *Provincial Lady in America,* 94–96.
15. Dallas Museum of Fine Arts, *1930's Exhibitions,* no pagination.
16. *Billboard,* September 2, 1933.
17. Chicago Historical Society, undated clipping, ACOP file.
18. New York *Times,* December 17, 1975.
19. *Ladies' Home Journal,* January, 1937.
20. *World's Fair Weekly,* June 3, 1933.
21. Roberts, *Black Magic,* 88–89.
22. *Fortune,* July, 1934.
23. Diggins, *Mussolini and Fascism,* 18.
24. *Ibid.,* 19.
25. Lincoln Steffens, *Century,* August, 1923.
26. Bertram D. Wolfe, *Strange Communists I Have Known,* 30.
27. Steffens, *The Autobiography of . . .,* 813.
28. *St. Nicholas,* April, 1923.
29. *Life,* October 18, 1923; July 15, 1936.
30. Tarkington, *Claire Ambler,* 85–87.
31. Roberts, *Black Magic,* 71.
32. Diggins, *Mussolini and Fascism,* 43–45.
33. *Fortune,* July, 1934.
34. Elsner, *The Technocrats,* 79.
35. Mead, *Blackberry Winter,* 187–88.
36. Raymond, *What Is Technocracy?,* 118–20.
37. Arkwright, *The ABC of Technocracy,* 65.
38. Raymond, *What Is Technocracy?,* 3–4.
39. Beard, ed., *Toward Civilization,* 3, 13.
40. Loeb, *Life in a Technocracy,* 97.
41. Wells, *The World Set Free,* 214–16.
42. Martin, *Prohibiting Poverty,* 4.
43. Charles A. Beard, intro. Laing, *Towards Technocracy . . .,* no pagination.
44. Raymond, *What Is Technocracy?,* 16.
45. Chase, *Technocracy,* 11.
46. Schlesinger, *The Crisis of the Old Order,* 463.
47. *Nation,* September 7, 1932.
48. New York *Times,* January 10, 1933.
49. Elsner, *The Technocrats,* 8.
50. William Soskin, intro. Sinclair Lewis, *Arrowsmith,* v–vi.
51. Lippmann, *Drift and Mastery,* 36.
52. Clurman, *The Fervent Years,* 121.
53. Beard, ed., *America Faces the Future,* 246.
54. *Ibid.,* 145.
55. *Ibid.,* 20 *et seq.*
56. *Ibid.,* 124.
57. *Ibid.,* 33.

58. Soule, *A Planned Society*, 206.
59. Beard, *America Faces the Future*, 397.
60. *Ibid.,* 118.
61. Soule, *A Planned Society*, 84.
62. Loeb, *Life in a Technocracy*, 75.
63. Quoted in Hallgren, *Seeds of Revolt*, 261.
64. *New Yorker*, June 10, 1974.
65. Scott, *Introduction to Technocracy by . . .*, 45–46.
66. New York *Times*, January 14, 1933.
67. Raymond, *What Is Technocracy?*, 28.
68. Elsner, *The Technocrats*, 37.
69. *Technocracy* magazine, December, 1935.
70. Elsner, *The Technocrats*, 85–86.
71. *Ibid.,* 144–46.
72. Norman, *Ezra Pound*, 175–76.
73. Schlesinger, *The Crisis of the Old Order*, 464.
74. Seidler, *Norman Thomas*, 50.
75. Kent, *Without Gloves*, 154.
76. Schlesinger, *The Politics of Upheaval*, 20.
77. Coughlin, *Eight Lectures on Labor, Capital and Justice*, 86, 95, 76.
78. Tull, *Father Coughlin and the New Deal*, 246.
79. *Ibid.,* 75.
80. Marcus, *Father Coughlin*, 157.
81. Kent, *Without Gloves*, 154.
82. Marcus, *Father Coughlin*, 127.
83. *Ibid.,* 8.
84. Tull, *Father Coughlin and the New Deal*, 114.
85. Marcus, *Father Coughlin*, 72–73.
86. Tull, *Father Coughlin and the New Deal*, 109.
87. Charles E. Coughlin, *Eight Lectures on Labor, Capital, and Justice*, 26–27.
88. Tull, *Father Coughlin and the New Deal*, 27.
89. West, *A Cool Million*, 59.
90. U.S. House of Representatives, HUAC, Vol. 6, 7255.
91. *Ibid.,* Vol. 6, 7256.
92. Rogge, *The Official German Report*, 113.
93. US House of Representatives, HUAC, Vol. 6, 7282.
94. Robert Lewis Taylor, *New Yorker*, August 24, 1940.
95. Hofstadter, *Anti-Intellectualism in American Life*, 132–33.
96. Geoffrey S. Smith, *To Save a Nation*, 69.
97. Detroit *Times*, April 18, 1934.
98. Detroit *News*, April 8, 1934.
99. US House of Representatives, HUAC, Vol. 10, 6069.
100. *Ibid.,* Vol. 6, 3713.
101. Joseph Dinneen, *American* magazine, August, 1937.
102. William Seabrook, *American* magazine, October, 1937.
103. American Civil Liberties Union, *Report*, January 24, 1938.

104. Spivak, *America Faces the Barricades*, 224.
105. Upton Sinclair, *Pearson's Magazine*, June, 1922.
106. Sinclair, *I, Governor of California*, 7.
107. Creel, *Rebel at Large*, 282–83.
108. Sinclair, "The Lie Factory Starts," in *The Epic Plan for California*, 38.
109. Sinclair, *I, Governor of California*, 16–17.
110. *Ibid.*, 61.
111. Sinclair, *I, Candidate for Governor . . .*, 174.
112. Holtzman, *The Townsend Movement*, 23.
113. Townsend Plan brochure, 7.
114. Holtzman, *The Townsend Movement*, 28.
115. Nicholas Roosevelt, *The Townsend Plan*, 13, 14.
116. Townsend Plan brochure, 3.
117. Nicholas Roosevelt, *The Townsend Plan*, viii.
118. Lippmann, *Interpretations*, 374–75.
119. Swing, *Forerunners of American Fascism*, 131.
120. Holtzman, *The Townsend Movement*, 13–14.
121. Pegler, *'T Ain't Right*, 216.
122. Creel, *Rebel at Large*, 284.
123. McWilliams, *Southern California Country*, 296.
124. Cleland, *California in Our Time*, 237.
125. West, *The Day of the Locust*, 165.
126. *Ibid.*, intro., xx, xxii.
127. Seldes, *The Movies Come from America*, 10–11.
128. Rosten, *Hollywood*, 5.
129. Charles A. Lindbergh, Sr., *Your Country at War . . .*, 34.
130. Pegler, *'T Ain't Right*, 158.
131. Carrel, *Man the Unknown*, 109–11, 271.
132. *Ibid.*, 220, 22, 153.
133. *Ibid.*, 62, 291–93, 244–46.
134. Cole, *Charles A. Lindbergh . . .*, 37–38.
135. Charles A. Lindbergh, Jr., *The Wartime Journals of . . .*, 3, 110, 78, 166, 75, 3.
136. *New York Times Book Review*, April 11, 1976.
137. Charles A. Lindbergh, Jr., *Reader's Digest*, November, 1939.
138. Charles A. Lindbergh, Jr., *Atlantic Monthly*, March, 1940.
139. Frank Lloyd Wright, *Scribner's Commentator*, October, 1941.
140. Diggins, *Mussolini and Fascism*, 346.
141. Adler, *The Isolationist Impulse*, 249.
142. Mosley, *Lindbergh*, 289.
143. Charles A. Lindbergh, Jr., *Wartime Diaries of . . .*, 485–86.
144. Mosley, *Lindbergh*, 268.
145. Anne Morrow Lindbergh, *Reader's Digest*, January, 1940.
146. Mosley, *Lindbergh*, 329.
147. Anne Morrow Lindbergh, *The Wave of the Future*, 12, 16–17, 18, 19, 37, 39.
148. *New York Herald-Tribune Books*, October 20, 1940.

149. Benét, *Selected Works of...*, 473–74.

150. Mosley, *Lindbergh*, 275.

151. Charles A. Lindbergh, Jr., *The Wartime Diaries of...*, 481.

152. *Ibid.,* 245.

153. Cole, *Charles A. Lindbergh...*, 162.

154. *Ibid.,* 173.

155. Adler, *The Isolationist Impulse*, 301.

156. *Ibid.,* 302.

157. Charles A. Lindbergh, Jr., *The Wartime Diaries of...*, 561.

158. *Ibid.,* 298.

159. New York *Times*, May 3, 1936.

160. New York *World-Telegram*, August 25, 1936.

161. Charles A. Lindbergh, Jr., *The Wartime Diaries of...*, 232.

162. Edmund Wilson, *Travels in Two Democracies*, 94–95.

163. *Time*, September 18, 1939.

164. *Time*, July 31, 1939.

165. New York *Herald-Tribune*, August 19, 1939; *Time*, August 28, 1939.

V.

1. New York *Times*, October 17, 1932.

2. Hallgren, *Seeds of Revolt*, 183.

3. Markey, *This Country of Yours*, 135.

4. *Ibid.,* 200–4.

5. *Fortune*, February, 1933.

6. *Ladies' Home Journal*, September, 1932.

7. Alvin Johnson, *Pioneer's Progress*, 85.

8. Steinbeck, *The Grapes of Wrath*, 64.

9. Lomax, ed., *The Penguin Book of American Folk Songs*, 140.

10. McWilliams, *California*, 157.

11. Duffus, *Queen Calafia's Island*, 166.

12. Parker Brothers' Monopoly brochure.

13. Joanna Colcord, *New Outlook*, December, 1932.

14. *Ibid.*

15. *Ibid.*

16. Borsodi, *Flight from the City*, 154.

17. Joanna Colcord, *New Outlook*, December, 1932.

18. New York *Times*, March 6, 1933.

19. *New York Times Magazine*, May 19, 1953.

20. *New Statesman*, June 29, 1935.

21. St. Clair McKelway and A. J. Liebling, *New Yorker*, June 13, 20, 27, 1936.

22. Calverton, *Where Angels Dared to Tread*, 340–41.

23. New York *Times*, March 6, 1933.

24. Parker, *The Incredible Messiah*, 205–6.

25. *Ibid.,* 241.

26. John Hoshor, *God in a Rolls Royce*, 131.

27. Cronon, *Black Moses,* 225.
28. Edmund Wilson, *The Shores of Light,* 665.
29. William Borsodi, intro. Hall, *A Little Land and a Living,* 31, 21.
30. Hall, *A Little Land and a Living,* 80, 78, 252.
31. *New Republic,* July 10, 1929.
32. Borsodi, *Flight from the City,* 52.
33. *Ibid.,* 16–17.
34. Borsodi, *This Ugly Civilization,* 338.
35. *Ibid.,* 398.
36. *Ibid.,* 217–18.
37. Harry Elmer Barnes, intro. Borsodi, *This Ugly Civilization,* vii.
38. Borsodi, *Flight from the City,* 2.
39. Schmitt, *Back to Nature,* 188.
40. M. G. Kains, *Five Acres . . .,* 2, 4–5.
41. *Down East,* November, 1970.
42. Nearing, *Living the Good Life,* v.
43. Paul Goodman, intro. Nearing, *Living the Good Life,* ix.
44. Waters, *B.E.F.,* 5.
45. *Ibid.,* 118.
46. *Ibid.,* 120.
47. Roger Daniels, *The Bonus March,* 75–76.
48. *Ibid.,* 66.
49. Quoted in Kramer, *Ross and the New Yorker,* 226.
50. Fleta Campbell Springer, *Harper's,* November, 1932.
51. *Ibid.*
52. Schlesinger, *The Crisis of the Old Order,* 261.
53. Roger Daniels, *The Bonus March,* 108.
54. Douglas, *Veterans on the March,* 152.
55. Waters, *B.E.F.,* 215.
56. *Time,* August 8, 1932.
57. *Collier's,* September 10, 1932.
58. Arthur Kallet and F. J. Schlink, *100,000,000 Guinea Pigs,* 38.
59. *Ibid.,* 193.
60. *Introduction to Consumers Research,* 1.
61. Don Wharton, *Scribner's,* November, 1937.
62. Consumers Research mimeographed statement, October 22, 1935.
63. Sorenson, *The Consumer Movement,* 48.
64. *Ibid.,* John D. Black intro., xi.

VI.

1. Cowley, *Exile's Return,* 225.
2. Draper, *Roots of American Communism,* 114–15.
3. Bryant, *Mirrors of Moscow,* 194.
4. Strong, *I Change Worlds,* 207.
5. Anna Louise Strong, *Hearst's International,* July, 1923.
6. *Ibid.,* January, 1924.

7. Strong, *I Change Worlds,* 207, 224.
8. *Ibid.,* 335.
9. *Ibid.,* 376.
10. Hindus, *Broken Earth,* 285–86.
11. Hindus, *Humanity Uprooted,* ix.
12. Davis, ed., *The New Russia,* 194–95.
13. *Ibid.,* 175.
14. Dreiser, *Dreiser Looks at Russia,* 83, 251.
15. Clurman, *The Fervent Years,* 161.
16. Seldes, *Years of the Locust,* 115.
17. George S. Counts, intro. Ilin, *New Russia's Primer,* v–vi.
18. Durant, *The Tragedy of Russia,* 53.
19. US House of Representatives, HUAC, Vols. 9–10 *passim.*
20. Durant, *The Tragedy of Russia,* 39–40.
21. *Nation,* May 1, 1935.
22. Advertisement in *Vanity Fair,* February, 1934.
23. Intourist, *A Pocket Guide . . .,* 3.
24. Lyons, *Assignment in Utopia,* 226.
25. Durant, *The Tragedy of Russia,* 27.
26. J. C. Furnas, *Saturday Evening Post,* November 19, 1935.
27. Kazin, *Starting Out in the Thirties,* 32.
28. Edmund Wilson, *Travels in Two Democracies,* 205.
29. Gibbs, "Big Nemo," in *More in Sorrow,* 205.
30. Edmund Wilson, *The Shores of Light,* 533.
31. Johns, *Time of Our Lives,* 340.
32. "Thirty Years Later," *American Scholar,* Summer, 1966.
33. Lillian Symes, *Harper's,* December, 1933.
34. Johns, *Time of Our Lives,* 322–23.
35. Gold, *Jews Without Money,* 303, 158, 214, 305.
36. Wakeman, *The Hucksters,* 133.
37. Edmund Wilson, *Travels in Two Democracies,* 164.
38. Steinbeck, *In Dubious Battle,* 206.
39. Steinbeck, *The Grapes of Wrath,* 210–11.
40. *Ibid.,* 324.
41. *The Nobel Prize Reader,* 10.
42. Sifton, *The Belt,* 143.
43. Elmer Rice, *We, the People,* 249–50, 252, 246.
44. Clurman, *The Fervent Years,* 12.
45. *Ibid.,* 27.
46. Jay Williams, *Stage Left,* 177.
47. Odets, *Awake and Sing,* 33.
48. Clurman, *The Fervent Years,* 147–48.
49. Ford, *The Time of Laughter,* 132.
50. Wilfred Sheed, *Life,* November 18, 1970.
51. *New York Times Book Review,* February 16, 1975.
52. Malcolm Cowley, *New York Times Book Review,* November 9, 1975.
53. Brown, *Dramatis Personae,* 84.

54. Brooks Atkinson, New York *Times,* March 13, 1938.
55. Lilienthal, *The Journals of . . .,* I, 236.
56. New York *Times,* July 6, 1975.
57. Clurman, intro. *Famous American Plays of the 1930s,* 10.
58. *New Yorker,* April 25, 1931.
59. Leonard Michaels, *New York Times Book Review,* December 9, 1974.
60. Wechsler, *The Age of Suspicion,* 172.
61. O'Hara, *Appointment in Samarra,* 219.

VII.

1. Fadiman, *Party of One,* 98.
2. Donald Davidson, in Couch, ed., *Culture in the South,* 206.
3. *Vanity Fair,* March, 1932.
4. Daniels, *A Southerner Discovers the South,* 7.
5. H. C. Brearley, in Couch, ed., *Culture in the South,* 679.
6. T. Harry Williams, *Huey Long,* 116–17.
7. Long, *My First Days in the White House,* 30–31.
8. *Ibid.,* 132.
9. Cason, *90° in the Shade,* 15.
10. Benton, *Artist in America,* 95–96.
11. Percy, *Lanterns on the Levee,* 20.
12. Glasgow, *A Certain Measure,* 68–69.
13. Thorpe, ed., *A Southern Reader,* 207.
14. Percy, *Lanterns on the Levee,* 116.
15. Carter, *Scottsboro,* 365.
16. *Ibid.,* 142.
17. Reynolds, *Courtroom,* 263.
18. *Ibid.,* 287.
19. Chalmers, *They Shall Be Free,* 222.

VIII.

1. Biddle, *An American Artist's Story,* 268.
2. Bush, *Ben Shahn,* 52.
3. Sherwood, *Roosevelt and Hopkins,* 58–59.
4. Flanagan, *Arena,* 16.
5. Houghton, *Advance from Broadway,* 199.
6. Flanagan, *Arena,* 9.
7. *Ibid.,* 18.
8. Whitman, *Bread and Circuses,* 17.
9. Houghton, *Advance from Broadway,* 137–38.
10. Mangione, *The Dream and the Deal,* 82.
11. Flanagan, *Dynamo,* 7.
12. *Ibid.,* 66–67.
13. Flanagan, *Arena,* 17.
14. Katharine Kellock, *American Scholar,* Autumn, 1940.

15. Sherwood, *Roosevelt and Hopkins,* 54.
16. Flanagan, *Arena,* 12.
17. *Ibid.,* 12.
18. Houseman, *Run-Through,* 183.
19. Mathews, *The Federal Theatre,* 114.
20. Flanagan, *Arena,* 161.
21. *Ibid.,* 161, 165.
22. Whitman, *Bread and Circuses,* 177.
23. Flanagan, *Arena,* 73.
24. US House of Representatives, HUAC, Vol. 4, 532.
25. *Federal Theatre Plays,* xii.
26. US House of Representatives, HUAC, Vol. 4, 2853.
27. Flanagan, *Arena,* 289.
28. *Ibid.,* 148–49.
29. Flanagan, *Dynamo,* 107.
30. Flanagan, *Arena,* 341–42.
31. US House of Representatives, HUAC, Vol. 4, 2857.
32. Gilbert Seldes, *Scribner's,* October, 1936.
33. *Fortune,* May, 1937.
34. Kazin, *Starting Out in the Thirties,* 119.
35. Broun, *Collected Edition of . . .,* 425–26.
36. Houseman, *Run-Through,* 258.
37. Whitman, *Bread and Circuses,* 165.
38. Mangione, *The Dream and the Deal,* 8, 47–48.
39. *Ibid.,* 81.
40. *Ibid.,* 8.
41. *Ibid.,* 97–98.
42. *Ibid.,* 87–88.
43. *Ibid.,* 37.
44. *Ibid.,* 373.
45. *Ibid.,* 14 *fn.*
46. Biddle, *An American Artist's Story,* 267.
47. *Time,* November 9, 1970.
48. Harold Rosenberg, *New Yorker,* June 3, 1973.
49. Biddle, *An American Artist's Story,* 270–71.
50. Bush, *Ben Shahn,* 58 *et seq.*
51. Biddle, *An American Artist's Story,* 279.
52. O'Connor, ed., *Art for the Millions,* 21.
53. *Fortune,* May, 1937.
54. Biddle, *An American Artist's Story,* 33.
55. *Fortune,* May, 1937.
56. Harold Rosenberg, *New Yorker,* June 3, 1973.
57. New York *Times,* March 9, 1930.
58. Nolan, *Marc Connelly,* 89.
59. New York *Times,* March 9, 1930.
60. *New Yorker,* March 8, 1930.
61. Broun, *Collected Edition of . . .,* 248.

62. Brown, *Dramatis Personae,* 88.
63. Taubman, *The Making of the American Theatre . . .,* 213–14.
64. *Ladies' Home Journal,* September, 1933.
65. McKay, *Harlem,* 196.
66. Gitlow, *I Confess,* 480–83.
67. New York *Times,* January 24, 1976.
68. *Ibid.*

IX.

1. Clarence Darrow, *Vanity Fair,* November, 1931.
2. *Ladies' Home Journal,* January, 1933.
3. *Vanity Fair,* August, 1932.
4. Corey Ford, *Vanity Fair,* January, 1931.
5. Boorstin, *The Americans,* 86.
6. DeVoto, *The Hour,* 80.
7. New York *Times,* November 8, 1933.
8. *Ladies' Home Journal,* November, 1933.
9. Elliott Roosevelt, *An Untold Story,* 266.
10. Advertisement, New York *Times,* December 17, 1975.
11. Adams, *The Wines of America,* 3.
12. Wagner, *American Wines and How to Make Them,* 64.
13. Sternsher, *Rexford Guy Tugwell and the New Deal,* 265.
14. Lewis Mumford, intro., Stein, *Toward New Towns for America,* 15.
15. Geddes Smith, in *ibid.,* 44.
16. *Greenbelt Towns,* Suburban Resettlement brochure, no pagination.
17. Arnold, *The New Deal in the Suburbs,* 36–38.
18. Stein, *Toward New Towns for America,* 166–67.
19. Greenbelt *News Review,* November 29, 1962.
20. Warner, *Greenbelt,* 33.
21. New York *Times,* March 15, 1938.
22. Dahir, *Greendale Comes of Age,* 9.
23. Arnold, *The New Deal in the Suburbs,* 182–83.
24. Chase, *Idle Money, Idle Men,* 187.
25. Owen, *The Tennessee Valley Authority,* 25.
26. Pritchett, *The Tennessee Valley Authority,* 17.
27. Sward, *The Legend of Henry Ford,* 148.
28. Jardim, *The First Henry Ford,* 150.
29. Nevins, *Ford,* 308.
30. Haynes, *Southern Horizons,* 227.
31. Franklin D. Roosevelt, *Selected Speeches . . .,* 102.
32. Lilienthal, *The Journals of . . .,* I, 245.
33. Arthur E. Morgan, *Atlantic Monthly,* September, 1937.
34. Duffus, *The Valley and Its People,* 50–52.
35. Lilienthal, *The Journals of . . .,* I, 120.
36. *TVA Today.*

37. James Remington McCarthy, *Sewanee Review,* 1934.
38. Lilienthal, *The Journals of . . .,* I, 236.
39. Owen, *The Tennessee Valley Authority,* opp. 85.
40. Jonathan Daniels, *A Southerner Discovers the South,* 67.
41. Lilienthal, *TVA,* 1, 9.
42. Franklin D. Roosevelt, *Selected Speeches . . .,* 103.
43. Lilienthal, *The Journals of . . .,* I, 94.
44. *Ibid.,* 102.
45. David E. Lilienthal, *New York Times Magazine,* January 7, 1945.
46. Stuart Chase, *Reader's Digest,* October 1944.
47. New York *Times,* January 7, 1945.
48. Tugwell, *The Democratic Roosevelt,* 287.
49. Hill, *The School in the Camps,* 1.
50. James, *The Writings of . . .,* 664, 669.
51. Harry H. Woodring, *Liberty,* January 8, 1934.
52. *New Yorker,* July 18, 1933.
53. Jay Williams, *Stage Left,* 160–71.
54. Couch, ed., *These Are Our Lives,* 412–13.
55. Hill, *The School in the Camps,* 66.
56. *Phi Beta Kappan,* May, 1937.
57. Cremin, *The Transformation of the School,* 320.
58. Hill, *The School in the Camps,* 62.
59. Cremin, *The Transformation of the School,* 321.
60. *Phi Beta Kappan,* May, 1937.
61. Lindley, *A New Deal for Youth,* 12.
62. Walter N. Parmenter, *Farm Quarterly,* Spring, 1967.
63. W. L. White, *Scribner's,* January, 1939.
64. Snyder, *Pare Lorentz and the Documentary Film,* 54.
65. *Ibid.,* 3.
66. New York *Times,* April 4, 1976.
67. New York *Times,* May 5, 1976.
68. Hutchinson, *The Imperfect Union,* 26.
69. Jacobs, *Rise of the American Film,* 149.
70. Howard, *The Labor Spy,* 96.
71. *Oxford English Dictionary.*
72. *Fortune,* October, 1938.
73. *Encyclopedia of Social Sciences* (1st ed.), VII.
74. Steinbeck, *In Dubious Battle,* 159.
75. Lippmann, *Drift and Mastery,* 55.
76. *Ibid.,* 60–61.
77. *Fortune,* January, 1935.
78. Hutchinson, *The Imperfect Union,* 142.
79. Pelling, *American Labor,* 161.
80. Beard, *America in Midpassage,* 518.
81. *Ibid.,* 538.
82. John T. Flynn, *New Republic,* April 11, 1939.
83. Hubbard, *Abe Martin's Almanack,* no pagination.

X.

1. William Harlan Hale, *Scribner's,* October, 1931.
2. New York *Times,* October 18, 1931.
3. Hubert Herring, *Harper's,* September, 1940.
4. Warren, *A New Design for Women's Education,* 276.
5. *Ibid.,* 17.
6. *Ibid.,* 20–21.
7. Cremin, *The Transformation of the School,* 312–13.
8. Warren, *A New Design for Women's Education,* 35.
9. *American Association of University Professors Bulletin,* May, 1933.
10. Duberman, *Black Mountain,* 28.
11. *Ibid.,* 29.
12. John A. Rice, *I Came Out of the Eighteenth Century,* 328.
13. Louis Adamic, *Harper's,* April, 1936.
14. John A. Rice, *I Came Out of the Eighteenth Century,* 32.
15. De Voto, *Harper's,* April, 1936.
16. Duberman, *Black Mountain,* 85.
17. *Ibid.,* 83.
18. John A. Rice, *I Came Out of the Eighteenth Century,* 330.
19. *Ibid.,* 331.
20. Kendrick, *Prime Time,* 116.
21. Harold Laski, *Harper's,* July, 1931.
22. Flanagan and Clifford, *Can You Hear Their Voices?,* 25.
23. Flanagan, *Dynamo,* 97.
24. Oliver La Farge, *Scribner's,* July, 1925.
25. Wechsler, *Revolt on the Campus,* 28–29.
26. Sevareid, *Not So Wild a Dream,* 62.
27. Wechsler, *The Age of Suspicion,* 36.
28. New York *Times,* December 30, 1932.
29. Sevareid, *Not So Wild a Dream,* 60.
30. Wechsler, *Revolt on the Campus,* 1934.
31. Kazin, *Starting Out in the Thirties,* 138.
32. New York *Times,* March 27, 1936.
33. Lash, *Eleanor and Franklin,* 546.
34. *Ibid.,* 549.
35. Wechsler, *The Age of Suspicion,* 71.
36. Lash, *Eleanor and Franklin,* 600, 611.
37. *Ibid.,* 604.
38. New York *Times,* December 29, 1973.

XI.

1. Trilling, *The Middle of the Journey,* 107.
2. Wilfred Sheed, *New York Times Book Review,* February 13, 1972.
3. Richard B. Morris, ed., *Encyclopedia of American History,* 388.

4. Matthews, *Half of Spain Died,* 25.
5. Westbrook Pegler, *New Republic,* May 11, 1938.
6. New York *Times,* June 6, 1937.
7. Rosenstone, *Crusade of the Left,* 214.
8. Knightley, *The First Casualty,* 215.
9. *Time,* October 5, 1936.
10. Fletcher Pratt, *American Mercury,* August, 1937.
11. Corwin, *Thirteen by Corwin,* 78.
12. Hellman, *An Unfinished Woman,* 55.
13. Hugh Thomas, *The Spanish Civil War,* 305.
14. Kazin, *Starting Out in the Thirties,* 108.
15. Clurman, *The Fervent Years,* 202–3.
16. Halper, *Good-bye, Union Square,* 212.
17. Baker, *Ernest Hemingway,* 400.
18. Clurman, *All People Are Famous,* 158.
19. Kazin, *Starting Out in the Thirties,* 187.
20. Sheean, *Not Peace but a Sword,* 103.
21. Baker, *Ernest Hemingway,* 425.
22. Behrman, *No Time for Comedy,* 204.
23. Paul, *The Life and Death of a Spanish Town,* 380–81.
24. *Ibid.,* 97.
25. *Writers Take Sides,* 74.
26. Muste, *Say That We Saw Spain Die,* 50.
27. Brown, *Dramatis Personae,* 271.
28. *AIM Report,* October, 1975.
29. Eby, *Between the Bullet and the Lie,* 146.
30. Rosenstone, *Crusade of the Left,* 88.
31. Matthews, *Half of Spain Died,* 82–83.
32. Fleischman, *Norman Thomas,* 175–76.
33. Rosenstone, *Crusade on the Left,* 23.
34. Mangione, *The Dream and the Deal,* 132.
35. Diggins, *Mussolini and Fascism,* 312 n.
36. Mangione, *The Dream and the Deal,* 176.
37. Bowers, *My Mission to Spain,* 418.
38. Hugh Thomas, *The Spanish Civil War,* 434.
39. *Ibid.,* 556–57.
40. Muste, *Say That We Saw Spain Die,* 128.
41. Hugh Thomas, *The Spanish Civil War,* 558.
42. Spivak, *America Faces . . .,* 214–15.
43. Howe, *World of Our Fathers,* 409.
44. Lilienthal, *The Journals of . . .,* I, 147.
45. Croy, *Country Cured,* 101.
46. Ferber, *A Peculiar Treasure,* 39–40, 55–56.
47. Jonathan Daniels, *A Southerner Discovers the South,* 258–59.
48. Cash, *The Mind of the South,* 334.
49. Thomas Wolfe, *Look Homeward, Angel,* 96.
50. Swanberg, *Dreiser,* 267, 412.

51. Sinclair Lewis, *Dodsworth,* 426.
52. Kramer, *Ross and the New Yorker,* 241.
53. New York *Times,* March 5, 1972.
54. Howe, *World of Our Fathers,* 600.
55. *Fortune,* February, 1936.
56. Glazer and Moynihan, *Beyond the Melting Pot* (2d ed., 1970), lx, xxxvi.

XII.

1. West, *Day of the Locust,* 134–37.
2. Parker, *The Incredible Messiah,* 52.
3. New York *Times,* February 12, 1976.
4. Henry J. Anslinger, *American* magazine, July, 1937.
5. US House of Representatives, Committee on Ways and Means, 1937; 33.
6. *Ibid.,* 24.
7. Brecher *et al., Licit and Illicit Drugs,* 458.
8. Nahas, *Marihuana—Deceptive Weed,* 39.
9. Goodwin, *Is Alcoholism Hereditary?,* 112.
10. Paul Popenoe, *Forum,* December, 1937.
11. Henry Pratt Fairchild, *Harper's,* May, 1938.
12. P. K. Whelpton, *Journal of Heredity,* September, 1939.
13. Lorimer *et al., Foundations of American Population Policy,* 25.
14. New York *Times,* January 21, 1939.
15. Kansas City *Star,* November 22, 1941.
16. *Business Week,* August 2, 1941.
17. Harlan T. Stetson, *Scientific Monthly,* July, 1936.
18. Lynes, *The Taste-Makers,* 250.
19. Henry F. Pringle, *Ladies' Home Journal,* June, 1939.
20. Stuart Chase, *Idle Money, Idle Men,* 179, 184–85.
21. *Time,* August 21, 1939.
22. Freeman Lewis, *Paper-Bound Books in America,* 13.
23. Frank L. Schick, *Library Trends,* July, 1938.
24. Butcher, *Many Lives—One Love,* 446.

XIII.

1. Adler, *The Isolationist Impulse,* 283.
2. Sherwood, *Idiot's Delight,* 189.
3. Brown, *The Ordeal of a Playwright,* 47.
4. *Ibid.,* 48.
5. *Ibid.,* 97.
6. Atkinson, *Broadway,* 224.
7. Brown, *The Ordeal of a Playwright,* 74.
8. MacLeish, *New Republic,* June 10, 1940.
9. Ernest Hemingway, *Esquire,* September, 1935.

10. Ernest Hemingway, *Ken,* August 11, 1938.
11. Eastman, *Love and Revolution,* 24.
12. *Ladies' Home Journal,* July, 1938.
13. *Ladies' Home Journal,* December, 1939.
14. Miller, *The White Cliffs,* 64, 70.
15. Sevareid, *Not So Wild a Dream,* 82–83.
16. Charles A. Lindbergh, Jr., *The Wartime Journals of . . .,* 561.

NONPERIODICAL SOURCES QUOTED

This list identifies where necessary books and pamphlets directly quoted in the foregoing text and distinguished by a number. A proper bibliography would be impossibly bulky. It must not be assumed that because a certain pertinent work is not mentioned here, it has not been consulted. The edition cited is always the one to which pages are referred.

ADAMS, LEON D. *The Wines of America.* Boston: Houghton Mifflin Company, 1973.

ADLER, SELIG. *The Isolationist Impulse: Its Twentieth Century Reactions.* New York: Abelard-Schuman, [c1957].

AMERICAN INSTITUTE OF PUBLIC OPINION. *Questions Often Asked About Published Polls.* Princeton, n.d.

ARKRIGHT, FRANK. *The ABC of Technocracy.* Based on Authorized Material. New York: Harper & Brothers, 1933.

ARNOLD, JOSEPH L. *The New Deal in the Suburbs: A History of the Greenbelt Town Program.* 1935–1954. N.P., Ohio State University Press, [c1971].

ATKINSON, BROOKS. *Broadway.* New York: Macmillan, [c1970].

BAKER, CARLOS. *Ernest Hemingway: A Life Story.* New York: Bantam Books, [c1970].

BARNOUW, ERIC. *The Golden Web: A History of Broadcasting in the United States,* Volume II–1933 to 1953. New York: Oxford University Press, 1968.

———. *A Tower in Babel: A History of Broadcasting in the United States,* Volume I–to 1933. New York: Oxford University Press, 1966.

BEARD, CHARLES A., ED. *America Faces the Future.* Boston: Houghton Mifflin Company, [c1932].

——, AND MARY. *America in Midpassage.* New York: The Macmillan Company, 1939.

——. *Toward Civilization.* New York: Longmans, Green and Co., [c1930].

BEHRMAN, S. N. *No Time for Comedy.* New York: Random House, [c1939].

BENÉT, STEPHEN VINCENT. *Selected Works of....* New York: Farrar & Rinehart, 1942.

BENTON, THOMAS HART. *An Artist in America,* new and revised edition. New York: University of Kansas Press-Twayne Publishers, 1951.

BERNAYS, EDWARD L. *Biography of an Idea: Memoirs of a Public Relations Counsel....* New York: Simon and Schuster, [c1965].

The Best of Life. New York: Time-Life Books, [c1973].

BIDDLE, GEORGE. *An American Artist's Story.* Boston: Little Brown and Company, 1939.

BIRD, CAROLINE. *The Invisible Scar.* New York: David McKay Company, Inc., [c1966].

BLAKE, PETER. *Frank Lloyd Wright: Architecture and Space.* [Baltimore]: Penguin Books, [c1960].

BOORSTIN, DANIEL J. *The Americans: The Democratic Experience.* New York: Random House, [c1973].

BORSODI, RALPH. *Flight from the City: The Story of a New Way to Family Security.* New York: Harper & Brothers, 1933.

——. *This Ugly Civilization.* New York: Harper & Brothers, 1933.

BOWERS, CLAUDE G. *My Mission to Spain: Watching the Rehearsal for World War II.* New York: Simon and Schuster, 1954.

BRECHER, EDWARD M., AND THE EDITORS OF CONSUMER REPORTS. *Licit and Illicit Drugs: The Consumers Union Report on Narcotics....* Mount Vernon, New York: Consumers Union, [c1972].

BROUN, HEYWOOD. *Collected Edition of....* Compiled by Heywood Hale Broun. New York: Harcourt Brace & Company, [c1941].

——. *The Sun Field.* New York: G. P. Putnam's Sons, 1923.

BROWN, JOHN MASON. *Dramatis Personae: A Retrospective Show.* New York: The Viking Press, [c1963].

——. *The Ordeal of a Playwright: Robert E. Sherwood and the Challenge of War.* New York: Harper & Row, [c1970].

BRYANT, LOUISE. *Mirrors of Moscow.* New York: Thomas Seltzer, 1923.

BUSH, MARTIN H. *Ben Shahn: The Passion of Sacco and Vanzetti.* With an Essay and Commentary by Ben Shahn. Syracuse: Syracuse University, 1968.

BUTCHER, FANNY. *Many Lives—One Love.* New York: Harper & Row, [c1972].

CALDWELL, ERSKINE. *God's Little Acre.* The Uniform Edition of the Works of. . . . New York: Duell, Sloan and Pearce, [1949].

CALVERTON, V. F. *Where Angels Dared to Tread.* Indianapolis: The Bobbs-Merrill Company, [c1941].

CANTRILL, HADLEY. et al. *The Invasion from Mars: A Study in the Psychopathology of Panic.* With the complete script of the famous Orson Welles broadcast. Princeton: Princeton University Press, 1940.

CARREL, ALEXIS. *Man the Unknown.* New York: Harper & Brothers, 1935.

CARTER, DAN T. *Scottsboro: A Tragedy of the American South.* Baton Rouge: Louisiana State University Press, [c1969].

CASH, W. J. *The Mind of the South.* New York: Doubleday Anchor Books, 1954.

CASON, CLARENCE. *90° in the Shade.* Chapel Hill: The University of North Carolina Press, [c1935].

CHALMERS, ALLAN K. *They Shall Be Free.* Garden City: Doubleday & Company, 1951.

CHASE, STUART. *Idle Money, Idle Men.* New York: Harcourt Brace & Company, [1940].

———. *Technocracy: An Interpretation.* No. 19 The John Day Pamphlets. New York: The John Day Company, [c1933].

CHORLEY, KENNETH. *Williamsburg in Virginia: Proud Citadel of Colonial Culture.* New York: The Newcomen Society in North America, 1953.

CLELAND, ROBERT GLASS. *California in Our Time.* New York: Alfred A. Knopf, 1947.

CLURMAN, HAROLD. *All People Are Famous.* New York: Alfred A. Knopf, [c1976].

———. *Famous American Plays of the 1930s.* The Laurel Drama Series. [New York]: Dell Publishing Co., [c1959].

———. *The Fervent Years: The Story of the Group Theatre and the Thirties.* New York: Alfred A. Knopf, 1945.

COLE, WAYNE S. *Charles A. Lindbergh and the Battle Against American Intervention in World War II.* New York: Harcourt Brace Jovanovich, [c1974].

COLONIAL WILLIAMSBURG. *The First Twenty-Five Years: A Report by the President as of December 31, 1951.* N.P., n.d.

CORWIN, NORMAN. *Thirteen by Corwin: Radio Dramas by.* . . . With a Preface by Carl Van Doren. N.P.: Henry Holt and Company, [c1942].

COUCH, W. T., ED., FEDERAL WRITERS PROJECT. *These Are Our Lives: As Told by the People and Written by Members of the.* . . . Works Progress Administration in North Carolina, Tennessee and Georgia. Chapel Hill: The University of North Carolina Press, 1939.

COUGHLIN, REV. CHARLES E. *Eight Lectures on Labor, Capital and Justice.* As broadcast by . . . over a National Network. Royal Oak, Michigan: The Radio League of the Little Flower, April, 1924.

COWLEY, MALCOLM. *Exile's Return: A Narrative of Ideas.* New York: W. W. Norton & Company, [c1934].

CRAVEN, THOMAS. *Modern Art: The Men, the Movements, the Meaning.* New York: Simon and Schuster, 1934.

CREEL, GEORGE. *Rebel at Large: Recollections of Fifty Crowded Years.* New York: G.P. Putnam's Sons, [c1947].

CREMIN, LAWRENCE A. *The Transformation of the School: Progressivism in American Education 1876-1957.* New York: Vintage Books, [c1961].

CRONON, E. DAVID. *Black Moses: The Story of Marcus Garvey.* . . . Foreword by John Hope Franklin. Madison: The University of Wisconsin Press, [c1955].

CROY, HOMER. *Country Cured.* New York: Harper & Brothers, [c1943].

CUMMINGS, E. E. *A Miscellany.* Edited with an introduction and notes by George J. Firmage. New York: The Argophile Press, 1958.

DAHIR, JAMES. *Greendale Comes of Age.* Milwaukee Community Development Center, 1958.

DALLAS MUSEUM OF FINE ARTS, *1930's Expositions.* . . . State Fair of Texas October 7–November 5, 1972. N.P., n.d.

DANIELS, JONATHAN. *A Southerner Discovers the South.* New York: The Macmillan Company, 1938.

DANIELS, ROGER. *The Bonus March: An Episode of the Great Depression.* Westport, Connecticut: Greenwood Publishing Corporation, [c1971].

DAVIS, JEROME, ED. *The New Russia: Between the First and Second Five Year Plans.* . . . With an Introduction by Edward M. House. Essay Index Reprint Series. Freeport, New York: Books for Libraries Press, n.d.

DELAFIELD, E. M., pseud. [Edmée Elizabeth Monica de la Pasture]. *The Provincial Lady in America.* London: Macmillan and Co., 1934.

DE VOTO, BERNARD. *The Hour.* Boston: Houghton Mifflin Company, [c1948].

DIGGINS, JOHN P. *Mussolini and Fascism: The View from America.* Princeton: Princeton University Press, [c1972].

DOUGLAS, JACK. *Veterans on the March.* Foreword by John Dos Passos. New York: Workers Library Publishers, 1934.

DRAPER, THEODORE. *The Roots of American Communism.* New York: Viking Press, 1957.

DREISER, THEODORE. *Dreiser Looks at Russia.* New York: Horace Liveright, 1928.

DUBERMAN, MARTIN. *Black Mountain: An Exploration in Community.* New York: E. P. Dutton & Company, 1972.

DUFFUS, R. L. *Queen Calafia's Island.* New York: W. W. Norton & Company, [c1965].

——. *The Valley and Its People: A Portrait of TVA.* New York: Alfred A. Knopf, 1944.

DURANT, WILL. *The Tragedy of Russia: Impressions from a Brief Visit.* New York: Simon and Schuster, 1933.

EASTMAN, MAX. *Love and Revolution: My Journey Through an Epoch.* New York: Random House, [c1964].

EBY, CECIL. *Between the Bullet and the Lie: American Volunteers in the Spanish Civil War.* New York: Holt, Rinehart and Winston, [c1969].

EDMONDSON, MADELEINE, AND DAVID ROUNDS. *The Soaps: Daytime Serials of Radio and TV.* New York: Stein and Day, [c1973].

ELSNER, HENRY, JR. *The Technocrats: Prophets of Automation.* N.P.: Syracuse University Press, [c1967].

FADIMAN, CLIFTON. *Party of One: The Selected Writings of. . . .* New York: The World Publishing Company, [c1955].

FARR, FINIS. *Fair Enough: The Life of Westbrook Pegler.* New Rochelle, New York: Arlington House, [c1975].

——, *Frank Lloyd Wright.* New York: Charles Scribner's Sons, 1957.

FARRELL, JAMES T. *A World I Never Made.* New York: World Publishing Company, [c1936].

Federal Theatre Plays. New York: Random House, [c1938].

FERBER, EDNA. *A Peculiar Treasure.* New York: Lancer Books, [1960].

FITZGERALD, F. SCOTT. *Three Novels of . . . The Great Gatsby . . . Tender Is the Night . . . The Last Tycoon. . . .* New York: Charles Scribner's Sons, [c1953].

FLANAGAN, HALLIE. *Arena.* New York: Duell, Sloan and Pearce, [c1940].

——, *Dynamo.* New York: Duell, Sloan and Pearce, [c1943].

——, AND MARGARET ELLEN CLIFFORD. *Can You Hear Their Voices? . . .* Based on a story by Whittaker Chambers published in the *New Masses.* Poughkeepsie, New York: Published by the Experimental Theatre of Vassar College, [c1931].

FLEISCHMAN, HARRY. *Norman Thomas: A Biography.* New York: W. W. Norton & Company, [c1964].

FORD, COREY. *The Time of Laughter.* With a Foreword by Frank Sullivan. Boston: Little, Brown and Company, [c1967].

FULTON, A. R. *Motion Pictures ... From Silent Films to the Age of Television.* Norman: University of Oklahoma Press, [c1960].

GALLICO, PAUL. *Farewell to Sport.* New York: Alfred A. Knopf, 1938.

GALLUP, GEORGE. *The Sophisticated Poll Watcher's Guide.* N.P.: Princeton Opinion Press, [c1972].

———, AND SAUL FORBES RAE. *The Pulse of Democracy: The Public-Opinion Poll. . . .* New York: Simon and Schuster, 1940.

GARWOOD, DARRELL. *Artist in Iowa: A Life of Grant Wood.* New York: W. W. Norton Company, [c1944].

GIBBS, WOLCOTT. *More in Sorrow.* New York: Henry Holt and Company, [c1958].

GITLOW, BENJAMIN. *I Confess: The Truth About American Communism.* With an introduction by Max Eastman. New York: E. P. Dutton & Company, [c1939].

GLASGOW, ELLEN. *A Certain Measure: An Interpretation of Prose Fiction.* New York: Harcourt Brace & Company, [c1943].

GLAZER, NATHAN, AND DANIEL PATRICK MOYNIHAN. *Beyond the Melting Pot: The Negroes, Puerto Ricans, Jews, Italians and Irish of New York City,* 2d edition. Cambridge, Massachusetts: The M.I.T. Press, [c1970].

GOLD, MICHAEL. *Jews Without Money.* New York: Horace Liveright, [c1930].

GOODWIN, DONALD. *Is Alcoholism Hereditary?* New York: Oxford University Press, 1976.

Greenbelt Towns. [Suburban Resettlement brochure] N.P., n.d.

GROPIUS, WALTER. *Apollo in the Democracy: The Cultural Obligation of the Architect.* New York: McGraw-Hill Book Company, [c1968].

GROSS, BEN. *I Looked and I Listened: Informal Recollections of Radio and TV.* New York: Random House, [c1954].

HALL, BOLTON. *A Little Land and a Living.* New York: The Arcadia Press, 1908.

HALLGREN, MAURITZ A. *Seeds of Revolt: A Study of American Life ... During the Depression.* New York: Alfred A. Knopf, 1933.

HALPER, ALBERT. *Good-bye, Union Square: A Writer's Memoir of the Thirties.* Chicago: Quadrangle Books, 1970.

HARMON, JIM. *The Great Radio Heroes.* New York: Doubleday & Company, 1967.

HARTMAN, WILLIAM, MARYLIN FITHIAN, AND DONALD JOHNSON. *Nudist Society ... Nudism in America.* New York: Crown Publishers, [c1970].

HAYNES, WILLIAMS. *Southern Horizons.* New York: D. Van Nostrand Company, 1946.

HECHT, BEN. *A Child of the Century.* New York: Simon and Schuster, [c1954].

HIGBY, MARY JANE. *Tune in Tomorrow ...* New York: Cowles, 1968.

HILL, FRANK ERNEST. *The School in the Camps: The Educational Program of the Civilian Conservation Corps.* New York: American Association for Adult Education, 1935.

HINDUS, MAURICE. *Broken Earth.* With an Introduction by Glenn Frank. London: T. Fisher Unwin, 1926.

———. *Humanity Uprooted.* New York: Jonathan Cape and Harrison Smith, [c1929].

HITCHCOCK, HENRY-RUSSELL, JR., AND PHILIP JOHNSON. *The International Style: Architecture Since 1922.* New York: W. W. Norton & Company, [c1932].

HOFSTADTER, RICHARD M. *Anti-Intellectualism in American Life.* New York: Alfred A. Knopf, 1969.

HOLTZMAN, ABRAHAM. *The Townsend Movement.* New York: Bookman Associates, [c1963].

HOSHOR, JOHN. *God in a Rolls-Royce: The Rise of Father Divine, Madman, Menace or Messiah.* New York: Hullman-Curl, Inc., 1936.

HOUGHTON, NORRIS. *Advance from Broadway: 19,000 Miles of American Theatre.* New York: Harcourt Brace & Company, [c1941].

HOUSEMAN, JOHN. *Run-Through: A Memoir by ...* New York: Simon and Schuster, [c1972].

HOWARD, SIDNEY. *The Labor Spy.* With the collaboration of Robert Dunn. New York: Republic Publishing Company, 1924.

[HUBBARD, FRANK MCKINNEY] *Abe Martin's Almanack.* [Indianapolis], n.d.

HUTCHINSON, JOHN. *The Imperfect Union: A History of Corruption in American Trade Unions.* New York: E. P. Dutton & Company, 1972.

ILIN, M. pseud. [Ilya Yaklovlevich Marshak]. *New Russia's Primer: the story of the five-year plan.* Translated from the Russian by George S. Counts and Nucia P. Lodge. Boston: Houghton Mifflin Company, 1931.

INTOURIST, *A Pocket Guide to the Soviet Union.* Issued by ... (State Tourist Company, USSR) Moscow. Moscow and Leningrad: Vneshtorgisdat, 1932.

JACOBS, LEWIS. *The Rise of the American Film: A Critical History.* New York: Harcourt Brace & Company, [c1939].

JAMES, WILLIAM. *The Writings of...: A Comprehensive Edition.* Edited, with an introduction by John J. McDermott. New York: Random House, [c1967].

JARDIM, ANNE. *The First Henry Ford: A Study in Personality and Business Leadership.* Cambridge, Massachusetts: The M.I.T. Press, [c1970].

JOHNS, ORRICK. *Time Of Our Lives: The Story of My Father and Myself.* New York: Stackpole Sons, [1937].

JOHNSON, ALVIN. *Pioneer's Progress: An Autobiography by...* New York: The Viking Press, 1952.

JOSEPHSON, MATTHEW. *The Money Lords: The Great Finance Capitalists 1925-1950.* New York: Weybright and Talley, [c1972].

KAINS, M.G. *Five Acres and Independence: A Practical Guide to the Selection and Management of the Small Farm.* New York: Greenberg, [1935].

KALLET, ARTHUR, AND F.J. SCHLINK. *100,000,000 Guinea Pigs: Dangers in Everyday Foods, Drugs and Cosmetics.* New York: Grosset & Dunlap, [c1933].

KAPLAN, JUSTIN. *Lincoln Steffens: A Biography.* New York: Simon and Schuster, [c1974].

KAUFMANN, EDGAR, AND BEN RAEBURN, EDS. *Frank Lloyd Wright: Writings and Buildings.* New York: The World Publishing Company, [c1960].

KAZIN, ALFRED. *Starting Out in the Thirties.* Boston: Little, Brown and Company, [c1962].

KENDRICK, ALEXANDER. *Prime Time: The Life of Edward R. Murrow.* Boston: Little, Brown & Co., [c1969].

KENT, FRANK R. *Without Gloves: A Realistic Running Comment on the Great Federal Experiments, Their Operations and Operators.* New York: William Morrow & Company, 1934.

KLEIN, ALEXANDER, ED. *Grand Deception: The World's Most Spectacular and Successful Hoaxes, Impostures, Ruses and Frauds.* New York: J. B. Lippincott Company, [c1955].

KNIGHTLEY, PHILLIP. *The First Casualty: From the Crimea to Vietnam: The War Correspondent as Hero, Propagandist, and Myth Maker.* New York: Harcourt Brace Jovanovich, [c1975].

KRAMER, DALE. *Heywood Broun: A Biographical Portrait.* New York: Current Books, Inc., 1949.

———. *Ross and the New Yorker.* New York: Doubleday & Company, 1951.

LAING, GRAHAM A. *Towards Technocracy.* Introduction by Charles A. Beard. Los Angeles: The Angelus Press, 1933.

LANDRY, ROBERT J. *This Fascinating Radio Business.* Indianapolis: The Bobbs-Merrill Company, [c1946].

——. *Who, What, Why Is Radio?* New York: George W. Stewart, [c1942].

LASH, JOSEPH P. *Eleanor and Franklin.* New York: W. W. Norton & Company, [c1971].

LEWIS, FREEMAN. *Paper-Bound Books in America.* New York: The New York Public Library, 1952.

LEWIS, SINCLAIR. *Dodsworth.* New York: Pocket Books, [c1941].

——. *It Can't Happen Here: A Novel.* Garden City: Doubleday, Doran & Company, 1935.

LILIENTHAL, DAVID E. *The Journals of...,* Vol. I. *The TVA Years 1939-1945...* Introduction by Henry Steele Commager. New York: Harper & Row, [c1964].

——. *TVA: Democracy on the March.* New York: Harper & Brothers, [c1944].

LINDBERGH, ANNE MORROW. *The Wave of the Future: A Confession of Faith.* New York: Harcourt, Brace & Company, 1940.

LINDBERGH, CHARLES A. *The Wartime Journals of...* New York: Harcourt Brace Jovanovich, [c1970].

LINDBERGH, CHARLES A., SR. *Your Country at War and What Happens to You After a War.* Philadelphia: Dorrance & Company, [1934].

LINDLEY, BETTY AND ERNEST K. *A New Deal for Youth: The Story of the National Youth Administration.* New York: The Viking Press, 1938.

LIPMAN, JEAN. *Calder's Universe.* A Studio Book. New York: The Viking Press, in Cooperation with the Whitney Museum of American Art, [c1976].

LIPPMANN, WALTER. *Drift and Mastery: An Attempt to Diagnose the Current Unrest.* With an Introduction and Notes by William E. Leuchtenburg. Englewood Cliffs: Prentice-Hall, [c1961].

——. *Interpretations, 1933-1935.* New York: The Macmillan Company, 1936.

——. *A Preface to Politics.* New York: Mitchell Kennerley, 1913.

LOEB, HAROLD. *Life in a Technocracy: What It Might Be Like.* New York: The Viking Press, 1933.

LOMAX, ALAN, ED. *The Penguin Book of American Folk Songs.* Baltimore: Penguin Books, [c1964].

LONG, HUEY PIERCE. *My First Days in the White House.* Harrisburg: The Telegraph Press, 1935.

LORIMER, FRANK, ELLEN WINSTON, AND LOUISE K. KISER. *Foundations of American Population Policy.* New York: Harper & Brothers, 1940.

LYNES, RUSSELL. *The Taste-Makers.* [New York]: Harper & Brothers, [c1954].

LYONS, EUGENE. *Assignment in Utopia.* New York: Harcourt Brace & Company, [c1937].

MACGOWAN, KENNETH. *Behind the Screen: The History and Techniques of the Motion Picture.* New York: Delacorte Press, [c1965].

MACLEISH, ARCHIBALD. *The Fall of the City: A Verse Play for Radio.* New York: Farrar & Rinehart, [c1937].

MANGIONE, JERRE. *The Dream and the Deal: The Federal Writers' Project, 1935-1943.* Boston: Little, Brown and Company, [c1972].

MARCUS, SHELDON. *Father Coughlin: The Tumultuous Life of the Priest of the Little Flower.* Boston: Little, Brown and Company, [c1973].

MARKEY, MORRIS. *This Country of Yours.* Boston: Little, Brown and Company, 1932.

MARTIN, PRESTONIA MANN. *Prohibiting Poverty: Suggestions for a Method of Obtaining Economic Security.* New York: Farrar & Rinehart, [c1932].

MATHEWS, JANE DE HART. *The Federal Theatre, 1935-1939: Plays, Relief and Politics.* Princeton: Princeton University Press, 1967.

MATTHEWS, HERBERT L. *Half of Spain Died: A Reappraisal of the Spanish Civil War.* New York: Charles Scribner's Sons, [c1973].

MAY, HENRY F. *The End of American Innocence: A Study of the First Years of Our Own Time 1912-1917.* Chicago: Quadrangle Books, [c1959].

MCKAY, CLAUDE. *Harlem: Negro Metropolis.* New York: E. P. Dutton & Company, [c1940].

MCWILLIAMS, CAREY. *California: The Great Exception.* New York: Current Books, Inc., 1949.

———. *Southern California Country....* Edited by Erskine Caldwell. New York: Duell, Sloan & Pearce, [c1946].

MEAD, MARGARET. *Blackberry Winter.* New York: William Morrow & Company, 1972.

MILLAY, EDNA ST. VINCENT. *Three Plays.* New York: Harper & Brothers, 1926.

MILLER, ALICE DUER. *The White Cliffs.* New York: Coward-McCann, [c1940].

MOSLEY, LEONARD. *Lindbergh: A Biography.* New York: Doubleday & Company, 1976.

MUMFORD, LEWIS. *American Taste.* San Francisco: The Westfield Press, 1929.

MUSTE, JOHN M., ED. *Say That We Saw Spain Die: Literary Consequences of the Spanish Civil War.* Seattle: University of Washington Press, [c1966].

NAHAS, GABRIEL G. *Marihuana—Deceptive Weed.* Foreword by W. D. M. Paton, CBE, FRS, DM, University of Oxford. New York: Raven Press, [c1973].

NEARING, HELEN, AND SCOTT NEARING. *Living the Good Life . . .* Introduction by Paul Goodman. New York: Schocken Books, [c1970].

NEVINS, ALLAN. *Ford: The Times, the Man, the Company. . . .* With the Collaboration of Frank Ernest Hill. New York: Charles Scribner's Sons, 1954.

[NEW SCHOOL FOR SOCIAL RESEARCH]. *The New School Murals of Thomas Hart Benton.* N.P., n.d.

NIELSEN, A. C. *Greater Prosperity Through Marketing Research: The First Forty Years of A.C. Nielsen Company.* New York: Newcomen Society in North America, 1964.

NORMAN, CHARLES. *Ezra Pound.* New York: The Macmillan Company, 1960.

OBOLER, ARCH. *Fourteen Radio Plays.* New York: Random House, [c1940].

O'CONNOR, FRANCIS V., ED. *Art for the Millions.* Boston: New York Graphic Society, [c1973].

ODETS, CLIFFORD. *Awake and Sing.* In *Famous American Plays,* Harold Clurman, ed. The Laurel Drama Series. [New York]: Dell Publishing Company, [c1959].

O'HARA, JOHN. *Appointment in Samarra.* With a new foreword by the author. New York: The Modern Library, [1963].

OWEN, MARGUERITE. *The Tennessee Valley Authority.* New York: Praeger Publishers, [c1973].

OWINGS, NATHANIEL ALEXANDER. *The Spaces in Between: An Architect's Journey.* Boston: Houghton Mifflin Company, 1973.

PARKER, ROBERT ALLERTON. *The Incredible Messiah: The Deification of Father Divine.* Boston: Little, Brown and Company, 1937.

PARRAN, THOMAS. *Shadows on the Land: Syphilis.* New York: Reynal & Hitchcock, [c1937].

PAUL, ELLIOT. *The Life and Death of a Spanish Town.* New York: Random House, [c1937].

PEGLER, WESTBROOK. *The Dissenting Opinions of Mister Westbrook Pegler.* New York: Charles Scribner's Sons, 1938.

———. *George Spelvin, American.* New York: Charles Scribner's Sons, 1942.

———. *'T Ain't Right.* New York: Doubleday, Doran & Company, 1936.

PELLING, HENRY. *American Labor.* Chicago: University of Chicago Press, [c1960].

PERCY, WILLIAM ALEXANDER. *Lanterns on the Levee: Recollections of a Planter's Son.* New York: Alfred A. Knopf, 1941.

PILAT, OLIVER. *Pegler: Angry Man of the Press.* Boston: Beacon Press, [c1963].

PRITCHETT, E. HERMAN. *The Tennessee Valley Authority.* Chapel Hill: University of North Carolina Press, 1943.

RAYMOND, ALLEN. *What Is Technocracy?* New York: Whittlesey House, 1933.

REMBAR, CHARLES. *The End of Obscenity: The Trials of Lady Chatterley, Tropic of Cancer, and Fanny Hill.* Introduction by Norman Mailer. New York: Simon and Schuster, [c1968].

REYNOLDS, QUENTIN. *Courtroom: The Story of Samuel S. Leibowitz.* New York: Farrar, Straus and Company, 1950.

RICE, ELMER. *We, the People: A Play in Twenty Scenes.* New York: Coward-McCann Inc., [c1933].

RICE, JOHN ANDREW. *I Came Out of the Eighteenth Century.* New York: Harper & Brothers, [c1942].

RICHARDS, WILLIAM C. *The Last Billionaire: Henry Ford.* New York: Charles Scribner's Sons, 1948.

RINGEL, FRED J., ED. *America As Americans See It.* New York: Harcourt Brace & Company, [c1932].

RIVERA, DIEGO. *Portrait of America.* With an explanatory text by Bertram D. Wolfe. New York: Covici-Friede, [c1934].

ROBERTS, KENNETH. *Black Magic: An Account of its Beneficial Use in Italy, of its Perversion in Bavaria, and of Certain Tendencies Which Might Necessitate its Study in America.* Indianapolis: The Bobbs-Merrill Company, [c1924].

ROGGE, O. JOHN. *The Official German Report: Nazi Penetration 1924–1942/ Pan-Arabism 1939–Today.* New York: Thomas Yoseloff, [c1961].

ROOSEVELT, ELEANOR. *If You Ask Me.* New York: D. Appleton-Century Company, [c1946].

ROOSEVELT, MRS. FRANKLIN D. [ELEANOR]. *It's Up to the Women.* New York: Frederick A. Stokes Company, 1933.

ROOSEVELT, ELLIOTT, AND JAMES BROUGH. *An Untold Story: The Roosevelts of Hyde Park.* A Dell Book. [1973].

ROOSEVELT, FRANKLIN D. *Selected Speeches, Messages, Press Conferences, and Letters.* New York: Rinehart & Company, [c1954].

ROOSEVELT, NICHOLAS. *The Townsend Plan: Taxing for Sixty.* Garden City: Doubleday, Doran & Company, [c1936].

ROSENSTONE, ROBERT A. *Crusade of the Left: The Lincoln Battalion in the Spanish Civil War.* New York: Pegasus, [c1969].

ROSTEN, LEO C. *Hollywood: The Movie Colony; The Movie Makers.* New York: Harcourt Brace & Company, [c1941].

SAARINEN, ALINE B. *The Proud Possessors: The Lives, Times and Tastes of Some Adventurous American Art Collectors.* New York: Random House, [c1958].

SANDBURG, CARL. *The People, Yes.* New York: Harcourt Brace & Company, [c1936].

SANDERS, MARION K. *Dorothy Thompson: A Legend in Her Time.* Boston: Houghton Mifflin Company, 1973.

SCHLESINGER, ARTHUR M. [JR.]. *The Age of Roosevelt: The Politics of Upheaval.* Boston: Houghton Mifflin Company, [c1960].

———. *The Coming of the New Deal.* Boston: Houghton Mifflin Company, 1958.

———. *The Crisis of the Old Order, 1919–1933.* Boston: Houghton Mifflin Company, 1957.

SCHMITT, PETER J. *Back to Nature: The Arcadian Myth in Urban America.* New York: Oxford University Press, 1969.

SCOTT, HOWARD. *Introduction to Technocracy by . . . and others. . . .* New York: The John Day Company, [c1933].

SEAVER, RICHARD, TERRY SOUTHERN, AND ALEXANDER TROCCHI, EDS. *Writers in Revolt:* An Anthology. New York: F. Fell, [c1963].

SEIDLER, MURRAY B. *Norman Thomas: Respectable Rebel.* N.P.: Syracuse University Press, [c1967].

SELDES, GILBERT. *The Great Audience.* New York: The Viking Press, 1950.

———. *The Movies Come From America.* New York: Charles Scribner's Sons, 1937.

———. *The Seven Lively Arts.* New York: Sagamore Press, [c1957].

———. *The Years of the Locust.* Boston: Little, Brown and Company, 1933.

SEVAREID, ERIC. *Not So Wild a Dream.* New York: Alfred A. Knopf, 1936.

SHEEAN, VINCENT. *Not Peace but a Sword.* New York: Doubleday, Doran & Company, 1939.

SHERWOOD, ROBERT E. *Idiot's Delight.* New York: Charles Scribner's Sons, 1936.

———. *Roosevelt and Hopkins: An Intimate History.* New York: Harper & Brothers, [c1950].

SIFTON, PAUL. *The Belt.* New York: The Macaulay Company, [c1927].

SIMONDS, WILLIAM ADAMS. *Henry Ford and Greenfield Village.* New York: Frederick A. Stokes Company, 1938.

SINCLAIR, ANDREW. *The Better Half.* New York: Harper & Row [c1965].

SINCLAIR, UPTON. *The Epic Plan for California.* NP, [c1934].

————. *I, Candidate for Governor; and How I Got Licked.* Pasadena, California: The Author, n.d., [c1935].

————. *I, Governor of California And How I Ended Poverty: A True Story of the Future.* Los Angeles, California: Upton Sinclair [no copyright, 1934].

SMITH, GENE. *The Shattered Dream: Herbert Hoover and the Great Depression.* New York: William Morrow & Company, 1970.

SMITH, S. GEOFFREY. *To Save a Nation: American Countersubversives, the New Deal, and the Coming of World War II.* New York: Basic Books, [c1973].

SNYDER, ROBERT L. *Pare Lorentz and the Documentary Film.* Norman: University of Oklahoma Press, [c1968].

SORENSON, HELEN. *The Consumer Movement: What It Is and What It Means.* New York: Harper & Brothers, 1941.

SOULE, GEORGE. *A Planned Society.* New York: The Macmillan Company, 1932.

SPIVAK, JOHN L. *America Faces the Barricades.* New York: Covici-Friede, [c1935].

STEFFENS, LINCOLN. *The Autobiography of . . .* New York: Harcourt Brace & Company, [c1931].

STEGNER, WALLACE. *The Uneasy Chair: A Biography of Bernard De Voto.* Garden City: Doubleday & Company, 1974.

STEIN, CLARENCE S. *Toward New Towns for America.* With an Introduction by Lewis Mumford. Chicago: Public Administration Service: The University Press of London . . ., 1951.

STEINBECK, JOHN. *The Grapes of Wrath.* New York: The Viking Press, [c1939].

————. *In Dubious Battle.* New York: The Modern Library, [c1936].

STERNSHER, BERNARD. *Rexford Guy Tugwell and the New Deal.* New Brunswick: Rutgers University Press, [c1964].

STRONG, ANNA LOUISE. *I Change Worlds: The Remaking of an American.* New York: Garden City Publishing Co., 1937.

SWANBERG, W. A. *Dreiser.* New York: Charles Scribner's Sons, [c1965].

SWARD, KEITH. *The Legend of Henry Ford.* New York: Rinehart & Company, 1948.

SWING, RAYMOND GRAM. *Forerunners of American Fascism.* N.P.: Julian Messner, Inc., [c1935].

TARKINGTON, BOOTH. *Claire Ambler.* Garden City: Doubleday, Doran & Company, 1928.

TAUBMAN, HOWARD. *The Making of the American Theatre.* New York: Coward-McCann, [c1965].

TENNESSEE VALLEY AUTHORITY. *TVA Today 1972.* Knoxville, January, 1972.

THOMAS, BOB. *Winchell.* Garden City: Doubleday & Company, 1971.

THOMAS, HUGH. *The Spanish Civil War.* Harper Colophon Books. New York: Harper & Brothers, [1961].

THOMPSON, DOROTHY. *I Saw Hitler!* New York: Farrar & Rinehart, [c1932].

THORPE, WILLARD, ED. *A Southern Reader.* New York: Alfred A. Knopf, 1955.

THURBER, JAMES. *The Beast in Me and Other Animals...* New York: Harcourt Brace & Company, [c1948].

The Townsend Plan. N.P., n.d. [Old Age Revolving Pensions, Ltd.]

TRILLING, LIONEL. *The Middle of the Journey.* New York: The Viking Press, 1947.

TUGWELL, REXFORD G. *The Democratic Roosevelt: A Biography of Franklin D. Roosevelt.* Garden City: Doubleday & Company, 1957.

———. *The Light of Other Days.* Garden City: Doubleday & Company, 1962.

TULL, CHARLES J. *Father Coughlin and the New Deal.* N.P.: Syracuse University Press, 1965.

TVA Today, N.P., n.d.

TWOMBLY, ROBERT C. *Frank Lloyd Wright: An Interpretive Biography.* New York: Harper & Row, [c1973].

US HOUSE OF REPRESENTATIVES. *Hearings before a Special Committee on Un-American Activities....* Seventy-fifth Congress, Third Session on H. Res. 282.... Washington: United States Government Printing Office, 1939.

———. Seventy-third Congress, Second Session. *Investigation of Nazi Propaganda Activities and Investigation of Certain Other Propaganda Activities.* Public Hearings of a Subcommittee of the Special Committee on Un-American Activities. Hearings No. 73-NY-7, 73-NY-12, 73-DC-4, 73-DC-6. Washington: United States Government Printing Office, 1935.

———. *Taxation of Marihuana.* Hearings Before the Committee on Ways and Means / House of Representatives / Seventy-fifth Congress, First Session on H.R. 6385. April 27, 28, 29, 30, and May 4, 1937. Washington: United States Government Printing Office, 1937.

VIERECK, GEORGE SYLVESTER. *Confessions of a Barbarian.* New York: Moffat-Yard, 1910.

WAGNER, PHILIP M. *American Wines and How to Make Them.* New York: Alfred A. Knopf, 1933.

WAKEMAN, FREDERIC. *The Hucksters.* New York: Rinehart & Company, [c1946].

WARNER, GEORGE A. *Greenbelt: The Cooperative Community.* With an Introduction by J. S. Lansill. New York: Exposition Press, [c1954].

WARREN, CONSTANCE. *A New Design for Women's Education.* By ... president, Sarah Lawrence College. New York: Frederick A. Stokes Company, 1940.

WATERS, W. W. *B.E.F.: The Whole Story of the Bonus Army.* By ... as told to William C. White. New York: The John Day Company, [c1933].

WECHSLER, JAMES. *The Age of Suspicion.* New York: Random House, [c1953].

——. *Revolt on the Campus.* Introduction by Robert Morss Lovett. New York: Covici-Friede, [c1935].

WECTER, DIXON. *The Age of the Great Depression. 1929-1941.* A History of American Life, Vol. XIII. Quadrangle Paperbacks. Chicago: Quadrangle Books, [c1948].

WEINER, ED. *Let's Go to Press: A Biography of Walter Winchell.* New York: G. P. Putnam's Sons, [c1955].

WELLS, H. G. *The World Set Free: A Story of Mankind.* London: Macmillan and Company, 1914.

WEST, NATHANAEL. *A Cool Million: The Dismantling of Lemuel Pitkin.* London: Neville Spearman, [c1954].

——. *The Day of the Locust.* N.P., The New Classics, [1950].

WHITMAN, WILLSON. *Bread and Circuses: A Study of Federal Theatre.* New York: Oxford University Press, 1937.

WILLIAMS, JAY. *Stage Left.* New York: Charles Scribner's Sons, [c1974].

WILLIAMS, T. HARRY. *Huey Long.* New York: Bantam Books, [c1970].

WILSON, EDMUND. *The Shores of Light: A Literary Chronicle of the Twenties and Thirties.* New York: Farrar, Straus and Young, [c1952].

——. *Travels in Two Democracies.* New York: Harcourt Brace & Company, [c1936].

WILSON, HARRY LEON. *Ruggles of Red Gap.* In *Ruggles, Bunker & Merton: Three Masterpieces of Humor.* Garden City: Doubleday, Doran & Company, 1935.

WINCHELL, WALTER. *Winchell Exclusive: "Things That Happened to Me—and Me to Them."* Introduction by Ernest Cuneo. Englewood Cliffs: Prentice-Hall, Inc., [c1975].

WOLFE, BERTRAM D. *Strange Communists I Have Known.* New York: Stein and Day, [c1965].

WOLFE, THOMAS. *Look Homeward, Angel: A Story of the Buried Life.* New York: Grosset & Dunlap, [c1929].

WRIGHT, FRANK LLOYD. *An Autobiography.* New York: Duell, Sloan and Pearce, [c1943].

WRIGHT, JOHN LLOYD. *My Father Who Is On Earth.* New York: G. P. Putnam's Sons, [c1946].

Writers Take Sides: Letters about the War in Spain from 418 American Authors. New York: The League of American Writers, [c1938].

WYLIE, MAX. *Radio Writing.* By ... Director of Script and Continuity of the Columbia Broadcasting System. Introduction by Lewis Titterton. ... New York: Farrar & Rinehart, [c1939].

INDEX

Aalto, Alvar, 35
Aberhart, William, 226, 233
Abraham Lincoln Brigade, 544, 550, 551–52, 553, 555–58, 559–60
Abrams, Albert, 248
Academic Gothic style, 35
Academy of Motion Picture Arts and Sciences, 98
Ackerman, Frederick L., 454
Acosta, Bert, 555
Actors' Equity, 416
Adamic, Louis, 523, 525
Adams, Franklin P., 136, 153
Adams, Leon D., 446
Addams, Jane, 170, 175, 440, 530
Addington, Lord John, 283
Adler, Dick, 115
Adler, Selig, 276, 282, 579
Aerocar Company, 46
Aesop Fables (movie), 97
Agee, James, 381
Aiken, Conrad, 421
Airmail, 15
Air transportation, 100–3, 202–4
Alabama Power Company, 405, 466, 468
Albers, Josef, 32, 522, 524, 525 n.
Albright Gallery, Buffalo, N.Y., 28
Alcott, Bronson, 320 n.
Alda, Robert, 569
Aldington, Richard, 598
Aldrich, Larry, 12–13

Aldrich, Nelson W., 27
Alfonso XIII, 539 n.
Algonquin Round Table group, 68, 160, 430
Algren, Nelson, 418
Ali, Muhammad, 43
Allen, Fred, 135, 150
Allen, Frederick Lewis, 184, 192
Allen, Gracie, 150, 154
Allen, Willis and Lawrence, 261–62
All God's Chillun Got Wings (play), 436
All People Are Famous (Clurman), 26
Alsberg, Henry, 402, 405, 418–19, 421, 422–23
Amalgamated Clothing Workers, 506
Amanda of Honeymoon Hill (radio serial), 123
Amateur hour radio programs, 132–35
America First movement, 236, 276–82, 285
American Association for the Advancement of Science, 219
American Association of Advertising Agencies, 107
American Association of Engineers, 223
American Association of University Professors, 519
American Christian Defenders, 239
American Civil Liberties Union (ACLU), 245, 246, 334, 397

American Fascist Organization of Black Shirts, 237
American Federation of Labor (AFL), 220, 334, 502, 508
American Federation of Television and Radio Artists, 148
American Guide series, 423
American Institute of Public Opinion, 107
American Laboratory Theatre, 365, 366
American Legion, 322, 323
American magazine, 17, 238, 244–45, 576
American Medical Association, 577
American Radiator Corporation, 46
American-Russian Chamber of Commerce, 349
American Student Federation, 531
American Sunbathing Association, 59
American Telephone & Telegraph Company, 23
American Vigilante Intelligence Federation, 239
American Women's Party, 170
American Writers Congress (1935), 356, 544, 546
American Youth Congress (AYC), 534–37, 559
Amkino, 353
Amos & Andy (radio serial), 118, 119, 385, 432
Amsterdam News, 309
Ancient Order of Hibernians, 208
Anderson, Marian, 432
Anderson, Maxwell, 156
Anderson, Sherwood, 356
Andrews, Robert Hardy, 125
Angelo, Joe, 329
Anglo-American Institute, 349
Anna Christie (movie), 95
Anslinger, Henry J., 576–77
Antibiotics, 70
Anti-Saloon League, 439, 440, 441
Anti-Semitism, 235–36, 238–39, 240, 243, 245, 284, 378, 466, 560, 561–62, 567, 570

Appointment in Samarra (O'Hara), 376
Aquitania, RMS, 14, 15
Architectural Forum, 41
Architecture, 29–46
Arden, Elizabeth, 194
Armored Cruiser Potemkin (movie), 353
Armory Show (1913), 27, 28
Armstrong, Hamilton Fish, 173
Army Corps of Engineers, U. S., 469, 479
Arnold, Joseph L., 463
Arp, Hans, 91
Arrowsmith (Lewis), 69
Art Deco style, 31, 32, 35, 195, 196, 198, 199, 589
Arthur, Jean, 168
Art News, 74
Arts, the, 26–103
Art Students League, 90
Asch, Nathan, 356
Asia magazine, 341
As I Lay Dying . . . (Faulkner), 377, 380
Associated Press, 136
Association Against the Prohibition Amendment, 439
Association of American Advertisers, 107
Association of Future War Propagandists, 533
Atherton, Gertrude, 549
Atkinson, Brooks, 288, 371, 409, 430, 431, 598
Atlanta *Constitution,* 109
Atlantic Monthly, 275, 340, 470
Atomic bomb, 602
Attitude sampling, scientific, 112–13
Auden, W. H., 73, 156, 551
Audit Bureau of Circulation (ABC), 112, 113
Authors' Guild, 420
Authors' League, 420
Autobiography (Steffens), 344
Autry, Gene, 130
Avon Books, 594–95

Awake and Sing (play), 366
Aydelotte, Frank, 520

Babies, Just Babies magazine, 179
Backstage Wife (radio serial), 124, 125
Back-to-the-Land movement, 311–20
Badzislawski, Hermann, 172 n.
Baer, Arthur "Bugs," 179
Baird, Bil and Cora, 415
Baker, George Fisher, 75
Baker, George Pierce, 163, 304, 403
Balbo, Italo, 204–5
Baltimore *Sun,* 109
Balzac, Honoré de, 159
Bambi (movie), 99
Bancitaly Corporation, 23
Bank of America, 23
Barbusse, Henri, 553 n, 598
Barkley, Alben, 470
Barnes, Albert C., 28, 525
Barnes, Harry Elmer, 317
Barnum, P. T., 270
Barr, Alfred H., 30
Barr, Donald, 145 n.
Barry, Philip, 183
Barthel, Kurt, 57, 59
Barthelme, Donald, 369
Bartlett, John H., 325, 327
Barton, Bruce, 252 n., 277
Baruch, Bernard, 215, 564
Bates, Ralph, 546
Bates, Ruby, 393, 396
Battle of Britain, 279, 599–600
"Battle of Washington," 329
Bauhaus, the, 32, 37, 522
Beard, Charles A., 17, 20, 206, 215, 218, 219, 220, 243, 423, 508, 509
Beard, Mary, 508, 509
Beecher, Henry Ward, 231
Behrman, S. N., 548
Bellamy, Edward, 214, 259
Bellow, Saul, 418
Bellows, George, 29, 88
Belmont, August, 565
Belt, The (Sifton), 363
Benchley, Robert, 161, 431
Bender, Lauretta, 427

Benét, Stephen Vincent, 156, 157, 280, 550
Bennett, E. H., 199
Bennett, Harry, 277, 506
Bennington College, 516–17, 518, 519, 521
Benny, Jack, 150, 158
Benson, Sally, 369
Bentley, Eric, 525
Benton, Thomas Hart, 11–12, 61, 81, 82–84, 90, 185, 387–88, 425
Benton, William, 277
Berg, Gertrude, 119
Bergen, Edgar, 143, 148
Bergensfjord, SS, 14
Bergoff, Pearl, 505–6
Bergoff Service Bureau, 505–6
Berle, Adolf A., 478
Berlin, Irving, 570
Bernays, Edward L., 193, 194
Best Years of Our Lives, The (movie), 265
Biddle, Francis, 236, 400
Biddle, George, 400–1, 424, 425, 427
Bilbo, Theodore G., 385
Billingsley, Sherman, 138
Bing, A. M., 454–55, 457
Bingham, Alfred, 188
Birkhead, L. M., 239–40
Birth control, 217, 587
Birthrate, 573, 581–89
Bishop, J. C., 130
Bismarck, Otto von, 37
Blackburn, Alan, 237
Black Friday, 57
Black Book magazine, 373
Black Majesty (play), 436
Black Mountain College, 520–26
Black Muslims, 434
Blacks, the, 432–37
Black theatre, 428–32
Black Thursday (1929), 19, 20, 26, 192
Blake, Peter, 41, 43
Bliss, Lizzie P., 27
Blitzstein, Marc, 409, 416
Bliven, Bruce, 222
Blum, Léon, 540

Blunden, Godfrey, 351 n.
Bodenheim, Maxwell, 418 n.
Bogardus, James, 42 n.
Bolshevism, 345
Bonnie, Richard J., 574 n.
Bonus Army, 77, 184, 237, 320–30, 336, 434
Book clubs, 26
Boone, Isley, 59, 60, 61
Boorstin, Daniel, 82, 442
Borah, William E., 209, 274
Borglum, Gutzon, 88–89, 401
Borsodi, Myrtle Mae, 315–16
Borsodi, William, 312–17
Boston *Globe,* 235
Botkin, B. A., 423
Boulder Dam, 477, 478
Bourgeois Gentilhomme, Le (Molière), 45
Bowers, Claude, 558
Bowes, Edward, 133–35, 144
Bowles, Chester, 277
Bradbury, Ray, 372 n.
Bradford, Roark, 429
Brady, Nicholas F., 439
Brandeis, Louis D., 206, 478, 561
Brearley, H. C., 383
Brecht, Bertolt, 413
Breuer, Marcel, 32, 33, 34
Brewster, Kingman, Jr., 277
Brice, Fanny, 570
Brinkley, Douglas, 243
Brinkley, John R., 226
Brisbane, Arthur, 160
Broadcasting. *See* Radio broadcasting; Television
Brogan, Sir Denis, 573
Broken Earth (Hindus), 341–42
Broken Lullaby (movie), 96
Bromberg, J. Edward, 365
Broom magazine, 214 n.
Broun, Heywood, 67, 159, 160, 161, 163, 165, 166, 417
Browder, Earl, 246, 321, 530, 546, 550, 567
Brown, John Mason, 551
Brown University, 531

Broyard, Anatole, 68
Bryan, Julian, 343, 349
Bryan, William Jennings, 227
Bryant, Louise, 338, 354
Buchman, Frank N. D., 282–87
Büchner, George, 417
Buckley, William F., Jr., 162
Bullitt, William C., 338
Burbank, Luther, 56
Burchfield, Charles, 27, 81, 87
Bureau of Labor Statistics, 112
Burnham, Hubert, 199
Burns, George, 570
Burns, Robert Elliott, 384
Burns Agency, William J., 505
Burroughs, Edgar Rice, 127
Butcher, Fanny, 595
Butler, Nicholas Murray, 196, 220, 223
Butler, Samuel, 40 n.
Butterfield 8 (O'Hara), 378
Byoir & Associates, Carl, 242
Bryd, Harry F., 274
Byrd, Richard E., 201, 555

Cacciatore, Maria, 37
Cadden, Joseph, 246
Caesar, Sid, 570
Cahill, Holger, 49, 402, 427
Calder, Alexander, 89–92
Caldwell, Erskine, 64, 82, 338, 356, 359–60, 377, 379, 380, 381
Calloway, Cab, 575
Calverton, V. F., 307
Camp, Walter, 435
Campbell, Mrs. Patrick, 435
Camp Nordlund, 244
Camp Siegfried, 244
Canaday, John, 73, 80 n., 84, 98
Candid camera, 70–73
Cannon, Joseph G., 468
Cantor, Eddie, 569
Cantrill, Hadley, 144
Capone, Al, 207
Carlyle, Thomas, 40, 44, 182
Carnegie, Andrew, 17
Carney, William, 539 n.

Carpenter, Edward, 57
Carrel, Alexis, 270–71, 275, 282, 283
Carrington, Elaine, 120
Carroll, Madeleine, 547
Carter, Dan T., 394 n.
Carter, Hodding, 390
Cartoons, animated, 96–100
Cary, Joyce, 74
Cash, W. J., 383, 389 n., 563
Cassatt, Mary, 90
Castle, William, 274, 281
Catchings, Waddill, 18
Catholic Legion of Decency, 60
Cedar Rapids *Gazette,* 276
Celotex Corporation, 46
Censored (Ernst), 496
Census Bureau, U. S., 112
Century magazine, 206, 341
Century of Progress Exposition, 42,
    43, 59, 83, 85, 86, 102, 197–202,
    204, 210, 433–34, 589
Chabas, Paul, 28
Chalmers, Allan K., 395, 398
Chalmers, Thomas, 496, 498
Chamberlain, Sir Neville, 139, 169
Chamberlin, William H., 345
Chambers, Whittaker, 361, 413
Chandler, Harry, 262
Chandler, Raymond, 282, 374, 575
Chaplin, Charlie, 96 n., 496
Charles, Perry, 133
Chase, Chris, 125 n.
Chase, Eugene, 246–47, 251
Chase, Stuart, 19, 57, 212, 213, 215,
    218, 331, 339, 454, 464, 591
Chaucer, Geoffrey, 64
Chavez, Cesar, 298
Cheever, John, 369, 418
Chicago Art Institute, 85
Chicago Civic Opera, 23–24
Chicago *Daily News,* 109, 171, 201
Chicago *Defender,* 434
Chicago *Tribune,* 69, 118, 162, 207,
    276, 282, 399
Chicago University, 53
Child, Richard Washburn, 205
Children's Bureau, U. S., 292

Christian Front, 231, 240
Christian Mobilizers, 240
Chrysler, Walter P., 196
Chumley, Lee, 212
Cincinnati *Enquirer,* 109
Citizen Kane (movie), 100
City, The (movie), 461–62
City College of New York, 531, 533,
    535, 566
Civilian Conservation Corps (CCC),
    330, 473, 480–87, 489, 494, 495, 512,
    525, 534
Civil Rights Congress, 397–98
Civil Works Administration (CWA),
    400, 401, 481
Clair, René, 95, 496
Claire Ambler (Tarkington), 207
Clapper, Raymond, 174, 598
Clara, Lu & Em (radio serial), 119–20
Clark, Champ, 275
Clark, D. Worth, 243, 275
Clark, Stephen C., 27, 28
Cleland, John, 360
Cleland, Robert Glass, 262
Clemenceau, Georges, 340
Clements, Robert E., 253, 256
Clurman, Harold, 26, 219, 344, 365,
    366, 372, 545, 547
Coates, Robert, 369
Cochran, Bourke, 227
Cohan, George M., 409
Cohen, Benjamin V., 561
Cohen, Octavus Roy, 118
Cold War, 140, 437
Cole, Wayne S., 278
Collage, 91
Collective bargaining, 507–8
Collectivism, 526
Collier's magazine, 70, 198, 330, 358
Colman, Ronald, 95
Columbia Broadcasting System
    (CBS), 139, 141, 143, 155, 156, 229,
    593, 601
Columbia Encyclopedia, 347
Columbia University, 531, 536
Columnists, newspaper, 159–81
Comic books, 126

Comic strips, 118
Coming American Fascism, The (Dennis), 222
Comintern, 552
Commission on Industrial Relations, 506
Committee for Industrial Organization, 416
Committee for the Nation, 514
Committee to Defend America by Aiding the Allies, 276
Common Sense magazine, 188, 226
Commonwealth Edison, 24
Communal movements, 303–11
Communist Party, 297, 330, 333, 336–37, 356–68, 394, 397, 421–22, 434–35, 436–37, 485, 506, 530, 538–39, 540, 541, 550, 551, 552, 556, 559, 568
Communists and Communism, 172, 222, 229, 244, 284, 286, 302, 327, 328, 330, 337, 338–39, 343, 345, 368, 411, 412, 419, 420–23, 428, 434, 528, 529, 539, 540, 542, 553, 559, 560, 567, 593, 601
Compulsory arbitration, 506–7
Congress, U. S., 111, 186, 257, 324, 326, 332, 406, 442, 507, 531, 533, 573, 596
Congress of Industrial Organizations (CIO), 508–9
Connelly, Marc, 430, 431
Conroy, Jack, 183
Conscientious objectors, 532
Constitution, U.S., 104, 105
Consumer movement, 331–35, 399
Consumer Reports, 335
Consumers' Bulletin, 335
Consumers' Distribution Corporation, 459
Consumers' Research, 331–35
Consumers' Union (CU), 334–35
Conte Biancamano, SS, 14
Cooke, Alistair, 403
Coolidge, Calvin, 104, 205, 468, 477
Cool Million, A (West), 237
Cooper, Gary, 325, 551 n.

Cooper, Hugh L., 212, 465
Cooperative Analysis of Broadcasting, 107, 113
Cooperative Movement, 459–60
Copeland, Charles Townsend, 163
Copland, Aaron, 461
Cornell, Katharine, 183
Correll, Charles, 118
Corwin, Norman, 149 n., 156, 157, 158, 545
Couch, W. T., 423
Coughlin, Charles E., 117, 172, 227–37, 241, 242, 251, 257, 386
Council of Social Agencies, Dayton, Ohio, 301–2
Country music, 130
Country of the Blind (Wells), 150
Counts, George S., 205, 344, 345, 346, 349, 350
Couzens, James, 386, 468
Covered Wagon Company, 46
Coward, Noel, 183
Cowley, Malcolm, 337–38, 346, 348, 356, 421, 548
Coxey's Army, 321
Cradle Will Rock, The (play), 409, 413, 414, 415, 416–17
Crane, Hart, 156
Crane, Jacob, 462
Crane, Mrs. W. Murray, 28
Craven, Thomas, 81, 83, 84
Crawford, Cheryl, 365
Credit unions, 460
Creel, George, 250, 251, 260, 420
Crews, Laura Hope, 95
Crichton, Kyle, 358, 411, 547
Crockett, Albert Stevens, 445 n.
Cronon, E. David, 310
Crosby, Bob, 148
Cross, Milton, 151
Crossley, Archibald M., 107, 108, 112, 117, 134
Crouse, Russell, 154, 360
Crowninshield, Frank, 28
Croy, Homer, 562
Crusaders for Economic Liberty, 239
Crusaders of Americanism, 239

Cubism, 91
Cudahy, John, 277
cummings, e. e., 197, 345, 357
Curran, Henry S., 65
Current History magazine, 178, 340
Curry, John Steuart, 81, 84–85, 425
Curtiss, Glenn H., 203
Customs, U. S., 62
Cutting, Bronson, 161, 225

Dabney, Thomas, 388
Dabney, Virginius, 390
Dada, 91
Daguerre, Louis Jacques Mandé, 73
Dahl, Harold, 555
Dahlberg, Edward, 356, 485
Daiches, David, 103
Daily News Building, New York City, 30
Daily Worker, 164, 334, 375, 551, 576
Damon, Anna, 246
Dana, H. H. L., 343, 365
Danforth, William H., 19
Daniels, Jonathan, 377, 382, 476–77, 563
Daniels, Josephus, 323, 327
Dante Alighieri Society, 209
Darrow, Charles B., 299
Darrow, Clarence, 251, 395, 439
Dartmouth College, 74, 75–76, 80
Daughters of the American Revolution, 432
Daumier, Honoré, 86
David Harum (Westcott), 121
Davidson, Donald, 380
Davies, Arthur B., 27
Davis, Elmer, 600
Davis, Jerome, 205, 343, 349
Davis, Richard Harding, 168
Dawes, Charles G., 197
Dawes, Rufus C., 197–98
Dawes Plan, 197
Day, Clarence, 360
Day of the Locust, The (West), 263
Dearborn, Michigan, 54–56
Dearborn *Independent,* 466
Deatherage, George S., 239

Debs, Eugene V., 553
Deep Throat (movie), 68
De Gaulle, Charles, 105
De Kruif, Paul, 69
Delafield, E.M., 199
Dennis, Lawrence, 222
Depression of the 1930s, 12, 13, 20, 26, 43, 46, 49, 50, 57, 61, 72, 80, 88, 98, 182–91, 192–95, 210, 220, 288–310, 317, 337, 346 n., 363, 369, 392, 399, 439, 455, 485, 488, 507, 512, 526, 529, 594
Dernburg, Bernhard, 243
Desert Song, The (movie), 95
Desmond, Olga, 58
Detroit *Free Press,* 77, 236
Detroit Institute of Arts, 79
Detroit *News,* 78
De Voto, Bernard, 65, 443, 513, 523, 525
Dewey, John, 35, 342, 350, 516, 525
Dewey, Thomas E., 108 n.
Diamond Lil (movie), 66
Dickstein, Martin, 239, 242
Dictionary of American History, 19
Dies, Martin, 242
Dies Committee. *See* House of Representatives Special Committee for Investigation of Un-American Propaganda
Dietrich, Marlene, 264
Diggins, John P., 205, 206, 209, 276
Dinneen, Joseph, 244
Dior, Christian, 30
Dirigibles, 202–3
"Dirty" words, 68–69
Disney, Walt, 97–100, 497
Divine, Father Major M. J., 261, 303–10, 311, 432, 539, 575
Dixon, Thomas, Jr., 379, 381
Dodge, Mabel, 58
Dollfuss, Engelbert, 229
Donnelly, Ignatius, 231
Doran, Dave, 556
Dos Passos, John, 81, 161, 338, 359, 363, 547, 548, 598
Douglas, C. H., 224, 225, 226

Douglas, Lewis W., 257
Downey, Sheridan, 252, 261
Draper, Muriel, 546
Draper, Theodore, 338
Dreiser, Theodore, 218, 226, 251, 344, 355, 522, 550
Dreyfuss, Henry, 590
Driberg, Tom, 284 n.
Drug addiction, 573–81
Duberman, Martin, 520, 521, 523 n., 524, 525
Dubinsky, David, 235
Dublin, Louis I., 183 n., 188, 585
Du Bois, W. E. B., 309
Duchamp, Marcel, 28, 91
Duffield, Marcus, 209
Duffus, R. L., 297
Dufy, Raoul, 29
Dunmore, Lord, 53
Dunne, Finley Peter, 162
Durant, Will, 345, 350
Duranty, Walter, 169, 343, 346 n.
Dust Bowls, 293–94, 295, 296, 386, 489, 490, 491, 492, 493, 495, 498
Dutt, Palme, 355
Dutton & Company, E. P., 58
Duys, J. E. W., 283

Earhart, Amelia, 196
Eastern States Cooperative League, 459
Eastman, Max, 599
Eaton, Cyrus M., 24
Eby, Cecil, 552, 556, 557
Eddy, Sherwood, 343
Edison, Thomas A., 21, 22, 35, 53, 56, 93, 194
Editorials, newspaper, 160
Edman, Irwin, 280
Edmondson, Madeleine, 125 n.
Education, 512–37
Edward VIII, 13
Eighteenth Amendment, 440 n., 443
Eilshemius, Louis, 27
Eimi (cummings), 345, 357
Einstein, Albert, 218, 572, 602
Eiseley, Loren, 418

Eisenhower, Dwight D., 329
Eisenstein, Sergei, 249, 353, 436
Elders of Zion, 560
Eliot, Charles W., 316, 338
Eliot, T. S., 157, 382, 408
Ellison, Ralph, 418
Elmer Gantry (Lewis), 239
Elsner, Henry, Jr., 224 n.
Emperor Jones (play), 429, 436
Empire State Building, New York City, 195
Emporia Gazette, 276
Encyclopedia of Sexual Behavior, 60
End Poverty in California (EPIC), 218, 219, 248, 249–52, 254, 255, 257, 258, 259, 260, 262, 302
Engineers and the Price System, The (Veblen), 211
Ernst, Morris, 61, 63, 173, 251, 395, 496, 509 n.
Erskine, John, 317
Esquire magazine, 65–66, 599
Ethel & Albert (radio serial), 123
Ethiopia, invasion of, 210, 242, 541

Factories in the Field (McWilliams), 296
Fadiman, Clifton, 153, 369
Fairbanks, Janet Ayer, 277
Fairchild, Henry Pratt, 582
Fall (radio show), 155–56, 158
Fantasia (movie), 99–100
Farm Security Administration, 295
Farrell, Frank, 137
Farrell, James T., 65, 356, 360, 375
Farson, Negley, 169
Fascist League of North America, 208–9
Fascists and fascism, 164, 172, 204–10, 222, 321, 368, 382, 484, 535, 539, 542, 545, 550, 599
Fashions and styles, 12–13, 30
Faulkner, John, 128
Faulkner, William, 82, 369, 377, 378–81
Fechner, Robert, 483

Federal Artists' Project (FAP), 402, 414, 418, 422, 424-29

Federal Bureau of Investigation, 245, 397

Federal Communications Commission (FCC), 128, 131, 143, 151

Federal Council of Churches of Christ in America, 220

Federal Deposit Insurance Corporation, 499-500

Federal Home Loan Bank (FHLB), 187

Federal Music Project (FMP), 402, 414, 428

Federal Summer Theatre, 411

Federal Theatre Project (FTP), 400, 404-18, 422, 423, 428

Federal Writers' Project (FWP), 184, 402, 405, 414, 418-24, 427, 428

Felix the Cat (movie), 97

Fels, Joseph, 459

Ferber, Edna, 562-63, 564

Field, Marshall, 375

Fields, Lew, 196

Fields, W. C., 43, 148, 150, 287

Fifth Column, 245

Fight for Freedom movement, 276

Filene, E. A., 459

Finland, invasion of, 598

"Fireside chats," Roosevelt's, 116-17, 227

Firestone, Harvey S., 192, 194

Fischer, Louis, 343, 349, 557

Fish, Hamilton, Jr., 209, 229

Fisher, Irving, 18, 194, 261

Fitch, John A., 503

Fithian, Marilyn, 59 n.

Fitzgerald, Ed, 591

Fitzgerald, F. Scott, 184, 337, 338, 378

Five Acres and Independence (Kains), 317

Five-Year Plan, 220, 295, 344, 346, 347, 529

Flagg, Ernest, 314

Flanagan, Hallie, 350, 365, 402-11, 422, 423, 513, 527

Flanders Hall (publisher), 242

Flight from the City (Borsodi), 317

Flying boats, 203-4

Flynn, John T., 21, 277, 282, 510

Folk songs, 80, 81

Fonda, Henry, 547

Fontanne, Lynn, 600

Ford, Corey, 368, 380, 442

Ford, Edsel, 78, 79

Ford, Ford Madox, 598

Ford, Henry, 17, 35, 39, 48, 53, 54-56, 101, 186, 193, 194, 216, 225, 230, 236, 274, 276, 282, 311, 363, 466-68, 470, 476

Ford, James L., 435

Ford, John, 95

Ford Motor Company, 506

Foreman, Larry, 417

Forestry Service, U. S., 452, 483, 486, 487, 493, 512

Forman, Henry James, 152

Fortune magazine, 16, 17, 19, 20, 71, 108, 109, 113, 119, 155, 185, 188, 205, 209, 288 n., 414, 427, 570

Forum magazine, 69

For Whom the Bell Tolls (Hemingway), 550, 551 n.

Fosdick, Harry Emerson, 396

Foster, Stephen, 56

Foster, William T., 18, 515

Foundation for Christian Economics, 238

Foundations of American Population Policy, 583, 584

Fountainhead, The (Rand), 45

Four Saints in Three Acts (Stein), 496

Fourth Estate, 104, 105

France, Anatole, 355

France, SS, 13

Franco, Francisco, 156, 164, 169, 539, 541, 542, 543, 546, 550, 552, 553, 558

Frank, Glenn, 341

Frank, Jerome N., 401, 500

Frankfurter, Felix, 235, 550, 561

Freberg, Stan, 157

Freeman, Joseph, 356, 530

French, Daniel Chester, 89

French Revolution, The (Carlyle), 182
Fresco painting, 75
Freud, Sigmund, 193
Friends of Democracy (FofD), 239–40, 241, 242
Friends of the New Germany, 243–44
Froebel, Friedrich, 40
Fuller, A. R., 96
Fuller, Buckminster, 45–46
Functionalism in architecture, 31, 32, 34

Gable, Clark, 264
Galahad College, 238
Gallegher, Michael J., 227, 229, 231–32, 234, 235
Gallico, Paul, 72
Gallup, George, 107, 108, 109, 110, 112, 113
Gallup Polls, 107, 109 n., 110, 433, 483, 510, 558 n., 586, 597
Gandhi, Mahatma, 169
Gangbusters (radio serial), 151–52
Garbo, Greta, 95, 270, 496
"Garden City" movement, 453–56
Garfield, James A., 520
Garfield, John, 570
Garibaldi, Giuseppe, 237
Garvey, Marcus, 309, 432
Gasoline Alley (radio serial), 123
Gates, John, 556
Gauguin, Paul, 29
Gauss, Christian, 513
Gauvreau, Emile, 136
Gehman, Richard, 263
Gellhorn, Martha, 543–44
General Education Board, 53
General Electric Company, 21
General Motors Corporation, 79, 80
George, Henry, 311
German-American Bund, 208, 239, 240, 244–46, 570
German White Book, 243
Gershwin, George, 409
Giannini, A. P., 23
Gibbons, Floyd, 168
Gibbs, Sir Philip, 168
Gibbs, Wolcott, 354, 368

Gibson, Charles Dana, 71 n.
Gilbert, Ruth, 142 n.
Gilbert, W. S., 157, 405
Ginsberg, Allen, 576
Gish, Lillian, 277
Gitlow, Matthew and Benjamin, 246
Glasgow, Ellen, 381, 389–90
Glass, Montague, 119
Glassford, Pelham D., 324–25, 326, 327–28
Glass Key, The (Hammett), 374
Glazer, Nathan, 572
Glyn, Elinor, 45
Goddard, Robert Hutchings, 13
God's Little Acre (Caldwell), 64
Gold, Mike, 81, 119, 357, 370, 372
Goldberg, Rube, 149
Goldberger, Joseph, 389
Golden, John, 407
Golden Gate Exposition, 80 n.
Golden Hour of the Little Flower, The (radio program), 228
Goldman, Sylvan F., 573
Gone with the Wind (Mitchell), 100, 379
Good-Bye, Union Square (Halper), 104
Goodman, Paul, 320
Goodwin, W. A. R., 49–51, 52, 54
Goodyear, A. Conger, 28
Gordon, Ruth, 395
Göring, Hermann, 272, 273, 275
Gorky, Maxim, 355
Gosden, Freeman, 118
Gossip columnists, 135–41
Grady, Henry, 378
Graf Zeppelin (dirigible), 202
Graham, Frank D., 302
Grand Coulee Dam, 478
Grapes of Wrath, The (Steinbeck), 294, 295, 311, 361–62
Graves, Robert, 15
Gray, Gilda, 66
Gray, Harold, 123, 126
Gray Shirts, 237
Great Bull Market, 16–19, 28, 183, 197, 443
Great McGinty, The (movie), 100

Great Plains, the, 489–93, 498
Great Radio Heroes (Harmon), 127
Great Technology, The (Rugg), 221
Greeley, Horace, 162
Green, Paul, 82, 366, 382, 415
Green, William, 506
Greenfield Village, Dearborn,
  Michigan, 53, 54–56
Green Pastures, The (play), 429–32
Greenspan, Magistrate, 68
Griffith, Raymond, 96 n.
Grinnell College, 403
Gropius, Walter, 30, 32–33, 34, 35, 38,
  44, 522, 525 n.
Gross, Ben, 133
Gross, Milt, 119
Group Theatre, 365, 366–67, 382, 485
Guggenheim Museum, New York
  City, 36, 92
Guild Studio, 365, 366
Gurdjieff, 41, 225

Haile Selassie, 164
Hale, William Harlan, 513
Hall, Bolton, 312, 313
Hall, James Norman, 264 n.
Hallelujah (movie), 95
Hallgren, Mauritz, 190, 290, 303
Halper, Albert, 104
Hambridge, Gove, 189 n.
Hammerstein, Oscar, 265
Hammett, Dashiell, 265, 356, 372–75
Hammond, Percy, 410 n., 496 n.
Hand, Augustus N., 63, 70
Hanfstaengl, Ernest, 284
Hapgood, Norman, 339
Happiness Haven (radio serial), 124
Harkness, Edward S., 439
Harmon, Jim, 127
Harper's Bazaar, 28
Harper's magazine, 193, 209, 340, 523,
  582
Harriman, Margaret Case, 172
Harrison, Frederic, 174
Harrison, Richard, 430
Hart, Lorenz, 378, 407
Hart, Moss, 569

Hartman, William E., 59 n.
Harvard Society of Contemporary
  Arts, 29
Harvey, Bill, 556
Hastings, Lord, 77
Hauptmann, Bruno, 411
Hauser, Philip M., 585
Hawaii, attack on, 601–2
Hayes, Roland, 429
Hays, Will H., 195
Hays Code, 67
Hays Office, 496
Hearst, William Randolph, 262, 548
Heaven's My Destination (Wilder),
  370
Hechinger, Fred M., 68
Hecht, Ben, 137, 167
Heflin, J. Thomas, 209, 385
Hellman, Lillian, 382, 545, 546, 547,
  548
Hemingway, Ernest, 169, 338, 368,
  370, 373, 378, 544, 547, 548, 550,
  551 n., 599, 600
Henderson, Donald, 530
Henry, Patrick, 51
Henson, Francis A., 343
Herbst, Josephine, 356, 548
Hershey, John, 369
Hibben, John Grier, 285
Hicks, Granville, 356, 421
Higby, Mary Jane, 120, 158
Hill, Frank Ernest, 481, 486, 487
Hill, George Washington, 139
Hill, Rowland, 400
Hillman, Sidney, 561
Himes, Chester, 418
Hindenburg (dirigible), 141, 202–3
Hindus, Maurice, 205, 341–43, 353
Hitchcock, Henry-Russell, 30, 34, 35
Hitler, Adolf, 73, 99, 158, 169, 171–72,
  236, 238, 240, 242, 243, 244, 245,
  273, 282, 284, 436, 532, 534, 536,
  539, 546, 559, 596, 597, 598
Hitler-Stalin Pact (1939), 165, 274,
  280, 535, 601
Hofstadter, Richard F., 76 n., 240–41
Holabird, John, 199
Holbrook, Stewart H., 515 n.

Holmes, John Haynes, 231, 251, 554
Holmes, Oliver Wendell, 34
Holt, Hamilton, 515, 519
Holtz, Lou, 570
Homer, Winslow, 88
Homosexuality, 57
Hood, Raymond, 29–30, 42
Hoover, Herbert Clark, 98, 104, 113, 116, 161, 173, 184, 186, 187, 188, 207, 213, 220, 240, 274, 283, 288, 289 n., 325, 326, 329, 400, 442, 477, 507
Hoover, J. Edgar, 138, 164
Hope, Bob, 149
Hopkins, Harry, 165, 176, 400, 401, 402, 403, 409, 453
Hopkins, Mark, 520, 524
Hopper, Edward, 81, 87–88
Hopson, Howard, 22
Hormel, Jay C., 277
Horse operas, 120–21
Horse's Mouth, The (Cary), 74
Houghton, Norris, 403
Houseman, John, 141, 410 n., 415–18
House of Connelly, The (play), 366
House of Representatives Special Committee for Investigation of Un-American Propaganda (HUAC), 238, 241, 246, 252, 266, 335, 412, 413, 421, 422, 535
Howard, Ebenezer, 37
Howard, Sidney, 502
Howard, Tom, 150
Howe, Irving, 561, 570
Howe, Quincy, 243
Hubbard, Elbert, 37, 43
Hull, Cordell, 283
Humanity Uprooted (Hindus), 342
Hummert, Frank and Ann, 120, 125, 126
Hundred Days, the, 178, 199, 438
Hunt, Frazier "Spike," 168
Hunter, Mary, 37
Hustler magazine, 66
Huxley, Aldous, 228, 548
Huxtable, Ada Louise, 33–34
Hydroelectric power, 464–80

Ibsen, Henrik, 438
I Change Worlds (Strong), 339
Ickes, Harold, 165, 176, 472, 475
Idiot's Delight (play), 597
Ile de France, SS, 14
Ilma, Viola, 534 n.
I Love a Mystery (radio serial), 152
Independent magazine, 340
In Dubious Battle (Steinbeck), 65, 297, 361, 366, 503
Industrial Management magazine, 211
Industrial Workers of the World (IWW), 500–1
Information Please (radio quiz show), 153–54
Informer, The (movie), 95, 96
Insull, Samuel, 18, 19, 20–23, 164, 500
Insull Utilities Investment Corporation, 22–23, 25
Inter-Church World Movement, 528
International Association of Theatrical and Stage Employees, 165
International Brigades in the Spanish Civil War, 551–60
International Congress of Architects (1937), 36
International Labor Defense (ILD), 394, 395, 396, 397
International Ladies Garment Workers' Union, 80, 371, 506
International News Service, 339
International Style of architecture, 31–32, 37, 49, 589
Intourist guided tours of Russia, 348–52
Isaacs, Edith, 403
Isherwood, Christopher, 247
Isolationism, 597, 600
It Can't Happen Here (Lewis), 65, 172, 173, 408, 409, 411
It's Up to the Women (Eleanor Roosevelt), 180
Ivens, Joris, 546

Jack Armstrong, All-American Boy (radio serial), 126

Jackson, Gardner, 185
Jacobs, Lewis, 501
James, Arthur Curtiss, 439
James, Henry, 65
James, William, 216, 482, 483, 487
Jarrell, Randall, 382
Jazz Age, 12, 13, 58, 218, 285, 356
Jazz Singer, The (movie), 93
Jeffers, Robinson, 207
Jefferson, Thomas, 51, 52–53
Jenkins, Susan, 333–34
Jennings, Paul, 31 n.
Jerome, William Travers, 505
Jessel, George, 570
Jessup, J. Charles, 130
Jews in America, 560–72
John Birch Society, 165
John Reed Clubs, 355
Johns, Orrick, 356, 418 n., 420, 537
Johnson, Alvin, 11, 292
Johnson, Andrew, 35
Johnson, Donald, 59 n.
Johnson, Hewlett, 224, 233
Johnson, Marietta, 312 n.
Johnson, Philip, 30, 34, 35, 237
Johnson, Sheila E., 59 n.
Jolson, Al, 93, 431 n., 570
Jones, Robert Edmond, 161, 430
Jordan, Virgil, 219
Josephson, Matthew, 21 n., 24
Joyce, James, 62
Judge magazine, 495
Just Plain Bill (radio serial), 123, 124

Kahn, Otto, 363, 564
Kains, M. G., 317
Kallet, Arthur, 332–33, 334
Kant, Immanuel, 379
Kantor, MacKinlay, 372 n.
Kaplan, Justin, 197
Kaufman, George S., 237, 407
Kaufmann, Edgar, 38, 40
Kaye, Danny, 570
Kazan, Elia, 354, 485, 531, 545, 547, 569
Keaton, Buster, 96 n.

Keegan, Wilbur C., 246
Keep America Out of War
    Organization (KAOW), 276, 278
Kelland, Clarence Budington, 121
Kellerman, Annette, 61 n.
Kelley, Florence, 176
Kellock, Katharine, 405
Kemble, Fanny, 154 n.
Kemp, Harry, 418 n.
Kempton, Murray, 11
Kennedy, Joseph P., 95, 230, 272, 500
Kent, Frank, 231, 257
Kent, Rockwell, 353
Keokuk Dam, 465
Kerr, Florence, 406 n.
Keynes, John Maynard, 37
Khrushchev, Nikita M., 300
Kielbasy, Matya, 95
Kieran, John, 153
Kilgallen, Dorothy, 137
King Features Syndicate, 136
Kingsley, Charles, 500
Kingsley, Sidney, 366
Kipling, Rudyard, 14, 168
Kirby, Rollin, 430
Kirkland, Alexander, 366 n.
Kirstein, Lincoln, 29
Klee, Paul, 32
Klein, Alexander, 21 n.
Knightley, Phillip, 544
Knights of Labor, 501
Knights of the White Camellia, 239
Kober, Arthur, 564, 569
Koch, Howard, 141
Kocher, A. Lawrence, 525 n.
Koestler, Arthur, 544, 547
Kooning, Willem de, 428
Kraft, Joseph, 162
Kramer, Hilton, 91
Kreuger, Ivar, 19
Kreutzberg, Harold, 196
Kreymborg, Alfred, 356
Kristol, Irving, 68
Kriza, John, 415
Kropotkin, Pyotr Alexeyevich, 311
Krowl, Henry C., 343
Kuhn, Fritz Julius, 243–46

Ku Klux Klan, 207, 227–28, 383
Kungsholm, SS, 14

Labor unions, 500–11
Ladies' Home Journal, 65, 70, 99, 109, 170, 173, 178, 180, 193–95, 203, 432, 440, 444, 597, 599
Lady Godiva: The Future of Nakedness (Langdon-Davies), 58
La Farge, Oliver, 528
Lafayette Escadrille, 555
La Follette, Philip, 135, 206
La Follette, Robert M., 243
La Guardia, Fiorello H., 308, 592
Lahr, Bert, 570
Lamont, Robert P., 192
Lamont, Thomas W., 19, 206
Lancaster, Osbert, 35 n.
Land-grant colleges, 532
Landon, Alfred M., 108
Landry, Robert J., 151
Langdon-Davies, John, 58
Lansill, J. S., 456
Lanterns on the Levee (Percy), 392
Lardner, James, 544
Lardner, Ring, 166, 375
Lash, Joseph, 177 n.
Lask, Thomas, 104
Laski, Harold, 526–27, 528, 530
Last Tycoon, The (Fitzgerald), 184
Latouche, John, 156
Laurel & Hardy, 96 n.
Laurencin, Marie, 29
Lavine, Harold, 308 n.
Lawrence, D. H., 247, 366 n.
Lawson, John Howard, 81, 265, 366, 485, 547
Leaf, Munro, 538
League Against War and Fascism, 242, 333, 556
League for Independent Political Action, 226
League for Industrial Democracy, 349
League for the Liberation of America, 238–39
League of American Writers, 169, 333, 421, 549

League of Nations, 231
League of Workers' Theatres, 411
Le Corbusier, 30, 35
Le Dain Commission, 575 n., 578
Lee, Gypsy Rose, 546, 592
Lee, Ivy Ledbetter, 270, 355
Le Gallienne, Eva, 406
Leibowitz, Samuel S., 395, 396, 397
Leider, Ben, 555
Leigh, Robert D., 516
Lenin, V., 221, 355
Leonard, John, 369
Let 'Em Eat Cake (Kaufman and Ryskind), 237
Let My People Come (movie), 68
Letter to Three Wives, A (movie), 265
Levant, Oscar, 153
Levine, Jack, 428
Lewis, Fulton, Jr., 281
Lewis, John L., 508–9
Lewis, Lloyd, 38, 201
Lewis, Mrs. Lloyd, 43
Lewis, Sinclair, 65, 69, 172, 239, 277, 381, 408, 411, 564
Lewis, Sir Wilmot, 172
Lewisohn, Sam A., 27, 28
Liberty League, 161
Life (comic weekly), 207
Life magazine, 71–72, 73
Life With Father (play), 360
Light of the World, The (radio serial), 121
Lilienthal, David, 176, 472, 475, 477, 478, 521 n., 561, 562
Lindbergh, Anne Morrow, 269, 278–81
Lindbergh, Charles A., Jr., 36, 101, 266, 268–83, 285, 598, 600, 601
Lindbergh, Charles A., Sr., 231, 266–68, 269
Lindley, Betty and Ernest, 488
Lindsay, Howard, 360
Lindsay, Vachel, 156
Lipman, Jean, 92
Lippmann, Walter, 17, 82, 160–62, 167, 170, 219, 258, 336, 504, 505
Literary Digest, 106, 108, 109

Literature, 61–65, 368–76, 377–83
Little Land and a Living, A (Borsodi), 313
Little Orphan Annie (radio serial), 123, 127
Little Review, 62
Lloyd, Harold, 96 n.
Lloyd George, David, 273
Lloyd-Jones, Jenkins, 39
Lodge, Henry Cabot, 278
Lodge, Nucia P., 344 n.
Loeb, Harold, 214 n., 215, 216, 221
London Economic Conference (1933), 230
London *Times,* 172
Long, Huey P., 117, 172, 226, 228, 231, 233, 236, 241, 249, 257, 384–86
Longfellow, Henry Wadsworth, 54
Longworth, Alice Roosevelt, 277
Looking Backward (Bellamy), 214, 219, 220, 221, 259
Look magazine, 72, 73
Loos, Anita, 183 n.
Lord, Philips, 151
Lord & Thomas (advertising agency), 252
Lorentz, Pare, 461, 495–99
Los Angeles *Daily Illustrated News,* 223
Los Angeles *Times,* 109, 255
Louisville *Courier-Journal,* 109, 160
Lovell, J. A., 132
Love's Coming of Age (Carpenter), 57
Lubitsch, Ernest, 95–96, 496
Luce, Clare Boothe, 179
Luce, Henry R., 16, 71, 72
Ludlow, Louis, 540
Ludlow massacre, 501
Luhan, Mabel Dodge, 338, 369
Lundeen, Ernest, 243, 275
Lynch, Peg, 123
Lynes, Russell, 28 n., 39, 589
Lyons, Eugene, 350

MacArthur, Douglas, 320, 330
MacCracken, Henry M., 281, 404, 527, 528, 535 n.

Macdonald, Dwight, 551 n.
Macfadden, Bernard, 136, 179
Macgowan, Kenneth, 96, 403
Mack, Julian W., 269
MacKaye, Benton, 453
Mackenzie, William Lyon, 553 n.
MacLeish, Archibald, 155–56, 225, 406 n., 598, 599
Macon *Telegraph,* 237
Mafia, the, 207
Magazines, 65–66, 118
Majestic, SS, 14
Major Bowes Amateur Hour, 133–35
Malcolm, Janet, 32
Malraux, André, 355, 545, 547
Maltz, Albert, 485
Manchester *Guardian,* 349
Mangione, Jerre, 418, 419, 421, 556
Man the Unknown (Carrel), 271
Mantle, Burns, 66
Mao Tse-tung, 355
Ma Perkins (radio serial), 125
Marcantonio, Vito, 428
March, Fredric, 546
March of Time, The (play), 72, 409, 410
Marcus, Sheldon, 228 n.
Marijuana, use of, 573–81
Marijuana Taxation Act (1937), 577, 579
Marin, John, 29, 88
Markel, Lester, 110, 111
Market research, 106–7
Markey, Morris, 134, 185, 290, 513
Marquand, J. P., 320
Marquand, Mrs. J. P., 277
Marsh, Reginald, 81, 88, 425
Marshall, Verne, 276
Martin, E. S., 207
Martin, Everett Dean, 221 n.
Martin, Prestonia Mann, 216–18
Marx, Karl, 37, 337, 355, 357, 381
Marx Brothers, 570
Mason, George, 52
Masses magazine, 236
Matisse, Henri, 29
Matthews, Herbert L., 542, 544

Matthews, J. B., 333, 334, 530, 539
Maupassant, Guy de, ⌣⌣1
May, Henry F., 16
Mayer, Arthur, 497
Mayer, Milton, 198, 199
McBride, Mary Margaret, 152–53
McCall's magazine, 495
McCarran, Pat, 275
McCarthy, Joseph, 140
McConnell, Lulu, 150
McCord, C. Stewart, 252 n.
McCormick, Anne O'Hare, 181
McCormick, Robert R., 276
McCullers, Carson, 382
McDonald, Forrest, 21 n.
McFee, William, 550
McGill, Ralph, 359, 390
McGinley, Phyllis, 369, 538
McGraw-Hill Building, New York
    City, 30
McGuffey school readers, 54, 56
McIntyre, O. O., 136
McKay, Claude, 418 n., 434
McKellar, Kenneth, 470
McKelway, St. Clair, 137, 138
McKenney, Ruth, 356
McLean, Evelyn Walsh, 327
McNamara, John T. and James, 501
McNaughton, Harry, 150
McPherson, Aimee Semple, 131, 260
McWilliams, Corey, 244, 247, 296
McWilliams, Joseph E., 240, 241, 242
Mead, Margaret, 212, 213
Media, the, 104–81
Meier, August, 433 n.
Mellon, Andrew, 18, 186
Mellow, James, 84
Memling, Hans, 87
Memphis *Commercial Appeal,* 109
Mencken, Henry L., 166
Men in White (play), 366, 569
Men Working (Faulkner), 128
Mercury Theatre, 141–46, 417–18
Merriam, Frank P., 252, 255
Metropolitan Museum of Art, 27
Mexican Renaissance, 73
Miami *Herald,* 109

Michigan Civic League, 78
Mickey Mouse, 97–99
Middle of the Journey (Trilling), 47
Middle West Utilities Corporation,
    22, 24
Mies van der Rohe, Ludwig, 30, 32,
    34, 35, 36, 37
Mill, John Stuart, 288
Millay, Edna St. Vincent, 28, 156
Miller, Alice Duer, 600
Miller, Arthur, 92, 415
Millet, Jean François, 200
Mills, Ogden, 193
Mills Brothers, 148
Minnesota University, 532–33
Minnewaska, SS, 14
Minor, Bob, 362
Miró, Joan, 90
Mirrors of Moscow (Bullitt), 338
Mitchell, Joseph, 368
Mitchell, Margaret, 379
Mitchison, Naomi, 306
Mobile homes, 46–49
Mobiles, 91
Modern art, 26–29, 49
Moellendorff, Fritz, 524
Molière (Jean Baptiste Poquelin), 45
Molnar, Ferenc, 183
Mondrian, Piet, 90, 91
Monopoly (game), 299–300
Monte Carlo (movie), 96
Montgomery *Advertiser,* 393
Moody, Titus, 116
Mooney, Edward, 232, 234, 236
Mooney, Tom, 76
Moral Re-Armament, 283, 285, 286–
    87
More, Sir Thomas, 259
Morgan, Anne, 534 n.
Morgan, Arthur E., 470, 472, 474
Morgan, Harcourt A., 472, 513
Morgan, Henry, 157
Morgan, John P., 79
Morgenthau, Henry, 207
Morgenthau, Henry, Jr., 561
Morris, Alice Elizabeth, 283, 290
Morris, William, 37

Morrow, Dwight, 269, 272
Moscow Art Theatre, 365
Moscow *News*, 340
Moseley, George van Horne, 240
Mosley, Leonard, 273, 280
Mosley, Sir Oswald, 237, 273
Motion pictures, 66–68, 92–100, 152
Motley, Willard, 418
Mount, Cati, 201
Mount Rushmore, South Dakota, 89
Moynihan, Daniel P., 572
Muggeridge, Malcolm, 351 n.
Mumford, Lewis, 30, 42, 454, 461, 464
Munson, Graham, 225
Mural paintings, 73–80, 83–84, 85, 88,
  425–26
Murphy, Frank, 230
Murray, Philip, 509
Murrow, Edward R., 600–1
Muscle Shoals Dam, 465, 466–69, 471,
  472
Museum of American Primitive Art,
  53
Museum of Modern Art (MOMA),
  New York City, 26–30, 31, 49, 237,
  428
Mussolini, Benito, 164, 169, 204–10,
  222, 242, 271, 385, 534, 541, 546
Mussolini and Fascism (Diggins), 205
Muste, John M., 551
Mutual Broadcasting System, 601
My First Year in the White House
  (Long), 386

Nacktheit, Die (Ungewitter), 58
Nahas, Gabriel G., 579–80
Nash, Ogden, 369
Nation, 57, 83, 185, 190, 211, 218, 353,
  349
Nation, Carry, 440
National Association for the
  Advancement of Colored People
  (NAACP), 309, 394, 395, 397, 433
National Board of Review, 99
National Broadcasting Company
  (NBC), 118, 119, 143, 151, 157, 593

National Commission to Advance
  American Art, 76
National Committee for the
  Limitation of Armaments, 528
National Consumers' League, 176
National Council of Social Work, 583
National German-American Alliance,
  208
National Labor Relations Board
  (NLRB), 334
National League for Social Justice,
  231, 232
National Recovery Administration
  (NRA), 189, 232, 332, 347, 399, 452
National Student League (NSL), 530–
  32, 533, 534 n., 537
National Union for Social Justice, 234
National Union Party, 257
National Youth Administration
  (NYA), 487–89
Natural Development Association,
  Salt Lake City, 301
Navy, U. S., 202, 203
Nazis and Nazism, 210, 239, 242–46,
  266, 272, 273, 278, 282, 283, 284,
  601
Nearing, Scott, 318–20, 452
Negri, Pola, 95
Neilson, William Allan, 440
Nelson, George, 41
Nelson, Steve, 556, 557
Neumann, John von, 572
Neutrality Acts (1935 and 1936), 541,
  558, 596
New Amsterdam, SS, 14
Newcomen Society, 115
New Deal, 21, 85, 88, 101, 116, 140,
  161, 163, 173, 176, 177, 178, 179,
  184, 187, 200, 220, 222, 233, 294,
  297, 311, 330, 332, 356, 386, 399–
  400, 411, 414, 438, 439, 452, 453,
  454, 456, 458, 469, 480, 481, 487,
  493, 495, 499, 507, 511, 513, 514,
  519, 561, 596
New Era, 13, 16, 18, 19, 20, 66, 170,
  183, 190, 192, 292, 317, 337, 356,
  365, 527, 586

New Masses, 83, 119, 164, 333, 352, 355, 358, 362, 412
New Republic, 83, 123, 220, 314, 333, 510, 543, 598
New Russia, The (Thompson), 171
New Russian Primer, 344, 345
Newscasters, 146–48
New School for Social Research, New York City, 11, 75, 83
News magazines, 26
Newspaper columnists, 159–81
Newspaper Guild, 161, 165
Newspapers, 118
New Student magazine, 528
Newsweek magazine, 106
New Theatre magazine, 413
New York *Daily Mirror,* 137
New York *Daily News,* 66, 69, 72, 137
New Yorker magazine, 71 n., 73, 95, 138, 156, 172, 174, 183, 323, 354, 369, 373, 378, 431, 483
New York *Evening Graphic,* 136, 137
New York *Evening Journal,* 137
New York *Evening Post,* 171
New York *Herald Tribune,* 99, 138, 161, 170, 173, 212
New York *Morning Telegraph,* 137
New York Stock Exchange, 20, 182
New York *Times,* 68, 82, 98, 109, 169, 170, 173, 181, 187, 297, 467, 480, 499, 513, 544
New York Times Magazine, 110
New York *Tribune,* 162
New York *World,* 119, 136, 160, 161
New York *World-Telegram,* 284
Nicholson, Harold, 272
Nielsen, A. C., 114–15
Night at the Opera, A (movie), 96
Nineteenth Amendment (1920), 440
1931 (play), 366
Nixon, Richard M., 105 n., 300
Nobile, Umberto, 202
Noble, Robert, 261
Nolan, Paul T., 430
Non-Partisan League, 234
Norman, Charles, 225
Normand, Mabel, 94 n.

Norris, George W., 467–68, 471, 476, 477
Norris, Kathleen, 277
Norris-La Guardia Act (1932), 507
North, Joseph, 550
North American Review, 178
Norway, attack on, 278
Notes on Virginia (Jefferson), 53
Nudism, 57–61
Nudist magazine, 60
Nudist resorts, 59, 60
Nudist Society (Hartman et al.), 59 n., 60
Nye, Gerald P., 274, 541, 558
Nystrom, Paul H., 190

Oboler, Arch, 116, 157–58
O'Connor, Francis V., 427
O'Connor, John J., 235
October Revolution, 348
Odets, Clifford, 183, 366, 367, 421
O'Farrell, Kirk B., 79
Office Workers' Union, 334
Of Human Bondage (movie), 96
O'Hara, John, 20, 373 n., 375–76
O'Keeffe, Georgia, 27
Olson, Cuthbert L., 252, 261, 262, 478
100,000,000 Guinea Pigs (Kallet and Schlink), 332
O'Neill, Eugene, 95, 183, 338, 407, 435
One-Third of a Nation (play), 411
On Liberty (Mill), 288
Only Yesterday (Allen), 184
Orage, A. R., 224
Orozco, José Clemente, 73, 74, 75–76, 80, 424
Osborn, Frederick, 583
Our Daily Bread (movie), 310–11, 325
Our Gal Sunday (radio serial), 125
Our Movie-Made Children (Forman), 152
Oursler, Fulton, 136
Our Town (Wilder), 367, 370–71
Owings, Nathaniel, 48, 198, 200
Oxford Group, 283–85
Oxford Pledge, 531, 534
Oxford Union, 527, 530

Pace, John, 328
Page, Thomas Nelson, 379, 385
Paley, William S., 139
Pal Joey (O'Hara), 378, 379
Palmer, Carleton H., 218
Pan American Airways, 203, 204, 269, 270
Panic (radio show), 155
Pantages, Alexander, 135
Paperback book industry, 594–95
Papineau, Louis Joseph, 553 n.
Parents' Magazine, 70
Parker, Dorothy, 68, 207, 356, 373, 375, 547
Parker, Theodore, 231
Parker Brothers Company, 299, 300
Parran, Thomas, 68, 69, 70, 411
Partners in Plunder (Kallet and Shallcross), 333
Part of Our Time (Kempton), 11
Pater, Walter, 359
Patman, Wright, 321
Patman Bill, 325, 326
Patten, Simon, 452
Patterson, Haywood, 397–98, 437
Patterson, William L., 394
Patton, George S., 329
Paul, Elliot, 548–49
Paul Reveres, the, 239
Paxinou, Katina, 551 n.
Payroll Guarantee Association, 261–62
Peck, George N., 277
Peets, Elbert, 462
Pegler, Westbrook, 24–25, 159, 162–67, 179, 180 n., 195, 258–59, 543
Pelley, William Dudley, 238–39, 241, 245, 246
Pemberton, Brock, 408
Pendergast, Thomas, 83
Pendleton, Edmund, 53
Pennland, SS, 14
Percy, Will Alexander, 388, 392
Perelman, S. J., 468
Perkins, Frances, 176, 401
Pershing, John J., 166
"Petty Girl," the, 65
Phi Beta Kappa fraternity, 50

Phillips, David Graham, 168
Phillips, Irma, 120
Phillips (Schlink), Mary Catherine, 331, 334
Phony War, 279
Photo-essay, the, 72
Photography, candid, 70–73
Photojournalism, 70–73
Picasso, Pablo, 545
Pilgrim's Progress, 16
Pinchot, Amos, 277
Pinchot, Gifford, 468
Pinkerton National Detective Agency, 505
Pinocchio (movie), 99
Pins and Needles (play), 371, 408 n., 570
Planned Society, A (Soule), 221
Playboy magazine, 66
Pleasure Man (movie), 67
Plow That Broke the Plains (movie), 461, 495, 496, 497–99
Plymouth, Massachusetts, 52
Pocket Books, 594
Poincaré, Raymond, 340
Poland, invasion of, 243, 274, 550
Pollock, Channing, 550
Pollock, Jackson, 428
Pomona College, 74
Ponzi, Charles 128
Poor, Henry Varnum, 81, 425
Pope, Alexander, 279
Popenoe, Paul, 582
Popular Front, 244, 541, 552, 553, 554
Porgy (play), 429
Pornography, 61–65
Porter, Katherine Anne, 381
Portnoy's Complaint (movie), 68
Post, Emily, 28
Post-Functionalism in architecture, 31–32, 34–35
Post Office, U. S., 60–61
Pound, Ezra, 41, 207, 225
Powell, Adam Clayton, Jr., 309
Powys, Llewellyn, 225 n.
Prairie States Forestry Project, 493–95
Pratt, Fletcher, 544
Prefabricated housing, 46

Preface to Morals, A (Lippmann), 336
Prendergast, Maurice, 88
Presidential press conference, 104–5
Price, Victoria, 393, 396, 397
Primitive art, 53
Pringle, Henry F., 573, 589–90
Profile, Prescott, 95
Progressive Education, 514–26, 528, 587
Progressivism, 206, 225
Prohibiting Poverty (Martin), 216, 259
Prohibition, 185, 200, 438–43, 447, 577, 578; repeal of, 443–46
Prohme, Rayna, 169
Prouty, Olive Higgins, 121
Psychological Review, 58
Public Health Service, U. S., 47
Public opinion polls, 105–12, 143, 433, 483, 510, 558 n., 597
Public Works Administration (PWA), 452
Public Works Art Program (PWAP), 425–26, 427
Pudovkin, Vsevolod, 353, 354
Pulitzer, Joseph, 160
Pulitzer, Ralph, 160
Pulp magazines, 372, 594
Putnam, Samuel, 421

Queen Elizabeth, RMS, 13
Quinn, John, 27
Quitman, John A., 392 n.
Quiz Kids (radio show), 154
Quiz shows, radio, 153–54

Radicalism, 526–37
Radio broadcasting, 26, 112–59, 600–2
Radio City Music Hall, New York City, 49, 195–97
Radwick, Elliott H., 433 n.
Railroads, 202
Rains, Claude, 395
Rand, Ayn, 45
Rand, Sally, 85, 201–2, 592
Randolph, A. Philip, 309
Randolph, Jennings, 243

Random House, 62
Rankin, John, 243
Ransom, John Crowe, 378
Rascob, John J., 18, 192, 500
Rating techniques, 114–16
Rautenstrauch, Walter, 213, 219, 223
Ravich, Duane, 489
Raymond, Allen, 212–13, 218
Reader's Digest, 69, 70, 275, 279, 310, 576
Reconstruction Finance Corporation (RFC), 186–87
Rector, George, 200, 445 n.
Red Bread (Hindus), 342
Red Cross, 186, 267, 326
Red Harvest (Hammett), 374
Red Virtue (Winter), 344
Reed, John, 161, 205, 338, 515 n.
Reed, Virgil D., 585
Reed College, 515
Regina *Daily Star,* 223
Regional art, 81–89
Regional Planning Association, 453–54, 455
Reis, Irving, 155
Religious radio broadcasts, 226–27, 228–29, 234–35
Remarque, Erich Maria, 598
Rembar, Charles, 62, 63
Reno, Milo, 561
Reserve Officers Training Corps (ROTC), 531–33, 534
Resettlement, 452–64, 495
Resettlement Administration, 400, 452, 453, 464, 495
Resolute, SS, 14
Restorations and reconstruction, 49–56
Reuther, Walter, 509
Rexroth, Kenneth, 418
Reynolds, Quentin, 70, 396
Reynolds, Robert R., 47
Rhymer, Paul, 123
Rice, Elmer, 183, 363
Rice, John Andrew, 519–20, 522, 523, 524, 525
Richards, Wallace, 456

Richards, William C., 55
Rickenbacker, Eddie, 277
Riefenstahl, Leni, 354, 497
Right to Happiness (radio serial), 125
Riley, James Whitcomb, 83
Rinehart, Mary Roberts, 194
Ringling Brothers-Barnum & Bailey Circus, 85
Ripley, Robert, 200
Rise of the Goldbergs, The (radio serial), 119, 120
River, The (movie), 461, 495, 497–99
Rivera, Diego, 49, 73, 76–80, 424
RKO-Roxy Theater, New York City, 195–97
Road of Life (radio serial), 125
Roanoke Island, North Carolina, 52
Roar China! (play), 366, 372
Roberts, Kenneth, 205
Robertson, Royal R., 327
Robeson, Paul, 156, 355, 420, 435–37, 530
Robins, Raymond, 346
Robinson, Boardman, 425
Robinson, Claude E., 107
Robinson, Earl, 156
Rochambeau, SS, 14
Rockefeller, Abby Aldrich, 27, 29, 49, 50, 53
Rockefeller, John D., Jr., 49, 51, 52, 54, 80, 195, 196, 439
Rockefeller, John D., Sr., 19, 26–27, 79, 80, 196, 316
Rockefeller, Nelson A., 49, 80
Rockefeller Center, New York City, 49, 79, 195
Rockefeller Foundation, 411
Rockwell, Norman, 88–89
Rodgers, Richard, 378
Rogers, Will, 219, 231
Rolland, Romain, 355
Rollins College, 515, 519–20
Romance of Helen Trent, The (radio serial), 121–22, 124, 125
Roosevelt, Anna, 179
Roosevelt, Eleanor, 102, 138–39, 159, 165, 170, 173–81, 184, 193–94, 216,

277, 330, 354, 371, 404, 405, 419, 432, 433, 460, 474, 481, 483, 487, 534–36, 537
Roosevelt, Elliott, 179, 446
Roosevelt, Franklin D., 47, 101, 104, 108, 116–17, 140, 162, 165, 173, 177, 178, 184, 186, 187, 193, 199, 224, 227, 230, 233, 239, 240, 281, 284, 308 n., 311, 330, 386, 399, 400–1, 404, 419, 424, 438–39, 442, 446, 460, 464, 468, 469, 475, 478, 481, 483, 489, 514, 533, 534, 535, 536, 541, 558, 596, 602
Roosevelt, Hall, 230
Roosevelt, Nicholas, 258
Roosevelt, Theodore, 399, 582
Roper, Elmo, 108, 109, 110
Rose, Billy, 591
Rosenberg, Harold, 419 n., 428
Rosenman, Samuel, 173
Rosenstone, Robert, 544
Rosenwald, Lessing, 277, 514
Ross, Colin, 246
Ross, Harold, 138
Rothafel, S. L. "Roxy," 196–97
Rothschild, John, 348
Rounds, David, 125 n.
Royce, Rosita, 592
Rubicam, Raymond, 113
Rugg, Harold, 215, 221
Ruggles of Red Gap (Wilson), 69
Rural Electrification Administration, 21, 476
"Rural living," 456
Ruskin, John, 37, 40, 44
Russell, Bertrand, 214, 216 n.
Russell, John, 92
Russell, Rosalind, 168
Russian-American Institute, 349
Russia's Iron Age (Chamberlin), 345
Rutgers University, 533
Ruth, Princess, 38 n.
Ryan, John A., 230 n.
Ryskind, Morris, 237, 570

Saarinen, Aline, 27
Saarinen, Eliel, 35

Sabin, Charles H., 439
Sabin, Mrs. Charles H., 277, 440, 441, 443
Sacco-Vanzetti case, 356, 394
Sachs, Paul J., 28
St. Gaudens, Augustus, 89
St. Nicholas magazine, 207, 209
St. Paul *Pioneer-Press,* 162
Salinger, J. D., 369
Salomon, Erich, 70, 73
Salt Lake *Tribune,* 109
Salvation Army, 290
Sanctuary, E. N., 239
Sanctuary (Faulkner), 380
Sandburg, Carl, 43, 156, 157, 182, 356
Sanders, Marion K., 171 n.
San Diego Exposition (1935), 223
San Francisco Art Institute, 76
San Francisco *Chronicle,* 211
Sarah Lawrence College, 516, 517, 518, 519
Sarg, Tony, 200
Saroyan, William, 373 n.
Saturday Evening Post, 118, 205, 428
Saturnia, SS, 14
Saxon, Lyle, 423
Schary, Dore, 569
Schiff, Jacob, 564
Schiok, Frank L., 595
Schlesinger, Arthur M., Jr., 105 n., 226, 229, 252 n.
Schlink, F. J., 331, 332, 333
Schoonmaker, Frank M., 448, 449
Schulberg, Budd, 264 n.
Schuler, Loring, 193, 194
Scientific Monthly, 588
Scopes trial, 383
Scott, Howard, 211, 212–13, 215, 218–19, 221, 222–24
Scottsboro Boys case, 392–98, 434
Scribner's Commentator magazine, 242, 276
Scribner's Magazine, 242, 497
Scripps-Howard newspaper chain, 160, 162, 165, 166, 170
Sculpture, 89–92
Scythia, SS, 14
Seabrook, William, 245

Sears, Roebuck & Company, 46, 193
Seattle Labor College, 300–1
Securities & Exchange Commission, 500
Seldes, George, 171
Seldes, Gilbert, 61, 118, 148, 154, 264, 414
Sergeant, John, 41 n.
Seuphor, Michael, 91
Sevareid, Eric, 529, 601
Shahn, Ben, 79, 81, 88, 426–27
Shallcross, R. H., 333
Share-Our-Wealth movement, 233, 386
Shaw, George Bernard, 43, 95, 349, 407
She Done Him Wrong (movie), 67
Sheean, Vincent, 168–69
Sheed, Wilfred, 369, 539
Sheeler, Charles, 31, 81
Shelterbelt Program, 493–95
Shelton, George, 150
Sherwood, Robert E., 93, 173, 597–98, 599
Ships and shipping, 13–15
Shipstead, Henrik, 230, 243, 275
Short-order diners, 34 n.
Show-Boat (play), 436
Shriver, Sargent, 277
Shuler, Bob, 131, 135
Sifton, Paul, 363, 366
Silly Symphonies (movie), 97, 98–99
Silverman, Henry J., 536
Silver Shirts, 238–39, 247
Simpson, Stephen, 102
Sims, William S., 166
Sinclair, Andrew, 439
Sinclair, Upton, 110, 216 n., 218, 248–53, 254, 255, 262, 302, 381, 386, 547
Siqueiros, David Alfaro, 73, 78, 424
Sirovich, William I., 414
Skariatina, Irina, 349
Skidmore, Louis, 198
Skidmore, Owings & Merrill, 48, 198
Skin Deep (Phillips), 331
Skin of Our Teeth, The (Wilder), 371–72
Slayton, William H., 439

Sloan, John, 76, 401
Smith, Alfred E., 178, 196, 231, 439
Smith, Gene, 183
Smith, Geoffrey S., 228 n., 233 n., 246
Smith, Gerald L. K., 233, 234, 241, 262
Smith, Kate, 148
Smith, Truman, 272
Smyth, William H., 211
Smythe, Edmund James, 239
Snow White (movie), 98
Soap operas, 118, 120–27, 144, 151
Sobol, Louis, 137
Social Credit, 224–26, 233, 249, 356
Socialist Party, 554
Social Justice magazine, 234, 235, 236
Social Security, 258
Social Security Act (1935), 307
Society for the Preservation of New England Antiquities, 33–34
Society for the Prevention of Vice, 64
Society of Independent Artists, 76
Society of the Friends of Beauty, 58
Sokoloff, Nicolai, 402
Sokolsky, George, 159
Solomon, David, 576
Sons of Italy, 208, 209
So Red the Rose (Young), 379
Soskin, William, 219
Soule, George, 18, 185, 220, 221
Soulé, Henri, 591–92
Sound track motion pictures, 92–100
South, the, 377–98
Southerner Discovers the South, A (Daniels), 377
Souvestre, Marie, 174–75, 534
Soviet Union, 205, 220–21, 266, 279, 282, 292, 295, 335, 336, 337, 338–56, 403, 413, 419, 436, 529, 536, 539, 540, 542, 550, 552, 555 n., 559, 560, 598
Spanish Civil War, 169, 236, 266, 539–60
Spanish Earth, The (movie), 169
Speakeasies, 442, 443
Spencer, Howland, 308 n.
Spengler, Oswald, 215
Spofford, William B., 343

Springer, Harvey, 132
Springtime (movie), 97
Stabiles, 91–92
Stage Left (play), 366
Stalin, Joseph, 139, 342, 346, 436, 559, 596, 598
Steffens, Lincoln, 206, 338, 346
Stegner, Wallace, 20
Steichen, Edward, 71, 72
Stein, Clarence S., 454, 455, 458
Stein, Gertrude, 496, 551 n.
Steinbeck, John, 65, 294, 295, 296, 297, 350, 361–62, 406 n., 503, 550
Steinmetz, Charles P., 56, 212, 213
Steinmetz, Harry C., 286
Stella Dallas (radio serial), 120, 121
Sten, Anna, 94
Sterling, George, 248
Sterne, Maurice, 425
Stetson, Harlan T., 588
Stevens, Mark, 91
Stevens Institute of Technology, 14, 90
Stevenson, Robert Louis, 29
Stewart, Donald Ogden, 265, 356, 546, 547, 550
Stickney, Dorothy, 360
Stock market crash (1929), 19–20, 24, 182–83, 192, 229
Stokowski, Leopold, 99, 196
Stone, Irving, 45
Stone Mountain, Georgia, 89
Stout, William B., 48
Stowe, Harriet Beecher, 170
Strachey, John, 221 n.
Strasberg, Lee, 365, 485
Stribling, T. S., 82, 372 n., 467
Strong, Anna Louise, 170, 171, 205, 277, 338, 339–41, 346, 349, 353, 354
Stuart, R. Douglas, 276–77
Student League for Industrial Democracy (SLID), 533–34
Students for a Democratic Society, 537
Sturbridge, Massachusetts, 52
Sturges, Preston, 100
Success magazine, 178
Success Story (play), 366

Sullivan, Mrs. Cornelius J., 27
Sullivan, Ed, 136
Sullivan, Louis, 30, 35–36, 37, 38
Sullivan, Mark, 165
Sullivan, Pat, 97
Sunbathing, 57, 58
Sunshine and Health magazine, 59
Supermarkets, 573
Supreme Court, U. S., 64, 170, 387, 397, 452, 470, 472, 507, 508, 510, 532
Survey-Graphic magazine, 69, 333
Swanberg, W. A., 339
Swanson, Gloria, 95
Swift, Philip T., 277
Swing, Raymond Gram, 258
Swope, Gerard, 218
Symes, Lillian, 356
Syndicated newspaper columnists, 159–81

Taft, William Howard, 503
Taillant, Robert, 423
Tales of a Wayside Inn (Longfellow), 54
Taliesin, 40
Tarkington, Booth, 207
Tarzan (radio serial), 127
Taste-makers, The (Lynes), 39
Tate, Allen, 378
Taubman, Howard, 431
Taussig, F. W., 193
Taylor, Elizabeth, 562 n.
Taylor, Frank J., 298 n., 548 n.
Taylor, Frederick Winslow, 511
Teague, Walter Dorwin, 31
Technical Alliance, 212, 213
Technocracy and the Technocrats, 192, 210–24, 226, 248, 302, 356, 454
Technocracy magazine, 223
Telephone, research by, 113–14
Television, 593
Teller, Edward, 572
Telling Tales magazine, 334
Tennessee Electric Power Company, 469
Tennessee Valley Authority (TVA), 22, 464–66, 468–80, 521 n., 526

Terkel, Studs, 201 n.
Terry, Paul, 97
Thaelmann, Ernst, 553 n.
Thaw, Harry K., 505
Theater Union, 366
Theatre Arts Committee for Democracy, 546
Theatre Arts magazine, 403
Theatre Guild, 365–66, 394
Theatre of Action, 485
There Shall Be No Night (Sherwood), 598
They Shall Not Die (play), 394–95
Thin Man, The (Hammett), 373, 374
Third Reich, 242, 243, 275, 280
Thirty-Nine Steps, The (movie), 96
This Is Nora Drake (radio serial), 125
This Ugly Civilization (Borsodi), 315, 316, 317
Thomas, Bob, 137 n.
Thomas, Elmer, 330
Thomas, Hugh, 552, 554, 559
Thomas, J. Parnell, 246
Thomas, Norman, 221, 277, 281, 550, 553, 554, 555, 567
Thompson, Dorothy, 99–100, 102, 143, 144, 154, 169–73, 277, 354
Thompson, William H., 198, 256
Thomson, Virgil, 496
Thoreau, Henry David, 167
Thorpe, Willard, 390
Three Acres and Liberty (Borsodi), 313
Three Little Pigs (movie), 98
Thunder Over Mexico (movie), 249
Thurber, James, 120, 125, 368, 369
Till the Day I Die (play), 367
Time magazine, 16, 19, 106, 252, 330, 369, 544
Tiomkin, Dmitri, 94
Titanic, RMS, 16
Tobacco Road (Caldwell), 67, 360, 569
Toller, Ernest, 413, 545, 547
Torio, Johnny, 207
To Save a Nation (Smith), 241
Toscanini, Arturo, 151
Touring trailer, 46–49
Toward Civilization (Beard et al.), 20

Townsend, Francis E., 253–58
Townsend Old-Age Pension Plan, 233, 248, 252, 253–58
Townsend Weekly, 256
Town Topics magazine, 136
Toynbee, Philip, 545
Tragedy of Russia, The (Durnat), 345
Trailer parks, 47–48
Travelers Aid, 290
Trilling, Lionel, 47, 538
Trotsky, Leon, 355
Trouble in Paradise (movie), 96
True, James, 276 n.
Truman, Harry S., 108 n.
Trumbo, Dalton, 96
Tucker, Sophie, 570
Tugwell, Rexford G., 176, 332, 401, 452–53, 480, 513
Tull, Charles J., 228 n.
Tunney, Gene, 196
Twain, Mark, 43, 168
Twenty-first Amendment, 443
Twombly, Robert C., 40 n., 43

Ulysses (Joyce), 62–63, 378
Ulysses case, 61–62
Unemployed Citizens League, 300
Unemployment, 596
Ungewitter, Richard, 58
United Automobile Workers, 509
United Mine Workers, 508
United Nations, 224
United Nations Building, New York City, 30
United States, SS, 13
Untermeyer, Louis, 86
Urban, Joseph, 11, 198
Urban League, 433
Usonianism, 40–42
Utopian Society movement, 254, 259–61

Valentiner, William P., 76–77
Valentino, Rudolph, 208
Vandenberg, Arthur, 275, 468
Vandercook, John, 436
Vanderlip, Frank A., 218, 223, 514
Van Doren, Carl, 65, 157

Vanity Fair magazine, 441, 495
Van Sweringen, Mantis and Oris, 23
Van Vechten, Carl, 575
Variety, 66, 137, 140, 151
Vaudeville News, 136
Veblen, Thorstein, 194, 211, 213
Vegetarianism, 58, 59
Venereal disease, campaign against, 68–70
Versailles Treaty (1919), 272
Veterans of Foreign Wars, 322
Veterans of Future Wars, 533
Vic and Sade (radio serial), 123
Vidor, King, 95, 311, 497
Viereck, George Sylvester, 58, 136, 242–43, 275, 365
Virginibus Puerisque (Stevenson), 29
Vitaphone, 93
Vogel, Arthur, 485
Vogue magazine, 495
Volstead Act, 200, 438, 447
Voorhis, Jerry, 246, 252
Vrooman, Carl, 283

Wagner, Philip, 451
Wagner, Robert F., 511
Wagner Act, 334, 508, 509
Wagner-Connery Act (1935), 507–8
Waiting for Lefty (play), 367, 408 n., 417, 569
Walker, Frank, 405
Walker, James J., 230, 378
Walker, Stanley, 138
Wallace, Henry A., 437, 561
Wall Street, 24, 182
Wall Street Journal, 478
Walsh, David I., 278
Wanger, Walter, 547
Ward, Harry F., 246, 343, 349
War Industries Board, 215
Warner Brothers, 93, 95, 98
War Production Board, 220
Warren, Carl, 69
Warren, Constance, 516, 517–18
Warren, George F., 514
Warren, Howard C., 58, 60
Warren, Robert Penn, 378
Warren, Wendy, 148

War Resisters League, 237
Washington *Post,* 117
Washington *Star,* 323
Waters, Walter W., 322, 325, 326, 327, 328
Watson, John B., 270, 583 n.
Watson, Thomas E., 231
Watterson, Henry, 160
Watterville-Breckheim, Baroness de, 283
Watts, Richard, Jr., 496 n.
Wave of the Future, The (Anne Lindbergh), 279, 280–81
Way of a Transgressor, The (Farson), 169
Wayside Inn, reconstruction of, 55
Way to Strength and Beauty, The (movie), 58
We, the People (play), 363–64
Weber, Joe, 196
Webster, Noah, 37, 56
Wechsler, James, 375, 529, 535
Weill, Kurt, 572
Welch, Robert, 165
Welles, Orson, 141, 142, 143, 155–56, 367, 415–18
Wells, H. G., 50, 97, 141, 150, 214, 216, 531
West, Mae, 66–67, 286–87
West, Nathanael, 237, 263, 356, 575
Westcott, E. N., 121
Wexley, John, 394
Whalen, Grover, 591, 592
What Happened to Harry (movie), 265
Wheeler, Burton K., 275
White, David McKelvy, 555
White, E. B., 368, 369
White, Stanford, 505
White, W. L., 497
White, William Allen, 276
Whitebread, Charles S., 574 n.
White Cliffs of Dover (Miller), 600
Whitman, Walt, 157
Whitney, Gertrude Vanderbilt, 29, 85
Whitney Museum of American Art, New York City, 29, 83, 85, 92
Whittier College, 223

Wickersham Commission, 207, 442
Wilbur, Ray Lyman, 189
Wilde, Oscar, 43
Wilder, Thornton, 97, 369–72, 377, 550
Wild Party, The (movie), 94
Wilhelm II, Kaiser, 243
Willard, Daniel, 293
Willard, Frances, 170, 440
William and Mary College, 49, 50
Williams, Albert Rhys, 171, 338
Williams, Aubrey, 176, 401
Williams, Carey, 260, 262
Williams, Harrison, 22
Williams, Jay, 366
Williams, T. Harry, 384
Williams, William Carlos, 550
Williamsburg, Virginia, restoration of, 49–54
Willkie, Wendell, 156, 173, 472
Wilshire, Gaylord, 248
Wilson, Earl, 137
Wilson, Edmund, 185, 285–86, 311, 356, 358
Wilson, Harry Leon, 69, 263 n.
Wilson, Woodrow, 386, 399
Wilson Dam, 465, 467, 469, 471, 479
Winchell, Walter, 135–41, 163, 167, 600
Wine industry, 446–52
Wines of America, The (Adams), 446
Winrod, Gerald, 132, 239, 241
Winslow, Thyra Samter, 369
Winter, Ella, 344, 344 n., 546
Wisconsin University, 85
Wolfe, Thomas, 15 n., 90, 91, 381, 421, 564
Woll, Matthew, 220
Women's Christian Temperance Union (WCTU), 441
Women's Home Companion, 189
Women's Organization for National Prohibition Reform, 440–43
Women's Wear, 87
Wood, Grant, 81, 85–87
Wood, Robert E., 277, 282, 514
Woodring, Harry H., 483, 484

Woollcott, Alexander, 42, 354
Woolsey, John M., 61, 62–63, 64, 68
Workers' Alliance, 412, 421
Workers' Ex-Servicemen's League, 321, 327–28
Works Progress Administration (WPA), 184, 400–3, 406, 412, 423, 481, 494
World Court, 231
World I Never Made, A (Farrell), 65
World of Tomorrow Exhibition (1939), 79, 462, 589–93
World Set Free, The (Wells), 50, 216
World's Fair Weekly, 204
World War I, 22, 215, 293, 378, 467, 528, 541, 552
World War II, 203, 204, 261, 279, 525, 540, 573, 597, 601–2
World Youth Congress, 535
Wren, Sir Christopher, 50
Wright, Ada, 395
Wright, Frank Lloyd, 29, 30, 34, 35–45, 83, 92, 255, 276, 453, 462 n.
Wright, Richard, 418
Wright, Wilbur and Orville, 56

Writers Take Sides (pamphlet), 549–50
Writers' Union, 421
Wunsch, William Robert, 522
Wylie, Max, 121
Wylie, Philip, 372 n.
Wythe, George, 51, 52

X-radio stations, 128–32

Yale, Frankie, 207
You Can't Go Home Again (Wolfe), 90
Young, Marian, 153 n.
Young, Stark, 379
Young Communist League, 556
Young Dr. Malone (radio serial), 125
Young Go First, The (play), 485
Young Widder Brown (radio serial), 123

Ziegfeld, Florenz, 198
Ziegfeld Follies, 61
Zimmerman, Wendell, 132